TH[E]
GOLDEN
PEN

PAST and PRESENT
BRASS COMPOSERS &
ARRANGERS of the
SALVATION ARMY

Written and compiled by
Steef Klepke Jr.

Dear Ken, Hope you will enjoy this book
thanks for your interest! There is nothing like SA banding!
may God Bless you!
Regards
Steef

Edited by David Miller and Glenn Horridge

Published by

SA Historical & Philatelic Association

In association with

Abernant Publishing
Alltmawr Fach
Builth Wells
Powys
LD2 3LJ

Printed and bound in the United Kingdom by

Think Ink Fine Art Printers
11-13 Philip Road
Ipswich
Suffolk
IP2 8BH

ISBN: 978-1-909196-03-2

First published 2012

CONTENTS

ACKNOWLEDGEMENTS

The idea for a book such as this was in my mind for many years and I had already started with it in my previous book 'Ever Heard the Sound?' where I wrote about several of my favourite composers and also Dutch Salvation Army composers. I have a deep affection and respect for all the people who are busy in a serious way with composing, in particular with the music I love so much, brass band music. In combination with a special purpose, writing good brass band music to spread the Gospel is one so very near to my heart.

To write a book like this is a journey through the complete musical history of the Salvation Army, one which is impossible to do on your own. Fortunately there is a strong bond within the Army, and even if you haven't seen or met a certain person, if you need him or her, this person is in principle always very willing to help. Therefore I would like to thank some people in particular:

Willi Erzberger from Zurich, Switzerland, a keen and enthusiastic bandsman (and composer!), who gave me a good start with this book, and who was of valuable help with information about Swiss Salvation Army composers; Colonel Robert Redhead for his much valued preface; Salvationist Herman A. Haverkate of RGB Research from Enschede in the east of The Netherlands. His database and knowledge about Army music became a good backup, help and source for this book; Amsterdam Staff Band archivist William Sprokkereef for his help on early composers, who were often very hard to cover. With his help a great deal of first class information has been rediscovered; also Composer Mark Freeh for his hard work to provide me with indispensable information about in particular the American Salvation Army composers, so much appreciated!

Also a huge thank you to Dr. Ron Holz, a true legend regarding Salvation Army banding knowledge; Composer Niels Silfverberg for help with and about Danish composers. Of interest is that he wrote a complete book about the Danish Staff Band while I was working on 'The Golden Pen'; Warren Baas for information about New Zealand writers; Former Amsterdam Staff Bandmaster Lieutenant Colonel Maurice Cooper; Songster Shirley Hutchinson from Worthing; Assistant Territorial Music Director and composer Andrew Blyth who, I am sure, is happy that the book is finally finished! Composers Dean Jones, Glenn Welch and Andrew Wainwright for their speedy and extended replies! Composer Brian Bowen for his valuable help, information and discussions! Peter Schrijver for his help on full score research; Pierre Coupienne for his help on the research of Belgian Salvation Army composers.

Salvation Army representatives:

Dianne Edwards of the Music Resources and Library Management in Australia. Susan Mitchem, National Archivist of The Salvation Army National Archives in Alexandria, USA. Karl R. Larson, Archives Secretary and Research & Volunteer Coordinator of The Salvation Army Archives in Canada. Harriet Jonkers of the Salvation Army Heritage Centre in the United Kingdom.

I also would like to thank the many composers, relatives, friends and other interested people who have shared their own files and information with me in order to give a little insight of who they are, what they have done, in relation to their compositions.

Also, or probably the biggest thank you to my lovely wife and encourager Paola with her incredible patience as I have been working on the computer so often. She knows what Salvation Army music means to me, but I owe her big time! Last but not least thanks to my daughters Melody and Brittany for helping me with putting the text in the right order and other relevant help with this book! I love you!

FOREWORD

By Gerard Klaucke

When Steef asked me to write this foreword I immediately thought about the many miles we were together in the car to Staff Band activities and talking about anything related to Salvation Army Brass Band Music.

It's a common fact that he was and still is totally committed to this type of music and that there is no other joy then playing, talking, listening and living Salvation Army music. So therefore I was not at all surprised that he told me about this book. Having read his first book I could imagine that it was not his last attempt to share his passion with us. And indeed it is a passion!

Let me make one thing very clear: his passion for Brass music and in particular Salvation Army music is not something everyone has. He has the motivation to sit down and work his way through his ideas, constantly fed by his everlasting passion. I remember the conversations about composers, arrangers, new published music and to define the content of these conversations, black or white! There was no grey area! It was superb music or total disaster! And still he managed to write a book about it. That makes you wonder if that passion is taking over in Steef's mind and his alter ego is writing this book.

I personally have the pleasure that Steef sometimes pops into the studio for a day and with loads of Dutch coffee he then starts re-organizing my CD collection in alphabetical order, something I hate doing, talking about passion!

In the past when Steef just joined the Amsterdam Staff Band in 1987 he was a boy who used his cornet to make statements. He never talked too much and he was modest, besides the fact that it is never wise to have a big mouth when you have just joined a premier Salvation Army Brass band.

Very soon Steef landed on the front row of the band and after a number of years he became the Principal Cornet player. That period of time is one of the most enjoyable in the band for me. As a percussionist you have the time to listen to solos from the soloists in the band when they perform and I have never heard Steef making a mistake. 'Solid as a rock' on the end chair of the Amsterdam Staff Band cornet section.

In our trips together we have shared so many nice stories that it would take at least another book to simply tell these ones, however, some of them are written in his previous book called 'Ever heard the Sound?' The lesson I have learnt from my friendship with Steef is that whatever you do, do it to the full. John Lennon used to say: Music is everybody's possession. It's only publishers who think that people own it. This book which you are about to read is everybody's possession, you don't own it, Steef shares this with us.

It is by sheer commitment of Steef and your interest that you are about to start reading this book, enjoy his and possibly your passion,

Gerard Klaucke is a former Amsterdam Staff Bandsman (tuned percussion) with over 20 years of International banding experiences. He has played as guest with the Canadian Staff Band as well as with the Black Dyke Band. He is owner and managing director of GK Design, an internationally recognized company in graphic design.

PREFACE

By Colonel Robert Redhead.

This is a remarkable book and I must first congratulate Steef, on behalf of all future readers, for his vision and tenacity in enabling the Salvation Army Band-world to come together in this way. It is a remarkable compilation.

All human beings have particular personal things which they love, and those who are linked with brass banding, and the Salvation Army version in particular, love to get together and simply enjoy sharing each other's company, with animated interest in this very unique genre. Banding is a joyful experience, part of which is the 'free-will' giving of time and practice, plus a desire to play better, coupled with the thrill of achieving new heights of performance.

The danger, of course, is that such genres can become 'beings' in themselves, and develop into self-serving, cliquish groups which, by their very nature, preclude 'non-members' from enjoying the experience. This has somewhat happened in Salvation Army banding, when the hard and yet satisfying experience of practice, rehearsal, performance, and camaraderie, has developed purely for one's personal pleasure, forgetting or ignoring, that the most satisfying joy comes when it is given to The Lord. To quote an old Salvation Army saying - 'The best for the Highest'. We are to preach the Gospel and bring people closer to our Saviour through our lives and music-making.

I believe that as you read this work, you will be inspired by the very personal expression of the writers. However, by its very nature, this book could provide quite a challenge to some. One might be tempted to first seek out some 'well-known' names and then be in danger of ignoring some of the rest. That would be a tragedy, for the personal history, and in many cases testimony, of these Salvationists, is part of the Army's mission. A life-long band member in a corps could reach our hearts just as much as a world renowned composer or performer.

Music is a very powerful influence on the human soul. The challenge is whether it is for good or bad. As Salvationists we can use this particular art-form to be a stepping-stone in a listener's experience of moving from Godlessness to the beauty of recognition of the very God they are denying. Just read some of the words expressed by our Salvation Army forefathers. There's no mistaking what Salvation Army Banding is about.

As you peruse the pages of this book, you will realise the work that Steef has done for our pleasure, and I thank him on your behalf, for being willing to take on this mammoth task, so he could share his passion with us. As you read, may you be inspired to be an even better musician for the Lord.

THE TITLE OF THIS BOOK

When thinking of a title for this book that would cover the complete content of it, a thought came into my mind that it should have something to do with the word 'writing'. To name it just 'Composers and Arrangers of the Salvation Army' would have been too easy. I also wanted to link it directly to composers.

So I have entitled this book appropriately (at least that's what I think) '***The Golden Pen***', referring to all the hard work the many composers have done in trying and succeeding to provide The Salvation Army bands with the thousands of works in all kind of styles. Remember that a good brass band can play many styles, and that many pieces have been written in various styles. In 'Ever Heard The Sound', my first book, I told that it is nearly impossible to explain what kind of music a brass band makes.

Of course the title 'The Golden Pen' isn't new at all. It is a very well known piece of music composed by one the greatest composers of all (with respect to all the others described in this book, all of whom are great composers!)' Wilfred Heaton (1918-2000). The Golden Pen is so typical of Heaton's innovative music in which can be heard unconventional rhythms and harmonic dissonances, but is nonetheless unmistakably light-hearted and vigorous. Wilfred Heaton was way beyond his time where composing is concerned and this is one of the many examples of his unbelievable skills in writing superb music for brass bands. So for more than only one reason I thought this to be the correct title of this book.

The dictionary gives many explanations about the word 'pen'. I would like to share three of them for various or better said obvious reasons:

1. any of various instruments for writing or drawing with ink or a similar substance.
2. the profession of writing: a master of the pen.
3. the pen as the instrument of writing or authorship: The pen is mightier than the sword.

When relating these three explanations, I would like to give all credits to the composers presented in this book. They are my heroes, they are my examples, they have taken the pen *'to use it as a sword'* by writing music for the Salvation Army!

MUSICAL QUOTES BY SIGNIFICANT PEOPLE

1. *Secular music, do you say, belongs to the devil? Does it? Well, if it did I would plunder him for it, for he has no right to a single note of the whole seven.... Every note, and every strain, and every harmony is divine and belongs to us.... So consecrate your voice and your instruments.... Offer them to God, and use them to make all the hearts about you merry before the Lord.*

William Booth

2. The theatre in Worcester was crowded for the visit of William Booth on January 22, 1882. Even the General himself 'had great difficulty in getting in'. The door was smashed by the crowd still trying to gain admission after the place was full. George 'Sailor' Fielder, the Commanding Officer, had been put up to sing. He had been a sea captain with a voice that had often been heard above the roar of the waves. He sang his testimony in the words, 'Bless His name, He set me free.' *'That was a fine song. What tune was that?'* inquired the Army's Founder later. '*Oh,*' came the reply in a rather disapproving tone, *'General, that's a dreadful tune. Don't you know what it is? That's 'Champagne Charlie is my name' '. 'That's settled it,'* William Booth decided as he turned to Bramwell. '*Why should the devil have all the best tunes?'*

The adoption of such music was soon put to full use. On Saturday afternoon, May 13, 1882, the congregation at the opening of the Clapton Congress Hall joined heartily in the chorus of Gipsy Smith's solo, '*O the Blood of Jesus cleanses white as snow*' to the music of *'I traced her little footsteps in the snow*'. There were no qualms of conscience. Many people gathered there knew none of the hymn tunes or gospel melodies used in the churches; the music hall had been their melody school. An early pamphlet made the Army's position clear by saying that it' considers all music sacred when used with holy purpose'.

William Booth

3. For his Christmas message to 'War Cry' readers of 1880 William Booth had already written: '*Bring out your comets and harps and organs and flutes and violins and pianos and drums, and everything else that can make melody. Offer them to God, and use them to make all the hearts about you merry before the Lord.'* Today, however, we have to take great care in the use of music originally written for other purposes. International laws of copyright forbid much that the Army was able to do in earlier times. Nevertheless, music is still one of God's most valuable gifts to mankind.

William Booth

4. *Music is for the soul, what wind is for the sail.*

William Booth

5. *Play your music to the Glory of God, the encouragement of your comrades and the salvation of the world.*

William Booth

6. 'How close to God beautiful music brings us, does it not? If you want to know one of the very good reasons why the world needs bands, just ask one of the Salvation Army warriors who for years have marched, carrying the message of the Cross, through the back alleys of life. Let him tell of the armies of men who have been turned toward a better life by first hearing the sounds of a Salvation Army band.

The next time you hear a Salvation Army band, no matter how humble, take of your hat!'

John Philip Sousa

7. *'I know of nothing in the Salvation Army that can be of more value in bringing blessing, arousing enthusiasm and building public opinion quickly than the consecrated efforts of a Staff Band'.*

Commissioner John J. Allen

8. *'There is no more effective method of evangelizing people than with a brass band. I confess I like brass bands and I like your brass bands!'*

President Theodore Roosevelt (of the United States of America, about the bands of the Salvation Army)

9. *'A nation creates music—the composer only arranges it'*

Mikhail Glinka

10. *As music is a language,*

the same in every land,

the hearts of men are reached by it,

for all they can understand

Author unknown

11. *Soul saving music, is the music for me!*

William Booth

12. *If God is to speak through music, He must have the best*

Eric Ball

13. *If there's only one brass player in the congregation, he should still play for the meetings, plain and simple.*

Major Jeffery Welch

14. *Armies of men have been turned toward a better life by first hearing the sounds of a Salvation Army band*

John Philip Sousa

15. *'We need torchbearers who not only play notes, but reach through those notations to the music those penned notes try to capture. For me, every time I play is a personal conversation...a prayer...between me and God...the Giver of the Gift. How privileged we are'*

Terry Camsey

16. General William Booth's first Order for Salvation Army bands, published in the 'War Cry', 27 March 1880 tells us the following:

Psalm 98: 6. - 'With trumpets and sound of cornet, make,' etc.

Psalm 150: 4. - 'Praise him with the timbrel,' etc.

Isaiah 38: 20. - 'The Lord was ready to save me; therefore we will sing my songs to the stringed instruments.'

Whereas, during the late Welsh and Cornish Councils, and before that time at Plymouth, Nottingham and elsewhere, we have proved the great utility of musical instruments in attracting crowds to our open-air and indoor meetings, we do here express our desire that as many of our Officers and Soldiers generally, male or female, as have the ability for so doing, learn to play on some suitable instrument. And as in many instances the obtaining of an instrument is a difficulty, we shall be glad if any friends who may have such instruments lying idle will consecrate them to this service, and send them to Headquarters. This includes violins, bass viols, concertinas, cornets or any brass instruments, drums or anything else that will make a pleasant sound for the Lord.

William Booth, General

17. *There is nothing better in all the world than real heart service in the ranks of The Army*

William Broughton

COMPOSERS GEOGRAPHICALLY

A British-style brass band is a musical ensemble comprising a standardised range of brass and percussion instruments. The modern form of the brass band in the United Kingdom dates back to the 19th century, with a vibrant tradition of competition based around local industry and communities. So it is obvious that the origins of Salvation Army composing and arranging centres in and around the United Kingdom. The Salvation Army not only started its work here, but as the real brass band movement is more or less the '*native musical form*' it is no surprise that the composers for the bands and therefore also the composers of the Salvation Army are still higher in numbers in the United Kingdom compared to other countries.

When we put the number of composers and arrangers described in this book together we see the following distribution. More than a half of them come from the United Kingdom, while the sum of the United States and Canada (so, North America really) take care of about 25%. When the Salvation Army bands started to develop it soon became clear that people from other parts of the world would start to write for this type of musical expression. Some striking facts are that now people from countries such as Japan are composing as well as from Africa (here shown as one, but there are already composers in the Congo, Kenya, Zimbabwe and South Africa amongst others, such as Richard Kimuya, Edward Lugonze, W.O. Shitandi, Kapela Ntoya, Don Aboka, Nick Omondi, George Mwiruki, Ben Owino, Peter Nyamala, Majanga and S. Otieno).

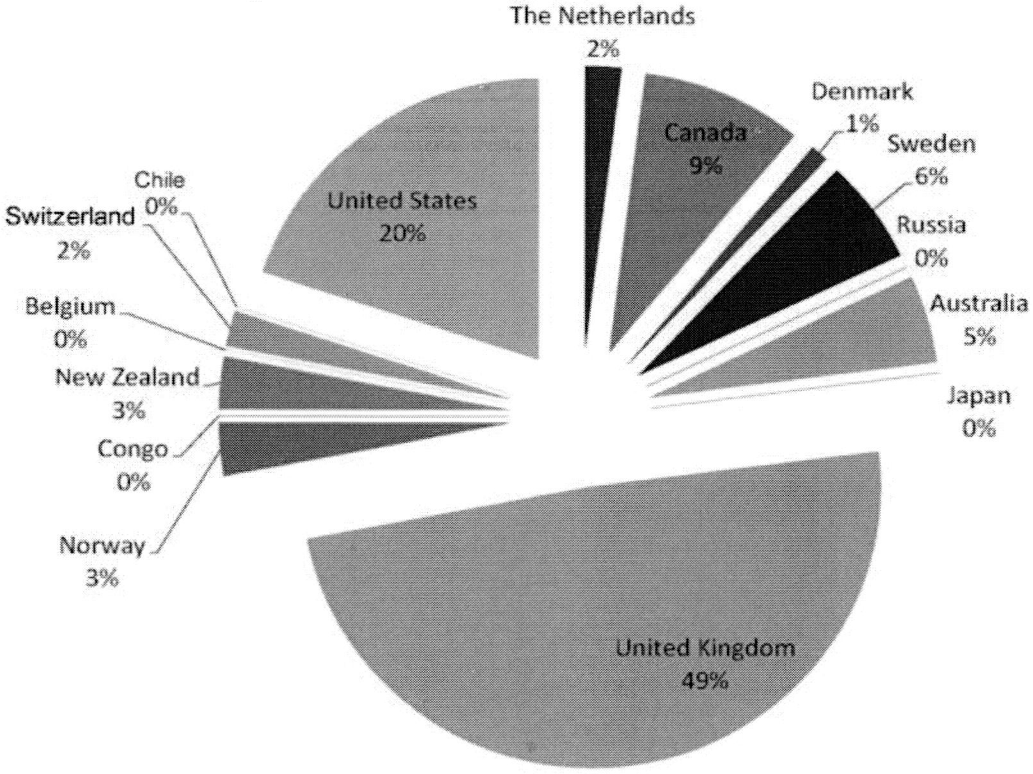

Unfortunately it was impossible to retrieve any personal information about any of these composers, and therefore it was chosen to name them as one here), as well as Chile and Russia write music for use and possible publication within the Salvation Army Journals. Not included are upcoming composers still unknown officially but trying to get their attempts played by local bands, from countries like Brazil and Argentina, just to name but two countries where brass banding is conquering. As the Army is still expanding also in countries such as India, the brass bands are getting supporters there, so it is only a matter of time before the first Indian people start composing for Salvation Army bands.

It is interesting to see that the Scandinavian countries take up to 8% percent of the composers, which is quite a lot compared to the rest of the world. Even better, some of the greatest composers in the history of the Salvation Army originate from Scandinavia and later moved to the United States of America*.

**Erik Leidzén and Emil Soderstrom just to name but two. Other composers with worldwide fame in the Salvation Army such as Erik Silfverberg from Denmark remained in their country and although the fact that the Salvation Army is not really large in numbers, his work has spread over the globe, making him an excellent representative for his native land.*

It is also surprising to see that more than 80 percent of all composers and arrangers within the ranks of the Salvation Army banding fraternity, including *secular* composers and arrangers but who also write music for the Movement, come from English speaking countries. The reason might be that these countries include some large countries (e.g. United States, Canada, Australia) and therefore are likely (but not necessarily proven) to have more composers compared to smaller countries. Whether or not this also influences the possible publications in the Journals of the Army is hard to say. It is a fact however that still the significant part of published composers are English native speakers.

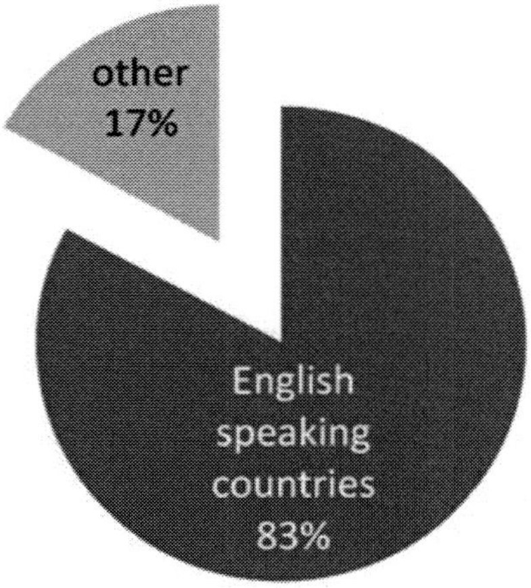

Even if you count composers from other origins (countries) to their own countries, the minor part of the graph will only show a slight move but the biggest part will remain English speaking people. The good thing about music (any music) is that it is an international language, so no direct local and or national verbal skills are required to play music from different parts of the world. A great example is of course the recent (2011) gathering of eight Staff Bands in London, England to celebrate the 120th anniversary of the International Staff Band, appropriately named 'ISB120'. Three out of the eight Staff Bands were from non-English speaking countries, but were able to play music together as if they always have done so. Also during this weekend probably the largest 'collection' of Salvation Army composers was seen. Norman Bearcroft, Terry Camsey, Dudley Bright, Paul Sharman, Olaf Ritman, William Himes, Ian Clarke, Ray Steadman-Allen, Erik and Niels Silfverberg, William Gordon and so on were all there.

COMPOSERS NAMES IN ALPHABETICAL ORDER

Countries written in *italic* are presumed correct.

A

1.	Abbott, Eric	Canada
2.	Agnew, May	United States of America
3.	Alish, Heinz	Germany
4.	Alan, J.D.	United Kingdom
5.	Allan, John	United States of America
6.	Allen, Herbert	United Kingdom
7.	Allen, Percy John	United Kingdom
8.	Alöw, Andreas	Sweden
9.	Anders, Ove	Sweden
10.	Alexander, Eric	United States of America
11.	Anderson, Folke	Sweden
12.	Anderson, Harry	United Kingdom
13.	Anderson, James	United States of America
14.	Anderson, W.	United Kingdom
15.	Andersson, Albert	Sweden
16.	Andersson, Bertil	Sweden
17.	Angwine, ??	United Kingdom
18.	Anefelt, Paul Viktor	Sweden
19.	Appleby, Harry	United Kingdom
20.	Arnott, Tom	United Kingdom
21.	Aspinall, John	United Kingdom
22.	Astbury, Mortimer	United Kingdom
23.	Audoire, Norman J.	Canada
24.	Ayling, Peter	United Kingdom
25.	Ayma, David	Chile

B

26.	Babb, Michael	United Kingdom
27.	Bainbridge, ??	United Kingdom
28.	Bale, Malcolm James	United Kingdom
29.	Ball, Eric	United Kingdom

30.	Ballantine, Leonard	Canada
31.	Balsnes, Olav	Norway
32.	Banks, Keith	United Kingdom
33.	Barlow, Glenn	Canada
34.	Barnes, Victor A.	United States of America
35.	Barrington, Andrew	United States of America
36.	Barry, Lorne	Australia
37.	Bartlett, Joe	United Kingdom
38.	Bateman, James Connor	United Kingdom
39.	Bates, Daniel	Switzerland
40.	Baxter, Leonard	Australia
41.	Bearchell, William	United States of America
42.	Bearcroft, Mark	United Kingdom
43.	Bearcroft, Norman	United Kingdom
44.	Beard, J.W.	United Kingdom
45.	Beer, Fred	United Kingdom
46.	Behrend, Kurt	Germany
47.	Beijer, Anders	Sweden
48.	Bennett, Emilee	United States of America
49.	Bennet, William	United Kingdom
50.	Berg, David	Sweden
51.	Birch, John	United Kingdom
52.	Birkett, Simon	United Kingdom
53.	Black, Thomas F.	United Kingdom
54.	Blanchard, Richard	United States of America
55.	Blomberg, Gunnar	Sweden
56.	Blott, Charles	United Kingdom
57.	Blyth, Andrew	United Kingdom
58.	Bøjstrup, Alf	Denmark
59.	Boon, Brindley	United Kingdom
60.	Booth, Evangeline Cory	United Kingdom
61.	Booth, Herbert	United Kingdom
62.	Booth, Lucy	United Kingdom

63.	Bosanko, Courtney	United Kingdom
64.	Bosanko, Ivor	United Kingdom
65.	Bowen, Brian	United Kingdom
66.	Bowes, Ray	United Kingdom
67.	Boyd, William	United Kingdom
68.	Brevik, Tom	Norway
69.	Bradley, William	United Kingdom
70.	Braine, Alfred	United Kingdom
71.	Bright, Clive	United Kingdom
72.	Bright, Dudley	United Kingdom
73.	Bright, James	United Kingdom
74.	Brakstad, John	Norway
75.	Bristow, Arthur	United Kingdom
76.	Brooks, Noel	Canada
77.	Brooks, Ray	Canada
78.	Broughton, Bruce	United States of America
79.	Broughton, Bill	United States of America
80.	Broughton, Ryan	Canada
81.	Broughton, William	United States of America
82.	Brown, Arnold	Canada
83.	Buchan, Craig	United Kingdom
84.	Bull, Ole	Sweden
85.	Bulla, Stephen	United States of America
86.	Burgess, Caleb	United Kingdom
87.	Burgmayer, Harold	United States of America
88.	Burrel, Howard J.	United Kingdom
89.	Burton, F.	United Kingdom
90.	Broadstock, Brenton	Australia

C

91.	Calvert, Morley	Canada
92.	Campbell, Timothy	United States of America
93.	Camsey, Gordon	United Kingdom
94.	Camsey, Terry	United Kingdom

95.	Carroll, W.	Canada
96.	Catelinet, Philip	United Kingdom
97.	Catherwood, David	United Kingdom
98.	Caudle, Graham	United Kingdom
99.	Challinor, Albert	United Kingdom
100.	Chase, Clarence	United States of America
101.	Chaulk, David	Canada
102.	Chesham, Howard	United States of America
103.	Cheyne, James	United States of America
104.	Christiansen, Mark	New Zealand
105.	Christmas, Jeff	Canada
106.	Clack, Michael	United Kingdom
107.	Clarke, Ian	United Kingdom
108.	Clarke, Mervyn	United Kingdom
109.	Clemons, Robert	United States of America
110.	Cocker-Hunt, Anita	United States of America
111.	Coggle, G.H.	United Kingdom
112.	Cole, Christopher	United Kingdom
113.	Cole, Nathan	United Kingdom
114.	Coles, Bramwell	Canada
115.	Coller, Charles	United Kingdom
116.	Collins, Gordon C.	United Kingdom
117.	Collins, Gordon	Australia
118.	Condon, Leslie	United Kingdom
119.	Cook, Kenneth	United Kingdom
120.	Cook, S.	United Kingdom
121.	Cooper, Frederick	United Kingdom
122.	Cooper, Maurice	United Kingdom
123.	Cordner, Martin	United Kingdom
124.	Cotterill, L.W.	United Kingdom
125.	Court, Douglas	Canada
126.	Cox, Sidney E.	Canada
127.	Craig, Charles	United Kingdom

128.	Crane, George	United Kingdom
129.	Crane, Kenneth	United Kingdom
130.	Creamer, Sam	Australia
131.	Cresswell, Raymond	New Zealand
132.	Crocker, J.	*Canada*
133.	Cruft, Adrian	United Kingdom
134.	Cuell, Edward	United Kingdom
135.	Cuell, Raymond	United Kingdom
136.	Curnow, James	United States of America
137.	Curnow, Paul	United States of America
	D	
138.	Dadson, E.V.	*United Kingdom*
139.	Dalziel, Albert	Canada
140.	Dahlstrøm, Haakon	Norway
141.	Darby, George	United States of America
142.	Davies, Howard	Australia
143.	Davis, Michael	United States of America
144.	Davis, Trevor	United Kingdom
145.	Denham, F.	United Kingdom
146.	Dennison, Robert	United Kingdom
147.	Dimond, Victor	United States of America
148.	Dickens, George M.	United Kingdom
149.	Ditmer, Bernard	United States of America
150.	Ditmer, Philip	United States of America
151.	Ditmer, Stanley	United States of America
152.	Dockerill, Frederick	United Kingdom
153.	Dockray, J.	United Kingdom
154.	Doe, Gurney	United Kingdom
155.	Dokter, Johan	The Netherlands
156.	Dorow, Reginald	United Kingdom
157.	Dove, Charles	United Kingdom
158.	Downes, T.	*United Kingdom*
159.	Downie, Kenneth	United Kingdom

160.	Drury, Albert	United Kingdom
161.	Drury, Paul	United Kingdom
162.	Dytham, Edward	United Kingdom
E		
163.	Ebbs, H.	United Kingdom
164.	Ebbs, Willaim Alex	United Kingdom
165.	Edmonds, David	United Kingdom
166.	Edwards, Alice	United Kingdom
167.	Edwards, Ernie.	United Kingdom
168.	Elgar, Edgar	United Kingdom
169.	Ellis, J.	United Kingdom
170.	Elloway, Kenneth	Canada
171.	Erzberger, Willi	Switzerland
172.	Eunson, Jeremiah	Australia
173.	Eustace, G.	United Kingdom
174.	Evans, Howard	United States of America
175.	Evans, Howard	United Kingdom
176.	Evja, Morgan	Norway
F		
177.	Fairbairn, W.	United Kingdom
178.	Farrington, H.	United Kingdom
179.	Feltwell, Ian	United Kingdom
180.	Fisher, Irwin	United States of America
181.	Fletcher, A.	United Kingdom
182.	Fletcher, Walter	United Kingdom
183.	Foote, Joseph	United Kingdom
184.	Fowler, W.	United Kingdom
185.	Francis, Les	New Zealand
186.	Freeh, Mark	United States of America
187.	Freeman Black, T.	United Kingdom
188.	Frei, Markus	Switzerland
189.	French, Edward	Australia
190.	Fristrup, Kristian	Denmark

191.	Frödèn, Rune	Sweden
192.	Frödin, Eric	Sweden
193.	Froude, H.	United States of America
194.	Fry, Fred William	United Kingdom
G		
195.	Garsegg, Bjørn Arne	Norway
196.	Gates, Dorothy	United States of America
197.	Gay, Albert	United Kingdom
198.	Gertsch, Gottfried	Switzerland
199.	Getz, Robert	United States of America
200.	Gibson, John	United Kingdom
201.	Goffin, Dean	New Zealand
202.	Goffin, Henry Charles	New Zealand
203.	Goldsmith, Arthur	United Kingdom
204.	Goldsmith, Otto	*United Kingdom*
205.	Gordon, William	United States of America
206.	Gore, William	Australia
207.	Gorling, Nathan	Sweden
208.	Gott, Barrie	Australia
209.	Goutcher, E.B.	United Kingdom
210.	Govaars, Gerrit	The Netherlands
211.	Graham, Peter	United Kingdom
212.	Grainger, Ron W.	United Kingdom
213.	Grant, D.	*United Kingdom*
214.	Grant, William	United Kingdom
215.	Gravett, Charles	United Kingdom
216.	Gray, A.	United Kingdom
217.	Gray, Harold	United Kingdom
218.	Green, James Paul	Canada
219.	Green, Walter	United Kingdom
220.	Greenfield, Albert	New Zealand
221.	Greenhorne, D.	*United Kingdom*
222.	Gregson, Edward	United Kingdom

223.	Greig, Alex	United Kingdom
224.	Greig, Cecil	Australia
225.	Griffith, Keith	United Kingdom
226.	Grindsted, Edgar	United Kingdom
227.	Groves, Peter	United Kingdom
228.	Grozinsky, Gustave	Russia/United Kingdom/Canada
229.	Gullidge, Arthur, W.	Australia
230.	Gustafson, Harold	United States of America
H		
231.	Haddon, David	United Kingdom
232.	Hague, Herbert	United Kingdom
233.	Halcrow, Lowery	United Kingdom
234.	Hall, Adam	United Kingdom
235.	Hall, Henry	United Kingdom
236.	Hall, Norman	United Kingdom
237.	Hall, P.R.	United Kingdom
238.	Hall, W.	United Kingdom
239.	Halpin, William	United States of America
240.	Hansen, Karl	Denmark
241.	Hansen, Audun	Norway
242.	Hanson, Andreas	Sweden
243.	Hanson, J.H.	Sweden
244.	Hanson, Torgny	Sweden
245.	Hannevik, John Philip	Norway
246.	Harris, James	Canada
247.	Hartill, Les	United Kingdom
248.	Harvey, Harry	Australia
249.	Hawkes, Frederick	United Kingdom
250.	Hawley, William	Canada
251.	Haydon, Claude	New Zealand
252.	Hayward, Kevin	Canada
253.	Hazell, Terry	United Kingdom
254.	Heath, George	United Kingdom

255.	Heathcote, Agnes	Canada
256.	Heaton, Wilfred	United Kingdom
257.	Hedgren, Viktor	United States of America
258.	Hedin, Elias	Sweden
259.	Heintzman, Ronald	Canada
260.	Herd, J.C.	United Kingdom
261.	Herikstad, Eiliv	Norway
262.	Himes, William	United States of America
263.	Hill, Edward H.	United Kingdom
264.	Hill, Henry	United Kingdom
265.	Hill, Sidney J.	United Kingdom
266.	Hingley, Barrie	United Kingdom
267.	Hodson, Albert E.	New Zealand
268.	Hogg, Brian	Australia
269.	Hollis, Daniel	Australia
270.	Holz, Richard	United States of America
271.	Hooton, Clifford	United Kingdom
272.	Hopkins, Duncan	Canada
273.	Hopkins, William	United Kingdom
274.	Hopkins, L.	United Kingdom
275.	Horden, Peter van der	Canada
276.	Horsey, Henry	*United Kingdom*
277.	Hubbard, Sidney Robert	United Kingdom
278.	Huguenin, Willy	Switzerland
279.	Hurley, W.J.	United Kingdom
280.	Hynd, John	United Kingdom
I		
281.	Inglis, Frank	Australia
282.	Ingram, Matthew	United Kingdom
283.	Irwin, Ross	Australia
284.	Ives, Charles	United Kingdom
J		
285.	Jackson, 'Ebbie'	New Zealand

286.	Jackson, George	New Zealand
287.	Jackson, T.	United Kingdom
288.	Jakeway, Albert	United Kingdom
289.	Jacobs, Bram	United Kingdom
290.	James, Ken	United Kingdom
291.	Johansson, Fritz	Sweden
292.	Johnson, Stuart	United Kingdom
293.	Jones, David E.	United Kingdom
294.	Jones, Dean	United Kingdom
295.	Jones, Ian	Australia
296.	Jones, Marlon	United States of America
297.	Jones, Noel	Australia
298.	Jones, Ralph	Australia
299.	Jones, Sidney	United Kingdom
300.	Jordan, Derek	United Kingdom
301.	Joy, Edward	United Kingdom

K

302.	Kane, Derick	United Kingdom
303.	Keeler, Robert	United States of America
304.	Kelley, Stanley	United States of America
305.	Kellner, Paul	United States of America
306.	Kellner, Steve	United States of America
307.	Kendrick, Wesley	United Kingdom
308.	Kenyon, Michael	United Kingdom
309.	Ketteringham, Keith	Canada
310.	Ketteringham, Kenneth	United Kingdom
311.	Key, Jack V.	United Kingdom
312.	Kiff, Douglas	United Kingdom
313.	King, H.	Canada
314.	Kippax, Milton	United States of America
315.	Kimberley, Nicolas	United Kingdom
316.	Kirk, Harry	United Kingdom
317.	Kirk, Michael	United Kingdom

318.	Kirk, Peter	United Kingdom
319.	Kirkland, Camp	United States of America
320.	Kitching, Wilfred	United Kingdom
321.	Kjellgren, Gunnar	Sweden
322.	Kjellgren, Gustav	Sweden
323.	Knight, Alec	*United Kingdom*
324.	Knight, Leonard	Canada
325.	Krinjak, Karen	United States of America
326.	Krommenhoek, Dick	The Netherlands
327.	Krommenhoek, Dirk	Canada

L

328.	Laken, Alan	United Kingdom
329.	Lamplough, Gavin	United Kingdom
330.	Langley, F.C.	*United Kingdom*
331.	Langworthy, Bert	United Kingdom
332.	Laurie, Andrew	United Kingdom
333.	Larsson, John	United Kingdom
334.	Larsson, Karl Edvin	Sweden
335.	Larsson, Kevin	United States of America
336.	Larsson, Nils	Sweden
337.	Law, W.H.	*United Kingdom*
338.	Lawson, Edward	United Kingdom
339.	Le Butt, Edwin	United Kingdom
340.	Leak, David	United Kingdom
341.	Legg, F.A.	*United Kingdom*
342.	Legg, G.F.	*United Kingdom*
343.	Leggett, Edwin	United Kingdom
344.	Leidzén, Erik	United States of America
345.	Lichtenberg, Wim van	The Netherlands
346.	Liddle, R.	United Kingdom
347.	Liechti, Walter	Switzerland
348.	Lodge, Edward J.	United States of America
349.	Lovatt-Cooper, Paul	United Kingdom

350.	Lowcock, Edward	United States of America
351.	Lundahl, Otto	Sweden
352.	Lundgren, Olof	United States of America
353.	Lundholm, Lennart	Sweden
354.	Lundkvist, Krister	Sweden
355.	Lynne, A.S.	United Kingdom
356.	Lyons, Alan	United States of America

M

357.	Macdonald, Tom	United Kingdom
358.	MacGeorge, ??	*United Kingdom*
359.	MacMahon, ??	*United Kingdom*
360.	Mack, Thomas	United States of America
361.	Mackereth, Andrew	United Kingdom
362.	Magnusson, Tobias	Sweden
363.	Main, Hector	United Kingdom
364.	Major, William	United Kingdom
365.	Mallett, Chris	United States of America
366.	Malm, Aexl	Sweden
367.	Malpass, Leslie	United States of America
368.	Malpass, Tom	United States of America
369.	Mann, ??	*United Kingdom*
370.	Manners, Keith	United Kingdom
371.	Marshall, George	United Kingdom
372.	Marshall, T.C.	*United Kingdom*
373.	Marti, Paul	Switzerland
374.	Martin, Diane	United States of America
375.	Martin, William	United Kingdom
376.	Mastin, George	United Kingdom
377.	Massarella, J.E.	*United Kingdom*
378.	McFarlene, Neville	United Kingdom
379.	McLoughlin, George	United States of America
380.	McNally, Robert	Australia
381.	Matthews, Cliff	United Kingdom

382.	Meakin, Arthur	United Kingdom
383.	Mehling, Charles	United States of America
384.	Mellins, ??	*United Kingdom*
385.	Meredith, John	United Kingdom
386.	Merritt, Henri	Canada
387.	Merritt, James	Canada
388.	Merritt, Percy	Canada
389.	Metcalf, Kevin	Canada
390.	Meyer, Donald	United States of America
391.	Millard, Arthur	New Zealand
392.	Miller, Andrew	United States of America
393.	Mills, David	Canada
394.	Millward, Cliff	United States of America
395.	Mitchell, Charles	United Kingdom
396.	Mitchell, Hubert	United States of America
397.	Morgan, David	United Kingdom
399.	Morgan, Harold	Australia
400.	Morrison, Don	United Kingdom
401.	Mott, Charles	United Kingdom
402.	Mountain, Herbert	United Kingdom
403.	Mowat, Christopher	United Kingdom
404.	Muller, Hans	Germany
405.	Munday, A.	United Kingdom
406.	Munn, Jonathan	United Kingdom
407.	Mylechreest, Edward	United Kingdom

N

408.	Needham, Phil	United States of America
409.	Nevard, E.	*United Kingdom*
410.	Newbiggin, John	United Kingdom
411.	Nieuwland, Cor	The Netherlands
412.	Noble, Andrew	United Kingdom
413.	Noblitt, Tom	United States of America
414.	Norbury, Kevin	United Kingdom

415.	Nordin, Hans	Sweden
416.	Norris, F.	Australia
417.	Ntoya, Kapela	Congo
418.	Nunn, Geoffrey	United Kingdom
419.	Nuttall, Richard	United Kingdom
420.	Nuttall, Thomas	United Kingdom

O

421.	Ogg, Ray	United States of America
422.	Okpebholo, Shawn	United States of America
423.	Olsson, Bertil	Sweden
424.	Oliphant, Celestine	United Kingdom
425.	Osborne, S.J.	*United Kingdom*
426.	Osgood, Donald	United Kingdom
427.	Otway, Harry	United States of America
428.	Østby, Klaus	Norway
429.	Owen, Edward	United Kingdom
430.	Oxley, J.	United Kingdom
431.	Ozanne, Maurice	United Kingdom

P

432.	Paine, Annie	United Kingdom
433.	Paine, W.	*United Kingdom*
434.	Palm, Ruby	United States of America
435.	Palmer-Barnes, Raymond	United Kingdom
436.	Parkins, William	United States of America
437.	Parr, Ernest	Canada
438.	Pascoe, Chelsea	United Kingdom
439.	Pattison, John	United Kingdom
440.	Payton, Orville	United States of America
441.	Pearce, Ralph	United States of America
442.	Pearson, Frederick	United Kingdom
443.	Pearson, Leonard	United Kingdom
444.	Pearson, William	United Kingdom
445.	Penberthy, Albert	Australia

446.	Pengilly, Alan	Australia
447.	Peterson, Sture	Sweden
448.	Pethybridge, Matthew	New Zealand
449.	Phillips, Richard	United Kingdom
450.	Pilley, Michael	Australia
451.	Pitcher, Grant	New Zealand
452.	Pitteway, Charlotte	United Kingdom
453.	Pittock, Dale	United States of America
454.	Pittock, Jon R.	Canada
455.	Poirier, Andrew	Canada
456.	Ponsford, Kevin	United Kingdom
457.	Ponsford, Steven	United Kingdom
458.	Post, Vernon	United States of America
459.	Poulton, Geoffrey	United Kingdom
460.	Press, Greame	Australia
461.	Prestage, ??	United Kingdom
462.	Priest, Christopher	United States of America
463.	Pullin, Stuart	United Kingdom
R		
464.	Raikes, Stan A.	United Kingdom
465.	Rance, Ernest	United Kingdom
466.	Rawlin, George	United States of America
467.	Rawlins, Kenneth	Canada
468.	Rayment, Phil	Canada
469.	Rayner, Iain	United Kingdom
470.	Redhead, Robert	Canada
471.	Reid, William	United States of America
472.	Reilley, J.	*United Kingdom*
473.	Reslow, Lloyd	United States of America
474.	Richardson, Rennie	United Kingdom
475.	Richardson, Robert	United States of America
476.	Ridenour, Mark	United States of America
477.	Ringle, Edward	United States of America

478.	Ritman, Olaf	The Netherlands
479.	Rive, Herbert	New Zealand
480.	Rive, Thomas	New Zealand
481.	Rivers, Patrick	United Kingdom
482.	Roberts, J.	*United Kingdom*
483.	Robinson, G.P.	*United Kingdom*
484.	Robinson, Graham	United Kingdom
485.	Robinson, Ian	United States of America
486.	Ros, Cornelis T.J.	The Netherlands
487.	Ross, Donald	United States of America
488.	Rowlands, ??	*United Kingdom*
489.	Rowsell, David J.	Canada (Newfoundland)
490.	Rowsell, Jonathan	Canada (Newfoundland)
S		
491.	Saggers, Herbert	United Kingdom
492.	Salt, Nigel	Australia
493.	Samuel, Nicholas	United Kingdom
494.	Samuelson, Otto	Sweden
495.	Sandberg, Amanda	Sweden
496.	Sanders, Mark	*United Kingdom*
497.	Saywell, Edward	United Kingdom
498.	Scheibner, Thomas	United States of America
499.	Schmidt, Ruben	Germany
500.	Schramm, Robert C.	United States of America
501.	Scotney, Arthur	New Zealand
502.	Scotney, Harold	New Zealand
503.	Scott, Lloyd	United States of America
504.	Sharman, Paul	United Kingdom
505.	Shaw, Darren	United Kingdom
506.	Sheldon, W.H.	*United Kingdom*
507.	Sherriff, Chas.	United Kingdom
508.	Shiels, James Jr.	United States of America
509.	Scholes, William	United Kingdom

510.	Shoults, Gerry	United States of America
511.	Shotton, Ray	United Kingdom
512.	Siddle, M.	*United Kingdom*
513.	Silfverberg, Erik	Denmark
514.	Silfverberg, Niels	Denmark
515.	Simmons-Smith, Nick	United States of America
516.	Skinner, Charles	United Kingdom
517.	Skoog, Bjorn	Norway
518.	Skoog, Jens	Norway
519.	Skyvulstad, Leif	Norway
520.	Slack, James	United Kingdom
521.	Slater, Richard	United Kingdom
522.	Slater, William	United States of America
523.	Slettholm, Yngve	Norway
524.	Smith Anthony	United Kingdom
525.	Smith, Bernard	United States of America
526.	Smith, C.	*United Kingdom*
527.	Smith, Ernest A.	United Kingdom
528.	Smith, G.S.	United Kingdom
529.	Smith, Jeremy	Canada
530.	Smith, Kenneth	Canada
531.	Smith, Stephen	United States of America
532.	Smith, Orrin	United States of America
533.	Snell, Malcolm	United Kingdom
534.	Snelson, Robert	United States of America
535.	Spencer, William	United Kingdom
536.	Spicer, Richard	United States of America
537.	Soderstrom, Emil	United States of America
538.	Sousa, John Philip	United States of America
539.	Staines, ??	*United Kingdom*
540.	Stanyon, Edwin S.	United States of America
541.	Stavik, Morgan Juel	Norway
542.	Steadman-Allen, Ray	United Kingdom

543.	Stevenson, William	United States of America
544.	Stone, Mark	New Zealand
545.	Storey, Abraham	United Kingdom
546.	Storey, T.H.	*United Kingdom*
547.	Storm, Helge	Norway
548.	Streeton, W.L.	*United Kingdom*
549.	Strehle, Kenneth Jr	United States of America
550.	Strombeck, George	United States of America
551.	Suziku, Hajime	Japan
552.	Swansbury, John	United Kingdom
553.	Swanson, ??	*United Kingdom*
554.	Squibb, Richard	Australia

T

555.	Talbot, J	*United Kingdom*
556.	Taylor, Alastair	United Kingdom
557.	Taylor, Dennis	United Kingdom
558.	Taylor, E.W.	*United Kingdom*
559.	Tebb, G.	*United Kingdom*
560.	Thomas, Martyn	United Kingdom
561.	Thomas, Martin Scott	United States of America
562.	Thomas, Percy	United Kingdom
563.	Thomas, Walter	United Kingdom
564.	Thornett, David	United Kingdom
565.	Tiberg, Wiktor	Sweden
566.	Titshall, Brian	United Kingdom
567.	Toft, Josef	United States of America
568.	Tovey, Bramwell	United Kingdom
569.	Tremain, Ronald	New Zealand
570.	Trigg, Roger	Australia
571.	Tucker, Thomas	*United Kingdom*
572.	Turkington, William	United States of America
573.	Turner, Edmund	United Kingdom
574.	Turner, Gordon	United Kingdom

575.	Turrin, Joseph	United States of America
576.	Twitchen, George	United Kingdom
577.	Twitchen, Herbert	United Kingdom
V		
578.	Vanderkam, Jules	Belgium
579.	Vaughan Williams, Ralph	United Kingdom
580.	Venables, Marcus	Canada
581.	Venables, Robert	Canada
582.	Verkaaik, Bernard	The Netherlands
583.	Verhelst, Steven	Belgium
584.	Vermeij, Ruud	The Netherlands
W		
585.	Wainwright, Andrew	United Kingdom
586.	Walkden, W.	United Kingdom
587.	Walker, Alan	United Kingdom
588.	Walker, Harold	United Kingdom
589.	Wallace, W.V.	United Kingdom
590.	Wallteng, Gustaf	Sweden
591.	Ward, Ken	United Kingdom
592.	Watson, Ty	Canada
593.	Watson, Stuart	United Kingdom
594.	Way, William	Canada
595.	Webb, Joy	United Kingdom
596.	Webber, Samuel	United Kingdom
597.	Weigle, C.F.	*United Kingdom*
598.	Welch, Glenn	United States of America
599.	Welch, J.	*United Kingdom*
600.	Wells, David	United Kingdom
601.	Wells, John	United Kingdom
602.	Werry, R.S.	*United Kingdom*
603.	Whitehouse, Alan	Australia
604.	Whitehouse, John	Australia
605.	Whitehouse, Gavin	United States of America

606.	Widmer, Werner	Switzerland
607.	Wiggins, ??	*United Kingdom*
608.	Wiggins, Archibald	United Kingdom
609.	Wilby, Philip	United Kingdom
610.	Willering, Alfred	The Netherlands
611.	Wilkinson, A.	*United Kingdom*
612.	Wilkinson, Keith	United States of America
613.	Williams, ??	*United Kingdom*
614.	Willson, Meredith	United States of America
615.	Wood, David	United Kingdom
616.	Wood, T.	*United Kingdom*
617.	Woodland, Craig	Canada
618.	Woods, G.H.	United Kingdom
619.	Worthington, Trevor	United Kingdom
620.	Wrieden, William	United States of America
621.	Wright, James	United Kingdom
622.	Wright, G.	*United Kingdom*
623.	Wright, W.H.	*United Kingdom*
Y		
624.	Young, Arthur	New Zealand
625.	Young, Herbert	United Kingdom
626.	Young Terence	United Kingdom
Z		
627.	Zealley, Harold	United States of America
628.	Zhuravlyov, Sergei	Russia
629.	Zimmerman, Martin	Switzerland

ABBREVIATIONS

A.Mus.A.	Associateship in Music, Australia
A.Mus.T.C.L.	Associateship in Music, Trinity College London (Theory)
A.T.C.L.	Associate of Trinity College of Music London (Instrument)
A.R.C.M.	Associate of the Royal College of Music
A.R.C.O.	Associate of the Royal College of Organists
B.Mus.	Bachelor of Music
D.Mus.	Doctor of Music
F.T.C.L.	Fellow of Trinity College of Music London
L.G.S.M.	Licentiate of Guildhall School of Music
L.R.A.M.	Licentiate of Royal Academy of Music
L.Mus.T.C.L.	Licentiateship in Music, Trinity College London (Theory)
L.T.C.L.	Licentiate of Trinity College of Music London (Instrument)
P.G.C.E.	Postgraduate Certificate in Education
R.N.C.M.	Royal Northern College of Music
IMED	International Music Editorial Department
PtG	Promoted to Glory – is a term used by The Salvation Army to describe the death of a Salvationist.
FS	Festival Series (SP&S) London
GS	General Series (SP&S) London
TS	Triumph Series (SP&S) London
US	Unity Series (SP&S) London
JC	Judd Street Collection (SP&S) London
AF	American Festival (USA) New York
AJ	American Band Journal (USA) New York
AE	American Instrumental Ensemble (USA) Atlanta
CM	Canadian Music Series (CND) Toronto
SF	Svensk Festmusik (SWE) Stockholm
NM	Norwegian Music Series (NOR) Oslo
SB	Scan Brass (NOR) Oslo
M/S	Manuscript (not [yet] published)
NJS	Noel Jones Series (Melbourne, Australia)
AGS	Arthur Gullidge Series (Melbourne Australia)

NZBBJ	New Zealand Brass Band Journal
NZEJ	New Zealand Ensemble Journal
MLB	Maple Leaf Brass (Toronto, Canada)
O.F.	Order of the Founder (highest praise within the Salvation Army for a a person who has served in a significant way to the Salvation Army)
The change from	1st Series (Ordinary Series) to General Series – March 1953 - No 1373
The change from	2nd Series to Triumph Series – January 1953 – No 493
The end of the	Festival Series, September 2005 – no 600
The new	'Judd Street Collection' – March 2006

INTRODUCTION

com·pos·er

1. a person or thing that composes.
2. a person who writes music.
3. an author.

'A composer (Latin com+ponere, literally 'one who puts together') is a person who creates music, either by musical notation or oral tradition, for interpretation and performance, or through direct manipulation of sonic material. The term 'composer' is often used to refer to composers of instrumental music, such as those found in classical, jazz or other forms of art and traditional music. In popular and folk music, the composer is usually called a songwriter, since the music generally takes the form of a song.'

Only but one simple question has made me started with this book:

Who is that person on the right top corner of the sheet music we play?

I have done all I can within my capabilities to answer that question. I hope that you not only enjoy reading this book but also that it explains more about that 'invisible' person.

When people ask about musical preference, you probably end up with as many different preferences as there are people you ask. Music is divided in countless styles and ways to express it. Music speaks to the hearts of people, music lives, music is emotion, music speaks, music has power, music reveals, music heals, music brings comfort, music brings joy, music… there is probably no subject that can give such endless conversations, arguments, discussions, preferences, news and knowledge as about music. People can talk about that 'one' note in a piece that makes it, or destroys it. Who wasn't impressed by the last chord of an impressive composition? Who didn't get goosebumps when hearing that first entry of a particular song?

Music has been used for thousands of years. In the Bible you can find examples of people who were either musicians or used and listened to music. Think of Saul, who invited David to play the harp for him to relax and to get calm… think of the trumpets used to destroy the mighty walls of Jericho (how powerful an instrument can be!)… Miriam who played the tambourine… and so on…

The Scriptures recognizes music as:

- a means for praise (Acts 16:25; Rom 15:9)
- a means of expressing joy (James 5:13)
- thanksgiving (Psalm 92:1-3)
- sorrow for sin (Isaiah. 16:10)
- a means of prayer (1 Corinthians 14:15; Psalm 72:20)
- and a means of teaching and spiritual communication (Colossians 3:16; Ephesians 5:19).

Biblical music makers are professional (1 Chronicles 15:22; 25:7; Isaiah. 5:11-12; Ezra. 33:32), as well as nonprofessional (Psalm 100; 1 Kings 1:39-40; 1 Chronicles 14:26; Ephesians 5:19; Colossians 3:16). There are those who direct music (Psalm 4:1, 5:1, 6:1, etc.;

Nehemiah 12:8) and teach music (1 Chronicles 15:22). The people of the Bible overflow with music in every circumstance, including cultural uses placed in positive (1 Samuel 18:7) and negative terms (Ezekiel 33:32). Music sounded in every aspect of life and work, play, celebration, and even war (Isaiah. 16:10; Jeremiah 48:33; Matthew 11:17; Luke 15:25; Genesis 31:27; Exodus 32:17-18; Ecclesiastics 2:8; Judges 11:34-35; 2 Samuel 19:35).

Jewish musicologist Abraham Idelsohn says, *'As many references in the Bible to the music performed in secular life testify, Israel enjoyed life through music both vocal and instrumental, and associated music with dance and wine in which men and women participated'.*

God has clearly His own preference for music as he gave many animals and birds in particular the gift of music. Later even music sung by birds inspired composers like Wolfgang Amadeus Mozart in their compositions. Recent research has shown that comparisons can be made and amazing similarity found in what some birds sing and what some composers trusted to the paper. A very interesting fact!

It is known that music also has been used in churches for centuries. It is also known that music was used just for fun for probably an even longer time. In my humble opinion there is no better way to make music than in service of God, through a church, and in my case, the Salvation Army. So, what is the difference between making music in church and in making music in daily life for non church related purposes. From experience one can tell the difference between playing in a group of musicians in Church and playing with a group of musicians outside church, although the musical ensembles are built up of the same instruments, and sometimes even play the same music! So if the ensembles are – more or less - the same, and the music can be the same, what can be the reason to choose either the secular way or the Church route. What are the key differences between these 'two worlds'.

Recently I spoke to a bandsman who told me that he only remained in Church 'for the music'. That was at least an honest statement! When I asked him what that (Salvation Army) music than means for him, he struggled somewhat to give an answer. *'That's a tough question'* he said, *'but it is probably that certain X factor, which makes it obviously clear for me that this is the place where I belong, even as I am not happy at the moment in the non-musical surroundings here in Church, but I never could play in a secular band, as the Salvation Army music has made me who I am today'.* The human life is a continuous development and people have to work hard to stay focused on their believes, their own rules and the things that keeps them busy. Some people have thought about music a little deeper than others and started to put some notes on paper. This resulted in music. Some composers are doing it to provide people with joyful music, other composers write music to honour God, and hope that their music will solely used for Church (or/and Salvation Army) engagements. Some became good, some became not so good, others became brilliant. The Church composers started to write musical lines for the words to be sung. Here, I assume, comes that X factor! When music is set to words that speak straight to the heart, then there will be an emotional additive. Music and words from Scripture… here you go! When someone says the prophetic words *'it is meant to be'*, I truly believe this.

People who are skilled in writing music always have fascinated me as from a very young age I can remember my own trial and errors from behind my desk at my old home. It all became a big error and soon after I realized how difficult it really is to write music. The real composers can sit for hours behind a piano playing around with chords, browsing through their own ideas, designing and shaping their own thoughts and eventually put them on paper. Some of these people deserve to be called great people, or even heroes. They are my heroes. No doubt.

Great people deserve great honour. Strong and energetic words are 'hero', 'heroes' and 'heroic'. These words alone are already powerful. Nobody can do without a hero in his or her life. Whether it is your father or mother, your teacher, your example in sport or someone else, every child needs a hero, an example to look up too. The definition of a hero is a person who is idealized for possessing superior qualities in any field. Let's say or imagine in the field of music. How many youngsters do have a hero, or idol if you like, whom they sometimes even worship? I think there aren't many without.

What does the dictionary say about the word 'hero'?

1. *a man or women of distinguished courage or ability, admired for his brave deeds and noble qualities.*
2. *a person who, in the opinion of others, has heroic qualities or has performed a heroic act and is regarded as a model or ideal: He was a local hero when he saved the drowning child.*
3. *the principal male character in a story, play, film, etc.*
4. *Classical Mythology.*
   a. being of godlike prowess and beneficence who often came to be honored as a divinity.
   b. (in the Homeric period) a warrior-chieftain of special strength, courage, or ability.
   c. (in later antiquity) an immortal being; demigod.

So, this is quite an enumeration of high profile people. Some people are born heroes or born leaders. Others become one accidentally and develop upon their achievement(s) or action(s). Real heroes are people who have done great actions but prefer to stay anonymous. Of course this is not always possible. When you have made a huge achievement publicly, you are known within certain communities, or within the world you live in. A simple fact is that if a world leader makes a positive move, he will be judged as a 'hero' the world over, while if your neighbour saves your kitten from drowning, he is either your hero or, if he or she is lucky, a local hero. Still, these people mean something to one another. Another view on a 'hero', might be that this person can do something that you can't.

When the Salvation Army started its work in darkest England in the 19th century as a humble *Christian Mission*, no one could ever imagine that one day this would be a worldwide organization, active in more than hundred countries. When the founder of this Army of Salvation started to spread the Gospel on the streets and corners of the West End in London, without any form of musical assistance, no one could ever imagine that one day, their bands would have conquered the world. When William Booth some time later met the Fry family, who became the first recognized Salvation Army band*. Even though there were only four of them (two cornets, an euphonium and a valve-trombone), he must have been very surprised when the somewhat aggressive and screaming bystanders, always willing to damage and hurt these early Salvationists with little stones, rotten fruit and eggs, became quiet when they started to play music. So in musical terms it could have been that these four people, who joined William Booth primarily to protect him from aggressive folk around, became his heroes. When at a later stage in the history of the Salvation Army the music sections begun to develop, one of the biggest needs was sheet music. It is known that much popular music had Christian words put to it (as William Booth expressed so well

'*Why should the Devil have all the good music?*'), so the songs soon became known, and were easy to sing along with. This was easy going, but soon after some early composers started to write music exclusively for the Salvation Army. For some of these people, like Richard Slater, who later became known as the 'Father of Salvation Army music', but also Arthur Goldsmith and Frederick G. Hawkes, it became part of their daily jobs, to provide the bands and bandsmen of the Salvation Army with decent and useful music. These first composing gentlemen were all part of the music department at the headquarters of the Salvation Army in London in the early 19th century.

'Father of Salvation Army music' was General Bramwell Booth's description of Richard Slater, O.F., whose story, together with much of the early history of Salvation Army music and song, was written by Arch R. Wiggins, in a booklet called '*Father of Salvation Army music*' (published by Salvationist Publishing and Supplies Ltd [SP&S], Judd Street, King's Cross, London, W.C.1 – 1945). Slater was foremost among many music makers of a Movement whose singing and playing has encircled the globe. '*Won from infidelity through a simple but eminently practical testimony*', says General Carpenter in his foreword in this book, 'this brilliant man lived among us for nearly sixty years as an example of humility, unselfishness and devotion to Christ our Lord'. The vast influence of his compositions will become a little clearer to Salvationists and others through his life story. Truly a remarkable man, and a true hero as well. A hero without knowing he was one.

**the Fry ensemble actually was the first Salvation Army band ever, however the first official Salvation Army brass band was the Consett Band.*

About the Consett Band: *'The first chord is enough to convince you of its excellence, the tone is remarkably fine, the ensemble is compact, and the solo work is marked by fine phrasing and artistic expression.' S.C. (The Bandsman and Songster, April 20, 1907).*

In the book '*Ever Heard the Sound?*' I have already mentioned several of my personal heroes. People like Eric Ball, Thomas Rive and Erik Leidzén, just to name but three of the many mentioned. Several Dutch heroes are also described, such as Dr. Bernard Verkaaik - and what about the Danish/American Emil Soderstrom, who could write music everywhere and at any moment, and who could also write the parts first before putting it together in a full score! Imagine what a genius this man must have been to do so! They all excelled in their own way in writing gorgeous, brilliant and fascinating brass band music which also has stood the test of time, as even nowadays their music is played by many bands in and outside the Salvation Army, the world over. People like these men are my heroes. In the continuation of this book, I will try to tell something about the lives of other composers as well.

Herbert Twitchen

Another hero who comes to mind but in a completely different way was Herbert Twitchen. Herbert was brought into the Salvation Army by his parents and soon had his eye on the band in which he would love to play. Although he had practiced the whistle at home, when he saw Trumpeter Sheard playing the cornet to accompany William Booth he was in the spell of this instrument and promised himself to take every chance he got to learn to play this instrument. When he found an opportunity to sit within the band he suddenly found a cornet from one of the bandsman who went to the Mercy seat. He took the instrument and during an accompaniment put the horn on his lips and tried to blow. Surprisingly he got a sound and it was even in tune, so he tried it a second time and also this time he could produce a tone that was in tune. He then thought immediately that he had mastered the instrument. When he had to give back the cornet to its owner he watched every cornet player he could find to see how they did it. How they played this instrument. Just trying to learn by watching. It didn't take long before he had written down a scale sheet and learnt how to use his fingers on the instrument. Each time a cornet player went away for any reason during a meeting, Herbert would fill the vacancy in the band. Sometime later he bought a little booklet for two pence, on harmony and counterpoint, trying to master the rules and laws of music theory. A circumspect band sergeant was watching young Herbert, and soon after the two became friends, meaning that this person guided him and taught him how to play music and explaining all he want to know about it. When he reached the age of nine, Herbert Twitchin joined the solo cornet section of the band. Persistence and lots of patience brought him further success and it was only a matter of time before he was known for his musical capabilities.

When the Regent Hall Corps had its jubilee in 1932, Herbert Twitchen took the Regent Hall Band to Buckingham Palace to play for the royal family. Another special fact was that he often was featured during concerts and other engagements playing the cornet with his right hand while accompanying himself on the harmonium! For many years this feature remained on the band's program. Somewhere in 1910, after nearly thirty years in the band, most of the time as its deputy bandmaster, Bert was asked to take up the position as bandmaster. This was much more difficult than it looked and therefore he asked for some time for consideration and reflection. His long association with bandmaster Blowers had shown that even as deputy, there was far more than being his assistant for musical matters. It was also about taking care for his fellow bandsmen, including spiritual welfare. Although he became aware of this immense task, he accepted it with pride. As a firm believer in the Army's principles and practices, he knew his men would keep in step with him as the band now entered a new era in its already colourful history and career.

When Herbert became the bandmaster, several bandsmen wished that he would re-organize the band, by removing the lesser skilled players and make it strong like a contest band. But he didn't. He was by far first and foremost a Salvationist, only the Kingdom of God was his priority. They were his bandsmen, by now all good Salvationists, with many of them having a impressive amount of years with service within the Salvation Army and the Regent Hall Band. So with a kind attitude towards the men, but managing the band with firm hand, he led the band until his retirement, some thirty-seven years later. Soon after he had accepted the baton of the Regent Hall Band, the band begun to move forward and the quality of playing increased. Their fame became known in and far beyond the borders of London. When King Edward VII died in 1910, no civilian band was allowed to play on the forecourt of Buckingham Palace, although Herbert Twitchin managed to get his band there to play suitable music for this sad occasion, including favourite hymn tunes of the King. This was the band's first visit to Buckingham Palace, and opened many possibilities for future visits of the Salvation Army. Often people asked Herbert Twitchen how he managed to get the band where it was now. He always saw this as a huge opportunity to put his local officers (band board) to the front explaining that he wouldn't be anywhere without them. His geniality made him almost a genius at bringing the best out of all types of people. When the band decided to do an open air concert in one of London's better neighbourhoods, one of the wealthy people living there didn't like what he saw and heard and tried to disturb the activities of the Salvationists on the street by turning the amplifier of his radio to the max.

When some moments later he tried to contact the bandmaster, all he got was a big smile and a wave. There upon he decided to call the police to end the noise of this Salvation Army band. The police officer then told him *'look, this band was playing on this corner before you were born, and the King himself has had them at his palace. Now, be advised by me, switch off your radio and make friends with the bandmaster and his lads'*. Fortunately the good man saw the wisdom of those words and surrended. Later, he became one of the best friends of the band in that area.

Not many problems came on his way during his tenure as bandmaster. However one is very well worth mentioning. After an accident bandmaster Twitchen was hospitalized and had to stay there no less than eleven weeks. Far from home, his work, his activities, and of course his band. This was a tough and trying experience for him, and one he didn't liked at all. But in the hospital several opportunities arose to get in touch with other people and to spread the Gospel in an easy and simple way. When he was able to change his bed for a wheel chair, people soon found him behind the piano, practicing his fingers, meanwhile blessing people with his music. On a certain day in hospital he requested some manuscript paper and started to compose a march. To write music in such an environment is really a 'tour de force' and needs lots of discipline. Here he managed to finish his first ever composition, a march called *'Deliverance'* (band journal 725). The life of bandmaster and composer Herbert Twitchen was full of good deeds, not only for his band, his bandsmen and music in general, but even more so for his fellow men and neighbours.

This resulted in the fact that during a farewell meeting to General Evangeline Booth he was called up on the platform to receive the highest honour within the Salvation Army a soldier can get, 'The Order of the Founder' (O.F.). The accompanying text says:

'Bandmaster Herbert W. Twitchin, Regent Hall Corps, London, has rendered exceptional service in Regent Hall Corps for over fifty years as bandsman and bandmaster; has shown unwavering loyalty to the flag; has faithfully adhered to regulations, and brought the band to a high standard of musical efficiency and personal religion; has set an example of true Salvationism to the world; and was honoured by Their Majesties King George V and Queen Mary in 1932 on the occasion of a visit by Regent Hall Band to Buckingham Palace'.

Although still young at heart, the bandmaster started to realize that the years had taken its toll, and in March 1947 he retired as bandmaster of probably one of the most famous Salvation Army bands ever, the Regent Hall Band. Many people payed tribute to this great man –a hero to many- which even included a message from a prisoner in Parkhurst Prison which was signed with *'One of your unknown friends'*. In his last appearance as bandmaster of the Regent Hall Band Herbert conducted the band in Bramwell Coles' *'Stand by the Flag'.* When he was finally released from his duties as bandmaster of the Regent Hall Band or Rink Band as it was better known - the Regent Hall had been a ice skate rink before it became a Salvation Army hall - Herbert Twitchen gladly responded to many requests to appear at concerts, festivals and meetings as a guest. And although he was no longer in charge of the band, his successor insisted that as often as he could, he would march with the band. To the end of his eartly journey Herbert W. Twitchen remained in step.

Herbert Twitchen is one of the early composers within the Salvation Army, and a true hero by means of his life. One of his most well known pieces is the solo *'Silver Threads'* which was published in 1928.

He even got the unique opportunity to record a solo featuring himself as soloist! His heritage is huge, leaving other people in awe about the way he lived and the way he took care for others, his fellow men. A true example how to live right! His musical heritage however is not as large as one would wish for. Despite his limited musical output he certainly deserves the title of 'hero'!

Looking back to the definition of a hero, or a heroic figure, the link to what follows in this book is clear and would speak to everybody's imagination. I have collected the following information as a kind of reference material when bands, people, bandmasters, musicians, or any other interested people are looking for info about a 'certain' Salvation Army composer and composers who have written special compositions for the Salvation Army or its bands. In doing so, I have tried to cover many current and past composers. In most cases the information is brief, but here you know in only a few lines the most significant information about the person. Some other composers have contributed to this book with an extended story about their own life, for which I am grateful.

REQUIREMENTS

As there are many more composers within the ranks of the Salvation Army than '*only*' – saying this with utmost respect- the well known writers such as Ray Steadman-Allen, Norman Bearcroft, Eric Ball, Erik Leidzen, Kenneth Downie etc I have tried to capture as many as possible. Some requirements were taken in account before I included them:

1. they had to be published composers/arrangers or
2. they were/are well known through there many manuscripts or
3. they are recorded composers/arrangers or
4. they are of another musical significance

In this high tech era many people are trying to write music using modern equipment such as computers and often forget that it is a must to know something about music rather than just start writing and see how it sounds. Therefore I have chosen to only describe some selected names of composers and arrangers who have proven by means of the –*my*- four requirements to be of value. Of course I may have not included all of them but I have tried to do so in the hope of producing an interesting read for everyone who is interested in more than playing notes, but who likes to see something, often very briefly, about the person *behind* the music.

RECORDINGS - SINGLE COMPOSER RECORDINGS

Recordings with music from only one composer:

There were and always will be some composers whose music is more popular than others. In a perspective of time you can also clearly distinguish composers who were and are favourites with the listeners and players alike. Many of these composers therefore were honoured with recordings featuring only their own music. Almost without any exception all of these recordings became very popular because of the common interest in a person's work. Whilst most composers are honoured, proud, and excited that their music could be or would be recorded, it is hard to find a recording *without*, again you should see this over time, any of the composers named here. It is quite remarkable that many of these highlighted composers are more of less 'old school' writers. Obviously they have written music that stood the test of time. Many compositions can nowadays be called 'old fashioned', or 'faded glory', however the fact is that many of these composers and their work are having a revival, seeing the amount of new recordings using their music.

Many pieces by many composers aren't recorded, used or published so to have a recording with solely the output of a single composer is a real bonus. Not only for the composer him (or her!) self but also for historical point of view as too often only a handful pieces of the same composer is used. When someone says the name of Eric Ball, people immediately think directly to his *'Resurgam', 'King of Kings'* or *'Clear Skies'* or a dozen others of his well known output, when the name of Arthur Gullidge is named, his famous cornet solo *'Jubilate'* or his timeless *'Divine Communion'* are the first titles that show up. The same goes for other composers of course. Think on Leslie Condon with *'The Present Age' and 'Call of the Righteous'*, Ray Steadman-Allen with *'The Holy War'*, George Marshall with *'Mighty to Save'* or Klaus Östby with *'The Jolly Salvationist'* and so on. But all these composers have written so much more that is far more worth listening, playing and publishing than only their popular works! One of my personal achievements would be if bands, bandmasters or musicians who are interested or are responsible for the content of a new recording would dig into the complete library of single composers just to find out that there is more than 'just' the known and popular pieces. In fact the biggest treasures are yet to be discovered!

Below are some of the most well known composers with *their* recordings, performing groups, title of the recording and names of the tracks. This list is incomplete, although most significant recordings are named. Information about the composer himself can be found elsewhere in this book.

GEORGE MARSHALL

One of the heroes in Salvation Army music. His story is well known, being paralyzed due a tragic accident in the mines, he was in a wheelchair the rest of his life. A composer of great influence to other composers he was recognized as one of the greatest of all. Some of his compositions such as *'Mighty to Save'*, *'Army of the Brave'* and *'Horbury'*, just to name but three are timeless classics and still used very often in the current era.

'Bramwell Coles and George Marshall were inspired in their march writing by the compositions of John Philip Sousa. When Sousa and his civilian concert band toured Europe in 1905 the teenaged Coles, already a music student and a member of the Chalk Farm Band's saxophone section, was taken by Bandmaster A.W. Punchard to Queen's Hall to hear and see the American visitors. Of that occasion Bramwell Coles later wrote; 'The playing of 'the Stars and Stripes for Ever' stirred every pulse and fibre in

my body'. After their London triumph Sousa and his band went to Newcastle, where 17 year old George Marshall was in the audience. He too fell under Sousa's spell and was fired with the ambition to write marches. Fortunately, the banding suspension he received for attending the 'worldly' concert did not deter him. His first march 'The Citadel' was published in 1912. In 1930 Sousa and Coles met at an Army jubilee in New York. The great man congratulated the Salvationist most warmly after hearing massed bands play his 'In The Firing Line'. Colonel Coles has long been recognized as the Army's 'march king'. Bandmaster George Marshall OF must have been a close runner up'. (source; The Salvationist, 6 November 2004).

- INTERNATIONAL STAFF BAND* – **Soldier of Christ**

(Mighty To Save, My Treasure, Ransomed, Jesus Himself Drew Near, Army Of The Brave, The Lord Is My Shepherd, The Liberator, The Greatest Of These, O Glorious Morn, Horbury)

*and massed songsters

A part of the text on the sleeve of this LP says the following (written by Ray Steadman-Allen, at the time Head of the International Music Editorial Department): *'the music of George Marshall (1887-1956) continue to be an inspiration to those who know his story and work. When he was a young man of thirty, a Salvation Army Bandmaster and already making his mark as a composer, his back was broken when a portion of roof collapsed at a coal face three miles under the North Sea. The reminder of his life became an epic of courage in disability. Although confined to a wheel chair, the lower part of his body being paralysed, he poured out the fruit of his creative gift in a triumphant song of faith in Christ, also accepting public engagement whenever possible'*, to proceed somewhere else on the sleeve, *'As a composer George Marshall's personal idiom and craftsmanship have put an identifiable stamp on his music, the bulk of which was produced between the two world wars'.*

THOMAS RIVE

A very neat recording made by Thomas Rive's corps band in cooperation with the Auckland Congress Hall Songsters in memory of his life and music, recorded after his passing. A brilliant and almost unlimited composer, with unfortunately a quite limited output due to his untimely passing. By far his best work, and also his most recorded is *'A Pilgrim Song'*, that even is used amongst the best bands inside and outside the Salvation Army.

- NEWTON CITADEL BAND and Auckland Congress Hall Songsters – **A Pilgrim's Songs**

(Newton Chorale, Be in time, Show me Thy face, Christ the Lord is risen, A Pilgrim Song, Rondo, Come Thou Holy Ghost, Our Blest Redeemer, Redeeming Love, I know a fount, Jesus shall reign)

KLAUS ÖSTBY

This recording is an accompanying CD that comes with the book with the same title. Unfortunately the book is (only) in Swedish, but the music is interesting enough to include it here.

- VARIOUS BANDS – **Skandinavisk Musicpionjar** *
- *(Kabelvag, For fulla segel, Jag tror pa Gud, Weber, Davids 121 Psalm, Passacaglia, Flyttfaglar, Rondo Pomposo, Den Glade Salvationisten, Da solen sjonk I vasterled, Sorgmarsch, O Herre till vem skulle vi dag a han, Till harlighetens land)*)

RAY STEADMAN-ALLEN

Much can be said about Ray Steadman-Allen and his music and it is without any doubt that a book will be written about his life and work in order to honour a man who is equally at home with any style of music. The fact there are hardly any recordings without at least a few of his compositions, and the fact that his music has became as much as popular within the secular movement of brass bands as within the Salvation Army, shows that this is a versatile composer. His output to date contains more than four hundred published works, and probably at least the same amount of compositions are still in manuscript format. Several recordings have been made with his output, amongst these are:

- INTERNATIONAL STAFF BAND & STAFF SONGSTERS – **By Love Compelled**

(The Evangelist, Blessed Be The Lord My Strength, The Ransomed Host, Remember Me, Youth's Adventure, The Christian Mission, By Love Compelled, The Christ, O Come and Adore, This Age of Rockets, Water's Edge, Gone My Care, O Lovely Name, Victorian Snapshots - On Ratcliff Highway, God Be In My Head)

- INTERNATIONAL STAFF BAND & STAFF SONGSTERS – **At the Edge of Time**

(The Scarlet Jersey, Whosoever Will, Simple Gifts, Childhood Suite, In Quiet Pastures, Humbly I Wait, Why I Love Jesus, At the Edge of Time, God of all Wonders, Evening Hymn)

An interesting recording is the following DVD. Not only Ray Steadman-Allen and his wife Joy and daughter Rosemary are seen on this celebration recording, but also Ray's other daughter Barbara, who, although raised within the ranks of the Salvation Army where she remained for more that 30 years, later on became a Reverend at Church. For more information about her, see the 'Female Composer' chapter.

- INTERNATIONAL STAFF BAND & STAFF SONGSTERS – **RSA 85 - A Birthday Celebration in Music**

(Silver Star, O Lovely Name, Blessed Be The Lord My Strength, Fantasia for Piano and Band on 'Christ is the Answer', Serenity, By Love Compelled, My New Day, The Holy War, He Giveth More Grace, Wonders Begin When The Lord Comes In, The Christian Mission, Lyric Variations, Remember Me, Romans 8 - A Brass Celebration, Vesper)

- YORKSHIRE BUILDING SOCIETY BAND – **Alpha & Omega**

(Hymn at Sunrise, In Quiet Pastures, The Beacons, Romans 8 - A brass celebration, At the Edge of Time, Evening Hymn)

- INTRADA BRASS – **Music of Ray Steadman-Allen**

(Hadleigh Camp; Go Down Moses; Pavilions of Praise; Rhapsody on Negro Spirituals - Russell Gray (Cornet): Floodtide; Southdown; Lord of the Sea; Happy in the Fight; God's Soldiers; Daystar; St Magnus (Hymn Tune))

ERIC BALL

The amount of recordings devoted to the music of Eric Ball shows clearly how much his music is loved and appreciated. His music always has been written with one goal in mind: to spread the Gospel and enlarge the Kingdom of Jesus Christ. Of course all other Salvation Army composers have done the same with the same goal in mind, but Eric Ball stands out above all of these other giants. His music is loved, played, recorded inside and outside the Salvation Army and still today he serves as an example to many composers and composers-to-be. His music is in fact loved and appreciated so much that even composers like Professor Peter Graham have composed a test piece based on a theme by Eric Ball. His march *'The Torchbearers'* was the basic idea for Peter Graham to create a major work to be featured at the National Brass Band Championships and *'The Torchbearer'* was the result, with nearly 15 minutes in length it is clear that Eric Ball is of an endless inspiration to the giants of today.

- INTERNATIONAL STAFF BAND – **Resurgam**

(Exodus; Star Lake; Clear Skies; Hold Thou my Hand; Song of Courage; Resurgam; Song of Faith from 'Songs of the Morning'; The Kingdom Triumphant)

- INTERNATIONAL STAFF BAND & INTERNATIONAL STAFF SONGSTERS – **Salute to Eric Ball**

(Torchbearers, Morning Song, The Eternal Presence, Magnificat, King of Kings, Psalm 150, Eric Ball speaks, Songs in Exile)

- INTERNATIONAL STAFF BAND & INTERNATIONAL STAFF SONGSTERS – **Highlights from A Thanksgiving Festival for the life and work of Eric Ball OBE**

(Torchbearers, Begin the day with God, Peace in our time, O Lord, Sound out the Proclamation, Pilgrim Song, In the secret of Thy presence, Love stands the test, Song of courage, Songs in Exile, The Benediction)

- BLACK DYKE BAND – **Festival Music**

(Torch of Freedom; Introduction to High Peak, spoken by Eric Ball, Star Lake; Rhapsody for Brass Bands High Peak; Festival Music; Introduction to Journey into Freedom, Spoken by Eric Ball; Journey into Freedom; A Kensington Concerto; September Fantasy Tenor Horn; Sinfonietta for Brass Bands: The Wayfarer)

- INTERNATIONAL STAFF BAND and BLACK DYKE BAND – **A Celebration in Brass**

(Torchbearers, Song of Courage, Torch of Freedom, September Fantasy, Sound out the Proclamation, Journey into Freedom, Never Give Up!, Resurgam, Songs of the Morning, Clear Skies, The Kingdom Triumphant, Star Lake)

- SOUTH LONDON FELLOWSHIP BAND – **Ball meets Leidzen**

(Good News!, To A Wild Rose, Sanctuary, The Challenge, The Kingdom Triumphant)

- MELBOURNE STAFF BAND – **Salute to Eric Ball O.B.E. A.R.C.M**

(Torchbearers, Songs of the Morning, The rock of ages, Songs in Exile, The Triumph of Peace, The Warriors Sanctuary, A greeting from Eric Ball, The Eternal Presence, Star Lake No.2, Departure, O Tell Once again, Resurgam)

- BRIGHOUSE AND RASTRICK BAND – **The Music of Eric Ball**

(Torchbearers, Melody in F, The Challenge, Prelude to The Dream of Gerontius, Petit Suite de Ballet, Song of Courage, Jewels, The Undaunted)

- CAMBRIDGE CITADEL SILVER BAND – **Profile, the music of Eric Ball, O.B.E.**

(Star Lake, Songs of the Morning, Happy Prospect, Jewels, Never Give Up, The World So Deceiving, Songs in Exile, Pledge for Service)

- HENDON BAND – **An Eightieth Birthday Tribute**

(Main Street, September Fantasy, Sunset Rhapsody, Softly Sounds the Little Bell, Andaluza, Romance, *The English Mainden)*

- CHALK FARM BAND – **Eric Ball Conducts**

(Torchbearers, The King of Kings, Sound out the proclamation, Star Lake No.2, Clear Skies, The Eternal Presence)

HAROLD SCOTNEY

The title of the LP is 'The Harold Scotney Memorial Record' and was recorded at the Sydney Opera House during the early 1970's when Brigadier Holz was the Chief Secretary for the Australian Eastern Territory. He conducted a massed band consisting of four corps bands from the Sydney area: Dulwich Hill Temple, Earlwood Citadel, Petersham Citadel and Sydney Congress Hall. All ten tracks on the album are compositions of Band-Inspector Harold Scotney:

- DULWICH HILL TEMPLE BAND, EARLWOOD CITADEL BAND, PETERSHAM CITADEL BAND and SYDNEY CONGRESS HALL BAND - **The Harold Scotney Memorial Record**

(March 'Heralds of Australia', Selection 'The Prince of Peace', March 'The Wellingtonian', Male Chorus 'Marching On', March 'Feilding', March 'The Quest', Meditation 'Nearer to Thee', March 'Wellington Citadel', Trombone Quintette 'Happy Comrades', March 'The Rally')

WILFRED HEATON

Although many compositions of Wilfred Heaton (in older Salvation Army journals [publications] indicated as 'bandsman Wilfred [or *Wilf*] Heaton' and later 'Deputy Bandmaster Wilfred Heaton') have been recorded the world over, it took until after his passing that two of the finest bands in the world –Black Dyke Band and the International Staff Band- finally recorded most of his brass band works on no less than four volumes of 'The Heaton Collection'.

- INTERNATIONAL STAFF BAND and BLACK DYKE BAND – **The Heaton Collection**

(vol.I, II, III, IV) *(Le Tricot Rouge; Contest Music; The Children's Friend (In Memorium); Victory For Me; Passing By; Partita; The Golden Pen; Just As I Am; Wonderful Words; My Treasure; Glory! Glory!; Celestial Prospect; Martyn; Praise; My Master's Will; Mercy's Light; Toccata, Oh The Blessed Lord, Five Little Pieces; Trombone Concerto; French; Annie Laurie; Beulah Land, Sinfonia Concertante for Cornet and Band, Music for Brass Sextet (Toccata - Oh, the Blessed Lord), Variations)*

A part of a concert review (2002) by the Eikanger Bjorsvik Mussiklag, one of Norways leading bands tells the following: *'The brass band world owes a great debt to Wilfred Heaton. His music - for too long almost criminally overlooked and ignored remains a musical monument to one of the greatest talents brass bands have ever come in contact with'.*

- EIKANGER BJORSVIK BAND – **Heaton**

(Celestial Prospect, Contest Music, Glory Glory, Just as I am, Mercy's Light, My Treasure, Praise, Toccata - Oh the Blessed Lord, Victory for Me)

ANDREW MACKERETH

One of the younger generation composers, Andrew made a speedy name for himself as a composer writing modern (compared to others) brass band music, which is used the world over. He became known with pieces like *'On a mission'* (great recording by the Household Troops Band) and *'Fall Afresh'*.

- COVENTRY CITY CORPS BAND – **Standard Bearers**

(Forward, Walking in the Light, Fall Afresh, Pilgrimage of Youth, Exaltation, I'll be a Light, Keep Me Praising, Standard Bearers, Time to Shine, Deep and Wide, Celebrate, Mackereth, Millennium Flourishes, Cheer Up)

LESLIE CONDON

Strangely enough only a few complete recordings have been made featuring the music by one of the greatest, and most well known of all, Leslie Condon. His compositions are legendary and still today his output is amongst the very best in the brass band world. Who doesn`t know his *'The Present Age'* or his timeless *'The Call of the Righteous'*, not to mention the solo which brought him eternal fame, *'Celestial Morn'*. He is also the composer of another speciality having written a duet for Eb Bass and BBb Bass! Only his two bands –he was vocal and Eb Tuba soloist and deputy bandmaster with the International Staff Band, and bandmaster of the Croydon Citadel Band- have recorded his music on a dedicated recording.

- INTERNATIONAL STAFF BAND – **The Music of Major Leslie Condon**

(Splendour of Youth, A Song of Praise, Fakenham Temple, Peace of Heart, Bognor Regis, The love of my Lord, Prayer of Childhood, A Call to Care, Easter Glory)

- CROYDON CITADEL BAND – **Celebration**

(Celebration, The Call of the Righteous, In Wonder Beholding, Festivity, Peace of Heart, The Present Age, Universal Message, Gift for His Altar, Song of the Eternal, Lord, How I Love You)

DEAN GOFFIN

Also one of the leading composers within the ranks of the Salvation Army, still so many years after his passing. His music is legendary and despite all the fantastic music he has written, his name will always be connected to what probably is the best known piece in the brass band history in the Salvation Army, his beloved composition, based on the hymn tune *'Aurelia'*, of course I am writing here about *'The Light of the World'*.

- CAMBERWELL CITADEL BAND – **Symphony of Thanksgiving**

(Introduction by Mr Norman Goffin, Anthem of the Free, Symphony of Thanksgiving, The Light of the World, Victorious, Wonderful Healer, Lift up Your Heart, Rondo for Euphonium and Band, The Road to Emmaus, My Strenght, My Tower, The Shadow of the Cross)

- WELLINGTON CITADEL BAND and SONGSTERS – **Where Glory Dwelleth**

(Anthem of the Free, Jesus loves me still, Where Glory Dwelleth, Ask and it shall be given you, Wonderful wonderful Jesus, Crusaders, Have you seen the Crucified, The Light of the World, Mercy, Tylney Hall, Jesus is so wonderful)

- WELLINGTON SOUTH BAND – **'Dean Goffin'**

(Alderny, Songs by the Rhine, Happy Harmony, Come Alive in Christ, Anthem of the Free, The Path of Glory, Rock of Ages, Rotorua Young People, Wonderful Jesus))

- REG VARDY BAND – **Crusader**

(My Strength, My Tower (2008 contest revision), Tylney Hall, The Compassionate Christ, Victorious, [Guest soloist: Richard Martin (principal trumpet of the Northern Sinfonia)], Neapolis, Symphony of Thanksgiving, Crusaders, Lift up your Heart, Shepherd's Carol, Alderney, Rhapsody in Brass, Wonderful Healer)

ARTHUR GULLDIGE

Arthur Gullidge is still regarded as one of the greatest composers from the southern hemisphere, his music often found on new recordings. In particular his marches are still immensely popular, but also his timeless cornet solo *'Jubilate'* and his everlasting popular devotional *'Divine Communion'* are still on the repertoire list of many bands today.

'Arthur Gullidge was in his early teens when he mastered the rudiments of music at the Melbourne City Temple Salvation Army Corps, where he eventually became deputy bandmaster. Would anyone have imagined then that he become internationally known as a composer of outstanding merit? Undertaking the responsibilities of bandmaster at Collingwood, a flourishing Melbourne inner suburban corps, his talent as a composer began to reveal itself. The 'Melbourne Temple' march was his first to be published by the Salvation Army, and its appearance was followed by other marches, selections and arrangements of national airs which captured the interest of Salvation Army musicians in many countries. He had succes in Salvation Army international music competitions, on one occasion gaining first prize in both the selection and the march sections. Among Arthur Gullidge's best known works are 'Army of Immanuel', 'Divine Communion' and 'British Melodies'. He also wrote prolifically for bands outside Salvation Army circles, where his music has always been highly popular.

When World War II broke out Arthur Gullidge was Melbourne Metropolitan's Divisional Bandmaster and bandmaster of the Brunswick Corps Band, where he directed a first class musical combination. He was the moving spirit behind the idea of a group of Salvation Army bandmen enlisting as a band. More than a score of them enlisted together and with a few non-Salvationists soon formed the 2/22nd battalion band. Arthur was appointed battalion bandmaster and given the rank of sergeant. His marked abilities as a composer and a band trainer were matched by his high standards as a Salvationist. In military camp life, as well as under the tests of warfare, he lived the life of a fully-committed Christian. Taken prisoner by the Japanese at Rabaul in 1942, Arthur Gulldige and 15 of his Salvationist comrades of the 2/22nd band were later transported by sea to a prison compound. The crowded ship was sunk in northern Pacific waters in July 1942 and the thousand or more prisoners, including the Salvationists, all lost. Of the other seven Salvationist members of the band six laid down their lives in New Britain. One managed to escape and eventually reached Australia. At the Militairy School of Music at Balcombe, Victoria, the character and courage of Arthur Gullidge have been recognised by the introduction of an annual award named 'the Gullidge Medal'. This record has been produced to honour the memory of Australia's outstanding Salvation Army Composer.'

(text: LP sleeve notes – Melbourne Staff Band 'Gullidge Festival' 1966)

- MELBOURNE STAFF BAND – **Gullidge Festival**

(The Heaven Bound Throng, Jubilate, Thoughts Divine, Army of Immanuel, Exuberance, British Melodies, Divine Communion, The Fount, Praise Him with Melody)

At the time of writing this, finally a second recording with Gullidge music is being made as it has been 70 years since the boat on which Arthur Gullidge and his comrades were captures was torpedoed by a Japanese war ship.

ALBERT JAKEWAY

Also one of the 'old school' famous Salvation Army composers, he is known, without any doubt, for his world reknowned march *'Rosehill'* which is played and recorded still today. The New York Staff Band did a full recording featuring Albert's music as part of their 'Profile Night' concert series of which the sleeve notes says; *'It is scarely credible that, during a long and distinguished career in Salvation Army music making, Colonel Albert H. Jakeway (R) had never visited New York. Nevertheless this was the case and despite torrential rain a goodly crowd of Salvationist musicians gathered in the Centennial Memorial Temple, New York City, to pay tribute to this amazing man. Colonel Jakeway celebrated his 86th birthday in 1979. He was a member of the International Staff Band for 18 years and as well as being conductor of the famous Rosehill Band for nine years, in addition of being bandmaster of the Tottenham Citadel Band and Clapton Congress Hall Bands. Additionally he spent a number of years as band instructor of Cambridge Heath SA Band. For many years Colonel Jakeway was a member of the International Music Editorial Department. He succeeded to the Headship following the retirement of Colonel Bramwell Coles. He has over hundred published vocal items and well over one hundred and forty band compositions. Throughout his retirement years, music has continued to flow from his pen and several compositions have been published. Any attempt to capture a true cross-section of the Colonel's work would be well-nigh impossible on just one record. However, we feel sure that this selection of highlights will make pleasant listening'.*

- NEW YORK STAFF BAND – **Profile II, the music of Colonel Albert H. Jakeway**

(Rosehill, Wonderful Joy, Sweetest Hallelujahs, The Joyful Pilgrim, O Happy Day, Ecstasy, Polonaise, The Great Call, Land Beyond the blue, Joyous Heart, Melody in Ab, A Song of Praise, Wings of Prayer, Wings of Joy)

RONALD HOLZ Sr

A legendary man from a legendary family. Richard Holz is still known today as the composer of *'Heralds of Victory'* just to name but one of his famous works. Also he was the 'guest of honour' in one of the New York Staff Band's 'Profile Night' series of which the sleeve notes says: *'A fourth generation Salvationist, Commissioner Richard Holz (R) has often been called 'Mr. Music' here in the Eastern Territory. He held many positions in his career as a Salvation Army officer, including three years as Chief Secretary in Australia. He retired from Chicago in 1981 where he was Territorial Commander for the USA Central Territory. He served for eighteen years as head of the Music Department of the Eastern Territory and as Bandmaster of the New York Staff Band. His compositions and arrangements are used by Salvation Army bands and choruses throughout the world. We were indeed honoured to have had Commissioner Richard E. Holz as our guest on this occasion and we feel that the highlights from this program will make pleasant listening'.*

- NEW YORK STAFF BAND – **Profile V, the music of Commissioner Richard E. Holz**

(Beneath the Cross, Connecticut Youth March, O How Glorious, Gabrielettes, Old Time Religion, Come Holy Spirit, God our Fathers)

BRINDLEY BOON

Colonel Brindley Boon has been a Salvation Army officer since 1950. He was internationally known as a journalist, songwriter and composer of vocal and brass band music and has more than 150 published works to his credit. The colonel's appointments have included the editorship of *'The Musician'* at two separate timings, the Canadian *'War Cry'* and the International *'War Cry'*. He was editor in Chief at International Headquarters and retired from active service in 1979 after serving as Chief Executive Officer for the 1978 International Congress. From 1966 to 1972 Brindley Boon served as National Secretary for Bands and Songsters in the British Territory, during which time he was a member of the International Music Board. He was a member of the International Staff Band (1952-1960), and during this time he visited The Netherlands, Switzerland, The United States of America and Canada. He is the author of some extraordinary books such as *'Play the Music, Play!'*, *'The Best of Both Worlds'* and *'ISB, The Story of the International Staff Band'*. Also Brindley was one of the long list of guest of honour in the 'Profile' series organized first by Terry Camsey, later continued by Gordon Ward, both principal cornet players with the New York Staff Band.

- NEW YORK STAFF BAND – **Profile III, the music of Colonel Brindley Boon**

(Hillside, Stand up for Jesus, A Starry Crown, To Save a Sinner, Christ of the Loom, Altar of Praise, Lay up treasures in Heaven, Lift up the Flag)

NORMAN BEARCROFT

There is hardly a Salvation Army recording known without any work by Norman Bearcroft. His marches are legendary, his solos are feared and his writing for in particular the euphoniums brought many players to exhaustion! His creatively with regarding to enjoyable 'crowd pleasing' music is nearly endless and therefore it was just a matter of time before a band would devote a complete album to him and his music. The first were the Household Troops Band, by then led by his old friend Major John Mott. In particular during Norman's tenure as Canadian Staff Bandmaster his output was huge and seemingly unlimited. It was also during this time that many of his most well known pieces were written, pieces like *'Golden Slippers'*, *'Just Like John'*, *'Sounds of Britain'* and so on.

- HOUSEHOLD TROOPS BAND and INTERNATIONAL STAFF SONGSTERS – **Tribute**

(Wreath of Courage, Just Like John, Bound For The Promised Land, Joyous Proclamation, The Better World, We're A Band That Shall Conquer The Foe, Reflections, Stories of Jesus, The Sound of Britain)

- HOUSEHOLD TROOPS BAND – **Troops Salute**

(*Wreath of Courage, Song of Exultation, Day of Jubilee, Green Hill, The Seafarer, Jesus I come to Thee, Shoes, Every time I feel the spirit, The Gospel Train, Share your faith, Wonderful story of love, On the sunny side, High fidelity, Bournemouth Centennial, The King's trumpeters, Westward Ho!*)

- HOUSEHOLD TROOPS BAND –**Tribute (DVD)**

(*Wreath of Courage, Just Like John, Stand Up And Bless The Lord, He Careth For Me, Bound For The Promised Land, Joyous Proclamation, The Better World, Down Memory Lane, We're A Band That Shall Conquer The Foe, Reflections, Stories of Jesus, The Sound of Britain, Happy Song*)

- CANADIAN STAFF BAND – **In Tribute**

(*Just Like John, The Word of Grace, Songs of Newfoundland, To Regions Fair, Londonderry Air*)

ROBERT REDHEAD

There are numerous recordings with compositions by Robert Redhead and his name is widely spread, even outside the Salvation Army, when only the name of the test piece *'Isaiah 40'* has to be named, however no full recording has yet been made. Even the one mentioned here is only but fifty percent of one, but important enough to put it down. Definitely a composer of huge significance and one who deserve at least a full recording of his compositions.

- CANADIAN STAFF BAND – **In Tribute**

(*Picton Citadel, Reflections in Nature, Shout Salvation, Jesus, Keep Me Near the Cross, Quintessence, I Know a Fount*).

- NORRIDGE CITADEL BAND and SONGSTERS – **Revelation Hope**

This CD contains a worship experience created by Colonels Robert and Gwenyth Redhead for the Norridge Citadel Band's tour of England in 1999.

01. Narration 02. All Hail The Power Of Jesus' Name Medley 03. Narration 04. Eternal God 05. Holy, Holy, Holy Is The Lord - Soloist: Ira Thomas 06. Narration 07. Thou Art Worthy (Mills) - Lamb Of God (Paris) 08. Narration 09. Power In The Blood 10. Celebrate Jesus! (Oliver) 11. Narration 12. Omega 13. Narration 14. Man Of Sorrows! - Soloist: Joan Spencer 15. Narration 16. Lo! He Comes With Clouds Descending 17. Glory To The Lord 18. Narration - Lamb Of God (Paris) 19. Glory To The Lord

KENNETH DOWNIE

Although Dr Kenneth Downie has been composing for several decades, it is only of the last two decades or so that his music was being recognized of great value to the music fraternity. Since then it has come in a fast flow and there are only few recordings these days without one or more compositions or arrangements from this well skilled man. His compositions are very popular with the best bands around the globe as well as others.

- INTERNATIONAL STAFF BAND – **St Magnus - The Music of Kenneth Downie**

(*The Joybringer, He Can Break Every Fetter, Music for a Joyful Occasion Revisited, Lord of all Hopefulness, The Father's Blessing, Concerto for Euphonium, St Magnus, Take Time, Praise Tribute, Peace , King of Heaven*)

- BRIGHOUSE AND RASTRICK BAND – **Purcell Variations**

(Bridgewater Intrada, Choose Freedom, Deep Harmony, Lord of all Hopefulness, Make Jesus King, My Father's World, Princethorpe Variations, Purcell Variations, St Austell Suite)

The International Staff Band has plans for a further compact disc with the music of Kenneth Downie, to be released in 2012, with pieces like *'Brother James' Air'*, *'Myfanwy'* and *'Oasis'*. This Downie recording will be a combination of pieces already recorded and newly recorded material, as a combination of SP&S and Kantaramusik publications.

WILLIAM HIMES

Chicago Staff Bandmaster for over three decades and extremely creative in his output. The sleeve notes accompanying this recording, written by his principal solo cornet for over three decades – Peggy Thomas- says: *'William Himes was born and raised in Michigan, where he attended the University of Michigan in Ann Arbor, receiving his Bachelor's and Master's degrees in music education and performance. Since that time he has appeared throughout the United States and Canada, Australia, New Zealand, England, Scotland Switzerland, Norway and Sweden as soloist, clinician and conductor. Well known for his compositions and arrangements Bandmaster Himes has more than 100 publications to his credit. These along with numerous manuscripts awaiting publication, are continually featured on international broadcasts and recordings. As conductor of the Chicago Staff Band, he has produced many recordings and led this outstanding 36-piece ensemble in successful concert tours of Panama, Mexico, Chile, Singapore, The Philippines, Hong Kong, New Zealand and Australia. Prior to assuming his present responsibilities as Music and Gospel Arts Director for the Salvation Army's USA Central Territory, he taught instrumental music in Flint, Michigan and was an adjunct lecturer in low brass at the University of Michigan Flint Campus'*. Next to that he also has been the bandmaster of the Flint Citadel Band prior to becoming the bandmaster of the Chicago Staff Band. This recording by the Household Troops Band (UK) is the first recording solely with his compositions and arrangements, although his music in general is recorded by countless bands around the world.

- HOUSEHOLD TROOPS BAND – **Himes (re-visited)**

(The Witness, Caprice for Cornet, Nicaea, God of Wonders, Aspects of Praise, Jericho (Re-Visited), My Christ is all in all, How majestic is your name, Festival Fanfare on St Francis, To know Thee, Milestone, Bolero, I have decided to follow Jesus, So Glad, God's Children)

RAY BOWES

One of the longest serving members of the International Staff Band, Ray was bandmaster of this great band for approximately fifteen years and a member for over four decades! He was a well respected composer with many compositions to his credit. At the end of his tenure as Staff Bandmaster, the International Staff Band recorded an album with his compositions. After his passing, his good friend Major George Wittingham, bandmaster of the South London Fellowship Band, recorded another disc with his works.

- INTERNATIONAL STAFF BAND – **The King's Crusader**

(Rhapsody for Cornet and Band, Joyous Song, Jesus Loves Me, Winterthur Centenary, The King's Crusader, The Invincibles, Youth's Ambition, Lord Show Me What I Need, Crown Of Gold, A Light Came Out Of Darkness, Song Of Triumph, Sunshine Mountain)

- SOUTH LONDON FELLOWSHIP BAND – **Crown of Gold**

(A Testimony of Praise, My Heart's Desire, Rhapsody for Cornet and Band, Abide With Me, Song of Triumph, Winterthur Centenary, Jubilant Faith, David of the White Rock, Sunshine Mountain, Armadale, Crown of Gold, Ask the Saviour to Help You, Harlesden)

ERIK LEIDZEN

Erik Leidzén stands amongst the greatest of all when in concerns composers in the Salvation Army. He was a very close friend of Eric Ball, another doyen in Salvation Army composing. Eric Ball wrote about Erik Leidzen: *'Born in Denmark, Erik Leidzén composed, taught and conducted for the greater part of his life in the United States of America. His work as composer and arranger for wind bands became widely known, but for Salvationists his music suited their particular form of Christian service, a matter of the greatest importance. Following the tradition of including within his compositions well known hymn and song tunes, he clothed these in fine harmonic and contrapuntal sounds, with immaculate scoring well worth study by all interested in brass bands. Yet the simple tunes were never overwhelmed, they can be heard clearly amidst the most involved of his works. It is said that he cared for 'The little old lady in the back row of his concerts''.* Although many bands around the world have recorded his music –Erik Leidzén's music is still today incredible popular- only a handful of recordings have seen daylight, with the most current one from Imperial Brass (USA).

- INTERNATIONAL STAFF BAND – **The Invincible Army**

(The Invincible Army; Song of the Brother (Derick Kane - Euphonium); Sweet Hour of Prayer; None Other Name; Steadily Onward; A Robe of White; The Cleansing Stream (Kevin Ashman: Soprano Cornet & Stephen Cobb: Bb Cornet); The Children's Friend; On The Way Home)

- SOUTH LONDON FELLOWSHIP BAND – **Ball meets Leidzen**

(Pressing Onward, Songs in the Heart, On The King's Highway, Concertino for Band and Trombone, The Call, The Children's Friend)

- NEW YORK STAFF BAND - **The Erik Leidzen Memorial Album**

(The Gift of God's Love, March of the Hours, Danish Rhapsody, Steadily Onward, We Have An Anchor, Joyful Duty, On the Way Home)

- STOCKHOLM 7 BAND – **This man Leidzén**

  (Den Oövervinneliga Armen, Hjartats Sanger, Intet Annat Namn, Ljuva Bonestund, Standigt Framat, Barnens Van, Concertino for Musikkar och Trombone, Botturno Religioso)

- IMPERIAL BRASS (USA) – **Leidzén**

(Jesu, Joy of man's desiring, Air in D, Sarabande, Preludes and Fugue, Toccata & Fugue in D Minor, Fantasia in G Major, Siciliano, Gigue Fugue – [at the time of writing it was not hundred percent known what the final repertoire would be, while also the title of the recording itself was not known])

- LEYLAND BAND – **Songs in the Heart**

(Pressing Onward, Songs in the Heart, Post Bellum Rhapsody, What a Friend, Concertino for Band and Trombone, Jesu Joy of Man's Desiring, EFG, Sinfonietta, Humouresque, The Children's Friend, The Song of the Brother, Abide with Me, Manhattan, The Old Rugged Cross, None other Name)

WILLIAM GORDON

His many arrangements and compositions for brass and concert bands are performed world-wide and their popularity is evidenced by the numerous recordings they receive. His music is included in the repertoires of some of the world's top bands, including the International Staff Band of the Salvation Army and The Black Dyke Band. Having served as conductor of the The Pasadena Tabernacle Band of The Salvation Army, he now travels extensively as a guest lecturer and conductor and is a member of ASCAP. (source: gordon-music.com)

- AMSTERDAM STAFF BAND – **Christmas in Brass**

(A Christmas Festival, Angels of Christmas, Away In A Manger, Carol Of The Bells, Christmas Bolero, A Christmas Canon, A Christmas Fanfare, The Christmas Song, Deck The Halls, Fiesta Navidad, Huron Carol, Il Est Ne, Jingle Bells, Let It Snow, Midwinter Carol, O Little Town Of Bethlehem, O Ye Merry Gentlemen, Rudolph, The Red-Nose Reindeer, Silver Bells, The Sounding Joy, Still, Still, Still, The Twelve Days Of Christmas, What Child Is This?)

- PASADENA TABERNACLE BAND – **Brass Praise**

(Make His Praise Glorous, In His Presence, Great is The Lord, Oh How He Loves You and Me, O Magnify the Lord, Because of who you are, He Liveth, Shine Down, In Moments like these, Messiah Choruses, Healing Stream, In Majesty He will come, King of Glory, Be Thou my vision, Holy Ground)

- INTRADA BRASS – **Apocalypse for Brass**

(Apocalypse for Brass, Assurance Variations, Big Band Spirituals, Church Windows, Fortress, Hommage Hymn, O Sacred Head, Processional for an Occasion, Saint Gregory the Great, Soon and Very Soon, Yankee Doodles)

- MONTCLAIR CITADEL BAND – **Spirituals for Brass**

(Chariots; I Got Shoes; He Never Said a Mumblin' Word; Old Time Religion; cornet duet - A Balm In Gilead; Amen; Amazing Grace; Steal Away; Go Tell It On the Mountain; Last Tango In Jericho; trombone solo - My Lord, What a Morning; Somebody's Knocking at Your Door; This Little Light; Give Me Jesus - trombone feature; Go Down Moses; Deep River; Wade In the Water; Nobody Knows; Sometimes I Feel Like a Motherless Child; I'm Gonna Sing 'Till the Spirit Moves In My Heart)

EMIL SODERSTROM

One of the most extravagant composers of all. For years a misunderstood man, yet brilliant in all his compositions. He got the opportunity to conduct the International Staff Band a few times during band practices and immediately made an impression by telling people exactly what they did wrong and how he wanted it. Emil could write music anywhere, anytime and under all circumstances. He was also known as the brilliant mind who could write parts before writing down a score! The recordings accompanying the book about his life are of great value to the Salvation Army banding history, with some unique and rare recordings.

- Three free recordings of rare and historic compositions come with the book '**Anecdotal Snapshots of Genius**', (the Music of Emil Soderstrom) written by Robert Getz. Significant pieces that are on the these recordings (played by various bands):

Song of Israel, Fighting for the Lord, On the Sea, Army of God, Deep Passage, Gartnergade, O Love that wilt not let me go, Minneapolis IV, Long Beach, Down From His Glory, O God our help, Southland Memories, California, American Rhapsody, March of the Hours, Low in the Grave He lay, Coronation,

Central States, Beautiful Canaan, Chicago Staff Band Jubilee, Swoneky, Rockford Temple, The Jubilee, Tranas.

PETER GRAHAM

One of the most important composers in the current brass band repertoire, currently with an emphasis on the secular movement. Dr. Peter Graham started his career within the Salvation Army in Scotland. For some years he lived in the United States of America where he played cornet with the New York Staff Band, meanwhile writing many new compositions for the band. Back in the United Kingdom he became bandmaster of the Regent Hall Band in London. After this he moved on working at Salford University where he is still teaching. His music is equally popular within the Salvation Army as elsewhere, proven by the fact that the probably two best bands of 'both worlds' have recorded CDs with his music.

- INTERNATIONAL STAFF BAND and BLACK DYKE BAND – **The Peter Graham Collection**

(Montage [1. Intrada, II. Chaconne, III. Rondo], Harrison's Dream, In League With Extraordinary Gentlemen [I. The Time Traveller, II. The Adventure of the Final Problem, III. The Great Race], The Torchbearer, The Ambassadors, Ad Optimum, St Teresa, The Last Amen, Blazon, Shine As The Light, The Dawning, Seize the Day)

- BLACK DYKE BAND – **Call of the Cossacks**

(Summon the Dragon; Windows of the World; Whirlwind; Swedish Folk Song; Shine as the Light; The Name; Gaelforce; Cartoon Music; The Whistler; Hine e Hine; Slavisch Fantasie (Hohne); Call of the Cossacks)

- BLACK DYKE BAND – **Music composed by Peter Graham**

(Dimensions; Prisms; The Essence of Time; Montage; On Alderley Edge; Crimond)

EILIV HERIKSTAD

For a long time a composer and arranger who is trying, with success to drive the brass band movement towards different directions. He was one of the very first composers to step aside from the normal route regarding writing as he was and still is a fan of the lighter music. His *'The Lily of the Valley'* and *'A Joystrings Review'* are good examples of this. He also shocked the Salvation Army banding world when he released his *'On Parade'* which was quite controversial at the time. He is a highly appreciated composer the world over. Finally a recording was made with only a 'Herikstad' tracklist, recorded by the Norway Territorial Band and conducted by the composer.

- NORWAY TERRITORIAL BAND – **Take it on Trust**

(On Parade, In the Sanctuary, Oh, How Quickly Time Fleets By, Thou Art!, A Joystrings Review, Heaven Came Down, Grace There Is My Every Debt To Pay, I'll Trust In Thee, I See You Through The Window, Joyful Follower, The Lily of the Valley, Be Not Afraid!, We Shall Sing, Schaffhausen, Teach me)

BARRIE GOTT

Barrie Gott, composer of many works with a lighter character, although he also wrote music in the more traditional way such as his uplifting march *'Collaroy'* (named after a

Australian music camp). He was bandmaster of the Sydney Congress Hall Band (Australia), Pasadena Tabernacle Band (United Stated of America) and the Brisbane City Temple Band (Australia) in that order. Although for many years a published composer, he got world recognition with his pieces such as *'Daniel'*, *'Godspell'* and his immense popular *'Lightwalk'*. The recording named below isn't played by a Salvation Army band, though still a great tribute to a great composer!

- THE RANSOME BAND – **Mumbo Jumbo**

(Declaration Overture; Mumbo Jumbo; Godspell, Adagio; Let there by Praise; Jazz Suite; Adagio; Lightwalk; Glasshouse Sketches; Daniel; Danny Boy; Gospel Train; Appalachian Overture)

EDWARD GREGSON

Like Peter Graham, Edward is currently primarily writing for non Salvation Army groups, with an emphasis even outside the brass band movement. A one time bandsman of the Tottenham Citadel Band (now Enfield Citadel Band). Although writing for nearly half a century, his first publication was the march *'Dalarö'*. He became known to the wider audience when his brother Bramwell brought the Salvation Army London Citadel Band (Canada) to the United Kingdom for which event Edward wrote his probably best known piece '*Variations on Laudate Dominum*'. The 'early' Edward Greson is particularly known for his Salvation Army repertoire. Of particular interest is his '*Concertante for Piano and Band*' which is a rarely heard piece but recorded on the first ever LP by the London Citadel Band.

- BLACK DYKE BAND – **The Trumpets of the Angels**

(An Age of Kings; Symphonic Rhapsody for Euphonium and Band; Concerto for Tuba and Band; The Trumpets of the Angels)

- BLACK DYKE BAND – **The Edward Gregson Collection**

(Dalarö, Voices of Youth, March Prelude, Essay, Concerto for French Horn and Brass Band, Partita, Chalk Farm No. 2, Variations on Laudate Dominum (revised), Tuba Concerto, Connotations, Dances and Arias, Of Men and Mountains, The Trumpets of the Angels, Before The Cross, An Age of Kings, Rococo Variations)

- WILLIAMS FAIREY BAND – **Gregson**
- *(Chalk Farm No. 2, Intrada, March Prelude, Music for Greenwich, Occasion, The Pacemakers, Patterns, Processional, A Swedish March, Voices of Youth)*

JAMES WRIGHT

James was a former bandmaster of the Sheffield Citadel Band and earned huge respect from his bandsmen. Although not a composer with the largest output of all, he certainly has made an impression on many. His arrangement of *'As The Deer'* has been played numerous times around the world by countless bands.

- SHEFFIELD CITADEL BAND – **Legacy**

(Clowne Centenary, As the deer, Fantasia for Children, Breathe, To Praise the Lord, Burdens are lifted, Lord of all, Lost in Thee, Dimensions of Youth, Move in my life, The sound of glory, You raise me up, Shine on Us, St Clements)

LLOYD W. SCOTT

Too little is known and published of Lloyd Scott, an American Salvation Army officer and a one time baritone player with the New York Staff Band. Although his name was known and recognized, the recording by the Montclair Citadel Band of *'The Solid Rock'* (cornet soloist Ron Waiksnoris) on the 1990 double CD released for the International Congress certainly helped him to expand his name as composer. Fortunately also Lloyd Scott was honoured in the United States with a recording (only released on Cassette tape) of his own music as part of the 'Profile Night' series.

- MONTCLAIR CITADEL BAND – **The Music of Lloyd Scott - All My Work is For the Master (**TRC-131)

Montclair Citadel Band and Songsters: Philip Smith, Bandmaster, Lindsay Evans, Songster Leader: I'll Stand for Christ (Band March) Songs of Joy and Praise (Band Selection) The King's Domain (Comments - Mrs. Major Lloyd Scott, Band Selection) I Have No Claim on Grace (Comments by Major Lloyd Scott, Songsters) I Will Follow Thee, My Saviour (Songsters) St. Bees (Band Meditation), Near to the Heart of God (Comments - Major Lloyd Scott, Band Song Arrangement), All My Work is for The Master (Songsters) The Solid Rock (Sheila Smith, Vocal, Philip Smith, Trumpet) Endless Day (Band March) God is Stronger Than His Foes (Songsters) Jesus, Where'er Thy People Meet (Songsters) The Disciples' Call (Congregation and Brass Ensemble) Old Orchard Centenary (Comments - B/M Philip Smith, Band March)

PHIL CATELINET

Who doesn't know the famous cornet duet *'Deliverance'* by Phil Catelinet? So many upcoming soloists have played this unique duet, making their first appearance on the 'Path of Soloists'. *'Deliverance'* has been a great piece for so many years but 'easy' music (if such a thing exists) was not his only strength. Many other pieces were written with great craftsmanship, with *'A Sunbeam'* being one of his master pieces.

- MONTCLAIR CITADEL BAND - **PROFILE IV, The Music of Retired Bandmaster Philip Catelinet** (TRLPS 38)

March 'Pittsburgh Temple' (Montclair Band), Vocal Selection 'Hallelujah to the Lamb' (S.F.O.T. Ensemble), Piano Solo 'Sonata' (Retired Bandmaster Philip Catelinet), Air Varie 'A Sunbeam' (Montclair Band), Piano Solo 'The Little Letters' (Retired Bandmaster Philip Catelinet), Vocal Selection 'Morning and Evening' (Temple Chorus, accompanist Patricia Geese), Comments of Retired Bandmaster Philip Catelinet Air Varie 'The Valiant Heart' (Montclair Band), Congregational Song 'Make the World with Music Ring'.

HOWARD DAVIES

One of the most significant musical figures within the Salvation Army in his homeland Australia, although he has worked in the United Kingdom and New Zealand as well. An enormous output definitely enriched the total musical repertoire of the Salvation Army worldwide. He has a long connection with his home corps Camberwell, where he was also bandmaster for a short period prior to becoming a Salvation Army officer. It is no surprise that it was decided to record a complete album of his music.

- CAMBERWELL CITADEL BAND and SONGSTERS – **Joy and Devotion**

(Joy and Devotion, On the way to Heaven, Bounty Down, Songs of Encouragement, How can I thank You?, He Found Me, Soldier Saint, God can do the impossible, He never said a mumbling word, The Wonder of His Grace, Praise Him with song, Behold the Saviour)

BRAMWELL COLES

One of the most recorded composers, with on many recordings at least a march penned by him, it has taken too long before a complete recording saw daylight featuring his music. Fortunately a book about his life and music was accompanied with a full recording, with much of his huge output. Many of his pieces were and still are incredibly popular, such as *'Victors Acclaimed', 'In the Firing Line'* and *'The Divine Pursuit'*, just to name but three. As just mentioned, it is a real bonus to have a recording available with only his music on it. The 'unfortunate' factor here is that they are all old recordings, digitalized and put on a new CD. Therefore it would be interesting to have a complete new recording scheduled with solely the music of Bramwell Coles. Until that time, see below.

- VARIOUS BANDs – **In the Firing Line**

(In the Firing Line, Atonement, The man of sorrows, Discipleship, The old rugged Cross, Divine Sufficiency, Victors Acclaimed, Here at the Cross, The Divine Pursuit, Portraits from St. Paul's Epistles, The King's Musicians, Departed Heroes)

*This recording is an accompanying CD which comes with the book of the same title (In the Firing Line).

While Bandmaster Marshall was preparing his march for publication Captain Bramwell Coles, in charge of the corps at New Barnet, was working on 'Under Two Flags'. The march took a year to write and, when it was completed, the captain, not trusting the precarious postal service of the day, committed it to the tender care of Corps Secretary Wilfred Coward, an SP&S employee. To ensure its safe arrival on the music editor's desk, Bramwell Coles met Wilfred's train at the local station that evening for confirmation! 'Under Two Flags' published in September 1919, became an immediate hit, with its skilful weaving of patriotic airs. It was intended as a tribute to Salvationist military personnel. The composer repeated his success during the Second World War with 'Victors Acclaimed' when he specially remembered his own seven children serving with the Forces. Gordon, the eldest, spent more than three years in Japanese prison camps. His daughter, Joan, served with the Wrens. All but one of them became Salvation Army officers and two of them, Alan and Dudley, serving as commissioners (source; The Salvationist 6 November 2004).

EDGAR GRINDSTED

Although by no means a recording with band music, this is still music by and for one single composer and therefore more than worth a mention here. This LP was produced by Stewart Edgar Grinsted, son of Edgar.

- **Edgar T Grinsted… The People's Mate... Come to Jesus… Echoes of…**
    1. Happy, Happy Day (Edgar and his wife Olwyn)
    2. A Bright Side Somewhere (daughter Susan, 1976 at home around the piano)
    3. Dudley Carol Service 1959 (Edgar, piano, Susan and Roger, soloists)
    4. Bromley Youth 1973
    5. New Abbott 1975 (Edgar at the Piano)
    6. Precious Jesus (Edgar and his wife Olwyn 1976)
    7. Come to Jesus (Edgar and his wife Olwyn 1976)

8. The Clean Heart Engineering Company (Farewell Sunday as Divisional Officer of the South London Division at Bromley Temple 1973)
9. Benediction (Fairfield Hall 1972)

RECORDINGS - COMPOSER TRIBUTE RECORDINGS

Other approaches to highlight the music of certain and specific composers can be found on recordings especially made for in particular overseas tours or in praise of composers for a special reason, or composers from a certain region or country. The International Staff Band (ISB) and International Staff Songsters (ISS) did this on several occasions, like their 1983 (joint) recording featuring music from New Zealand composers. The New York Staff Band did this to honour three of their countrymen, who all became famous by means of compositions, and the Camberwell Citadel Band from Australia did this also to two of their 'own'. Information about these composers can be found elsewhere in this book.

Trevor Davis, himself a noted composer and at the time working as a Salvation Army officer in New Zealand, wrote the accompanying text for a recording which says: *'When the first Salvation Army open-air meeting in New Zealand was conducted in Dunedin on 1st April 1883, the singing was accompanied by the lone concertina of Captain George Pollard, pioneer along with Lieutenant Edward Wright. By December of the same year, five well established brass bands, plus a drum and fife band, participated in the first Congress to be held, also in Dunedin. Every-day musicians like Bandmaster Tucker, George Jackson and his brother Ebby Jackson, Albert 'Wingy' Hodson (all composers, and described in this book later on) and many others established Salvationist music making on a firm footing, and through one hundred years of Salvation Army service in the islands of New Zealand, music has been used efficiently and effectively'.* He then proceed with; *'Amongst musicians, one can of course identify performers of great virtuosity, conductors of distinction and composers of note. This Album ('Heritage of Praise') serves to highlight the contribution of this last group of people (the composers), for there have been many from the relatively small population of New Zealand who have rightly earned world-wide repute. One only has to refer to the Cresswells, the Goffins, the Millards, the Rives, the Scotneys or the Tremains to attract international and immediate recognition. The International Staff Band and International Staff Songsters join forces to present music from New Zealand composers (though not all can be included on a single recording!)'.*

Indeed composers like Dean Goffin and Thomas Rive, just to name but two can be counted to the very best the Salvation Army ever has produced. The fact that they came from a thin populated country makes it even more special.

RONALD TREMAIN [1]

HAROLD SCOTNEY [2]

HENRY C. GOFFIN [3]

THOMAS RIVE [4]

HERBERT RIVE [5]

RAY CRESWELL [6]

DEAN GOFFIN [7]

- INTERNATIONAL STAFF BAND and STAFF SONGSTERS – **Heritage of Praise**

  A Tribute to New Zealand Salvationists by the International Staff Band and International Staff Songsters - :

Praise [1], The Wellingtonian [2], Maidstone [3], Christ the Lord is risen today!, Look Ye Saints!, Redeeming Love, Be in time [4], The King's Command [5], The Happy Heart [6], Shepherd's Carol, The Shadow of the Cross, Lo! He comes with clouds descending [7]

In 1995 the New York Staff Band, the oldest Staff Band in the world and probably also the most recorded Staff Band, decided to do a recording completely devoted to 'a few of their own', namely famous members of the Broughton family. Three of them, Brigadier William Broughton (1884-1950) and two of his grandsons, William and Bruce would feature on their new CD. Brigadier William Broughton has been a huge influence on many within no less than three territories in the USA as he was for a time bandmaster of the New York Staff Band, the Chicago Staff Band and the Western Territorial Staff Band (California) which was for a long time defunct but was reinaugerated some years ago and now renamed as the Western Territorial Band.

WILLIAM BROUGHTON Sr [1]

WILLIAM (BILL) BROUGHTON [2]

BRUCE BROUGHTON [3]

- NEW YORK STAFF BAND – **The Broughtons**

(The Santanian [2], Come and Get Saved [3], Take Up Thy Cross [2], In the Garden [3], Wonderful Words [2], The Gold Old Way [3], America [1], In Perfect Peace [2], Big Little Light [2], Now I Belong to Jesus [3], Swing That Door [2], The Prayer Meeting [3], Thinking of Jesus [3], Covenant [3], Carry On [1])

Australians are always proud on their own 'sons' and history shows that in that part of the world a significant number of Salvation Army composers have provided music for the Army's purposes. Apart from several well known men two are highlighted on a (cassette tape) recording *'The Joy of Service'.* The text in the sleeve notes already gives a good idea of the profile of these two composers; *'Noel is the son of officer parents, Brigadier and Mrs John Jones. Together with his wife Mary and children they soldier at the Ringwood Corps in Melbourne, Australia. He gained the A.Mus.A for pianoforte teaching when only a teenager and since then has devoted a lot of time to teaching young folk particularly within the ranks of the Salvation Army. Noel enjoyed twelve years in the Melbourne Staff Band on the solo cornet bench and was also the band's pianist. He continues to serve in the Ringwood Corps senior music sections (band and songsters) and is also the Young People's Band Leader. Numerous young lads have benefited from his loyal and devoted service and the YP Band has provided him with the opportunity of using his manuscripts. Noel was employed in the banking industry for several years and then followed a four year term with the Victorian Education Department as a music teacher. He was appointed by Commisioner Eva Burrows as the Territorial Music Director for the Southern Territory here in Australia. This position enabled Noel to share his love of music making for the Lord with Salvationist Musicians throughout this vast nation. His continual aim since a lad has been spread the Gospel story through the means of sanctified music'. The other composer who is featured here on this recording is Howard Davies of which the text says; 'A Salvation Army officer, Howard Davies is well known throughout the Army world for his songs and brass band compositions. At the age of seven he began studying the violin, then years later receiving his A.Mus.A from the Melbourne Conservatorium of Music. Prior to entering training for Salvation Army officership in 1964 he served for a short period as bandmaster of the Camberwell Citadel Band. Married in 1967, he and his wife were appointed to corps work in rural Victoria. In 1972 an appointment to the International Music Editorial Department in London further developed his skills in composing and arranging. During this four year period he was a member of the*

International Staff Band as principal first baritone, also serving as bandmaster of the West London corps of Ealing. Major Davies has travelled widely in the interest of Salvation Army music, not only in all states of Australia, but also in Britain, Switzerland, Holland, South Africa and Zimbabwe. He currently has over seventy vocal and brass compositions published in Army journals'.

NOEL JONES [1]

HOWARD DAVIES [2]

- CAMBERWELL CITADEL BAND and SONGSTERS – **The Joy of Service**

(Service our joy *[1],All the world is waiting [2], Rally round the banner [1[, Make me more like You [2], Memories of Childhood [2], Building a new world of love [2], Fewster [1], Launceston [1], He's everything to me [2], Praise Him [1], Give the Glory to Jesus [2], Pleasure in His Service[2], There is Power [1], Now the day is over [2]*)

RECORDINGS - PRAISE AND RECOGNITION

Alongside several internationally famous Salvation Army Staff and corps bands, both The International Staff Band and (as an example) the Enfield Citadel Band are known for their many tours abroad. Both bands have made recordings with compositions from noted composers by means of praise and recognition. When the International Staff Band was to tour the United States of America in 1989, they re-released several tracks from past recordings onto one single CD, so that a complete album with American composers saw daylight. This became their tour recording and was named 'American Band Classics'. The Enfield Citadel Band latest American tour dates from 2007, for which they recorded several known and well chosen works from American Salvation Army composers.

INTERNATIONAL STAFF BAND – **American Band Classics**

- **WILLIAM HIMES** [1]
- **STEPHEN BULLA** [2]
- **JAMES CURNOW** [3]
- **BRUCE BROUGHTON** [4]
- **IVOR BOSANKO** [5]

St. Francis [1], Crossroad [2], To Know Thee [1], The Cleansing Power [2], The Great Salvation War [3], Milestone [1], O How I love Jesus [3], The Firing Line [4], Aspects of Praise [1], Marching Onward [5]

ENFIELD CITADEL BAND – **American Anthology**

- **STEPHEN BULLA** [1]
- **BRUCE BROUGHTON** [2]
- **JAMES CURNOW** [3]
- **WILLIAM HIMES** [4]

Praise Him! [1], The New-born Babe [2], Faith is the Victory [3], Journey into Peace [4], Images for Brass [1], Guardian of our Way [3], New York 90 [1], Cause for Celebration, The Higher Plane [1], Covenant [2], I'd Rather Have Jesus [4], The Firing Line [2], A Psalm of Praise [3], Motivation [4]

Knowing that already quite a substantial part of the composers output has been used, either as published music or as manuscript, it is often a subject of discussion what could be still in the cupboards of these craftsmen, as well as in the cupboards of various households, bands, publishing agencies and Salvation Army music departments which never saw daylight, never will see a publication, or even is lost for some reason. It is known that many treasures of compositions have been in a dark drawer before they were (re)discovered!

Another praise and recognition to certain Salvation Army composers was when the Melbourne Staff Band (Australia) recorded a LP album featuring only Australian composers. The text on this special recording, which marked the 90th anniversary (1980) of the Melbourne Staff Band says:

'The Melbourne Staff Band of the Salvation Army is proud of its musical heritage. This disc, which is released for the 90th anniversary celebrations of the band, features music written or arranged by Australia Salvationists from the past and the present.

1. *The first march entitled 'Balga Citadel' was written for the opening of the Balga Corps in W.A. and* **Allen Pengilly** *of Western Australia is the composer.*
2. *1890 is the centenary of the Salvation Army in Australia and Captain* **Howard Davies**, *who is the Commanding Officer of Chelsea Corps, in Victoria, has written 'Songs of Australia', especially for the band. The selection includes some well known and typically Australian folk songs; 'the song of Australia', 'Jog Along till Shearing', 'Botany Bay', 'The Ryebuck Shearer', and both the standard and Queensland versions of Waltzing Matilda. The listener will feel the ruggedness of the young country, the loneliness of the bush and the joy of a new found life, in this descriptive writing.*
3. *The cornet solo 'Song of Experience' from the wealth of music composed by retired bandmaster* **Leonard Baxter** *of Brisbane City Temple Corps in Queensland, is presented in three movements, and includes the melodies; 'He came right down to me', and 'O Happy Day'. Staff Bandsman Robert Beasy is the soloist.*
4. *A Recording featuring Australian composers would not be complete without 'an* **Arthur Gullidge** *march' and 'Unconquered' has been selected.*
5. *Bandmaster* **Barrie Gott** *of Sydney Congress Hall is one of the younger generation of composers, and his march 'Gold Coast Temple' is included.*
6. *Gems from the Great Masters No.1 was a feature of Staff Band programs in the 1902's and it was during this period that* **Robert McAnally**, *the arranger of this selection was conductor of the Melbourne Staff Band.*
7. **Noel Jones** *is a member of the Melbourne Staff Band solo cornet section and he has arranged the hymn tune 'Jesus is real to me', as a trombone solo. This is played by Staff Bandsman Ken McClimont.*
8. *An Arrangement from the Classics by* **Gordon Collins** *of South Australia, 'Allegro Deciso' from Handel's Water Music Suite rounds off a recording which members of the Melbourne Staff Band trust will not only entertain, but will challenge, uplift and above all glorify God'.*

Whether the next recording belongs to the 'Tribute' range or to the 'Praise and Recognition', it doesn`t really matter. The fact is that this is yet another great recording to show a huge appreciation to probably three of New Zealand's most well known composers. Although the repertoire is nowadays a little predictable, it is always great to hear pieces as mentioned below in the repertoire list. Many bands has recorded music by Dean Goffin of course, and the three piece recorded here by his father Harry are also recorded several times, but in particular the music of bandmaster Ray Cresswell really deserves more attention and preferably a recording by one of the current bands of this era.

PRAISE IN BRASS

Music by New Zealand Salvation Army composers,

performed by the Christchurch Citadel Band of the Salvation Army.

RAY F. CRESSWELL

1. March - Motivation
2. Cornet Trio - Joyful Praise
3. March - Petone Citadel
4. Hymn Tune Arrangement - St Catherine
5. March - Motueka
6. March - Divine Guidance

HARRY C. GOFFIN

7. March - The Red Shield
8. Descriptive March - Salvation Army Patrol
9. March - New Zealand Warriors

J. DEAN GOFFIN

10. March - Tylney Hall
11. Hymn Tune - Peace
12. March - Anthem of The Free

RECORDINGS - SPECIAL THEMES

Next to the three earlier mentioned recordings from specific composers, there is another reason to highlight music. There are also several recordings available with a content by various composers, but which are all arranged by one arranger with the purpose to move the music towards a specific subject, target or idea. An excellent example of such a *theme recording* is the CD 'Connect' by the Swiss Staff Band, '*Brass of Praise*', where Mark Frei, one of the composers/arrangers within the country, arranged all the tracks for this particular recording in order to direct the music onto a specific story that the band is trying to tell through their music.

The notes for this recordings says (*source: heilsarmee.ch*)

'Songs of praise that emphasis the Greatness and Almightiness of God and His love have been extremely popular since the creation of the world. 'Connect' unites this original sense by combining music from the Bible with modern-day musical trends. Following in the footsteps of the original Salvation Army and the creative pioneering spirit, an innovative musical production has arisen based on favourite music, texts, pictures and personal thoughts of all of the band members. Markus Frei has arranged and composed the music on behalf of Brass of Praise. The intended music style can be described as Brass-Pop, which is a skilful combination of brass band instrumentation, rhythm section and song.

The CD tells of a Brass of Praise concert day with tumultuous arrivals from all corners of Switzerland, a chaotic dress rehearsal, a contemplative preparation for the concert and an intensive concert sound. With this in mind, the Brass of Praise would like to unite people with people, they tried and tested with the new, as well as portraying an exciting and innovative dimension. Music in the honour of God as a challenge for the present day!'

BRASS OF PRAISE - **Connect**

01 Warm up

02 He is able

03 The Gift

04 007 Light

05 Open your Eyes

06 Connect

07 King

08 Little Sunshine in Switzerland

09 Love can build a Bridge

10 Marching onward 2007

11 Deep Gratitude

RECORDINGS - CLASSICAL MUSIC

Already from an early stage, composers within the Salvation Army started to use music from the classical composers, just to provide playable and recognizable music for the fast increasing amount of brass bands within the organization.

Transcriptions and arrangements

Many 'transformed' classical works for brass bands do have either the (sub)title 'transcription' or 'arrangement'. *Transcription* may also mean rewriting a piece of music, either solo or ensemble, for another instrument or other instruments than which it was originally intended. The Beethoven Symphonies by Franz Liszt are a good example. Transcription in this sense is sometimes called arrangement, although strictly speaking transcriptions are faithful adaptations, whereas *arrangements* change significant aspects of the original piece.

It is generally recognised that Richard Slater held the torch for the use of the classics as an edifying, enriching and refining tool in the growth of Salvation Army bands. He soon expanded the options for bands to include medleys, the range of composers and sources used indicating a man well versed in operatic, chamber and symphonic literature. Bramwell Coles' famous *'Moments with Tchaikovsky'* and *'Treasures from Tchaikovsky'* led Salvation Army band music towards portions of symphonic or absolute music. This naturally provided more challenging musical experiences, an aspect that intensified after World War II.

Already some years ago The Norwich Citadel Band, then led by Bandmaster Robert Munn, was the first Salvation Army band who did a recording with only transcriptions and arrangements from classical pieces. This recording was released before many other bands would release their own CDs with classical music and the band was in that way beyond its time.

NORWICH CITADEL BAND – **Classics in Brass**

1.	**The Marriage of Figaro**	Mozart arr. William Himes
2.	**Symphonic Concert March**	Binelli arr. William Himes
3.	**Andante Cantabile**	Tchaikovsky arr. Brian Bowen
4.	**Concert Etude**	Goedicke arr William Broughton
5.	**Slavonic Dance no.8**	Dvorak arr. Ray Steadman-Allen
6.	**Chanson de Matin**	Elgar arr Wesley Kendrick
7.	**Finale from Symphony No.2**	Tchaikovsky arr William Gordon
8.	**Academic Festival Overture**	Brahms arr George Twitchen
9.	**Coronation March**	Meyerbeer arr Albert Jakeway
10.	**Minuet in E**	Boccherini arr Charles Skinner
11.	**Introduction & Allegro Spiritoso**	Senaille arr John Gibson and William Himes
12.	**Themes from 'The Italian Symphony'**	Mendelssohn arr Dean Goffin

13.	**Legen (Christ in His Garden)**	Tchaikovsky arr Bramwell Coles
14.	**Russian Folk Dance**	Shostakovisch arr Torgny Hanson

The recording with classical arrangements and transcriptions by the Enfield Citadel Band (Bandmaster Jonathan Corry) was released in 2009, just as the composers profiled and featured on this recording are celebrated for their anniversaries: Handel 250th (1685-1759), Haydn 200th (1732-1809) and Mendelssohn 200th (1809-1847). The choice of repertoire on this recording provides an excellent overview of the repertoire Salvationist transcribers have provided Salvation Army bands since World War I. Not only the Salvation Army was and is making use of classical transcriptions and arrangements, also the *secular* brass bands, with their rich history, still often make use of this genre. One of the leading brass bands is – almost *of course-* the world famous Black Dyke Band who have released a whole series of recordings with classical transcriptions and arrangements, think on their '*Spectacular Classics*' series, but also their ground breaking '*The Messiah*' double CD, or their '*Straus*', '*Verdi*', '*classical dyke vol 1 – Elgar*' and superb '*Fantastic Overtures*' releases. Another non Salvation Army brass band CD with classical music definitely worth mentioning is the recording by the Grimethorpe Colliery Band - *The History of Brass Band Music - Classical Arrangements.* Within the Army there are not many recordings with solely classical music, therefore a mention of Enfield's recording is definitely worth mentioning below. However, on many recordings released by the Salvation Army, classical works can be found.

ENFIELD CITADEL BAND – **Classically Enfield**

1.	**Fanfare 'La Peri'**	Paul Dukas arr. Richard E Holz
2.	**War March of the Priests**	Felix Mendelssohn arr. Frederick Hawkes
3.	**Come, Sweet Death**	J S Bach arr. Erik Leidzén edited. R W Holz
4.	**Overture to The Magic Flute**	Wolfgang Amadeus Mozart arr. Michael Kenyon
5.	**Queen of the Night's Aria**	Wolfgang Amadeus Mozart arr. Andrew Blyth
6.	**Morceau Symphonique**	Alexandre Guilmant arr. Ray Steadman-Allen
7.	**Poem**	Zdenek Fibich arr. Ray Steadman-Allen
8.	**Overture to Beatrice and Benedict**	Hector Berlioz arr. Keith Wilkinson
9.	**Lend Me Your Aid**	Charles Gounod arr. George Marshall
10.	**Themes from the 'New World' Symphony**	Antonín Dvorak arr. Ray Steadman-Allen
	I. Adagio - Allegro molto	
	II. Largo	
	III. Molto vivace	
	IV. Allegro con fuoco	
11.	**Trumpet Concerto in Eb**	Franz Joseph Haydn arr. Ray Steadman-Allen
	Movement II	
	Movement III	

12. **Sound an Alarm** George Frederic Handel arr. Frederick Hawkes

13. **Hallelujah Chorus** George Frederic Handel arr. Arthur Goldsmith

Other titles of music that have been written by the grand classical composers and that has been arranged, or transcribed are named below. The list isn't complete but these are the most significant. Many of these pieces could be found on earlier Salvation Army recordings with a few extremely popular works like *'Treasures from Tchaikovsky'*, *'Melody in A-flat'*, *'Solveigns Song'*, *'Marche Militaire Francaise'* and *'Concert Piece for Trombone'*, just to name but a few. The names between brackets is of the transcriber/arranger.

AJ0107	**Air from the Suite in D**	J.S. Bach (Erik Leidzén)
AJ0188	**Trepak from the Nutcracker**	P.I. Tchaikovsky (Keith Wilkinson)
AJ0196	**Troika from Lt.Kije**	Prokofiev (Andrew Blyth)
AJ0248	**Hallelujah**	G.F. Handel (Dorothy Gates)
CM0042	**Nocturne**	Felix Mendelssohn (J. Davies)
FM0071-1	**Largo**	G.F. Handel (Klaus Östby)
FS0028-2	**The Trumpet Shall Sound**	G.F. Handel (Frederick Hawkes)
FS0029	**Mount of Olives**	Ludwig van Beethoven (Frederick Hawkes)
FS0063	**O Thou That tellest to Zion**	G.F. Handel (Frederick Hawkes)
FS0068-1	**Sound an Alarm**	G.F. Handel (Frederick Hawkes)
FS0090	**Moments with Tchaikovsky**	P.I. Tchaikovsky (Bramwell Coles)
FS0128-1	**With Verdure Clad**	Joseph Haydn (Eric Ball)
FS0153-2	**Morning Tide**	Henry Purcell (Philip B. Catelinet)
FS0164-2	**A Pilgrim Prayer**	P.I. Tchaikovsky (Ray Steadman-Allen)
FS0174	**Treasures from Tchaikovsky**	P.I. Tchaikovsky (Bramwell Coles)
FS0184-1	**Trumpet Voluntary**	Henry Purcell (Albert Jakeway)
FS0195	**Trumpet Concerto**	Joseph Haydn (Ray Steadman-Allen)
FS0196-1	**Polonaise in A**	Frédéric Chopin (Albert Jakeway)
FS0196-2	**Melody in A-flat**	Johannes Brahms (Albert Jakeway)
FS0220-1	**Lend Me Your Aid**	Charles Gounod (George Marshall)
FS0254	**Italian Symphony**	Felix Mendelssohn (Dean Goffin)
FS0256	**Nimrod**	Edward Elgar (Dean Goffin)
FS0271 PR	**Sheep May Safely Graze**	J.S. Bach (Michael Kenyon)
FS0274	**New World Symphony**	Antonin Dvorak (Ray Steadman-Allen)
FS0275	**The Last Spring**	Edvard Grieg (Ray Steadman-Allen)
FS0276	**Royal Fireworks Music**	G.F. Handel (Charles Skinner)

FS0282	**Melodies of Dvorak**	Antonin Dvorak (Ray Steadman-Allen)
FS0284	**Solveigns Song**	Edvard Grieg (Ray Steadman-Allen)
FS0330	**Trumpet Concerto**	J.N. Hummel (Vernon Post)
FS0334	**Melodies of Grieg**	Edvard Grieg (Ray Steadman-Allen)
FS0359 TS	**The Swan**	Camille Saint-Saëns (Ray Steadman-Allen)
FS0374	**Marche Miltiare Francaise**	Camille Saint-Saëns (Michael Kenyon)
FS0383	**Concert Piece for Trombone**	F. A. Guilmant (Ray Steadman-Allen)
FS0410-2	**Panis Angelicus**	César Franck (Brian Bowen)
FS0421-2	**Theme by Brahms**	Johannes Brahms (Brian Bowen)
FS0443	**Second Hungarian Rhapsody**	Franz Liszt (Robert Redhead)
FS0453	**Elsa's Procession to the Cathedral**	Richard Wagner (William Himes)
FS0469	**Procession of the Nobles**	Rimsky Korsakov (James Curnow)
FS0474	**Appian Way**	Ottorini Respighi (Peter Graham)
FS0477	**The Little Russian**	P.I. Tchaikovsky (William Gordon)
FS0510	**Coronation March**	P.I. Tchaikovsky (Kevin Norbury)
FS0521	**The Flower Duet**	L. Delibes (Norman Bearcroft)
FS0525	**Finale from 'William Tell' Overture**	Gioacchino Rossini (Dean Goffin)
FS0546-1	**Pomp and Circumstance March No.2**	Edward Elgar (James Wright)
FS0546-2	**Chanson de Matin**	Edward Elgar (Wesley Kendrick)
FS0566	**Farandole**	Georges Bizet (Richard Phillips)
FS0585	**Les Toreadors from Carmen No.1**	Georges Bizet (Keith Manners)
GS0730-1	**Largo in G**	G.F. Handel (Frederick Hawkes)
GS0827	**The Hallelujah Chorus**	G.F. Handel (Arthur Goldsmith)
GS1215-1	**By the Cross**	Felix Mendelssohn (Bramwell Coles)
GS1237	**Coronation March**	Giacomo Meyerbeer (Albert Jakeway)
GS1447-1	**Glory to God**	G.F. Handel (George Marshall)
GS1719	**Allegro Spiritoso**	Jean Baptiste Senaille (William Himes)
GS1750-2	**Trumpet Tune**	Henry Purcell (Ray Steadman-Allen)
GS1807-1	**Poem**	Zdeněk Fibich (Ray Steadman-Allen)
GS1839	**Pavane**	Gabriel Fauré (Kevin Norbury)
GS1859	**Benediction**	Johannes Brahms (Brian Bowen)

GS1882	**Arrival of the Queen of Sheba**	G.F.Handel (Michael Kenyon)
GS1895	**Voluntary on Old Hundreth**	Henry Purcell (James Curnow)
GS1914-2	**Of Whom I Sing**	Edvard Grieg (Leonard Ballantine)
GS1972	**Sarabande**	Claude Debussy (Richard Holz Jr)
JC0606	**Swan Lake Act 1**	P.I.Tchaikovsky (Trevor Davis)
JC0607	**Rhapsody on a Theme by Purcell**	Henry Purcell (Kevin Norbury)
JC0635	**Excerpts from the Finale from Symphony No.4**	P.I. Tchaikovsky (Bill Gordon)
S0487	**Concert Etude**	Alexander Goedicke (William Broughton Jr)
TS0325-1	**March in Scipio**	G.F. Handel (Philip Catelinet)
TS0699-2	**Ballade**	Edvard Grieg (Brian Bowen)
TS0734	**Visions of Youth No 2**	J.S. Bach (Philip Catelinet)
TS0963-1	**Hornpipe from the Water Music**	G.F. Handel (Harold Burgmayer)
TS0981	**Thine is the Glory**	G.F. Handel (Harold Burgmayer)
TS1087	**Air from the 'Water Music'**	G.F. Handel (Derek Jordan)
TS1091	**Sarabande and Variations**	G.F. Handel (Graham Eacott)
TS1103-1	**Pie Jesu**	Gabriel Fauré (Kevin Norbury)
US0214	**From 'Judas Maccabeus'**	G.F. Handel (Kevin Norbury)
US0280	**If Thou Art Near**	Frédéric Chopin (Michael Babb)
US0285	**O Magnum Mysterium**	Tomas Luis de Victoria (Harold Burgmayer)
US0361	**Trepak**	P.I. Tchaikovsky (Martin Cordner)
US0365	**Largo (Aria from Opera 'Xerxes')**	G.F. Handel (Nick Simmons-Smith)
US0377-2	**Introduction from 'Dives and Lazarus'**	Ralph Vaughan Williams (Anthony Smith)

It is known, as mentioned before, that several composers have dug into classical music to see whether or not certain pieces were useful for possible transcription or arranging purposes. Such a composer was the Swedish/American Erik Leidzén who was known for his almost unlimited skills when it concerns to composing, arranging but also writing poems. His music is legendary and in particular his solos, written as 'theme and variations' (e.g. *'Tucker'*, *'Songs in the Heart'*, *'Home on the Range'* and so on) were timeless gems and are still high in the ranking of popular solos as of today. Erik Leidzén was in particular a fan of the music of Johann Sebastian Bach and used many of his compositions as material to be used in brass band circles. Probably the best well known example of this is his transcription of *'Jesu, Joy of Men's Desiring'*, which was used on many recordings, including those of the New York Staff Band and Amsterdam Staff Band. Erik Leidzén arranged around 20 Bach pieces during the 1950s and said he did them as exercises, but they all became real gems. Recently these transcriptions were found again, dusted off and the New York based 'Imperial Brass' band recorded them. Amongst the track list are *'Jesu, Joy of Men's Desiring'*, *'Air in D, Sarabande'*, and many *'Preludes and Fugues'*. This was not enough really to fill a complete recording so Mark Freeh, one of the founders of Imperial Brass, and also a noted Salvation Army composer, arranged *'Toccata & Fugue in D Minor'*, *'Fantasia in G Major'*, *'Siciliano'*, and the *'Gigue Fugue'*. It is a historic recording as most of the Bach/Leidzén music has never been played.

RECORDINGS - SECULAR TRIBUTES

That the compositions of all these Salvation Army composers are not only known and appreciated within our organisation but also outside the movement, is evident when you look at several first-class recordings of their music by leading non-Salvation Army brass bands in the UK and also in other countries with a rich brass band history. Ever since the music of the Salvation Army was made available to wider circles in the early 90's, it is almost impossible to find a brass band recording with no Salvation Army music on it. The most well-known recordings are named here, and have set an example to brass bands around the world. In these recordings, you can distinguish a significant proportion of the musical heritage of the Salvation Army. Names of composers are given in brackets after each title.

The Yorkshire Building Society Band, conducted by Professor David King, was one of the first with a series of real ground breaking recordings featuring the music of Salvation Army composers and arrangers, but already some years earlier, when David King was the conductor of the famous Black Dyke Mills Band, he recorded *'Toccata - Oh the Blessed Lord'* which was already a shock as this had not really been done before. His knowledge and preference for Salvation Army music is legendary as he has always been a great encourager of Army music and its composers. Although the content of the three recordings might be a little predictive when it comes to choosing a repertoire to record, when you actually hear the band playing the music, you instantly forget any prejudices.

YORKSHIRE BUILDING SOCIETY BAND - **Essays for Brass. 1**

- *The Call of the Righteous (Condon), Just as I Am (Heaton), The Kingdom Triumphant (Ball), The Light of the World (Goffin), The Lord is King (Steadman-Allen), My Strength My Tower (Goffin), On Ratcliff Highway (Steadman-Allen)*

YORKSHIRE BUILDING SOCIETY BAND - **Essays for Brass 2**

- *Children of the Heavenly Father (Steadman-Allen), For our Transgressions (Calvert), The Holy War (Steadman-Allen), I Know Thou Art Mine (Ballantine), In Perfect Peace (Downie), The Present Age (Condon), A Psalm of Praise (Curnow), Quintessence (Redhead), Toccata - Oh the Blessed Lord (Heaton)*

YORKSHIRE BUILDING SOCIETY BAND - **Essays for Brass 3**

- *Born to Battle (Broadstock), Festivity (Condon), Hymn for Diana (Turrin), My All is on the Altar (Calvert), A Pilgrim Song (Rive), Resurgam (Ball), Rhapsody in Brass (Goffin), Song of the Eternal (Condon)*

As the brass band music of the Salvation Army has a special place in any history of the secular brass band movement, it was no doubt that a specially dedicated recording by the Grimethorpe Colliery Band, as part of their historical recordings set of '*The History of Brass Band Music*' (complete set contains):

1. The History of Brass Band Music Vol 1 - The Golden Era
2. The History of Brass Band Music Vol 2 - The Salvation Army Connection
3. The History of Brass Band Music Vol 3 - The Early Years
4. The History of Brass Band Music Vol 4 - The Modern Era

5. The History of Brass Band Music Vol 5 - Classical Arrangement
6. The History of Brass Band Music Vol 6 - New Adventures

would include a disc completely with Salvation Army compositions and so they did. The repertoire is a little predictable although they are absolute gems in their own right. The track that really draws attention and is probably of significance for historical reasons is track 1 'The Founder's Hymn'.

GRIMETHORPE COLLIERY (UK Coal) BAND - **The Salvation Army Connection**

- *The Founder's Hymn (Ellis), The Liberator (Marshall), Exodus (Ball), Just As I Am (Heaton), Concertino for Band and Trombone (Leidzen), The Light of the World (Goffin), The Holy War (Steadman-Allen), Covenant (Broughton), The Present Age (Condon), Victors Acclaimed (Coles)*

BLACK DYKE BAND - **World Class Marches of The Salvation Army Volume 1**

- *The Red Shield (Henry Goffin), Star Lake (Eric Ball), Silver Star (Ray Steadman-Allen), The Invincible Army (Erik Leidzén), Soldiers of Christ (George Marshall), California (Emil Söderström), Anthem of the Free (Dean Goffin), Rousseau (Ray Ogg), Mighty to Save (George Marshall), Crown of Conquest (Ray Steadman-Allen), In the Firing Line (Bramwell Coles), Emblem of the Army (Arthur Gullidge), Torchbearers (Eric Ball), Wisbech Citadel (Albert Gay), Under Two Flags (Bramwell Coles), Rosehill (Albert Jakeway), Fighting for the Lord (Emil Söderström), Montreal Citadel (Norman Audoire)*

BLACK DYKE BAND - **World Class Marches of The Salvation Army Volume 2**

- *The Liberator (George Marshall), Minneapolis IV (Emil Söderström), Dalarö (Edward Gregson), The Flag of Freedom (Bramwell Coles), To Regions Fair (Norman Bearcroft), Victors Acclaimed (Bramwell Coles), Exeter Temple (Leslie Condon), Goldcrest (James Anderson), Motondo (Donald Osgood), Army of God (Emil Söderström), Spirit of Joy (Herbert Rive), The Roll Call (William Broughton), Indomitable (Herbert Mountain), The Redcliffe March (Daniel Hollis), Heroes of the Combat (Bramwell Coles), Cairo Red Shield (Arthur S Raikes), Spirit of Praise (George Marshall), The Wellingtonian (Harold Scotney)*

BLACK DYKE BAND - **World Class Marches of The Salvation Army Volume 3 -** Festival Marches

- *Departed Heroes (Bramwell Coles), The Canadian (James Merritt), Praise (Wilfred Heaton), Crusaders (Dean Goffin), Steadily Onward (Erik Leidzén), Celebration (Leslie Condon), March of the Hours (Emile Söderström), The Southern Cross (Brian Bowen), The High Council (Ray Steadman-Allen), Faith is the Victory (James Curnow), Chalk Farm No. 2 (Edward Gregson), The Ambassadors (Peter Graham), Milestone (William Himes), Choose Freedom (Kenneth Downie), Montclair Citadel (Stephen Bulla)*

YBS BAND - **Alpha and Omega - The Music of Ray Steadman-Allen**

- *Hymn at Sunrise, In Quiet Pastures, The Beacons, Romans 8 - A brass celebration, At the Edge of Time, Evening Hymn*

WILLIAMS FAIREY BAND - **Heralds of Victory**

- *Manhattan (Erik Leidzen), Heralds of Victory (Richard E. Holtz) , Lord of All Hopefulness (Kenneth Downie), Lord Make Calvary Real To Me (William Broughton), Heritage of*

Freedom (James Curnow), On The Kings Highway (Erik Leidzen), What a Friend (Erik Leidzen), Take Up Thy Cross (W. Broughton), Deep Passage (E. Soderstrom), My Jesus I Love Thee (David Catherwood), Hillcrest (B. Broughton), The Old Rugged Cross (Erik Leidzen), Beautiful Christ (Erik Leidzen), American Rhapsody (E. Soderstrom), Golden Jubilee (Milton Kippax), I Walked Today Where Jesus Walked (Peter Graham), Climb Ev'ry Mountain (Thomas Mack), A Psalm of Praise (James Curnow)

GRIMETHORPE COLLIERY BAND – **Hymns vol.I**

- *In Perfect Peace (Kenneth Downie) Dear Lord and Father (arr. Peter Graham) Ellacombe (William Himes) Lord of all Hopefulness (Kenneth Downie) St. Francis (William Himes) Praise My Soul (arr. Michael Babb) Reflections in Nature (Robert Redhead) As the Deer (arr. James Wright) Nicaea (arr. William Himes) Colne (Thomas Rive) Shine Jesus Shine (arr. Richard Phillips) How Sweet the Name (arr. Donald Osgood) Amazing Grace (William Himes)*

**six tracks by non-Salvation Army composers are not included here.*

GRIMETHORPE COLLIERY BAND – **Hymns vol.II**

- *Who is on the Lord's Side? (Rachie)(arr. Richard Phillips) His Provision(Ivor Bosanko) I Vow to Thee, My Country (Thaxted) (arr. Ray Steadman-Allen) There is a Redeemer (arr. Leonard Ballantine) A Gaelic Blessing (arr. Ray Steadman-Allen) Someone Cares (arr. Ray Steadman-Allen) Martyn(Wilfred Heaton) Cwm Rhondda (arr. Richard Phillips)The Potter's Hand (arr. Trevor Davis) Penlan (Charles Skinner) King of Kings (arr. Dean Jones) Mid all the Traffic (Shenandoah) (Leonard Ballantine) In Christ Alone (arr. Dean Jones) St. Columba (Keith Griffin)The Power of Your Love(arr. Richard Phillips) To God be the Glory(arr. Howard Evan) Share My Yoke (arr. Ivor Bosanko) When the Music Fades (The Heart of Worship) (arr. Leonard Ballantine)Consecration Hymn (arr. Ray Steadman-Allen) Light of the World (arr. Nicholas Samuel) Margaret (Peter Graham) Jerusalem (arr. Albert Jakeway)*

UNITED NORWEGIAN CHRISTIAN BAND – **Anthem of the Free**

- *Anthem of the Free, So Glad!, Jesus joy of man's desiring, I'd rather have Jesus, All to Jesus, The Eternal Presence, He is Lord, Shall we Gather, A Pilgrim Prayer, Sing Hosanna, Song of Exuberance, Hyldningsmarsj.*

BRASS OF THE POTOMAC – **American Rhapsody**

- *American Rhapsody (Emil Söderström) A Festive Prelude (Stephen Bulla), Erie Canal (Bruce Broughton), Wind Beneath My Wings (arr. Stephen Bulla), Harlequin (Bruce Broughton), Images for Brass (Stephen Bulla), Aura Lee (Bruce Broughton), California (Emil Söderström), To a Wild Rose (arr. Stephen Bulla), Deep Passage (Emil Söderström), My Country 'Tis Of Thee (Bruce Broughton), Post Bellum Rhapsody (Erik Leidzén), Shenandoah (Stephen Bulla), God and Country (William Himes)*

BETLEHEMSKYRKANS MUSIKKAR – **Joyful Journey**

- *Joyful Journey (David Glanneskog), Nicaea (William Himes), Vivat Regina (William Mathias), Quicksilver (Peter Graham), To the Chief Musician (William Himes), Rhapsody on Swedish Folk Songs (Hans Nordin), The Call of the Righteous (Leslie Condon), I need thee every hour (arr. David Glanneskog), The Southern Cross (Brian Bowen)*

NEW ENGLAND BRASS BAND – **In Concert**

- *Montclair Citadel (Stephen Bulla), Good Old Way (Bruce Broughton), Love Divine (Mozart/Jakeway), Cause For Celebration (William Himes), Sweet Hour Of Prayer (Erik Leidzen), Sinfonietta (Gordon Langford), Melodies Of Dvorak (Ray Steadman-Allen), Suite For Brass - Three Hymns (Stephen Bulla), Dance Before The Lord (Peter Graham), Charlotte Celebration (Stephen Bulla)*

NEW ENGLAND BRASS BAND – **Light of the World**

- *Old Hundreth (Geneva Psalter, 1511- Psalm 100), The Light of the World (Sir John Dean Goffin), Fortress (William Gordon), March: Crusaders (Sir John Dean Goffin), Be Thou My Vision - (James Curnow), Images for Brass (Stephen Bulla), Holy, Holy, Holy (arr. James Curnow), Swing Low (arr. Andrew R. Mackereth), Sweet Hour of Prayer (arr. Eric Leidzen), The Heralds (Phillip B. Catlinet), The Salvation Army (arr. Ray Steadman-Allen), A Psalm of Praise (James Curnow), God Be With You (Ralph Vaughan Williams, arr. William Gordon)*

RECORDINGS - VARIOUS

When someone noticed a lack of a good recording of *'The Red Shield'* march by New Zealander Harry C. Goffin, father of another well known composer, Dean Goffin, Egon Publishers, a publishing agency in the United Kingdom immediately came up with the idea to form a band with the purpose of bringing recordings of brass music by Salvation Army composers to the wider audience. The date was 1993 and Egon Virtuosi Brass was born. The conducter was also the Bandmaster of the Enfield Citadel Band, James Williams. The best way however to show how Salvation Army marches should be played, was to let them be played by Salvationist musicians! So, although Egon Virtuosi Brass is strictly speaking not a Salvation Army band, it existed entirely of Salvationists!

EGON VIRTUOSI BAND - **Classic Marches Of The Salvation Army**

- *The Liberator (George Marshall); Rosehill (Albert Jakeway); Celebration (Leslie Condon); Soldiers Of Christ (George Marshall); Motondo (Donald Osgood); Fill The World (Erik Silfverberg); The Red Shield (Harry C. Goffin); Spirit of Joy (Herbert Rive); Able (revised by William Himes); Anthem Of The Free (Dean Goffin); Under Two Flags (Bramwell Coles); Rousseau (Ray Ogg); Praise (wilfred Heaton); Montreal Citadel (Norman Audoire)*

During the planning of the second recording with marches, it became clear that the band's conductor, James Williams was not able to lead the band due to overseas commitments. Coincidentally Bram Gregson, brother of composer Edward Gregson, and former Euphonium soloist with the Tottenham Citadel Band, and at the time of planning this new recording bandmaster of the Canadian based London Citadel Band, was willing to lead the band during this recording.

EGON VIRTUOSI BAND - **Classic Marches Of The Salvation Army Vol 2**

- *Beaumont (George Dickens); Neath The Flag (George Marshall); Crusaders (Dean Goffin); Dalaro (Edward Gregson); Victorious (Arthur Gullidge); Heaven Came Down (Eiliv Herikstad); The Scarlet Jersey (Ray Steadman-Allen); Alderney (Dean Goffin); Wisbech Citadel (Albert Gay); Stapleford Citadel (Charles Dove); The Joy-Bringer (Kenneth Downie); Youth Undaunted (David Thornett); Goldcrest (James Anderson); Dovercourt Citadel (Percy Merritt); Temple 85 (Norman Bearcroft); The Salvation Army (Sousa, arr. Ray Steadman-Allen); Flag Of Freedom (Bramwell Coles)*

EGON VIRTUOSI BAND – **Music for a Joyful Occasion!**

- *Silver Star (Ray Steadman-Allen), The Glorious Fountain (Bernard Smith), Quintessence (Robert Redhead), Never Give Up (Eric Ball) Music from Kantara (Kenneth Downie), Finale from Horn Concerto No.1 (Straus, arr Lee Baker), Wonderful Words, Wilfred Heaton), Crown of Conquest (Ray Steadman-Allen), Home on the Range (Erik Leidzén), Music for a Joyful Occasion (Kenneth Downie)*

EGON VIRTUOSI BAND - **Brillante** (The Music Arrangements of Peter Graham)

- *The Ambassadors; Fantasia Brillante on Rule Brittannia; Las Lluvias Grandes; The Amzing Mr Leidzen; I Walked Today Where Jesus Walked; Shine As The Light; The Guardian; Whirlwind; Dear Lord And Father; Glorious Ventures; The Dawning; Fanfare and Prelude on Kilmarnock*

EGON VIRTUOSI BAND - **Deep Harmony**

- *Service Above Self (Ray Steadman-Allen) Flourish For Trombone (Kevin Norbury) Deep Harmony (Kenneth Downie) Swingtime Religion (Barrie Gott) Joyous Proclamation (Norman Bearcroft) Just Like John (Norman Bearcroft) Dance Of The Comedians (Smetana Arr. Iain Rayner) The Eternal Presence (Eric Ball) Deep River (William Broughton) French Military March (Saint-Saens Arr Hargreaves) None Other Name (Erik Leidzen) Rosseau (Ray Ogg)*

EGON VIRTUOSI BAND – **The King of Kings**

- *The King of Kings (Eric Ball), To set the People fee (Bruce Broughton), Songs of the Morning (Eric Ball), Concertino for Band and Trombone (Erik Leidzén), New Zealand Warriors (Henry C Goffin), Wondrous Day (Erik Leidzén), The Penitent (Harry Kirk), The Holy War (Ray Steadman-Allen)*

In the meantime Egon Brass, as they were called, had also started to perform at brass band contests and gala concerts, and doing additional concerts, which was not the main purpose of having set up this group of avid brass players. The sometimes complex crossover activities interfered with Army regulations and a solution was sought to end this difficult situation. So after these six great recordings, Egon Virtuosi Band was disbanded.

Another such band which saw a somewhat strange start was the New York based Metro Brass. As the explanation in its until now only recording says; *'having been established in 1998 to provide Salvationist brass musicians with an additional outlet of service and musical ministry'* and *'Metro Brass draws its musicians predominantly from the Greater New York metropolitan area, hence its name. All participants are volunteers as well as members of The Salvation Army with a few exceptions'*. They chose an excellent repertoire for their recording, having invited probably the greatest trombonist of all times, New York Philarmonic Principal Trombone Joseph Alessi to feature several trombone solos. These included probably the two most well known and difficult solos for this instrument in the entire Salvation Army repertoire, *'The Eternal Quest'* and *'Song of Exuberance'*. Although not a real Salvation Army band in my opinion, they chose to feature the great music of composers from the organization.

METRO BRASS – **Song of Exuberance**

- *Olympic Fanfare and Theme (arr. Peter Graham), Soing of Exuberance (Leslie Condon), Folk Festival (Shostakovich, arr Martin Cordner), Let the Beauty of Jesus (William Broughton), Partita on 'St. Theodulph' (Kevin Norbury), The Eternal Quest (Ray Steadman-Allen), Beaumont (George H. Dickens), All I ask of You (Webber, arr Christopher Mowat), He is exalted (Robinson, arr Martin Cordner), Morceau Symphonique (Guiltman, arr Ray Steadman-Allen), Since Jesus (Leonard Ballantine), The Day Thou Gavest (Philip Wilby), Renaissance (Peter Graham)*

A third band that began with the main purpose to only record brass music was the Toronto based 'Intrada Brass'. Led then and now by its founder and conductor (bandmaster is a typical Salvation Army terminology) this band started in 1995 and soon after recorded their first CD featuring the music of one of the giants within the Salvation Army music ministries, Ray Steadman-Allen.

The idea was to record on a regular basis although this became far more difficult than they expected it to be. The band started with only Salvationist musicians, with a few exceptions but over the years has changed their personnel in such way that it is now a band of players with some exceptions, of non-Salvationists. The band includes some professional brass players.

INTRADA BRASS – **Music of Ray Steadman-Allen**

- *(Hadleigh Camp; Go Down Moses; Pavilions of Praise; Rhapsody on Negro Spirituals - Russell Gray (Cornet): Floodtide; Southdown; Lord of the Sea; Happy in the Fight; God's Soldiers; Daystar; St Magnus (Hymn Tune))*

Yet another feature that has been held to honour composers and arrangers in the movement was the '*Meet the Composer*' concert as part of the 1978 International Congress of the Salvation Army, held in London, in the United Kingdom. Here various bands played special tribute to a composer. Although only but one item of each featured composer was played or sung, the aim of this particular recording was to highlight the effort the composers had made in the past time. The Congress Choruses here was led by two noted composers (one of which was also featured on this recording); Major Norman Bearcroft and Captain Trevor Davis, while a third Salvation Army composer, Peter Ayling, played the organ. A fourth composer –Terry Camsey- was featured as cornet soloist (at the time he was the principal solo cornet of the International Staff Band) in Ray Bowes' cornet solo '*Rhapsody for Cornet and Band*', a solo that contains one of his own tunes '*A Christmas Lullaby*' that Ray Bowes wrote for Terry, who had made a name for himself not only as composer but also as cornet virtuoso.

Bandmaster Brian Bowen;

1. The Southern Cross – Manchester Citadel Band

Young People's Band Leader Erik Silfverberg

2. Jesus, the name high over all – The Congress Choruses

Major Norman Bearcroft

3. Just Like John - Enfield Citadel Band

Major Ray Bowes / Staff Bandsman Terry Camsey

4. Rhapsody for Cornet and Band - International Staff Band

Lt. Colonel Stanley Ditmer

5. I'm in His hands – Congress Choruses

Lt. Col. Ray Steadman-Allen

6. Lord of the Sea – Upper Norwood Band

Retired Bandmaster Herbert Mountain

7. Sheffield Citadel – The massed bands

Lt.Colonel Ernest Rance

8. The Reason – The congregation and International Staff Band

Commissioner Richard Holz

9. Heralds of Victory – Cornet ensemble and the massed bands

Major Leslie Condon

10. The Call of the Righteous – Govan Citadel Band

Eric Ball

11. The Kingdom Triumphant – the massed bands and congress choruses

Another significant recording that might fit under this chapter *'recordings – various'* is certainly one by the in Washington D.C. based National Capital Band, one of the staff bands that are in existence in the United States of America. In 1990 this band made a recording appropriately entitled 'Monuments' (which can be referred to either the musical content as well as to the composers). A part of the inlay/explanation about the CD tells us that *'the extensive literature of the modern brass band includes many 'classics', music that endures the test of time, providing a fresh and vibrant experience for every new listener, even decades after the works were conceived'*. The text continues with *'This (particular) recording recognizes and pays tribute to three such men; Eric Ball, Dean Goffin and Erik Leidzén'*. A very important sentence follows and says *'Their substantial output of divinely-inspired work continues to be studied, performed, recorded and broadcast throughout the world today'*. This is very true as their music is indeed, still today and after all these years, studied, performed and recorded.

These three men belongs to the *hardcore* of Salvationist composers and have been examples to generations of composers, in and outside the Salvation Army as they were and are known not only for their huge output, magnificent compositions, fearless ideas within their writings, but also of their sterling Salvationism. When Eric Ball commenced the task as International Staff Bandmaster, likely the highest (if there is such a thing, because the last chair second cornet player in a insignificant corps band located in the outskirts of the globe is certainly and definitely not less important) and most important position within the musical forces of the Salvation Army, he said *'The International Staff Bandmastership is not my highest ambition. I have another ideal. It is to attain Christ. Toward that I press forward'*. Eric Ball was a sincere honest man, with a huge motivation of serving his Lord. When you listen to his music then it is soon clear how moving and spiritual this is. Think on his most well known work *'Resurgam'* (meaning: I shall rise again!) or his *'Songs of the Morning'* (unfortunately his plans for a parallel piece/sequence *'Songs of the Evening'* was accomplished), his *'Songs in Exile'* with the unmistakable song included *'I'm the child of a King'*, or his popular *'King of Kings'*, just to name but a few of his masterpieces.

National Capital Band – Monuments

1. **Suite for Brass – Three Hymns ; O Worship the King** (Stephen Bulla)
2. **Suite for Brass – Three Hymns ; Amazing Grace** (Stephen Bulla)
3. **Suite for Brass – Three Hymns ; How Firm a Foundation** (Stephen Bulla)
4. **The Old Wells** (Eric Ball)
5. **Variants on St. Francis** (David Chaulk) Euphonium solo, David Church, soloist
6. **The Cross** (Erik Leidzén)
7. **The Pilgrim Way ; The Pilgrim Song** (Eric Ball)
8. **The Pilgrim Way ; Invocation** (Eric Ball)
9. **The Pilgrim Way ; Joy of Heart** (Eric Ball)
10. **The Holberg Suite, Op. 40 ; Praeludium** (trans. Steven Kellner)

11. **The Holberg Suite, Op. 40 ; Sarabande** (trans. Robert C. Schramm)
12. **The Holberg Suite, Op. 40 ; Gavotte/Musette** (trans. Robert C. Schramm)
13. **The Holberg Suite, Op. 40 ; Rigadoun** (trans. Eric Alexander)
14. **From Every Stormy Wind** (Brian Hogg)
15. **Victorious** (Dean Goffin) Cornet solo, Lars-Otto Ljungholm, soloist
16. **My Strength, My Tower** (Dean Goffin)
17. **In the King's Service** (Erik Leidzén)

The annual 'Profile Night' series, held in New York, mostly featuring the New York Staff Band, but also the Cambridge Citadel Silver Band and Montclair Citadel Band, is to highlight the work of a single composer who has made a name for himself over previous decades, providing music that is used the world over. The series had been set up by composer Terry Camsey, the then Divisional Music Director for the Greater New York Area, and who was succeeded by Gordon Ward, principal cornet and deputy bandmaster of the New York Staff Band and still the driving force behind the idea and the organization of the Profile Night Series. Gordon hails from the United Kingdom but immigrated to the United States and soon after his arrival started involvement with this concert series. Several recordings saw daylight since that first Profile Night featuring what probably can be named as the 'Godfather' of Salvation Army (and even in secular circles) brass band music, Eric Ball. More details about these recordings can be found on the 'Recordings – Single Composer Recordings' chapter.

Special guests for the Profile Night Series:

1979 - Profile Night Series 1, Eric Ball

1980 - Profile Night Series 2, Albert Jakeway

1981 - Profile Night Series 3, Brindley Boon

1982 - Profile Night Series 4, Phillip Datelined

1983 - Profile Night Series 5, Richard E. Holz

1984 - Profile Night Series 6, Ray Steadman Allen

1985 - Profile Night Series 7, Leslie Condon

1986 - Profile Night Series 8, Stanley Ditmer

1987 - Profile Night Series 9, Ray Bowes

1988 - Profile Night Series 10, Robert Redhead

1989 - Profile Night Series 11, William Himes

1990 - Profile Night Series 12, James Curnow

1991 - Profile Night Series 13, Michael Kenyon

1992 - Profile Night Series 14, Erik Silfverberg

1993 - Profile Night Series 15, Howard davies

1994 - Profile Night Series 16, Ivor Bosanko

1995 - Profile Night Series 17, William and Bruce Broughton

1996 - Profile Night Series 18, Noel Jones

1997 - Profile Night Series 19, Peter graham

1998 - Profile Night Series 20, Stephen Bulla

1999 - Profile Night Series 21, Kenneth Downie

2000 - Profile Night Series 22, Kevin Norbury

2001 - Profile Night Series 23, Trevor Davis

2002 - Profile Night Series 24, Norman Bearcroft

2003 - Profile Night Series 25, Terry Camsey

2004 - Profile Night Series 26, Harold Burgmayer

2005 - Profile Night Series 27, Brian Bowen

2006 - Profile Night Series 28, Leonard Ballantine

2007 - Profile Night Series 29, Sir Dean Goffin

2009 - Profile Night Series 30, Andrew Mackereth

2010 - Profile Night Series 31, Richard Phillips

2011 - Profile Night Series 32, John Larsson

2012 - Profile Night Series 33, Paul Lovatt-Cooper

Already earlier than the aforementioned concerts for and with composers, in 1927 some Salvation Army composers were presented in a 'composers festival' held at the famous Clapton Congress Hall. Bands such as the International Staff Band, Chalk Farm Band, Regent Hall Band, but also Croydon 1 Band (later renamed in Citadel Band) and the Clapton Congress Hall Band itself feature the music of composers and contemporary composers of their time, Richard Slater (often referred to as the 'Father of Salvation Army music'), Frederick Hawkes, Arthur Goldsmith, Bramwell Coles, Wilfred Kitching, Herbert Twitchin, Edward Saywell and Eric Ball. Except for Richard Slater and Bramwell Coles, they also were able to conduct their own compositions. Another concert was held a year later in the presence of General Bramwell Booth. Both Frederick Hawkes, Richard Slater and Eric Ball were again present and conducted their own compositions but in this year's version of the composers festival also three composing bandmasters were present; Harry Kirk of Leeds, George Marshall of Southall and Jules VanderKam of Belgium.

As from the start of Salvation Army music, the early Salvationists were always encouraged to submit their compositions for possible publications in the Army journals. They were however not really recognized because of their efforts and it might have been the case that the editors at the music department thought that it was not a good decision to publish their name on the music sheets. So for many years the names of the composers did not appear on either the full scores as well as on the band parts. It took until 1935 that it was decided to put the names on the sheets in order to give credit to the composer. One main thought behind this idea was that it would be good, especially for youngster, to have their own heroes in music writing within the Salvation Army.

Another example:

Quite often a composer is invited for a band weekend, festival or concert. These concerts do not necessarily contain only music by that particular composer but of course he or she is a significant part of the happening. Occasionally the composers, who are often skilled on an (several) instrument(s), will feature as guests soloist too, besides conducting (their own) compositions and giving a lecture about their compositions and the background of it. In October 1993 the Melbourne Staff Band (Australia) organized a concert featuring composer Stephen Bulla as special guest. Stephen is of course a world renowned composer, not only within the Salvation Army but also far beyond. Apart from being a composer he is also a first class pianist and an excellent trombone soloist.

Melbourne Staff Band (conducted by staff bandmaster Colin Woods)

1 Praise Him – Stephen Bulla

2 Lowell Anniversary – Stephen Bulla

3 Canaan's Land – Stennet, arr Stephen Bulla

4 Blessed Assurance – arr Stephen Bulla

5 Call of the Seasons – Philip Catelinet

6 Jesus, Thou art everything to me – arr William Himes

7 Music of Thanksgiving – Kenneth Downie

8 Handel in the Strand – Grainger, arr Robert Schramm (soloist Stephen Bulla)*

9 The Cleansing Power – Stephen Bulla

10 Improvisation – Stephen Bulla**

11 Beyond the Sunset – arr. Stephen Bulla

12 Crowns of the Spirit – Stephen Bulla

13 He walks with God – Chadwick arr. Stephen Bulla

14 Chorale and Toccata – Stephen Bulla

*Piano solo

**Piano duet with Staff Bandsman Michael Harding

RECORDINGS - BRASS ENSEMBLE

One of the most underestimated forms of brass playing is definitely those of the brass *ensemble*. The brass ensemble music has been written for various settings, but unmistakably the most well known is the brass sextet (*Cornet 1, Cornet 2, Eb Horn, trombone, Euphonium, Eb bass*). With this setting you can, when well written, almost cover a whole brass band! So several Salvation Army composers have dedicated themselves not only to write for full brass bands but also to write for this unique and very pleasant form of music making. There have been and still are some fantastic ensembles within the Salvation Army such as the 'Jubilant Brass' from Camberwell, Australia. They made a fantastic recording –Jubilation!- and they used not only compositions written for brass ensemble but also 'full band' compositions, which they just played with the seven of them (six plus percussion). The official statement says *'Jubilant Brass was formed in 1983 by seven members of the Camberwell Citadel Band. The group plays bright and attractive music, and emphasises entertainment, humour and variety in its performance, but also features devotional musical and personal testimony. The aim of the group is to communicate the joy and fulfillment of a Christ centered life by excellence in music, presentation and personal witness. To that end this recording is offered'.*

Another fantastic brass ensemble what really did set new levels of quality playing with this limited amount of players is the Toronto based 'Sovereign Brass', where its members came from past and present Canadian Staff Bandsmen. Their recording *'Toccata'* was simply the best ever. Also they choose compositions which were written not only for brass ensemble but also for complete band 'occupation'. One of these compositions is also the title track, Wilfred Heaton's *'Toccata'.* This piece was once written as a brass ensemble version but somehow the music was lost, therefore Sovereign Brass chose to use the full band version and just play it with the six of them. A few years later the music was fortunately found again and even recorded by an ensemble of the famous Black Dyke Band on their 'Heaton Collection'.

Nowadays the Birmingham (United Kingdom) based 'Vision Brass' is the leading ensemble in the Salvation Army world when it comes to ensemble playing. Formed in 2001 with the intention only to play in this setting as a onetime venture, they were soon in the spell of this way of 'brass banding'. Composer and International Staff Bandsman Paul Sharman was one of the founder members. The group has recorded two CDs featuring a wide mix of styles and music with a significant contribution of Salvation Army composers. Both recordings are excellent examples of first class ensemble playing.

CD1 – **Amazing Grace**

Toccata (Bach, arr. Ray. Farr) Holy Ground (arr. James Curnow) Amazing Grace (trad., arr. Luther Henderson) Star Lake (Eric Ball) Alleluiah (Mozart, arr. Gavin R Lamplough) Fall Afresh (arr. Andrew Mackereth) Ask (arr. Peter Graham) Yesterday (arr. R. Willis) Rondeau (Mouret) Wonderful Day (Peter Graham He is Lord (arr. Robert Redhead) Music Maker (arr. Peter Graham) Manhattan (Erik Leidzén) Mr. Jums (C. Hazel) All that I am (William Himes) Canadian Folk Song Suite (Morley Calvert) Just a closer walk (trad., arr Gillis)

CD2 – **In His Joyful Service**

Hillcrest (Bruce Broughton) More than a song (arr. Nicolas Samuel) Glory, look away! (Luther Henderson) Prelude to Te Deum (Marc-Antoine Charpentier) Nothing but Thy Blood (Donna Peterson) Mighty to save (George Marshall) When I'm 64 (arr. Chris

Dedrick) Shekinah (Kenneth Downie) Santa Barbara Sonata (Bramwell Tovey) I dreamed a dream (Claude-Michael Schonberg) Arrival of the Queen of Sheba (arr. Gavin Lamplough) Nearer My God to Thee (Luther Henderson) Written in Red (arr Dean Jones) The Queen of the Night Aria (arr. Gavin Lamplough) Gabriel's Oboe (Ennio Morricone) Kraken (Chris Hazell) In His Joyful Service (William Broughton)

New York Brass Sextet Journal

A brilliant series of brass ensemble music is published by the Salvation Army in New York, United States of America. Composers such as Stephen Bulla, James Curnow, Bruce and William Broughton and others like David Chaulk, Kenneth Downie and Mark Freeh, just to name but a few, joined forces to produce a fantastic brass ensemble series, and the 'New York Brass Sextet Journal' was born. Nowadays no less than eight volumes with in total forty-five compositions have been produced. In 1995, John Street, founder and owner of 'Egon Publishers' thought it would be great to record this music, and so 'Principals play New York' was released. About this album: *'The New York Brass Sextet Journal contributes significantly to the chamber brass literature. This recording demonstrates not only an excellent sample of that repertoire, but gives an excellent model for its performance and interpretation. The sextet players are Roger Webster (cornet), Matthew Baker (cornet), David Horn (tenor horn), Andrew Barryman (trombone), Robert Childs (euphonium) and David Nesbitt (tuba)'.* Of significant not are the two cornet players, both are former principal cornets with the famous Black Dyke Band, where Matthew Baker is also a former solo cornet with the Enfield Citadel Band.

The interest of this kind of compositions was and is huge and so these six principal brass players from the secular movement –although one has a Salvation Army background- are the featuring soloists. Although when you look at the composers featured on this recording, the geography shows a substantial part which comes from the United States of America, while the United Kingdom is poorly represented, let alone other parts of the world. This has nothing to do with whether or not composers are interested or not, but rather with the convenience of having first class composers at hand, or near the publisher.

Tracklist – 'Principals play New York'

1	A Shining Light	Stephen Bulla
2	In The Garden	William Broughton
3	Sheaves	William Broughton
4	French	David Chaulk
5	Manhattan	Erik Leidzén
6	Swing Low	Emil Soderstrom
7	Sunshine	William Broughton
8	Little Washington	Clemons
9	The Heavens Declare - Psalm XIX	Marcello / Mark Ridenour
10	Trumpet Tune	Purcell / Stephen Bulla
11	Intrada XII - A Mighty Fortress	Altenburg
12	Intrada V	Hassler

13	Ave Verum Corpus	Mozart / James Curnow
14	Marche Militaire	Schubert / Mark Freeh
15	Rondeau	Mouret / James Curnow
16	Gloria!	Kenneth Downie
17	Carol Of The Bells	Stephen Bulla
18	God Rest You	Jones
19	Faithful Follower	Ditmer
20	Rhapsody For Trombone	David Catherwood
21	Journey	Stephen Bulla
22	Praise And Thanksgiving	Brian Bowen

Another well known brass ensemble was the Bloomington Brass Quartet, based in Bloomington, in the United States of America, and attached to the local Salvation Army corps there. It soon became the Bloomington Brass Ensemble, an octet. This ensemble was led by Glenn Welsh, an American composer (see 'WELSH, GLENN'), who also writes a significant amount for this ensemble. Yet another ensemble, the Blue Water Brass Sextet, is by composer Orville Payton, with himself on the trombone.

Composers used the brass ensemble really well and in particular within the New York Staff Band and Chicago Staff Band, where several brass ensembles, mainly sextet's, over the years were used to develop the music of these writers. Of course, the sextet as such is not the only form for which music was written. One of the much used ensemble-forms was also the quartet –cornet 1, cornet 2, Eb Horn and Euphonium, with for example Eric Ball's *'Jewels'* as probably the (current) most well known example of composition for quartet. The Salvation Army has published complete books with compositions for quartet, with people such as Bramwell Coles, Ernest Rance, George Marshall, Fred Dockerill, Percy Merritt, Arthur Gullidge and Albert Jakeway, just to name but a few of the suppliers of this kind of music. Other forms were the 'trio', existing of cornet, horn and euphonium, or larger scale ensembles (septet or more). Nowadays the smaller ensemble form is hard to find within the Salvation Army. There are however still contests of brass quartets (for that matter) in the secular banding world, and also within the Salvation Army, in particular, the sextet form of music making seems to be having a revival.

RECORDINGS - PROMOTIONAL PURPOSES

Almost every publisher of music releases now and then recordings to challenge possible buyers to purchase their products. This fact can be divided into several options. There are publishers of sheet music who request bands to record their publications, which often sees world renowned bands feature in a style or quality of music they usually wouldn't normally play and there are publishers who gather a few talented musicians with whom they record newly available sheet music. The recording eventually will see either complete or incomplete tracks, to trigger possible customers. One way or another and perhaps strangely enough, many of these recordings became real collector's items too.

Besides the several examples given above, composers also try to get their music known to people, bands etc, beyond their immediate range of influence. This could be done by requesting bandleaders and conductors to perform their music on a (more) regular basis, or set up concerts featuring their own compositions. Another way to promote their efforts is to somehow produce promotional recording which gives that single composer a chance not only to highlight his or her writings but also to choose his or her own preferred musicians in order to get the most decent performance recorded. In the early 90's the music of Ty Watson, at the time principal Euphonium and deputy bandmaster with the Salvation Army Mississauga Temple Band, as well as euphonium with the Canadian Staff Band, became popular around the (Salvation Army) world and for this purpose he collected his own favourite compositions by his own pen, asked some of his friends, without any exception all past and present members of the Canadian Staff Band, to perform exclusively on a recording featuring the music of Ty Watson, with the composer himself conducting.

TY WATSON MUSIC LIBRARY

1. March: Botwood Centenary
2. March: Mississauga Spirit
3. March: Shout the Victory.
4. Classical Transcription: Finale from Shostakovich's the 'Bolt'
5. Swing Arrangement: Swing Hosanna – cornet soloist Kevin Metcalf
6. Solo: Mid-Winter (cornet) – soloist Melody Watson
7. Solo: Joyful Song (cornet) – soloist Melody Watson
8. Solo: Vigilant (bass trombone) – soloist Len Ferguson
9. Solo: Eyes Upon Jesus (horn) – soloist Ian Watkinson
10. Duet: Fire Divine (Euph Duet) – soloists Mark Hall & Robert Miller
11. Congregational Accompaniment: Thou Great Jehovah

Also on this recording are pieces written for small ensemble (four parts with optional euphonium fifth). These include: *'He's Able'*, *'The Lord's Army'*, *'We Shall Win'* and *'Swing Hosanna'*.

This recording has helped Ty Watson to also make a name for himself outside of his native Canada, and even outside the Salvation Army, as his music was used, performed and recorded by even the best contesting bands in for example the United Kingdom. Star soloists like Douglas Yeo (bass trombone Boston Symphony) and Brett Baker (principal trombone Black Dyke Band) and David Robertson (principal cornet London Citadel Band and Canadian Staff Band) recorded his music and even as recent as 2010 his music was recorded by the Norwich Citadel Band in the United Kingdom.

One of the most special and vibrant compositions of Ty is his bass trombone solo *'Vigilant'* which is dedicated to Len Ferguson, former bass trombonist of the Canadian Staff Band and Ottawa Citadel Band of the Salvation Army, and draws thematic material from the traditional children's song, *'God Sees the Little Sparrow Fall'* of which the words say:

God Sees the Little Sparrow Fall (Author unknown)

God sees the little sparrow fall,
It meets His tender view;
If God so loves the little birds,
I know He loves me too.

(Chorus)

He loves me too, He loves me too,
I know He loves me, too;
Because He loves the little things,
I know He loves me too.

He paints the lily of the field,
Perfumes each lily bell;
If He so loves the little flowers,
I know He loves me well.

God made the little birds and flowers,
And all things large and small;
He'll not forget His little ones,
I know He loves them all.

Other promotional recordings are the annual complimentary recordings to promote new sheet music that is published within the Salvation Army both in the United States Central Territory (American Brass Ensemble Series) and in the United Kingdom (Unity Series). These recordings have proved to be very effective not only in helping to choose new music from particular composers and arrangers but also to get an idea how the music should or and can be played.

SUPPORTING RECORDINGS

Although not focussed on one or more specific composers, the Salvation Army has released several recordings to help either small corps, or just congregations to sing along, having a good accompaniment, or better said, an accompaniment anyway! Some of the titles that has been relaesed are:

Melbourne based corps bands and Melbourne Staff Band – Songs to Sing

The text of the following recordings says: '*Hymn Tune Accompaniment: This collection is an invaluable worship resource. In addition to its obvious use as accompaniment to congregational singing where no live accompaniment is available, this CD series can be used to expand the tune repertoire of worship leaders, serve as a performance model for instrumental groups, and be used as preliminary music to enhance the mood for worship and praise services. Comprehensive indexes are provided to assist in locating tunes to the hundreds of songs they accompany - Alphabetical Tune Index, Metrical Index and Topical Index. Songs are listed in the order in which they appear under the appropriate songbook headings and themes*'.

There are no less than ten discs divided/recorded between the two bands below.

Chicago Staff Band – Hymn Tune Accompaniment (10 CDs)

Norridge Citadel Band (USA) - Hymn Tune Accompaniment (10 CDs)

And than there are also no less than 18 volumes *Hallelujah Choruses*, also recorded by the Norridge Citadel Band, often with the assistance of other performing Salvation Army artists.

RECORDINGS - TRIBUTE THROUGH THE YEARS

The bands of the Salvation Army can boast a rich heritage and for a very long time people have composed and arranged music. For more than a century this has happend and even today many of these early written pieces are often played. To show that these compositions are still in demand and can still give many bands a real challange, the International Staff Band started a series of recordings in 2009 which pay tribute to many people who have served the musical fraternity in the Salvation Army so well. Although most pieces have been recorded before, it is a great collection and one after another gem can be heard.

Of a significant note is that on each of these discs, the last track is a conversation/discussion between International Staff Bandmaster Stephen Cobb and Lt. Colonel Ray Steadman-Allen. This might give mixed feelings to many listeners as it is quite a long debate, time in which they also could have record one or two pieces, but when you consider the age of RSA (born 1922) it is fantastic to hear his voice, so it's also preserved for the future. This reminds one of the introduction Eric Ball gave on the International Staff Band and International Staff Songster LP *Salute to Eric Ball* where Eric himself started off before his best piece is played (Songs in Exile) with the words; *By means of this recording*.... Once you have heard this, you never will forget the influence of his voice.

At the time of this writing three volumes were released with at least a further two volumes (Heritage Series vol.4 – music from the 1960s and Heritage Series vol.5 – music from the 1970s) in the pipeline. There even might be some successors to this series, so that in total a good overview on the Army's brass music heritage can be had.

Here follows the content and composers (and soloists) of the 'volumes' one to three.

Heritage Series vol. 1 – music from the 1930s

Southern Australia (Arthur Gullidge), Sound Out The Proclamation (Eric Ball), The Cleansing Stream (Erik Leidzén) [Gary Fountain (Soprano Cornet) and Kevin Ashman (Cornet)], The Old Wells (Eric Ball), Praise and Exultation (Eric Ball), The Song of the Brother (Erik Leidzén) [Derick Kane (Euphonium)], Bravest of the Brave (Bramwell Coles), Great and Glorious (George Marshall), A Never-Failing Friend (Erik Leidzén) [Andrew Justice (Trombone)], A Sunbeam (Philip Catelinet), The Triumph of Peace (Eric Ball), In conversation (Lieut-Colonel Ray Steadman-Allen and Bandmaster Stephen Cobb)

Heritage Series vol. 2 – music from the 1940s

Praise (Wilfred Heaton), A Pilgrim Prayer (Tchaikovsky arr. Ray Steadman-Allen) [Andrew Justice, Lyndon Moorby, Stuart Hall and Bradley Turnbull (Trombones)], Wells of Gladness (Ray Steadman-Allen), Ransomed (George Marshall)[Derick Kane (Euphonium)], Portraits from St Paul's Epistles (Bramwell Coles), I. The Happy Man, II. The Supplicant, III. The Man of Valour, IV. The Triumphant Man, Hadleigh Camp (Ray Steadman-Allen), Divine Communion (Arthur Gullidge), Star Lake (Eric Ball), Jubilate! (Arthur Gullidge) [Kevin Ashman (Cornet)], Just As I Am (Wilfred Heaton), The Crusade of Youth (Philip Catelinet) I. The Torchbearer II. The Witness III. The Reverie IV. The Challenge, Minneapolis IV (Emil Söderström), In conversation (Lieut-Colonel Ray Steadman-Allen and Bandmaster Stephen Cobb)

Heritage Series vol. 3 – music from the 1950s

Motondo (Donald Osgood), My Heart's Desire (Ray Bowes), Heroes of the Faith (Charles Skinner), The Eternal Quest (Ray Steadman-Allen) [Andrew Justice (Trombone)], The Light of the World (Dean Goffin), Lord of the Sea (Ray Steadman-Allen) I. Water's Edge II. Seascapes III. Seafarer's Song, To Regions Fair (Norman Bearcroft), For Our Transgressions (Morley Calvert), Symphony of Thanksgiving (Dean Goffin), Wondrous Day (Erik Leidzén) [Roland Cobb (Cornet)], In conversation (Lieut-Colonel Ray Steadman-Allen and Bandmaster Stephen Cobb)

RECORDINGS - CHANCES

It is most unfortunate that so many compositions and arrangements were never used for recording purposes, or only were used once or twice or were used when they were new, and therefore popular but that after a certain period they never were used again. This implies that music is dependent - dependent on people, and/or on the time. Music which once was new and modern, could be received nowadays as old fashion and uninteresting, sometimes even boring. Performing bands, band leaders, players and other musicians don't always take the time to dig into the high quality of certain pieces. They rather play what is new in order to play the newest compositions by the -current- most popular composers and arrangers, although 'popular' is a very transient understanding of course.

Men and women, who made the Salvation Army music big, are often now forgotten. Sometimes composers such as Eric Ball and Wilfred Heaton to name but two of the greatest, are still being played, but definitely the biggest part of their often huge output is still forgotten. When one say Eric Ball, only his *'Resurgam'* and *'Clear Skies'* are being played...when one say Robert Redhead, only his *'Quintessence'* is being played...of course this is rather downplaying of what is actually played by bands but still.

Fortunately there are also bands, with the International Staff Band as excellent example, who have decided that indeed this music deserves a new chance. Their *Heritage Series* recordings (music from the 1930's, 1940's and 1950's to date) is absolutely a great idea, however when you look at the choice of repertoire on these discs they remain on the same idea and only recorded what is known very well. What once was popular and what always has been popular, even today.

Also a very much underestimated part of the high quality compositions are the Unity Series (the simplest band journals, followed by the Triumph Series, General Series, Festival Series and currently the Judd Street Collection, being technically most demanding of all). Probably not the most challenging production for full scale bands, but definitely an underestimated series of compositions and worth exploring on recordings.

Some music which could be considered for new CD recordings are for instance the following pieces:

1 Eric Ball - Challenge and Response, Good News, Streams in the Desert, Rhapsody on American Gospel Songs, The Prospect Before, Praise and Exultation

2 Robert Redhead - He Gave Me Joy, We are an Army

3 Erik Leidzen - Danish Rhapsody, Where Flowers Never Fade

4 Brian Bowen - Day of the Spiritual, The Suppliant Heart

5 Dean Goffin - Duke Street, Songs of the Faith, The Shepherd's Psalm

6 Col. Frederick Hawkins - Deadmarch in Saul

7 Erik Leidzén - First Swedish Rhapsody

8 Ray Steadman-Allen - Kum Bah Yah, Logos, Neath Italian Skies, The Netherlands Rhapsody, The Kings Minstrel, The Netherlander

9 George Marshall - Neath the Flag, Sons of the Army

10 Kenneth Cook - Songs of the Seasons, The Passing Years

11 Emil Söderström - Selection of American Folk Songs, Chicago Belmont Corps, A Song of Israel, Down from His Glory, Low in the Grave He lay

12 Charles Dove - Stapleford Citadel

13 Terry Camsey - Sing Hallelujah Shout Hallelujah

14 Richard Slater - The Stilling of the Storm

15 Norman Bearcroft - The Power and the Glory

16 George Marshall - The Citadel, Visions

17 Percy Merritt - The Golden West

18 Howard Davies – Beyond the Blue Horizons

19 Jules vanderKam – My Fortress

20 Bernard Verkaaik - Je Maintaindrai, Battle Spirit, Victory of the Light

Of course this is just a minor selection –only 20 composers are listed- of the seemingly endless list of great choices and one that obviously has no end as well, and which is of course very personal. Still it is an important part of the heritage of the Salvation Army history and one that must not be neglected.

Apart from the fact that it is also important to record this kind of music and appreciate the efforts that composers have put in creating this music, it is also a way of motivation for lesser qualitative and quantitative bands who can use this kind of recordings as an example of how it should and could be played. Another good reason is that *'aunt Betty, one of these silent and seemingly invisible people, and for years on the backrow of the hall'* would appreciate this kind of music probably more than any other. The following limited list might give an indication of interesting compositions worth to be explored, played, explained and definitely recorded.

Unity Series:

Eric Ball	In the Light
Eric Ball	Songs for Pilgrims
Dean Goffin	Stories of Jesus
Kenneth Downie	Sing Hosanna
Kevin Norbury	Mission
Richard Phillips	The World's Greatest Love Songs
Ray Steadman-Allen	It Happened to Me
David Rowsell	Out of His Wounded Side
Brian Bowen	The Happy Land
Dudley Bright	As I Am
Martyn Thomas	Spiritual Rock

Norwegian Junior Series

Paul Marti	Great Day
Niels Silfverberg	The Gospel Train
Erik Silfverberg	Perfect Peace

Brass Music for Young Bands (USA East)

Bruce Broughton	Powerful and Free
Eiliv Herikstad	Just a Closer Walk

Canadian Band Journal

Emil Söderström	The Coming Army
Bramwell Coles	I Will Guide Thee

Brass Ensemble Journal (USA East)

Erik Leidzén	Crusaders Hymn

American Brass Ensemble Series (USA South)

William Himes	A Gospel Song Sing-Along
William Himes	A Caribbean Sing Along

Another chance that definitely deserves a go is to record just more of the single composers recordings as described in 'Recordings – Single Composer Recordings'. It is quite difficult to understand why brass bands of the Salvation Army who are in a way connected to one or more composers, haven't done all that is in their capabilities to bring such a person to the fore front. Without wanting to point directly to a band, certainly composers like Terry Camsey, Arthur Gullidge and Bernard Verkaaik, just to name but three significant people, deserve to have their own album. Hopefully this book triggers the appropriate people to do so!

FEMALE COMPOSERS

Although most music is written by male composers, there is no doubt that female composers have also brought a wealth of musical compositions. Music composed by women started to appear in the 1500's already however there is music known from even earlier times composed by women. Their compositions gradually increased by the years and around the second half of the 18th century they were a significant presence in a world which was dominated by men.

Historically, women in music have been considered unusual and sometimes even unwelcome. Now compositions of previous centuries are being heard again, and female composers, performers and musical directors are beginning to get accepted. However they still seem to receive a critical approach which relates to gender rather than ability. In parallel; if we look at female bandmasters, and three well known come up immediately; Maissie Wiggins (UK), Peggy Thomas (USA) and Carole Reinhart (USA), we are certainly proud on them and on their achievements, but still think it's a bit out of the 'normal' route.

In the secular brass band scene –in particular in The Netherlands, Saskia Apon is one of the leading female brass composers. Amongst the many pieces she wrote is her '*Rainforest Concerto*', a trombone duet in three parts that has been recorded by Brass Band Rijnmond, one of the leading brass bands in the Netherlands, with Jörgen van Rijen and Ivan Meylemans, two international well known trombone virtuosi, as soloists.

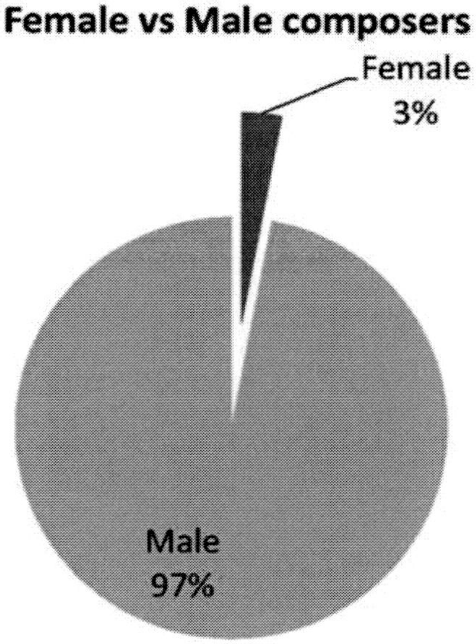

Also within the Salvation Army female composers are present and known for their skilled output. When thinking of female composers people would immediately recall the name of Joy Webb, who has contributed very well to the Army's repertoire. But there are others as well. Two of the earliest in Salvation Army history might be Lucy Booth and Evangeline Booth, two daughters of the Army's founder, William Booth.

Another female composer of note was Captain Ruby Palm of the United States, she was the first female Salvationist, as Mrs. Brigadier Ruby Adams, to have a band arrangement published. In the 1960's one of Erik Leidzén's students was a female Diane Martin (Jamaica, New York). She made a name for herself as a composer and still composes today. All of these women are described below (see: PALM, RUBY and MARTIN, DIANE).

One of the most popular cornet solos in and outside the Salvation Army is unmistakably Joy Webb's '*Share My Yoke*', which is recorded by many bands inside and outside the Salvation Army and still today is regarded as one of the most popular cornet solos within the 'global' brass band repertoire. The Chelmsford Citadel Songsters recorded a CD with solely the music of Joy Webb.

Although Joy Webb is still around, it is Dorothy Gates who is currently 'leading the team of female composers' where brass music by female composers is concerned. Dorothy hails from Northern Ireland and is a former member of the Southern Territorial Band, the National Capital Band and Spiritual to the Bone. Currently she is principal trombone with the New York Staff Band, and their 'composer in residence'.

Another name already related to the New York Staff Band is Emilee Bennett, who for a while was the band's baritone player. She also played Euphonium with the New Jersey Youth Band with whom she recorded one of her own compositions. Although not a brass composer, ever since the King's Singers recorded June Collin's *'The Quiet Heart'*, she became known as a composer for the wider audience as she composed this great piece way back. Her compositions have been published by the Salvation Army for many years already but it was because of this vocal group that she really became known to the wider audience. June is the wife of a former Songster Leader at Staines, UK. The fact that in particular this piece came into life because of the King's Singers made other arrangers such as Olaf Ritman (Ede, The Netherlands) and John Meredith (Boscombe, United Kingdom) realise that this might be a great addition to the brass band repertoire, which resulted in two separate arrangements of this brilliant piece, coincidentally also recorded around the same time (John's version with the Boscombe Citadel Band –first half of 2011, Olaf's version with the Amsterdam Staff Band – first half of 2011).

Yet another female composer is Charlotte Sharman (neé Pitteway) from Regent Hall, London, United Kingdom. She is married to composer and cornet soloist/deputy bandmaster of the Regent Hall Band and International Staff Bandsman Paul Sharman. One of the younger female composers, she was featured as composer in the *The Power of your love* and we look forward to her composing more music for use within the Salvation Army.

One of the younger women composers is Chelsea Pascoe of the Belfast Sydenham Corps (UK). She has already written for Salvation Army bands, including for the (Northern) Ireland Divisional Youth Band (bandmaster John Murdock) of which she is a member (solo horn) before she was 'discovered' by Jonathan Corry, bandmaster of the Enfield Citadel Band and a native of Northern Ireland, who recorded the piece, *'Prayer Gently Lifts Me'*, written by Chelsea, on the latest recording (Enfield Connection, SPS284CD, 2011) as part of the encouragement towards the younger composers within the Salvation Army.

Barbara Steadman-Allen

Barbara started her musical life as a 4 year old pianist, daughter of a Salvation Army composer and international music editor, and was enticed into trombone playing aged eleven when the local Salvation Army young people's band needed a trombonist. At the time she was one of nine living family trombone players (not all at once). Blowing one brass instrument almost automatically enables you to have fun with other brass instruments so she quickly developed trumpet playing for descants and sax for fun. She has a music degree from Birmingham University and has been a secondary school music teacher, church choir director, both youth choir and adult, band conductor, arranger and composer. She wanders into the world of strings on a violin. Barbara believes passionately in the Holy Spirit's inspiration of music from the earliest times of the Old Testament to the present day and on into tomorrow and that all stages, eras and styles should be embraced, with the proviso that the participants are able to worship and enjoy doing their best for the glory of God. That means hymns and songs have to be chosen with a view to the suitability of the accompanying instruments and voices. She loves 'crossover' music in worship e.g. trad hymns set to up tempo accompaniments! *(source: cofeguildford.org.uk)*

The inclusion of Barbara Steadman-Allen does not entirely fit with the aim of this book but I found her background interesting enough to include, as she has also had music published -as a composer- by the Salvation Army. Next to her daily duties and work, she is currently writing a book, together with her sister Rosemary, about the life and music of their father, Colonel Dr. Ray Steadman-Allen.

Another significant female composer, although not of any known brass work but still highly regarded is Miriam Mary Richards, who was born in New Barnet in Hertfordshire on 12 April 1911. She was the daughter of Brigadier William J. Richards and grew up in Indonesia and Korea where her father died in 1920. She entered the International Training College in 1932 after having worked for five years at International Headquarters in the Editorial Department. She retired in 1971 as a lieutenant-colonel. She wrote many songs of which some one hundred and twenty five were published by the Salvation Army.

Even more; Salvationist Anita Cocker-Hunt is originally from Cleveland, Ohio in the USA. She earned her Bachelor of Music Education and Bachelor of Music in trumpet degrees from the University of Cincinnati College-Conservatory of Music. She has held positions as high school band and orchestra director in the Cleveland area, as private trumpet instructor at the Cleveland Music School Settlement, and was a member of the Cleveland Women's Symphony Orchestra. It is almost unbelievable in this current era that in earlier times women were not allowed to play in a band. Slowly they conquered this and nowadays the bands -worldwide- can't do without them. That even female bandmasters and fortunately also female composers and arrangers now have joined the until recently regarded as men-only fraternity, is of real significance. William Booth, the Founder of the Salvation Army already recognised this by saying that *his best men are women*! The women mentioned here are just a minor enumeration of the many women who has contributed significantly to the repertoire of the Salvation Army.

Regent Hall Salvationist Penny Babb, daughter of composer Michael Babb, has in collaboration with her father also had some publications in the Army band journals. Although the music was published with her name on it, she is not in this book in the Composers chapter as her work was really a joint effort rather than completely sole compositions.

CHOICE OF MUSIC - MUSIC IS MAGIC

By Garmt Dijksterhuis, June 2011

Music is so much more than just a series of notes. I'm not quite sure what this 'more' is, it must be hidden in the many different aspects of music. There's a very important social aspect to playing music. Even the solo artist wants an audience to interact with, and those lucky enough to play in a band know the importance of the social aspect. When playing music together with someone, you're becoming friends instantly. It is impossible to play with people you don't like, and if the music turns out right, you'll like them. And the audience hears it. It's also much fun to play together. Personally I enjoy the little musical jokes between the band-mates, like secretly copying a drum riff on the guitar, and watching the reaction of the drummer, or trying to echo the singer... Sometimes it goes wrong, but that's part of the fun, and very often the audience will not notice, at least I hope so... It all adds to the intimacy between the members in a band. Music is at the same time cerebral and visceral.

There are great intellectual challenges to overcome. Learning specific phrases involves practise, but not just of the motor system. It's a demanding intellectual task to master a piece, e.g. playing unexpected tempo changes or notes that sound dissonant at first. Only after a lot of physical and psychological work will the task be mastered. The subtlety of the interplay between what the mind tells you what it should sound like, and what the fingers actually carry out is enormous. It's on a millisecond scale and the tiniest changes in pressure of the lips, position of the fingers, or force on the keys, can make all the difference.

At some point it's impossible to think in such detail, and one has to start feeling the music, which is accomplished by many cycles of rehearsing and listening, rehearsing, listening, rehearsing, listening, etc. Obviously there's a lot of psychology in music. Recent studies in time perception have indicated that upon hearing a simple rhythm, just a series of clicks, subsequent scoring on some cognitive tasks increases. It may have something to do with attention, maybe making you more alert. As every musician knows, even the simplest of rhythms will resonate inside you. You not only hear the clicks, you can feel them. You just have to tap your feet, sway your body or just your head, and when the rhythm feels right, you want to grab your instrument and play along. The clicking also seems to influence time perception. Musicians will know this. While playing good music there is no sense of time, other than the metre. You're flowing on the stream of music, and as everything is flowing on the same beat, time stands still. When the piece is finished, time seems to have flown by too fast, it's always a pity it's over, and to be thrown back again in the now. Obviously there is a huge creative aspect in music.

It's not only the composers who show creativity, also the players have to be creative. If it were just a matter of playing the notes from the score, music would sound dull and boring. Have you ever listened to a symphony orchestra playing rock-songs? Very often they just don't get it, they play the notes but lack the feel of a good rock band. It's the creativity the players have to add to the written music, that makes for a great performance.

The magic of creativity is that one is able to make something out of nothing. One moment there's silence, the next moment there's a beat and before you know you are mesmerised by this fantastic sound. It may sound so simple, one person likes brass, another the clavichord, yet another can listen to rock day after day, but an individual's musical choices are probably as difficult to explain as consumers' choice of food and personal care products. One idea about musical preferences is that the music that you heard during an important change period in your life (typically puberty with its increase in independence) may stick with you forever. This means that you may agree to the preferences of your peers, through what friends played you, or from the radio.

For many people born in the 30's or 40's that means jazz and be-bop, for those from the 40's and 50's it will be rock and rockabilly, people from the 60's, as myself, often are lovers of American and British rock music. I must say, personally, reggae, rap or dance music doesn't touch me. According to this theory, it's an age thing I'm afraid. In this book the religious aspect of music plays an important role. I could call this the 'magic' of music. You can decide to honour a deity with your music, or you can celebrate the fact that a group of people who enjoy themselves through music becomes more than just a collection of individuals. This 'more' I call magic.

Professor Dr. Garmt B. Dijksterhuis is professor of Sensory Science at the University of Copenhagen (Denmark) and Research Center (The Netherlands) and Science Leader at Unilever Research and Development, Vlaardingen, The Netherlands.

In his spare time he is an avid amateur musician in the field of Blues Rock, playing electric guitar. He is a colleague of the author of this book.

DIFFERENT MUSICAL FORMS

To write music for any group of musicians or bandsmen is not something you can do easily. Many compositions have been written with a purpose and with a particular goal in mind. This already indicates the direction towards a composer should think when writing a new work. Is it for use on the street, should it be a 'show off' solo work, should it be an orchestration of a classical work or perhaps a rhapsody type of work etc. Below several of the used forms of music within the Salvation Army are mentioned together with a brief explanation.

MARCH

The march is definitely one of the eldest forms of brass band music. These compositions were (are) meant for use on the streets to walk on in a steady and organized way. They are probably also one of the most well known form of band music too, and also with the biggest impact on composers, each of whom has at least a few marches in their output. The usual form is in a 4/4, but favorites are also 6/8 and 2/4. Most of the marches were written with a special purpose in mind, hence the titles of these music forms which are direct indications to names of corps (e.g *'Exeter Temple'*, *'Hadleigh Temple'*, *'Amsterdam Congress'*), music schools and music camps (e.g *'Cobham Hall'*, *'Tylney Hall'*, *'Camp Akatarawa'*) or other Salvation Army camps (e.g *'Motondo'*), or even regions (e.g *'The Golden West'*, *'Spirit of the West'*). Other purposes for writing marches are to honour people, bands and departments with marches entitled *'The Red Shield'* (social service of the Salvation Army) and *'Cairo Red Shield'* (the Salvationist soldiers in Egypt during the Second World War). Good quality marches never lose the interest of players and so even marches written a long time ago, in particular by the 'march king of the Salvation Army', Bramwell Coles, are still immensely popular today. Variants on the usual march form are the so called 'descriptive march' such as *'The Salvation Army Patrol'* and of course the 'quick march' of which Paul Drury's *'Jubilee'* is the best known example.

FESTIVAL MARCH

Not like the so called street march the Festival March was created for use during concerts which within the Salvation Army are generally 'Festivals'. Festival Marches are not written for use in a march, which is shown in many compositions as it is 'allowed' to use different time signatures. Great examples of Festival Marches are William Himes' *'The Witness'*, which was his first entrée in the Festival Series of the Salvation Army and although accepted with a certain reluctance as they thought that in this work he would have spoiled all his creativity, it is of course known now, years after he wrote *'The Witness'*, that his creativity is nearly endless. Another great example of a good well written Festival March is *'The Southern Cross'* by Brian Bowen. Named after a famous star in the southern hemisphere, this piece also became very popular. Other good examples to showcase the difference between a normal march and a Festival March are *'The Ransomed Army'* (Kevin Norbury), *'Chalk Farm No.2'* (Edward Gregson), *'Able'* (William Turkington, revised by William Himes), *'Motivation'* (William Himes) and probably the most well known of all, Leslie Condon's *'Celebration'*. Another comparison with the Festival March is the so called 'Concert March' and even the 'Symphonic Concert March' are names given to marches which aren't meant to be for marching purposes but for the 'Festivals' (concerts) given by the Army.

TONE POEM

Usually the larger type of concert works, this type of work was introduced in the 1930's during the cooperation of Eric Ball with General Evangeline Booth. The General was inspired by her own song *'Songs of Evangel'* (SP&S 1936) to write a brass band work and in a discussion with Eric Ball she suggested that it should be written in the style of a tone poem. As a result of the creativity of these two people, Eric Ball's first Tone Poem *'Exodus'* was written in 1937. Other well known Tone Poems are Eric Ball's *'Resurgam'* and Ray Steadman-Allen's *'D-Star'*.

FANTASIA

The fantasia form was created by the composers likely as any other form would not be sufficient enough or and when the form would not be of primary importance. There are not many of the fantasias around and *'Fantasia on Lobe den Herren'* (Eric Ball) is perhaps the best well known example of this although James Wright's *'Fantasia for Children'* is also very good example. It shows differences with Eric Ball's masterpiece but is also brilliant in its own right. In the current era composers gradually call new large solo works a 'fantasia' (e.g. Fantasia for Cornet).

RHAPSODY

A rhapsody is a more difficult phenomenon to describe as it is usually also a larger concert work, although it is not a tone poem. Rhapsodies are more the story telling kind of compositions and good examples of this are *'Rhapsody on American Gospel Songs'* and *'Challenge and Response'*, both great compositions by the pen of Eric Ball. A rhapsody also can be a more extended solo work, and probably the best example for this is *'Rhapsody for Cornet and Band'* by Ray Bowes. A variant on the 'rhapsody' are the 'rhapsodic variations' like *'My Strength My Tower'* (Dean Goffin).

SELECTIONS

In the beginning of the existence of the Salvation Army William Booth, its founder, soon already saw that there was a need to develop the Army's band music. He then asked Richard Slater, the 'Father of Salvation Army Music', to produce a 'selection' of music that could be set as a standard and example for all what would follow. The first selection was *'Old Song Melodies'* and was published in 1902. The selections used in the Salvation Army are usually a number of Salvation Army song treated in various ways with interludes between each melody line, but over the years more and more challenging changes are being used which could make them small concert works. Some good examples of this are *'Selections from Godspell'* (Barrie Gott), *'Songs in Exile'* (Eric Ball) and *'The Light of the World'* (Dean Goffin).

AIR VARIE

The Air Varie is one of the eldest forms used to describe the music used in the Salvation Army. It is usually a type of 'theme and variations' although this is not always the case. Some good examples to illustrate this are *'A Sunbeam'* (Philip Catelinet), which has no real variation form compared to *'The Old Wells'* (Eric Ball).

OVERTURES

Although the word 'overture' is used to the full in classical music (e.g *'Le Carnaval Romain, Finlandia', 'Le Roy d'Ys', 'Russlan and Ludmilla'*), this form is not used often within the Salvation Army and probably the only real example that does justice to the use of it is *'God with us'* (Kevin Norbury).

MEDITATIONS

To consider giving a composition the name of a 'meditation' it is obvious that the piece should be in a kind of meditative or devotional manner. It is also very clear that when you listen to this type of music the word 'meditation' is the only appropriate name, especially when you listen to pieces like *'Just as I am'* and *'My Master's Will'*, both brilliant additions to the Salvation Army repertoire by Wilfred Heaton. Ray Steadman-Allen said about the term: *'It implies the setting of devotional material in a subjective way, treated either in accordance with the sentiment, and perhaps a sequence of associated words, or allowing his own response to dictate the manner of expression'.*

SONG SETTING

A song setting or any related form (e.g hymn tune setting, chorus setting) is closely connected to the 'selections' with the difference that the song settings are simpler in set up and usually shorter in duration. Good examples are e.g. *'In perfect peace'* (Kenneth Downie), *'Light up the sunshine'* (arr. Maurice Ozanne) and *'Lord, with my all I part'* (Brian Bowen).

ARRANGEMENTS

There are really countless examples to show the real meaning of an arrangement. Probably the first that comes to mind is the arrangement of classical music. Often mixed up with a 'transcription', when using the word 'arrangement', the composer or in this case the arranger can take another route with the original music and can add his own ideas to it, which is really the big difference between this and a transcription. A great example to describe what is meant here is the piece *'Kaleidoscope'*. The original tunes comes from music by the classical Russian composer Rimsky Korsakov, but Brian Bowen has weaved several bits and pieces together to make a great concert type of work, which also became very popular amongst bands. Another way to describe an 'arrangement' is in principle the use of any melody line from (preferably) well known music or songs and change it into a way the composer/arranger likes. An arrangement as such can vary in length and duration. Apart from the earlier mentioned *'Kaleidoscope'*, there is also Leslie Condon's masterpiece *'The Call of the Righteous'* which is called an 'arrangement' although the first suggestion for this piece was to name it a *'Tone Poem'* although Leslie simply found it too short to do so. Other variants on 'arrangement' such as 'Hymn tune arrangement' and 'festival arrangement' are also in existence.

VARIATIONS

An important form that appeared lately in the Salvation Army journals is the 'Variation'. Although this one is of course also closely related to the Tone Poem and perhaps also to the Rhapsody and even the Arrangement it definitely earns its own place in this brief enumeration of musical forms used in the sheet music of the Army. A piece like *'A Pilgrim Song'*, which is probably Thomas Rive's greatest piece, is called a 'variation' but probably one of the most recent compostions, Kevin Norbury's *'Variations on Maccabeus'* is the best example of this form. The variation as such is easily recognizable as it usually starts with the (hymn) tune which is often also the title of the piece, followed by several variations on this tune. The musical ideas of tune, set as variations, can be quite extended, difficult and developed in musical terms.

SUITES

When the Army started the publications of its music, the 'Suite' form was already popular. In most cases it is a piece of music divided in -usually three- parts, with the middle part being the minor key part and the last part again in the major key. Some suites such as *'On the Road'* (Howard Davies) have appeared in the Festival Series (the most advanced level of Salvation Army publications) while others like *'Splendour of youth'* (Leslie Condon) and *'Joy and Devotion'* (Howard Davies) have appeared in the more intermediate publications. Other great examples of suites are Eric Ball's *'Songs of the Morning'* and Bramwell Coles *'The Divine Pursuit'* with its -certainly at that time- unusual 5/4.

TRANSCRIPTIONS

Other than with the earlier mentioned arrangements, the transcriptions are basically just the brass band versions of music that was originally written for other musical combinations. The most common one here is the 'translation' from classical music to the setting of the brass band, with some great example like *'Procession of the Nobles'*, *'Festive Overture'* and *'Jesu, Joy of Man's Desiring'*. Nowadays, in particular in the secular movement, music from other orchestral forms (big band, wind band, jazz etc) is used for making transcriptions.

SOLOISTS

To highlight the often extraordinary skills of soloists within bands, composers have written special music to show this to the audience. Over the years some notable players have proven to be of great value to composers, and acted as fantastic representatives for these writers. Worth mentioning are players such as Roland Cobb and David Daws (ISB, Cornet), Deryck Diffey (CSB, Cornet), Robert Merritt, Clarence White (CSB, Trombone) and Leslie Condon (ISB, E*b* Bass) just to name but five of them, but of course many other highly skilled players have done justice to the full in performing music written by the often invisible people, the *composers* and *arrangers*. The many variants of instruments for which composers have written solo music reflects almost every instrument in the brass bands of the Salvation Army, E*b* Soprano Cornet, B*b* Cornet, Flugelhorn, Tenor Horn, Baritone, Euphonium, Trombone, Bass Trombone, E*b* Bass and even Tuned Percussion. To the knowledge of the author there is -within the repertoire of the Salvation Army- no solo written for BB*b* Bass (yet). Some other great combinations were also born out of the creative brains of the composers, such as for:

Cornet: duet (either two B*b* cornets as well as duets for Eb cornet and Bb cornet), trio, quartet, quintet, ensemble (or feature) but also duet between Eb cornet/Bb cornet and flugelhorn. All forms mentioned here are often in use and countless pieces in this setting have been written.

Horn: duet, trio, ensemble (or feature). Rarely used in this way, however the tenor horn as solo instrument is becoming more and more to the forefront when the use of a solo instrument is required.

Trombone: duet, trio, ensemble (or feature). The trombone has always been a great source of inspiration to many composers and arrangers, which resulted in many additions for this instrument, also as a solo instrument. Popular composers are often great trombonists themselves, and some familiar names include: Dudley Bright, Roger Trigg, Ray Steadman-Allen and David Catherwood just to name but a few.

Euphonium: duet. Although the euphonium is one of the most popular solo instruments next to the cornet, the use of this great instrument in another setting such as a duet is still rare.

Bass: duet for Eb Bass, but also duet for Eb bass and BBb bass. The Eb bass is going through a real revival as solo instrument. It is a fact that several brass soloists from the secular brass band movement have brought a wealth of experience and new solos into the repertoire for Eb bass, and slowly also the Salvation Army repertoire is enriched by compositions especially written for this great instrument.

Percussion: the drum kit is often used as a solo instrument but usually this happens in or during a piece of music rather than as a real solo instrument. The 'tuned' part of the percussion (glockenspiel, xylophone, marimba, and even timpani etc) is in use as real 'stand up' solo instrument.

Other combinations have also been the result of the seemingly endless brain waves of the composers. Examples of this are: Double quartet for cornets and trombones (e.g. *'Never Give Up'* - Eric Ball), duet for cornet and euphonium (e.g. *'I'll Not Turn Back'* – Ivor Bosanko), duet for cornet and trombone (e.g. *'Joy in my Soul'* – Erik Silfverberg). Some solo compositions have been written so that, unintentionally, other instruments have been able to use them. To illustrate this, there are compositions such as the cornet solo *'Golden Slippers'* (Norman Bearcroft) that was previously played on trombone! The immensely popular flugelhorn solo *'So Glad'* (William Himes) has been played on Cornet, Trombone, Saxophone and Clarinet, just to name but a few. Other solos have even been written to be played on even more instruments; *'The Old Rugged Cross'* (Erik Leidzén) – Trombone or Cornet, *'The Eternal Quest'* (Ray Steadman-Allen) – Trombone or Euphonium.

Salvation Army Composers Conference at Salvationist Publishing & Supplies, ca 1965.

When this conference happened, this might have just been 'another' occasion for the participants, and perhaps for everyone around them as well. When we look back now some forty plus years further, it is almost unbelievable that so many significant giants of the Salvation Army music have (at least once) gathered together in this way. The men in this picture represents a great deal of the complete Salvation Army journals ever published! Although grateful -which is a heavy understatement- for what they have written, it is most unfortunate that people such as Thomas Rive and Leslie Condon, just to name but two, have passed away far too early. Imagine what they could have written if living a 'normal' lifetime!

The real story behind this photo is that the Centenary of the Salvation Army was held in London in the summer of 1965. There were such things as marching displays and a huge parade of countries in national costume, bands and so on at the Crystal Palace. There was also a rally on Trafalgar Square and meetings in the Royal Albert Hall led by General Frederick Coutts. As many composers and song writers were going to be in London for this event it was suggested that SP&S (where the International Music Editorial Department was then located) might organise and host an afternoon conference for them. Of the people that came are in the photograph, Colonel Charles Skinner was the Music Editorial Head at that time. He is on the front row together with Eric Ball and Philip Catelinet. Catelinet gave a talk (and spoke of trying to involve USA ex-high school band people under the Salvation

Army 'umbrella') but other speakers are unknown. Doubtless Skinner and Ball would have taken part. The event was really more a soul get together than a technical conference.

Front row (from left to right):

Ernest Rance, Herbert Mountain, Norman Bearcroft, Phil Catelinet, Frederick Harvey (Head of Salvationist Publishing & Supplies), Charles Skinner, General Wilfred Kitching, Eric Ball

Second row (from left to right):

Haakon Dahlstrom, Donald Osgood, Kenneth Cook, Herbert Young, Edgar Cuell, Eddy Dytham, Harry Kirk, John Birch

Third row (from left to right):

Thomas Rive, Harry Stilwell, Terry Camsey, Ivor Bosanko, Brindley Boon, Dean Goffin, Leslie Condon, Sidney Hubbard

Fourth row (from left to right):

Unknown, Unknown, **Robert Redhead, Neville McFarlane, Michael Kenyon (not confirmed) Ray Bowes, Brian Bowen, Ray Steadman-Allen**

Back row (from left to right):

Unknown, Unknown, Unknown, Unknown, Unknown, Unknown, **George Crane, Terry Hazell**

Currently there has been a Composers Forum running in the United States of America led by noted composers like William Himes, Stephen Bulla and James Curnow and so on. These happenings were very successful and will likely be continued in the future. Still the photo here remains very significant, not the least for historical purposes.

COMPOSERS OF THE SALVATION ARMY

In Alphabetical order you will now encounter many composers who either are:

- Salvationists, who have written for the Salvation Army.
- Salvationists, who have written for the Salvation Army and for secular bands.
- Non-Salvationists, who have written for the Salvation Army and for secular bands.
- Non-Salvationists, who have written music not for the Salvation Army as such, but whose compositions are being used within the Army.
- As extra a limited amount of new upcoming composers have been included here. Through this writing the author hopes to be of encouragement to this new generation of brass composers and arrangers.

ABBOTT, ERIC

Dr. Eric (Oscar) Abbott. Bandmaster, cornetist, pianist, organist, composer, arranger, born in St John's, Newfoundland, Canada, on 4th August 1929. ATCL 1949, LTCL 1950, L MUS (Acadia) 1951, B MUS (Acadia) 1952, L MUS TCL 1955, M MUS (Acadia) 1956, D ED (Boston) 1969, FTCL 1970. His teachers included Edwin Collins, Janis Kalejs, Hugo Norden, and Gardner Read. His doctoral thesis was 'The evolution of the Canadian festival movement as an instrument of music education'. He began teaching music in St. John's schools in 1948 and became band director for the Avalon Consolidated School Board in 1968. His broadcasting career, which began in 1949, has included several hundred piano, organ, and cornet recitals. He was choral arranger and conductor for eight years on CBC radio's 'Come All Ye Round' and music director 1960 -1962 for CJON radio and CJOX-TV, St John's. He led Salvation Army bands in St John's and in Massachusetts and became director of the Booth Memorial Brass Band in 1968. In 1983 the onset of Ménière's disease forced him to retire from full-time teaching, but he maintained his position as instructor with the Salvation Army Training College, and the Salvation Army Cadet's Band. He also continued to teach privately and conduct the Silver Chords, a senior's choir. He was Promoted to Glory on 9th February 1988.

Important compositions

St.John's Citadel (GS1705) 1978, Surrender (AJ109) 1980, Invitation (CM45) 1963

AGNEW, MAY

May (Kingston, Canada 1865 – New York, USA 1935) became a Salvation Army officer from the New York 3 Corps and worked for a time as an editorial for The 'War Cry' and in the Candidates Department. In 1902 she married the reverend Harold Stevens, who became pastor of Parkdale Alliance Tabernacle in Toronto, Canada. Together they served for some 25 years as evangelist throughout the United States, the British Isles and Canada. The first songs that she contributed to 'The Musical Salvationist' were in 1887 and 1888.

Important compositions

Have faith in God (GS0352) 1897, Jesus is looking for thee (GS0356) 1898

ALISH, HEINZ

Heinz Alisch was born on 23 February 1934 in Tuttlingen, Germany. Captain Heinz Alish is the composer of the March *'German Congress'* which was the first band composition by a German Salvationist to appear in the Salvation Army band journals. He was a Salvation Army officer. He suffered a severe illness which interrupted his service and so had to relinquish his officership. Had some positive comments by colonel Albert Jakeway saying he would got far as a composer. He is the son of Officer parents and at one time all four Alish children were officers. Heinz started composing music as a teenager and never stopped composing music. He is now retired and lives, together with his wife, in Pfullingen, Southern Germany.

Important compositions

Camp Plon (TS0679) 1966, German Congress (TS0571) 1957, On the Pilgrim Path (US0072) 1964

ALLAN, J.D.

One of the early composers (late 1800's). No further information could be retrieved about him.

This is the first composer in this book of which no information is available. Despite all efforts unfortunately of many of these early composers, no information is preserved. It was also a habit in those days that the name of the composer did not appear on the composition as such, hence the difficulty to find any valuable information back, which could be used in this writing.

Important compositions

Closer to Thee (GS0201) 1892, A Crown of Peace (GS0100-1) 1888

ALLAN, JOHN J.

John Allan, born as son of Salvation Army Officers in the USA, was an excellent cornet player. He was a member of the New York Staff Band and later became an officer of The Salvation Army. He was the founder of the summer music camps. As a Staff-Captain and Youth Secretary, he and his wife started and directed with music camps in the Eastern and Central Territories at Star Lake, New Jersey, and at Wonderland, Wisconsin. During World War 1 he served as a Chaplain in the US Army. As a Commissioner, John J. Allan served General Orsborn as Chief of the Staff from 1946 to 1950. In sending a message to the Melbourne Staff Band upon the occasion of its diamond jubilee in 1950, he said: *'I know of nothing in the Army that can be of more value in bringing blessing, arousing enthusiasm and building public opinion quickly than the consecrated efforts of a Staff Band'.* Probably his most well known work is the cornet solo *'Memories'* which saw publication in 1946.

Important compositions

Memories (FS140) 1946

ALLEN, HERBERT

Henry Allen (18 February 1865 – 2 February 1943) was a bandmaster of the New Brompton (later Gillingham) Corps Band for about seven years and afterwards was junior soldiers sergeant major. He played a variety of musical instruments, including several non-brass instruments. He formed several alternative bands in particular young people. He was Promoted to Glory from Great Horton, and was the first Household Troops Bandsman to become an Officer. He was converted at Wensbury, Staffordshire, in 1883, and on June 28, 1887, left home to join this famous musical Combination. His first training for Officership was received in the 'Integrity' Van, which was then situated in a field of cabbages at Great Marlow. Soon afterward he was sent to his first appointment at Maidenhead, in April 1888. During his active career Major Allen commanded some fifty Corps, which included Burnley Citadel, Carlisle, Lincoln, Oldham and Leeds West Hunslet. He was always a Band enthusiast and his cornet was often heard in the open-air. He retired from Great Horton, and the writer, when a Young People's Band member at this Corps, will remember the sterling worth of this grand Salvationist who was much loved and respected in the district. His son, Bandmaster Herbert Allen, of Great Horton, is a talented cornetist, concertina player, and composer. His song *'Living in Jesus'* is universally popular. *'Glad Surrender'* a Second Series march was also written by him. ('The Musician' 19-3-1938)

Important compositions

Glad Surrender (TS0098) 1927, The Path is very narrow (GS0396) 1900, That means me (GS0313) 1896

ALEXANDER, ERIC

Born on April 23, 1959, Eric Alexander is a Trombonist and composer/arranger by profession. He currently belongs to the staff of the arrangers for the Church of Apostles, the largest television ministry around the globe. His compositions can be heard no over 250 recordings, including his own solo recording *'Credo'*. He was a member of Spiritual to the Bone ensemble, led by Stephen Bulla, another noted composer, the Southern Territorial Band and the National Capital Band of the Salvation Army.

Important compositions

Lord, Lord You sure been good to me

ALLEN, PERCY JOHN

A newspaper article of 1946 tells us: Death of Mr. P.J. Allen – Late bandmaster to Rugby Salvation Army and Talented Composer. Nineteen years bandmaster of the Rugby Salvation Army band, Percy John Allen, L.Mus., L.C.M., who died at his home in Rugby on Friday, was also a composer of band music, and was the son of a Salvation Army bandsman of years service. Percy Allen who was a boot and shoe repairer by trade, carrying on businesses in Sheep Street and Cross Street in Rugby, was in 1927 appointed Sub-Postmaster at the Sheep Street Post Office. He was sixty years of age. Mr. Allen was the son of Mr. John Allen, a railway goods guard who was killed in tragic circumstances on the railway in 1925. His father was for many years an enthusiastic member of the local corps of the Salvation Army and played in the corps band as a bass player from his earliest days. The whole family shared Mr. John Allen's interest in the Salvation Army, and by their musical talent rendered the organization signal service.

Compositions: In 1926 Mr. Allen was one of the sixty Salvation Army bandmasters chosen to attend a special bandmasters' training, and high Salvation Army executives including the late General Bramwell Booth were present. On another occasion he conducted a band weekend at Manchester Salvation Army Temple, when his own march *'Activity'* was played, and his father conducted the services. Mr. Allen composed a number of vocal compositions and brass band selections which were accepted by the Salvation Army Musical Board in

London and were highly praised. His first brass band selection *'Wonderful Love'* was given its first public performance in Rugby Recreation Ground in 1928. His second band composition *'Walking with Jesus'* was played by the International Staff Band in 1934. He retired from the position of bandmaster in September 1944, and was presented with an electric clock by the members of the band.

Percy John Allen started his Salvation Army banding career as a boy on the triangle. He then took up the tenor horn, but an affliction of the throat caused him to discontinue playing a brass instrument. He turned his attention to the drum and there are few places in the country where the name of Percy John Allen is not associated with that instrument. He formed a Drum and Fife Band in 1907 and in 1922 became bandmaster, filling that position until 1944, with only a short interval.

Important compositions

Activity (GS0870) 1921, Walking with Jesus (GS1091) 1935, Wonderful Love (GS0977) 1928

ÅLÖW, ANDREAS

Andreas was born in 1979, in Gothenburg, Sweden. Practically born into the Salvation Army, it's no wonder he turned to music early on. The family belonged to Gothenburg 1, also known as Gothenburg Temple Corps. His father was the corps bandmaster, and his mother played piano and sang solos. At age 7, he started playing cornet in the youth band, switching to horn within a few years. Throughout his childhood, Andreas also played plenty of football, and music was simply one of his interests. At age 13, he began discovering rock music and took up bass guitar, the instrument that he, to this day, considers his main instrument. Together with his friends, Andreas started a heavy metal band that, for a few years, was a peculiar but interesting addition to the corps' music life. Today Andreas says that this period was a great learning experience, as it taught him that even forms of music that, on the surface, might seem to have little in common, are connected and part of the same language.

Whilst cutting his teeth in rock bands, Andreas kept playing his Eb horn and started going to some music schools. It began to dawn on him that there were some true treasures in the repertoire of SA brass music. Experiences like playing William Himes' *'To the Chief Musician'* or Leslie Condon's *'The Present Age'* at music camp touched something deep inside, and Andreas knew that he wanted to create the same kind of music. By the time he left Gothenburg to study music in Stockholm, he had already made his first attempts at arranging music for band.

In Stockholm, he joined the then Stockholm 7 band, led by Torgny Hanson. Torgny and others encouraged Andreas to write more band music, and in 1999 the first full band piece, a song arrangment on a swedish worship chorus, saw the light of day. Andreas credits the late James Anderson (composer of the march *'Goldcrest'*, among other pieces) for encouragement and advice when finishing this piece. The arrangment, based on Psalm 139 and titled *'Du omsluter mig'* was well received and played by various bands during the following years. Andreas continued by writing marches, cornet solos, meditations and so on. He brought piece after piece to band practice, and recorded them to keep track of his progress. During this time, Anders Beijer was also in the band, and many discussions were had about the music they were both writing. They encouraged each other and exchanged ideas. In 2001, Andreas entered the Royal College University of Music in Stockholm, studying musc theory and arranging. This gave him the opportunity to widen his ambition and he started writing music for string orchestra, and brass quintet, to name a few examples. He graduated in 2006, earning a Masters degree in music theory.

After 7 years in Stockholm, Andreas felt his hometown calling. He felt that it was time to move back to Gothenburg. During the following years Andreas concentrated more on his bass playing and composing/writing rock music. He never did stop writing band music, though. In 2005, *'There is a redeemer'* was published in the ScanBrass series. Currently, there are several other pieces published and Andreas is writing more music than ever. He is still playing bass guitar and writes and records progressive rock in his home studio. Brass-wise, he's come back from a hiatus and opted to switch to trombone, a move he secretly wanted to make for years. Even whilst playing horn in the TMI Band at the Territorial Music Institute in Texas back in 1999, he wondered if not the loudest instrument of the band was the most fun... Now that he's made the switch, he agrees that it IS fun.

Andreas had a few musical heroes when starting to compose, such as Leslie Condon and Wilfred Heaton, but his main influence was Eric Ball. There was something about the depth of Eric's music, and the strength of his melodies that captured Andreas' imagination. Listening to massed band recordings of *'The Kingdom Triumphant'*, *'The Eternal Presence'* and *'Resurgam'*, Andreas knew that this was his aim. A great, full sound, haunting melodies and a firm foundation in Scripture. The most important impression left by Eric Ball's music, to Andreas, was the spiritual depth. Music, in the ideal world, HAS to mean something. It always says something, about the person who composes it, but also about his Creator. The exceptional spiritual aspect of Salvation Army band music can sometimes be almost overwhelming, something that Andreas can testify to. Sometimes, in the middle of a piece, he's found it hard to keep playing, as the message delivered through the music has hit home. This is surely something that others have experienced, too. When it comes to the more technical side of band music, Andreas points to people such as Donald Osgood, Morley Calvert and Peter Graham as examples of how to use the band efficiently. He remembers in particular playing Graham's *'Shine as the light'* and being struck by how awesome the sound of just basses playing the chords in the 4th bar of the cornet solo was. Peter Graham, like Heaton and Ball before him, really showed the richness of sound that the brass band is capable of. Another influence on Andreas' arranging has been Philip Wilby's 'Black Dyke Tune Book', where Wilby makes the band sound almost organlike and regal. There are many things that the brass band does well, but the choral quality is Andreas' favorite. *'All the fast runs and loud chords in the world can't overshadow the warmth and serenity of a good hymn, played by a brass band'*, he says.

Andreas hopes to develop his writing and to further explore the brass band medium, all for the glory of God.

Important compositions

There is a redeemer, Immanuel – God with us, Stunden har kommit, Stockholm South Citadel,

FMV 2008, Lament of the forgotten, Trinity Fanfare

ANDER, OVE

Ove was bandmaster on the Stockholm Temple Corps for several years in the 1980´s and 1990´s. Born in 1956, he is a Swedish music researcher working at the Swedish University and Stockholm Music Institut. Ove did his doctorate at Stockholm University in 2000 where his thesis was about instrumentation and composition techniques in symphonies written by 19th century composers. Ove Ander has published editions of older Swedish music: Franz Berwald Sämtliche Werke (Bärenreiter Verlag) samt Monumenta Musicae Suecicae. He has, together with Mattias Lundberg, made some extensive research on older music sources in Sweden.

Important compositions

Stridsman ar jag (SF0006) 1986

ANDERSON, FOLKE

Folke is a Swedish composer and was also bandmaster of the Orebro Corps Band in Sweden. His selection *'The Joy of Salvation'* was awarded 3rd place in section One of the international music competition in 1947. It was published in the General Series journal in March 1949 and serves a useful purpose in the general ministry of army bands.

Important compositions

The Joy of Salvation (GS1311) 1949, Sound the battle cry (GS1533) 1964, Orebro 1 (GS1601) 1969

ANDERSON, HARRY *(also known as Henry)*

Apparently a native of Belfast, he is believed to have been the organist at the Carlisle Circus Methodist Church there. When his music appeared in 'The Musical Salvationist' in 1887 he was designated 'Auxiliary H. Anderson', and his father, William Anderson, of Queen Street, Belfast is said to have helped in Salvation Army meetings when the Academy Street Corps opened in Belfast.

(source: Companion to the Songbook – 1988)

Important compositions

Oh, Live thy life in me (GS0324) 1896

ANDERSON, JAMES

James Anderson was born 1946 in Glasgow, Scotland, a fourth generation Salvationist. Jim graduated from the Royal Scottish Academy of Music, and Jordanhill College of Education in 1974, and has built a fine reputation as an educator, conductor and composer both in his native Scotland and throughout The Salvation Army world. As a composer and arranger, Jim has over 60 band and choral works in publication, many of which are performed and recorded internationally. Jim felt privileged to be given the opportunity in 1992 to move to Texas in the United States to work full-time for The Salvation Army in ministry and was until his untimely passing the Divisional Music Director for the National Capital and Virginia Division and Bandmaster of the National Capital Band. Before that he was Territorial Music Director for the West and Bandmaster of the famous Pasadena Tabernacle Band.

Important compositions

Goldcrest (GS1841) 1989, Flying High (GS1848) 1990, Jesus Loves Me (TS759) 1973, The Words of the Amen (m/s), Camp Happyland (GS2088) 2010

ANDERSON, W(ILLIAM?)

One of the early composers (first half of 19th century).

No further information could be retrieved about him.

Important compositions

Mercy (GS1072) 1933

ANDERSSON, ALBERT J.

Albert was born in 1874 and Promoted to Glory in 1904. He played in the Swedish Staff Band during the 1894 -1895 season, assumed playing Eb Cornet. Between 1895 and 1900 he was the Bandmaster of the Jönköping Corps Band (Frälsingsarméns musikkar Jönköping) and also composed the *'Jönköping March'* (svensk Festmusik 10). He was a Trader by profession.

Important compositions

Festmarsch (FM0039) 1906

ANDERSSON, BERTIL

Bertil Andersson was born on May 13th 1915 in Sala, Västmanlands län, in Sweden. As a child he visited the Salvation Army and eventually became a soldier and bandsmen at the Södertälje corps. In 1935 he entered the training college for officers in Stockholm. In 1940 he married Lieutenant Mildred Ingeborg Nygren. As officers they served in different corps in Sweden. Later Bertil became the National Band Secretary of Sweden and was Promoted to Glory in 1982.

Important compositions

March Looking Heavenward (GS1437) 1956

ANEFELT, PAUL VIKTOR

Colonel Paul Viktor Anefelt was born on May 29, 1900 in Stockholm. As a child of 10 years he became a member of the Young People's Band of the Salvation Army at Stockholm 1 (Templet), and in 1916 he moved on into the Senior Band. From 1917 to 1918 he was a member of the Swedish Staff Band in Stockholm. In 1919 Paul joined the Training College for Officers of the Salvation Army. As an Officer-Assistant he served in 6 Corps in Sweden, before he had as an Officer the responsibility for 16 different Corps. From 1931 until 1933 Paul was the Bandmaster of the Swedish Staff Band and from 1942 to 1957 he was the Chief of the Department for Music at the Headquarter in Stockholm. He was Promoted to Glory in 1985.

Important compositions

Jerusalem (FM275), Wallteng Melodier (FM282) 1986

ANGWINE, (first name not known)

One of the early composers (late 1800, early 1900).

No further information could be retrieved about this person.

Important compositions

Thine, Thine I will be (GS0332) 1897

APPLEBY, HARRY

Harry Appleby was one of the most colourful of early Army musicians. Trained as a professional musician by age fourteen, he become a cornetist in a military staff band. Major Thomas Blandy, the Salvation Army Divisional Officer, introduced Appleby to General William Booth, requesting that 'The Musician' serve on his staff. After military discharge, Appleby worked for 18 months for Blandy organising and supervising bands of the Eastern Division, thus being perhaps the first 'Divisional Music Director' in the history of Salvation Army music. In May 1885, when the Household Troops Band was founded, Harry Appleby became their first bandmaster. By 1891 he was no longer leading the Household Troops but took over the leadership of the Home Office Band (Headquarters Band London) and continued his supervisory work of all staff bands until 1894. He retired from active service by the early 1900s but did see further service as corps bandmaster at Southend.

Important compositions

A Great Salvation [also refereed too as '*Appleby's March*'] (GS213) 1893, The Absent Guest (GS251-2) 1894, My burden at Thy feet I jay (GS384-2) 1900, The Veteran's March (AJ61 – adapted by Erik Leidzén) 1964

ARNOTT, TOM

Thomas Arnott was born in Pentre, South Wales into a coal mining family in 1897, his father being a Salvationist and his mother a Congregationalist. He commenced to learn the cornet under the guidance of a Lieutenant Worthington and at the age of nine played 2nd cornet in the time of Bandmaster A. Morse. Tom Arnott held the positions of Deputy Bandmaster and Band Secretary alternately before reaching the age of eighteen. He was then playing euphonium and passed a searching practical test on this instrument under the late Mr. William Rimmer and Mr. T.H. Seddon, of Kettering, also in theory under Dr. David Evans of Cardiff University. At the age of twenty he transferred to Pentre, in the Rhondda Valley, where he spent two very happy years, and at once recognized in Bandmaster J. Simmonds a musician of outstanding quality and a teacher of the first order. Under his direction banding became a greater joy than at any time previously. Whilst at Pentre he composed his first march, which he named after the Corps. At the end of two years he went to South Africa to seek his fortune in the goldmines and spent the first eight months working on a sinking-shaft, roughing it in single quarters being many miles from a town. He had a longing to see Johannesburg, and one Sunday morning found himself in that city, where he was thrilled at the sight of a woman Salvationist in full uniform. Within a short space of time Tom moved into Johannesburg, and to his great surprise found that during the interval between his first visit Bandmaster Tom Milligan, whom he had played under at Pontycymmer, had come to Johannesburg from the USA and was in charge of the Band. Tom Arnott became his Deputy and for the last eight of his fourteen months in the Corps acted as Bandmaster during Tom Milligan's absence.

At the wish of the Bandsmen he wrote a march, which bears the name of the Corps. He stayed almost two years in South Africa but during the period contracted a serious illness from which the doctor said he was unlikely to recover, but the doctor was emphatic that he must return to his native land, as a recurrence of the complaint would surely prove fatal. In due course he sailed for home, and within a short period got married, settling down in Pentre. For seventeen years he labored through 'thick and thin' for all that's best in the 'good old Army' which he said he loved with all his heart. In turn he became Deputy Bandmaster, Young People's Band Leader, and Bandmaster during his stay in Pentre where he also wrote the *'Heavenly Mansions'* and *'Reliance'* marches. His work then took him to Pontypool, in the Monmouthshire valleys, where he spent twelve very happy months as a Bandsman in the neighbouring Corps of Abersychan.

About this time Pontypool Corps lost its Bandmaster by transfer and for a while was without a Leader. Bandsman Arnott was asked to become Bandmaster, which position he held for five years. Later he was offered employment in Worthing and after spending three years there as a Bandsman, during which time he was extremely happy amongst his comrades, he became Bandmaster although he would gladly have excused himself and would have preferred freedom from such responsibility. His loyalty to, and his love for, The Salvation Army, however, was always his first consideration. Furthermore Tom said *'I should like to encourage all young Salvationists to lay themselves out for the fullest possible service early in life as I am convinced it is the best way to secure maximum joy and happiness'.* Only a few compositions were published, although he composed extensively. He was Promoted to Glory in 1960 at the age of 72.

Important compositions

Heavenly Mansions (GS0767) 1917, The Pentre (GS0602) 1910

ASPINALL, JOHN

Former member of the Household Troops Band, Home Office Band, and International Staff Band. Lieutenant-Colonel John Aspinall M.B.E., was the eldest son of the late Brigadier Frank Aspinall, whose fascinating life-story appears in Mrs. General Carpenter's book, 'Three Great-hearts'. Appointed as Lieutenant to Maidstone in 1890, John Aspinall commenced an active career of forty-three year's service, which ended when he retired from the Staff Secretaryship of Salvationist Publishing and Supplies Ltd., in 1933. Among Corps which he commanded were Upper Norwood (Crystal Palace), Long Eaton, Basingstoke, and Camberwell. For a period the Colonel served in Germany, and during the last war he was in charge of a Motor Ambulance Unit in France, and also was attached to the War Department at N.H.Q. for which war service he was awarded the M.B.E. Colonel Aspinall was for many years a member of the International Staff Band, and before that came into being, of the Household Troops Band, visiting Canada and the U.S.A., and Home Office Band. In addition to playing the cornet, he was an acceptable singer, banjoist, and concertina exponent. Another link with The Salvation Army's music was his Secretaryship of the old National Headquarters Music Board. He was the brother of Mrs. Major William Hodgson and of the wife of Rev. W. A. Ashby. John Aspinall was a keen business executive, despite his breezy, jovial disposition and, particularly as a Staff Bandsman, and during the years when he accompanied Mrs. General Higgins on her campaigns, the General was then the Chief of the Staff, was noted as a zealous soul-winner.

'I insist on the equality of women with men. Every officer and soldier should insist upon the truth that woman is as important, as valuable, as capable and as necessary to the progress and happiness of the world as man '. So said William Booth, founder of the Salvation Army, in 1908. He proved that he meant what he said when he placed Brigadier Mary Murray in charge of the Salvation Army's 'Naval and Military League' at the time of the Great War. She, together with Staff

Captain John Aspinall, went to Belgium and France in 1914 to see what help could be given to the men of the British Expeditionary force.

Important compositions

He drew me by His love (GS0413-1) 1902

ASTBURY, MORTIMER A

Mortimer Astbury was one of the first flugel players with the International Staff Band (early 1900) as well as a Salvation Army officer, and composer. Captain Astbury was a long-serving flugelhorn player in the band and did a great deal in helping to popularise that instrument, especially when an independent part in the scoring was provided for it.

Important compositions

Consecration (GS0559) 1908

AUDOIRE, NORMAN J.

Bandmaster Norman Audoire L.T.C.L., F.C.C.M., was born at St. Albans, England in 1898, of Salvation Army Officers of sterling Channel Island stock, who were then in command of the Corps. His father Major J.J. Audoire (R.) is a splendid type of early school of Salvationist, whose zeal and devotion made The Army the power it is in the world today. The Channel Islands have a significant French influence in their history, and this explains the French nature of the family name Audoire. As a younger person he was involved in music ministry at both Cambridge Heath Corps (in London) and Carlisle Citadel corps before he moved to Canada, settling in Toronto. Shortly after that he became Bandmaster at Earlscourt Citadel in Toronto. Earlscourt Citadel is known today as Yorkminster Citadel. In 1930 he was transferred by his employer, Canadian National Railways, to Montreal where he linked up with the Montreal Citadel Corps. That same year he became Bandmaster at Montreal Citadel - a position he held continuously until 1960 when he retired and Morley Calvert (another gifted composer) became corps bandmaster. During his time the band had a star studded history, maintained a membership that at times was a high as fifty five and doing a lot of travel in Eastern Canada, New York, Boston and other points in the USA. Norman is known for his compositions - the marches *'Montreal Citadel'*, *'Earlscourt Citadel'* and *'Aggression'*, a series of solos such as *'We'll all shout Hallelujah'* (euphonium) *'The Priceless Gift'* (trombone) and *'An Irish Melody'* (soprano cornet). The solos were all written for members of the Montreal Citadel Band. Interestingly, if you were to look at *'Montreal Citadel'* and *'Earlscourt Citadel'* you would see that the plan of the march and the rhythmic structure were virtually identical. Norman Audoire served as corps organist at the Citadel for years. The Citadel was in a church which The Salvation Army had purchased and it had a great pipe organ. He was a natural musician with a great gift of melody and a sense of colour and he did some marvelous playing on the organ whilst the younger members of the band took up the offering in the meetings. In retirement, he did the rehearsals for the Park Extension Band (another smaller corps in Montreal) and left his mark in that corps. He continued to be the corps organist at Montreal Citadel during all this time. Norman Audoire died in 1964. The Montreal Citadel Band played at his funeral the hymn tune setting *'Martyn'* by Wilfred Heaton and *'On the Way Home'* by Erik Leidzen. Those who played under him remembered his as a leader who inspired confidence and helped a band believe it could do things. His quality of being able to inspire people may well have been greater than his musical ability - not to minimize his musical gifts.

Important compositions

Montreal Citadel (GS1084) 1934, Earlscourt Citadel (GS1020) 1930, The priceless gift (GS1116-1) 1936, We'll Shout Hallelujah (GS1264) 1945

AYLING, PETER

Peter Ayling (13 october 1953), a former Salvation Army officer, was a member of the International Staff Band (percussion, horn, piano soloist) for more than a decade and an acclaimed international Salvation Army pianist. He studied harmony and counterpoint at the Middlesex Polytechnic, Morley College, and the Royal Academy of Music in London. Later he moved to the Netherlands (1991-1994) to become the Territorial Music Director and conductor of the Amsterdam Staff Band and Amsterdam Staff Songsters. When moving back to the United Kingdom he became a member of the Music Ministries Unit (MMU) in London and was conductor of the International Staff Songsters. Although he mainly wrote songs he also provided some compositions for several band journals.

Important compositions

Lord, With My All I Part

AYMA, DAVID

David Ayma (1968) started his study in music by The Salvation Army under Major Edward Ringle and Commissioner (later General) John Larsson. A native of Chile, David Ayma gained his musical education at the National Music Conservatory and Faculty of Arts of Chile University. He has composed for brass ensemble and band, choir, and full orchestra. Some of Ayma's brass band compositions have been published by The Salvation Army (both in London and New York) and Muso's Media of Australia. Since 1998 David has been conductor and composer-in-residence of the Temuco Philharmonic Orchestra in Temuco (Southern Chile) and Orchestral Conductor adviser for the Young Musician Society (SMJ).

Important compositions

Kings of Orient (TS1112), Praise's Power (GS1981), St. Denio (FS531), New Direction (FS559)

BABB, MICHAEL

Michael Babb studied at Trinity College of Music in the early 1950s with teachers such as Henry Geehl and Phil Catlinet. He also worked alongside Salvation Army composers such as Ray Steadman-Allen and Les Condon as a proof-reader in the Music Editorial Department.

During his long teaching career, he wrote many works for school performances, including music dramas and an Easter Cantata. Since retirement he has written the music for an opera, *'Avalon'*, performed on tour in Yorkshire by a professional group supported by the Arts Council.

Although most of his published works have been written for The Salvation Army, many more have been performed in manuscript with considerable success. These include works for symphonic wind band as well as brass and vocal, and remain available. Latterly he has been instrumental in preparing The Salvation Army Classics series, writing 13 out of the first 16 arrangements to be published. Thus major works such as Eric Ball's *'Constant Trust'* have become accessible to bands of limited numbers.

Bandsman Michael Babb was commissioned songster leader of the Regent Hall Songsters in April 1963 and at the same time David Sewell was appointed his deputy. Michael Babb, as a well-known composer of Salvation Army music, maintained a very high standard of musicianship. During his leadership the brigade undertook several fruitful weekend campaigns in the British Isles. During the early 1960's the National Songsters were inaugurated at the Regent Hall and the Regent Hall Songsters contributed by supplying four songsters to the splendid new brigade: Veronica Cuthbert, Mary Edge, Patricia Holmes and Gillian Denham. Veronica, Mary and Patricia were all soloists with the National Songsters, and Gillian the elocutionist. Songster Leader Babb willingly released these songsters to fulfil their services with the National Songsters. One of the outstanding occasions of the leadership of Michael Babb was when the Regent Hall Songsters were invited to be the solo brigade at the Fairfield Halls for the Songster Leaders' Councils Festival. The songsters sang *'The wonder of His grace'*, which brought great blessing to those who heard them sing and also those privileged to sing. Songster Leader Babb resigned in 1970 and was followed by Elgar Gambling. Under the leadership of Songster Leader Gambling the songster brigade grew greatly in numbers and continued to undertake engagements for the Lord. One of the invitations extended to the brigade under the leadership of Elgar Gambling is to annually represent The Salvation Army in the 'Sir Malcolm Sargent Cancer Fund for Children' MESSIAH evening at the Royal Albert Hall. Nationally famed soloists, orchestras and conductors gave their services free of charge for this very worthy cause and the Regent Hall Songsters represent The Salvation Army in the chorus of 500, attending in their uniforms, a wonderful opportunity for witness amongst all the evening dress.

Important compositions

The Crimson Stream (FS420) 1982, The Golden Cord (FS232) 1958, Before the Altar (FS301) 1967

BAINBRIDGE, (first name not known)

One of the early composers (late 1800, early 1900).

No further information could be retrieved about this person.

Important compositions

Jesus come down (GS0345) 1897

BALE, MALCOLM JAMES

Malcolm James, born on 7 May 1934, grew up in the corps at Branksome and, after two years national service, went to the International Training College to become a Salvation Army Officer in 1954. He served in various appointments before he was transferred to the International Headquarters in 1964. Whilst serving at IHQ he was editor of several of the Army's issues as well as editor for *'The Musician'* (1974-1977). Malcolm was also known for his poem writing, and had already won a prize at age eight. Apart from publications in the Army's band journals he has also published in *'The Musical Salvationist'*.

Important compositions

Monkland (TS0716) 1969, Jonah and the Whale (TS0802) 1976

BALL, ERIC

Eric Walter John Ball was born on October 31, 1903 at Kingswood, near Bristol in England, eldest son of Salvation Army officers. As a child, he was taught the piano, but gained much of his musical education in The Salvation Army, particularly the Young People's Band in Ealing. In Buckinghamshire he extended his musical studies to the organ. His teacher also schooled him in harmony and counterpoint and gradually a talented composer began to emerge. In 1919, Eric obtained a position at The Salvation Army Musical Instrument Department in Judd Street in London. His interest in composition led to a move into the Musical Editorial Department. Eric married Olive Dorsett who was a Singing Company Leader in Southall Citadel. In 1927, he had gained an ARCM and was commissioned as a Salvation Army officer. Around this time his conducting career began and, after serving as bandmaster with a number of corps bands plus the Salvationist Publishing and Supplies Band (SP&S Band), he was appointed Bandmaster of The International Staff Band (ISB) in July 1942. Unfortunately, Major Eric Ball and The Salvation Army were soon to part company. He had become very interested in psychic research and began to investigate Spiritualism, which the Army strongly proscribed. In 1944, Eric Ball resigned his commission. In 1977, he was thanked publicly in a Royal Albert Hall gathering for 50 years of service to Salvation Army music, and the Salvation Army took Eric back. He was Promoted to Glory on October 1st 1989.

About Resurgam

(resource: Dr. Ronald Holz, copied with permission)

Eric Ball's tone poem Resurgam (R. Smith, 1950; FS 302; January, 1967) can be considered the first truly masterful brass band composition by a composer nurtured exclusively within the brass band movement. Composed as the test piece for the 1950 British Open Brass Band Championship, it was also printed years later in the Salvation Army Festival Series, a unique distinction for a 'secular' brass band work. Taken in its historical context, 'Resurgam' may be seen to represent a continuation of the series of tone poems Ball wrote the 1930s—early '40s for the SA while a member of the Music Editorial Department. In fact, Ball even self-references himself by quoting from an earlier work, Exodus. The piece is symbolic of the merging of his SA roots and training with his new career in the brass band contesting scene, having resigned in 1944 as an officer in the SA. By the time of its release in the SA journals, 'Brother' Eric Ball had become reintegrated into SA fellowship.

While Ball did not intend a 'descriptive fantasia' nor did he intend to directly illustrate a given text, the scripture passage from the Apocrypha, Wisdom III: 1—3, appended to the score does provide clues to the music. Knowing the vast quantity and style of choral music Ball wrote for the SA, allows me to emphasize Ball's later comments [FS score notes] that the opening of the piece is a setting of the first half of the passage, the portion he called the faith motive. The listener may join these words to the principal melody right up until the first pause: The souls of the righteous are in the hand of God and no torment shall touch them (and no torment shall touch them). In the eyes of the foolish they seemed to have died... It would not be surprising if at some time a choral or vocal source were found for this noble theme. The next two lines provide the basis for so much of the angry, disturbing, dissonant music of the tone poem that will alternate back and forth with the faith motive: And their departure was accounted to be their hurt, And their journeying away from us to be their ruin. The music reflects frustration, despair, pain, and lament (cornet solo). Ball described the music [analysis printed in the British Bandsman] then moving on to an atmosphere of fear and even hysteria, interspersed with sudden silences and a sinister 'fateful knocking at the door.' The Gregorian chant sequence Dies irae [Day of wrath..] from the Requiem Mass appears, followed by a direct quotation from his earlier tone poem Exodus, the Death motif. After the tumult is finished and a soft yet ominous gong is sounded, the faith motive returns, but in a new key symbolic of resurrection [The Latin 'Resurgam' may be translated I shall rise again] The glorious climax, surely one of the finest moments in brass band music, subsides gently into a Coda where the trombones intone what must be the final line of the scripture: But they are in peace. Ball hoped the effect of a good performance would be 'one of serenity achieved in the face of sorrow and fear.' 'Resurgam' is intensely personal and yet universal, the composer intending that the work be understood on a variety of levels and not as propaganda of any one sect or religion.

Test piece or work to draw an audience towards higher things? Perhaps both. Eric Ball's 'Resurgam', first a test piece (British Open, 1950) and then allowed into the Festival Series (FS 302, Jan. 1967) would represent a reversal of such a process, though the latter not only had a scriptural base, but also had a vocal origin. This can be made clear by placing the text of the scripture attached to the 'Resurgam' score cover – 'The souls of the righteous are in the hands of God…' -- putting these into the main melodic lines of the first section. I would not be surprised if at some time a manuscript part-song is found of that setting. The ontology of such a work of instrumental piece of music is a fragile, mysterious thing, and so its ability to be aligned with spiritual thoughts after the fact is not so earth-shattering a disclosure.

One little anecdote about Eric Ball; Many years ago he was the compare at a festival/concert in which the International Staff Band played *'Toccata'* (Wilfred Heaton). At the end of it Eric said '*I give that 9 out of 10. I can't give it 10 out of 10 because there is no such thing as perfection this side of heaven.*'

Important compositions

Resurgam (FS302) 1967, Challenge and Response (FS381) 1977, King of Kings (FS67) 1931, Exodus (FS117) 1937, Song of Courage (FS285) 1961, Songs of the Morning (FS114) 1937, The Challenge (FS482) 1990, Songs in Exile (GS1460) 1958, Star Lake (GS1200) 1941, Star Lake 2 (GS1555) 1965, Songs of Pilgrims (US71) 1964

Book 1 - **The Man and his music** - by Peter M. Cooke

An extensive and interesting book about the doyen of all Salvation Army composers and beyond, Eric Ball.

Book 2 - **His Words and his Wisdom** - by Peter M. Cooke

A compilation of his writings from the pages of The British Bandsman & The Bandsman & Songster.

Book 3 – **'The Musical Salvationist'** – The World of Richard Slater – by Gordon Cox

Page 165 to 185, Richard Slaters vision on Eric Ball as also a general view by Gordon Cox on several aspects in the musical live of Eric Ball.

BALLENTINE, LEONARD

Leonard Ballantine (Len) was born 23 July 1950 and studied music at the University of Toronto. He worked five years as a freelance composer and was leader of the 'New Life Singers'. He also wrote music for publicity spots. For three years he was leader of the Department for Music of The Salvation Army in Canada and Bermuda. Len served as Bandmaster and Songster Leader before he entered the School for Officers of The Salvation Army. As an officer he was chef of the Music Department of the British Territorium of The Salvation Army and became Songster Leader of the 'International Staff Songsters' (ISS) and composed music for Brass Bands and Songsters. He is in particular well known for his contemporary output. Nowadays he is a corps officer in Canada.

Major Len Ballantine is well known for his choral and brass compositions in The Salvation Army. His leadership of the International Staff Songsters from 1992-1998 brought a decidedly contemporary note to main stream vocal ensemble work within our culture. Len is comfortable with a wide range of musical expressions from the Classics to Pop, and he welcomes modern material as a helpful necessity in the fashioning of worship. In his role as Music and Gospel Arts Secretary for Canada and Bermuda, Len gave oversight and vision to the department's efforts in resourcing the Territory at a time of great change. He became appointed to the renamed 'Music and Gospel Arts' department at Territorial Headquarters for Canada and Bermuda in July, 2002. To that point their ministry had been split between corps officership in Canada and music ministry in the UK. Len's background in vocal music and composition has prepared him for leadership in a broad range of Salvation Army music making. At a time of great change in Salvation Army culture and practice, Ballantine brings a balanced and heartfelt approach to the outward expression of faith in our Lord Jesus.

As a graduate of the University of Toronto Faculty of Music, Len Ballantine is known widely as an arranger and composer of both choral and brass music. Throughout his career he has travelled extensively in Europe and North America as a guest clinician and conductor. From 1992-1998 he directed The Salvation Army's premier vocal ensemble based in London, England. During this period the group made four international tours and seven recordings. Each December at Roy Thomson Hall Len brings together musicians and singers from Ontario to perform in a spectacular community festival called Christmas with The Salvation Army. Len and his wife Heather are the current pastors the Army's Yorkminster congregation where he founded and continues to direct the GTA Community Choir.

His first love, however, was the pianoforte. He began studies with his father at the age of four when other teachers felt him too young to take serious lessons. His advancement was quick and determined, and by the age of 16 he had earned the Associate of Music Diploma in performance piano and pedagogy from the University of Western Ontario's Conservatory of Music (A.W.C.M.). By this point he was competing regularly in Kiwanis Music Festivals in Windsor, Chatham and Toronto, eventually winning top honours in all locations, and at the C.N.E. music festival as well. His scholarships and prizes afforded him other opportunities for study and advancement. At 17 he spent the summer in Montreal at L'Ecole Vincent D'Indy where he studied with Yvonne Hubert, herself a student of Nadia Boulanger. Later that same year he performed the Schumann *'Piano Concerto in A minor'* with the Windsor Symphony Orchestra. As part of his recognition as top winner in the Windsor Kiwanis Festival, Len was featured in a half hour radio broadcast recorded in the CBC affiliate's Windsor studios. In that broadcast, one of his piano compositions, *'Shades of Charlie Brown'*, was first recorded. He continued studies at the University of Toronto where he won a piano scholarship to study with the venerable Swiss teacher, Pierre Souveran. Although his composition studies have led him to discover a broader musical path, his love for the piano continues, and his arrangements for piano bear the marks of one who understands the instrument with the soul of a performer.

Important compositions

Daniel's Band (m/s), Shall we gather (FS470) 1989, The Etobican (FS495) 1992, Since Jesus (FS518) 1995, Abram's Praise (FS513) 1994, Joyful, Joyful (AF011) 1990, I know Thou art mine (GS1890) 1993

BALSNES, OLAV

Olav was born on 5 November 1936 in Aalesund on the west coast of Norway. He lived there until 1964 when he moved north to the town of Tromsoe. He returned to Aalesund in 1967 before leaving the town again in 1988. He also lived in Denmark for three years. A banker by profession, he worked in banks from 1955 until 1987. After that, Olav worked in his own one-man company as a business advisor.

It was by accident that he became involved with the Salvation Army. His school was trying to set up a school band and here Olav failed to impress the conductor that he 'had it in him' to be a band member. Olav was disappointed, wanted to play, and the only option was the small junior Salvation Army band. This experience however led him to a wish to learn more about music. He soon joined correspondence courses in musical theory and harmony. Olav early thought of writing his own music and he was encouraged to continue his music study. He was blessed with the opportunity to early try out his music writing with the band he played in. Over the years having that same possibility with other bands he was involved in was a great help in his music making, as he consider himself an autodidact in that area.

From his early junior days until 1964 Olav was engaged in the Salvation Army in Aalesund, both with the junior band and later as bandmaster in the senior band. He did his military service in Oslo in 1957 to 1958, and in that period he played in the well-known Oslo III Band of the Salvation Army. In the first half-year of 1960 he studied banking in London, England and had the privilege of playing in the Upper Norwood Band, alongside many of the then International Staff Band members. In Tromsoe he helped with starting a new junior Salvation Army band – the first ever in that city. Both in Aalesund, and later in places in Eastern Norway, and Denmark, where his work took him to, Olav was also involved in musical activities outside the Salvation Army. He conducted bands as well as choirs, and wrote music for these entities as well as for other ensembles.

Important composition

Come (US0062), 1964

BANKS, KEITH

Commissioner Keith Banks entered The Salvation Army training college in 1962; his sessional name was 'Heroes of the Faith'. Commissioner Pauline Banks entered training in 1963; her session was 'Proclaimers of the Faith'. Keith and Pauline were married in 1965, Pauline was at the time a member of The Joystrings, The Salvation Army's internationally-famous pop group who achieved two singles in the UK national charts. They served together as corps leaders in the UK Territory at Enfield, Crouch End, Skegness, Clapton (London) and Carlisle before taking up the commission of Divisional Youth Secretary and

Area Director for Guides and Brownies in Nottingham and South London. They remained in these posts until 1985 when they became Senior Training Officers at the William Booth Training College in Denmark Hill, London. In 1988 they became the divisional leaders of the North London Division until 1994 when they took up the challenges of Officer Commanding and Command President of Women's Ministries for The Salvation Army in Papua New Guinea. They were transferred to Japan in 1998 where they served as Chief Secretary and Territorial Secretary for Women's Ministries until Pauline's ill health dictated a return to the UK Territory in 2000. As Pauline's health improved, Keith was appointed Secretary for International Personnel in 2001 and subsequently became the International Secretary for Personnel in 2002. During this time Pauline served as the International Statistician, Assistant Secretary for the General's Consultative Council and Assistant Secretary to the International Management Council. Both these appointments enabled them to witness the work of the Army across the globe. Following further health concerns for Pauline, they both stepped back from international demands and in 2004 they were appointed the UK Territorial Commander's Representative in Scotland.

(source: salvationarmy.org.uk)

Important compositions

I'll be a light (GS1968) 2000, A New World (TS1127) 2003

BARLOW, GLENN

Glenn Barlow (14 November 1974) was appointed Bandmaster in April 2004, following six years of service as a member and two years as deputy bandmaster at the North York Temple Corps in Canada. Educated at the world renowned Royal Academy of Music in London, England, he gained his Bachelor of Music (Honours) and LRAM, FTCL, LGSM and ALCM diplomas. During his tenure at the Academy, Glenn was a member of the Enfield Citadel Band as its Soprano cornet player under the direction of Bandmaster James Williams MBE. He grew up as a member of the Boscombe Corps in the South of England.

His conducting has not been limited to the brass band idiom, having conducted the Colorado Symphony and the Vancouver Symphony and a performance of the rarely heard Mahler Symphony No.8 (Symphony of a Thousand) at London's Royal Festival Hall. He has produced events in Toronto including the '1000 Children's Voices' at Massey Hall and most recently the 'Concert for Asia' Tsunami benefit concert at Roy Thomson Hall with the Toronto Mendelssohn Choir, Elmer Iseler Singers, massed choirs and the North York Temple Band.

Important compositions

Let Nothing Disturb Thee (m/s), More than Wonderful (m/s), Down in the Kingdom (Trombone Feature) (m/s), When You Believe (m/s)

BARNES, VICTOR A.

He was for many years bandmaster of the New Haven (Connecticut) Corps Band, and a real stalwart. He also led for a number of years a division-wide band (Southern New England Division, Connecticut and Rhode Island) during the late 1950's early 1960's. He was also, as a younger Salvation Army musician, an accomplished cornetist.

He was active in divisional (Southern New England) musical programs such as band schools and camps. He led the divisional band for several years, was a fine cornetist and did some composing, mostly for the corps band. For a while in the fifties the New Haven (BM Vic Barnes), Hartford (BM William Reid) and Manchester (BM Peter Carlson) bands would present an occasional tri-band festival at one of the corps. Victor was always very much involved in the planning of this.

Important compositions

The Constant Friend (TS0240) 1936, Exhortation (TS0375) 1945, Southern New England (TS0663) 1965

BARRINGTON, ANDREW PHILIP

Andrew (24 October 1973) served as the Divisional Music Director for The Salvation Army Arkansas and Oklahoma Division in the United States and is the Bandmaster of The Cherokee Brass Band of the Salvation Army and the Principle Eb Tuba Player for the USA Southern Territorial Band. He has had a number of pieces for Brass band published and considers himself a product of The Salvation Army's music program. Andrew has studied informally with James Curnow, Steve Bulla and Eric Alexander.

Important compositions

March – Victory (ARJ66-283)

BARRY, LORNE

Lorne Barry was born in Hamilton, Bermuda on April 30, 1970 a son of Salvation Army Officers (Canada and Bermuda Territory). He first started playing piano at age five after his parents heard him playing melodies on an old piano in the basement. It was around the same time that he began singing solos in church. First exposed to a full Salvation Army brass band at the age of ten at the corps in Kingston, Ontario, he began playing the cornet at that time and was a cornet/trumpet player for the next six years. In 1994 his parents were transferred to the Ontario South Division to the city of St Catharines, which is when brass band music really began its influence on him. Lorne moved to flugelhorn at the age of 17, which is the same age he began conducting (youth choir then youth band). Lorne Barry attended both divisional music camp at Camp Selkirk and national music school at Jackson Point and the influence of Brian Burditt on his interest in brass bands cannot be overstated. Of course there were other notable guests as well, including Len Ballentine, Robert Redhead, Bill Gordon, Bill Broughton, Per Ohlsson, to name a few, with each bringing his own strengths from which he has drawn influence from. Lorne Barry began writing brass band arrangements at this time as well, although had been creating original piano arrangements for a number of years before that (basically from when he began learning piano at age five).

Part of the divisional music school was a daily theory lesson, however there were a few who had finished all the levels, so the faculty created a class for them to try their hand at brass band compositions. His first piece was an arrangement on *'May Jesus Christ be Praised'*. There were a few original pieces in the following years and the corps band that Lorne Barry attended were very willing to give them a run through. He attended McMaster University in Hamilton, Ontario and went to Argyle Citadel for three years, followed by Hamilton Temple for a further two, moving to Euphonium in the brass band at Argyle and then Eb Bass at Hamilton Temple. It was in Hamilton where he met his wife who was from Brisbane, Australia, and emigrated to Australia in 1994. He attended Brisbane City Temple from that time at the suggestion of Barrie Gott, and became the deputy Bandmaster there shortly after in 1995. In that band Lorne Barry at times played Eb Bass, BBb Bass, Euphonium, Flugelhorn Horn, Trombone and even percussion, which he believe gave me a better understanding of how each instrument fits within the brass band structure.

Arrangements for brass band were born out of necessity, and there are many arrangements in files hidden away in boxes that range from the traditional to contemporary, which were made to work in conjunction with the contemporary group at the church. One of the more unusual arrangements he scored was the national anthem for the Republic of China (Taiwan) for a band trip, performed for the President as part of a short concert in the Presidential Hall, a concert which he was fortunate enough to conduct the band for. The first piece of music he had published was also used as part of the repertoire on that band trip: *'Credo'*. Since then there have been a few more published pieces, but perhaps the most significant is *'God has Healed'*, which was written to commemorate the birth of his firstborn son Raphael, whose name also means 'God has Healed'. At present Lorne Barry still resides in Brisbane with his wife and family although he is no longer associated with the Salvation Army there and has been inactive from participating in brass bands for a few years now.

Important compositions

Trinity (FS599) 2005, Credo (FS591) 2004, God has healed (GS2067) 2008

BARTLETT, JOE

Joe wrote the march *'Heavenward Bound'* dedicating it to the Red Shield at Barie in Italy where he spent two years of his army service. This march was originally written for general series but he was asked by Colonel Albert Jakeway, who was then Head of the music board of the Salvation Army, to write it in a lower key for triumph series. Whilst in Barie he formed the Red Shield Band but there was a problem, they had no music to play from! Therefore Joe wrote some twenty or more pieces from memory. Strangely enough, this march was the only piece of music that was ever accepted for publication. Joe was a superb arranger and on a Sunday morning the congregation would hear a new melody to a song at the Salvation Army service and by the evening, there was a full band arrangement ready to be played. When you consider in those days there was little help i.e. computers, photocopiers etc., everything was done in written manuscript. Joe Bartlett was Deputy Bandmaster at Poole in the 1950's and during the 1960's was Bandmaster at Branksome. An outstanding musician, he was an exceptional player and euphonium soloist besides playing the trumpet, cornet and trombone. Even shortly before his 80th Birthday he was playing the famous solo *'Rule Britannia'* which he had also arranged for full orchestra. Since then, the musical talents of his family have been carried on in fine tradition. Joe is the grandfather of composer Darren Bartlett.

An article which appeared in '*'The Musician'*' on JULY 16th 1955 says:

MEET THE COMPOSER - Introducing a New Contributor to the Band Journal

DEPUTY BANDMASTER J. BARTLETT, of Poole Citadel.

Born of Salvationist parents - his father, then Bandmaster of Poole, was killed in action in the early days of the first world war - Deputy Bandmaster J. Bartlett played cornet at a very early age. Whilst serving in the middle east and Italy during the second world war, the Deputy Bandmaster took an active part in the Bari Red Shield Band. Deputy Bandmaster

Bartlett is well known as a euphonium soloist and is a keen bandsman. He has a son (Joe Bartlett Junior) who plays euphonium in the band of the Royal Tank Corps, serving in Germany. The Deputy Bandmaster is the composer of the Triumph series march, *'Heavenward Bound'*, recently published.

Important compositions

Heavenward Bound (TS0532) 1955

BATEMAN, JAMES CONNOR

Born as the son of James senior on 18 November 1854, James junior became a music hall entertainer, known for his singing and banjo playing. He was seriously injured whilst working at an oil mill. He got into a depression and there after a friend of his suggested that he should join The Salvation Army by means of cure. So, one day he followed the early Salvationists back into the corps hall at Sculcoates and became converted. He was a soldier for only a short time as he soon became an officer in 1882. He served in no less than 14 corps appointments in the short time of only six years. Except for writing band music he also contributed to "The Musical Salvationist". James Bateman died on 5 June 1888.

Important compositions

Joy Without (GS0094) 1888

BATES, DANIEL

Daniel Bates was born on April 7th 1967 in Vevey, Switzerland, as eldest son of Salvation Army officers. When he was five he was sent to piano lessons at the Music Conservatory School in Bern. A year later he started playing the Cornet in the YP Band of Bern1 Corps which the family attended. In 1982 his father was sent to Harare, Zimbabwe as the Financial Secretary. The whole family moved to Zimbabwe, where Daniel finished his O-Levels in Music at the Music School of Zimbabwe in Harare. He also played in the Harare City Band and was made the Songster and Corps pianist. During this time he wrote arrangements for Brass Band and also several piano pieces which he usually played himself at the Corps. In 1986 the family moved to London, Bromley where Daniel attended Bromley Temple Corps, playing Solo Cornet in the band. He soon became the songster and Corps pianist.

In 1989 he moved to Zurich where he attended the Zurich Central Corps. In Zurich he took lessons at the Jazz School of Zurich for two years whilst working in a Swiss Bank as an Oracle Database Engineer. During this time he wrote several Band arrangements which Zurich Central played. A few songs for songster were written too which were published in the Swiss Territory. Since 2000 Daniel is the bandmaster of the Zurich Central Band. In 2007 Daniel founded the relief organisation 'SwiZimAid' which has the intention of helping Salvationists in Zimbabwe. Since then one to two containers full of clothes, instruments, hospital material etc. have been sent yearly to Zimbabwe. He has also travelled to Zimbabwe with a group from Switzerland various times, including leading the Zimbabwe Territorial Music Camp in 2010.

Important compositions

He Reigns, I Want to Praise You, Save me O Lord

BAXTER, LEONARD

Leonard Stanley Baxter was born in Brisbane, Queensland, Australia in 1910 and died in Brisbane, in 1998, aged 88 years. His lifelong passion was music: music dedicated to the glory of God. Len's parents were Salvation Army officers and were stationed at the Brisbane Palace Hotel when Len was born, one of six children. All brothers and sisters were gifted musically: Len's eldest sister, Sophie, sang opera at Covent Garden, another sister, Florence, played piano beautifully, his brothers, Norman, Les and Roy, were talented brass band players, with Les, holding the position of Bandmaster of the South Brisbane Federal Band for many years. Len met his wife, Katherine, at music lessons where they were taught by the same music teacher, and he would walk her home after these. They married in 1933, for 64 years until his death. They have one daughter, Helen, who lives in Brisbane, Australia.

Len, a third generation Salvationist, spent all his life at the Brisbane Temple Corps where, for 45 years, he was Bandmaster of the Brisbane Temple Band. Len was asked to take the Brisbane Temple Band in 1932 at the age of 22, having been a Bandsman in the band, playing tenor horn, since he was 14. He then served in Australia and overseas for four years during World War 2, in the 1st Armoured Division AIF, and when the division was posted to Morotai, to push back Japanese troops, he went as the Bandmaster of the 1st Armoured Division AIF Band. When he returned from overseas duty, he was offered the position of bandmaster of the newly formed Northern Command Defence Force Band. He declined because he had dedicated his musicianship to the glory of God, and in those days, Salvationists were not permitted to be part of both a Salvation Army band and a secular band. Len continued as Bandmaster for 45 years in total and, following his desire for the best for God, developed the band into a world class musical combination with a reputation for excellence in musicianship and Salvation Army mission. He was awarded an MBE for his contribution to Salvation Army Music in 1973.

Len Baxter was a brilliant musician, gifted in composition, a masterful bandmaster and spiritual leader for his group. Len's home was always filled with music: Len loved the classics and wrote many brass band arrangements of the works of the masters; he also loved brass band music played well, and was a special devotee of the British colliery bands; but mostly, he loved his God and his church, the Salvation Army, and committed his musical ability to the honour and glory of God through his ministry in the Army. He was a prolific writer, even during the war on active service, where his soldier friends always knew that if Len was not around, he would be writing music, where he quickly wrote band parts for a national anthem for visiting dignitaries from a soldier's rendition of whistling the anthem, and where he and his military band took part in the official surrender ceremony at Morotai at the end of the war.

After the war, he composed and arranged many pieces for the sole use of the Brisbane Temple Band. Len wrote all the music, full scores and full parts, by hand with a simple pen with nib and Indian ink, sometimes with a piano and sometimes without, and his meticulous craftsmanship is evident in his manuscript. When asked how he wrote, he said, 'I hear all the parts in my head'. His philosophy was evident in that he wanted his music to be played according to his interpretation and to be played well, and so he was quite protective of it. His music has only ever been used by the Brisbane Temple Band, except for some individual pieces that were sent to Bandmaster friends who specially requested copies. His arrangement of Spirit of the Living God has been used by several Army bands in Australia. He never wished for fame, and so all of his compositions remain unpublished, and most have only ever been played by one brass band, the Brisbane Temple Band of the Salvation Army.

Leonard Baxter was for 44 years the bandmaster of the Brisbane City Temple Band in Australia. He was quite reluctant to send his work to the Music Department for possible publication. Instead he rather kept it for his own band and a limited selection of other interested bands. His challenging cornet solo 'Song of Experience' was recorded by cornet soloist Robert Beasy and the Melbourne Staff Band on the 1980 'Songs of Australia' recording, featuring Australian composers.

He became bandmaster in 1932 of the Brisbane City Temple Band. During World War 2 he served with the Australian Imperial Forces and was bandmaster of the band of the 1st Armored Brigade. A rigid disciplinarian, Baxter got the most out of his musicians. A typical example of this is the arrangement of his cornet section. Usually the top cornets, or soloists, occupy the front row nearest the conductor. Not so in the band of Leonard Baxter. The first chair players are at the rear and the first and second cornets are in the front row nearest the conductor. 'In this way', explains bandmaster Baxter, 'I can keep an eye on them, giving them special attention to the inner harmonies assigned to these players'.

Important compositions

Path of Duty, Song of Experience

BEARCHELL, WILLIAM E.

Born of pioneer officer parents in Deseronto, Ontario, the Bearchells received their 'marching orders' for the USA in the early 1900's. Following Corps appointments that took the family to seven states, putting the children in eleven different schools, Bill graduated from Butler, Pa. Highschool in 1917. He continued his studies at the University of Pittsburgh and the Westinghouse Corporation in the field of Mechanical drafting. This was interrupted by a short tour of duty in the US Army. Bill's corps life came first as was demonstrated by his active leadership as a bandsman, songster and in all phases of the Young People's and Senior Soldier's activities. In 1920 came the call of God to full-time service and an officer and he entered the Salvation Army Training College in New York City.

In 1926 Captains William Bearchell and Robina Ladlow were united in marriage by Commissioner Samuel L. Brengle. This union was blessed with twin sons, both who became active in full time service for the Salvation Army. No matter what his official assignment might be, William Bearchell found outlet in extracurricular activities for the Army, particularly in the field of music where he brought his exceptional talents to a variety of leadership challenges. He served as Songster Leader of the New York No.1 Corps and for eight years was bandmaster of the Brooklyn Citadel Band, brining the band to new heights of musical excellence. He was a member of the New York Staff Band during his tenure at THQ, serving in turn as the leader of the Staff Band Male Chorus, Deputy Bandmaster and finally for five years as Staff Bandmaster. He also led the Staff Songsters and the great 125 voice Temple Chorus. Whilst carrying his assigned duties in a praiseworthy manner, Colonel William Bearchell wanted to go that extra mile, to make that further dedication of the talent God had given him. To fully detail this stewardship here defies accommodation, but some highlights need another look for indeed his contributions will forever be a part of the Army's illustrious musical history. The Colonel was a writer, composer, arranger and accompanist with few peers, songster leader and bandmaster. His wedding of the tune *'Wells'* with the familiar lyrics of *'Rock of Ages'* has been sung by male choral groups all over the world with unusual effectiveness and blessing. Frequently played marches composed by the Colonel include *'Brooklyn Citadel'* and *'Marching to Zion'.* He contributed numerous choruses to Army hymnody and his choral compositions have been published in 'The Musical Salvationist'.

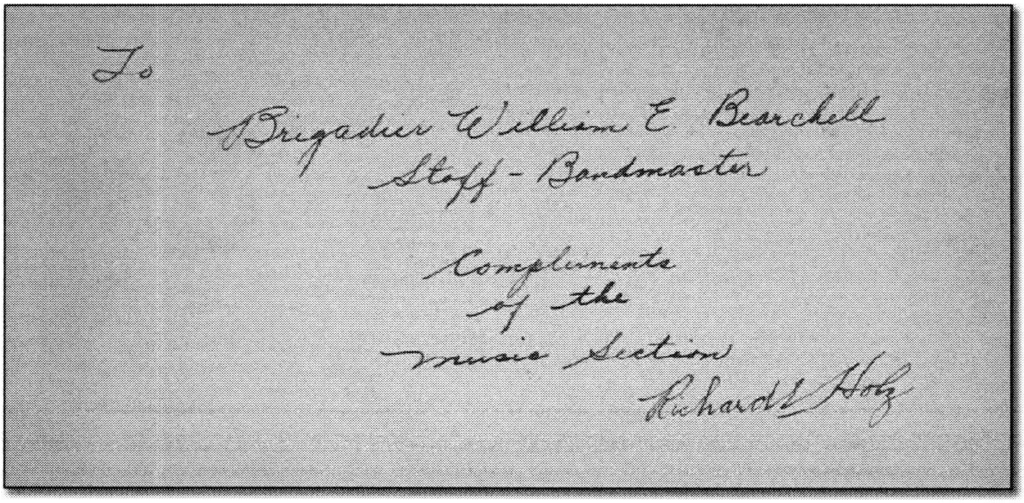

The first page of the 1948 score of the Salvation Army 'Band Music for Evangelism Competition Numbers' – with a personal message from colleague composer Richard Holz to William Bearchell.

Important compositions

Brooklyn Citadel (GS1137) 1938, Marching to Zion (GS1281) 1947

BEARCROFT, MARK

Mark was born in Twickenham on 21 July 1960, where his parents, Norman and Jill Bearcroft, were the commanding officers of that corps. Shortly afterwards his father was appointed as National Bandmaster so they moved! Salvation Army music has obviously been highly influential on him, he has listened to the composing process of many of his father's pieces! Mark was sent for piano lessons as a kid because it is useful! This led to him forming his own musical taste and style. Learning the cornet in the band and playing together as a family is also part of his heritage. It is difficult being the offspring of a composer who is so well known. People are always making comparisons. Also, there was often the suggestion that *'Norman wouldn't have done it that way'* - and, in fact, although he was always ready and willing to help, he cannot help but judge a piece by his process and style.

Mark always has been a bit of a functional composer. He ran a Salvation Army barbershop quartette made up of friends from the South London area and he quickly learned that it would add interest to the programme if the group had things to sing that were written especially for them - taking into consideration strengths and weaknesses, styles they were good at and those they should avoid.

Similarly, when he married Tracy her somewhat unique (especially in the Salvation Army) singing style needed material that was written especially for her, and often for a specific purpose. Mark's most well known song *'In Me'* was written because they needed a song of that style for a CD they were making. They were recording on the Monday and nothing had happened so he took a selection of Harry Read's poems with him to an annual event entitled *'A Day with the General'*. The International Staff Songsters (ISS) were on duty and he set about writing the song whilst trying to look as if he was listening to the General!

More recently he has written pieces for specific events. When he was the Territorial Music Director in Australia Southern Territory, he was asked to write marches, incidental music for big events and celebration music etc.

Since their return from Australia his music writing has taken a bit of a different turn. A creative artist must have an output and as Music Editorial in London didn't seem too interested in what he sent them he decided to try his hand at different ensembles. They formed an ensemble from some friends and family and he wrote a complete cantata based around the story of the Trial of Jesus. This was presented at Brighton Congress Hall during Holy Week 2011. The ensemble consisted of 2 flutes, an oboe, cello, piano, narrator and Mark put in a brief trumpet part.

His current thinking is that he will develop this sort of writing - for the groups that he know and are a bit different from the mainstream. Published songs – *'Boundless Love', 'Happy in Him', 'In Me'* (in various forms!) and *'Heaven'* is in this stable

BEARCROFT, NORMAN

Norman Bearcroft was born on 24th January 1926 in England as youngest of four children to officer-parents. After becoming Salvation Army Officers in 1950 with his wife Jill, (in the same session as Leslie Condon) they served as Corps Officers for 10 years before Norman was appointed to the Department of Music in London (and worked alongside the late Commissioner Dean Goffin, another prolific Army Composer) in 1960. They were then appointed to Canada where he served as Music Secretary for that territory and managed to reform the Canadian Staff Band (CSB). The original band had been almost literally wiped out in 1914 when on a journey to the International Congress in England, their ship collided in fog with a Norwegian collier and sunk. Normand and Jill both returned to the United Kingdom in 1976 to help in preparations for the 1978 International Congress. In 1980, he was asked by the General to form the International Staff Songsters (ISS) which he conducted until 1992, when he and his wife retired from active service to Winton Corps. After Jill passed away, Norman married Major Kathleen Getz (sister of USA composer Robert Getz) and moved to the USA where he still lives. He has an enormous output and many of his compositions have been published within the Salvation Army. Norman is known amongst bandsmen for his challenging solos and cornet and euphonium parts in particular.

The Household Troops Band made a complete recording with Norman Bearcroft's music called 'Troops Salute' (HTB2) and the Canadian Staff Band did a 'shared' recording of his music (the other half featuring the music of Robert Redhead) called 'In Tribute'.

Important compositions

Share your Faith (GS1748) 1981, Sound of Britain (FS429) 1983, Song of Exultation (FS403) 1983, The Seafarer (GS1736) 1980, Three Spirituals (Shoes, Every time I feel the Spirit, The Gospel Train) (m/s), Golden Slippers (FS402) 1979, High Fidelity (GS1852)

1990, The King's Trumpeters (FS408) 1980, Just Like John (FS360) 1974, The Word of Grace (FS376) 1976, To Region's Fair (GS1458) 1958.

Book: **In Good Company** - by Norman Bearcroft

In Good Company covers a wide expanse of time and space in Salvation Army history. The author, Lieut-Colonel Norman Bearcroft, was born in the UK in 1926 and now lives in retirement in the USA. His memoirs take you on an interesting journey from the UK, to the USA, Canada, Russia, Zimbabwe and Australia. The book covers a lot of the Army's musical history, such as the first National School of Music, the re-formation of the Canadian Staff Band, the founding of The International Staff Songsters etc. His personal insights and powers of storytelling bring historical events to life.

BEARD, J.W.

Born in 1898, Promoted to Glory in 1967. Former Bandmaster of Worksop, Nottinghamshire. He passed away during the preparation of the march *'Ceaseless Praise'* he composed. News of it's publication arrived on what would have been his 71st birthday. Usually a new writer makes his debut with a less involved type of composition e.g a march, but Beard made his debut with a selection form composition, '*Thy will be done*'. The journal says that the bandmaster has certainly succeeded in giving us an easy, effective piece, of devotional character, which will be found within the reach of most bands.

Important compositions

Banner of Love (TS0592) 1959, Ceaseless Praise (TS0707) 1968, Redeemed (TS0552) 1956, Thy will be done (TS0186) 1933

BEER, FREDERICK

'A King's Musician', is the title of an article taken from 'The Musician' of 15 June 1940. It continues with: *One of the King's best trumpeters, Brigadier Frederick Beer, of Toronto, Canada, has answered the heavenly call. The vibrant notes of his ever-present cornet, though stilled so far as Army meetings are concerned, will continue to ring in the hearts of his fellow Bandsmen who knew and loved him. He was engaged in his work as Trade Secretary at the Toronto Headquarters on the day of his sudden Promotion to Glory, and died as he would have wished, on active service. Brigadier Fred Beer had practically a lifelong association with The Army, was employed on International Headquarters in London, before becoming an Officer, and became a member of the International Staff Band. He entered the work from Exeter, and was commissioned an Officer in 1905. After a period in South Africa he returned to IHQ and resumed his duties as a Staff Bandsman. At different times he was associated with Southend Citadel Band, Wood Green Band and Exeter Temple Band. In 1915 the Brigadier was appointed to the Finance Department of the Toronto Headquarters and later held the positions of Territorial Auditor, and Chief Assistant to the Financial Secretary. Through his career Fred Beer's love of Army music persisted and he was a well known figure at Canadian Congress gatherings, being the leader of the massed bands. He was an active Bandsman to the last and was a member of the North Toronto Band. He was also associated at various times with several well known Canadian Bands as cornet soloist and bandmaster, including the Calgary I Band and the Peterborough Temple Band.*

Important composition

Wanted Soldiers (GS0413-2) 1902

BEHREND, KURT

Kurt Behrend is a trombonist with the Salvation Army Solingen Corps Band in Germany. Apart from playing with the corps band, he has arranged a substantial amount of music, including the biggest part for the Christmas recording of the Solingen Corps Band entitled *'O Bethlehem, du kleine Stadt'*. The most important part of his work are the arrangements of tunes to be used by the small German Salvation Army bands in his own country. He is a former bandmaster of the West-Germany Divisional Band.

Kurt was born in 1936 in Solingen, West Germany. His parents and grandparents were also Salvationists. Other family members were Salvation Army officers in East Prussia. Kurt became a bandsman in the Senior band when only twelve years of age. He started as a tuba player but soon moved on to euphonium and later trombone. Jurt followed music studies with professor at Weiand in Wuppertal for composition and orchestration. He was in charge of processing new hymns for the Salvation Army song book *'Lasting Happiness'*.

Important compositions

Silent Night (For solo horn and brass), Horn Solo No. 1 in E flat major (Richard Strauss)

BEIJER, ANDERS

Anders Beijer was born 1983 in Stockholm to a Salvation Army family. His father, Sture Beijer has an established reputation as an excellent trombonist in the Stockholm 7 Band (now Stockholm South Citadel Band), where Anders' grandfather, the well known Erland Beijer, has been the Bandmaster for many years. Anders is a Salvation Army Officer in Sweden. As a young Boy he has learned to play different instruments. In his spare time he writes music, mainly for the Salvation Army and to some extent in 'Kulturskolan', an after-school education in arts for young people in Sweden. Before Anders became an officer he was a bandsman in the Stockholm 7 Citadel Band, and probably he wouldn't be composing music today if it wasn't for them.

Important compositions

The Water of Life (GS2076) 2009

BENNETT, EMILEE

Emilee Bennett is born on July 9, 1983 and is a Salvationist of the Montclair, NJ Citadel where she attends with her family. She is a Bandsman (Solo Euphonium), Songster (Soprano), YP Band Instructor, Youth Chorus Leader and a Sunday School Teacher. She served for 5 years as a member of the New York Staff Band and for 10 years, as a member of the New Jersey Youth Band. For many years, following her days as a camper, she has been on the staff of the Army's prestigious Star Lake Music Camp. She enjoys composing both brass band and vocal compositions which allowed her to attend the National Composition Seminar at Asbury College.

Emilee was classically trained as a Euphonium soloist while an undergraduate student at Montclair State University where she also studied piano, music theory and composition. Her mentors were professors Dr. Mary Jane Craig and Dr. Pat Burns.

Emilee is currently employed as a teacher at the Montclair Cooperative School. She lives at home with her parents and sibling in Clifton, New Jersey, USA

Important compositions

More to Give (m/s)

BENNETT, WILLIAM S.

This might have been Brigadier Bennett, who was known as The 'Black Prince'. William was born on 1 March 1851 in Limehouse and Promoted to Glory on 14 January 1923 from the Cottage Hospital in Staines. An illustration is known of this man playing the violin. He became an officer in 1876 and was send to Whitechapel to take up command of this corps and retired in 1920. He served in a total of 52 years as Salvation Army officer.

Important compositions

God is a Spirit (GS1143-1) 1938

BERG, DAVID

David Berg was born on 22nd December 1902 in Stockholm. He became a soldier of the Salvation Army in 1926. In 1930 he became Bandmaster of the Stockholm Temple Citadel Band (Stockholm 1). His compositions are published in the Swedish Music Series.

Important compositions

Templets Sorgmarsch (FM267), Skurar av Välsignelse (FM247) 1960

BIRCH, JOHN

Major John Birch is a retired Salvation Army Officer living in Liverpool, in the North West of England. His wife and he soldiers at the Walton Citadel Corps.

John was born in Ilkeston, Derbyshire, on the 9th September 1928, the 5th child to his parents Albert & Elsie. When he was 18 months old his mother died and he had to go and live with an Aunt in London. His Aunt loved watching the Parades with the bands marching down 'the Mall' to Buckingham Palace. It was watching and hearing the bands that he developed an interest and love for music.

Eventually his father re-married and he was able to return back to the family home. At the age of 7 his father taught him to play a Brass Instrument. John's father then received promotion with his work, and the whole family moved to Stapleford (Near Nottingham). It was there that his love for the Salvation Army developed and he eagerly joined in the activities of the Young People's Band, Singing Company and Corps Cadets. It was here that he met Joy, whom he later married.

Eventually he became a Bandsman at Stapleford, Nottingham, and later he was appointed as Deputy Bandmaster to Bandmaster Charles Dove (Snr). He was a well-known Composer, who encouraged John in the art of Composition. This led him to undertake a course in harmony and Band arranging with the Parr School of Music in Manchester. Later he studied Harmony at Goldsmith College in London.

John and Joy were married on the 8th March 1952, in full Salvation Army uniform and have three children, Robert, Jennifer and Lorraine.

In 1957, John and Joy entered the Salvation Army International Training College in London, and in 1958 were commissioned as Salvation Army Officers. After 13 years serving as Corps Officers (in Friar Park; Erdington, Oakengates, Radcliffe, Droitwich, Kidderminster, Leamington Spa, Hockley and Walsall) they were then appointed to Headquarters in London and soldiered at the Thornton Heath Corps in South London.

Eventually John became the Young People's Band Leader, then Deputy Bandmaster, and finally Bandmaster.

His compositions have been mostly written for the 'Triumph Series' Band Journal apart from a March written for the 'General Series' and a March written for the 'Unity Series'. He has one song published for Songster Brigade's entitled *'Unlimited Forgiveness'*. John was also asked to arrange the band accompaniment to two songs for United Singing Companies to sing at a Congress held at the Wembley Stadium. It was also a great honour to be asked by Lt.Col. Ray Steadman-Allen to arrange 10 tunes for use in the present Band Tune Book. John was Promoted to Glory on April 14th 2012.

Important compositions

The Crowning Day (TS0506) 1953, Happy Journeying (TS0598) 1959, Themes of Gladness (TS0728) 1970, Consistency (TS0796) 1976, Thornton Heath (TS0920) 1986, Springburn Citadel (TS0688) 1967, Centennial, Youthful progress (GS1636) 1972

BIRKETT, SIMON

Simon was born in Darlington, England in 1970 and started playing the piano and euphonium at 10 years old. At school he studied euphonium with Paul Smith (then the principal Tuba player with the BBC Symphony Orchestra), going on to study Music at the Birmingham Conservatoire where he was taught Euphonium by Steven Mead. He came to work for the Salvation Army Music Department at THQ straight after university (1993) and he is still there. Simon played in the International Staff Band for almost ten years. He has always preferred to perform music rather than write it, which is why his output is very limited! He only writes music when they need a piece in the office for one of the publications, and there are many much better composers than him (according to Simon himself!) who get asked before he does! When Simon wrote *'Gladness'* (US 187), it was never really intended for publication, he only wanted Ray Steadman-Allen to look at it for him and give him some ideas on how he might change things and improve it, but to his surprise it was put into the journal and published! He currently works as the Music Originator and Technical Manager in the editorial section of the Music Ministries Unit at THQ London, so he oversees the editorial section from where originates most of the music published, and looks after the technical side of the office (computer hardware/software, photocopiers etc etc).

Important compositions

Gladness (US187) 1995

BLACK, THOMAS FREEMAN

Very little is known about Tom Black, however some interesting facts were written in The Bandsman and Songster of 1907, which is: *The Salvation Army Bandmaster who, in his nineteenth year, composed the popular 'Sheffield' March, and is now the leader of Bonnie Dundee 2, came up from the Juniors. In other words, Bandmaster Thomas F. Black is 'Army made.' It was at Heeley where, as a Salvation Army Junior, he had formed a resolution to be a Bandsman, that he was given his first instrument. It was not a plated one, and would in fact have done credit to a scrap heap, but The Army Junior saw as many possibilities in it as the Bandmaster saw in him. Fired with enthusiasm, young Black made such progress that he soon became a valuable acquisition to the Band. The Bandmaster gave him every opportunity of acquiring an all round knowledge of the various instruments in the Band, and the young*

Bandsman, when only eighteen years of age, had a practical knowledge of all of them. The instruments on which he displayed more than ordinary skill were the euphonium, the tenor horn and bass trombone. At this period of his life, having spent five years with the Heeley Band, he was transferred to Sheffield Citadel, where he played G (bass) trombone.

In twelve months' time he was made Deputy-Bandmaster, which position he held for eighteen months. It was about this time he thought he would try his hand at composition, with the result that he produced the 'Sheffield' March. Eventually he was appointed Bandmaster, and during his command the Band made rapid progress. The time came when the Bandmaster felt that a change from Sheffield would be beneficial, and in this connection he found his Army service very useful. Godliness is profitable for both worlds, and although our comrade has always given his services to The Army with a single eye to God's glory, yet he found, with gratitude, that his talents were blessed to his earthy advantage. He saw an advertisement for a Bandmaster at Dundee 2 Corps, offering at the same time a good situation. His application was successful, and very soon the comrades at Dundee 2 were welcoming Brother Black. At that time the Corps had 'a comparatively young Band' of sixteen players. Now there are twenty-four uniformed Bandsmen, and six waiting to be drafted into the Band. The instruments are new 'Army made,' and plated, 'Class A,' a recent presentation. Our correspondent writes: 'The Band and their playing are now the talk of the city.

Where they used to draw their hundreds, they now attract thousands. Every Sunday afternoon large crowds of people listen to the delightful rendering of Army music on the Shore Terrace.' Bandmaster Black is not only an accomplished musician, but an out-and-out Salvationist. He is ever ready to do anything that lies in his power likely to be he means of extending the Kingdom of God and leading souls to seek the Saviour he loves. Still a young man, Bandmaster Black has, we hope, many years in which to carry on the good work.

(The Bandsman and Songster, June 15, 1907)

Important compositions

Wareham (GS1062) 1933

BLANCHARD, RICHARD

No information about this composer is available. There is reason to believe that he was from the United States of America. His only known published composition is in the USA Eastern Territory Music Publications American Soloists Albums No.4.

Important compositions

Fill my cup

BLOMBERG, GUNNAR

Gunnar Blomberg was born in Sweden and was the Bandmaster of the Stockholm Temple Band (Stockholm 1 Band) from 1936-1940. He took his organist exam but was self taught as a composer and arranger. His *'Swedish Festival March'* is probably his most well known piece and was written somewhere in the 40's of the previous century. His *'Swedish Melodies'* was recorded on the 'Vintage' recording by the Stockholm 7 Band.

Important compositions

Hyfydrol (GS1278) 1947, Silver Hill (GS1307) 1948, Swedish Festival March (FS157) 1949

BLOTT, CHARLES

He was born on 25 February 1894 and Promoted to Glory on 26 May 1969. He was equally at home on the horn, cornet and euphonium and was a member of the Eston Corps all of his life. Charles was taught to play by a bandsman Robottom. Later he taught himself music theory and harmony from books he purchased.

When he was 5 his father was killed in the Eston Iron Stone Mines at the age of 34. Charles left school at 14 (because he had to be the man of the house) and went to work as an errand boy for the local grocer. From his wages he was able to save enough money to buy himself a piano which he taught himself to play. He also played the Accordion/Banjo and Mandolin. He seemed to have a gift for music.

He wrote several pieces of music but did not feel they were good enough for publication until on one occasion, Captain Dean Goffin was staying at Charles' house on his tour of the Durham & Tees Division in his capacity as National Bandmaster, looked at some of his music and decided to take three pieces back to the Music Department for consideration for publication. They were the march *'Eston'*, the songster piece *'Room at the Cross'* and a song for women's voices *'Precious Name'*. All were subsequently published around the same time. He did send other pieces to the Music Board which they kept for consideration at later dates but they were never published.

Important compositions

Eston (GS1522) 1963

BLYTH, ANDREW

Andrew Blyth, born in 1971 in Margate Kent, is a fifth generation Salvationist. During his formative years he was captivated by the Salvation Army and its music making and started to work for the Salvation Army in 1988. He joined the International Staff Band in 1988 and then the Music Editorial Department in 1989. Here he came under the influence and teaching of Michael Kenyon whilst taking private compositional lessons with Phillip Catlinet. In 1999 he left the ISB and continued his corps responsibilities at Margate as Songster Leader. It was in 2001 he became the leader of the International Staff Songsters (ISS), the Salvation Army's premier choral group which he led for two years. In 2005 he was commissioned as the Bandmaster of the Enfield Citadel Band following the legendary Bandmaster James Williams. At present Andrew has over 40 published brass and choral works by the Salvation Army and is the Assistant Territorial Music Director for the Salvation Army.

Important compositions

Shine Down (FS539) 1998, The Great Celebration (FS563) 2001, Compelled by Love (GS2026) 2005

BØJSTRUP, ALF

Alf Bøjstrup was born 28 January 1925 in the city of Aalborg where he grew up and met the Salvation Army. He became a Salvationist and bandsman. He showed musical skills and in 1950 he became the corps Bandmaster. In the 1960's he moved with his wife to Copenhagen to work at the Army's social institution Hørhuset, and they became soldiers at the Copenhagen Temple Corps where Alf for many years played Cornet in the band. For many years Alf would also be leader of a chorus at the Army's social services. He wrote a number of songs for songsters and young people in a very recognisable rhythmic style. He wrote some arrangements for congregational singing (tune book style) and a Eb Bass solo, but his only published music for band is in the Norwegian Junior Series.

Important compositions

Nørholm Camp (NMSJ 53)

BOON, BRINDLEY

Brindley Boon has been a Salvation Army officer since 1950. He is internationally known as a journalist, songwriter and composer of vocal and brass band music and has 150 published works to his credit. The Colonel's appointments have included the editorship of 'The Musician' (1955 - 61, 1965 - 66); the Canadian edition of The 'War Cry' (1962); and the International 'War Cry' (1972-76). He was Editor-in-chief at International Headquarters (1973-77) and retired officially from active service in 1979 after serving as Chief Executive Officer for the 1978 International Congress. From 1966 to 1972 Colonel Boon served as National Secretary for Bands and Songster Brigades in the British Territory, during which time he was a member of the International Music Board. Since 1976 he has been a member of the Song Book Council and in retirement has given valued assistance to the International Music Editorial Department in preparing the new song books and the corresponding tune books. Brindley Boon was a member of the International Staff Band (ISB) from 1952 to 1960. Colonel Boon was Promoted to Glory in March 2009.

Book - **The Best of Both Worlds** - by Brindley Boon

In The Best of Both Worlds, Salvation Army composer Colonel Brindley Boon delves deep into memories covering nine decades to provide a record of an extraordinary life. His twin loves of music and journalism provide the framework for this fascinating autobiography.

Important compositions

Altar of Praise (FS307) 1967, Count your blessings (GS1376) 1953, Croydon Citadel (GS1506) 1961, Troyte (GS1644-2) 1973

BOOTH, EVANGELINE CORY

Evangeline Cory Booth (1865-1950), General of the Salvation Army, born in England, daughter of General William Booth. At the age of 17, she began evangelistic preaching. She was field commissioner of the Salvation Army in London for five years, commander of the Salvation Army in Canada from 1895 to 1904, and commander in the United States from 1904 to 1934. Evangeline Booth was General of the international Salvation Army from 1934 to 1939. Her works include *'Love is All'* (1925), *'Songs of the Evangel'* (1927), and *'Woman'* (1930). Her *'Streams in the Desert'* was the first published composition by a woman composer!

Important compositions

Streams in the Desert (FS113) 1937, The wounds of Christ (GS283-2) 1895 , While the Light from Heaven (GS225) 1893

BOOTH, HERBERT

Herbert Henry Howard Booth (26 August 1862 – 25 September 1926) was the third son of William and Catherine Booth. Herbert received little formal elementary education but became a student at Allesly Park College and the Congregational Institute at Nottingham. At the age of twenty, Herbert began helping his sister Kate Booth in building up The Salvation Army in France. Two years later, he was given charge of England's cadet officer training. He wrote many songs for The Salvation Army and became a bandmaster and a songster leader.

Important compositions

Jesus is strong to deliver (GS41) 1886

BOOTH, LUCY MILWARD

Lucy Milward Booth was born on 28 April 1868 as youngest daughter of General William Booth. She became an officer of The Salvation Army and married the Swedish Salvation Army officer Emanuel Hellberg. They served for the Salvation Army in India, France, Switzerland, Denmark, Norway and after her husband was Promoted to Glory, Lucy worked for the Salvation Army in South America. She received the Order of the Founder. Lucy was Promoted to Glory on 18th July 1953.

Important compositions

Keep on believing (GS130-1) 1890, Only One Intention (GS130-2) 1890

BOSANKO, COURTNEY

The Festival which marked the retirement of Bandmaster Herbert Mountain also saw the commissioning of bandmaster Courtney Bosanko A.L.C.M. He was a member of the well known Salvation Army musical family, his father being the retired bandmaster of the Bargoed Citadel band, and his brother bandmaster at Cardiff Canton. In his teens he played solo euphonium in the Men's Social Headquarters Band, under the leadership of Colonel Arthur Goldsmith, and at the age of 21, he was commissioned bandmaster at Walthamstow. After two years he transferred to Salisbury, continuing to serve there as Bandmaster for 17 years. During the War he was bandmaster of the 7th (Haytor) Battalion of the Devonshire Regiment stationed in Italy, and was congratulated by Field-Marshall Alexander upon the performance of his band in Rome.

In early life he was greatly influenced by his mother's Godly example and was converted during his school days. A lifelong Salvationist, he held very sacred the fundamental principle of Salvation Army banding. In writing to a friend in 1946, the bandmaster stated that he had rededicated his life to God some three years ago, on the eve of going to Tunisia, and later followed with *'A little musical ability is only one of the many things needed to be a bandmaster'*. With experiences gleaned from 19 years as bandmaster and expertise acquired from Colonel Goldsmith's instruction, Courtney Bosanko soon proved his capabilities as a band trainer. His was the ability to give confidence to those who doubted their own abilities, to extract from ordinary players extraordinary musical performances. As a result the band was soon in much demand sometimes with engagements being requested up to two years in advance.

Important compositions

The Bargoed March (TS168) 1932, Joyful Testimony (GS1308) 1948

BOSANKO, IVOR

Ivor Bosanko was born in Cardiff, Wales. He attended the Welsh College of Music and Drama studying trumpet and piano. He is an Associate of the Royal College of Music, a Licentiate of the Royal Academy of Music and a Fellow of Trinity College of Music. Ivor commenced playing in a brass band at the age of eight and since then brass banding has been an important part of his musical expression. He was a member of H.M. Irish Guards Band from 1957-1960. During his stay in London, Ivor had the opportunity to play with many of the major orchestras, including The Covent Garden Opera, The BBC Symphony, and The BBC Concert Orchestra. He was the principal trumpet with the National Youth Orchestra of Wales for seven years, returning in 1958 as the soloist for their summer tour. In 1975 he emigrated with his family to Philadelphia. In 1979 he accepted the position of Territorial Music Secretary for The Salvation Army, covering the thirteen Western States. He is known as a prolific composer of both instrumental and vocal music.

Important compositions

Glorious Liberation (FS538) 1997, In this Quiet Moment (FS578) 2002, His Provision (GS1864) 1991, Strathallan Suite (GS2022) 2004, Rocky Mountain Centennial (AF005) 1989.

BOWEN, BRIAN

Brian Bowen was born on 27 September 1940 in Staines, England, and from an early age was very early interested in music. After study music he received the L.T.C.L in 1962, and F.T.C.L. in 1969 in conducting Brass Bands. From 1961 to 1986 Brian was the Bandmaster of the Staines Citadel Band. From 1964 to 1976 he was a member of The International Staff Band (ISB) on Flugel Horn. He then moved to New York where became the bandmaster of the New York Staff Band from 1986 until 1992. With the New York Staff Band he visited Australia, Canada, Denmark, Germany, Great Britain, Japan, Korea, Holland. New Zealand, Norway, Singapur, Sweden, Switzerland and ofcourse the USA. During this time Brian Bowen worked at the Music Department of the Salvation Army in New York.

Important compositions

My Comforth and Strength (FS305) 1967, Hope Variations (FS403) 1980, The Southern Cross (FS353) 1973, The Warriors (GS1682) 1976, Themes from Schubert's Fifth Symphony (FS326) 1970, Kaleidoscope (Rimsky-Korsakov), Day of the Spiritual (1973) Folk Heroes (1992) The Suppliant Heart (FS357) 1974, Salem Variations (FS548) 1999.

BOWES, RAY

Ray Bowes was born on 12th January 1925 in England. He studied music theory with a private teacher and passed the exam at the 'Trinity College of Music' in London with the qualification A.Mus. T.C.L. He then entered the Training College of the Salvation Army in London to become an officer. As an officer he became a member of the International Staff Band (ISB) where he played Cornet and Flugel Horn. In 1970 he was made deputy bandmaster before in 1975 becoming bandmaster of the ISB, a position he held until 1989. In 1980 he was made responsible for the Music Department of the Salvation Army in London, retiring in 1990. Later he served as an adjudicator for Brass Band contests and composed music for Brass Band, choir and piano. He once said: *'It is not easy to determine why somebody composes music. Expressing my thoughts through music causes me to have profound emotions, sometimes as an act of praise and worship, or sometimes trying to encourage others to worship'*. He was Promoted to Glory on February 13th 2010.

He became know in particular for a number of pieces including; *'Rhapsody for Cornet and Band'*, euphonium solo *'Song of Triumph'*, *'The King's Crusaders'*, *'Jesus loves me'* and *'The Prodigal'* which are also his most recorded pieces.

The International Staff Band recorded a full CD of his compositions while he was in his last year as Bandmaster of this band. The CD is called 'The King's Crusader' (SPS074CD). After Ray Bowes passed away in 2010, the South London Fellowship Band conducted by his friend Major George Whittingham, recorded another CD with his works, with guests soloists Keith Hutchinson (cornet) and Simon Birkett (Euphonium) (SPS258CD).

Important compositions

Rhapsody for Cornet and Band (FS410-1) 1981, The King's Crusaders (FS239) 1959, The Prodigal (FS415) 1981, Winterthur Centenary (GS1837) 1989, Lord, show me what I need (TS951) 1989, Crown of Gold (FS293) 1966, Harlesden (TS861) 1981.

BOYD, WILLIAM

Commissioned as the second official Bandmaster of the Paisley Citadel Band around 1905 as successor of Edward Rowe, who was Bandmaster from 1895 until 1905. William Boyd was born around 1880. Although the Corps of Paisley has records of every Corps Officer going back to 1882, no records were found which could lead to more information about William Boyd.

Note the different address of Publishing Offices, although the same piece!

One interesting fact about Boyd's *'The Paisley March'* is that over the years it was played so many times that the people at the corps developed a 'local whistle', based on the opening 'chromatic like descending scale' as seen in the first three bars and one beat of the march i.e. the first two bars are whistled quickly, (descending) with each note punctuated individually and the second and third bars whistled as a rising glissando. This is still today known in the Paisley Corps as the 'Paisley Whistle'!

Important compositions

The Cadet March (GS0508) 1905, The Paisley March (No.484) also published around 1905.

BRAKSTAD, JOHN

Brakstad was born in 1940 in Bergen, Norway where he still lives. A live long Salvationist Brakstad has written special compositions and arrangements for many Salvation Army bands, including the Bergen 1 Band of which he is the bandmaster.

John Brakstad gained much of his musical experience as bandmaster, composer and arranger for the Salvation Army, and from studies at the Bergen Musikk Konservatorium. He has also been working as a conductor for several Norwegian Contest bands, and is regularly used as an adjudicator at the Norwegian Band Association's Contests and Championships. Brakstad has written many compositions for brass and concert bands published by primarily Norsk Noteservice and Warner Chappel Music. Several of these are test pieces for the national championships and later performed regularly at the same competitions. Among his most known original works are *'Variations for Band'*, *'The Old Railway Station'*, *'Musica Tripartite'* and *'Cobalt'*. He has written music for the Military band in his native Bergen and the Staff Band of the Norwegian Armed Forces which has been performed at the Bergen International Festival. Brakstad also wrote music (Prelude Olympic) for the opening ceremony at the 1994 Olympic Winter Games in Lillehammer, Norway. He also wrote a large work for choir and band for the Arne Garborg 150th Anniversary in 2001. His last work *'Toccata e Corale'* is used as qualification piece for the top section in the Norwegian championship 2012. Apart from this work he has written many transcriptions on the music of Edvard Grieg as well as in particular many Christmas arrangements and marches. Within the Salvation Army his music is published in the Norwegian Series and ScanBrass.

Important compositions

Han Frelste en Synder (SB2010-02)

BRADLEY, WILLIAM

William Bradley was a Yorkshireman who became a School Headmaster at Carlisle and Bandmaster of Carlisle Citadel. He wrote a March of that name published in the 1200's Ordinary series. He also wrote a trombone solo published in the Trombone Solo with piano accompaniment Book used by all Salvation Army trombonists in the 50's and 60's. William was a fine trombonist himself. He later moved to Hanley, Staffs where he was made Bandmaster. He served as an Instructor at the Army's North West School of Music in the mid 1960's.

Important compositions

Carlisle Citadel (GS1289) 1947, Invitation (TS0203) 1934, Pardoned and Free (GS1047) 1932, The Ransomed (TS0164) 1931

BRAINE, ALFRED

An officer of the Salvation Army, Colonel Alfred Braine was the first official National Secretary for Salvation Army Bands and Songsters Brigades in the United Kingdom when it was announced in 1921 to set up such a department. He was already a corps bandmaster at Battersea 1, at age seventeen. He was a member of the International Staff Band and later was the leader of the Salvation Singers (forerunners of the International Staff Songsters). He also issued the Salvation Army's first tune book.

Important compositions

Get ready for the harvest home (GS0168) 1891, Whosoever will may come (GS0214) 1893

BREVIK, TOM

Was born in Fredrikstad, Norway in 1948. He had his musical studies in Bergen and took exams with The Highest Degree of Music Performance from Bergen Music Conservatory, with flute recorders as main instruments. He has been one of the most active and central persons in the Norwegian band movement over the last decades, both as an administrator, musician, composer, arranger, publisher, conductor and jury member. Tom Brevik has been both Musical Director and President of The Norwegian Band Federation (NMF). As a conductor he has conducted top renowned Norwegian Brass Bands like Manger Musikklag and Eikanger/Bjørsvik Musikklag. He is an international brass band jury member and is one of three members of The Music Commission of the European Brass Band Assosiation (EBBA).

(source: musikkped.no)

Important compositions

Wondrous Truth (FS339) 1971

BRIGHT, CLIVE

Son of one of the seven Bright Brothers (composer James Frederick Bright is one of them). His father was the Young People's Band Leader and Clive at eighteen became the Hadleigh Temple Singing Company Leader. There is still a photo of the Singing Company about 1950 showing Clive holding the baton. Clive was a very competent trombone soloist and went on to become the manager of Boosey and Hawkes, the music publishers and instrument makers.

Clive Bright moved to Harpenden from Hadleigh in 1957 and soon after this date he became the corps Bandmaster. He held this position for a few years. He then resigned and left the Salvation Army. Whilst Bandmaster at Harpenden, Clive worked at the Music Editorial Department at Judd Street. From here, he went to work for Chappell's Music in Regent Street, London before moving on to Williams school of Church Music. He is now long since retired and lives in South Wales. During Clive's term as Bandmaster a number of 'Composer Festivals' were organised over a period of time involving such personalities as Ray Steadman-Allen, Leslie Condon and several others. These events raised money for a new instrument scheme at that time for the Harpenden Citadel Band.

Important composition

Festive Praise (FS0589) 2004

BRIGHT, DUDLEY

Dudley Bright (23 April 1953) had the first cornet lessons with his father, who was Young People's Bandleader at his Salvation Army Corps. At the age of 10, Dudley won the first price at a School Contest of Music. Later Dudley became the Principal Trombone of the London Symphony Orchestra since 2000. Before that he was for many years in the same seat at the Philharmonic Orchestra. He studied at the Guildhall School of Music and Drama, graduating in 1974, later becoming Professor of Trombone at the Royal Academy of Music. Dudley is held in high esteem in the music world and is regarded as one of the world's leading trombone players. He also has a wealth of experience in playing and conducting brass bands, both in Salvation Army circles and in the brass band movement as a whole. As a Soloist and lecturer he visited the USA, Canada, Japan, Germany, Sweden,

Scotland and Switzerland. Dudley once said: '*We always have to remember that we are first of all Christians, then Salvationists and in the end Musicians. With Salvation Army music we can continue to build God's kingdom. My aim is to make music with this in mind.*'

Of all his compositions his rarely heard *'Near the Cross'* jumps out in originality, creating a mystic atmosphere and brings the Message to the full.

Important compositions

Near the Cross (FS395) 1978, Spirit of the West (GS1772) 1983, Confrontations (FS423) 1982, Excelsior (FS499) 1993, The Greatest of These (GS1832) 1988

BRIGHT, JAMES FREDERICK

James Bright was born on 3 August 1888 at Mozart Street and was Promoted to Glory on 4 January 1976 aged 87. He was one of seven brothers who were all Salvationists. James also wrote songster music. He was Bandmaster at Kilburn until 1928 when he moved to Wealdstone and before him Clive Bright's father was the bandmaster. Clive was the cousin of Dudley Bright's father (and so a son of James Frederick Bright). He was later Deputy Bandmaster until he was removed by the corps officer as he had done a little deputising in The Home Guard Band for Denis Wright. He had a few Second Series pieces and a few songs published (one in the last months of his life!). He regarded the 'moderns' with deep suspicion as his music is more antiquated. His grandson, Dudley Bright's one and only Triumph Series piece *'Within the Sanctuary'* is a sincere tribute to James Bright and is an arrangement of his song of the same name, written to words of Arch Wiggins for the rededication of rebuilt Wealdstone corps (now closed).

Sometime around 1903/1904 James' father bought some fish and chips wrapped in newspaper which happened to be the 'War Cry'! The reading of this greasy paper interested him enough to visit the local Salvation Army hall, leading on to becoming a Salvationist. His sons also joined, including James who was the eldest. James started to play the cornet when he was about seventeen years of age. At Kilburn Corps he was the Young People's Bandleader and later Bandmaster with a band numbering around twenty five. A move of house meant a transfer to Harlesden Corps, where he took on the position of Young People's Bandleader, and two of his sons became also part of his band. Another house move saw them go to Wealdstone where he was commisioned Deputy Bandmaster in the early 1940's.

James Frederick Bright was completely self-taught musically through books like G.A. MacFarren's *Rudiments of Harmony* and other books he could lay his hands on. Besides band music he also wrote vocal music such as *'Within the Sanctuary'*, *'The Greatness of love'* and *'Surrender Complete'*.

'Within the Sanctuary' was written for the re-opening oft he Wealdstone Corps Hall from which Dudley Bright (grandson of James) composed a meditation putting in a cornet obligato for Dudley's father (son of James). *'Surrender Complete'* was never heard by James but Tommy Wilson (now a longstanding member of the London Citadel Band in Canada) went to Northwick Park Hospital and played the melody to James on his cornet.

Important compositions

Invitation and comfort (TS0470) 1951, My faith looks up to thee (TS0450) 1950, Prayer and eventide (TS0502) 1953

BRISTOW, ARTHUR

At fourteen years of age a Doncaster born grocer's assistant he took his first lessons in cornet playing. Little did Arthur Bristow then dream that one day he would become a Salvation Army officer, composer, song-writer, instrumentalist, Bandmaster, instructor, Songster Leader, expert tuner of brass instruments and manager of three affiliated 'musical' departments of The Salvation Army. Lieut.-Colonel Bristow, has been an officer for forty-six years and music, 'his sweetest recreation', has run parallel with his service for the Kingdom. While still in his teens, Arthur was appointed to Heely Corps, Yorkshire, where he was instructed to take charge of the Band. Here Lieutenant Bristow received his first lessons on the concertina. Then followed opportunities for conducting various bands in connection with the Founder's motor tours, officers' councils and weekend campaigns. Later on General Bramwell Booth and General Higgins made use of his gifts in the same way. Three eminent teachers who had tutored the young cornetist must have been exceedingly proud of their pupil when he played the first Salvation Army broadcast cornet solo from the BBC Manchester Studio in 1923. For twenty-one years Arthur Bristow served as a Corps officer and commanded such Corps as Manchester Temple, Halifax, Rugby, Cambridge and, lastly, Darlington. In 1925 the Colonel was appointed to the International Music Editorial Department as assistant to Colonel F.G. Hawkes. This was during one of the busiest and most historic periods in the department's history, for it involved the preparations and publication of the Band Tune Book for congregational singing, which took three years to complete. Appointment to the Musical Publications Department followed. "The Musical Salvationist", tune books, band music and a few instrumental albums comprised the publications of that day. The Colonel 'dreamed up' the idea of providing everything a Salvationist musician needed and, working toward this end with Colonel Hawkes (until 1936) and later with Colonel Bramwell Coles and his colleagues, made the dream come true. A wide range of subjects of interest to bandsmen and songsters has been dealt with in articles by the Colonel. 'The cornet and how to play it', 'The Drum', 'The Power of Sacred Song', 'Points for Beginners', 'Intermediates', 'Advanced Students' and 'Teachers' are among them. His detailed descriptions of instrument manufacture in the 'Our Own Make' series in "The Musician" were widely read. The Colonel devoted himself in his younger days to the study of the concertina and gained proficiency certificates. In a concertina competition for officers he secured first prize and was invited by the Education Secretary to prepare concertina lessons for officer-students. These were eagerly sought after and the name Bristow became the hallmark of this course of instruction for twenty-six years. At the request of Commissioner Mildred Duff a concertina correspondence class was conducted in 'The Warrior' for twelve years. The Colonel was also responsible for the revision and enlargement of the English and Triumph Concertina Tutors in use today. The 37,000 Salvation Army gramophone records sold annually at 'Judd Street' have been produced under Lieut.-Colonel Bristow's supervision. He has attended rehearsals and was always present in the studio. The Musical Instruments Department came under the Colonel's management upon the retirement of Brigadier Archie Burgess in June, 1938. Opportunity knocked with no uncertain sound and received a hearty welcome from this indefatigable task-tackler. The manufacture and tuning of brass instruments at the Army's Instrument Factory at St. Albans formed a further important responsibility requiring the skilful handling of Lieut.-Colonel Bristow. Reference was made to the factory by the well-known broadcaster Richard Dimbleby during his St. Albans 'Down Your Way' program. After being initiated into some of the mysteries of instrument manufacture, Mr. Dimbleby listened to the Colonel's able playing of a flugelhorn and then attempted to broadcast a 'tune' himself! The syllabus of the National Youth Music Camps would have been incomplete without the Colonel's informative talks. For five years Lieut.-Colonel Bristow was Bandmaster at Ilford, the band playing 'solo' under him at a Crystal Palace Festival. His men regarded him as a model of punctuality, keenness and 'a stickler' in his adherence to Army principles. During the war he rendered yeoman service with his cornet. He also led the Ilford Songsters for nearly six years. (Freely adapted from "The Musician" 15 April 1950)

Important compositions

Stepping Heavenward (TS89) 1927, My all in all (TS207) 1934, A Soldier of the Army (TS154) 1931

BROOKS, NOEL

A native of Newfoundland, Noel was born in St. John's, Newfoundland, Canada on March 24, 1972, and raised in Grand Falls, which is also on 'The Rock', as Newfoundland is known. He joined the Grand Falls Corps Band in 1986 where his father, Ray Brooks was bandmaster. Noel started his music degree at Memorial University of Newfoundland in 1991 and majored in Theory and Composition. He played in the St. John's Temple Band from 1991 to 1994 and graduated in 1995. In that same year he moved on the Canada's mainland and settled in London, Ontario.

In London he started his Master's of Music degree at the University of Western Ontario in 1995 and joined the London Citadel Band where he still plays trombone. He graduated from the University in 1998. After that he started at the Teacher's College in 2000, and graduated in 2001. Since then he has been working as an elementary school music teacher which he is still today.

Noel Brooks started writing Salvation Army music in 2001, and his first piece was *'Born for You'* (published in the American Band Journal), and as such recorded by the London Citadel Band. Other pieces he got published are *'Love So Amazing'*, in the Triumph Series, and also recorded by his corps band, and *'Oh, How He Loves You and Me'*, in the Triumph Series, and recorded by the Canadian Staff Band.

Four other Salvation Army pieces still unpublished are *'Cwm Rhondda'* and *'Do You See What I See?'* both recorded by the London Citadel Band and *'God Be With You Till We Meet Again'* which was recorded by the Meadowlands Citadel Band from Hamilton, Ontario. Noel also wrote several other pieces written for elementary school band and are still awaiting publication.

Important compositions

Born for you (AJ240) 2005

BROOKS, RAY

One never knows when a genius could be lurking in the back of the band in the tuba section. That's Ray Brooks. Not only is he a composer but also a poet. He recently wrote a beautiful number for the band titled *'In His presence'*. In 2005 he published a book of his poems *'As seen through glass'*.

Ray was born in Green's Harbour, Trinity Bay in 1940. A son of Salvation Army officers, he grew up in various Newfoundland communities, graduating from the Salvation Army high school in Windsor in 1956. After attending university for one year, he returned to Windsor and began his teaching career as a classroom teacher. Continuing his university studies, he received degrees in Education (1962) and Arts (1966) from Memorial University. He has held teaching positions at Peterview, Hare Bay (B.B.), Middle Brook (Gambo), Grand Bank, St. John's and Grand Falls-Windsor. Whilst teaching in St. John's he pursued an interest in music. A student of Mrs. Carla Furlong and the late Dr. Eric Abbott, he received a Licentiate in Tuba performance from Trinity College of Music (1970). He continued further studies in Music theory and Brass pedagogy at Mount Allison University and completed a year's study in Music history at the University of Toronto. He received his Masters of Education degree from Boston University in 1975. From 1971 until his retirement in 1992 he taught instrumental music at Grand Falls Academy. He now resides in London, Ontario with his wife Elsie. He is the father of composer Noel Brooks.

Important compositions

In His Presence (m/s)

BROUGHTON, BRUCE

Bruce Broughton was born in Los Angeles on March 8, 1945. His banding activities were all as a child and teenager. He began composing when he was twelve and studied composition several years later at the University of Southern California and privately with fellow composer Emil Soderstrom. He began working for CBS Television after graduating from college in 1967 and became a freelance composer in 1977. Over the last 40 and more years, although the majority of his work has been for film and television, he has written band pieces, but most of his Salvation Army music was composed before he became a professional composer.

Bruce Broughton is one of the most versatile composers working today, and writes in every medium, from theatrical releases and TV feature films to the concert stage and computer games.

With over 20 Emmy nominations, Bruce Broughton has received a record 10, most recently for HBO's Warm Springs. He's also won Emmys for Eloise at Christmastime; Eloise at The Plaza; Glory & Honor; O Pioneers!; Tiny Toon Adventures Theme Song; The First Olympics, Athens 1896, Part I; Dallas: Ewing Blues; Dallas: The Letter; and Buck Rogers: The Satyr.

Numerous TV credits include the main titles for JAG, Tiny Toon Adventures, and Dinosaurs, as well as scores for Amazing Stories, Quincy, and How The West Was Won. Movies for television include Lucy, Bobbie's Girl, and O Pioneers!; and the miniseries Roughing It, The Blue and the Gray, and the Emmy nominated True Women.

An accomplished composer of concert music, Broughton has conducted and recorded numerous original works, including *'Mixed Elements'*, commissioned by and premiered at the Sunflower Music Festival, *'Modular Music'*, composed for the Los Angeles Chamber Orchestra; *'The Magic Horn'*, commissioned jointly by the Chicago, Seattle and National Symphonies for the Magic Circle Mime Company; *'Excursions'*, commissioned and premiered by The United States Air Force Band in Washington, D.C.; *'Fanfares, Marches, Hymns and Finale'*, commissioned by The Bay Brass; *'English Music'* for Horn and Strings;

'And on the Sixth Day' for oboe and orchestra; *'Tyvek Wood'*, commissioned by the Debussy Trio; a piccolo concerto; a tuba concerto; several solo works for winds; numerous chamber works, and the list goes on.

As a conductor, his recordings of Miklós Rózsa's *'Ivanhoe'* and *'Julius Caesar'* for Intrada records, performed by the Sinfonia of London shortly before the composer's death, have received rave reviews, as has his recording of Bernard Herrmann's riveting score for *'Jason and the Argonauts'*.

Broughton is a board member of ASCAP, a governor of the Academy of Motion Picture Arts and Sciences, a former governor of the Academy of Television Arts and Sciences, and past president of The Society of Composers and Lyricists. He has taught film composition in the Advanced Film Music Studies program at USC and is a frequent lecturer at UCLA.

In 1995 the New York Staff Band recorded a CD with compositions from the three Broughton family members, simply entitled 'The Broughtons' TRCD1053

Important compositions

To Set The People Free (m/s), The New Born Babe (FS327) 1970, Covenant (FS459) 1987

BROUGHTON, WILLIAM

William Broughton was born in Los Angeles to Salvation Army Officers. He found his interest to Salvation Army music in the music camps of the Salvation Army, where he met Erik Leidzén. He began his career as trombonist. As a studio trombonist, he has performed for most of the television and motion picture studios in Hollywood, California. As a composer and producer for television, his work includes compositions for *'Hawaii Five-O'*, *'Buck Rogers'*, *'BJ and the Bear'*, *'The Hardy Boys'*, *'Misadventures of Sheriff Lobo'* und *'Quincy'*. As a Salvationist Bill has a keen interest in Salvation Army music education programs and is a popular guest at summer music camps throughout North America. He wrote music for choir, orchestra, Concert Band and Brass Band. William is President of S.G.M. Productions based in Atlanta, Georgia and active Salvationist in Atlanta Temple Corps.

He once said: *'The Salvation Army presents for me the Word of God. On this are based all my song arrangements. I feel a deep connection to this works which are my favourites.'*

In 1995 the New York Staff Band recorded a CD with compositions from the three Broughton family members, simply entitled 'The Broughtons'TRCD1053)

Important compositions

Deep River (GS1953) 1999, Gowans and Larsson Overture (AF003) 1988, Take up Thy Cross (AJ127) 1984, In perfect peace (AJ141) 1989, Glory Be (FS491) 1992.

BROUGHTON, RYAN

Ryan was born on April 12, 1988 in Guelph, Ontario, Canada. He grew up in Guelph, attending the Guelph Citadel. He did the usual progression from the Young People's Band to the Senior Band, where he started on baritone, then moved to bass trombone. When Ryan was 14, he joined the Ontario South Divisional Youth Band, which is now called 'Impact Brass', where he would play for the next seven years, playing baritone for 4 years, before moving to bass trombone for the last 3. Ryan then moved to North York Temple in 2009, where he joined the band on bass trombone, and still plays to this day. He is currently studying bass trombone performance at the University of Toronto.

He first showed interest in composition when he was 10 years old, when he wrote a short string quartet. Around the same time he wrote a short etude for piano, just trying to figure out what sounded interesting. He then didn't write anything for quite a while until around 2006, when he wrote a few short arrangements for Young People's Bands, and wrote a few pieces for wind ensemble. Since starting university, Ryan hasn't had a lot of time to dedicate to composition, so his output has been relatively low, only producing a few short arrangements, mostly when requested. He has been working on a few new ideas recently, and hopes to have his first major work for brass band completed over the summer 2011.

Important compositions

Silent Night (m/s), Come to Jesus (m/s)

BROUGHTON, WILLIAM

William Broughton was born in 1884 to a Salvation Army Officer parents in England. In the age of fourteen he started to compose music and won several 'Music Awards'. One of his first works was the march *'Chicago March'*, published in 1908 in the General Series No. 568 (former Ordinary Series). In 1902 he became an Officer of The Salvation Army and emigrated to the USA. In America, William was responsible to introduce the brass bands and promote the brass band music in the Salvation Army. He served also as Bandmaster of the Flint Citadel Band, the Chicago Staff Band and the New York Staff Band. 1949 he retired as Band Secretary of the U.S.Western Territory. He was Promoted to Glory in 1950. In 1995 the New York Staff Band recorded a CD with compositions from the three Broughton family members, simply entitled 'The Broughtons' (TRCD1053).

William Broughton, a son of the late Major William Broughton, commenced writing music in his youth, and at the age of fourteen had his first composition published in "The Musical Salvationist". It has been written of him that 'he is musical from head to toe,' and when a boy, was often billed as 'the eleven-and-a-half-year-old cornet player'. At sixteen he won a prize in an International Music Competition, and since that time he won eight prizes in similar competitions. When eighteen years of age he entered the International Training College, and in 1904 received an appointment on the Chicago Headquarters, USA. He became leader of the Territorial Band, and in that capacity participated in the 1914 International Congress. The *'America'* march was specially written for this event. For nine years Major Broughton was in charge of Flint Citadel Band, and in 1919 his father, then retired from active service in the homeland, went to America to be near his son. The veteran Officer fast became a much-loved and respected Soldier at Flint Corps, and one Sunday night, accompanying himself on the concertina, he sang, as a solo, *'At the Cross there's room'*. It was to be his last solo on earth, for a few days later he was stricken with illness and Promoted to Glory. In honour of his beloved father's memory, his son composed the meditation, *'At the Cross there's room'*, which he regards as one of the most outstanding of all his compositions. *'It was not made to order'*, the composer declares; *'It came by inspiration, and it has a message'*. As many souls were won for the Kingdom by the singing of this grand old song by William Broughton, junior., in the Salvation of countless souls. William Broughton has been Bandmaster of the New York Staff Band, and in this connection it has been written of him: *'he has the knack of bringing out of his men more music than some of them ever imagined they possessed. He insists on a high standard of efficiency in every detail of Band life, including deportment and uniform wearing. In addition to his natural ability William Broughton has worked hard at himself. As a youthful Captain he studied harmony, counterpoint, fugue, and canon, and won a scholarship entitling him to free tuition at the Chicago College of Music'.* Of the cornet duet, *'Lover of the Lord',* he wrote; *'This was written about as quickly as anything I have ever done. I received a letter from Colonel Hawkes about three weeks prior to the General's Motorcade, asking for a cornet duet on the theme, 'You must be a lover of the Lord'. I received the message at 11 a.m. and immediately sat down to write, by 5 p.m. I had completed the whole score and posted it off to London'.* Later William Broughton was in charge of the Social Institution of Cleveland, Ohio, but continued to be busy with his musical composition. His solo, *'Sound the Battle Cry',* written for the trombone, was fast becoming universally popular. The true word of this well-known Army musician can be better understood when it is known that he wrote these words in a message to the Bandsmen of Australia: *'There is nothing better in all the world than real heart service in the ranks of The Army'.* (freely adapted from 'The Musician' 19-2-1938)

Important compositions

The Golden Gate (FS020) 1925, Santa Lucia (FS094) 1934, The Chicago March (GS568) 1908.

BROWN, ARNOLD

Arnold Brown was born in London, England, on 13th December 1913, the son of Salvation Army Officers parents who were stationed at that time at the Tottenham 2 Corps. While he was a young boy his family emigrated to Canada, and it was from Belleville Corps that Arnold Brown entered training, becoming an officer in 1935. A two-year corps command was followed by 10 year's service in the editorial department at Territorial Headquarters, where he became assistant editor of The 'War Cry'. During that time he compiled a history of the first 50 years of Salvation Army ministry in Canada, entitled *'What Hath God Wrought?'* On 15th September 1939 Captain Arnold Brown married Lieutenant Jean Barclay. In 1962 the then Brigadier Brown was appointed as territorial youth secretary of Canada and Bermuda. In 1964 there came a return to public relations work, this time at International Headquarters, where Lieut-Colonel Arnold Brown was appointed as secretary for public relations, being promoted to the rank of Colonel just a few months later. In his capacity as a Rotarian he was invited to address many international conferences. Commissioner Arnold Brown was appointed Chief of the Staff in October 1969, where he served for five years before returning to Canada as territorial commander in 1974. Three years later, the 1977 High Council of The Salvation Army elected him to become the 11th General of The Salvation Army. Arnold and Jean Brown gave 42 years of joint service before they retired from active leadership. He was Promoted to Glory 2002, at the age of 88.

Important compositions

The world set free (TS284) 1939, Glad entrance (TS404) 1947.

BUCHAN, CRAIG

Born in Mirfield, West Yorkshire on 28 March 1974, Craig attended The Salvation Army from birth. His home corps was Heckmondwike, where he became Singing Company Leader at the age of only seventeen.

After leaving school he moved to Scarborough, and gained a BA (Hons) in Music from York University. His tutors encouraged him leaning towards composition and conducting and after graduating he went to Salford University to study for a Masters in Composition with Professor Peter Graham. Craig had met Peter at a music school in 1993 in the Central and West Yorkshire Division and to meet up again and study was a great privilege for him.

It was during this time that his Unity Series arrangement of *'Pastime with Good Company'* (2002) was published by the Salvation Army. As part of the course he arranged many new pieces. *'Made in America'* (2002) was an eclectic arrangement of US music commissioned by Bandmaster David Nicholson of Birmingham Citadel Band for their 2003 tour of the USA. Featuring many genres, the piece included native American music and snippets of Sousa's Salvation Army March. This has been Craig's largest piece of music to date.

'Music of thy Voice' (2002) reflects the compositional tutelage of Peter Graham. A through arrangement with a slower middle section featuring Joy Webb's songster piece *'The First Step'* the piece ends with an exuberant arrangement of the hymn *'Beethoven'*. This piece was featured at the Western Territorial Music Institute (USA) in 2002.

In 2003 Craig moved to Washington, DC to work for The Salvation Army as the Associate Divisional Music Director, and joined the National Capital Band on flugelhorn. He wrote several pieces that were used by the Divisional Youth Band during this time for which he had responsibility. These arrangements were very much seen as 'utility' pieces, written for specific groups and meetings.

On returning to the United Kingdom, he was commissioned as Deputy Bandmaster at the Leeds Central Corps, becoming Bandmaster on the retirement of Bandmaster Jack Flounders. He went on to study with Ray Farr at Durham University in 2005 and has maintained contact with him since. Ray led a recent Leeds Central Band retreat. The band has enjoyed a busy program over the past few years with highlights including a tour of Ghana in August 2010 and being the first Salvation Army Band to appear in an established concert series at The Sage, Gateshead.

By profession Craig is an Independent Financial Adviser and owns a national United Kingdom advisory practice who deal with doctors and dentists. He is married to Ruth and they have two boys, Ewan and Cameron. With the arrival of the boys and the establishment of a successful business Craig found it difficult over the past 6 years to sit down and compose. However, encouraged by two friends and colleague composers, Dean Jones and Kenneth Downie, he has started to write again.

Important compositions and arrangements

Prelude to a Theme (2000), A Coventry Fanfare (2000), Shine on us (2001), Pastime with Good Company [US0274] (2002), Music of Thy Voice (2002), YSCA 2002 (2002), Holy, Holy, Holy (2003), Made in America (2003), Cornet Solo - If you call me, Lord (written for International Staff Bandsman Rob Gill) (2003), March - from The Love for Three Oranges (Prokofiev) (2003).

BULL, OLE

Born in (around) 1810 and was Promoted to Glory on 17 August 1880. Ole was one of the people who accompanied General William Booth on the violin during the early years of the Salvation Army in particular when William Booth visited the United States where Ole lived in Cambridge. He was a Norwegian by birth.

Important compositions

Säterjäntens Söndag (FM0072-1) 1906

BULLA, STEPHEN

Bandmaster Stephen Bulla (30 January, 1953) received his degree in arranging and composition from Boston's Berklee College of Music, where he developed an interest in jazz/pop styles that eventually led him to the freelance commercial music field. In 1980, Stephen joined 'The President's Own' U.S. Marine Band and White House Orchestra as Staff Arranger. He is responsible for producing music that encompasses all styles and instrumental combinations, most of which is performed for Presidential functions and visiting dignitaries. Stephen's brass and vocal compositions are published and performed internationally, and he travels frequently as a guest conductor, soloist and clinician. Stephen Bulla has conducted the National Capital Band (one of the Army's Staff Bands in the United States) since 1985 and is also a member of the Trombone-Ensemble 'Spiritual to the Bone'. For some time he was also a member of the Southern Territorial Band and the New York Staff Band.

Important compositions

Crossroad (FS467) 1988, The Higher Plane (FS517) 1995, The Cleansing Power (GS1844) 1989, Star Lake 70 (AJ251) 2007, Montclair Citadel (FS582) 2003

BURGESS, CALEB

After Fred Fry, the International Staff Band was reorganized in 1893 and Jabez Lyne became the Bandmaster because of his huge experience and knowledge about banding. Lyne was an officer, but soon relinquished this position and left the Salvation Army for a career in politics. Caleb Burgess then became the new bandmaster of the International Staff Band after a stint as Bandmaster of the 2nd Household Troops Band. He didn't remain for long in this capacity as he was replaced soon after by George Mitchell who took charges of the ISB age 22.

Important compositions

Marching to a better land (GS0215) 1893, My Pilot (GS0247) 1894

BURGMAYER, HAROLD

Harold Burgmayer was born on 18th May 1955. He began his musical journey with cornet lessons from his father who was an avid junior band leader. At age 14, Harold began conducting and arranging music for his small corps band in Levittown Pennsylvania, while benefiting from the music program of the Pendel Division under the leadership of bandmaster Kenneth Strehle and later, Ivor and Janette Bosanko. In the fall of 1973, Harold began architectural studies at the prestigious Cooper Union and was invited to join the New York Staff Band under B/M Derek Smith. For the final two years at Cooper, Harold assumed leadership of the Philadelphia Citadel Band and Songsters. Since 1981, Harold has served as the Divisional Music Director for The Salvation Army in Eastern Pennsylvania and Delaware. During this time, Harold completed a Master and Doctor of Musical Arts degree music composition from Temple University. Harold lives in Philadelphia, Pennsylvania with his wife Priscilla and two daughters Carissa and Erin. The Burgmayer family worships at The Salvation Army Philadelphia Pioneer Corps, where they have soldiered for the past 23 years. Harold and Priscilla have set three priorities in their lives: the first, to love God; the second, to love each other; and the third, to disciple their daughters in the faith. Their ministries in music, discipleship and evangelism flow out of and have worked harmoniously with these.

Important compositions

We have an anchor (FS476) 1990, All your anxiety (TS963-2) 1990

BURRELL, HOWARD.J

Howard Burrell (1944) has his roots in the Salvation Army. He is Emeritus Professor of Music at the University of Hertfordshire where he was appointed in 1972 to commence music activities. When he retired from his academic post in December 2005 he left behind a thriving Department embracing composition, technology and music industry business studies. He continued his connection with the University until July 2010 in his role in developing UH Recordings which he founded in 2006.

Prior to coming to Hatfield he had spent five years as a student at Queen's University Belfast, and a year at Nottingham University before taking up an appointment to commence music studies at Norwich City College. His move to the Hatfield Polytechnic was to do likewise!

From 1978 until 2005 he was conductor and Artistic Director of the Hatfield Philharmonic Orchestra (later the Philharmonic at UH and then the deHavilland Philharmonic). In that time he conducted over 250 concerts giving many first performances. Among the highlights was the concert in which with John Lill, they played all five of the Beethoven Piano Concertos. Others included *'The Rite of Spring'* (Stravinsky) and the *'Turangalîla Symphony'* (Messiaen).

From 1974 to 1994 he toured the country first with Operabout (amateur) and then with the professional company Opera East. With the latter he gave over 400 performances of operas ranging from *'The Marriage of Figaro'* (Mozart) to *'La Boheme'* (Puccini).

In 1988/9 he was instrumental in organizing a community opera project in Heddingham (NE Essex). The opera was *'Carmen'* (Bizet) and involved over 250 local people, an artist in residence at Heddingham School, the USAF and Essex County Council. It culminated in four performances in Cressing Temple Barns, C14th tithe barns recently restored and used for the first time for these performances. The project was filmed and broadcast as a documentary on Anglia Television.

From 1986 to 1995 he also ran and conducted the very successful student big band 'Tuesday Night'. Not only did the Band do regular gigs locally but also toured to Germany and France, the latter three times.

Burrell's compositions including two symphonies (1998/99 and 2000) have been widely performed and three of his string quartets, Nos 3 (1974), 4 (1981) and 5 (2007/8) were issued on the UHR label 2008. Commissions have included 'Occasion' for brass band (Besses o' the Barn 1975), 'Visions for Chorus, brass and percussion' (Harlow Chorus 1978), 'Kings Variations' (Kings School Cambridge 1985), 'Kaleidoscope' for flute, harp, violin and cello (Pearce School Cambridge 1987). In October 2009 his Anniversary for orchestra was premiered by deHavilland Philharmonic in celebration of that orchestra's 40th anniversary. A number of his works for brass are included on Fanfares, Fancies and Fugues UHR 020011017 including The Hatfield Procession used in the graduation ceremonies of the University of Hertfordshire for the academic procession. Howard Burrell was elected to Stevenage Borough Council in May 2007 on which he currently serves as portfolio holder for Children and Young People, Culture, Sport and Leisure.

Burrell's parents (now both Promoted to Glory) were Salvation Army Officers. There are a number of other compositions – Songster and Singing Company pieces and a fanfare piece which was done at a Royal Albert Hall occasion somewhere around 1975.

Important compositions

A Child's prayer (US0068) 1964

BURTON, F

One of the early composers (late 1800's).

No further information could be retrieved about him.

Important compositions

In the cause of the Lord (GS0293-1) 1895, Is my Cross too much for me (GS0293-2) 1895

BROADSTOCK, BRENTON

Brenton Broadstock was born in Melbourne, Australia. He studied History, Politics and Music at Monash University, and later composition and theory with Donald Freund at the University of Memphis in the USA and with Peter Sculthorpe at the University of Sydney. The University of Melbourne awarded him the Doctor of Music degree in 1987. In 1991 he signed a publishing contract with G. Schirmer, Australia (Music Sales). He has won numerous prizes for composition including First Prize in the 1981 Townsville Pacific Festival's National Composition Competition for his orchestral work Festive Overture; the Albert Maggs Award; two APRA Music Awards for his orchestral works *'The Mountain'* and *'Toward The Shining Light';* First Prize in the Hambacher Preis International Composers' Competition, West Germany for his Tuba Concerto; and in 1994 he received the Paul Lowin Song Cycle Award, Australia's richest composition prize, for *'Bright Tracks'* for mezzo soprano and string trio. His orchestral work *'Stars In A Dark Night'* (Symphony #2) received four 'Sounds Australian' National Music Critics' Awards including 'Best Australian Orchestral Work in 1989' and was the Australian Broadcasting Corporation's entry to the prestigious Paris Rostrum of Composers in 1990. In 2001 he received the Australian Music Centre's Victorian Award for Best Composition – Dark Side Symphony #5, and in 2002 his *'Federation Flourish'* was nominated for an APRA/AMC 'Orchestral Work of the Year'.

His music has been performed at many international festivals including The Stroud Festival, England; the 11th Berlin Biennale; the Festtage fur Musik in East Berlin; Darmstadt Summer School, West Germany; the Music Today Festival, Tokyo; the Hong Kong and Oslo World Music Days; Asian Music Festivals in Japan and Korea; Musica Nova Festival in Munich; the BBC Proms; the European Brass Band Championships in Birmingham; and in Australia at the Adelaide Festival, Musica Nova Festival, Brisbane; Summer Music, Moomba and Spoleto Festivals in Melbourne and the Townsville Pacific Festival. There have also been performances in England, Germany, New Zealand, Canada, Russia, Sweden, Spain and China. He has had performances by all of the major orchestras in Australia: the Melbourne, Sydney, Adelaide, Queensland, Tasmanian and West Australian Symphony Orchestras, the Australian Youth Orchestra and Camerata Australia, and by the Sendai Philharmonic Orchestra in Japan, the BBC Symphony Orchestra, the Bavarian Radio Orchestra in Munich, the Pacific Ocean Orchestra and the Krasnoyarsk Orchestra in

Russia, the Philharmonic Orchestra of Moldova, the Ulster Orchestra, and the Tampere Philharmonic Orchestra in Finland. In July 1994 The Australian Youth Orchestra conducted by Yakov Kreisberg performed Festive Overture on their world tour, including the BBC Proms at the Royal Albert Hall and the Concertgebouw in Amsterdam.

Brenton has also written several major brass band works; he was commissioned to write *'Winds of Change'*, which was premiered at the 2000 European Brass Band Championships in Birmingham by the Yorkshire Building Society Brass Band, conducted by David King, and broadcast, on BBC Radio (see Reviews). This work was the A Grade Test Piece at the 2002 Australian Brass Band Championships held in Geelong. Brenton's 30 minute work *'Gates of Day'* was premiered as the final work in the 2001 Melbourne International Festival of the Arts. Scored for 100 brass players (4 brass bands), military band and 400 bellringers playing 2001 bells it was played at the outdoor Sidney Myer Music Bowl to an audience of several thousand.

In 2001 he was one of seven composers commissioned to compose a work, *'Jagged Tears'*, for the Field of Bells - a computer controlled interactive installation (a public music instrument) - at Birrarung Marr in Melbourne.

In 1988-89 he was the Melbourne Symphony Orchestra's Inaugural Composer In Residence. In 1997 he received the Jean Bogan Prize for his solo piano work Dying of the Light and in 1998 he received the Michelle Morrow Memorial Award for Composition and an Explorations Opera Project grant. In 1998 he spent three months in Italy on fellowships awarded by the Civitella Ranieri Foundation and a Bellagio Study Center Award from the Rockefeller Foundation. In November 2005 he returned to Italy as a fellow at the Ligurian Study Center in Bogliasco, Italy.

In 1999 he received the prestigious Don Banks Award from the Australia Council, for his contribution to Australian Music, which enabled him to compose for most of that year, including visits to the USA (Visiting Professor of Composition at Indiana University), England and Russia. His five symphonies were recorded by the Krasnoyarsk Symphony Orchestra (Russia) conducted by Andrew Wheeler and released on the Etcetera label in 2000 receiving excellent reviews in England and Australia (see Reviews). The CD was named as one of The Recordings of the Year 2007 by Music Web International editor Rob Barnett (see Reviews). Brenton's solo piano work *'Torre di Forza'* was one of two Australian 'test' pieces commissioned for the 2004 Sydney International Piano Competition, and in 2005 ABC Classics released a CD of orchestral works performed by the Tasmanian Symphony Orchestra conducted by Ola Rudner (see Reviews). His chamber opera based on Ray Bradbury's Fahrenheit 451 was performed in Bonn, Germany in April 2006.

Brenton has been a member of many boards, committees and competition panels, including The Australia Council, Arts Victoria, the Australian Music Centre, Symphony Australia's Reading Panel, the Paul Lowin Prize, The Maggs Prize, APRA Classical Music Advisory Committee, The Victorian College of the Arts Committee, Australian National Academy of Music, Australian Composers' Orchestral Forum, National Music Camp, Chamber Made Opera et al, and adjudicator at several national music competitions and eisteddfods. In 1995 the Australian Music Centre published his book Sound Ideas (with Linda Kouvaras) that documented 95 Australian composers (see Articles - Rites of Passage). Brenton has written 5 symphonies, concertos for tuba, piano and saxophone, several orchestral works, a chamber opera, 4 string quartets and much chamber, choral and solo music. His compositions are available on 43 commercial CDs worldwide (see discography). From 1982-2006 he was employed in the Faculty of Music, University of Melbourne where he was Professor of Music and Head of Composition. In 2007 he was one of 4 musicians short-listed for the Melbourne Prize and he was appointed as a Vice Chancellor's Fellow at the University of Melbourne. From 2008 he has been a freelance composer and in 2009 was Composer in Residence with the Melbourne Symphony Orchestra.

Important compositions

Born to Battle, Meditation on Rapture, Take all my sins away, Nearer my God to thee, Rutherford Variations, St. Aelred (Rhapsody for Band), Vision of the Lost, Song of the Pilgrim, Every harmony is Divine

CALVERT, MORLEY

Born in Brantford, Ontario in 1928, Morley Calvert moved to Montreal with his sister and parents, and later graduated from McGill University with a Bachelors Degree in Music. He was the founder and director of the McGill Concert Band, the Lakeshore Concert Band, and Monteregian Music Camp. From 1960 - 1970 he was bandmaster of the Salvation Army Montreal Citadel Band. His career as music director spanned 28 years and touched hundreds of young lives in Montreal and Barrie. As composer, Morley leaves a wonderful legacy of published and recorded works, including *'An Occasional Suite'* commissioned by Expo '67; Suite for the Montergian Hills, composed for the Montreal Brass Quintet and recorded by the Canadian Brass among others and *'Introduction, Elegy and Caprice'* as test piece for the 1978 European Brass Band Championship. Much of Morley's music was written for and published by the Salvation Army and if *'Introduction, Elegy and Caprice'* represents the pinnacle of his works for brass band, then the devotional *'For Our Transgressions'* illustrates the depth of his spiritual experience - a journey with his Lord to the victory of perfect peace. He was Promoted to Glory on September 6, 1991.

Important compositions

Canadian Folk Song Suite (FS331) 1970, My all is on the Altar (GS1400-2) 1954, For our transgressions (GS1440) 1957, Nearer to the Cross (GS1554)1965.

CAMPBELL, TIMOTHY

Timothy Campbell was born on October 21, 1976 in Guelph, Ontario, Canada. Like many young people in the Salvation Army he began playing cornet in the junior band at an early age. This led to regular attendance at music camps and eventually a spot with the Divisional Youth Band. Though brass banding was a primary part of his Salvation Army upbringing, Timothy refined his musical abilities on piano through the Royal Conservatory of Music. Just short of getting his letters in piano performance, Timothy went on to study piano and composition at Asbury College where he spent much time with James Curnow and Ronald Holz. He went on to complete his master's degree in theory at the University of Connecticut and also managed a festival orchestra where he worked with many prominent musicians in the New York and New England areas.

Aside from an original work for children's voices (i.e., *'Whatever'!*) Timothy mostly arranges music. His titles include: *'Awesome God'*; *'King of Kings'*; *'Love, Love'*; *'Praise the Name of Jesus'*; and *'Celtic Folksongs for All Ages'* – a jointly arranged play-a-long book with James Curnow published by Hal Leonard.

He currently resides in Mt. Pleasant, Michigan, USA with his wife and son where among other things he is the bandmaster for the Central Michigan University Brass Band.

Important compositions

King of Kings (AE200421) 2004, Lead me to Calvary (AE200924) 2009, Love, love (AE200514) 2005, People need the Lord (AE200812) 2008, Praise the name of Jesus (AE200632) 2006

CAMSEY, GORDON

Born on May 22, 1947 and a former trombonist with the International Staff Band (27 years with the band), Gordon succeeded Christopher Priest (also a composer) as Bass Trombonist within the ISB. Gordon was Songster Leader at Leighton Buzzard Corps from 1986 until 2006. Since 1960 the Leighton Buzzard Salvation Army Band has had four Bandmasters. Richard Guess, a music teacher in Leighton Buzzard has led the Band for the past ten years but passed the baton on to Retired Songster Leader Gordon Camsey in September 2011.

Important compositions

The wondrous Story (US0140) 1990

CAMSEY, TERRY

Raised in the Army since birth at Cheltenham Corps in the UK. a self-taught composer/arranger with over one hundred compositions published by The Salvation Army in UK, USA West and east, Sweden and elsewhere. Many more are as yet unpublished. A children's musical, *'Get on Board Children'* was been published by Lillenas and was re-issued after 10 years as a gold star edition because of its popularity. Also a cornet soloist with such well-known Salvation Army bands as Cambridge Heath, Uppper Norwood, the ISB, Hollywood Taberncle, the NYSB plus principal cornet soloist of HM Irish Guards Band. Many solos composed at the request of leading Salvation Army soloists around the world and recorded by them. He became a Salvation Army officer in 1985 specializing in the health and growth of churches, a passion he still pursues avidly.

Terry Camsey was born on the 23rd of June 1935 in Cheltenham, Great Britain. He taught himself what he wanted to know about music. Terry was the principal cornet player of the Upper Norwood Band, International Staff Band , New York Staff Band as well as the Band of H.M. Irish Guards. He was also a member of the National Youth Orchestra of Great Britain. Terry Camsey travelled the world as guestteacher and soloist and made recorded for radio, LP cassette and CD. As officer of the Salvation Army he was responsible for Corps Growth. His motivation is the inspiration and the wish to write functional, playable and interesting music for the Salvation Army. Terry was Promoted to Glory on 30 June 2011.

Derick Diffey, the legendary cornet soloist, tells about Terry: *'He and I were quite close as we served in the guards together. He was in the Irish Guards as Principal Cornet and I was in the Welsh Guards doing the same. He was Principal of the International Staff Band and I was the same in the Tottenham Citadel Band (Enfield). He was once introduced as the finest cornetist in Great Britain by his Music Director, Major Jeager who continued to tell the audience that he was very proud of Terry 'for he is a very good Lad, he doesn't smoke, doesn't drink, and doesn't swear. The worst thing he has ever done is go into Marks & Spencers and shout, 'Woolworths'. '*

Important compositions

Life's Pageant (FS364) 1974, Happy Land (JC621) 2007, Happiness and Harmony (GS1618) 1971, A Joy Untold (GS1708) 1978, Longings (GS1856) 1990, Sing Hallelujah, Shout Hallelujah (GS1669) 1975.

CARROLL, WILL(IAM)

One of the early composers. Former bandsman with the International Staff Band. He immigrated later to Canada. After his immigration to Canada he became deputy bandmaster of the (then famous) Winnipeg Citadel Band, but passed away suddenly on returning to his home in Winnipeg. He wrote the march *'Canada West'* which was the first composition from the Canada West Territory to appear in the Ordinary Series Band Journal.

Important compositions

Canada West (GS0962) 1927, Roll On (TS0145) 1930, Simplicity (TS0125) 1929, The Victor's Crown (GS0991) 1929

CATELINET, PHILIP

Philip Bramwell Catelinet was born on December 3, 1910 to Philip Arthur and Mabel Alice (nee Bowen) Catelinet. Educated at Gregg Business College, he received music scholarships to Trinity College of Music in London and The Tobias Matthay Pianoforte School, also in London. He received diplomas from the Royal Academy of Music, Trinity College of Music, and the Incorporated London Academy of Music. Trained as a pianist, he became an arranger for the Salvation Army and composed and arranged over 100 vocal and instrumental pieces just for the Salvation Army. He taught himself to play the tuba and euphonium. His abilities on these instruments earned him a position with the BBC Military Band from 1937 to 1942, a job which was interrupted by service in the British Army from 1942 to 1946. Stationed in North Africa and the Middle East during World War II, Phil was a medic and played piano for the entertainment of his fellow troops.

After his return from the military, Phil returned to find that the BBC Military Band had been disbanded during the war. He sought a position as an accompanist but there were no openings. Instead, the BBC arranged for him to audition as a tubist for several prominent British conductors, including Sir Adrian Boult. As a result he became the principal tubist for the BBC Theatre Orchestra and performed with the London Symphony and Philharmonia Orchestras as well.

In 1954 composer Ralph Vaughan Williams asked Phil and the London Symphony Orchestra to premiere his new tuba concerto at the orchestra's Jubilee Concert. Phil met with the composer at his residence and played through the work and consulted him during the preparations and rehearsals. The work's world premiere came at the Royal Festival Hall on June 13, 1954 with Sir John Barbirolli conducting and Vaughan Williams in attendance. Unsure of the audience's reaction to the new piece, Phil asked his wife Rosalind not to attend the concert. In an article for The TUBA Journal, Phil wrote of the *'belittling image invariably linked to both the tuba and tubists'* and *'...I did not know how the public would react. If I had to suffer, I would rather suffer alone.'* The music and Phil's performance were both well received, and the orchestra and soloist held a recording session the following day. This recording is available on CD from EMI Records.

In 1956 Phil and his family left England and moved to Pittsburgh, PA, where he took a position as assistant professor of music at Carnegie Institute of Technology (now Carnegie

Mellon University). Phil also served as conductor of the Brass Choir, director of the Kiltie Symphony Band, conductor of the Honors Band, Chairman of the Music Extension Department, and founded and performed with the Pittsburgh Brass Quintet. He created and organized the annual Carnegie Awards Festival for individual musicians, bands, and choruses. He also performed with the Pittsburgh Symphony Orchestra as an extra and as an accompanist for student soloists in the music department.

Throughout his life, Phil was an active member of the Salvation Army, both in England and in the United States. In addition to his work as a composer and arranger for the Salvation Army, he served as conductor of the Pittsburgh Temple Band and as organist. He also worked as a guest conductor, clinician and soloist (both piano and tuba) for the Salvation Army throughout North America and spent time working with Salvation Army youth.

Following his retirement in 1976, Phil and Rosalind returned to their native England. Phil remained active as a composer, arranger, adjudicator and writer in his later years. He died on November 21, 1995.

(source: philipcatelinet.com – used with permission)

Philip Catelinet – by Robert Getz

Philip Bramwell Catelinet was my dear friend. I visited him and Rosalind, 'Rosie' to me, at their home which was in the English way named 'Peveril'. It was in Broadstairs, Kent on Fordoun Road.

Upon arriving and immediately enjoying tea and scons, he played for me my piano transcription of Heaton's 'Praise!' He then did something amazing. He started playing the scherzo from 'The Valiant Heart'... in thirds! (a technical tour de force to be sure!) He did so as easily as someone else playing 'Chopsticks'! I have the arrangement and plan to publish it soon.

The Dean Goffin Wikipedia refers to Dean as the first (1950) important Salvation Army composer to hold a bachelor degree in music, which is in error. Phil did well before the second World War! He was a most amazing pianist (Played accompaniments for the great hornist Brain), a first class (real) conductor, Composer, arranger, and the world's leading tuba virtuoso of his age. In his early years he played euphonium. He eventually came to the USA and was on the faculty of Carnegie Tech in Pittsburg and principal tuba with the Pittsburg Philharmonic.

In 1958 I was at CMI (Central Territory music camp) and Phil was the guest. My brand new Boosey Imperial euphonium was delivered to the camp as I got there. Needless to say, I was thrilled! Phil was my biggest hero in those days and had recently recorded the new Vaughan Williams Tuba Concerto with the London Symphony Orchestra. Phil immediately started calling me 'Euph' rather than Bob, which I kind of liked. He looked my new horn over and praised its quality. Then he said 'Come on, Euph, and bring your mouthpiece!' As I caught up with him I asked where we were going. 'To the carpenter shop to fix that bloomin' mouthpiece!' 'FIX?' Yikes, it was brand new! I was afraid to complain as he took a pipe reamer and started to carve away at the bore until he could easily drop an wooden pencil through it! 'There. Now you can get a real sound and not that pinchy mouthpiece sound they provide!' I was struck dumb by this event, but when I put the mouthpiece into my horn and played, I couldn't believe my ears! It worked! As I matured as a player and went professional, I finally ended up using the largest bass trombone mouthpiece made by Schilke Company. A lesson well learned from a real pro. Just as a gag, and as a salute to Phil, I sometimes played solos using a Salvation Army Eb Bombardon (bass) mouthpiece that I had the shank shaved to fit the euphonium ... it raised the eyebrows of the bandsmen to say the least!

Decades later I received a call from Captain Ernest Miller, then Central Music Director. He had an emergency vacancy in the Faculty Band on Eb Bass and could I come and fill it? Camp started the next day, and my friend Eric Ball was the guest, so how could I say no? I had no access to a good Eb Bass, but our corps had just purchased a small model Boosey Bb bass, which I took, figuring to transpose. When I got to the first rehearsal, who should be sitting in the Eb Bass section but Phil! What a time we had! He was transposing on his F Boosey and I transposed the Eb part on the little Bb bass. Ray Wright, a profoundly gifted player, sat next to me on Bb Bass and between his and Phil's banter all week, I was kept in stitches laughing. Major Victor Danielson, a musician of redoubtable stature provided the other Bb bass part, and we reckoned this was the bass section of the century, which toward the end of camp Eric also pronounced. Phil came from Pittsburg to be with his old friend Eric for the week, and did not conduct or otherwise take the spotlight.

When I became a professional player and was principal euphonium in the Detroit Concert Band under the great cornet/trumpet virtuoso Dr. Leonard B. Smith, Phil wrote a euphonium duet for me with concert band accompaniment, 'Plus Two'. I found at that time that Leonard, a man very tight with a dollar, funded a scholarship at Carnegie Music Department in honor of Phil. Leonard was not easy with praise and even less free with a dollar, so this meant very significant affection and respect he held for Phil!

It should be noted that Phil was the single funniest person I ever experienced and when he got wound up could easily rival Victor Borge. The difference was that with Phil it was all spontaneous. He could keep an audience entertained, inspired, amazed and laughing themselves sick all at the same time!

He was a wonderful and deeply spiritual man, Christ-centered totally.

During the Second World War he was home with his two sons when a concussion bomb hit near the house and sucked all the air out, killing the two boys and injuring Phil severely. Emergency workers found the boys dead and took Phil away to hospital. When Rosalind arrived home there were her two sons dead and her husband missing! They were SA Officers at the time and she conducted the funerals for her boys not knowing where Phil was! Eventually she found him and they were reunited. Shortly thereafter, their daughter died of cancer! Their faith was not shaken and they went on to have a second family of Barry and Annette, both of whom reside in the States today.

In his final years Phil had put on a great deal of weight, and suffered ulcers on his calves necessitating his sleeping in a chair. He fell several times and Rosalind could not help him up, so emergency workers had to be summoned. This greatly embarrassed him, but neither he nor Rosalind ever complained. They rather kept their happy dispositions and encouraged and inspired me greatly. I dearly miss out long phone chats! Oh, how we laughed together! I miss my dear, dear friends much more.

Philip Bramwell Catelinet, Professor Emeritus, USA Citizen, British dual Citizenship. Born 3rd December 1910. Died 21st November 1995. Education, matriculation standard followed by courses at Gregg Business College. Music Scholarships to Trinity College of Music, London and The Tobias Matthay Pianoforte School, London, student of Harold Craxton and Vivian Langrish. Diplomas awarded: Licentiate, Royal Academy of Music (Pianoforte- Performers); Associate Trinity College of Music (Teachers Diploma); Incorporated London Academy of Music (Pianoforte- Performers); Gold Medal Award, Pianoforte 1926.

Important compositions

A Sunbeam (FS115) 1937, Winnipeg Citadel Jubilee (FS272) 1963, The Heralds (FS144) 1947, The Valiant Heart (FS147) 1947, The Warrior (FS124) 1938.

CATHERWOOD, DAVID

Catherwood, David (Belfast, 7 May, 1956). He studied music at Queen's University Belfast (BMus Hons.). His main instrument is trombone. He is Director of Music at Campbell College, Belfast and closely involved with the music of the Salvation Army, having been bandmaster at Belfast Temple, Ireland Divisional Youth Band and Belfast Sydenham. He guests regularly in summer music camps in Canada and USA. As a composer he has written music for band, band soloists and choirs. He is published by SP&S, Alfred Publishing Company, Warner Brothers and Belwin Mills, and through his own company, Opus 3. His seven sets of graded band music for young people From the Beginning are published by Opus 3, and he has also made many arrangements of orchestral and ensemble music for school orchestras. His music has been recorded by a number of brass bands, including Williams Fairey Band and the International Staff Band (The Salvation Army's premier brass band based in London). His solos have been recorded by many leading trumpet, cornet and euphonium virtuosi in Europe, Australia and in the USA. He is a member of ASCAP and since 1996 has received an annual award from ASCAP for his contribution to church choral music in the USA. Married to Wilma – one daughter, Tess

Important compositions

Cornet solo When I remember (ABJ 173) 1997, Forward! (Opus 3 Music), A song of Sharon's rose (GS1860) 1991, Everybody should know (GS 1840) 1989, Spirit of Life (GS 1951) 1998, In His Presence (GS1984) 2001.

CAUDLE, GRAHAM

Born in the Salvation Army Mothers Hospital, Clapton in London England on 22 September 1938 to Arthur and Lily Caudle. Dedicated at Homerton Corps. He was taken to Walthamstow Central Corps at eight years old, and learnt to play the Tenor Horn in the Young People's Band conducted by Henry Willis. He was privately taught piano until the age of twelve, when his parents could no longer afford lessons. He accompanied the corps Singing Company at age of twelve and at fourteen took up the euphonium in the Senior Band. Brigadier Burnell Webb of the Drummers Fraternal asked him when he was fourteen, to be the pianist for this group, and Graham used to also accompany his daughter Joy, (vocal) and also Susan Hanscombe (flute). At seventeen, Graham became Young People's Band Leader and was called up for National Service Christmas in 1956 and served for three years as principal euphonium in the Royal Electrical and Mechanical Engineers Staff Band.

On demob, he returned to Walthamstow and married Hazel Herrick (from Reading Central Corps) in 1961. At age of twenty two, he was made Bandmaster of the Walthamstow Central Band and fulfilled this position for twenty one years, and during this time was pianist at East London Music Schools and East London Youth Chorus, led by Keith Prynn. In 1980 Graham Caudle was asked by Jacqui Proctor to join the International Staff Songsters, and enjoyed six years of happy service, under the leadership of Colonel Norman Bearcroft. He sang tenor and played the piano and the glock. Many weekend visits were undertaken up and down Britain and also a visit to Canada, as well as special meetings such as The Royal Albert Hall. The Caudels then transferred to Wood Green Corps, and he was asked to be Deputy Bandmaster. There he was Corps pianist, Singing Company pianist and Songster pianist until they moved to Wisbech in 1993 (because of redundancy). Here they served for ten years at Wisbech Citadel where again he was Corps pianist and Deputy Songster Leader, and during the last five years, led the Songsters. Once again they then transferred to Peterborough Citadel in 2003, and both are now Songster Sergeants, and Graham is also the Band Sergeant. Corps pianist, Singing Company pianist and Songster pianist again, and continuing throughout his banding - playing euphonium.

Graham commenced composing and arranging when in the Royal Electrical and Mechanical Engineers Staff Band, and was encouraged by such people as Colonel Albert Jakeway, Colonel Charles Skinner and Colonel. Ray Steadman Allen.

Important compositions

Lewisham Young People (TS0840) 1979

CHALLINOR, ALBERT EDWARD

The composer of the new Second Series march *'Launch Out!'* No.268, Bandmaster Albert Edward Challinor (L.R.A.M., A.R.C.M.), of Rock Ferry, is a product of the Young People's Corps, and commenced Banding at the age of thirteen on an Eb bombardon. He made such rapid progress that he was given the euphonium, and until a few years ago was a very capable soloist. Forsaking the instrument for the score, he studied musical history under George Mastin, and collaborated with him in writing songs, a number of which have appeared in "The Musical Salvationist", including *'The Flag of Honour'*, published in the issue dated October 1932. The Bandmaster was compelled to give up his studies for four years owing to long business hours, he took up the study of harmony, under Bandmaster George Marshall, and a close analysis of our best writers inspired him to attempt composition. ('The Musician' 26-5-1938).

Important compositions

Launch out (TS0268) 1938

CHASE, CLARENCE

Served for years as bandmaster at the Binghamton, New York Corps, and played an active role in both community and Salvation Army band activities in Eastern New York. A student of the famed trumpeter Ernest Williams, he served on the staff of Williams' Summer Music School, as well as on the staff of Star Lake Musicamp in the late 1940s-early 1950s. Contributed pieces to the Eastern Territory's youth band publication, *'First Marches and Selections'*.

Important composition

Joyful Song (ABJ0034) 1957

CHAULK, DAVID

David Chaulk, a native of Canada (New Foundland), was introduced to brass playing in The Salvation Army. After successes in Canadian national competitions, David studied euphonium and trombone at Asbury College and Northwestern University (USA). His principal teachers included Arnold Jacobs, Edward Kleinhammer, James Curnow and Charles Vernon. While a student, David was a finalist in the 1980 ITEC Euphonium Solo Competition and, in 1979, was winner of the prestigious Penniston Concerto Competition. Following graduation, David was a freelance orchestral and commercial musician in Chicago and Atlanta. He regularly performed with leading orchestras and in recording studios. In 1985 David and Stephen Bulla released the highly acclaimed euphonium and piano recording *'Variants'*. Maintaining links with the Salvation Army brass band world,

David served as Principal Euphonium of both the Canadian and Chicago Staff Bands, as well as being Bandmaster of the famous Hamilton Temple Band of The Salvation Army (Canada).

Important compositions

Corner Brook Temple (GS1781) 1984, I Surrender All (GS2038) 2006.

CHESHAM, HOWARD

The late Lt. Colonel Howard Chesham of The Salvation Army was a groomsman in my parents' wedding, June 16, 1938, and one of my dearest friends in life. I played in the Chicago Staff Band with him for over ten years and knew him well until his dying breath. He was undoubtedly the greatest alto horn player of all time. His last working position was as Treasurer for the National Salvation Army in America, a most considerable position of trust and responsibility. Most importantly, he was a Christ-centered gentleman of the highest order.

First, Howy is the only person I know of who (seventy years ago!) received a performance degree in alto horn. He took up the alto horn as a solo instrument when Sousa (under whose baton Howy played once) was in his last years of banding. This was an era when the cornet was the darling of all soloist instruments (keep in mind that Sousa's band was far more prominent and popular than Symphony orchestras of the day). When all the boys were trying to be like Herbert L. Clarke, Howy Chesham was charting territory that none since has explored – the alto horn as a true virtuoso instrument.

Let me vouchsafe my claims regarding his virtuosity by quoting some truly great musicians. I saw a letter to Howy from the redoubtable Erik Leidzen stating that Howy was 'the greatest alto horn player in the world' . . . and Leidzen was hardly given to faint praise! Later, in the late 1960', while Howy was my guest for lunch at famous The Cliff Dwellers' Club in Chicago, my party (consisting of Howy, Lt. Colonel William Scarlett, Eric Ball and myself) encountered Will Scarlett, trumpeter with The Chicago Symphony Orchestra, who was accompanied by the world renowned principal trumpeter Adolph Herseth. Will introduced Howy to Bud Herseth as 'The greatest alto horn player in the world'. Many years later while entertaining the great brass band composer/ conductor Eric Ball in Cambridge, Massachusetts I recounted these two incidents and Eric quickly added 'Add my name to that list!' In addition to this, both Emil Soderstrom and Irwin Fischer adored Howy's playing. Sodertstrom wrote a solo for Howy, and Leidzen wrote the now famous 'Old Rustic Bridge' for Howy. Fischer, when writing his 'Wonderland Camp' march, used the alto horn as most composers would use the solo cornets, because Howy played solo horn in the band for which it was written. Chesham commissioned me to write a solo for him which resulted in my profoundly difficult 'Fantasy Suite for Horn and Piano – Aberystwyth' which he played with disarming ease and profound artistry. In 1935 the great Bernard Smith wrote a solo for Howy for the first Central Music Institute of The Salvation Army, 'Robes Of White', which Howy alone ever played. Half a century ago Howy wrote a horn trio, 'Wonderful Words of Life' which was rejected for publication because The Salvation Army in England could not find three horn players to audition it for the Music Board! The Chicago Staff Band horns routinely played it through several generations of players, always with Howy in the lead.

Howy was an artist. His greatest asset was his tone. It sounded like he was playing from the bottom of a deep well or inside a cave. Unlike other hornists, he had power beyond imagining. His technique was flawless and his stamina unbelievable. He played like a poet, with phrasing and dynamic nuance never to be equaled. The late Ren Schilke created a Howard Chesham model mouthpiece because of his respect for Chesham. Fifty years after the fact I looked at a score that Howy and I played together and the mere recollection of his playing a portion of it brought me to sobbing tears . . . so beautiful was his playing. This from one playing the lowly 'peckhorn'!

I have been privileged to count among my closest friends many musical giants, and I hold none in higher veneration than Howy. I thank God for his very being and for his counting me (in his words, see photo) one of his 'finest friends'. I have been blessed.

(source: injofferings.com, used by permission of Robert Getz)

Renowned horn soloist Howard Chesham lead the Chicago Staff Band as bandmaster during the Second World War years 1943-1945 and kept the band in an excellent shape, despite the fact that several bandsmen were away serving their country.

Important compositions

Wonderful Words of Life (horn trio)

CHEYNE, JAMES

James Cheyne was born in Galesburg, Illinois. His early music training came from his father, James Cheyne, Sr., and through the music and music programs of The Salvation Army. Growing up in eastern Michigan, he attended the Detroit Citadel Corps, Echo Grove Music Camp, and the Central Music Institute in Wisconsin. James attended Michigan State University, receiving a Bachelor's Degree in Music Theory and Composition in 1978; and the University of Illinois, receiving a Master's Degree in Music Theory and Composition in 1981. His composition teachers have included Irwin Fischer, David Liptak, Salvatore Martirano, and Ben Johnston. James is a composer and conductor, among other interests. His approaches to creating music are both traditional (established techniques and procedures toward a desired result) and experimental (untried techniques and procedures toward unpredicted results, and also traditional methods and materials in non-traditional contexts). These approaches have included excursions into electronic music (magnetic tape-based, analog synthesis, and digital) and microtonal music, with a special emphasis on extended just intonation.

Most of his current compositions are for brass band, brass ensembles, choirs, & soloists. Some were written for, and published by, The Salvation Army. As a conductor, he has led several ensembles, including The Salvation Army's Clearwater Citadel Corps Band and Florida Divisional Band. Since 1999, he has served as music director for the Sunshine Brass Band. As a pianist, he performs regularly with his wife, Deanna.

Important compositions

Thine is the Glory (AE200024) 2000, An American Journey (m/s)

CHRISTMAS, JEFF

Canadian composer Jeff Christmas is no Salvationist although he has written several pieces especially for Salvation Army bands. He is often featured by the London Citadel Band and the Canadian Staff Band. He is Composer in Residence of the Orchestra London (Canada). Jeff is a Canadian-based composer, arranger, conductor, drummer and percussionist. He studied at York University, Toronto, Canada, the University of Western Ontario, London, Ontario, Canada, and Berklee College of Music, Boston, where he majored in Film Scoring and Composition.

Important compositions

Living Flame (m/s), Songs of Erin (m/s)

CLACK, MICHAEL

Michael Clack first learned a brass instrument as a child at the local Salvation Army where his father was bandmaster. Piano tuition was followed by the organ before moving on to study at the London College of Music (GLCM, Hon FLCM) and London University where he gained a B.Mus.(Hons) degree. Michael Clack was awarded the MBE for his services to music in education. Clack was bandmaster of the Salvation Army Chalk Farm Band for over thirty years, commencing in 1963. During his leadership, the band toured through most of Europe - including playing to the Pope in the Vatican City, Australia, and even to Japan where it took part in the Midosuji Parade in Osaka in 2000. He is a published composer in the Salvation Army and outside for Winwood Music, with a particular interest in the solo repertoire for alto-trombone.

Important compositions

Thy Welcome Voice (US0103) 1987, Beautiful Light (US0130) 1990

CLARK, IAN

Ian and his four siblings were fourth generation Salvationists. He was born in 1948, in Reading, Berkshire, United Kingdom. Malcolm, Ian's older brother, was three. Two years and eight months later, their mother gave birth to triplets; two girls and a boy. (It was Mervyn, who penned the song *'Precious Jesus'*, which became, and remains, very popular.) When things in their small terrace house became a little cramped, Malc and Ian moved in with their grandparents, just a few doors away; an arrangement that lasted until the early 1960's, when their parents bought a larger home, in Caversham, a couple of miles away.

Most of their extended family, on father's side, were also Salvationists; among them, two officers. Ian's granddad played 'Double B' (Bb bass) in Reading Central, which is a miracle, he having received near-fatal wounds in the Somme, in WW 1. During the 2nd World War Ian's father had been in the RAF, serving, for a time, in Egypt. He'd been a member of the Cairo Red Shield Band (of which he often spoke very fondly.)

His other grandparents lived in Birchington, near Margate in Kent, having been bombed out of their Ilford home during the Blitz. During the same period, the blast from a doodlebug left his grandfather totally and permanently blind. Although they too, were staunch Salvationists, in his grandfather's case this hadn't always been so. Being of Jewish stock, his conversion to Christianity, and subsequent enrolment as a Salvationist, so angered some of his family, they burned his first Salvation Army uniform. Granddad played bass drum in Margate corps band, even on the march, Nan (much shorter than him) walking beside him, holding his arm, leading him.

Ian joined the Young People's Band on cornet, and the Singing Company. In the senior band he never progressed beyond first cornet. He showed no particular musical tendencies. In fact, through lack of practice, Ian had a poor embouchure and weak lip; something he later regretted. More than thirty years later, he finally admitted cornet wasn't his instrument but horn was.

On leaving school, with just two, mediocre qualifications (one of which was art: painting remains his second love, as far as hobbies go), Ian became an apprentice book-binder at a local printing works. In the mid-sixties, five lads in his corps formed a 'pop group' (The

Pioneers; later becoming Change – meaning the change God can make in one's life.) When the drummer left Ian took his place, a first for him, but practice and determination got him through. However, Ian became more interested in guitar, and inspired by such guitar greats as Clapton, Hendrix, Beck, etc., spent many hours practising chords and riffs. When the rhythm guitarist, Peter, left, Ian took over, eventually swapping with Malc, to play lead guitar. (Peter's young brother is Commissioner John Wainwright.)

Among the many and varied venues they played in, up and down the country, was the Centenary Celebrations at Chrystal Palace, in 1965. Ian began writing some of the group's songs (the aforesaid guitarists strongly influencing his style.) it was during this period that his desire to compose/arrange began to surface, and grow. Ian began to hear vague ideas in his head – brass band pieces mainly – usually triggered by some specific theme, usually a religious one like, for instance, certain events in The Bible (something that continues to this day). Actually they were more inspiration to write than specific musical ideas as he discovered, when trying to transfer some of these 'ideas' onto manuscript.

His first submission to Salvation Army Music Editorial resulted, not surprisingly, in a rejection letter (his first of many), Ray Steadman-Allen tactfully pointing out its many faults and shortcomings. Now, some forty-five years on, Ian still remember his advice, quote: '...*Be adventurous...*'. Fast forward to the early 70's, the then bandmaster, seeing one of his efforts, suggested he take some lessons in harmony and counterpoint. (Counterpoint? What the heck was that?). For various reasons, this never happened, unfortunately nor has it, to this day. The fact that Ian couldn't play the piano didn't help with his writing. Even the simplest hymn tune was beyond him. For him, the instrument has only ever been a tool for checking chords. For some years now, his hands being deformed by arthritis, Ian has been unable to do even that. In January 1972, he joined the Thames Valley Police. Months later, Ian joined their brass band (which included three other fellow Salvationists.) The fact that he was made principle cornet is an indication of the band's standard! (Incidentally, as he was now in an 'outside' band he was forbidden from playing in the Salvation Army band at Reading). This is when his desire to compose really began to take hold. However, he still knew nothing about harmony, and even less about counterpoint. Getting professional tuition was out of the question, so he decided to teach himself. From the couple of books he bought, he learned the basics – the 'rules of thumb'. He was already writing music (not very well), when a new Music Direcotor was employed. Gordon Saunders was ex-RMA Sandhurst Band, and a fine cornet/trumpet player (who, in his younger days, was a Salvationist at Tadley Corps, where his, now late father was Bandmaster). Gordon, who did a lot of arranging for brass band, really encouraged Ian in his writing, and began playing his music (with Tadley – not Salvation Army – his other band, also). In 1992 ill-health forced Ian to retire from the police. Unable to afford house prices in the south, Ian moved to Birmingham where he lives today.

His musical turning point came like many others with computer music software, Sibelius 1 (plus a reasonable soundcard). Having always thought that, as a budding composer/arranger, getting published was the be all and end all, it still it eluded him; each rejection letter bringing fresh disappointment. To avoid this, Ian began writing solely for his own enjoyment, with no sights on publication. The computer gave him a virtual band that could play anything he wrote which meant he could write anything he wanted. His writing improved, and ideas flowed. In 2000 he won much to his own amazement the Band Piece category in a (global) competition for non-published composers, run by Leeds University

(Prof. Phillip Wilby) in association with Black Dyke Band, and others. As a winner, Ian had the privilege of hearing 'Dyke' perform it.

He still did submit to the Salvation Army, but for no other reason than *why not*? His breakthrough came with the publication of *'Always Cheerful'*, what a lift that gave him! On a sad note, there was a delay in the printing, during which time both his parents passed away, and never got to see his first published piece although they did know it was pending. Writing directly onto virtual manuscript, from scratch, and hearing it played back – his only option – is a slow, but enjoyable, process. He now also dabbles in orchestral writing for his own enjoyment. Although Ian has had secular pieces published, 'Army' music, with its ability to touch people's hearts and minds – associated words often a factor in this, of course – means much more to him. And when he think of some of the earlier and present-day Salvationist composers, he feels extremely humbled.

Important compositions

With Shield and Banner Bright (TS1183) 2008, Have Faith (US0366) 2010, Just as Thou Art (m/s), Soldiers of the Cross (m/s), The Cantonian (m/s), Rhapsody for Euphonium and Band (m/s), Sunshine Way (m/s)

CLARKE, MERVYN

Mervyn Clarke was born in 1951, a triplet with 2 sisters. He has two older brothers, Malcolm and Ian. Ian also being a composer as described in this book. His parents were Salvationists and he is a fifth generation Salvationist. Times were hard during those early years but somehow his mother found the money for Mervyn to have piano lessons. He joined the Young People's Band at about the age of seven and learned to play the cornet. He has no recollection of these early years and showed no interest in music. Mervyn was only interested in football and cricket as most young boys are and represented the school at both. He had no musical interest and gave up the piano lessons. This really upset his mum and she said it was something he would regret for the rest of his life. How right she was. When Mervyn was about 12, he moved on to tenor horn from the cornet. He still had no musical interest but was enjoying the tenor horn. When the time came to join the senior band his playing was improving and the solo horn player in the band at that time took him under his wing and they met most Thursdays before the band practice for an hour's tuition. Reading Central Band at that time was a large band with some 13 horns and Mervyn went in on second horn. His interest in playing was growing and he was practising for at least an hour and a half every day and finally made it to solo horn in the band.

Mervyn left school at the age of fiftheen. He still didn't really have any real musical interest. Jobs were plenty in those days and he had no idea what he wanted to do. Eventually he chose to be an apprentice motor vehicle mechanic which he did for two years. During that period he suddenly had a very strong desire to become a member of the International Staff Band. Why he had such a desire he'd no idea to this day. Friends in the Army band thought he was mad with no hope whatsoever of achieving his aim. One day Mervyn saw an advert in 'The Musical Salvationist' for a vacancy in the Music Department in SP&S, Judd Street. This was the department selling music and instruments and not the Music Editorial Department. He applied for the position and was successful and went to work for the Army in late 1968. When Mervyn first went to work there, Bernard Adams was the head of the Department and Roland Cobb, the legendary principal cornet of the International Staff Band was second in charge. The ISB had recently conducted a Tour of Australia and that was the year Roland left the ISB. Following the Tour other members of the ISB decided to leave and there was a vacancy in the horn section. Mervyn had attended ISB rehearsals and made his wishes known that he wanted to join the band and in 1969 he was invited to have an audition which was conducted by Bernard Adams and Charles Skinner. The audition took place just before one o'clock on a Friday lunchtime just before the rehearsal started at one so band band members were gathering for the rehearsal. So it was quite an ordeal but Mervyn felt he had done reasonable well. It took a while for him to be informed but all looked good and in December 1969 he became a very proud member of the ISB. He started playing out with the band in January 1970. These were some of the happiest days of his life and he made some very good friends. Two of his billeting partners were Stephen Cobb, the present ISB bandmaster and for several years Mervyn was a close friend and billeting partner of Peter Ayling, who later became the Musical Director of the Amsterdam Staff Band, Amsterdam Staff Songsters and International Staff Songsters.

He is proud to have served with band members such as Brian Bowen, Ray Bowes, Howard Davies, Robert Redhead and Leslie Condon to name but a few. Derek Kane joined the band during his time and is still playing with the ISB today. It was during this time that he became much more interested in music and started to learn more about the Theory of music and Composition. Whilst working at Judd Street he met his future wife Carol who had travelled up from Bristol with her mother to buy some Singing Company music. Mervyn got her address and wrote to her and so their relationship started. For a period of time Ray Bowes became the Head of the Department and Mervyn and Carol became close friends. Ray conducted their Marriage Ceremony in Bristol in 1976. During this time he started to dabble at music composition and had the song *'Precious Jesus'* published. This song has recently been recorded by the King's Singers. Unfortunately Army pay during those days was poor and it was evident that he was going to have to find himself a career which would support a wife and family and so Mervyn decided it 1977 to leave the ISB and become a policeman. His last engagement with the ISB was at the Bandmaster's Councils in 1977. He was very proud of this achievement. Strangely his last weekend away with the band was in Bristol, the home of his wife. During his time with the band, it made two tours; one of Switzerland and the other of Holland. Mervyn was fortunate to play in many great venues such as the Royal Albert Hall and the Royal Festival Hall. They made a number of recordings and were featured both on the radio and television. He was very sad to leave the band but had to move on.

In June 1977 Mervyn joined the Thames Valley Police as a constable. At this time he was still playing in Reading Central Band but shifts made it difficult for him to attend as others wanted and so after a period of time pressure was put on him to attend more which he wasn't prepared to do and so Mervyn left. He also stopped attending the Army on a regular basis even though his wife and young family were still going. During this period of time he did nothing musically. Thames Valley Police had at that time a brass band and Mervyn was asked on several occasions to join but declined. Gradually such was his musical interest that he started to get back into music and when asked in about 1984 to join the Police band he did and eventually he became the band secretary and deputy bandmaster holding both posts at the same time! Mervyn also started writing music which the band regularly preformed. In 1996 the then Chief Constable decided to end the Police Band and Mervyn returned to the Army and joined the band once again. In December 2007 he retired from the police service in the rank of sergeant after 30 years service. In April 2008 he rejoined Thames Valley Police where he is today working as a Warrants Officer.

Mervyn has written a number of pieces and have been very fortunate with the support locally and several of his compositions have been recorded. On the last Reading Central Band CD he had three of his compositions recorded. His parents would have been very proud and it is sad that both had passed away before this had happened. He has not had any proper musical theory tuition which is much to his regret as he often wonders what he might had achieved had he done so. Mervyn has had many happy years making and writing music. He has had many opportunities and experiences he would never have had had it not been for the fact that he learned to play a brass instrument. He does have one regret and something he has never forgotten when his mother told him as a little boy that he would regret not keeping up his piano lessons. She was so right and he can only wonder how his life had been had he kept up those lessons so many years ago now.

Important composition

Precious Jesus (GS1938-1) 1997

CLEMONS, ROBERT

Captain Robert Clemons is a corps officer in the United States of America. One of his duties was as the commanding officer of the Orange Corps in Texas, USA Southern Territory. He composed *'Fanfare for a Dignified Occasion'* which was performed during the 1978 International Congress 'Symphony of Praise' festival at The Royal Albert Hall in London, in which the New York Staff Band, Melbourne Staff Band and International Staff Band participated. It is the first fanfare to be published in the band journals and also the first to be published for full band.

Important compositions

Biloxi (TS0908) 1985, Fanfare for a dignified occasion (GS1728-2) 1980

COCKER-HUNT, ANITA

Anita Cocker Hunt is originally from Cleveland, Ohio. She earned her Bachelor of Music Education and Bachelor of Music in trumpet degrees from the University of Cincinnati College-Conservatory of Music. She has held positions as high school band and orchestra director in the Cleveland area, as private trumpet instructor at the Cleveland Music School Settlement, and was a member of the Cleveland Women's Symphony Orchestra.

Anita returned to Cincinnati to serve as Divisional Music Director for the Salvation Army in Southwest Ohio and Northeast Kentucky until 1997, when she moved back into public education as director of bands in the Pendleton County, Kentucky School System. She also earned her Master of Music degree in Instrumental Wind Conducting at the University of Cincinnati College-Conservatory of Music. She worked for Buddy Roger's Music from 2001 until 2007 and is presently Divisional Brass Ministries Director for the Southwest Ohio/Northeast Kentucky division of The Salvation Army. She keeps active with guest conducting and instructing at various music camps.

She is Associate Conductor of the Commonwealth Brass Band, an ensemble in residence at Indiana University Southeast, and on staff as an adjunct faculty member at IUS. Anita serves on the Board of Directors of Cincinnati Brass Band and also served as President of the North American Brass Band Association (NABBA) from 2001 to 2007. She continues to be an active member of the NABBA Board.

Important composition

I do believe (US0170) 1993

COGGLE, G.H.

G. H. Coggle was actually Cecil and strangely enough his brother George was called Will. A very strange set-up! Cecil was a former Young People's Band Leader of the Salvation Army Beccles Corps in the United Kingdom approximately between 1955 and 1960. One of his most well known pupils was Robin Bryant, later to be the Army's photographer.

Cecil is credited as having written the *'Beccles March'*, in fact he did put a lot of work into it. Most certainly the melody line was his, but it was rumoured at the time that he had simply tried to copy from various band scores, the other brass parts. One can imagine just what it sounded like. However, a friend of his, Bandmaster Fred Dockerill, came to Cecil's aid and helped him score it. Cecil left the Salvation Army sometime after that and formed the Beccles Town Band.

Important composition

Beccles (TS0491) 1952

COLE, CHRISTOPHER

Soldiered at Penge in South London, played Eb Bass and euphonium in the Salvation Army, and was a very talented musician, in particular on the piano and organ. He died tragically young. He was a member of the Music Editorial Department in the seventies and also served in the International Staff Band on Eb Bass.

Important compositions

The Reason (GS1681) 1976, Life's Dedication (TS828) 1978

COLE, NATHAN

Nathan Cole, born on 23 July 1981, was appointed bandmaster of the Bristol Easton Band in 2008. He is a music teacher by profession and studied at the Birmingham Conservatoire. Nathan origins from Australia where he was taught to play cornet as a member of the Camberwell Citadel Youth Band. In 1997 he moved to the United Kingdom where he joined Bristol Easton Band on flugelhorn, however his focus soon became more on playing percussion which got him a place in the percussion section of the International Staff Band in which he played for eight years.

Important composition

Candlelight Carol

COLES, BRAMWELL

Bramwell Coles was born on 11 February 1887, in a modest officer quarters in Cambridge, England, where his Salvation Army Officer parents were serving. He exhibited an early interest and talent for music. Bramwell's first cornet lessons, at age thirteen, came from Bandmaster Will Bolton at the Shipley Corps in Yorkshire, where his parents were the corps officers. With no young people's band at the corps, he took his place in the senior band. In 1906 he has won the third prize at an international Composers Contest of the Salvation Army. Three years later he won the first price on a similar occasion of the Salvation Army. In 1914 he attended the School for Officers of the Salvation Army. As an officer he served on the International Headquarters in London as a journalist, and in 1925 he moved to Toronto to work in the same function. In 1936 he had to go back to London as successor of Colonel Frederick Hawkes, as Chef of the Music Departement. In 1943 to 1944, Bramwell was the temporarily Bandmaster of the International Staff Band (ISB). He was asked to take the band permanently but refused as he thought his daily job at the Music Department was already busy enough to do it right. Erik Leidzén once said that when Bramwell Coles arrived at the gate of Heaven, John Philip Sousa, the great American march writer, would be waiting to greet him and say: '*Bram, on earth I was called the March King, but now, in Heaven, I must be honest and hand the crown to You*'.

Book - **In the Firing Line** - by Wally Court

This is a biography of Colonel Bramwell Coles. The book's title comes from Coles' World War I march '*In the Firing Line*' which ranks with the best marches ever written. Bramwell Coles was basically self-taught and his life and service bridged the period between pioneering Salvationist composers and the emergence of degreed music professionals in the Army's ranks. During his lifetime Coles served as an ordained minister, composer, arranger, instrumentalist, bandmaster, choir leader, journalist, editor, critic, educator and head of the Army's Musical Editorial Department for 16 years, with responsibility for all music performed by Salvation Army musicians worldwide

Important compositions

The Divine Pursuit (FS143) 1947, True Comrades (GS691) 1913, Undaunted (GS832) 1919, In the Firing Line (GS935) 1925, Bravest of the Brave (GS1013) 1930, The Maple Leaf (GS1021) 1930, Deeds of Valour (GS1193) 1941, Victors Acclaimed (GS1253) 1945, Heroes of the Combat (GS1277) 1947.

COLLER, CHARLES

Charles Coller became a Salvationist at Regent Hall in 1885. He was a member of the Household Troops Band on its first campaign in 1887. Adjutant Charles Coller was a trombonist with the International Staff Band in the beginning of the previous century. He didn't write much for brass bands. In fact, during that time is was common that when a composer submitted his composition to the International Music Department for possible publication, the band would play it through to see whether or not it would be usable within the Salvation Army. The name of the composer however was not known while the band played it. When the band played his composition without knowing that it was his, lots of arguments and comments came up, and even his colleague in the trombone section mentioned that it was nearly impossible to play! What the composer felt can only be imagined, especially as he also could not play it himself. Charles Coller never submitted another band piece for possible publication, but he became known for his excellent vocal compositions.

Important compositions

The Three Bidders (GS0289) 1895, Death's Rolling Tide (GS0353) 1989, The Holy Waters (GS0416) 1902

COLLINS, GORDON C.

One of the early composers (late 1800, early 1900).

No further information could be retrieved about this person.

Important compositions

Before I got Salvation (GS0064) 1887, I'm Bound for Canaan's Shore (GS0112) 1889, A Wonderful Joy (GS0322) 1896

COLLINS, GORDON

Gordon was born in 1934 in Melbourne to Salvation Army parents and commenced his playing career when only eight years old. Over the years he has given service in several Corps and has held different positions such as Corps Sergeant Major, Male Voice Leader, Deputy Bandmaster and Bandmaster (now retired after 21 years). He also commenced a Youth Band at Ingle Farm, which group developed into a very useful combination within the Corps, with its own ministry of outreach and service. About 10 years ago Gordon commenced a small group of retired musicians called 'Brass From The Past' and they very quickly became known in the local community and received many requests to play at various functions such as Companion clubs, Probus and other similar social groups. These types of social functions required a different type of repetoire which the Salvation Army didn't provide so he quickly had to turn out arrangements that suited their needs including arrangements from the classics and musicals. The result has been an accumulation of sundry arrangements which suited their needs at the time and proved very acceptable to the audiences. This group has now unfortunately had to dispand with the inevitable passage of time and subsequent unavailability of players.

Gordon did undertake formal music studies to A.Mus.L.C.M. and A.MusA. level, the former being London College of Music and the latter Australian Music Examinations Board. He has a personal interest in the study of counterpoint and composition and has accumulated a good collection of text books and reference material over the years to which he still refers. Before retirement Gorodn was the manager of the management consultancy branch in Australia Post. Both Gordon and his wife Marie still soldier at the Ingle Farm Corps, Adelaide in South Australia. They have two grown children and two grandchildren. Gordon's musical influences have without doubt been Eric Ball and Leslie Condon.

Important compositions

Allegro Deciso from Handel's Water Music Suite, Majesty, Farandole from L'Arlesienne Suite No. 2

CONDON, LESLIE

Leslie Condon, born on 28 October 1928, was, before he entered the Salvation Army training college to become a Salvation Army officer, a humble postman but eventually attained qualifications (diplomas, not Degrees) from The Trinity College London. He received a 'Licentiate of The Trinity College London' (L.T.C.L.) for Brass Band Conducting, Arrangement and Musical Knowledge in July 1956. Then in July 1959 he passed a 'Licentiate in Music of The Trinity College London' (L.Mus. T.C.L.) for Harmony, Counterpoint, Orchestration, Principles of Teaching, Form and History of Music. He was then awarded a Fellowship of the College (F.T.C.L.) at the same time. He does not have qualifications in Piano (in fact he taught himself to play!) and was not a Doctor of Music, what some people assume. He died tragically and suddenly on Christmas Eve while conducting his Croydon Citadel Band. Probably his best pieces are *'The Present Age', 'Song of the Eternal', 'Festivity'* and, of course, his tuba solo *'Celestial Morn'*.

While living in West-London Leslie Condon was evacuated to Fakenham, Norfolk during the 2nd World War. It was there that, while attending a Salvation Army meeting, he decided to live a life in accordance with the ground rules of the Bible. At the Salvation Army he received his first music lessons. Later on in life he received his qualification as F.T.C.L. and L.Mus.T.C.L. He enlisted in the Royal Air Force and whilst serving in the Persian Gulf he decided to dedicate his life to God as a Salvation Army officer. After leaving military service he returned to Fakanham and entered the Salvation Army Training College in 1950. He married Ruth Mitchell in 1957. In this period the young officer also started to make a name for himself as composer. In 1957 he was transferred to the Music Editorial Departement in London. Since 1958 he played Eb Bass with the International Staff Band (ISB) of which, later on, he became deputy bandmaster. He was a guest conductor in Salvation Army Music Camps in the USA, in European countries, South Africa and Zimbabwe.

Leslie Condon was, before he entered the Salvation Army training college to become a Salvation Army officer, a humble postman but eventually attained qualifications (diplomas, not Degrees) from The Trinity College London.

Book - **Les Condon, He Just Couldn't Say No** - by Dot Condon

For many years, the name of Leslie Condon could be found in the various journals of Salvation Army Bands. Whether it was a simple hymn tune arrangement to a detailed tone poem, the message would still be there. His pieces have gone on to become undisputed classics and are still loved whether you hear them for the first time or for the hundredth time!

Important compositions

Celestial Morn (FS264) 1962, Easter Glory (FS285) 1965, Call of the Righteous (FS294) 1966, Celebration (FS311) 1968, Song of Exuberance (FS320) 1969, The Present Age (FS342) 1972, Radiant Pathway (FS371) 1975, Festivity (FS439) 1984.

COOK, KENNETH

Kenneth Cooke was born on 20 July 1926 and passed away on 27 October 2007, aged 79 years. Kenneth became Bandmaster of the Regent Hall Band from 1951 until 1959 and was a former Bandmaster of the Boscombe Citadel Band which he conducted from 1964 until 1971. He wrote history in the Salvation Army when he came with what is considered as the first bass trombone solo in the Salvation Army repertoire *('The Passing Years')* which was published halfway the previous century.

During his time at Regent Hall he attained his F.T.C.L. in band conducting – the first person to do so because he pioneered that qualification which he helped to establish. He was examined for this qualification with the Regent Hall (Rink) Band of the Salvation Army.

Sadly his composing skills were cut short when he succumbed to a brain tumour in the early sixties prior to his bandmaster appointment; so while he was able to cope with those duties his illness denied him the ability to continue writing. His widow still lives in Bournemouth.

Just a snippet – the opening few bars of *'The Passing Years'* were taken from Wagner's *'The Master Singers of Nuremburg'* – very skilfully done!

Important compositions

The Passing Years (FS243-1) 1959, The Trumpeters (GS1540) 1964, Spirit of Christmas (GS1402) 1954.

COOK, S

One of the early composers (late 1800, early 1900).

No further information could be retrieved about him.

Important compositions

Salvation is for all (GS0257) 1894

COOPER, FREDERICK W.

Fred was born on the 27th of March 1905 in Shirebrook, Derbyshire. He was Promoted to Glory on the 19th August 1993. He was the eldest son of the family of seven children. The Cooper Family moved from Derbyshire to Goldthorpe after World War I for work in the coal mines.

They lived in house near to Salvation Army hall so all family went to Sunday school. Fred learned to play a trombone and older members of the band took an interest in him. Coming from a very poor large family money was very scarce but he was encouraged to maintain his link with the Corps by the older members of a very sizeable band. In Yorkshire at that time the coal mining villages had a large proportion of Salvationists who had come to work in the South Yorkshire coalfields and the band was made up of men from all parts of the UK. Goldthorpe in the 1920's had a band of forty five men and Fred was soon established as a very good trombone player

From Goole at this time came a family called Spencer. William, the father of this family, was a Salvationist and soon became the Bandmaster and Fred fell in love with his daughter Harriet (Doll) and they were married in 1928. Maurice was born in 1929 and younger brother Douglas in 1931.

Fred worked in the coal mine but was always active in the Corps and became Songster Leader in his early 20's, a position he held for over forty years and was also deputy bandmaster (to his father in law) for nearly thirty years. In his spare time he studied harmony and composed two trombone solos *'Glad in the Lord'* and *'Glory to His name'* which were both published in the Salvation Army journals.

On his retirement from the coal mines Fred became a peripatetic music teacher for the local authority and formed several choirs in the local community. The choir at his hometown of Goldthorpe gave over 40 public concerts to raise funs for all manner of charitable causes, and he was still involved with this teaching when he died in 1993.

Maurice, the eldest son became a Salvation Army officer and after a period of Corps Officership was appointed to the International Staff Band as Euphonium soloist. and also served as Bandmaster of the Amsterdam Staff Band. The younger son became a mining and civil surveyor and served for a number ears in musical leadership in the Goldthorpe Corps before retirement.

Important compositions

Glad in the Lord (GS1389) 1953, Glory to His name (TS0551-2) 1956

COOPER, MAURICE

Lt. Colonel Maurice Cooper (born June 8, 1929, Goldthorpe, Yorkshire, England). Born in the Yorkshire mining village of Goldthorpe, Maurice Cooper is a 5th generation Salvationist. The earliest photo of Maurice shows him at the age of two stood at a music stand with a baton in his hand. His Grandfather was Bandmaster Spencer (who wrote *'Jesus is Strong to Deliver'*); his Father also having 2 trombone solos published by the Salvation Army.

Describing himself as an occasional arranger, Maurice recounts that whilst he has written a lot of material, only fifteen of these pieces have been published by the Salvation Army *('a lot presumably remaining in the cupboards at Headquarters')*. His published arrangements include for Songsters and Band, Congregational Songs ('the Blessing' in BTB), his Sessional Song ('Marching Evangelists') and music for the Dutch National Congress.

Taught by his father, Maurice started playing tenor horn at the age of 6. With no Young People's Band at the Corps, Maurice's first engagement (at the age of 6½) was Christmas carolling on 2nd horn in the Corps' Senior Band. His first solo at the age of ten on tenor horn was the trombone solo *'Priceless Gifts'*. At the age of fifteen, he joined the Senior Band (officially) on 2nd chair Euphonium, and for a period of three months then became the band's only Euphonium in a band of some thirty+ players. By this time he had already written his first piece of music (aged sixteen) performed by his School Orchestra. Maurice recalls that at the age of twenty he thought of giving up Salvation Army banding to play with local colliery bands but quite the reverse happened and Maurice responded to the call to officership. Thereafter Maurice continued his Salvation Army banding and carolled with various bands every Christmas for seventy continuous years before his retirement! After a year of piano lessons in his teens, Maurice was called into the armed forces from school. Furthering his musicianship, Maurice joined the Staff Band of the Corps of Royal Electrical and Mechanical Engineers on G Trombone for two months then transferring to Euphonium, serving until July 1949.

In November 1949, Maurice was invited to meet with another Staff Band, the International Staff Band, during the band's visit to Sheffield. Following an audition on Euphonium in December 1949 Maurice was offered a position in the International Staff Band and a job at International Headquarters but declined. In 1952 Maurice was commissioned as a Salvation Army Officer and served in Liverpool, Glasgow and the Isle of Man which put his playing on hold until a move from Glasgow to IHQ in London in 1960, at which point Maurice joined the ISB on Euphonium. During this time Maurice also wrote various published pieces for Singing Companies including *'Gideon's Band'*, *'Elijah'* and *'Oh Blessed Lord'*. Whilst serving at IHQ (in various positions), Maurice and his wife Eva, soldiered at Lewisham Corps in London. In 1967 Maurice became Bandmaster at the Corps and also of the South London Divisional Youth Band. As Bandmaster of the South London Divisional Youth Band, the Band toured extensively across Scotland, England and in 1974 Holland (including a national radio broadcast). Maurice also undertook various Divisional Music School Directorships.

In 1975 Maurice left the ISB and was appointed as Dutch Secretary for Music and Bandmaster of the Amsterdam Staff Band. His enthusiasm for music-making was soon evident in that Territory with the establishment of four Divisional Youth Bands in Holland in January 1976. Whilst serving in Holland, Maurice also undertook further Music Schools in Germany, France, Italy and Belgium. 1980 saw a move back to IHQ and in 1982 Maurice assumed the position of Bandmaster at Bromley Temple Corps in South London. In 1987 (having not played regularly for 12 years!) he was approached to rejoin the ISB on Euphonium and did so staying for a further two years. Further music schools in England followed prior to his retirement from IHQ in 1994. However, even in retirement he was approached to return to Holland to resume for five years the post he originally undertook in 1975. Maurice eventually returned for a period of three months before Bandmaster Don Jenkins' appointment.

In retirement (in Bromley) Maurice continues to play the Organ at a local Crematorium and has been asked whether he was interested in becoming the resident pianist on a cruise ship. His musical highlight in his 80th year was being privileged to conduct the Leeds University Symphony Orchestra in Gustav Holst's *'Planets Suite'*. So far as his musical influences are concerned, Maurice is largely self-taught (possessing perfect pitch) but in particular notes the significant contribution of Bandmaster Bernard Adams (ISB) to his Salvation Army musical development. Maurice has a Son (a Medical Consultant and a semi-professional trombonist) and a Daughter (working in Law and Finance); 2 of his 4 grandchildren have also played as members of the National Youth Orchestra of Great Britain on Cello and Viola. Maurice has no regrets over the decisions he has made as both an Officer and a Musician and believes that in every avenue of service he has been fulfilled. His wife Eva was always supporting him in everything he did as a musician and Officer during their 55 years of happy marriage.

CORDNER, MARTIN

Martin Cordner (born in 1973, Chichester, United Kingdom) is a husband, father, officer (minister) in The Salvation Army, and a musician. He is married to Leanne and they have two sons, Oliver and Zachary.

Martin has been writing music since 1988 (first published piece in 1994) and to date he has more than 40 published works. In 1989 he commenced work as an employee at The Salvation Army's International Headquarters and this brought him under the influence of some of the Army's leading musicians at that time; Col. Ray Bowes, Stephen Cobb, Peter Graham, Cols. Robert Redhead and Ray Steadman-Allen among others. Since that time a variety of leadership roles in brass tuition, brass bands, choral groups, an appointment to the ISB in 1997 and opportunities as a Salvation Army officer have further developed his writing.

Since their commissioning as officers in 2002, Martin and Leanne have enjoyed a variety of appointments to corps (churches) in England and Scotland. In August 2010 they were appointed as leaders to Belfast Sydenham corps, Northern Ireland. Martin tries to balance family life, corps responsibilities and music ministry, and sees no conflict in being an officer and musician - believing one complements the other.

Important compositions

Lord of Sea and Sky (JC620) 2007, Crossbearers (FS586) 2004, Fanfare and Flourishes (FS598) 2005, In Christ Alone (GS2039) 2006 , Round-Up (GS2079) 2009.

COTTERILL, L.W.

One of the early composers (first half of 19th century). All what was found is that he was a bandmaster. No further information could be retrieved about him.

Important compositions

The Advance (GS0967) 1927

COURT, DOUGLAS

Douglas Court is a native of Toronto, Canada and received his early musical training in The Salvation Army. His formal training was received at the University of Toronto where he studied trumpet and graduated with a Bachelor of Music Education degree. Douglas has also studied composition at the University of South Florida. While living in Toronto, he worked as a freelance trumpet player performing with groups such as the Canadian Opera Company orchestra. From 1986 through 1995 Douglas held the position of Divisional Music Director for The Salvation Army in the state of Florida. This position allowed for extensive work with young musicians, running summer music conservatories, teaching private lessons as well as conducting both adult and youth ensembles. Douglas also has many instrumental and vocal pieces published by The Salvation Army.

Important compositions

Peace like a river (US143) 1991, Ding Dong Merrily on High (AJ233) 2004.

COX, SIDNEY E.

As a young man Sidney Cox (1887-1975) was attracted to The Salvation Army in Calgary, and in 1909 entered the training college in Toronto, where he met Violet Henderson, who later became his lifelong partner. After his commissioning as an officer, he served on the training college Headquarters in Winnipeg. It was in Winnipeg where he began to write songs and choruses. His initial chorus written in 1914 was *'You Can Tell Out The Sweet Story.'* In 1922 he went to Chicago to join the staff of the Moody Bible Church. In 1929 he returned to The Salvation Army and accepted an appointment in the Southern Territorial Headquarters in Atlanta where for fourteen years he served, first as territorial youth secretary, later as principal of the training college and finally as territorial evangelist. He once again left the ranks of Salvation Army officership *'because of an increasing desire in his heart to find himself wholly occupied with Bible teaching and preaching.'* Following the Promotion to Glory of his beloved Violet in 1967 he continued his travelling ministry until 1972. In his semi-retirement years prior to the Promotion to Glory of his dear wife Violet they both lived in The Salvation Army Eventide Home in Detroit, Michigan. This became the base from which 'God's Melody Maker' and his devoted wife conducted campaigns in the Army's five North American territories and beyond. Violet and Sidney Cox were laid to rest in The Salvation Army plot in Westview Cemetery in Atlanta Georgia and as Sidney's casket was being brought into the cemetery the Cadets from the Atlanta CFOT formed an Honour Guard thus marking the high esteem accorded to Sidney by The Salvation Army.

(source: salvationist.ca)

Important compositions

Freely He'll Forgive (GS0384-1)

CRAIG, CHARLES

Charles Craig was born in February 1939 in London, brought up in the small Norfolk Corps of Thetford where he learn to play the Tenor Horn in the Young People's Band and Senior Band until, at 18 he joined the Royal Air Force as a musician playing French Horn. During the next 22 years he soldiered at several Corps as he travelled throughout Europe and the Middle East. His interest in composing and arranging began during his 2½ years duty with the Middle East Air Force Band based in Cyprus under Denzil Stephens, a noted Euphonium player.

Charles first published composition was a march *'Bright Canaan'*, no 619 in the Triumph Series Journal in May 1967 whilst he was Bandmaster of the Oakengates Corps Band. Following service in Lincolnshire and Somerset he moved in October 1974 to the Royal Air Force Germany Band for 3½ years where, despite language difficulties, he soldiered at Solingen Corps, playing under Bandmaster Heinrich Schmidt, the present Bandmaster of the German Staff Band. By this time, and with the rank of Sergeant he was playing trombone. The RAF band often performed in Holland and broadcast from Hilversum. Charles enjoyed visiting Gouda Corps with the Solingen Corps Band.

On leaving the Royal Air Force in 1979 he then spent more then 10 years working for The Salvation Army social services in hostels and eventide homes in Belfast, Birmingham, Jersey (in the Channel Islands) and London before a breakdown forced him to resign and move to Kent where he has lived with his wife and three children since 1989. Since 1997 he has been assistance Young People's Band Leader at Margate Corps and continues to compose both vocal and band music which is used in various parts of the world. At present he has over 20 compositions published by The Salvation Army.

Important compositions

Lincoln Citadel (GS1640) 1972, Social Services (GS1777) 1984

CRANE, GEORGE C.

Was Bandmaster at Twickenham in the 1960's, in West London for many years. George Crane was a member of the executive committee at the National Association of Brass Band Conductors from 19th November 1966 to 6th December 1975. He was enrolled as a soldier in May 1943 by Major Marshall. He was Promoted to Glory early in 1988, the officer at the time was Major Patricia Bowthorpe. His wife's name was May. George was also the Over 60's secretary for many years, besides his duties as a Bandmaster and Bandsman. He is remembered as a pleasant, courteous, gentlemanly kind of person.

George Crane was born in Wandsworth, South London, in about 1905. He later moved to Thornton Heath, where he was songster organist, and then to Upper Norwood, where he was songster organist. In about 1942 he was called-up for War service. Round about this time his home was bombed (twice) and so the family moved to Twickenham, in south-west London, and when George was discharged from War service he joined them there. He was bandmaster at Twickenham twice, retiring, and then taking up active service again.

George Crane was an accomplished musician, playing piano, organ and cornet, later trombone. He obtained an LTCL in brass band conducting, and wrote numerous pieces for bands and songsters. He supplied the music for my first published song, *'Service and praise'*, Musical Salvationist January 1961.

Important compositions

Forward be our Watchword (TS0208) 1934, I'll Follow (TS0296) 1940, Marching to Canaan (TS0128) 1929, The Wandsworth March (GS1004) 1929

CRANE, KENNETH

Ken Crane was Songster Leader of the Luton Temple Songsters and solo euphonium player of the Luton Temple Band in the 1960s. His parents were officers at the corps in the 50s and he stayed at the corps when they moved on. He also was a member of the International Staff Band for some years in the early 1950's. Here he was also the band's youngest member and replaced the illustrious Josh Walford as Euphonium soloist with *'Ransomed'*.

Important compositions

Accrington (US0045) 1960, Glorious Invitation (US0012) 1957, To the Glory Land (TS0568) 1957

CREAMER, SAM

Sam Creamer (September 27, 1985) is a young Australian Salvationist, attending the Carindale corps in Brisbane, Queensland. He is married to Rhiannon. Sam is actively involved in the Carindale Music section playing Percussion in the Band, accompanist for the Songsters, and assisting Sunday worship on the music team. He is also currently the musical director for the Salvation Army South Queensland's Divisional Youth Big band, and has also been involved with the Salvation Army Queensland Performing Arts School on several occasions, both as staff and as a camper.

Sam Creamer was born into a Salvationist family in Toowoomba and was actively involved in the corps' ministry until moving to Brisbane at age 22. His Primary and High school education was achieved in Toowoomba, in which he gained most of his musical knowledge and experience. He started learning drums from the age of 4. During his career he has also learnt to play the Piano, Brass (through YP band), Guitar & Bass Guitar (through school), and Saxophone. Sam's composing and arranging has developed over time basically through trial and error. Studying theory through the Australian Music Examinations Board (AMEB) was a crucial implement to his writing which has helped it develop to what it is today.

Sam Creamer is a great believer in not writing without inspiration and not forcing pen to paper, however sometimes this is hard not to do when certain deadlines are to be met. He is regularly arranging music for worship in his corps (modernised hymn tune & worship arrangements), which has also spread to some other corps in Brisbane and beyond. He also arranges secular popular music for the Divisional Youth Big Band.

It has just been in the last couple of years that his full length brass band pieces have started to appear in the repertoires of more famous Army bands such as the Melbourne Staff Band, Brisbane City Temple band, and Adelaide Congress Hall Band. On top of this, the Australian Southern Territory has started publishing two new brass Band series for which many of his arrangements have been submitted for publishing, and in many cases published in the series.

Important compositions

In the Love of Jesus (Arthur Gullidge Series AGS1003), He hideth my soul (Noel Jones Series NJS1003), Faith is the Victory (m/s), My Prayer (m/s)

CRESSWELL, RAYMOND FRANCIS

Raymond Francis Cresswell, was the son of Salvation Army Officer parents, and started playing in the St. Alban's Corps Band as from a very youthful age. Ray transferred to Newton Corps where he undertook private music study with a retired music professor. His first pieces were written and rehearsed with the Petone Citadel Band when he moved there as a fitter in the New Zealand Railway Workshops. *'Maori Melodies'* was his first success. Although it was not well received in London by the International Music Edition Department of the Salvation Army, it was published in 1950 by the Music Department of the Salvation Army in New Zealand. It found a ready audience when it was played and broadcast over the radio. When Ray Cresswell moved to Motueka (north of the South Island) upon seizing an opportunity to work the family farm, he doubled the size of the Corps band from one to two. He became bandmaster of a band that never exceeded twelve in number. Ray was presented with a special Centennial Award in 1983 in recognition of his small band compositional efforts. In 1985 the Wellington Citadel Band performed a festival consisting entirely of his music as a gesture of thanks on his retirement. Raymond Cresswell was Promoted to Glory in 1990.

Important composition

Petone Citadel (GS1360) 1952

CHRISTIANSEN, MARK

Mark was born in 1969 in Rotorua, New Zealand and was brought up in The Salvation Army. He started his banding life in the Rotorua Young People's Band on 2nd Cornet and then moved into the Senior Band at the age of 14-15 on 2nd Horn (and was a part of a Horn Section that was 6 in total and he was the only male). He spent a year on this part, was then moved to the Baritone section and developed his playing skills within this section for approximately two years. An opening then came on the Euphonium section and because he developed a very keen interest in the Euphonium (and having his Father as the Bandmaster, who was also a Euphonium player) the transition to this part was somewhat easier.

He auditioned and was accepted in The Salvation Army New Zealand National Youth Band in 1987 under the Bandmaster Mike Craven, who taught Mark a great deal about banding and more importantly, his spiritual life. He was involved in this group for 14 years and had the following Bandmasters – the late Eric Geddes (Bandmaster of Wellington City) & Stephen Stein (current Bandmaster at Carina Corp – Australia) and Lt. Colonel Robert Redhead (when he was appointed Chief Secretary in NZ), who all provided different elements to his banding life and Christian walk.

After finishing school Mark moved from Rotorua to Auckland (approx in 1991) where he became a member of the then Auckland Congress Hall Band on 3rd Euphonium (now known as Auckland City) and spent his times under various Bandmasters and under the great guidance and influence of his fellow Euphonium team members, Jim Clarke and the late Retired Bandmaster & Songster Leader Ken Mahaffie. After serving his apprenticeship within the Band he was appointed Bandmaster in 2002 and still holds this position.

The only composition he have written/arranged during his banding career was recorded on the NYB CD – *'Shine'* (for its USA Tour) and *'My Fathers World'*

CROCKER, JETHRO

Jethro (Jet) Crocker was born in Heart's Delight, Trinity Bay, on 28 January 1913. He moved to St. John's (Newfoundland) when he was a young man and later opened his own business; City Radio and Music Company Ltd. He served 34 years as a Soldier of the Salvation Army at Adelaide Street and St. John's Citadel and at Corner Brook. He served in several Local Officers' positions including those of assistant Sergeant major, Songster Leader and Bandmaster. Jet had several musical compositions published by the Salvation Army including *'Jesus Knows and Cares'*, which won second place in an all-Canada competition in 1946-47. He was also active and involved in the provincial Music Camps. Jet had just returned from instructing the Corps Band at Dildo-New Harbour when he took ill on 27 January 1963. He died later that night at the Grace Hospital in St. John's. The funeral at St. John's Citadel was conducted by the Corps Officer Brigadier K. Graham, assisted by Provincial Commander Colonel G. Higgins.

Important compositions

The Prodigal (CM0044) 1963

CRUFT, ADRIAN

Adrian Francis Cruft (10 February 1921 – 20 February 1987) was a British composer and not related to the Salvation Army as such. Cruft, the son of the double-bass player Eugene Cruft, was educated at Westminster Abbey Choir School, Westminster School, and as a Boult conducting scholar at the Royal College of Music from 1938, completing his studies there briefly in 1946-1947 after service in World War II. He was a composition student of Gordon Jacob and Edmund Rubbra but also studied double bass with his father. Cruft became chairman of the Composers' Guild of Great Britain 1966.

In the score notes of Festival Series 422 is written: *'we are grateful to Adrian Cruft for his contribution to our (Salvation Army) repertoire. Adrian Cruft is a professional Composer and a distinguished musician, and expressed the desire to write something for our band journal and this composition [Meditation on Passion Chorale] is the result. The work is different from the usual compositions we publish and may cause difficulty in the initial stages because of the unfamiliar style'.*

Important composition

Meditation on Passion Chorale (FS0422-2) 1982

CUELL, EDGAR JAMES

An Army Composer Edgar (Eddie) James Cuell was born on 3rd December 1900 in Portsmouth, Hampshire England, to parents Jacob and Harriet Cuell. Both parents were Salvationists, his Father having served as an early day Salvation Army officer. Interest in music led to the boy learning the organ and receiving lessons in brass band playing from the then Bandmaster at Portsmouth Citadel, Alfred Simmons. He later studied theory and harmony with Bandmaster George Marshall, the noted Army composer. Edgar (Eddie) Cuell became the youthful Young People's Band Leader at Portsmouth Citadel in the early 1920s and held that position for six years before transferring to Chalk Farm. At that well known Corps he served closely with Bandmaster (National Bandmaster) A.W.Punchard OF, first as a valued member of the cornet section of the Band, and then in successive appointments as Young People's Band Leader (for eight years) then as deputy bandmaster and acting bandmaster. After a period as acting Songster Leader at Worcester, he became Songster Leader at Rugby, an appointment he held with distinction until his transfer to

Eastbourne Citadel, where he took up the responsibilities as bandmaster in 1960. Eight years later he was among the first area bandmasters appointed when he took up this duty for the Brighton area. Later in an organisational re-arrangement which saw the transfer of this area to the West London division, the title was changed to that of Divisional Bandmaster. This was an assignment which he respected and relished and smaller bands on the Sussex coast had reason to be grateful for his kindly interest and patient instruction. He arranged a number of 'Small Bands Festivals' and at these events he did not take the baton, preferring the 'small band bandmasters' to have centre stage.

For thirty three years he was engaged in the Fire Service. Thirteen of those years were spent in the London Fire Brigade, when he attended all the London blitzes in the Second World War. Because of his specialised training and intimate knowledge of Portsmouth and Southampton, he was also selected to carry out duties on fires caused by major raids on those cities. In 1942/43 he was appointed as Staff officer to the Regional Commissioner Lord Dudley, and was responsible for much of the National Fire Service organization in the Midlands. His final appointment was Deputy Chief Fire Officer for the County of Warwickshire from which post he retired in 1958. When he was on duty, he would come to the Sunday meetings in his fire chief's uniform, conduct the songsters, and then go to work.

As a composer he wrote more than 20 published compositions including eleven for 'The Musical Salvationist', six Band songs, two marches *('Reunion'* and *'Eastbourne Citadel')* three pieces for Home League Singers and two songs for Young People's Singing Companies. A number of his vocal compositions were written in conjunction with Major Doris Rendell and Adam Hall both notable Army poets. Eddie was a firm believer in the power of prayer both in his personal experience and in his encouragement and influence of others. The family have several memories of physical healing as an answer to prayer.

Eddie married Edith at the age of 19 and there were five children – Raymond, Bernard, Iris, Ruth and Rosemary. Edith was Promoted to Glory in 1951. He then married Miriam Hollock on 18th October 1952. Miriam passed away on18th March 1977. He married Ella Burns in May 1979. Eddie was one of a number of Army composers selected to work re-arrangement of tunes for the then 'new' Salvation Army Tune Book in 1978/9. He was Promoted to Glory on 18th November 1979 after a very short illness. On the music stand of his piano was the part finished arrangement of the tune *'Prepare me'*, some of the Song Book words of which are:

'Prepare me now, prepare me here,
To stand before thy throne
That I, without a doubt or fear
May stand before Thy throne'

Important composition

Eastbourne Citadel (GS1612) 1970

CUELL, RAYMOND EDGAR JAMES

Raymond Cuell of Highgate, commenced cornet lessons at the age of six years, when his father was Young People's Band Leader at Portsmouth Citadel. In 1927 he joined the Chalk Farm Young People's Band and after transferring to the senior band was appointed Deputy Bandmaster in 1946. The new Bandmaster payed tribute to the help given him by National Bandmaster A.W. Punchard in general band training and business life. A successful student in theory and harmony under Bandmaster George Marshall, he also gained high marks in the Bandmasters' Correspondence Course. Ray Cuell has visited nineteen Continental countries with Salvation Army and R.A.F. bands, including 5,850 miles travelled by air. He toured Germany as cornet soloist with the Wood Green brass quartet. Prior to his appointment Ray Cuell was the Young People's Sergeant-Major at Highgate. His father and younger brother were Songster Leaders at Rugby ad Wealdstone respectively.

Raymond Cuell was born on the 17th June 1920 in Portsmouth, Hampshire and was Promoted to Glory on 26th December 2008, after a long battle with illness, at his home in Lincolnshire. He was married to Evelyn Gladys Stevens in 1939 and they had two Sons, Kenneth and Howard. Raymond was the eldest of five children born to Eddie and Edith Cuell. Ray inherited his love of music from his Father (composer Edward Cuell). He joined the senior band at Chalk Farm becoming the youngest player, under Bandmaster A.W. Punchard. Ray was 'called up' during the Second World War, serving in the RAF Central Band, some of the time in Italy. He was also based in the United Kingdom and spent some time in Scarborough, Yorkshire. He wrote his first March *'Scarborough Citadel'* which was published in 1946, as a tribute to the Corps who looked after him whilst stationed in that area.

At the end of the war, following his 'demob', Ray became Deputy Bandmaster at Chalk Farm and during that time wrote his second March *'Field Service'* as a tribute to serving Salvation Army Officers. The march was published in 1961, by which time Ray had become Bandmaster at Highgate building the Band from two players to twenty-one!

Ray also played in the International Staff Band for some time including a tour of America. For some reason his music was not packed with that of the rest of the Band and he played the repertoire for the tour entirely from memory. He had a photographic memory for music, and would spend hours at the piano playing from memory, not only Salvation Army music, but secular as well. He simply lived for his music! In later years Ray was not an active Salvationist for many years but would attend regularly at either Chalk Farm, Regent Hall or Hendon.

Important compositions

Salvation Banner (TS0364) 1944, Field Service (GS1348) 1951, Scarborough Citadel (GS1272) 1946

CURNOW, JAMES

James Curnow is an active Salvationist, and received his early musical training at The Salvation Army Royal Oak, Michigan Corps in the USA. He has served as Bandmaster of the Flint, Michigan Citadel Corps and Bandmaster of the Asbury College Salvation Army Student Fellowship Band. James Curnow, a composer of international renown, is currently a resident of Stone Mounzain, Georgia where he composes and arranges full-time and is an educational consultant for Jenson Publications Corporation. His formal training was received at Wayne State University / Detroit, MI) and Michigan State University (East Lansing, MI) where he was a euphonium Student of Leonard Falcon and a conducting student of Harry Begian. As a conductor-clinician-composer, he has traveled throughout the United States, Canada, Australia and Europe where his music has received wide acclaim. He has won several awards for band compositions including the American School Band Directors Associaton/Volkwein Award in 1977 *('Symphonic Triptych')* and 1979 *('Collage for Band'),* the American Bandmasters Association/Ostwald Award in 1980 ('Mutanza') and 1984 *('Symphonic Variants for Euphonium and Band'),* the 1985 Sixth International Competition for Original Compositions for Band, and has received annual A.S.C.A.P. awards for significant contributions to the band literature of America since 1979. James Curnows has more than 200 published works.

Important compositions

Saints of God (FS388) 1978, The Great Salvation War (FS463) 1988, Variations on Terra Beata (FS489) 1991, A Psalm of Praise (FS407) 1980, Guardian of our way (GS1673) 1975, The depths of His love (GS1836) 1989.

CURNOW, PAUL

Paul Curnow has served as a Salvationist music leader for many years, and recently this has included leadership of the 'Intermountain Divisional Band' (Denver) and the 'Southwest Divisional Band' (Phoenix). Paul Curnow has been writing music for many years, having studied with Normand Lockwood while earning a Master of Arts in Composition and Conducting at the University of Denver. He taught at the same institution as well as the university system in California. He has written for voice, orchestra, brass ensembles, brass bands, solo instruments, and is published by Singspiration / Zondervan and Medici Music.

Important compositions

The Festive Season (AJ239) 2005, Angels watching over me (AE199123) 1989.

DADSON, E.V.

A former bandsman of the Wood Green Band in London, England. No further information could be found about this composer.

Important compositions

Decision (TS0140) 1930, Through doubt to Triumph (TS0167) 1932

DALZIEL, ALBERT ERNEST

Was the son of Alexander Dalziel, a Salvationist at King's Cross Corps. He was born on 10 April 1892. He became corps secretary and then deputy bandmaster there before going to the International Training College in 1912 to become a Salvation Army officer. During the following year he was commissioned as Assistant Cadet's Sergeant-Major and became conductor of the cadet's band. After several appointments in the United Kingdom he moved to Canada around 1930 as Training Principal in Winnipeg, during 1930-1932. After this he became Divisional Commander for British Columbia and Training Principal in Toronto during 1937-1939. Later he returned to the United Kingdom where he became Chief Side Officer for the men at International Training College, followed by an appointment as General Secretary for Scotland and Ireland. His last appointment was as Provincial Commander of Newfoundland, Canada and retired as a Colonel in 1957. He was Promoted to Glory on 29 December 1974.

Important compositions

Pioneers (CM0039) 1963, Testimoney (CM0017) 1958, Worf of life (CM0026) 1958

DALSTRØM, HAAKON

An odd one out in this list of composers and arrangers is the Norwegian Haakon Dahlstrøm. Not a real composer, but significant enough to mention here. Haakon Dahlstrøm, born on 7 February 1907, was a very gifted piano player, composer and arranger. He used to be bandmaster of the Norwegian Staff Band in the early days, and did a lot of arrangements and small compositions for them. The Norwegian Staff Band was shut down in 1940, but re-established as National Band and later Norway Territorial Band in 1994, and is still running today. Haakon Dahlstrøm arranged the Norwegian Band Tune Book in the 1970's. He did a marvelous service as an officer and became Territorial Commander in the Norway, Iceland and Faeroe Island Territory with the rank of Commissioner.

In many senses Dahlstrøm was one of the greatest characters in Salvation Army, but he was not really a composer. He wrote just some small uninteresting pieces of music. One said: *'He did not have the fantasy to write'* and many think that is correct. But first of all he was a hymnologist, one of the absolute best in Norway, and probably in Europe. He had a great knowledge about classical Christian hymns and also, of course, hymns from the Salvation Army. Haakon was Promoted to Glory on 31 October 2006, just some months before his 100th birthday.

DARBY, GEORGE

A former New York Staff Bandmaster (1912-1931), George wasn't educated in composing but learned it *'on the job'*. Just after the turn of the century he immigrated from the United Kingdom to the United States, and became bandmaster of the Fall River Salvation Army Band. From here he was recognised as possible musical leader, which eventually led to his appointment first as Deputy Bandmaster (1911) and later, in 1912, as Staff Bandmaster of the New York Staff Band.

Important composition

Bible picture – The Prodigal Son

DAVIES, HOWARD

Howard Davies was born to Salvationist parents Ruth and Fred Davies on 12th November 1940. His father was a cornet soloist in the Melbourne Staff Band during the 1940s/50s. Howard's older brother, Brian, also later played cornet in both the ISB and the Melbourne Staff Band and served as Bandmaster at Camberwell Corps for over 30 years. From the very start of life Howard grew up in a musical environment. He began studying violin at the age of seven and in 1959 achieved his A.MUS.A. (Violin – performing) degree from the Australian Conservatorium of Music. During the 1950's piano accompaniments for the two cornet players and one violinist were ably provided by Aunt Phyllis who came to live in the family home around 1946. The Davies family soon became well known and used at Corps programmes around Melbourne. This musical environment served to develop Howard's keen ear for music and a love for melody and harmony.

From quite an early age Howard showed some interest in poetry, particularly poems with strong rhyme and metre. He began to write humorous limericks about some of his Aunts. Several short poems of his were published in the children's page of the Melbourne Argus Newspaper in the early 1950's. That interest in writing rhyming poems was to develop in later years. Howard's early years were at Canterbury Corps. Having had a brief (but unsuccessful) start on cornet, Howard had made good progress on the violin. However, the

YP Band Leader gave him an old baritone. Transferring to Camberwell Corps a few years later led to a move to trombone. Howard's first efforts at music composition and arranging came in his late teens. Musical influences were Salvation Army brass and vocal music. His violin studies had also grounded him in classical music. However, he also enjoyed Dixie-land jazz. In the late 1950s Pee Wee Hunt LP records were quite popular.

With several other young bandsmen of Camberwell Corps a small, informal 'dixie-land group' came into being. Having a 'good ear' for harmony, Howard discovered he was able to arrange various bright Salvation Army songs and Christmas Carols in a similar style. This appears to have been the starting point for more serious composition and musical arrangements in the future.

Around 1959 Howard served as YP Band Leader at Camberwell Corps. Then at the age of 21 he became Bandmaster of Camberwell Citadel Band, following his father into that position. Since 1957 he had been employed with the National Australia Bank, He resigned in March 1964 to enter The Salvation Army Officer Training College in Melbourne as a Cadet in the 'Proclaimers of the Faith' Session. The Training Principal at that time was Brigadier Geoffrey Dalziel. He soon put Howard's music abilities to work. Within a short time he was appointed as Bandmaster of the Cadets' Band and asked to write the Cadet's Dedication Song. This latter task also required him to write suitable poetry.

Other songs were soon needed, this time for a Cadet's Rhythm Group. Songs produced included *'On the road to Heaven'* (later published in "The Musical Salvationist"). Also, a Christmas song *'The angels sang the story'* that eventually appeared in the Salvation Army Christmas Carol Book. Further songs were written (rather in the style of Gilbert & Sullivan!) for an annual Salvation Army History Pageant held at the Training College in November 1964. A short musical entitled *'Army without guns!'* was featured in the programme.

In 1972 Howard wrote music for a full length Musical entitled *'Soldier Saint'*. This was based on the colourful life of George Scott Railton, a pioneer Officer of The Salvation Army. As well as being presented in Australia this musical was also staged in London, New York and Los Angeles.

In January 1967 Lieutenant Howard Davies married Captain Muriel Hewitt. Their first married appointment was to Broadford, a small Victorian country town. It was here that one of Howard's best-known songs, *'The wonder of His grace'*, was written. The inspiration for this song came from the glorious night skies where the stars and 'milky way' are so much clearer than are often possible to notice in large cities full of street lights. In 1969 Captain and Mrs. Davies were appointed to Shepparton, a fruit-growing region of Victoria. Songs written at Shepparton included *'Not if I owned the world'* and *'Long way to travel alone'*. In September 1972 the Davies (and their three young children) arrived in the United Kingdom where Howard commenced an appointment at the International Music Editorial Department at Judd Street, Kings Cross. The Head of the Department at this time was Major Ray Steadman-Allen. Also working in the department at that time was Captain Robert Redhead.

The Davies family attended Ealing Corps in West London where Howard was asked to become Bandmaster. In May 1973 he was appointed to the International Staff Band where he played 1st baritone for the next three and a half years. His first engagement with the ISB was Bandmaster's Councils Festival at the Royal Albert Hall. Soon after the ISB toured Switzerland. The Staff Bandmaster at that time was Colonel Bernard Adams.

For the first few months after arriving in London, Howard was reluctant to write brass band music. (Who wouldn't be – with Ray Steadman-Allen and Robert Redheard sitting at the other desks!) Howard felt his forte was song-writing. But after just a few months of his arrival in the Music Department Major Steadman-Allen gave him a very specific assignment. He was to write a 'straight-forward melody cornet solo' using the old Army song *'Nearer to Thee'*. This short piece was needed to 'fill a half page' in the forthcoming Triumph Series Journal. Howard was given two weeks to produce the finished arrangement!

By the due deadline Howard nervously passed the arrangement to RS-A for vetting. He was relieved that only one note in the bass line apparently needed changing! *'Nearer to Thee'* was Howard's first brass band publication. Once over the hurdle of self-doubt, Howard slowly began writing further music for brass bands. Other pieces that followed included the song arrangement *'He found me'*, then *'Selection from Soldier Saint'* and eventually a Festival Series selection *'On the Road'*. Songs written in London included two short YP songs *'Caring for me'* and *'Friends of Jesus'* (both found their way into the 1987 SA Tune Book), *'Search for a new world'* and *'How can I thank You?'*

In 1976 Major Les Condon was Secretary for Bands and Songsters. He invited Howard to join him and other staff at the annual Music School, then held at Tylney Hall. Unfortunately on the third day Howard, feeling unwell, and was dismayed to discover he had the measles! (Some weeks earlier two of his ownchildren had measles!)! Very disappointed, he returned home, not wishing to cause an epidemic of measles at Tylney Hall! Fortunately, at that time Major Norman Bearcroft was visiting the UK on furlough from Canada. He kindly agreed to step in and take over Howard's duties at the Music School.

At the end of 1976 Howard and his wife Muriel, along with their four children, Jennifer, Stephen, Christine and Fiona (the latter born in London) returned to Australia where they took up a new appointment at the Melbourne Corps of Chelsea. During the next four years at Chelsea, band music Howard wrote including: *'Songs of Australia'* (commissioned by Staff Bandmaster Colin Woods for the Melbourne Staff Band's visit to the U.K) - an Easter meditation – *'He never said a mumblin' word'*. Vocal music included God can do the impossible! Then followed a three-year appointment at Ringwood Corps. Among the wide range of healthy corps sections was the YP Band and learners group. Numbering over 25 players and learners, their encouraging and capable leader was Noel Jones.

Vocal music written during that Ringwood period includes – *'All the world is waiting'*, *'Lord, you know that we love You!' and 'Far more than I deserve!'* In 1984 the Davies' were appointed to the Melbourne Training College staff. Howard was to be Senior Training Officer (and later, Assistant Principal) this demanding four-year appointment proved to also be a creative period of music production.

Annual requests for Commissioning songs produced *'We have peace'* and *'Here am I, my Lord!'* Some bright songs were needed for the Male Voices, which led to *'God's still the One!'* being written. In addition to 'normal' duties, time had to be found (usually after mid-night!) to write songs and complete orchestrations for the musical *'Southern Cross'*. This was first presented as a 'try-out' in Melbourne and then taken to Sydney for the Bi-Centenary Congress led by General Eva Burrows.

In January 1988 Majors Howard and Muriel Davies were appointed to Waverley Temple Corps in Melbourne where they remained for the next seven years. This was one of the largest Corps in Australia, formerly the Hawthorn Corps, which successfully relocated to the outer growing suburb of Glen Waverley in November 1987. Band music written during this period included the Easter meditation – *'Jesus Dying on the Tree'.*

In 1995 the Davies' were appointed to Perth Fortress in Western Australia where they greatly enjoyed the typical warmth of 'west-australian' Salvationists. The benediction *'As we leave this place'* was written while the Davies' were Corps Officers at Perth Fortress. In January 1997 the Davies' were appointed as Divisional Commanders of the Northern Division in New Zealand, situated in Auckland. This was a wonderful experience and the warm friendship of New Zealand Salvationists was greatly valued. Again, this was a busy, but enthralling appointment. There was little time to write music. However, as guest of the annual music school in Wellington, time was somehow found to write a piece for the Music Students Band – *'I love you, Lord!'*

As Divisional Commander in Auckland Howard was conscious of following in the steps of Dean Goffin, one of the truly great Salvationist composers and musicians. Sadly, by the time the Davies' arrived in New Zealand Dean Goffin had 'left this world for a far better one!' Majors Howard and Muriel Davies returned to Melbourne with brief appointments at THQ before appointed as Divisional Commanders for Eastern Victoria Division in September 2001. After a brief illness Major Muriel Davies was 'Promoted to Glory' in April 2002. Together they had served the Lord for 35 years.

In June 2003 Major Sheina Henderson of the United Kingdom and Ireland Territory and Major Howard Davies were married at the Springburn Corps in Scotland. Returning to Australia they served two years before retiring in December 2005. They now live in retirement in the country town of Drouin where they are active in the nearby Warragul Corps. Major Howard Davies has also been the Executive Officer and playing member of the Melbourne Veterans Band for the past five years.

Important compositions

On the Road (FS384) 1977, Soldier Saint (GS1678) 1976, Beyond Blue Horizons (GS1766) 1983, People Need the Lord (GS1935) 1997.

DAVIS, MICHAEL

Michael Davis was born on 26 November 1946 to Colonel and Mrs. Aston Davis, Salvation Army officers in the Caribbean Island of Jamaica. Michael started his musical studies piano and theory- at age eight at the Royal School of Music in London, England. In 1968 they immigrated to the United States were he did further studies at the Brooklyn Conservatory, in piano and composition. Cornet lessons were started in 1958 when he was twelve years of age. His teacher at that time was Major Winifred Garner (Bromley Temple). When in the USA, Michael was fortunate to study music under Ray Steadman-Allen, Bruce Broughton and Robert Redhead, at Star Lake. He still writes music for brass and vocal and is connected to the Salvation Army Bedford Temple Corps in the USA. He also played baritone in the New York Staff Band from 1972 to 1975.

Important composition

Jesus, I come (TS1217) 2011

DAVIS, TREVOR

Trevor Davis (1944?) is one of the more well known Salvation Army composers with some excellent compositions which have appeared on many recordings. He went to the International Training College from 1965 to 1966 and after some corps appointments became National Bandmaster for the British Territory around 1974, a position he held until 1981. In this year he was send to New Zealand as Territorial Music Secretary. This lasted to 1981 when he came back to the United Kingdom. From 1992 to 1994 he was Editor in Chief for the International Editorial Musical Department. In 1977 he was also one of the first at the faculty of the then Cobham Hall Territorial Music Camp in the United Kingdom, where he led for some years the 'Trevor Davis Band'. The last period as an active officer he was Executive Officer of the International Staff Band, a position he held on two different periods. In 2009 he retired and is, although retired, active at the Leicester South Salvation Army Corps.

Important compositions

Elation (FS451) 1986, Where I am (FS584) 2003, Shepherd Song (GS1939) 1997, Ruth (GS1943) 1998.

DENHAM, F

Not much is known about F. Denham except that he was Bandmaster at the Pontypool Corps in the United Kingdom. No further information could be retrieved about him.

Important composition

The Pontypool March (GS0882) 1922

DENNISON, ROBERT

Robert was a conductor of contesting bands before he became to lead the South Shields Corps Band. As none of the bandsmen at South Shields could read or write, either English or musical notation, he taught his band members to do both.

Important compositions

The Shields March (GS0564) 1908, The Tyneside March (GS0550) 1907

DIMOND, VICTOR H.

Born on July 7, 1900 in Staines, Middlesex, London, United Kingdom and was Promoted to Glory on January 23,1981 in Biddeford, Maine, United States of America. Brig Herbert Victor Dimond was associated with Salvation Army music his entire life. His earliest memory was being carried on his bandmaster father's shoulder on the way to band practice. When Victor retired, the English 'Musician' referred to him as the well known and award winning American composer. During Victor's 50 years of composing The Salvation Army published over 25 of his songs, and two marches.

Forgiveness With Thee. This 1932 song with words and music by Victor, was his first song to be published by The Salvation Army. 'Condemnation fills my mind, Stained with sin my record stands; Can I not a refuge find? Cleansing for my heart and hands? There is forgiveness with Thee, There is forgiveness for me. God's Holy Word declares it. There is forgiveness for me.'

Blessing On The Pilgrim Way: Victor described the inspiration for this song in the 'Musical Salvationist' (October 3,1959) Late one night while driving through the Nevada desert, on their way home after attending the Annual Congress of Corrections, Victor and his wife Edna suddenly found a herd of cattle blocking the road. *'Turning sharply from the road, balanced for part of the time on two wheels, we managed miraculously to avoid the livestock and were soon on our way again.'* Shortly after returning home the song was formed. 'Footsore, weary, wandering along, Thoughtless, dreary, In my heart no song: Then I met the Saviour, I heard Him kindly say: 'There are blessings on the Pilgrim Way.''

My Pledge: With words and music by Victor this was a prize winner in the 1964 USA Salvationist Songs of a Century contest. 'O Lord, when will I understand that life is not to please, and pamper me with luxury nor make a way of ease? But as the candle grows less tall in shedding helpful light, so must I spend my strength and time to aid the cause of right.'

Ask the Lord: Victor wrote the words to a melody by his son, Major Edward V Dimond (Executive Director Harbor Light Complex, Cleveland Ohio). In the April 1967 Musical Salvationist Lt Col Charles Skinner described it as a 'rhythmic' appeal song that, with the added guitar chords, would have a wider appeal and 'there is little doubt it will catch on quickly.' It was also published in 'New Songs for Male Voices' Issue 36 January 1966. Thanks to the Cleveland Harbor Light Combo's recording, which was distributed via the Salvation Army Tape Fellowship, it soon became popular in Australia 'Ask the Lord, He'll hear your prayer Is not His presence everywhere? Every burden He will share: Jesus the Friend of sinners! Bring your doubts and bring your fears, Bring your heartaches and your fears, All the sins of bygone years Bring to the Friend of sinners.'

On This Day: With words and music by Victor it was written for Male Chorus. It became a yearly favorite of the New York Staff Band and was included on their 1974 LP A Christmas Gift of Music (TRLPS20). 'Angels are singing in the sky Anthems of praise; Shepherds to Bethlehem draw nigh, Marvel and gaze.'

Atkinson, Edna F: Born October 21, 1902 Troy New York. Died May 26, 1969 Biddeford Maine. Some 50 years after her pioneer Salvation Army officer parents were stationed in Troy, Edna returned as the wife of the corps officer Major Herbert Victor Dimond. To commemorate these events, Victor composed the popular march 'Troy Temple'. It was published in the USA 'East Brass Band Journal' and was premiered by the New York Staff Band (October 3, 1969). Lt Commissioner J Clyde Cox, the meeting leader said 'I'm sure that march will be played many, many times over again.' It was also recorded by the Stockholm VII Band for their 1970 USA Tour (Triumphonic TRLPS-13)

The 1926 marriage of Victor to Captain Edna F Atkinson joined one of the Territory's foremost contralto soloists to one of its most sensitive piano accompanists. Edna's signature solo was *'Sharon's Rose'*. They were married in Hartford Connecticut where Victor, as a soldier, had been the corps bandmaster before leaving for Salvation Army Officer's Training in 1921. Victor's march *'Hartford'* recalled those events and was played at the famous Old Orchard Beach Maine Camp Meetings of 1968

Victor was converted in 1911 at Kilburn London, He was a Junior Soldier and was active in the Scouts and the Senior Band. Victor immigrated to the USA in May 1921, living in Manchester Connecticut and later in nearby Hartford. He worked as a tool and die maker for the aircraft engine manufacturer Pratt & Whitney in Hartford. In September 1923 he became a cadet in The Salvation Army Training College for Officers in the Bronx New

York and was commissioned in June 1924. As corps officers the Dimond's ten USA East field appointments included: White Plains (NY) where General Evangeline Booth Ret was a soldier, and premier corps like the New York Temple, and the Boston (Massachusetts) Palace. Victor was the founding manager of the Army's Retired Officer's Residence in Asbury Park New Jersey, and later the manager of the Evangeline Residence in Cleveland (Ohio). Brig Dimond retired in 1965 after serving for 10 years as Director of the Eastern Territory's Correctional Services where he was the Army's liaison to the American Congress of Corrections. Victor was elected a fellow of the College of Fellows of the American Protestant Correctional Chaplains Association. He received their highest award, and was a visiting chaplain at the famous American Sing Sing Prison in New York State.

Following the Promotion to Glory of Victor, the USA 'War Cry' described him as a Prison worker extraordinary and used a photo of him counseling two prisoners on the cover of the 'Correctional Services' issue of May 2, 1981. It quoted his philosophy that work with offenders should concentrate on *'growth, creativity, affection, mutual sharing, understanding and gaining an experience of God.'*

The Philadelphia Orchestra under the leadership of Eugene Ormandy was world famous. Victor's oldest daughter Frances, a lifelong resident of Philadelphia, fondly remembers taking her father to a concert where he quietly explained a complicated chord progression that ended in a D Major. Victor had perfect pitch and could write down a melody after hearing it once. Victor composed melodies to words of Will J Brand, Charles Wesley, S B Simpson, and Rev Thomas T Lynch, and collaborated with Army musical giants Erik Leidzén and Emil Söderstrom.

There is no death!: Emil Soderstrom composed the melody to Victor's words 'There is no death! But only life unending. To those who thru' the years identified their lives the past, the present, and the future, with Christ the Son of God, who for them died.' Soderstrom also supplied the melody for *'My Soul Is Thirsting'* and *arranged 'Out On Life's Ocean'.*

My Master wills!: Erik Leidzen arranged the melody and the words of Victor. 'My Master wills! I can but bow submissive, And tender all that life vouchsafes, and use In willing service time and talents gladly, And follow Him, through rewards I lose.'

Also numbered among Victor's Army musical friends were Harold Zealley and Eric Ball.

Father: Edwin Henry Dimond, Bristol England - died Willesden London England

Mother: Ada Clapp: Born November 30, 1864 - Died January 18, 1937 Kensal Rise London England

Victor's father Edwin became a bandsman in 1882, along with Sidney Cox. Edwin later served as bandmaster, passing the baton to Cox in 1893. Edwin was also the bandmaster at Dawlish, Dartford, Staines, Kilburn, Kensal Rise and Harlesden Corps where Arch R Wiggins (of later SA literary fame) was one of his bandsmen. (See The 'War Cry' UK August 15, 1936 and 'The Musician' October 15, 1973 page 580)

Important composition

March - Troy Temple (AJ0077) 1969

DICKENS, GEORGE M.

George Dickens was the son of officer parents in Australia. He joined the Melbourne Staff Band in 1918 after serving as conductor at Collingwood and Brunswick Salvation Army bands. He was appointed Deputy Bandmaster of the Staff Band in 1927, and Bandmaster in 1929. In 1936, George moved to Sydney where he was employed by a musical publishing firm. He then served as Bandmaster at the Rockdale Citadel Band for 19 years and was an active leader in the musical life of Australia's Eastern Territory Music Department until his pension.

Important compositions

Collingwood (GS918) 1924, Beaumont (GS1001) 1929,

DITMER, BERNARD BRAMWELL

A brother of composer Stanley Ditmer, and once a Salvation Army officer and as such in command of the Lancaster Corps in Pennsylvania. Bernard was born on 23 April 1915 and was Promoted to Glory on 24 March 1988.

Bernard's daughter Kathi recalls: *'Letters from Erik Leidzén, correspondence with Eric Ball, Memories of Emil Soderstrom staying at our house. Stories of funny things he would do at Band Camp, [Bernard was very well known for his sense of humour], sermons that to this day I think of at least once a week. He wrote an alto horn solo while at Camp Nathan Hale one summer, while it was to be arranged for full band, but the ONLY copy of the piano part was lost. Dad never rewrote it. I still have the solo horn part though.'*

There are still many manuscripts of music written and some partially written that he did nothing with. He was such a perfectionist, probably meant to go back over it again before submitting. Unfortunately this never happened.

Important compositions

March – Gladness, Selection - Alstone

DITMER, PHILIP

Philip, born on November 23, 1953, was a bandsman and cornet soloist with the Cambridge Citadel Silver Band. He also served as Divisional Music Director for the Salvation Army's Massachusetts Division with headquarters in Boston. He is the oldest son of commissioner and composer Stanley Ditmer.

Important compositions

Kremser (AJ0120) 1983, I Surrender (ABJ109)

DITMER, STANLEY

Stanley was born in Youngstown, Ohio to Salvation Army officer parents on November 6, 1924. After graduating from high school, he entered the United States Navy in 1943 and served for 36 months as a radio school instructor. Upon discharge from the Navy, Commissioner attended Oberlin College Conservatory of Music. After completing his studies he entered The Salvation Army School for Officers' Training and was commissioned in 1949 with the Peacemakers Session. He was also awarded a Bachelor of Science degree from Skidmore College and did graduate work at New York University and the Psychological Corporation of New York. In February 1953 Commissioner married his first wife, Catherine. Together they served for many years in various appointments. He was appointed as territorial chief secretary in the Southern Territory in 1982. In 1985 he became the territorial commander of the Central Territory and in 1986 the territorial commander of the Eastern Territory. It was from the Eastern Territory he and Catherine retired in 1990. Commissioner Ditmer wrote many musical compositions. A favourite is *'I'm in His Hands,'* written in 1956, which has been translated into more than 20 languages. He was a creative musician and had the ability to write both simple, instantly appealing songs and also developed works to challenge musicians. His songs came from a vast and rich experience of service and devotion to Christ.

Important compositions

Triumphant Faith (FS191) 1953, Ceaseless Service (GS1568) 1966, I'm in His hands (AJ243) 2006

DOCKERILL, FREDERICK J.

Fred Dockerill, from the Dartford Corps was one of the participants in the 1926 International Music Competition, which was held for the first time in no less than seventeen years. He was mentioned by winning a price in this competition. Frederick Dockerill was also bandmaster at Woolwich (South East London). He worked for many years at Salvationist, Publishing and Supplies (SP&S) and probably played in the SP&S Band under Eric Ball, although this is not confirmed. Frederick Dockerill was also Bandmaster of the Plumstead Citadel Band, before Cyril Brisley was bandmaster there.

Important compositions

Joyful Experience (FS159) 1949, The Army Drum (GS1163) 1939, Arizona (TS602-2) 1960

DOCKRAY, J ('Titch')

A fine exponent of the piano accordion, he came to London around 1932 and joined the Tottenham Citadel Band. By his personality he had captured the hearts of the people there, which was even better as he soon became the new bandmaster of the Tottenham Citadel Band in succession of Bandmaster Dry. He soon proved a popular leader. His tenure as bandmaster however did not last long as a visit to Luton Temple in 1937 proved to be Bandmaster Dockray's last public engagement for he was stricken with an illness from which he never recovered. He died suddenly the following September.

Important composition

Tottenham Citadel (GS1108) 1936

DOE, GURNEY

One-time bandmaster of Norland Castle Corps (which no longer exists), West London. He was a member of the SP&S Band (under Eric Ball) and one of its only two secretaries during it's life time, the other one being Lt. Col. William Cozens. Besides his activities in the Salvation Army, he was for a period also active outside the organisation and became Secretary of the National Association of Brass Band Conductors (which still exists today). This was around 1947-1948. He also might have been a member of the Southall Corps. He had a Diploma of the Guildhall School of Music.

Important compositions

The Army Colours (TS0116) 1928, My Refuge (TS0251) 1937, A Surrendered Life (TS0215) 1935

DOKTER, JOHAN

Johan Dokter (5 December 1968) was born in Ridderkerk in the South-west of the Netherlands. He learnt to play the cornet on a young age and soon was under the spell of Salvation Army music. In 1990 he joined the Amsterdam Staff Band on 2nd cornet and worked his way up eventually ending as Principal Cornet in 2000. He started composing in the early 90's, mainly for use within small bands, however he soon expanded his output which results in some recorded music by his hand.

Important compositions

All the time in the world (m/s), Egmont Overture, Opus 84 (m/s)

DOROW, REGINALD E.

Reginald E. Dorow was from Norfolk, England, and is a former bandsman of the Cambridge Heath Band of the Salvation Army.

He moved to Cambridge in the 1960s with his job, where among other things he played trombone in the Kings College orchestra. During the 2nd world war he was a signaller on the flag ship of a minesweeper in the Royal Navy and was often loaned to the Royal Marine Band in Portsmouth.

Important composition

The pure in heart (GS1667) 1975

DOVE, CHARLES

Bandmaster Charles Dove was a name that was to be known throughout Salvation Army circles, and a name that was revered for the integrity it commanded. Charles Dove was born to parents Frederick and Ann in Stapleford in 1907 and was the youngest of five children. Charles' older brother, Mark, was born two years previous and was later to become a fine bass player. It is known that all five children were active in the Stapleford Corps. Charles was a member of the Young People's Band from an early age and became an accomplished cornet player.

Tragedy was to strike the Dove family on 18th July 1918. An explosion at the shell filling factory at Chilwell, Nottingham, killed 117 people, including Frederick Dove, Charles' father. This must have put a lot of strain on the family and made it difficult for Mrs. Dove senior to cope with the bringing up her young family. As a boy of eleven the tragedy seemed to strengthen Charles, and he continued with his musical and spiritual training in the Corps. At the age of fifteen Charles was transferred to the Senior Band and two years later, in 1924, he was commissioned deputy to Bandmaster E. Linsdell. This was a commission that was carried out with joy and enthusiasm and was to prepare him for the future.

It was in 1928 that Charles Dove's name first featured in the 'Bandsman and Songster' magazine. Charles, who was a self taught composer, had his first composition accepted by the Music Board – the march *'I'll Stand for Christ'*. The following were the editorial comments. '*We are glad to welcome into our ranks of Composers a new composer in the person of Deputy Bandmaster C. Dove of Stapleford Citadel, and if his future efforts compare with the one under review we forecast a great future for him in this field*. When Bandmaster Linsdell retired in 1930 Charles accepted the full responsibility of the band. Bandsmen who served under him remark what a pleasure it was. He has been described as a great band trainer and an encourager of his men, particularly the younger bandsmen. One bandsman said, '*if you played a wrong note Charles didn't need to say anything. The look he gave made sure you played it correctly next time*'. He led by example and did not need to preach to his bandsmen, working on the theory that only the best was good enough for the Lord. His example led him to always appear at an Open Air Meeting a few minutes before the appointed time, only illness would keep him away. It was under the baton of Charles Dove that Stapleford Citadel Band grew in stature and became well travelled in the Salvation Army world.

Charles Dove gave all his energies to his task as Bandmaster and to composing, not an easy matter as he carried out a demanding job as a moulder at the local Stanton Iron Works. He was also a devoted family man. His children speak of the times he spent with them, taking them on what they describe as 'Nature Walks'. Family time meant a lot to Charles. It has been said that music 'oozed' from Charles Dove. As he walked along the street he would be humming a melody that would help him formulate his next composition. Composing became second nature to him and he devoted a great deal of energy and time to his compositions. One comment was that Charles was determined to set himself a target of one composition per month. This was very demanding on the creative spirit of a composer who only had his spare time to devote to writing. Charles could be seen after a day at the Iron Works working on his manuscripts at the kitchen table. Saturdays were also good days for him to concentrate on his writings. The compositions of Charles Dove have appeared in almost all of the Salvation Army's publications, not only in the band journals but also in publications for singing groups. Charles' wife, Mabel, provided the words to some of the songs, notably 'My Prayer' which was published in "The Musical Salvationist" in July 1963, with Charles composing the melody.

It was in 1946 that Charles Dove first submitted a manuscript to the Salvation Army Music Department for the march '*Stapleford Citadel*'. The comments he received from the Music Department on the rejection of the march are as follows. '*The cornet parts are far too high. The piece was not sufficiently original and the International Staff Band had been playing something similar for the past two years*'. The score was revised slightly and re-submitted in 1947. At the Bandmaster's Councils Festival at London Clapton Congress Hall in 1947, General Albert Orsborn announced that Bandmaster Charles Dove had won two First Prizes in the International Music Competition of that year, with the march '*Stapleford Citadel*' and his selection '*Friend of Friends*'. The International Staff Band was later to record '*Stapleford Citadel*' on a '78 disc. Charles originally wanted to name the march '*Hazeannal*' incorporating the names of his twin daughters, but this was rejected and he then decided on '*Stapleford Citadel*'.

In all his compositions Charles was concerned that they would have the right effect on his listeners. He wanted what he wrote to be useful, not showy, or merely clever and decorative, but a real contribution to the music of the Salvation Army. It has been said that his Sunday night Selections were real sermons in music and could bring a devotional and reverent atmosphere to a Meeting. Charles Dove retired as Bandmaster in 1964 and handed the baton over to his son, who was respectfully known as 'young Charlie'. Although Charles had been a brilliant cornet player he took up his position on the trombone section, playing 'G' trombone. Here he was as conscientious, playing his part well with humble and

Christian spirit. Charles and Mabel visited Canada while retired and Charles had the privilege of conducting one of the Canadian Corps Bands in his selection *'My Song of Joy'* in preparation for the 'Great Falls Festival'. Two of Charles' manuscript marches are named after Canadian corps.

Charles' Promotion to Glory in 1974 was sudden and unexpected. On his way home after a band practice he felt ill. He put his beloved trombone on a hedge for safe keeping, then collapsed and died. His contribution as an outstanding Salvation Army musician was evident, not only by the number of people who attended his funeral service, but also by the number of ordinary people who stood and paid their respect as his funeral cortege passed through the streets of Stapleford. The quote *'Servant of God, well done'*, is a fitting tribute to the man who wrote *'A Constant Friend'.*

(source; A. Stevenson)

'The Musician', of March 14, 1942 tells us:

Bandmaster Charles Dove was born of Salvationist parents and at the age of seven and a half started to learn music under the late Bandmaster Richardson at Stapleford. About a year later, when the Young People's Band was formed, he was commissioned a member. He was converted in a Young People's Meeting at the time and sought and found the Blessing of Full Salvation at the age of fifteen. Shortly after his transfer to the Senior Band, at the age of seventeen, he was made Deputy-Bandmaster. Six years later he was appointed Bandmaster, which position he has now held for ten and a half years. After studying other people's music he decided to 'do a spot of composing on my own,' to use his words. His first attempts at composition were very crude, nevertheless he managed to get a piece published when he was twenty years of age, the march, 'I'll stand for Christ.' The Bandmaster always takes a delight to Open-Air Meetings and is never happier than when 'dabbling in some kind of music either writing it, playing it, or listening to it. Strange to relate,' he says, 'I have to confess that I cannot play any musical instrument than brass.' Following is a complete list of his published compositions: 'I'll stand for Christ', 'Press Onward' and 'Boston' marches, the selections 'Coming Home' and 'Glad Tidings' which obtained third place in the 1939 Second Series Music Competition and the meditation 'The Name of Jesus' (Second Series), the selection 'Joyful Tidings' (Ordinary Series), and two quartets 'Glory and Praise' and 'Calvary' (which secured first and second prizes in the International Music Competition). In conjunction with other comrades he had the following pieces published in "The Musical Salvationist": 'All I have is Thine', 'Sunshine', 'The message of Salvation', 'Songs of the Cross', and 'With Jesus in my heart'. Both words and music of 'Peace and Satisfaction' are the compositions of the Bandmaster, who has also had published the cornet solo, 'All through the nigh', which appears in the latest Instrumental Album. The selections, 'The Cross of Jesus' (Second Series) and 'Perfect Submission' are awaiting publication. Mrs. Charles Dove, who composed the words of 'With Jesus in my Heart', which appeared in "The Musical Salvationist" in July, 1941, is the daughter of the retired Band-Sergeant Gough, of Stapleford, but was born in Catford, London. Cradled in The Army, she was enrolled Junior Soldier in the William Booth Memorial Hall, Nottingham, by Commssioner Hurren. She is a member of the soprano section of the Stapleford Songster Brigade and is also a Company Guard. Only of recent years has she attempted song-writing, and although, as she says, her songs are of simpler type, they have been written with the object of bringing blessing and cheer. Her greatest desire is to have a Salvation Song published that will be the means of leading some lost soul to Christ. Her other published songs are 'All I have is Thine', and 'Sunshine'. One or two are also awaiting approval.

Important compositions

The Seeking Heart (GS1643) 1973, The Divine Call (GS1569) 1967, Perfect Submission (GS1202) 1942, Stapleford Citadel (GS 425) 1948, A Constant Friend (US66) 1964

DOWNES, T

No information was found about this composer.

Important composition

Allegro from the Water Music

DOWNIE, KENNETH

Kenneth Downie was born in Glasgow in 1946 and educated at Greenock High School, the Royal Manchester College of Music and Durham University. He then became a specialist music teacher in schools, culminating in an appointment as head of music at Poole Grammar School, before leaving his position to move into the jewellery business in 1976. His published compositions, now numbering over 50, many of which have been recorded and broadcast on national radio, span a period of 30 years and are mainly for brass bands or songsters. Kenneth lives in Winchester with his wife Patricia, who is also a musician, teaching pianoforte and singing. Together they attend the Winchester Salvation Army Corps, where Kenneth is Bandmaster and Patricia Songster Leader. Kenneth's involvement in The Salvation Army's music scene has afforded him the opportunity to travel throughout the world as, along with Patricia, he has been involved in music schools, clinics etc. in the USA, Canada, France, Sweden and Holland. In 1999, Kenneth was honoured by the New York Staff Band, when he was selected as the featured composer for their annual 'Profile Night'. In 2001 Kenneth was appointed 'Creative Consultant' to The Salvation Army's Music Ministries Dept. in the United Kingdom, where it is anticipated that, as well as continuing to write for The Salvation Army, he will be active in encouraging and mentoring a new generation of composers.

Important compositions

The Joybringer (FS337) 1971, Through the Blood of the Lamb (FS390) 1978, Princethorpe Variations (FS473) 1989, The Pilgrims (FS536), Festive Praise (FS589) 2004, The Promised Land (JC629) 2008, Visions of Gerontius (JC630) 2008, Reverie (GS1875) 1992, Stars of the Morning (GS2072) 2009, Quiet Time (GS1887-1) 1993.

DRURY, ALBERT

Born 21 september 1908, Promoted to Glory 12 August 1992. The Drury family have served faithfully at the Norwich Citadel Corps for many years. Albert was one of five brothers who grew up in the corps and attended the Young People's Corps from around the first world war era. Lt. Colonel Florence Drury was born at Thetford in Norfolk, and grew up in the thriving corps at the historic little market town. Albert entered the Salvation Army International Training College in 1938, and Florence in 1939. Although this was affected by the outbreak of WWII, they were married in 1940. Prior to entering the Training College he was for a short time, probably no longer than a year, bandmaster at Norwich Citadel, his home corps. Albert later also served at the ITC and conducted the cadets Bands for many years. He was the Cadet's Bandmaster in 1950/51 along with Norman Bearcroft and Leslie Condon.

A brief synopsis of his Salvation Army appointments is as follows: Corps Officers at Lewes, Brighton Edward Street, Portslade, Tonbridge, all between 1940 and 1946. Then Liverpool Congress Hall, Southport and in 1948 William Booth Memorial Training College. First as a Side Officer then Field Training Officer. They were then fortunate as a family to stay in

London until 1958, following which they moved to Dundee, Scotland, as Divisional Youth Officer, 1961 to Glasgow as Divisional Youth Secretary, then promotion to Territorial Youth Secretary for Scotland before being sent to Bristol in 1967 as Divisional Commander. His final appointment was as National Youth Secretary based in London, the oldest officer to hold that position and to retire from it! After his official retirement they took on responsibility for Kettering Corps for two and a half years, moving back to Scotland to be near family in 1976.

It is unclear as to when *'Norwich Citadel'* was composed, it might have been during the time that he was the Cadet's Bandmaster at the training college. It is known however that, having submitted the march to the Music Board in London, it was rejected (according to Albert's wife, by Wilfred Kitching, later to become General). The story continues that many years later, while in Scotland, Leslie Condon approached Mrs Drury and asked if she could find the score of the march and send it to him, without Albert's knowing. This she duly did and it was subsequently published and has been played on many occasions. So also many thanks to Les Condon, a wonderful composer and true disciple of the Lord.

Of interest, Albert Drury was largely self taught, although he had won a scholarship to the City of Norwich School as a boy. It is not known how old he was when he completed his education but he was a great reader all his life and a dedicated Salvation Army Officer. It is said that he had yellow, red & blue blood in his veins!

Important composition

Norwich Citadel (GS1652) 1973

DRURY, PAUL

Paul Drury (grandson of previous composer Albert Drury) was born in Dundee, Scotland in 1967 and received his early musical education at school and at the Salvation Army. Paul studied tuba with Anthony Swainson of the BBC Scottish Symphony Orchestra for four years, becoming an Associate of the Royal College of Music aged 17 (one of the youngest tubists to achieve this award). He was also principal tuba of the National Youth Orchestra of Great Britain and principal euphonium of the National Youth Orchestra of Scotland. Whilst at school Paul also performed as a concerto soloist with the Royal Scottish National Orchestra. Paul has played with many leading bands in both the Salvation Army and contesting worlds, and for many years was Eb Bass soloist with Edinburgh Gorgie SA Band, as well as being Deputy Bandmaster from 1994-2001. Paul was also a member of the Household Troops Band in 2001-02.

Paul is well known as a composer and arranger and has had many compositions published by the Salvation Army in the General, Triumph and Unity Series, as well as the Sing to the Lord Series for Singing Companies and Songster Brigades. Paul has also been a busy composer and arranger for contesting bands and has a number of works for contesting bands available. Paul has been invited to compose works for many of the world's leading bands, including Grimethorpe Colliery Band, Carlton Main Frickley Colliery Band, Sellers International Band, Unison Kinneil Band, The New York Staff Band and the Household Troops Band of the Salvation Army, as well as being commissioned to write solos for virtuoso soloists Phillip McCann and Les Neish.

In 2003 Paul was the winner of the inaugural Longridge Composers' Forum, and his circus march *'Jubilee'* won the Best March Prize for the Sellers International Band at the 2004

Brass in Concert contest at Spennymoor. He was the composer of the title track on the 2004 recording by the International Staff Band.

In 2009, Paul was asked to arrange a piece of music for the popular singer Hayley Westenra, accompanied by the Black Dyke Band. This piece, an arrangement of *'Hine e Hine'*, received its premiere performance at the Glasgow Royal Concert Hall in May 2009.

In 2010, Paul was the winner of a competition organised by the Salvation Army in Southern California to write a march to be played at the world famous Tournament of Roses Parade in Pasadena, California, a parade watched by a live audience of 1 million on the streets of Pasadena, and a worldwide television audience of 250 million. In 2011, Paul was also commissioned by the Scottish Brass Band Association to write a march to celebrate the 10th anniversary of the popular West Lothian Festival of Brass entertainment contest.

Paul has held a number of conducting positions within the brass band fraternity, including Resident Conductor with both Kirkintilloch and Whitburn Bands and he has also appeared as conductor with the Bon Accord, Newtongrange and Bathgate bands. Paul enjoyed a very successful 3 year period as the Musical Director of the Lochgelly Band, and in March 2010 led them to the 1st Section Title at the Scottish Championships, which lead to an appearance with the band at the National Finals in Harrogate in September 2010. As well as currently being Resident Conductor with Unison Kinneil Band, in January 2010 Paul took on the leadership of the Songster Brigade at the Salvation Army Corps in Gorgie, Edinburgh.

By profession Paul is a Director of a Christian charity working with homeless and vulnerable people, is married to Fiona, a trombonist with Unison Kinneil, and has two young sons with a further child expected in November 2011.

Important compositions

Such Love (GS2046) 2006, Jubilee (GS2006) 2003

DYTHAM, EDWARD (Eddie)

Eddie Dytham's early days (1940s/50s) were at the Hendon Citadel Corps where he was the Young People's Bandleader. He was also a member of the Music Editorial Board. He was a greatly underrated musician and good Christian gentleman. Most of his life was spent in Rugby where he was the Bandmaster. His band training skills were superb. The band's fortunes wavered between being a top-notch Army band when he was fortunate enough to receive transfers into it (Rugby was a headquarters town for major electronics/design companies) but the opposite also happened when over the years bandsmen and their families moved out of the area.

During the sixties the band stabilised with some good 'corner' men but overall no 'stars'. Thanks to Eddie's skills and leadership he was able to make the band play well above themselves and maintained a creditable standard. His later years in retirement were spent at Bristol Easton Corps but his retirement and life came to a premature end when he contracted cancer. Born in 1917 and retired in Bristol to be near family, he died about 1985. Employed by the General Post Office, (which included telephones) at the Radio Station near Rugby which housed the Telephone masts which sent messages all over the world.

About 1943 he was transferred to work at Hendon and was appointed as Young People's Band leader at Hendon Corps. One of his boys was Roland Cobb, father of Steve Cobb, the current International Staff Bandmaster. Roland became Bandmaster at Hendon and Principal Cornet in the ISB for many years. Eddie was also deputy bandmaster at Rugby and studied conducting and score reading with Eric Ball. Surprisingly, when the Rugby bandmaster retired in 1945, Eddie was appointed bandmaster although he still worked in Hendon 80 miles away. He travelled up from Hendon every week for Band practice and also nearly every weekend. He was transferred back to Rugby in 1946 but continued to study with Eric Ball. Naturally they played a lot of Eric's compositions. John Hynd was appointed as his Deputy in 1951 and for 12 years until he went to Zambia, learned most of his conducting and interpretation skills from Eddie. He had a well deserved reputation as a very good band trainer and was invited to many Salvation Army Music Schools. He was John's close friend and mentor. He taught him harmony and encouraged him to consider teaching. He was a very good pianist and accompanied John many times when he played solos. He led the Rugby Citadel Band on two overseas tours of Denmark. The first in 1949 was the first band to tour Denmark after the 2nd World War and broadcast in the presence of the Queen of Denmark. In 1970 Eddie did a Teacher training course at Birmingham University specializing in Music. He was then appointed to the Music Department at Rugby School, but continued to be the Corps bandmaster and Corps pianist. He retired in Bristol to be near his family and studied with Open University for a Music Degree. He died around 1985.

Bandmaster Ralph Pearce recalls: *'Edward Dytham was the Bandmaster of the Rugby Citadel Band. I played in this band during the year my father was the Corps Officer. A consummate musician the sad fact is that he did not contribute more. The two publications would have been produced when he was in his 20's. During meetings his piano preludes and offertories were wonders of creativity. Some of us would ask if he could put them down on paper but he would claim that they were of the moment and as such were gone. If only cassette or digital recorders were around!*

As a bandmaster his was a gentlemanly approach but his style of man-management produced high level results. The band, which at the time played at a very high level- touring Norway, was always very musical and refined – rough playing was the one thing likely to cause him to anger! I recall one rehearsal of Eric Ball's 'The Old Wells' where the cornets played rather too loud in the final variation. Rather than being chastised, Ted the Red, as he was affectionately known, asked them for more - again and again - until they could give no more. That was the end of the matter and the bad play was never repeated.

His ear for detail was phenomenal. Once during a long Easter Weekend in Leeds where we finished up on the Monday with a massed band event, he had the second cornet striking with fear as he told which of them had played a wrong note, what the note played was and what it should be. We of the Rugby Band smiled in sympathy – we had been there.

It was a privilege to know him and play under his leadership and listen to his piano magic. One of his chord progressions remained in my mind and I have used it since - where? - I'll never tell!'

Important compositions

Happy Song (GS1326) 1950, Only Thee (GS1291-2) 1947

EBBS, H(AROLD/HARRY?)

One of the early composers (late 1800, early 1900). He was an early Salvation Army officer (Adjutant at the time of the publishing of his compositions) and might have been related to the next composer, William Ebbs, although this could not be confirmed. No further information could be retrieved about him.

Important compositions

The Soldier (GS0607) 1910, Over life's Ocean (GS0310) 1896

EBBS, WILLIAM ALEXANDER

William Alexander Ebbs, born on 20 September 1890, was a son of early-day Officers (major William Alfred Ebbs and Jessie Parker Ebbs), Commissioner Ebbs became a bandsman in his teens in Cambridge and after serving as an office boy and shorthand typist at International Headquarters, was commissioned an officer from Wandsworth in 1908, only eighteen years of age. After corps, divisional and National Headquarters responsibilities, 1919 saw the first of his many overseas appointments. In France he served as Divisional Commander, in Belgium he was A.D.C to the Territorial Commander, in Italy he commanded the Territory for five years. Following membership of the Army's first High Council he commanded three Divisions in the USA until appointment Chief Secretary in charge of the Australia Eastern Territory. Duties as Director of the British Red Shield Services preceded his command of the South Africa Territory and in 1950, responsibilities as Editor in Chief and Literary Secretary International Headquarters. Two years later he became Secretary of the Public Relations Department and for Parliamentary and Migration Affairs. He took up his last appointment as Secretary for Trade in 1956. He was the Army's representative on the Central Committee of the World Council of Churches and Chairman of the Advisory Council to the General. All in all he was a Salvation Army officer for fifty-two years.

It has been said that he was a man of *'artistic conceptions, a musician, and a lover of the arts'.* William Alexander Ebbs, or Wm Alex Ebbs as he was known, was Promoted to Glory on 22 August 1960.

Important composition

Lord, Speak Once Again (GS0329)

EDMONDS, DAVID

David Edmonds was born in November 1982 in Colchester, England. He grew up in the Salvation Army and is currently soldering at the Dunstable Corps where he lead the worship group playing piano and keyboard and in the Young People's Band. He grew up playing the Cornet and got involved in all kinds of music events as a youngster. As he got older, he had a go writing music and got his 1st publication at the age of 21 in the Scripture Based Hymns *('In the tomb so cold').* After plenty of coaching and support from Kenneth Downie, Andrew Blyth and the Music Ministries Unit, he developed his skills and has had music published every year since in the 'Sing to the Lord Children's Voice Series', 'General Series' and 'Unity Series'. David has continued to play and develop as a musician and now plays principal cornet for his corps band, the divisional youth band and 2nd cornet in the Salvation Army's Household Troops band. He continues to write, play and arrange for the glory of God and *'thank Him for the gift he has given and to be able to help others to find Him through his music and his outward sign of love for the Lord'.* He is also a secondary music teacher and his degree was in music composition and technology. David Edmonds studied at the University of Hertfordshire.

Important compositions

A Christmas Mambo (US0323) 2006, Exalted! (GS2063) 2008, In His time (US0356) 2009, A Traditional Christmas (US0347) 2008

EDWARDS, ALICE GEORGINA (née PURDUE)

The composer of the piece mentioned below is likely Alice Edwards, but this is not hundred percent confirmable. Alice was born on 25 October 1878 as Alice Georgina Purdue. Only four years later the whole family moved on to Notting Hill, where she became a convert at the Salvation Army, age twelve. Besides playing the cornet, she was equally at home on the piano and mandolin. For a time she was the pianist of a musical group which was led by Richard Slater, however her profession was music teacher. In 1896 she entered the Training College to become a Salvation Army officer. In 1899 she married to Robert W. Edwards, who also was an officer. After several corps appointments including Birmingham Citadel and Portsmouth Citadel, they were appointed to the Public Relations Bureau in 1925. They retired from active service in 1932. Alice Edwards was Promoted to Glory on 22 October 1958, age eighty.

Important composition

The Lord will be gracious (GS0294-2) 1895

EDWARDS, ERNEST WALTER.

Ernest Edwards was born in 1912 and was Promoted to Glory in 2002 when he was 90. In 1938, Ernest Edwards accepted the position of bandmaster of the Tottenham Citadel Band after the sudden deaths of Bandmaster Dockray and Songster Leader Jackson in the same week, and rapidly gained the respect of the band through his unstinting service and dynamic personality. He was to lead the band for 16 memorable years. In April 1954 the band toured Holland and upon its return Bandmaster Edwards retired from the key position. At that point, he transferred to Wood Green (where he became Songster Leader) and several months later he was succeeded as Bandmaster of the Tottenham Citadel Band by the then Captain Ray Steadman-Allen. Edwards, was the son of the late bandmaster Edwards of the Tunbridge Wells Corps Band. Ernest Edwards had achieved the L.R.A.M. and A.R.C.M. diplomas.

Walter Ernest William Edwards, L.A.R.M., A.R.C.M., bandsman of Tunbridge Wells, Pianist, piano-accordionist, trombonist, organist etc. Son of the Bandmaster. Brothers are also versatile instrumentalists, Norman playing xylophone, violin, marimba, and tenor horn, and Percy the piano, organ, xylophone, and flugelhorn. Ernest Edwards originally played trombone in Tunbridge Wells Band, of which he was Deputy Bandmaster when sixteen years of age. He transferred to Tunbridge Wells eight years ago. Whilst Ernest had received music lessons at school, he did not start to study the subject seriously until he was eighteen years of age, when he commenced under Mr. E.R. Miller, F.R.C.O., for organ, pianoforte, and theory. He pursued his studies at the Royal Academy of Music under Professor B. Knott, F.R.A.M., for pianoforte. Our comrade's enthusiasm is evidenced in that he made a journey of sixty miles for every lesson. Most of his studies have, within recent years, been made in the train whilst travelling the thirty miles to and from London officer of an insurance company, where he is well known to his colleagues as a Salvationist-musician. He persevered with such success that in 1935 he secured his L.R.A.M. and A.R.C.M. diplomas at the first attempt, and, as far as con be ascertained, is still the only Salvationist to have secured both distinctions. Described as a young composer showing great promise, his published pieces include, *'Behold, God is my Salvation'* ('The Musical Salvationist') and 'The Great Review' (Instrumental Album). ('The Musician' 1-1-1938)

Important composition

Forward to Victory (TS0479) 1952

ELGAR, EDGAR

Edgar Elgar was not a Salvationist nor in any way related to the Salvation Army as such. He was however one of the greatest composers in the English history and wrote phenomenal music. Sir Edward William Elgar (2 June 1857 – 23 February 1934) was an English composer, many of whose works have entered the British and international classical concert repertoire. Among his best-known compositions are orchestral works including the *'Enigma Variations'* and the *'Pomp and Circumstance Marches'*. His music inspired Salvation Army composers and arrangers to use it for Army purposes and they started to transcribe and arrange his music for use within brass bands. His *'Pomp and Circumstance No.2'* was skilfully arranged by James Wright, bandmaster of the Sheffield Citadel Band, while his beautiful *'Nimrod'*, which was taken of his probably most famous work, the *'Enigma Variations'* was arranged by Dean Goffin, another noted composer who could claim the title 'Sir'.

A remarkable thing happened when Dr. Clement C. Palmer, organist and conductor of the choir of the Canterbury Cathedral heard Eric Ball's *'The Old Wells'* played by a Salvation Army band. Dr Palmer sent the score to his friend, Sir Edgar Elgar. He then made the effort so send a letter with compliments to the composer, Eric Ball.

Although not a Salvation Army band, the world famous Black Dyke Band did a complete recording with music of Sir Edward Elgar (Classical Dyke vol.1 'Elgar').

Important compositions

Enigma Variations, Severn Suite Opus 87

ELLIS, J

Very little is known about J. Ellis. He is the composer of the hymn tune *'O Boundless Salvation'*, which has appeared in the 1900 Band Music No.1, in the brass tune book (BTB) accompaniment to the songbook of 1899 by the Salvation Army.

Important compositions

The Founder's Hymn

ELLOWAY, KENNETH

Kenneth (Albert) Elloway. Conductor, teacher, born in Weymouth, England, 17 Jan 1916, died in Halifax, Nova Scotia, 22 Sep 1980; ARCM 1943. He first played cornet and later took up the trombone and string bass. He graduated in 1945 from the RMSM (Kneller Hall). In 1950 he passed the school's advanced examination for military bandmasters. Following a career with British military orchestras and bands, Elloway moved to Halifax in 1955 as music director of the Royal Canadian Artillery Band and became inspector of bands for the Canadian Army Eastern Command. He frequently guest-conducted the Halifax Symphony Orchestra, adjudicated at music festivals across Canada, and lectured at Mount Saint Vincent University, Halifax. Retiring from the army in 1965, he moved to Toronto as head of music at Emery Collegiate Institute. He returned to Halifax in 1966 as conductor of the CBC Halifax Chamber Orchestra (formerly the CBC Halifax Strings). He was acting director 1959-65 and director 1966-70 of the Maritime Conservatory of Music and was associate conductor 1967-8 of the Halifax SO. He guest-conducted the Halifax Wind Ensemble, the Atlantic Symphony Orchestra (in concert and on the recording CBC SM-215), and the Edmonton Symphony Orchestra. Elloway became co-ordinator of instrumental music for Dartmouth schools in 1969, music director of the Dartmouth Choral Society in 1971, and the founding conductor of the Chebucto Orchestra in 1975. He taught at Dalhousie University from 1974 until his death.

(Author: Jack Kopstein)

'Bandsman Kenneth Elloway son of Bandmaster and Mrs. A. Elloway was the solo cornet player on Weymouth Band before enlisting in the Band of the 2nd Battalion Dorsett Regiment, at the age of sixteen. A year later he became the solo euphoniumist, and started to learn the string bass. From 1936-38 he attended a Pupil's Course at the Royal Military School of Music, Kneller Hall, and whole there gained several prizes in the annual competitions. These included a certificate for euphonium playing, a bronze medal for annual training, and prizes for string bass playing and harmony. During this period Kenneth Elloway enjoyed a happy association with Southall Citadel Band. When war broke out he was Band Corporal of the Dorset Regimental Band, and after the first year of the war became Band Sergeant of the newly-formed Dorset Regimental L.T.C. Band. In 1942 he was called back to the wartime Royal Military School of Music, to start on the three-year Bandmasters' Course. He is now a member of the famous Kneller Hall Band, playing BBb bass and string bass. A few months ago he took the Royal College of Music examination for Military Band Conducting, and is, we believe, the first Salvationist to gain the A.R.C.M. diploma for Military Bandmastership. With Mrs. Elloway and two-year-old Mary, he is at present associated with Aldershot Corps, where he is the temporary Songster-Leader. Our comrade has had a number of songs published in "The Musical Salvationist'.'' ('The Musician' 31-7-1943)

Important compositions

Athens Red Shield (GS1397) 1954, Greensleeves (GS1565-2) 1966, Halifax Young People (CM0021) 1958, Weymouth Citadel (GS1300) 1948, Weymouth Young People (TS0408) 1947, Wonderful love (TS0367) 1944

ERZBERGER, WILLI

Willi Erzberger was born on 28th of November 1940, in Thalwil near Zurich, Switzerland, and is the eldest of four sons of Salvation Army Officers. He played cornet in several bands at corps where his parents served as Officers. Since 1959 he is a member of the Zurich Central Hall Band where he was the Principal Cornet for over fourty years.

From 1960 to 1964 he served as Young People's Band Leader, and from 1964 to 2001 he was the Deputy Bandmaster and during this time he also served, from 1972 to 1991, as Bandmaster of the Divisional Youth Band of Zurich (DJM). From 1985 to 1991 he was a member of the National Band of the Salvation Army in Switzerland 'Brass of Praise', where his youngest brother Ernst Erzberger (a former bandmaster of the Salvation Army in Basel) was the Bandmaster.

In 1986 he started to collect numbers and titles of Salvation Army Music from over the whole world, to compile an Instrumental Music Index. Later, after an idea of Colonel Ray Bowes, he began to compile the Salvation Army Composers Dictionary.

Important compositions

Flugel Horn Solo - A Prayer, Hymn Tune Arrangement - Saints of God, March - DJM Zürich* (Divisions Jugend Musikkorps), March - Keep in Step, March - Revival (J.P.Sousa, arr. W.E.), Instrumental Quartet – Sandon

** This march was written for the Divisional Youth Band Zurich (DJM = Divisions Jugend Musikkorps), where Willi was the Bandmaster from 1972 to 1992. Well known melodies out of the 'Zurich Niederdorf Opera' (a story about Zurich) are included. In sections D and F we hear the song, the Salvation Army sings in a pub (in this opera). The march finish with few bars of a well known melody that is very popular to hear every year on the 'Spring Festival' in Zurich when they 'burn the winter'.*

EUNSON, JEREMIAH

Jeremiah Eunson was an early Salvationist in Australia. He was the first bandmaster of the Melbourne Staff Band, which started to function officially in 1890. Jeremiah was born in the United Kingdom and had played in William Booth's meetings in England. Soon after his emigration to 'Down Under' he joined the Salvation Army and taught new Salvationists how to play a brass instrument. When composing is concerned, no titles are known but from what he wrote it is known that he wrote the parts out by hand, with his cornet on the same table. Taking it up when necessary to try out what he just had written.

EUSTACE, G

One of the early composers (late 1800, early 1900).

No further information could be retrieved about him.

Important compositions

Dash on, ye waves (GS0398) 1900, The march to Bethlehem (GS0298) 1895, The message of the Bells (GS0438-2) 1903

EVANS, HOWARD (USA)

Lt.-Colonel Howard Evans was raised in what could probably be considered a traditional Corps. His father was the Corps Sergeant Major and his mother the Home League Secretary. There was also the Corps Band and Songsters, with a tutoring program for beginners on brass instruments. He played first in the beginners band before becoming a member of the Senior Band. His musical training in the Corps became very important when he joined the United States Navy - especially since he was chosen as the Company Bugler and therefore played the drills on the bugle as the rest of his Company did their physical exercises! After being discharged from the service Howard returned home again to attend University and also took his place in the Corps Band.

The year 1948-49 was undoubtedly the most significant year of his life. He moved to New York City to serve as the Divisional Music Instructor for the Greater New York Division. He was also given the opportunity to play Eb Tuba in the New York Staff Band (incidentally his son-in-law Ron Waiksnoris is now the New York Staff Bandmaster). Howard attended the Tremont Corps in New York City and served as the Corps Bandmaster. In addition he had the opportunity of meeting every week with Erik Leidzén, whose tutoring in music and philosophy was of inestimable value.

Howard had already done some arranging and composing, and meeting with Mr. Leidzén provided the opportunity to refine what he had already done as well as attempt more creative efforts. Out of this came the march *'Tremont'* with the theme *'I'm living on the mountain'* and named to recognize the historic New York City Corps where he was serving as the bandmaster.

It was also at this time that he wrote the cornet trio *'Sweetest Name'* with the very familiar chorus as the theme. It was suggested that this should be submitted to the International Music Board for publication consideration. However, Brigadier Richard Holtz was the Music Secretary for the United States Eastern Territory and had established what is commonly referred to as the 'Yellow Book Series'. He asked Howard to consider letting him publish the cornet trio in that series to provide some repertoire variety. Needless to say, he yielded to his friend Dick Holtz's request, although it meant combining two of the variations into one to meet publication restrictions.

For many years the Friday Evening at the Temple series meetings in New York City were held every week from October to May with very few exceptions. The New York Staff Band and Temple Chorus were on duty for almost every meeting. The usual platform arrangement meant that the tuba section of the band was directly in front of the first row of the Temple Chorus. In that front row was a beautiful soprano soloist named Betty Valentine. It didn't take long for a friendship to develop between a young tuba player in the back row of the band and the beautiful soloist in the front row of the chorus.

However, there was one serious problem, the young lady was an accepted candidate! Howard's hidden thoughts of such a commitment for him soon had to be revealed and they were married at the end of that Summer before returning to University. Although Betty worked that year for the Corps Officer, Howard enhanced his veterans student income by teaching students who bought brass instruments from a local store.

A year later they left for the New York Officers Training College, along with a perspective New York Staff Band trombone soloist, Lindsay, their son, who at the time was four months old. Since then they have made further contributions to the music and arts programs of The Salvation Army through, Craig, Carolee (married to the Staff Bandmaster) and Ian in the Territorial Arts Ministry Program.

Through the years they have encouraged others through their Corps ministry, divisional leadership appointments and the training college to consider music in every form as an offering to God, and to give the very best whether writing, performing or listening to music.

Important composition

Sweetest Name (AJ028) 1954

EVANS, HOWARD (UK)

Howard Evans was born on March 15th 1958 in England. He has a well-established musical career as a pianist, music teacher, conductor as well as composer. This began with a varied musical education, commencing with brass at the age of seven. By the time he was ten, he was also studying the piano, together with the French horn and the cello. He later graduated with a Mus.B (Hons) degree from the University of Manchester, and also obtained LRAM, LTC and ARCM (Hons) diplomas in piano teaching and performing, as well as brass teaching. In 1982 Howard entered the International Training College and become an Officer of the Salvation Army in 1988. He served as 'National Bandmaster' of the Salvation Army in England, and later as Bandmaster of the Amsterdam Staff Band in the

Netherlands. He finished his career as an Officer and became in April 2002 Bandmaster of the Boscombe Citadel Band of the Salvation Army.

Important compositions

Starlights (FS502) 1993, Elegiac Variations (FS524) 1996, Chassidic Dance (FS588) 2004.

EVJA, MORGAN

Born on December 16, 1948 to officer parents in the Norwegian Salvation Army. As a child Morgan attended as a soprano the Norwegian Broadcasting Corp. Boys Choir, a professional choir used for the Corp. plus singing in funerals, weddings and Christmas concerts. Here he learned to appreciate vocal music, classical and modern. Learned also to read music and group discipline. He had also classical piano lessons for about six years. However he got bored in the long run and dropped out at the age of twelve. Morgan became a Salvationist in the Salvation Army when he was sixteen years old and attended the Band in the Oslo Temple Corps, playing trombone.

As teenager he became interested in contemporary pop music, particularly The Beatles, Rolling stones and others. Played along with their records on piano, bass guitar and acoustic guitar. He learned to play the (bass) guitar and was involved in the first Norwegian Army pop group, called 'The S-Team', inspired on the British 'Joystrings'. He later joined also other Christian pop groups within the Salvation Army where he played mostly bass guitar, but also piano and acoustic guitar.

In 1972 he started studies at the University of Oslo with music and English. He finished this in 1979 with a Masters Degree in Music, much concentrated in the fields of composing and arranging contemporary music, jazz and choral music. Additional courses were followed in music production. Classical guitar and trombone as main instruments. English studies ended with a Bachelor Degree.

Morgan was asked in 1979 to build and be responsible for a music studio, run by the Territorial Headquarters. He has since then arranged, produced and engineered approximately 200 albums for Army and non-Army customers in the Salvation Army-studio. He has also played the piano in several sessions and has also been responsible for the maintenance of the technical gear. All together for more than 30 years. In addition to this full time job Morgan has also worked at the THQ (Music Editorial Department) as arranger, composer, proof-reading music etc.

He is active (technical) and responsible in the Oslo Temple Choir for all the sound and also plays the piano on demand in the corps. Morgan Evja is currently a Music Adviser for the Salvation Army in Norway and the Faroe Islands.

Important composition

Happy Juniors *[Glade Juniorer]* (NMSJ23)

FAIRBAIRN, W

One of the early composers (late 1800, early 1900).

No further information could be retrieved about him.

Important composition

Forward March (GS0282) 1895

FARRINGTON, H

One of the early composers (late 1800, early 1900).

No further information could be retrieved about him.

Important composition

A Sinner's resolve (GS0680) 1913

FELTWELL, IAN

Ian was born in Nuneaton (UK) in 1966 where he still lives, and he worships at Nuneaton Citadel Corps. He plays euphonium in the band and since 2006, has also been the Songster Leader. In the past he has also been the YP Band Leader and 13+ leader in the Sunday School. Ian is a 4th generation Salvationist and music has been an important part of his life. He started composing relatively late in life, inspired to do so by the playing of the Melbourne Staff Band at the Gospel Arts Festival, at the Royal Albert Hall in 2001, in particular, their playing of *'Exaltation'*, written by his close friend and Bandmaster at Nuneaton, Andrew Mackereth. The piece was inspired by Psalm 92, with the central theme 'great is the Lord and worthy to be praised'. He said that *'God spoke to me so strongly that day, and I knew that composing was something I was being called to do, to help me be a more effective Christian'*.

Whilst he has had no formal training, Ian has worked hard to develop his talent as a composer, and has been fortunate enough to have several pieces of music (both brass and vocal) published, and has never lost his desire to produce music to the best of his ability for the glory of God. Ian loves the way the God can use music to bless and inspire people all over the world and never ceases to be amazed at the way God can touch the hearts of those that hear music. To date Ian has had the following pieces of music published by the Salvation Army:

Vocal: *'Peter, James & John'* (Male Voices), *'He's Standing Here'* (Female Voices), *'God is Love'* – *'Sing to the Lord'* (Mixed Voices)

Brass: *'Reasons Why'* – General Series (recorded on the Melbourne Staff band's 'Fiesta' CD), *'We Saw Love'* - General Series, *'Great Big God'* – Unity Series, 'Kids *Alive'* – Unity Series

Also recorded but not yet published: *'Full Surrender'* (recorded on the Melbourne Staff Band's *'Battle Ready'* CD)

Important composition

We saw love (GS2068) 2008

FISHER, IRWIN LEROY

Born July 5, 1903 in Iowa City, Iowa, died in Wilmette, Illinois May 7, 1977. Although not a Salvationist, Irwin wrote several pieces for the Salvation Army while being a guest conductor at Central Institute of Music (CMI).

In 1942 Colonel Harry Otway, of The Salvation Army, came to The American Conservatory to study composition with Irwin. Otway was Music Director for the eleven central states in the Army and in charge of their top music camp – The Central Music Institute – at Wonderland Camp, Camp Lake, Wisconsin. Otway invited Irwin to be a special guest faculty at the ten day Institute that year. This happy arrangement lasted for thirty two years. Features of the camp were his faculty-band readings of transcriptions of the music of the masters always under Irwin's baton. Irwin never charged for his services or for his expenses in all those years. It was among the most beloved of all of his activities in life. His family was always invited and often attended, enriching the experience for all, which enthralled the campers for years. Irwin was profoundly respected by all, and adored by those he touched at CMI. In the early 1950's he wrote an unusual, descriptive march, '*Wonderland Camp*' for the faculty band. It became an annual feature of the Institute. The piece features a theme based on the tritone, because of the 'wonder' of the interval. It may well be the world's first use of a muted alto horn, which opens the march on the augmented fourth, answered by flugelhorn, cornet and finally soprano cornet, each entrance higher than the last. The effect was to represent the sun rising over the camp, reflecting on the lake. As the sun is finally up, the activity of the camp is represented by the non-stop thematic energy. This non-typical march ends with a majestic group of chords representing the joy and love Irwin felt for each person there. It is a masterpiece of scoring and innovation.

In 1970, the Bandmaster of the Massachusetts Salvation Army Cambridge Citadel Silver Band commissioned Irwin to write a major piece for our band. The bandmaster said *'I told him of the strengths of each player and offered other ideas for the piece. The result was a wondrous and, in the words of musicologist Edith Borroff, 'Most Majestic!' meditation, The Strength Of God's Love. It is a big work that will test the endurance of any band, which effort will be reward to any who persevere. It features Praise To The Lord The Almighty in addition to a rich mix of original material. At one point, if the acoustics are just right, one of Irwin's original themes emerges due entirely to overtones. The piece has received very few readings due to its difficulties, and the Cambridge band no longer exists.'*

On the evening of May 5, 1977, while seated at his work-table working on what was to be his Second Piano Concerto, he peacefully fell into his final sleep. His memorial service featured tapes of Jean Hayden and Alan Rogers singing some of Irwin's sacred songs, accompanied by the master himself at the organ.

It was a long, challenging and satisfying career, but much more it was a personal ministry in music and life that touched thousands of lives, making them better in the process. Irwin was a rare talent and an even rarer man who served God in everything he did from being a father and husband and friend to performing to composing to teaching .

(source: injofferings.com, used by permission from Robert Getz)

Important compositions

Wonderland Camp, The Strength Of God's Love

FLETCHER, A

A former bandmaster of the Rock Ferry Corps Band. No more information about this composer could be found.

Important compositions

Rock of ages (TS0191) 1933, Soldiers true (TS0165) 1931

FLETCHER, WALTER JAMES

Walter Fletcher was born on 22 May 1905 and Promoted to Glory on 10 April 1988. He was an officer eventually with the rank of Brigadier. Apart from his corps appointments, he worked for the Salvation Army Assurance Society in the Liverpool District, but also held International Headquarters appointments. He retired from active service in 1975. Walter Fletcher whose family originated in Ripley and his father Francis Fletcher was the Bandmaster at Ripley before moving to Rossington. When a Captain, Walter Fletcher composed the '*Rossington*' march.

Important composition

The Irish Salvationist (GS1645) 1973

FOOTE, JOSEPH

A Newspaper of 11 February 1933 says:

'Brigadier Joseph Foote (1860), who died on Thursday night, was one of the oldest officers of the Salvation Army. He was 73 years of age. He helped to lay the foundations of the Salvation Army's work in many parts of England. He was one of the party of officers which began the work of the Salvation Army in India. After completing 44 years of continuous service he settled in Sydney at Dulwich Hill. The funeral took place at Rookwood Cemetery, following a service conducted at 1.45 p.m. at the Dulwich Hill Citadel by Commissioner William McKenzie'.

Important composition

Let the waves wash me (GS0366-2) 1898

FOWLER, W

One of the early composers (late 1800, early 1900).

No further information could be retrieved about him.

Important composition

The Heavenly pilot (GS0409) 1901

FRANCIS, LES

His grandfather was a Palmerston North Salvation Army bandsman in the 1880s. His father, Bill Francis, was a champion soprano cornet player from Wanganui Garrison Band (non-SA band). Les learned cornet from his father and commenced contesting in the Nelson Garrison Band in 1920. He started conducting in 1930 in Westport then Greymouth with B-grade bands. In 1937 he conducted A-grade band St Kilda (Dunedin) for eleven years. He competed in nineteen New Zealand contests winning seven championships. During WWII he conducted the Burnham Camp Band until 1943 when Norman Goffin (Dean Goffin's older brother) took command. Francis graduated Bachelor of Music from Otago University in 1942 and taught music at King's High School, Dunedin and Palmerston North Boys High School. He retired from conducting in 1966.

Important composition

Hawera (NZBBJ 11)

FREEH, MARK

A son of Salvation Army officers, Mark Freeh, born on August 22, 1939 in Newburgh, New York has been involved with brass music since a very early age. He studied tuba with William Bell of the New York Philharmonic while attending Manhattan School of Music and for two years studied arranging with Erik Leidzén. When eighteen years of age, he moved to New York to play tuba and bass trombone with the New York Staff Band for the next eight years and spent two years traveling throughout Central and South America performing with a United States Army Band.

As the conductor and founder of the Manhattan Brass Choir, he recorded with Clark Terry and Urbie Green for A.B.C. Records. At that time, Mark also conducted the MBC at Radio City Music Hall and at Carnegie Hall sharing the stage with Duke Ellington. Involved in the studio recording business in New York City for over thirty years, he received Gold and Platinum records for Billy Joel's *'Innocent Man,' 'The Bridge,'* and Chaka Khan's *'I Feel for You.'* During this time, a project, *'Sundae in New York'* received an Oscar for Best Animated Film in 1984. Also he designed and built seven recording studios.

As a recording engineer, he has recorded albums with Philip Smith, Kirk Nurock, Pendel Brass, Santa Ana Corps Band, The Bones of Contention and several with the New York Staff Band. In addition, he produced two CDs, *'Pittsburgh On Parade'* and *'Footlifters'* for River City Brass Band and 'FREEH-WAY' with Bramwell Tovey and the G.U.S. Band. Mark Freeh has taught at Star Lake Music Camp, the New School of Social Research in New York City and conducted special brass classes at Brooklyn College. In addition, he was on the faculty of Manhattan School of Music for 11 years and the arranging staff of Warner Bros. He has arranged over 160 pieces for brass band and several hundred more for different size brass ensembles.

Mark Freeh has arranged for the following:

Philip Smith, David Daws, Steven Mead, Warren Vache, Roger Webster, Trevor Groom, Chris Jaudes, Brian Grant, James Morrison, Patrick Sheridan, James Shepherd's Versatile Brass, Canadian Brass, New York Philharmonic Brass, Milwaukee Symphony, Norfolk Symphony, Manhattan Brass Choir, River City Brass Band, Brass Band of Battle Creek, G.U.S. Band, Imperial Brass, New York Staff Band, Halle Brass, Augustana Brass Choir, Brooklyn College Brass Ensemble, N.Y Electric Chamber Ensemble, Orchestra by the Sea, Warner Bros. Publications, Crabtree Music Publishers, The Salvation Army – USA, Eastern Territory Music Publications

Although he has his most of output published outside the Salvation Army, he is of significant importance when Salvation Army music is concerned, not at least because of his famous cornet solo, which is published in the American Band Journal, '*What a Friend*', which is recorded, amongst others, by former New York Staff Bandsman, and current principal trumpet of the New York Philharmonic Orchestra, Philip Smith. In 1991 Mark, together with two friends, founded the Imperial Brass (band) in New Jersey. One of the legendary recordings they made with this band include *Bone-A-Fide Brass*, featuring New York Philharmonic Principal Trombonist Joseph Alessi. Amongst others are some Salvation Army tracks including *'Someone Cares'* and *'Home on the Range'*.

Together with Robert E. Richardson, Mark was the founder of '*The Enthusiast*', a brass band news magazine. Some information from one issue is published elsewhere in this book (see: Erik Leidzén).

Mark, as a composer and performer, was highly influenced in his life by people like Erik Leidzén, Johnny Richards, Derek Smith and Richard Holz.

Important composition

What a friend (AJ131) 1985

FREEMAN BLACK, T

One of the first Salvationist-musicians to apply himself to diligent study was Dr. T. Freeman Black. Appointed Bandmaster at Sheffield Citadel at twenty-one, he sought to equip himself for the task of directing thirty-eight bandsmen and in the years 1908, 1910 and 1911 took senior honours at the Trinity College of Music in London, the certificates of the Royal Academy and Royal College of Music for advanced harmony and counterpoint, and the diplomas of A.Mus L.C.M and A.Mus., B.C.M., London. He was the composer of the march *'Sheffield'* amongst others. When the family moved to Scotland, he became Bandmaster at Dundee II Corps (now Dundee Central). When his widowed mother was taken suddenly ill and died the same day, Black, then a lad, was so distressed at not being able to help her that he resolved to study medicine and become a doctor. Whilst employed on the engineering staff of the Dundee Water Works he gave up every available moment of his spare time to his studies.

In 1915 Bandmaster Black answered the call for skilled engineers to help the war effort and upon demobilization in 1919 lost no time in continuing his medical education, qualifying as a physician and surgeon in the summer of 1923, three months under the prescribed minimum time. The bandmaster later devoted much time and study to dental surgery, gaining expert knowledge which qualified him to advise Salvation Army bandsmen in securing dentures that would enable them effectively to continue their playing. This advice came in for great demand and a series of articles on the subject, with diagrams, which were first published in 'The Bandsman and Songster' in 1932, has been reprinted in booklet form. Dentists have expressed admiration of the Bandmaster's prescription. Bandmaster Black's interest in musical affairs was by no means over in 1934, when he added to his F.T.C.L. diploma for cornet playing that of L.G.S.M. (Bandmaster), a newly founded examination of the Guildhall School of Music for brass band conducting. Many Salvationists followed the Bandmaster's example/ When he was Promoted to Glory in 1941 the letters M.B., Ch.B., F.T.C.L., L.G.S.M. and M.R.S.T. could be added to his name.

(source: Play the music, play! Page 213-214)

FREI, MARKUS

Salvationist from Bern, Switzerland, Markus (21 July 1970) works for the Music and Gospel Arts at Territorial Headquarters in Switzerland. Analumni of the Swiss Jazz School. Markus' speciality is certainly not the 'old school' Salvation Army brass music, but exploring new ways to provide the Army of good material to attract more people who are not familiar with brass band music. As a result of this, the Swiss Staff Band 'Brass of Praise' recorded a full CD with this music entitled 'Connect', in 2007.

Markus Frei was born in 1970 Frauenfeld, Switzerland and is the son of Werner Frei (1940) and Paula Frei (1936), Salvation Army Officers who retired in 2005 as Commissioners. As an Officer's son, Markus moved to several places in Switzerland which included Frauenfeld, Amriswil, Basel, Langnaund and Bern. At the age of eight he started to play he cornet nd received lessons in the Corps where he was at that time. At the age of ten he started to play piano nd got private lessons and attended music school. The period 1986-1989 brought him in contact with synthesizer keyboards. During this time he also relinquished his brass instrument for the benefit of the piano. In 1993 Markus started to work in the Music

Department of the Salvation Army in Bern in the 'Contemporary Music' area and only one year later he begun studies at the 'Academy of Contemporary Music' in Zürich. After 2003 he worked as Project-Leader for The Salvation Army Music & Gospel Arts as well as freelance musician, and has credits for about 25 CDs and uncounted concerts.

Important compositions

Warm up, He is able, The Gift, 007 Light, Open your Eyes, Connect, King, Little Sunshine in Switzerland, Love can build a Bridge, Marching onward 2007, Deep Gratitude

FRENCH, EDWARD

Little is known about Edward French. Edward, whose nickname was 'Teddy', but he was a bandsman at the Sydney Congress Hall Corps in the 1930's. Edward composed a march and named it *'Sydney Congress Hall No.1'*. He sent it off to London for possible publication approval. They looked at it and said it was a good march and they would publish it, however they did not like the name so they did re-name it *'Army Legions'*.

Unfortunately during WWII the place in London where the music was kept was bombed and the original score was lost. After the War a second score and parts were given to Ted Bamford so that the Rockdale Salvation Army Band (Conducted by Bandmaster George Dickens) could play it. After a few months Ted asked when would they be playing the march *'Army Legions'*, which was the new title of the march, after which George Dickens told him he didn't know anything about it. It was then that Ted realized that he must have left it in the train and that was the last it was ever heard of.

Important composition

Freedom from Sin (GS1044) 1932

FRISTRUP, KRISTIAN

Kristian M Fristrup, was born 1887 in Denmark and died in 1947. He was an officer of the Salvation Army, song writer and composer. Fristrup was trained as an officer of the Salvation Army school in Chicago in 1908. He worked as a music instructor in the Central Territory of the United States. He also worked for a time in America's Western Territory, where he was an officer at various Swedish corps. He was also editor of 'The Young Soldier', Trade Secretary and Divisonal Officer for two divisions. He also worked for a time in Honolulu, Hawaii. From 1935 until 1942 he was head of the Salvation Army's music department in Sweden.

Important compositions

Even me (FS066) 1931, General Evangeline Booth (FM0201) 1936

FRODEN, RUNE

Rune Frödèn was born in Sweden and became officer of the Salvation Army. After several years as corps officer, Rune became National Music Secretary for Sweden and served on the Headquarters in Stockholm. After his time at National Headquarters he became a headmaster of the Solna Music School.

Important compositions

O, jag vet ej en van lik Jesus (FM0304-2) 1960, Kommen, I herdar (FM0306) 1960

FRÖDIN, KNUT ANDERS ERIC

Eric Frödin was Bandmaster of the Karlstad Corps Band for some years. He was born on 18 April 1909 in Karlstad and Promoted to Glory 30 July 1970, also in Karlstad. On 9 april 1938 he married Wivi Elisabeth.

Important compositions

Segrande Kampar (FM0288) 1987, True for ever (TS0511) 1954

FROUDE, H

H. Froude was the deputy bandmaster of the New York Temple Band in the United States. The march *'Matchless Love'* was his first publication in the band journals of the Salvation Army. He was a pupil of Erik Leidzen.

Important composition

Matchless love (GS1220) 1943

FRY, FRED WILLIAM

Fred Fry (3 July 1859 – 24 June 1939) is a son of Charles William Fry, the first Salvation Army bandmaster. As a boy he played cornet in the Wesleyan Chapel Orchestra in Alderbury, and at the age of eight played the harmonium. He was a member of the Fry Family Band, which was formed in Salisbury in 1878 and toured Britain extensively until 1882 when his father died after a short illness. Fred was then appointed secretary to Herbert Booth and for several years travelled on musical campaigns with the Training Home Songsters and other various groups, including the Household Troops Band. He worked in the Music Editorial Department preparing band music and the music typesetting for *"The Musical Salvationist"* during the years 1886-1892. In 1891 he was appointed bandmaster of the International Staff Band, which made him the real first bandmaster of the illustrious band. He did not remain long in this capacity as one year later he went to Canada as private secretary to Herbert Booth. When returning to the United Kingdom he worked for many years in the Town Clerk's Department in Gillingham.

Important compositions

With Sword and Shield (GS0061) 1887, Spread the News (GS0237) 1894

GARSEGG, BJØRN ARNE

Bjørn Arne Garsegg was born on the 20th of July 1949 in the small town of Askim, 50 km south of the Norwegian capital Oslo. Bjørn learned to play Eb horn, later baritone, Eb bass and euphonium in the Askim Junior Salvation Army Band under the baton of bandmaster Paul G. Lier. He joined the senior band 'Askim Hornmusikk' as a euphonium player under the baton of Paul G. Lier and later bandmaster Egil Gundersen. He also played under the band's frequent guest conductor Eiliv Herikstad, the composer and arranger who later became and still is (2012) the bandmaster of Askim hornmusikk (Askim Corps Band). For a period he played baritone with the united Salvation Army band Kongressmusikken and euphonium with the Oslo III Salvation Army band. Bjørn joined The Royal Norwegian Navy Band as a euphonium player, also playing trombone in their big band, for three and a half years in the 1970's. From 2007 he resumed some modest composing, writing nine small compositions in traditional style for different ensembles, as a tribute/homage to his home district of Indre Østfold. Some of the music is written for brass band, others for choir, further for accordion, for piano, for big band and for string orchestra. Most of the music has *'Indre Østfold'* in its title. Among the arrangers of his music are the Salvation Army composers of Askim, bandmaster Eiliv Herikstad and deputy bandmaster Morgan Juel Stavik. By profession Bjørn has been and still is a night watchman/security guard in Oslo through more than three decades.

About *'The Battle Cry'*: When Bjørn was about 17 years old, still attending high school, he wrote a little march which he called *'1883'*, since he had found out that 1883 was quite an important year in the history of SA music making. The march included a Sunday School song *('I am happy')* and a few bars of the song *'The Battle Cry'*. Because Bjørn's favorite brass composition was *'Resurgam'* by Eric Ball, he asked Eric Ball to arrange his little march. Eric, always a very busy man, suggested that Bjørn should ask Michael Kenyon to arrange it. But Bjørn asked Eric Ball a second time. Eric than said yes and arranged the march a couple of years later, when he got time. The International Music Department, at that time under the direction of Ray Steadman-Allen, changed the title from *'1883'* to *'The Battle Cry'* and published it in the General Series in 1974.

Important composition

The Battle Cry (GS1656) 1974

GATES, DOROTHY

Dorothy Gates (April 1, 1966) received her Bachelor of Music degree in composition and trombone performance from Queens University Belfast, from where she won a scholarship to attend the University of Michigan in 1988. It was there she received her Master of Music degree in Trombone performance. As a composer her works have been featured throughout the world and many of her works have been published and recorded. As a member of the jazz ensemble 'Spiritual to the Bone', Dorothy has performed in Switzerland, Australia, New Zealand, Canada, Great Britain and throughout the US. Dorothy has served as the Music Editor for The Salvation Army's Eastern Territory in New York and Composer in Residence for the New York Staff Band since 2002. She is the first woman Editor/Composer to be employed by The Salvation Army in this role. Dorothy, her husband Mark, and beagle Dougal live in Warwick, NY and attend the Spring Valley Salvation Army, where Dorothy is the Songster Leader (Choir Director).

Important compositions

Breathe (AJ0221) 2003, Hope (m/s), Freedom (m/s)

GAY, ALBERT

Little is known about Albert Gay. Albert Gay was the Mayor of Wisbech during 1954-1955 and wrote the march *'Wisbech Citadel'* to celebrate the opening of the new Salvation Army hall. Albert Gay was also honorary Musical Director and Chorus Master of the The Wisbech Amateur Operatic and Dramatic Society. Albert Gay once was a Salvationist bandsman, but didn't remain with the organization although he always was proud on his Salvation Army heritage. As a tribute to the memory of his former bandmaster, Albert Veal of Abertillery, he wrote the march *'Western Valley'*. It also appears that Albert Gay was a partner in the firm of Sutterby & Gay, a trade directory. Their premises in Wisbech were on the corner of Union Street and Hill Street.

Important compositions

Wisbech Citadel (GS1442) 1957, His Royal Banner (GS1196) 1941, Western Valley (GS1152) 1938

GERTSCH, GOTTFRIED

Gottfried Gertsch was a young Salvation Army officer, when he was send to Zurich 2 Corps. Here he found a small corps band, although quite skilled and working in an efficient way. The music that this small band used were no more than songs from the 'War Cry', so Gottfried decided that this should improve somehow and soon after he was composing and arranging the melodies for the brass instruments. This was mostly done on Friday, learned on Saturday and performed on Sunday! In order to be skilled enough for this task the captain undertook a series of studies on harmonization. When he was promoted to the rank of Adjutant he had to move to Bern, to establish a Music Department at the Territorial Headquarters. One of the first things there he had to do was to visit all the (then) seventy corps bands within the Territory to tune the instruments! Gottfried Gertsch was Promoted to Glory in 1960, age 91.

Important composition

Band arrangements of songs from The 'War Cry'

GETZ, ROBERT

Robert Getz was born on Mother's Day, May 11, 1941 in Parsons, Kansas, USA, in a Salvation Army corps building, during the Holiness Meeting. His parents were corps officers and his father had to interrupt his sermon to deliver Robert. Robert (Bob) was the earliest commissioned senior bandmaster in the history of the Central USA territory, when he was at the age of 14. He started a band at the Milwaukee South Corps. Later Bob became a bandmaster of the Chicago Belmont Corps Band and started the Northern Illinois Youth Band, both of which were the best bands in the USA then. In 1967 the Chicago Belmont Corps (CBC) organised a concert salute to Emil Söderström. Emil composed the march *'Chicago Belmont Corps'* as a commission of Bob. This march features the hymn tune *'Belmont'* but in 4/4 time, and a clever opening motive figure didactically using the notes C-B-C for 'Chicago Belmont Corps'. Bob served as bandmaster of the Dearborn Heights Citadel Band in Michigan, a total of 37 years plus 10 years as euphonium soloist with the Chicago Staff Band (CSB). He was asked 3 times to be bandmaster of the CSB but it didn't work out. Bob played professionally as well with the Detroit Concert Band under Dr. Leonard B. Smith.

Important composition

Ellers (FS363) 1974

GIBSON, JOHN

Bandmaster John Gibson was born in England in 1922. As a young man of 27 he assumed leadership of the Norwich Citadel Band. He was leading the Band for 37 years (1949-1986). During his working years John was Head of Brass for Norfolk Education and was a well-known figure in the Norfolk musical scene, conducting the Norfolk Symphonic Wind Band. John (or Jack as he is known to many) played the piano each Sunday during the services. A measure of his continuing interest in the Band is that he was in the recording studio recently, providing assistance and advice, particularly with two of his own compositions that were recording. During John's leadership, the Band was privileged on three occasions to give performances at London's Royal Albert Hall and also another at the Queen Elizabeth Hall. Overseas tours were made to the Netherlands (1959), Sweden (1971) and the USA and Canada (1985) in addition to several recordings, TV and radio broadcasts.

Important compositions

The Traveller (m/s), General's Command (m/s), The name of Jesus (m/s), Futurists (US0291) 2003

GOFFIN, DEAN

Dean Goffin was born on the 9th of July 1916 in Wellington, New Zealand as son of Henry Goffin, a Salvation Army officer and composer. When Dean was 19 year old he was appointed bandmaster of the Wellington South Band. At this corps he met his Wife Marjorie. When the 2nd World War started Dean enlisted in the New Zealand Armed Forces. He became bandmaster of the newly formed band of the 20th Infantry Battalion and later on the 4th Brigade Band. He served with them in the Middle East and Europe. During this time he composed and arranged numerous pieces for this among which *'Rhapsody in Brass'* and the parade march for the 4th Brigade *'Bel Hamid'*. This march was later on adapted for Salvation Army use and renamed *'Anthem of the Free'*. After the War Dean kept on composing and his work was featured by the Wellington South Band. He transferred to Timaru to take up another job and became bandmaster there. He was studying music at the time. As he wanted to take part in a competition for devotional selections for Salvation Army use, he sent some of his compositions to International Headquarters. When in 1949 *'Rhapsody in Brass'* was chosen as the test piece for the British Open Championships in Manchester, people at the Salvation Army started asking questions about the lack of publications of his work. It was discovered that the pieces he had sent for the competition had been put in a drawer as they did not meet the exact criteria. Among these pieces was one of his most appealing works: *'The Light of the World'*, which was published a year later. In that same year, 1950, he completed his bachelor of Music studies at Otagu University. In 1951 Dean and Marjory entered the Salvation Army Training College in Wellington. He became a corps officer and in 1956 he was appointed National Bandmaster in the British Territory. Later on he became National Secretary for Bands and Songster Brigades. In this period he organised the yearly festival in the Royal Albert Hall and was responsible for the national music schools in the UK. In 1966 he returned to New Zealand and after serving as Divisional Commander and Chief Secretary he became Territorial Commander in 1980. To mark the centenary of the Salvation Army in New Zealand the Queen bestowed the honour of Knight Bachelor to Dean and Marjory. Sir Dean Goffin was Promoted to Glory on the 23rd of January 1984.

Book - **Symphony of Thanksgiving** - by Cyril R. Bradwell

'The life and music of Commisioner Sir Dean Goffin, Symphony of Thanksgiving, as stated on the back of this tremendous interesting book about one of the leading band figures within the Salvation Army, is the fascinating story of a man whose life's purpose was forged in the violent crucible of war, and was worked out, intensely and gloriously, through music and service in the Salvation Army'.

Important compositions

Crusaders (FS173) 1951, My Strength, my Tower (FS270) 1963, Victorious (FS288) 1965, The Light of the World (GS1329) 1950, The road to Emmaus (GS1380) 1953, Challenge of the Cross (GS1408) 1955, Camp Akatarawa (GS1698) 1977, Alderney (TS0500) 1953

GOFFIN, HENRY CHARLES

Henry Charles Goffin was born in Plymouth, England on the 8th of March 1885. When he was 16 year old he was commissioned bandmaster of Plymouth 2 Band. When he entered the Salvation Army Training College in 1903 he was made bandmaster of the Cadet's Band and on several occasion directed this band in meetings led by General William Booth. After he left Training College he was corps officer in London, Scotland and Lancashire. He married Captain Kate McLean Ferguson. After a while he relinquished his duty as an officer and lived in Rohesay, where his wife grew up, and took up work as an insurance agent. Wellington City Corps sponsored the family as immigrants and Henry accepted the offer of Bandmastership of that corps. After a while they were re-accepted as officers and served several corps in New Zealand. Later on he was put in Charge of the Band and Songster Department in Wellington. He is the father of Dean Goffin. He was Promoted to Glory in 1973.

Henry C. Goffin became a Bandmaster at the age of fifteen at Plymouth, in which town his father carried the Army Flag for fifty years. In the year 1907, the youthful musician won second prize in the International Music Competition, with a march entitled *'Plymouth'*, and he has been closely associated with Army Bands and music from those early days right up to the end of his life. He held the position of National Secretary for Bands in New Zealand. In 1914, after a period of Officership in the British Territory, Harry Goffin immigrated to New Zealand, where he assumed control of the Wellington City Band. Major Leslie T. Glover, of the International Headquarters, and a member of the Band at that time said, 'He was a great disciplinarian', and also speaks most highly of his inspiring leadership and example. A period as Assistant Officer at the Corps, with special responsibility for Band affairs, followed. Henry Goffin was not only well known throughout the Dominion as an excellent musician, Band trainer, and organizer, a man who gets things done, but also as a lover of the souls of men.

Three times Commanding Officer of Wellington City, and Auckland Congress Hall, Corps, the Major has in no small way helped to firmly established the work of The Army in those large and important centers. Following the disastrous earthquake at Napier, Hawkes Bay, on February 3, 1931, Major Goffin was appointed to take command of the Corps there. In a surprisingly short space of time, although the newly-erected Citadel had been razed to the ground, the Major nobly grappled with and overcame the innumerable difficulties. After two years of strenuous toil in that ill-fated town, he received orders to farewell, and many were the petitions made begging his superior Officers to let him remain. The town authorities revealed their great appreciation of the Major's work by stating that his assistance was *'absolutely necessary to the rehabilitation of the town'*. Henry C. Goffin is a most versatile man, for in addition to his successful periods of Corps leadership, he has also been Private Secretary to the Territorial Commander, and the Editor of the New Zealand Band Journal. Four of his Brass Band arrangements published in the English Band Journals are outstanding: *'The Red Shield'* march, its title suggested by the badge of the Naval and Military League, *'The Salvation Army Patrol'*, representing the march past of a Troop of Life-Saving Scouts or Guards, *'The New Zealand Warriors'* march, and the cornet solo, *'Maoriland'*. Harry succeeded Bandmaster Harold Scotney in the leadership of Wellington City Band, when that well-known composer transferred to Australia to take up the position of Band Inspector to the Eastern Territory.

About his March 'Plymouth', composed in 1907 (GS558);

Henry's first composition; named after his home town; written when stationed at Harpurhey, Manchester; won 2nd prize in 1907 international SA music competition. '*My first attempt at putting to paper the musical thoughts which occasionally came to my mind... This march was sent to the Music Editorial Department as an entry for a world-wide competition for SA bandsmen and to my great surprise the competition was voted excellent and I was awarded the second prize. I obtained an illuminated certificate signed by General Bramwell Booth and Colonels G. Mitchell and William Eadie.*' (HCG memoirs)

Important compositions

New Zealand Warriors (GS1041) 1932, The Red Shield (GS986) 1928, The Salvation Army Patrol (GS1012) 1930

GOLDSMITH, ARTHUR

Arthur Goldsmith was born in England in the year 1875 and was Promoted to Glory in 1948. In 1888 he started to work at the Music Department of the Salvation Army International Headquarters in London. In the same time he studied music in London and also was the bandmaster of the Poplar Citadel Band. In 1901 he became a member of the International Staff Band (ISB). He played with them for 28 years. Arthur was a gifted soprano cornet player. When they started to publish the magazine 'The Bandsman and Songster' (which later became 'The Musician') Staff-Captain Arthur Goldsmith became the Ediot in Chief, A Year later he was transterred to the Music Editorial Department where he worked together with Brigadier Richard Slater and Staff-Captain Frederic Hawkes. He worked here until 1921, from 1931 onwards as music-editor.

Staff-Captain Arthur Goldsmith.

For some years now, Staff-Captain Goldsmith has been one of The Army's best London musicians. Not only as a Bandsman, Bandmaster, Band teacher, and as a member of the Rink Male Quartet, but in theory and general musical knowledge, he has been reckoned among The Army's front rank men. He was a member of the Poplar Band either as Bandsman, Bandmaster, or Instructor, for about sixteen years, and also a Bandsman at Regent Hall for four years. In addition to this he has, at various times, been attached to the International Junior Staff, Home Office, and International Trade Headquarters Bands, and is at present a member of the Staff Band, playing the soprano. As a composer he is not as yet so widely known, but his Prize Melody (which, by the way, has taken on excellently on the Continent), and his excellent Prize Selection will aid considerably in this direction. The Staff-Captain's appointment to the Editorship of 'The Bandsman and Songster' will bring him into close touch with Bandsmen and Songsters in every part of The Army musical world.

(The Bandsman and Songster, April 6, 1907)

Colonel Arthur R. Goldsmith retires.

'Colonel Arthur R. Goldsmith, Chief-Secretary of the Men's Social Work, composer and conductor, and first Editor of our predecessor, 'The Bandsman and Songster', retired from active service at a memorable service at a memorable Meeting arranged in his honor at the Victoria Homes, Whitechapel, and presided over by the Chief of the Staff. After prayer by former Chaplain, Lieut.-Colonel Frank Wotton (Retired), the Chief, at the conclusion of his warm, personal tribute to Colonel Goldsmith's forty-three years of Officer ship, announced that the General had decided that he should remain a member of the International Music Board and of the Doctrine Council, and should early in April, undertake a tour of Canada and the U.S.A. in the interests of our musical forces. This announcement was greeted with applause which betokened delighted approval, from an audience of Men's Social Officers gathered from all parts of the United Kingdom, and will be welcomed by all who know and appreciate the Colonel's worth to The Army as a musician and lecturer.

The Chief spoke of the Colonel's good work as a fellow-Soldier with him at Ilford in years gone by, and described him as a man with a mind well furnished with Biblical and theological knowledge, and of clear judgment. Lieut.-Commissioner John F. Lewis, the Governor, made the mention of Mrs. Goldsmith, and wished that she could have lived to have shared in the retirement of the Colonel, whose long years of uninterrupted service he said, had given him the affection all who knew him. Following a vocal solo by Brigadier Percival McLean, the Captain, and a former Deputy-Bandmaster of the Men's Social Work Headquarters Band, provided reminiscences of his command of Ilford Corps, when Brigadier Cunningham used to bring up the rear of the march, Major Goldsmith 'tootled' away on his cornet, and Ensign and Mrs. Tickelpenny led the forces forward.

The Colonel was 'the light of the activities in the open-air' and often brought men to the Hall in order to get them saved. 'We regard you as a workman who needed not to be ashamed', he concluded. Bandmaster H.W. Twitchin, of Regent Hall, spoke of four boys who started their Army career at about the same time, ad who had each achieved success in the realm of Army music. George Fuller, Arthur Goldsmith, Fred Punchard and himself, and of two who had many things in common. When a Bandsman at the 'Rink', Captain Goldsmith and he were the only solo cornetists. The Captain had encouraged him to study music, they were members of the first Male Voice Party formed in The Army, both had broken their legs, both had won a prize in the same section of a Music Competition in the early years of the present century, and finally, he, the Bandmaster, had blazed the trail for the Colonel's visit to Canada and the States. As a former International Staff Band colleague and billeting partner, Colonel Alex Mitchell had known Colonel Smith for more than thirty years, and had never seen him nonplusses.

He had followed the Colonel in some of his appointments, and had seen 'the hall-mark of quality' in all that he had done. 'His music, of course. is imperishable', Colonel Mitchell remarked. With an accuracy of date and detail Colonel Goldsmith reviewed his life of sixty-five years, most of it spent in God's service, and the majority of that in the Salvation Army. He had, he said, been fortunate in his personal contacts with great Salvationists, and in his variety of appointments. As we hope to publish in brief the story of the Colonel's life and service in an early issue, we purposely omit relating his account of it, as given at the Valedictory gathering, in connection with this report. The proceedings, most intimate and interesting, were brought to a conclusion by the benedictory prayer of Mrs. Commissioner Cunningham.'

('The Musician', February 2, 1940)

Arthur R. Goldsmith member of the International Music Board, and former International Staff Bandsman and Bandmaster of the Men's Social Headquarters Band. Throughout his Salvation Army career, Colonel Arthur R. Goldsmith, the boy from a Poplar chapel who was to become one of our leading musicians, has been extremely reticent in the matter of talking about himself of his work. Indeed, it is only within the past few weeks we have been able to glean certain interesting facts concerning his career, and most of these have been obtained as the result of much questioning of comrades associated with him.

It was the writer's privilege to be the first to interview the Colonel, whose name will always be closely linked with that of Lieut.- Colonel Slater and Colonel Hawkes in the production of Salvation Army music, on the day of his retirement after forty-two years of unbroken service as an Officer. No better tribute can be paid to any man than to state that his influence for good defies tabulation, and this is certainly true of Arthur R. Goldsmith. For instance, who can measure the far reaching results of the encouraging words he spoke to a diminutive Halifax Young People's Band-member, when visiting that town with the International Staff Band many years ago? The 'Stick it, Sonny!' inspired that youngster to greater efforts, and kept him plodding on through many dark experiences. To-day, Major Alfred J. Gilliard, Editor of 'The 'War Cry", still speaks appreciatively of those simple, but encouraging, words, probably long since forgotten by their author.

Early days.

Arthur Robert Goldsmith was born at Poplar in 1875. His father, a sailor for twenty-four years, was a Sunday-school teacher at the Bath Street Chapel in this East London district, and wielded a wonderful spiritual influence over his scholars, many of whom revere his name to this day. Arthur Goldsmith's father did not know a note of music, and always sang out of tune, but he was a great student and was well informed on many subjects. It was from his mother that Arthur inherited his gift for music, for she came of a family of musicians, and was a capable singer. Already converted in a chapel revival, it was at the age of ten that young Goldsmith became a cornetist in the 'Invicta' Military Band, which was associated with the chapel. Soon he was more proficient on his instrument than his bandmaster!

The 'Invicta' and Poplar Salvation Army Bands were on very friendly terms, and it was after his being loaned to the Army Band for a Sunday that he decided to remain for good! When only fifteen years of age the young cornetist, as the result of diligent study, hard practice, and commendable Salvationism, was given the position of Corps Bandmaster at Poplar. At first his efforts at conducting were rather resented by the older men, but Bandmaster Goldsmith quickly established himself by dint of his capable leadership and sheer musical ability. His elder sister Esther, who had been a 'Little Solider Captain', a title long since extinct, was already an Officer and subsequently married Captain James Dermott.

In later years Mrs. Dermott became Home League Secretary at Barking, a position she until her promotion to Glory. The present Bandmaster at Barking is her son, and Major Dermott, of International Headquarters, is a daughter. The Colonel's sister is also remembered at Southall Citadel, where, as Captain Goldsmith she was the Commanding Officer fifty years ago, and at other Corps, including Barking. A number of Sister-comrades were members of the Poplar Band in those early days, one of whom was Emma Turner, a sweet singer, who, in the course of time, became of the then Bandmaster, and another was the Colonel's younger sister. The mother of Bandmaster George Friday, of Grimsby Citadel, was also a Bands woman at Poplar. Mrs. Goldsmith, although working behind the scenes, and comparatively unknown, was through the years a great source of strength to her musician-husband. She was Promoted to Glory, after a long and trying illness, in 1936. All the members of the Goldsmith family op Poplar eventually became Salvationists, except the father.

The Colonel's second sister, Emily, afterward Mrs. Will Wellard, wife of the first Ilford Bandmaster, and Home League Secretary at that Corps for many years, was Promoted to Glory in 1938. Her son, Adjutant Will, is serving on the British Field, and a daughter, Mrs. Harold Thorough good, was the young People's Singing Company Leader at Southend Citadel. Retired Bandmaster Ben Goldsmith, the Colonel's brother, is now Songster Leader at Romford, and it speaks well for the first Salvationists of the Goldsmith family that, with one exception, all the children and grandchildren are Salvationists. Of Colonel Goldsmith's children, Major Albert, of International Headquarters, is Songster Leader at Bexleyheath and a composer of ability. Adjutant Ben is a pioneer Officer in Tanganyike, where he has been laboring for the past five years, and Edith is a Songster at Barking. Much could be written of Colonel Goldsmith's Poplar days, but let it be put on record that, although the Poplar chapel boy has risen in the Salvation Army musical world, and concluded his career in the position of Chief Secretary of the Men's Social Work, after periods as an International Headquarters Auditor, Secretary of The Army's Fire Insurance Corporation, and Financial Secretary of Salvationist Publishing and Supplies Ltd., he has retained that humility of spirit which marked his early endeavor, and won the esteem of his first Bandsmen. Poplar Corps, now No.1 in Salvation Army history, is 'Home' to Colonel Goldsmith and is much beloved by him. Making a name.

In December, 1888, Arthur Goldsmith, a very shy and timid boy, commenced employment on International Headquarters. It was not long before his musical ability was recognized, and he was found a place in the Junior Staff Band, forerunner of the International Staff Band. Contemporary members of the Junior Staff Band included George Mitchell, afterward Commissioner and Bandmaster of the International Staff Band, Alfred Benwell, now Commissioner and Territorial Commander in Holland, Samuel Hurren, now Commissioner and Principal, International Training College, Joshua Smith, now Colonel and Staff Secretary at I.H.Q., Harry Haines, now Colonel, Retired and formerly Leader and Secretary of the International Staff Band, Alfred W. Punchard, now National Bandmaster, and for forty-odd years Bandmaster at Chalk Farm, and others who later became well known in The Army. What stories could be written of their boyhood's escapades! During his late teens and early twenties, Arthur Goldsmith was fast making a name for himself as a cornetist. He played in the Home Office Band, which was then under the direction of Bandmaster Appleby, and was a member of the erstwhile Trade Band under Colonel F.G. Hawkes, Retired, who first introduced the Colonel to the soprano.

When nineteen years of age young Goldsmith attracted the attention of the late Lieut.-Colonel Slater, who asked his to write a Christmas song for "The Musical Salvationist'.' Although his first effort was rejected, budding composers, please note! His second attempt met with the editor's approval, and *'Why Jesus came'*, his first published song, appeared in the December 1895, number. From then on, a steady flow of vocal compositions appeared under Arthur Goldsmith's name. Early songs were 'then and now', written especially for the Trade Band, and a setting to *'We're travelling Home.'* The Colonel speaks most appreciatively of the help and encouragement given to him in those far-off-days by Lieut.-Colonel Slater and Colonel Hawkes. A period at Ipswich as Scribe on the Divisional Headquarters brought the youthful composer into contact with the Citadel Band, then, as now, a fine combination. Later, service on the Trade Headquarters in Glasgow paved the way for his pioneering of Springburn Band, to this day one of Scotland's leading musical selections. In 1897 Arthur Goldsmith, an established musician and accountant, became an Officer. Musicianship and accountancy have gone hand in hand through almost the whole of his career, and there have been few men who have achieved success in both spheres.

Appointed to the Men's Social Work, the Colonel served on its Headquarters for ten years.

It is a coincident that his first and last ten years of Officership should have been spent in this particular Department. During his first period of service on the Social Headquarters the Colonel experimented in arranging music for a party of five instrumentalists, and thereby gained knowledge in the art of scoring, which later was to stand him in very good stead. Whilst a Captain, Arthur Goldsmith was a Bandsman at Regent Hall, and shared the solo cornet with Herbert W. Twitching, now the Bandmaster, who is never tired of making it known that Captain Goldsmith was the first to encourage him to make a closer study of music. While at the 'Rink', the then Captain was also a member of the first Army Male Voice Quartet, which made quite a name for itself. An International Staff Bandsman. Captain Arthur Goldsmith entered the International Staff Band as a recognized member in 1901, and was associated with The Army's premier combination for nearly thirty years, winning renown in the brass band world as a soprano cornetist. He first played the part in the Staff Band in 1903, succeeding Bandsman Will Faux, who was also a great player.

It was Arthur Goldsmith's refined musicianship as an instrumentalist which left such an indelible impression upon his hearers. Whilst he always knew how to make his part effective, he could also lend weight with his soprano cornet to the solo cornets when the need arose. Colonel Edgar Dibden, who played solo cornet in the Staff Band for many years, corroborates this fact. Another associate, Colonel Joshua Smith, says that his outstanding memory of Colonel Goldsmith's soprano playing in the manner in which he rode over the Band, on the octave, in playing hymn-tunes on the march. Often the late Commissioner Mitchell, the Bandmaster, would ask his soprano cornetist to play *'Madrid'* and other such hymntunes as a solo whilst the Band went marching through the streets. Commissioner Mitchell's name is revered by all Salvationist-musicians, but by none more than Arthur Goldsmith. The Commissioner encouraged him to write music for the Staff Band, and always gave opportunities to the composer of some of his Band's finest pieces to conduct them in the practice-room, and to explain their construction. The International Staff Band is bound up in no small way with the Colonel's career, and his association with it has undoubtedly colored the greater part of his life. As a Staff Bandsman he toured the Continent on several occasions, and campaigned at scores of places in the British Isles. The writer (Douglas J. Rolls), when a boy, recalls the Band's visit to Northampton. The outstanding memory for him is not the excellent playing of the Band although this *'brought the house down'* with *'Army of the Brave',* but Brigadier Goldsmith's Bible-reading and exhortation on the Sunday afternoon. The text was, *'Ho, every one that thirsted, come ye to the waters.'*

Arthur Goldsmith was not only an enthusiastic Bandsman in every sense of the word, but was, and is, a most enthusiastic soulwinner, a capable leader of Prayer Meetings, and a very respectable platform speaker. The Colonel is no spoilsport, nor his he devoid of humor, as the following tribute from Brigadier Andrew Jones will prove: 'Being a former member of the International Staff Band, I have long known the Colonel as a good companion, a really good comrade, always cheerful, even when personal sorrow dogged his steps. He has a ready smile and can produce at any time a humorous incident culled from a rich mine of interesting and varied experiences; he is a frank but kindly counselor; and is never behind with practical help when the need arises.' It was while in the International Staff Band that Colonel Goldsmith blossomed forth as a composer, the Band being the vehicle through which he was able to express himself. His first published Brass Band piece, the *'Mercy'* selection, was a big success. It was written of the 1907 International Music Competition. The arrangement gained first prize and established the name of the then Staff-Captain Arthur Goldsmith as a front-rank composer. Lieut.-Colonel Slater gave the selection its name, it being entered for the Competition without a title. 'The Father of Salvation Army music' thought very highly of this arrangement, and was especially fascinated with the unusual finale, which he likened to clamoring souls besieging the Throne of Grace for mercy. *'At J'*, he wrote, *'begins a short finale, opening as with a sigh from the trombones, followed by a finely-conceived series of chromatic chords for cornets only, like a group of departing angels who have given invitation and warning, but sorrowfully question to what issue.'* In the same competition the Colonel also won first prize for a song.

His music.

The *'Mercy'* selection secured for the Colonel a reputation for high musical efficiency, and the quality of that initial success was no flash in the pan, as the following complete list of his compositions for Brass Band proves:

Marches:

Come Away (BJ 572) Kettering (BJ 561) The Victor (BJ 610) The Wonder-working Blood (BJ 636) The Coming of Jesus (BJ 653) Glorious Tidings (BJ 663) The Joyful Army (BJ 686)

The Happy Soldier (BJ 696) Army Song Marches 1 (BJ 705) Army Song Marches 2 (BJ 793)

Come and be a Soldier (BJ 771) In the Fight (BJ 709) On the March (BJ 737) The President (BJ 828) Marching Homeward (BJ 865) Marching Onward (BJ 840)

Selections:

Mercy (BJ 534) My Saviour (BJ 570) Battle Strains (BJ 580) Pardoned (BJ 595) Come Home (BJ 614) Happy in the Lord (BJ 635) Harvest Praises (BJ 624) The Pleading Sinner (BJ 645)

Following the Lord (BJ 657) My Keeper (BJ 660) My Guide (BJ 676) Salvation (BJ 689)

Saving Grace (BJ 693) My Light (BJ 703) The Sinner's Doom (BJ 715) The Better World (BJ 719) Rejoicing in the Lord (BJ 722) Echoes of the Congress (BJ 726) To God on High be Glory (BJ 731) Nearer to the Lord (BJ 735) The Cleansing Current (BJ 742) Congregational Tunes No.1 (BJ 749) The Lord is my Shepherd (BJ 753) Young People's Songs (BJ 757)

Selections for Salvationist Meetings No.1 (BJ 760) Cheerful Songs (BJ 765) O Rest in the Lord (BJ 769) The Absent Guest (BJ 769) White as Snow (BJ 772) God is Near Thee (BJ 778) The Risen Saviour (BJ 778) The Glorious Fountain (BJ 779) Adeste Fideles (BJ 782)

A Crown of Peace (BJ 783) I am the Resurrection (BJ 783) I think of all His Sorrow (BJ 783)

At the Cross (BJ 790) Favourite Hymn Tune No.2 (BJ 791) Abide with Me (BJ 794)

The Peace of God (BJ 794) Congregational Tunes No.2 (BJ 802) The Lamb of Calvary (BJ 803) Jesus Lives (BJ 806) Song Book Selection No.1 (BJ 807) The Wondrous River (BJ 815)

Matchless Grace (BJ 818) Still Unsaved (BJ 819) The Hallelujah Chorus (BJ 827) Song Book Selection No.2 (BJ 830) Oh, Worship the Lord (BJ 831) Rockingham (BJ 839) Conquering Faith (BJ 842) Strains of Victory (BJ 851) Favourite Hymn Tunes No.4 (BJ 855) My Protector (BJ 857) The Banner of Liberty (BJ 836) If With All Your Hearts (BJ 873) The Song that Reached my Heart (BJ 873) Jesus of Nazareth (BJ 885) Showers of Blessing (BJ 885) All we like Sheep (BJ 888) Memories of the Masters (BJ 896) And the Glory of the Lord (BJ 905) Cujus Animan (BJ 1130) Seek ye the Lord (BJ 1139)

Second Series:

March: Blessed be the Name (13) Selection: Early Memories (6)

Not only did Arthur Goldsmith write 'hot', but undoubtedly he wrote by inspiration, and seldom suffered from a lack of ideas. For instance, no fewer than thirty introductions were written to '*Adeste Fideles*' before he was satisfied. All the Colonel's work is characterized by thoroughness and that he possesses an ample knowledge of his subject is shown in almost every bar he wrote. He has a good knowledge of harmony and counterpoint, and reveals skill in his arrangements, the originality, melodic smoothness, and beauty of which are examples to be copied by all aspiring Salvationist-composers.

Arthur Goldsmith always had in mind the needs of The Army and the capabilities of its musicians when writing his music. Because his music is inspired it will feel a place on Salvation Army programs so long as The Salvation Army remains. Thrilling stories could be written about several Goldsmith pieces, but the following episode is a crowning tribute to their worth. The Men's Social Work Headquarters Band, conducted by the Colonel, was giving a Festival in the courtyard of Maidstone Prison to more than two hindered prisoners. The closing piece was '*Rockingham*', and every man put all he knew into its interpretation. The feeling that the music and its message 'went over' was unmistakable. A few days later the Bandsmen learnt that a former Bandsman, then a prisoner, had given his heart afresh to God as the Band had played its final piece. He had been allowed to absent himself from the Festival, and given a fatigue duty to do, he had knelt down in a kitchen surrounded by buckets and mops, and cried to God for forgiveness. The strains of '*Rockingham*' had vividly reminded him of the days when he himself had played in a Salvation Army Band. The late J. Ord Hume, one of the greatest arrangers of brass and military band music, considered '*Rockingham*' a first class arrangement.

150 published songs.

Colonel Goldsmith has had more than one hindered and fifty of his songs published in "The Musical Salvationist'.' '*Showers of Blessing*' is one of the most beautiful of his settings, others of outstanding merit being '*When the sky is blue*', '*Seek ye the Lord*' and '*United in Christ.*' One Christmas-eve a small carol party from Romford, under Bandmaster Ben Goldsmith, the Colonel's brother, paid a surprise visit to the Colonel's home, where its members rendered delightful seasonable music. This kindly gesture touched a responsive chord in the Colonel's heart. Still under the sweet influence of the carols, he was inspired to write a melody. Later, in looking for words to fit this tune undoubtedly caught from the heavens, he turned to the Song Book, and the first set of verses he noticed was, '*Lord, I hear of showers of blessing.'* It was most remarkable that the words fitted the tune exactly. Indeed, most people would declare that the tune was written with these words in mind.

His Music Editorial Appointment.

On his appointment to the Music Editorial Department in 1908 Colonel Goldsmith's real work as a composer commenced. Prior to this he had been the pioneer Editor of 'The Bandsman and Songster' the forerunner of "The Musician" which was first issued in 1907, and thus he can add a working knowledge of Army journalism to his many accomplishments. At this time he studied diligently to improve his understanding of musical form, brass band technique, harmony, counterpoint, and theory, and obtained the diploma of an A. Mus.L.C.M., obtaining ninety-six marks out of a possible 100.

Another significant thing which has only recently come to light is that a number of Colonel Goldsmith's compositions and literary articles were published under noms de plume. The following pen-names were used for the purpose, and many readers will remember them: J.H. Gray, J. Hargraves, Legrand, E. Sargeant, and G. Ambrose. In each of them one will find the Colonel's initials, 'A.R.G.' The Colonel had in mind their use as a means of experimenting in writings of differing styles. He was a member of the Music Editorial Department for thirteen years, and on Lieut.-Colonel Slater's retirement in 1913 was made jointly responsible for the management of the Department with Colonel Hawkes. To aptly describe the work of these thirteen years, and in order that we might give an expert's viewpoint of Colonel Goldsmith's music, Brigadier Bramwell Coles, the present Head of the Department, has written the following tribute: *'Since he won first place in the 1907 International Music Competition with the 'Mercy' selection, Colonel Arthur Goldsmith's name has been written large on the pages of the Army's musical history. His vocal and instrumental compositions and arrangements have been forthcoming on a liberal scale. But to speak of the volume of a composer's output, though evidence of industry is, after all, to say very little'.*

The value of any man's work is not assessed by the quantity but by the quality of his achievement. And it can be said without hesitation, that the name of Arthur Goldsmith at the head of a song or Band Journal has always stood for several things, for instance, sound workmanship. His scoring has a special attraction for the student, for his melodies are harmonized with a true touch and unerring taste. His is workmanship of a high order, and it is that which serves true inspiration. The his music testifies to originality of mind. Avoiding well-trodden paths, he has always sought to find new ways to explore new realms. More important still, he was kept in mind the real purpose of Salvation Army music. In much of his music there is an eager movement, as of a zealous preacher impatient to deliver his message. For he has always had something to say, and, happily, has had the means to express himself simply, clearly, and effectively. He has not only had the necessary building material, so to speak, but also the tools, the mental equipment, the technical knowledge to enable him to build, and to build well. He has left his mark on Army music for all time. An Interpreter of Music. Another important aspect of the Colonel's activities is his ability to teach and to interpret music, both as Band trainer and as a Songster Leader. He commenced serious Band training fifty years ago when a lad of fifteen, and made a success of it, and to-day as an interpreter of soul-saving music, he has few rivals. It was the writer's privilege to play the trombone under Colonel Goldsmith's baton for nearly three years in the Mens Social Works Headquarters Band, and never will he forget the patience and care the Colonel paid to every bar of music played. In two hours of practice, with not a spare minute or a washed second, he gave the Band all he could muster in mental, spiritual, and physical strength. By his method of teaching, his dynamic personality, and his knowledge he stamped every bar with sincerity. At the end of the practice he and his Bandsmen were almost exhausted, but it was worth it, for we Bandsmen had gained something which will constantly remain with us, a true perspective of the value God puts on Army Bandmastership. We must gain and do our utmost for the Highest.

Many young fellows have sat enthralled in the Colonel's practice rooms to go in turn to their own Bands, some as Bandmasters, taking with them an inspiration and spiritual technique which was gained by communion with the spirit of Arthur Goldsmith. The Colonel makes every bar of music played animate and sparkling, and clothes a theme or melody with a new meaning. He seeks to discover the spiritual implication of the music and endeavors to get the Band to interpret this in its playing. The Colonel possesses an excellent memory majority of the songs used in our Band Journals. He can also give *'chapter and verse'* of tunes long forgotten by those who played them in the days for yore. This knowledge, by the way, has made the Colonel a valuable member of the International Music Board, on which the General has requested him to continue to serve. He is chairman of the sub-Board which considers contributions to 'The Musical Salvationist'. Colonel Goldsmith considers his ability to interpret the soul of music a precious and Heaven-sent gift. Of some of his methods in the practice room and on the platform the critics may say, 'Pure emotionalism!' but there is much more in it than that. The world's greatest conductors must, of necessity, give emotional as well as intellectual readings of their scores.

Seeing the Colonel conduct such pieces as *'The King of kings', 'The Cross'*, or *'A Souls Awakening'* is a never-to-be-forgotten event. One memorable occasion he conducted the International Staff Band through the first-named piece at a Lecture Session in connection with the annual Bandmaster's Councils, and the reporter wrote the following vivid account: *'It was a technical display, and yet handled with such insight, such reverence, and mastery, that the congregation was brought to a pitch of high emotional sensitivity. As the conductor revealed the meaning of the music all again saw the King of kings scorned and buffeted, and yet triumphant in His silent suffering. The late Commissioner Charles Jeffries, when British Commissioner and presiding at an Associated Headquarters Festival, said of the Men's Social Work Headquarters Band's rendering of 'A Soul's Awakening', conducted by the Colonel: 'Immediately the Band commenced to play it seemed that a religious influence came over the whole people.' In addition of those already mentioned the following Bands have been instructed by the Colonel at different times: Wood Green Citadel, St. Albans, Chalk Farm, and Barking Senior, which combination he still instructs, and Young People's'.*

Yet a further example of the catholicity of his interests in his association with Raydon village. For more than thirty years he has been annually conducted the Corps Harvest Festival week-end, always giving the Band a practice and special tea-table talk on the spiritual aspects of their work. In this connection Bandmaster W.E. Tricker writes: *'Most of our men were afraid to go to the first Band practice conducted by Colonel Goldsmith, but what a difference in the last! Every available man listened with intense eagerness to the Colonel's words on the inner meaning of the music under consideration. He was always anxious that the music should make its spiritual appeal. Every note, every sign, was pointed out to the unobservant. The Colonel could address all the men by their Christian names. Then those Sunday after-tea table talks. The first one, I remember was on Work, for which, by the way, the Colonel was taken to task by our then Commanding Officer. 'Fancy', she said, 'lecturing about Work to men who rise at 5 a.m. and work till late at night!' But the spiritual and musical application was, of course, 'Nothing is achieved without hard work.' One of the last talks was around the same subject. 'Don't rest content', the Colonel said, 'because about 25 per cent of your village is covered, work hard, and never leave off till the other 75 percent is won for Christ. To you who are starting, I say, work! To you who have been working for years, still more work! To you who have nearly finished, work as long as you can and encourage the others.' Colonel Goldsmith has done much toward lifting our Band and Corps out of a rut and broadening our outlook. In the homes of our people he always gave the impression of being one of them, not one above them.'*

His influence.

One of Colonel Goldsmith's most important contributions to the welfare of our Organization is the influence he has had and has on the life of its youth. Many who today are Officers, Bandmasters, or Songster Leaders thank God that they ever came into contact with this humble Salvationist. Colonel Arthur Goldsmith is widely esteemed as one who combines appreciation of the ambitions of the present generation with firm loyalty to The Army's fundamental principles regarding its music. The Colonel says: *'All I have got belongs to The Army. It is The Army, under God, that I like to lift up, and not the individual, hence my objection to Composers' Festivals.'* Again and again he has stated that *'It was The Army which gave me my chance.'* And now this splendid Salvationist-musician, taken from ordinary clay, but fashioned by God into a vessel of distinction and usefulness, has retired from active service, but not from an active life. ('The Musician' July 6 - august 17, 1940)

Important composition

Rockingham (GS839) 1920

GOLDSMITH, OTTO

Early composer. Although his name could not be found in the history books of the Salvation Army in England nor Sweden, it might be a pseudonym. Fact remains that some pieces were published in the Swedish band journals to the credit of a person with this name.

Important composition

Marsch av Goldsmith (FM0063-1) 1906, Hur Salig är den Lilla FLock (FM0063) 1906

GORDON, WILLIAM

William Gordon (4 February 1942) is a resident of Southern California, where he received most of his musical training, having his degrees in both composition and conducting from California State University in Los Angeles. His many arrangements and compositions are performed worldwide and their popularity is evidenced by the numerous recordings they received. William, or Bill as he is known, was the Bandmaster of the Pasadena Tabernacle Band of The Salvation Army and travels extensively as guest lecturer and conductor. As a composer William, is one of the most creative and productive composers within and possible outside the Salvation Army. Many of his output is published by various publishers, including the Salvation Army. Also his own company Gordon-Music has released his music. Several CD recordings has appeared bearing solely his music, including the Pasadena Tabernacle Band, Cariboo Hill Temple Band (former Vancouver Temple Band), Intrada Brass and a Christmas recording by the Amsterdam Staff Band, featuring his Christmas book *'Christmas for Brass'*. He also released two recordings (Brass Sabbath) with his own music played by a composite band.

Important compositions

Salvation's Song (FS440) 1984, Laudes Domini (FS557) 2000

GORE, WILLIAM

William Gore was born in 1871 as son of Salvation Army Officers in Australia. He took his first lessons on the cornet very early, and as a 10 year old boy he played in the Adelaide 1 Citadel Band. In 1883 when his parents were asked to open a Corps in the South-Australien bush, he followed them. In Port Pirie the 14 year old William started his first Salvation Army band, and a second one in Port Augusta. On returning to Adelaide again he was involved in starting a band in Norwood. At the age of 16 years he was asked to start a Staff Band at the Southern Australia Headquarters. At this time he was the Bandmaster of the Adelaide 1 Citadel Band. In 1888 he moved to Sydney, where he was responsible for training all the bands in the Sydney area. In 1890 he was employed on the 'Music Editorial Department' in Melbourne. He became an Officer of the Salvation Army and married in 1895, and was transferred to the Field. Most of his compositions are published in Australia. He was Promoted to Glory in 1927.

Important composition

The Melbourne March (GS505) 1905

GÖRLING, NATHAN

Born in 1905, and a member of the Swedish Staff Band between 1920 and 1922. He played 1st Tenor Horn (which is translated in English, a valve trombone!). One of seven siblings, Nathan was one of the youngest member of the Swedish staff band ever. Before joining the staff band he was studying in Jönköping. One of his class mates was the late Secretary of United Nation Mr Dag Hammarskjöld. Nathan composed the march *'Med snabba steg'* (translated *'With fast steps'*). After being member of the staff band he studied music at the Music Conservatory (now the Royal Academy of Music) in Stockholm. Later he took up the responsibility as Head of Music at Europa Film. He wrote hundreds of original music, arrangements and melodies for hundreds of movies. He was Promoted to Glory in 2002.

Important compositions

Med Snabba Steg (FM0136) 1923

GOTT, BARRIE

Barrie Gott was born in England in 1947 and immigrated in 1951 to Australia. He was a member of the 'Sydney Symphony Orchestra' and studied Trompet and conducting at the Sydney Conservatorium of Music, obtaining his 'Orchestra Diploma', 'Bachelor of Music Degree' and 'Master of Arts Degree'.

In 1973 Barrie became the bandmaster of the Sydney Congress Hall Band. Later he emigrated again, this time to the United States of America where he became bandmaster of the Pasadena Tabernacle Band with whom he also recorded several releases including one with trombone virtuoso and colleague composer William Broughton, who now resides in Australia. When moving back to Asutralia he took up the vacant position as bandmaster of the Brisbane City Temple Band of The Salvation Army. He currently conducts the Queensland Pops Orchestra.

Important compositions

Daniel (FS444) 1985, Lightwalk (FS462) 1988, Collaroy (GS1677) 1976, Gold Coast Temple (GS1833) 1989, Moses Get Down (AF15) 1991

GOUTCHER, E.B.

No information could be retrieved of this composer, exept that he was a bandsman.

Important composition

The Better Land (TS0184) 1933

GOVAARS, GERRIT JURIAAN

Gerrit Jurriaan Govaars was the first Salvationist and officer in the Netherlands. He was born on 19 April 1866 in Amsterdam and was Promoted to Glory in the city of Soest on 22 October 1954. Gerrit Govaars commenced the work of the Salvation Army in the Netherlands together with the English officers Joseph Tyler and his wife. Gerrit received the Order of the Founder (O.F.) in 1947 when he had the rank of Colonel. The grandson of Gerrit Govaars is Dr. Robert Simpson, a well known English composer who spent his early years in the Salvation Army in Lewisham. Another descendant of Gerrit Govaars is Colonel Mrs. Barend van den Hoek (neé Govaars). She is Dutch, but worked almost her intire life in Asia. She is now retired and lives with her husband in Melbourne, Australia.

Composer Ralph Pearce wrote a great piece on the tune of '*Govaars*' properly entitled '*Dutch Variations*'. This was released as sextet version and later extended for full brass band.

Important composition

Hymntune – 'Govaars'

GRAHAM, PETER

Peter Graham was born into a Salvation Army family in Hamilton, Lanarkshire, Scotland. He was, from a very early age, interested in Salvation Army music. He studied brass-pedagogic in Edingburgh. He immigrated to USA and worked in The Music Department of The Salvation Army in New York, and became a member of the New York Staff Band (NYSB) where he played cornet. Peter was soldier and bandsman in the Manhattan Corps, there he served also as bandinstructor. In 1986 he returned to the United Kingdom where he lived with his family in London. Here he served in the Music Department of The Salvation Army in Judd Street, and became the bandmaster of the Regent Hall Band. Later he extended his study in music by Salford College in Manchester. Today Peter Graham is a Professor in Music and a professional composer. Outside the Salvation Army he became known for his great and significant output when it regards to contest works such as '*Call of the Cossacks*', '*Cry of the Celts*', '*Harrison's Dream*', '*Journey to the Centre of the Earth*', '*On the shoulder of giants*' and '*The Torchbearer*', just to name but a few.

Important compositions

The Ambassadors (FS430) 1983, Blazon (FS496) 1992, The Last Amen (FS583) 2003, Regeneration (GS1764) 1983, Ayr Citadel (TS1125) 2003

GRAINGER, RONALD W.

Lieutenant-Colonel Ron Grainger grew up as part of a Salvationist family in Bracknell, along with brothers David, Edwin and John. During National Service he linked up with the Nottingham Memorial Hall Corps, where he met May Smith, and they were married in

March 1944. As a Young People's Bandleader, a promising composer and bass soloist, Ron was able to nurture people in his circle of influence. During this time he served as a superintendent in the Salvation Army Assurance Society, and with May, entered the 1959 Greathearts Session for four months of training. Following their commissioning in December 1959 they were appointed back to the Assurance Society with their daughters Avril and Karen. Ron served as district superintendent in Porth, Hartlepool, Harlesden, Coatbridge and Swansea. In 1972 they were transferred to the Men's Social Service Headquarters, where Ron became Board Secretary and later Property Secretary. In retirement the Colonel continued to work in the Property Department at NHQ, following his wife's Promotion to Glory in 1987. Lt.Colonel Ron Grainger was a man of creativity and quiet influence. He invested in people and his life of integrity and faith was seen through simple acts of kindness and wise counsel. Family was important to him and he was enriched by seeing his grandchildren. In 1998 he married Major Grace Fox. In later years the Colonel had a number of significant health issues and life became more restricted. During these times of adversity he demonstrated resilience, strength of character and quiet confidence in the Lord. Ron was Promoted to Glory in 2010.

Important compositions

The Pleading Saviour (TS0625) 1962, The song in my heart (TS0538) 1955, Whosoever will (TS0516) 1954

GRANT, D

No information could be retrieved of this composer.

Important composition

The Lord's My Shepherd (Crimond)

GRANT, WILLIAM

Although not confirmed, this might have been William Grant, a former bandsman of the Upper Norwood Corps in London, who later became conductor of the Crystal Palace Band.

Important composition

Whole wide world for Jesus (US0009) 1957

GRAVETT, CHARLES W.

Charles Gravett (*'Bond of Friendship'* and *'The Brighton March'*) was the uncle of Neville Mcfarlane, another composer described in this book, his mother's eldest brother. He was born in Brighton in 1890 and died there about 1975. He was the first of seven brothers and two sisters born to Charles Gravett senior, a converted Skeleton Army leader. Charles was largely self-taught and was Bandmaster at Brighton Congress Hall for a period in the 1930's. In private life he was a window cleaner. He played in the Band certainly into the late 1960's and led the Male Voice group for many years.

Important compositions

Bond of Friendship (GS0902) 1923, The Brighton March (GS0811) 1919

GRAY, A

No information about this person could be retrived.

Important compositions

Ceaseless vigil (TS0655) 1964, Devotion (TS0357) 1944, Fortitude (TS0476) 1951, Forward Valiant Army (GS1208) 1942

GRAY, HAROLD J.

As a mere boy Harold Gray's outlook in life did not appear too rosy, his father being a great drunkard, who had a penchant for frequently falling into the hands of the police. Harold's only comfort was his mother, a hardworking little woman who was very anxious for her son's welfare. At the age of five Harold's parents moved into a new home, and by a strange coincidence a Salvationist couple named Stephens, who had moved into the district about the same time, took up residence next door. Harold Gray always thanked God for their bringing him into contact with The Salvation Army. Times out of number these Salvationists helped his mother by providing her with the necessities of life, for his father would often spend his hard-earned wages in the public-houses. This kindness soon ripened into friendship, and around the age of seven or eight young Harold Gray was taken to The Salvation Army and immediately *'fancied it'*. He had previously attended Church, the Baptist Sunday School, and also a small Mission, but was not contented at any of these, likening himself to a *'round peg in a square hole'*.

He well remembers, on a number of occasions, when he saw Brother Stephens in the street with his trombone, that he would imitate the movements of the slide in his boyish way. Little did he think that one day he would be a trombone player himself. He was quite happy now, and made up his mind to 'stick' to The Army. At the age of thirteen and a half he was given an instrument, and old baritone, and this was the day for which he had longed. He recalled that upon one occasion he left his instrument, as usual, in a corner of the kitchen, alas! what a shock he had next morning when he saw his baritone. His father had come home in a drunken stupor on the previous night and had fallen headlong into the corner on top of his instrument, adding crude outlines to its already poor state. Bandmaster Gray remembered, too, how his father, the worse for drink, would come around the Open-Air ring on Saturday nights and, putting his hands on the boy's shoulder, with tears trickling down his cheeks, would say, *'Stick it, my lad. I want you to grow up to be good'*. About this time his mother, too, joined The Salvation Army, and he felt very proud. The uphill fight still continued in his young life, however, for at the age of fourteen and a half his father passed away, in tragic circumstances, having died as he had lived. When he was sixteen Harold was given a flugelhorn, which he played for nearly two years, and was then promoted to 1st baritone, on which instrument he showed great promise.

By the time he reached eighteen he had a longing for a trombone, but this section being complete there did not seem any immediate hope of his being promoted to the 'Vanguard'. A little later young Gray got to hear of a man who had a few second-hand instruments for sale, including a tenor trombone. His mother, knowing how he has set his mind on this type of instrument, bought it for him, and he made rapid headway, believing he was on his right instrument at last. His first real test was now to come, for at the age of twenty he was recommended for the important position of Band Sergeant, but though so young he filled the post satisfactorily, being well supported by the late Bandmaster J. Davis. His knowledge of the trombone stood him in good stead when he 'joined up', especially his study of the bass and tenor clefs. In France, for more than three years, he was fortunate in being able to play in a band most of the time as a trombone soloist. Also with the Army of Occupation in the Rhine he filled the position of soloist. With demobilization he once more settled down in the Corps to take up the Band Sergeant's position again. A beautiful spirit was shown by Brother Stephens, who willingly stepped down as the soloist so that Gray might take his place. Being of studious mind, he continued to make a persistent study of the slide, also of the trombone family in general, ultimately becoming a player of no mean order. Eventually he relinquished the position of Band Sergeant to take up the Deputy Bandmastership, holding the Songster Leader's commission simultaneously. About this time Gray decided to take up harmony, and bought an old textbook from a second-hand bookshop. He became so interested that he thought he would like to probe into the mysteries of composition, a rather taxing problem at his time of life, now twenty-seven, but he was not afraid of hard work. The Bandmaster expressed deep appreciation of the help rendered him by Colonel Frederick Hawkes and Bandmaster George Marshall, under whom he studied. That the Bandmaster is made of the 'Warrior Grit' type of Salvationist, and a zealous plodder, is proved by the fact that at a time when a serious crisis descended upon the Corps, which practically rent it in twain. With only five stalwart Bandsmen left, Bandsman Gray (as he was then) was asked if he would take on the unenviable position of Bandmaster. What a task! But being made of the 'stuff that counts', he accepted, knowing full well the enormous amount of hard work and worry it would entail. The Lord has abundantly blessed the Bandmaster, despite lack of encouragement, which at times was manifest.

(freely adjusted from 'The Musician' 10-9-1938)

Important compositions

Ever loyal (TS0156) 1931, Forward to Conquer (TS0172) 1932, Joyful Meeting (TS0120) 1929

GREEN, JAMES PAUL

Born in Sydney, Nova Scotia, Canada on 15 April 1929, Paul got an ARCT euphonium 1957, B.MUS (Toronto) 1954, M.MUS (ESM Rochester) 1959, PhD (ESM Rochester) 1974. Following graduation from the University of Toronto he was head of the music department and conductor of the concert band 1955-65 at T.L. Kennedy Secondary School in Mississauga. He served from 1963 until 1965 as conductor of the Salvation Army's famous Dovercourt Citadel Band in Toronto and taught 1964 until 1966 at the Ontario Ministry of Education's Summer School of Music.

In 1965 Paul Green joined the faculty of music at the University of Western Ontario, where he has taught brass and woodwind techniques and conducting, has given graduate courses in the psychology of music and the philosophy of music education, and served 1969-79 as chairman of the music education department. He conducted the university's Symphonic Band 1969-70 and its Faculty of Music Brass Choir 1965-70. Green is the co-author and arranger, with Kenneth Bray, of the series of wind instrument instruction books *'Solos for Schools'* (Gordon V. Thompson 1978-81).

He is long retired and currently living in Toronto and attending the Etobicoke Temple Corps. While he was in London at the University, he also served as the Divisional Bandmaster for the Ontario West Division of the Salvation Army for several years.

Important composition

Stephanos (GS1703) 1978

GREEN, WALTER R.

Walter R. Green was converted, in 1895, at Clapton Congress Hall while Colonel Pugmire was in command. He became a Bandsman under Bandmaster Caleb Burgess, of Household Troops fame, which service he continued during the whole period of his two successors, Colonel S. Deverill and Bandmaster A.M. Prestage (later of New York) respectively. Having been made Band Secretary, Correspondent Green faithfully 'obeyed the baton' wielded by Lieut.-Commissioner W. Dalziel, then, owing to removal to another district and the changed conditions created by the war, he transferred to Romford Band, where he served as Band Secretary and, later, as Corps Sergeant-Major. On returning to the Congress Hall, Correspondent Green played under the direction, first of the late John Howard and them of Bandmaster Lieut.-Colonel A. Wellman, again taking up the duties of Band Secretary.

When reasons of health compelled him to relinquish his instrument (trombone) he was roped-in as Corps Secretary until 1931. A very serious breakdown in health now intervened, necessitating retirement both form business and strenuous Salvation Army work. 'After forty-three years' active service, I am really retired,' declares Brother Green, 'but I still do 'my bit' behind the scenes.' There breathes the true warrior-spirit! ('The Musician' 20-8-1938)

Important composition

Come with thy sin (GS0330-1) 1896

GREENFIELD, ALBERT

The son of Salvation Army officer parents. He was in 1935 bandmaster of the Wellington South Band immediately prior to Dean Goffin taking over as a teenager. Played both euphonium and cornet. He left the band as euphonium player eighteen months after Dean Goffin's appointment. *'Berhampore'* is the only composition he is remembered by. It would have been written in the mid-1920s for publication in the NZBBJ 12.

Important composition

Berhampore (NZBBJ12)

GREENHORNE, DAVID

A bandsman of the Yeovil Corps in Somerset, United Kingdom.

Important composition

Melcombe (TS0799) 1976

GREGSON, EDWARD

Edward Gregson, born 1945 to a Salvation Army Family in England, is among the newer school of British wind composers who are bridging the gap between the romantic music played by many of the brass and wind bands earlier in the 20th century and the more experimental avant-garde compositions written during the last twenty five years. A brass bander, Gregson began to take an interest in music at about the age of eight and was soon taking piano lessons and playing in a Salvation Army Band. At eleven, he started to write some piano pieces, and at eighteen, he entered the Royal Academy of Music, London. Gregson taught first at the University of London Goldsmith's College, and is now Principal of the Royal Northern College of Music, Manchester. His brother Bram moved to Canada where he became the bandmaster of the London Citadel Band with whom he recorded a lot of Edward's compositions including his ever favourite *'Laudate Dominum'* as well as his *'Concertante for Piano and Band'*. A ground breaking recording by the Black Dyke Band (The Trumpets of the Angels) featuring Edward Gregson's music was made in 2004 celebrating the fact of 40 years composing for brass bands.

Important compositions

Symphonic Rhapsody for Euphonium (FS379) 1976, Variations on Laudate Dominum (FS393) 1978, Chalk Farm No.2 (FS406) 1980, Before the Cross (JC644) 2010, Dalarö (GS1613) 1970

GREIG, ALEX

Alex was a bandsman of the Aberdeen Corps Band in Scotland. His brother James was a bandsman with the Salvation Army Coventry City Band for many years and was a poet, Alex setting a number of James words to music. Alex was the father of (composer) Cecile James Creig, who later moved to Australia. The Greig family used to think that they were decendances of Edvard Greig, the Norwegian composer, but there is no proof of this.

Important compositions

Coronation Day (GS0331-2) 1897, Tried, Faithful and Precious (GS0205) 1892, Why did He love me so (GS0444) 1903

GREIG, CECILE JAMES

Born on 22 February 1895 in the United Kingdom and died in Australia on 20 June 1968. He came to Australia in 1926 and became bandmaster of the Norwood Citadel Band in Adelaide, South Australia. He returned to Scotland in 1939 and because of World War 2 he did not return to Australia until 1941. Once again he took up leadership of the Norwood Citadel Band and retired from that position in 1948. He was the son of Alex Greig.

Cecil James Greig was awarded the D.C.M. with the British Forces in World War 1. He had the letters L.T.C.L; L.G.S.M. after his name. He had a strong strength of character and a firm disciplined manner when leading the band.

Important compositions

Happy Song (FS0132) 1939, The Luton March (GS0744) 1916, Norwood Citadel (GS1088) 1934

GRIFFIN, KEITH

Keith Griffin was a songster leader (choir conductor) for the Salvation Army in Cardiff Canton.

Born in Cardiff and educated at Canton High School for Boys and University College Cardiff under Alun Hoddinott, Keith Griffin studied early choral music as a research student before joining the Welsh Arts Council in 1971. In the same year he married a fellow student, who is now a retired head teacher and music consultant. They have two children, both of whom are active musicians in addition to their careers in corporate affairs, politics and journalism.

At the Arts Council, Keith Griffin had special responsibility for the development of amateur music throughout Wales through the Welsh Amateur Music Federation, now Ty

Cerdd – Music Centre Wales, and was also involved as a conductor or performer with a number of choral and instrumental ensembles; he is currently musical director of the Cardiff County and Vale of Glamorgan Youth Brass Band. He formed the National Youth Brass Band of Wales in 1982 and the National Youth Choir of Wales in 1984. National Youth Jazz Wales followed in 2000, the National Youth Wind Orchestra of Wales in 2001, National Youth Symphonic Brass Wales in 2002 and the National Youth Training Choir of Wales in 2005, these later groups under the auspices of National Youth Arts Wales, which is a partnership between Ty Cerdd and the WJEC (which runs the NYOW, Theatre and Dance).

By the '90s the Welsh Amateur Music Federation had developed to such an extent that it had become an independent organisation, and Keith Griffin moved from the Arts Council to be Director of Ty Cerdd-Music Centre Wales, which was itself a partnership between the Welsh Amateur Music Federation and the Welsh Music Information Centre, which Ty Cerdd re-formed in 1999. Ty Cerdd moved to the Wales Millennium Centre in 2004, and was expanded to include a recording studio and music research and performance library, in addition to new offices and public access facilities.

Ty Cerdd currently offers grant aid and other assistance to over 400 amateur music performing societies throughout Wales representing some 25,000 performers or associated members. Over 500 individual grants are administered each year, and there is a full programme of workshops and performances, 200 of which are provided as part of the WMC's free performance series on the Tesco stage. Support for Welsh composers is offered through promotion and commissions. Ty Cerdd is one of 42 Music Information Centres worldwide, and in 2008 will host the conference of the International Association of Music Information Centres, which visits Wales for the first time.

The Ty Cerdd recording studio works through a wide range of musical genres, including young rock groups, WNO, BBC, S4C, and a wide range of amateur and professional musicians, minority cultural groups, and with people with disability or special educational needs.

The Centre is also working with primary school teachers to provide the 'Young Composer' series, which will be a major Welsh music resource.

The Centre monitors trends in music, and works closely with other national music organisations in Wales, including CAGAC (the local authority heads of music services consortium), particularly in the delivery of music provision to young people. It continues to fund and administer 6 of the 7 national youth music ensembles in Wales, marking the 25th anniversary of the NYBBW in 2007 with a very successful tour of Canada, and celebrating the success of the NYCW with the first performances by a Welsh national music ensemble at the BBC London Proms in 2007 and 2009.

Important compositions

St. Peter (GS1611-2) 1970, Sweet Chariot (TS0863) 1981

GRINDSTED, EDGAR SWEARSE

Born in Wood Green, United Kingdom on 3 August 1897 to Colonel and Mrs. Grindsted, and his childhood was comparable with that of most boys and girls born to Salvation Army officers. Money was minimal, but with both parents of good report he early learned the value of other securities.

Edgar entered the International Training College in February 1919 and was commissioned as an officer five months later. He married Captain Louise Kitching (daughter of Commissioner Kitching) in 1921 with whom he got two children (Edgar Jr and Jane). Amongst his many corps appointments he also became Corps Officer of the famous Clapton Congress Hall from 1931 to 1934. As from 1951 he became Territorial Commander for the UK, British Commander, and finally Territorial Commander for Canada which was also his last appointment before his retirement in 1967.

Edgar Grindsted was loved by all with whom he worked, whether they were officer colleagues in the Salvation Army or fellow soldiers in Militairy service. He was known for his huge cultured voice which you could hear easily 50 yards away. Commissioner Edgar Swearse Grindsted was Promoted to Glory on 30 March 1979.

Important compositions

Faith of our Fathers (TS0410) 1947, Joyful Service (TS0813) 1977

GROVES, PETER

Former member of the International Staff Band and a son of Major and Mrs. Charles Groves. The hymn tune arrangement listed below is his only published work for brass band. He was from the Darlaston Corps in the United Kingdom. Peter Groves was a member of the the Music Editorial Department for a while, possibly in the 50's. He also wrote interesting songster pieces and was a very promising composer at the time. He later moved to Canada.

Important composition

Ottawa (GS1325-2) 1950

GROZINSKY, GUSTAVE ADOLF ALEXANDER AUGUSTINE

Gustave Grozinsky was born in Moscow around 1870 and died in Canada on 21 December 1936. He was the son of Julius Grozinsky, a tailer by profession. Likely political refugees, as his father had been sent to Siberia, they went to the United Kingdom and came to live in Camberwell. Here he became a convert after hearing a Salvation Army band playing on the streets. After being trained as a Salvation Army officer, he served in that capacity in several corps appointments including Northampton, Wandsworth, Catford, Dorking and Thurso. Later they moved on to Canada and became soldiers at Edmonton Citadel. He was a very musical figure and played violin, banjo and guitar, and contributed several songs to The 'War Cry' and "The Musical Salvationist" as well as his entrée to the General Series.

Important composition

I'll be true (GS0226) 1893

GULLIDGE, ARTHUR W.

Arthur W. Gullidge was born on 9th April 1909 in Broken Hill, New South Wales, Australia. He developed his musical talents in the Salvation Army in Melbourne City Temple Corps where he was Deputy Bandmaster. Later, Arthur became the Bandmaster in Collingwood Corps, where many of his Compositions were written. During the 2nd World

War, Arthur Gullidge, together with other Salvationists, offered for military service. He was promoted to Sergeant and Bandmaster of the Military Band 2/22, in which several Salvationists played. Arthur was captured and imprisoned and died in a prison camp on 1st July 1942. He wrote: *'Although many of my compositions, that have been used commercially, have a high technical standard, my compositions for the Salvation Army, have brought me more satisfaction, then I believe they are a special way in which I can serve the Lord'.*

Book 1 - **Brave and True** - by Lindsey C. Cox

In 1942, the biggest single loss of life suffered by Australia happened in one single wartime act. The number of lives lost was two-and-a-half times the total number of Australian soldiers killed in Vietnam. Amongst those who perished were 22 Salvation Army Bandsmen enlisted in the AIF under renowned Bandmaster Arthur Gullidge to form the 2/22nd Battalion Band. Just one bandsman survived the invasion of Rabaul.

Book 2- **Tuned to the Celestial Pitch** - by Leslie Rusher

It is timely to recognise the life and work of Salvationist composer and Bandmaster, Arthur Gullidge. At the age of 33, Arthur lost his life when the prisoner of war vessel on which he was being held was torpedoed. Twenty-one other Salvation Army bandsmen who were part of the 2/22nd battalion were lost on that day. This book will evoke tender memories of their service.

Important compositions

Jubilate (FS160) 1949, Divine Communion (GS1255) 1945, Southern Australia (GS1168) 1939, Unconquered (GS1485) 1960, Emblem of the Army (GS1572) 1967

GUSTAFSON, J. HAROLD

Arranger of several pieces published in USA East American Band Journal, Gustafson led for many years the large, active music program at the Swedish-American corps in Jamestown, New York. Interestingly, the corps gave him the designation 'music minister' due to the many responsibilities he held in the music program of the corps.

Important composition

Selection - Grand Old Gospel Songs, Selection - Songs of Salvation, March - The Hallelujah Way

HADDON, DAVID

Born on the 26th of December 1940 into a Salvation Army family. His father at the time was serving his country in the Armed Forces in India and what was then Persia, (now Pakistan) and Ceylon, (now Sri Lanka). David met him for the first time when the war was over in 1945. His mother was at this time attending the Northampton Citadel Corps, where her sister and sister-in-law belonged; her brother was also on active service overseas.

During this time they were virtually living with his grandparents. They had an old organ, it had a couple of pedals that you had to work constantly to make any sound, so it was more like a harmonium. From his earliest years he used to love to play on it. David would stand in front of it so that he could reach the keyboard, pedal with one foot while playing tunes with one finger at the same time.

Fast forward to 1945 and the return of his father. He was, of course, a stranger to David, and it was difficult for both of them to adjust. When within about three years it was decided that the Haddon's should move home to another part of the town of Northampton, they found themselves closer to Northampton Central corps than the Citadel, and therefore transferred to the Central. .

It was not long before David was invited to join the singing company. He would be about nine at the time and was soon persuaded to rsecite poetry on singing company programs. But that came to an end when on one such program he forgot the words and ended up in tears. David was good friends with the boy who sat next to him. He played drum in the Young People's Band. In the Sunday afternoon meetings that they used to have in those days, he would sit alongside him as he played the drum. Sometimes he would get him to play it instead, which David did. He learned that his friend was learning to play a brass instrument. So when he became proficient enough to move permanently on to baritone, David found himself the Young People' Band drummer! All of this happened without actually being asked to play by the Young People's Bandleader. But he was a kind Christian gentleman who would happily break the rules in order to help someone to become involved for the sake of the Kingdom. It wasn't long before he asked David if he would like to have a go at learning to play a cornet. He would be at least ten by now, so quite a late starter.

David took to the cornet immediately, (and still plays one today), and became fascinated with the musical language and wanted to know as much as he could about key relationships, and the way music was put together. It was all new to him and he would devour anything he could to help him learn about the theoretical aspect of music. He was also beginning to listen to classical music and it is true to say that he was about eleven when he learnt to read music, and by the age of twelve he was trying to compose it. At first he used to hide what he had written in a drawer, until his mother discovered it. She showed it to David's father, whose comment was *'Ugh, he's trying to run before he can walk!'* So his father was no great encouragement to him, despite being the Deputy Bandmaster at the corps.

Eventually David decided to take some of these early attempts at composition along to Young People's Band practice and got one or two of the lads to join him in trying it out after the official band practice had finished. When the Bandleader realized what they were doing, unlike his father, he was very encouraging. He had suggested earlier that he should go to the summer music school, held then at Grendon Hall, about ten miles from Northampton. He was one of the instructors at the school and used to take them over on the back of his lorry, which they thought was great fun. Before they went, he asked if he could have the music David had written up until then to have a good look at. Unknown to David his real purpose was to pass it on to the Musical Director, a young Captain Ray Bowes, later to become Lieutenant Colonel Ray Bowes, conductor of the International Staff Band, and Head of the Music Editorial Department for some years.

Characteristically Ray said nothing to David, but on the mid-week talent evening he got a big surprise. Ray had not been conducting the band that David was in, and unknown to him the band that he was conducting had been rehearsing a march that David had written. And they played it in front of parents and instructors at the talent evening! It sounded pretty awful, but it was an encouragement to keep at it. That was his first public performance. He was twelve or thirteen at the time.

Another person who influenced David in his early attempts at composition was Bandmaster Jack Key, originally from Bexleyheath. He was working for the Salvation Army Assurance Society and was sent to Northampton as the Superintendent. He came to soldier at the Central corps, and as soon as he heard that David had tried his hand at composing, he took him under his wing. David was thirteen at the time. He gave him regular lessons in harmony and other aspects of musical composition at his home on a Wednesday evening, and it was under his tutelage that David first submitted a composition to the Music Editorial Department, as it was then called, at Salvationist Publishing and Supplies Ltd in Judd Street, London. He recall that it was a cornet trio called *'God is Love'*, based upon the tune of the same name. Needless to say, it wasn't acceptable for publication, but he received an encouraging letter from Lieutenant Colonel Charles Skinner, the then head of the department. David was then sixteen.

It was later in his sixteenth year that Jack Key was informed by the Army that they were transferring him to Lincoln. David was devastated, but he was determined to continue to compose. It was a sort of inner compulsion which has remained throughout his life. David kept submitting music, most of which was rejected, but eventually his determination was rewarded, and his first publication appeared in "The Musical Salvationist" in April 1968. It was a setting of song number 711 in the Salvation Army Song book, with words by Lily Sampson which begin: *'As the varied way of life we journey'*. David called it *'The Road of Life'*. Two years later, he had a band piece published in the Triumph Series: a song arrangement based on the song *'I hear Thy welcome voice'*. He called it simply *'Thy Welcome Voice'*. It is gratifying to know that this simple arrangement is still being used by a number of smaller bands.

After these two pieces David had to wait thirteen years before his next publication. This was in the General Series, and was certainly the most ambitious and modern piece he had had published up to that time. He called it *'Soldiers of Salvation'*, and it is based on a tune that is no longer in the song book, called *'Turn to the Lord'*. David took the title from the words of the chorus of that song: *'Fighting beneath the Army colours, saved from sin through Jesus' love. We are soldiers of salvation. Marching to the realms above'*.

David only had to wait four years for his next publication. This was a Triumph Series march dedicated to the Young People's Corps that he had grown up in. It was called *'Northampton Central Young People'*. This was quite a simple little march. It was published in July 1987. Two years later, in 1989, due to adverse circumstances in David's life, he felt the need to transfer elsewhere. The obvious choice was the other Northampton corps, which he had left years before, the Citadel; though they had moved to the Eastern most part of the town, and the corps had changed its name to Northampton East. David immediately felt welcome at the East, and within two years he was asked to take on the position of Band Sergeant, a position David still holds.

Since transferring to the East corps he has had two further publications, the first in 1995 was a song in the 'Sing to the Lord' books for mixed voices. His only other publication since then has been a transcription for brass of Sir Edward Elgars lovely early work, *'Ave Verum'*. This was published in the Triumph Series in March 2009.

David does not limit his composing exclusively to the Salvation Army. He has written music for brass bands outside of the Army, and pieces for strings, for concert bands, for wind quintet, a serenade in four movements for French Horn and Strings, and even one piece for full orchestra.

Important composition

Northampton Central Young People (TS0932) 1987, Thy welcome voice (TS0727) 1970, Soldiers of Salvation (GS1762) 1983

HAGUE, HERBERT EDWARD

Herbert Hague (1900 – 1987) was a lifelong Salvationist and at an early age joined the local Salvation Army Band at Somercotes, Derbyshire. His mother was a Salvation Army officer in the 1890's and it was at Somercotes where she married. Both Herbert's parents were active in the Salvation Army throughout their lives. Herbert played the euphonium and, at twenty one, he entered for the London College of Music examinations for both theory and practice, his instrument being the euphonium. A few year's later he transferred to Ripley Corps where he became Songster Leader.

He was a coal miner, and in 1926 there was a severe depression in mining resulting in a general strike throughout the United Kingdom. Therefore, he decided to immigrate to Canada where he was associated with the Salvation Army at Glace Bay, Nova Scotia but only for a short time having returned to the United Kingdom within six months. On his return, he became deputy bandmaster at Ripley and about this time he composed *'The Ripley March'*, which became quite popular with Salvation Army bands.

Alongside brass banding, he became an exceedingly accomplished English Concertina player, recognized at national level, and this interest remained with him for the rest of his life. The Salvation Army published a tutor for the English Concertina used mainly by Officers when many played this instrument. Herbert contributed to this publication with a piece entitled *'Descriptive selection – Sunday Morn'*. He played the concertina as a solo instrument regularly over more than sixty years at Army festivals and for local charity efforts.

Other than in the Triumph Series of the Salvation Army musical journals he also had some publications in 'The Musical Salvationist' (respectively in 1930, 1932 and 1972).

Important composition

The Appeal (TS0524) 1954, Happiness (TS0620) 1961, Ripley (TS0196) 1933

HALCROW, LOWERY

Out of South Shields Corps, he was a band instructor as well as the Provincial Bandmaster in the Northern Province of the United Kingdom.

'Divisional Bandmaster Halcrow, in charge of South Shields 2, spoke strongly on the power of music. He was of the opinion, he said, that if music, consecrated, could not reach the heart, nothing could. He referred to an instance of a week or two ago when South Shields 2 were playing 'Nearer, My God to Thee' on a Sunday morning, a man, who was a first-class musician, followed the Band to the Hall and got converted.' (The Bandsman and Songster, April 13, 1907)

Important compositions

Glory to God (GS0264) 1894, Saviour's Birth (GS0326-2) 1896

HALL, ADAM

Adam Hall was born 22 Mar 1899 at Felling, Co. Durham, the eldest son of Robert Adam Hall and Jessie Dent. On 11 Sep 1923 he married Catherine May Winton at The Salvation Army, Cannock. They had nine children. Catherine died 28 Jul 1964, Hackney, London; Adam died 7 Jun 1979, Southampton. Throughout his Army banding, Adam always played Double B. He held a number of positions in Felling Corps; Band Sergeant, Corps Secretary and Songster Leader. In 1940 the family moved to South Shields, and transferred to South Shields Central Corps, where Adam served as Band Sergeant and Corps Sergeant-Major. Sometime in the late 1950's/early 1960's, they transferred to South Shields Saville Street Corps. It was while they were on holiday in London when Catherine died. Daughter Catherine was living in Leytonstone and offered Adam to stay with her and her family, and he soldiered at Leyton Corps, and was for a while Deputy Songster Leader. When Catherine and family moved back north to Peterlee, Co. Durham, Adam soldiered at Horden Corps. A further move took Adam to stay with eldest daughter Betty and family at Hatfield, Hertfordshire, and so Adam soldiered with them at St. Alban's Corps until his death. Adam had no musical training other than what he learnt at the Army, but was a prolific writer of verse and articles, and could write a good tune. As far as I know he never wrote a Band piece, but sometimes wrote melodies to link together in march style. He had quite a number of his songs published by The Salvation Army from 1926 through until the 1970s. In all there were 7 songs for Songsters; 2 songs for Male Voices; 2 songs for Soloists; 3 songs for Home League Singers and 19 songs for Young People.Grandfather of International Staff Bandsman and Maidenhead Citadel Bandmaster Stuart Hall

Important composition

Rejoice (US0053) 1964

HALL, HENRY R.

Henry Hall was born in Peckham in 1898, South London and served in both the Salvation Army and the British Army. His early musical career was slow to start but eventually he was engaged by the London Midland and Scottish Railway to be in charge of the music throughout their then large chain of hotels. This included Gleneagles, where he had formerly led the band. It was from there that the BBC took him in 1932 as successor to Jack Payne as leader of the BBC Dance Orchestra, and from Broadcasting House at 5.15 each week day Hall gathered a huge following. His signature tune was *'It's Just the Time for Dancing'* and he usually ended with *'Here's to the Next Time'*. In 1932 he recorded the song *'Teddy Bears' Picnic'* with his BBC Orchestra. The record gained enormous popularity and has sold over a million copies. He was Promoted to Glory in 1989.

Important composition

Holly (GS0787) 1917, The Norwood March (GS0922) 1924, The Nunhead March (GS0751) 1916, On the Ocean (TS0021) 1923

HALL, NORMAN

Very little is known about Norman Hall. He was a Deputy Bandmaster of the Higher Openshaw Citadel Band (Manchester Higher Openshaw was the 15th Salvation Army corps opened in Manchester, in 1903, in Fairfield Road.)

Important composition

Mancunian (TS0744) 1971

HALL, P.R.

A former Songster Leader

No further information about this person could be retrieved.

Important composition

Calvary (TS0286) 1939

HALL, W

A former Bandsman.

No further information about this person could be retrieved.

Important composition

Staines (TS0376) 1945

HALPIN, WILLIAM

Born on 20 November 1862, William was a British Salvation Army officer from Birkenhead #2 Corps who was a converted musician. His first appointment as an officer in 1883 was the Manchester #1 Corps, and six corps were to follow before he went to New York in 1885 and founded the New York 1 Corps Band and also led the Ohio Divisional Band. In 1888 he became Divisional Officer of the Southern Ohio, Indiana and Kentucky District. In 1901 he resigned from officership but was reaccepted in 1911 as Adjutant. After several positions he went to France in 1917 on War Service and returned a year later where he continued his work for the Salvation Army at the Divisional Headquarters in Baltimore. In 1924 he became Territorial Prison Secretary, which was his last appointment. In 1925 he was a Brigadier and retired two years later. Brigadier William Halpin was Promoted to Glory on 11 August 1941.

His Order of Service for his funeral tells us: *'Tempered in the heat of the organization's early days, and tried in the crucible of persecution and misunderstanding, the Brigadier, a gifted poet, preacher, and musician, was a contemporary of such Salvationist warriors as the late commissioner Thomas Estill, Colonel William Evans, and other esteemed Salvationist figures, equally well known and widely loved and possessed a sheaf of golden memories bearing upon the tempestuous days of the organization's early beginnings. However he never lost touch with the new generation and his friends were among the old and young, the famous and the obscure.'*

'The Old Orchard Beach camp meetings that year (1934) were blessed with the participation of seasoned 'Warriors of the Cross,' Commissioner Samuel Logan Brengle, Lt. Commissioner Edgar Hoe, Colonel William J. Morehen, Colonel Alfred Chandler and Brigadier William Halpin - all retired veterans of the camp meetings and of many hard-fought battles with the devil'.

(source: Salvation Army Museum, New York)

Important composition

Get ready for His coming (GS0204) 1892

HANSEN, KARL

Karl Hansen was from Copenhagen but learned his trade in Herning (Jutland). Here he met the Salvation Army and became a Soldier, and was put in charge of the first band at Herning Corps. This was probably around 1895. He became an Officer in 1897. He was

Corps Officer at a number of large corps, but got assigned to Territorial Headquarters, at the Finance Department, became National Auditor, and in the 1930's he became Head of the Property Dept. He became a Brigadier before his retirement.

In 1913 Ernst Söderström became Staff Bandmaster. In connection with the change of leadership, Karl Hansen (then an Adjutant) became the Band Secretary of the Staff Band. He was (at least at that time) playing Bass Drum. A positive identification of him is tell us that from 1911 he was a member of the band. (He may have entered the ranks of the Staff Band as early as 1909-1910, but not earlier). He was married in 1913 to Captain Lydia Nielsen and was with the band at the International Congress in 1914.

After this no information on his assignment on the Staff Band could be found, and it is very likely that he ended his duty around the outbreak of the war, because a lot of changes hit the Territorial Headquarters, partly due to many male Salvationists enlisting for military service. He could have been in the band for a longer period, but this is not likely.

Important composition

Barnens Fanvakt *(The Children's Colour Guard)* (FM0048-2) 1906

HANSON, AUDUN

Audun was born in Haugesund, Norway on 23 October 1943 and became involved with the Salvation Army first through Sunday school, youth and scouting, and later became a Salvationist, musician and music teacher. He and his wife went to the Training College in 1970 and they were Salvation Army officers until 1992. In this period they had been corps officers at Sandnessjøen, Vadsø, Vik i Sogn, Bryne and Bodo. For more than four years he worked at the Salvation Army's Territorial Headquarters in the Music Department in Oslo, and also as Institutional Manager of a protected home for homeless people in Stavanger. Later he worked in the county child welfare until his retirement in 2005. He has conducted various vocal and instrumental musical groups. Audun started composing music while he had a two-year leave as a Salvation Army officer between 1977 and 1979. He started to write music, mainly for the Bryne and Sandnes Corps to use in their meetings. It was thus a lack of appropriate music that was the reason he started writing while he was engaged as instructor in these bands. He has no background or training in composition, but used his enthusiasm and experience as a bandsman. During these two years he worked in the music department, along with Major Paul Marti (another composer).

Important composition

Barnevennen Jesus (NMSJ30)

HANSON, ANDREAS

Andreas Hanson (19 December 1969) is one of two sons of Torgny Hanson. In 1988 he founded the Big Town Brass of the Salvation Army, a regional band, mainly with younger players from the Stockholm area for whom he wrote several pieces. He studied trumpet with Philip Smith, principal trumpet of the New York Philharmonic Orchestra and is a professional conductor.

Important composition

Three Christian Songs (m/s)

HANSON, JOHN HUGO

John was born in 1890 and Promoted to Glory in 1965. He played in the Swedish Staff Band in 1913, being their Eb Cornetist. Next to this, he was the founder and Bandmaster of the Malmö 2 Corps Band, during 1911 and 1933, after which he transferred to Limhamn where he became bandmaster of the Limhamn Corps Band until 1948. He composed the marches *'Var glad'* (*'Be glad!'* Svensk Festmusik 125) and *'Var trogen'* (*'Be faithful!'* svensk Festmusik 212). He was a shoemaker by profession and was the grandfather of Torgny Hanson.

Important compositions

Var Glad! (FM0125) 1921, Var Trogen! (FM0212)

HANSON, TORGNY

Torgny Hanson started to play the cornet in the Salvation Army Band in his hometown Malmö at the early age of 11. Already when he was 16 he was appointed deputy bandmaster and started his musical education at 18 at the State College of Music in Malmö where the famous Danish trumpeter Knud Hovaldt was his teacher. Professor Arne Hammelboe was his teacher in conducting. In 1971 Torgny Hanson studied trumpet with Bernard Brown at Guildhall School of Music in London and also the brass band movement and it's repertoire under personal supervision of Geoffrey Brand and Eric Ball.

In his professional life Torgny Hanson is an educator and a performer. He has been a teacher at the State College of Music in Malmö as well as at the Royal College of Music in Stockholm, where he also was the director for the instrumental- and ensemble-teachers' education. His professional career as conductor has included positions as musical director of two fulltime professional wind orchestras, Östgöta Symphonic Winds and Stockholm Symphonic Wind Orchestra. During the 1990s he regularly conducted the National Youth Wind Orchestra of Great Britain and was an artistic adviser of that organization. Between 1992-2008 Torgny Hanson was the Inspector of Military Music in Sweden with the rank of lieutenant colonel. He is a founding member of the Swedish Society of professional orchestral conductors.

As brass band conductor he is well known in The Salvation Army after more than thirty years leadership for the Södertälje Salvation Army Band as well as the internationally renowned Stockholm VII Band. He is still active as bandmaster and conductor of Stockholm South Citadel Band (former Stockholm VII). He has been a guest conductor of Salvation Army bands in several countries but also directed courses for musicians and conductors in Scandinavia, Germany, UK, USA and Canada. In 1988 he was invited by James Watson and The Desford Colliery Band to spend a week of rehearsals and concerts as guest conductor which also meant the world-premiere performance of Robert Simpson's composition *'Introduction and Allegro on a Bass by Max Reger'*. He has on several occasions visited USA to conduct top brass bands in the states of Ohio, Kentucky and New York. As conductor of wind bands he has performed in countries as Denmark, Norway, Finland, Russia, The Netherlands and Canada.

Torgny Hanson is often invited as adjudicator of contest for brass bands as well as symphonic bands. He has adjudicated the top section of European championships for brass bands twice as well as several times in Norway and Sweden. His transcriptions and arrangements for brass band are much appreciated and played frequently.

From 2009 he is the musical director and conductor of the Solna Brass, Stockholm. He is now continuing his career as free lance conductor, teacher and lecturer.

Important compositions

Vallflickans Dans, Folk Dances

HANNEVIK, JOHN PHILIP

John Philip Hannevik was born in Tromso, Norway in 1970. His first experiences with music came when his parents became corps officers in Cardiff Canton (Wales) when he was only four months old. He soon showed a great interest for music, and when his parents farwelled from Wales, he was presented with his first conductor's baton from corps bandmaster Ivor Bosanko. Philip was three years old! Philip grew up as a Salvation Army bandsman. He got his first professional tuition from composer Eiliv Herikstad, who was Philip's music teacher when Philip went to the Salvation Army's Jeloy College. Philip completed a BA in Social Science at the University in Oslo in 1994. During that summer, something very important happened for him. He was appointed as the Commissioner Richard E. Holz Memorial Program Staff Chair winner at Star Lake Musicamp. This was a great inspiration to him. At the end of music camp, back home in Oslo, Philip decided to apply for a study in music at Oslo University. He completed his MA Musicology in 1998. Philip was bandmaster for the Oslo Temple Band between 1994 - 2006. He has also been bandmaster of the Norwegian Territorial Band since 2001. Philip has received tuition from some of Scandinavia's top professional conductors. He was prize winner at the European Young Conductor's Competition in 2003 and he has conducted some of the finest brass soloists in Europe in several of the best concert houses in Scandinavia. Philip now works as a professional conductor and is an active Salvationist in Oslo Temple Corps. He married to Trine-Lise in May 2009. Philip sees it as a great gift from God to be able to work as a musician and to be a member of a church that always wants to spread the message of God's love to all people. His greatest ambition is to be a witness for Jesus.

Important composition

Da ser jag dina hander (SB2006-02) 2006

HARRIS, JAMES

Bandmaster James Harris arrived in Canada from Lancashire, England where he had been bandmaster for 16 years. When in Canada he took over the Ottawa Citadel Band (formerly known too as the Slater Street Citadel Band) in May 1906. He was added to the Ottawa Citadel (Number 1 Corps) Roll on 1 July 1906. He served as Bandmaster for 34 years, being forced to relinquish his position in 1939 because of ill health. He was a successful Bandmaster, the Band making such good progress that several Band members were transferred to Ottawa Number 2 Corps (Gladstone) in 1910 to help start a Band there. By April 1911 Harris was leading a Band of 26 players, and this increased to 40 by 1920, Harris having successfully managed to hold the Band together while 24 Band members enlisted in the First World War.

After his retirement he was presented at a special Recognition event on 30 November to 2 December 1940 with an Honorary Bandmaster's Commission in recognition of his 50 years as a Commissioned Bandmaster. He was Promoted to Glory on 8 January, 1952.

Important composition

Gloryland (TS0224) 1935

James Harris, on the front row, far right

HARTILL, LES

Les was born in 1936, and dedicated in the Dudley Corps (No. 54), where he grew up in the Young People's Corps. His mother was for many years the Home League Secretary there. They were very fortunate to have excellent Young People's Leaders, particularly with the Young People's Band and Singing Company, so as Junior Soldiers, they received good training, musically and spiritually. Both Young People's Band and Singing Company maintained high standards and travelled widely throughout the United Kingdom conducting 'Special' weekends. Les was also a Corps Cadet, and a member of the Scout Group, so the overall the training received was such as to equip them for the future and ground them in their faith and they were always reminded of the necessity of giving 'the best for the Highest'. Les eventually became, in his early teens assistant Young People's Bandleader, and Corps and Songster pianist.

Apart from the Army musical training, Les began piano lessons at the age of eight, then a year later added the piano accordion; then a little later still, the violin. He gained his A.L.C.M diploma (piano) at the age of sixteen. The accordion became and still is a particular love, and in his youth he was frequently called upon as a soloist within the Birmingham Division and indeed further afield. He also had the experience of being invited into the Drummers Fraternal, organized by Major Bernal Webb (the father of composer Joy Webb). This was something of an institution in the United Kingdom, for many years conducting weekends at Corps all over the United Kingdom, focusing on the role of the Army Drum as the mobile altar of early days, and using music as a vehicle for evangelism.

Although Les was invited more for his accordion/ keyboard skills rather than his expertise with a snare drum! But it was quite thrilling to march with a Corps of Drums heading the various Corps bands. At eighteen years old, Les was called up to do two years National Service in the Royal air force. Although posted to R.A. F. Lyneham in the signals department, he did continue to play in the station band as a volunteer bandsman. More importantly, he met his future wife, Betty, whilst serving there, as she was also in the R.A.F at nearby RAF Hullavington. Shortly after returning to civilian life, they were married at Dudley Corps on August 18th. 1956. In 1959, they entered the William Booth International Training College, as Cadets in the 'Greathearts' Session. Les became the sessional pianist, and had the joy of playing together with the then Lieutenant John Larson (later to become General of the Salvation Army), John on the college organ, and Les at the piano during their times of worship in the Assembly Hall. Les and Betty were commissioned in 1960, with their first appointment being Saxmundham in Suffolk.

The accordion was very useful there with no band, and only a small songster brigade, as they were then able to conduct open-air meetings. Their first published composition for the Salvation Army was written there. Their daughter was born there, and was eight weeks old when they were moved right across the country to South Wales. They served at Neath and Swansea before moving to Tenby; a seaside town in West Wales and spent two years there, with very busy summer seasons with open air meetings, beach meetings, and a Sunday evening community hymn singing at the harbour. No Band, so the accordion had constant use. Out of season there were of course still the open-airs, and not forgetting carol singing around the streets of Tenby at Christmastime.

They had a quartet of teenaged girls, who bought guitars (this was the Joy Strings era) then informed Les to teach them. As Les had never played a guitar this was interesting. Thus a guitar was purchased. Les would learn a few chords, then teach the girls, then some more chords, etc. They added guitars to the accordion, and occasionally Les would borrow a string bass from a nearby club, just to vary the sound a little, and they used all their resources to attract the crowds and present to Gospel.

Later they moved up to Harrogate, then to Bradford in Yorkshire. But sadly, his wife's health broke down, and following their last move to Derbyshire, they regrettably had to end their officership. They then settled in Ilkeston, in Derbyshire, where Les served as Songster Leader for a period, and where their daughter Gay had her early vocal training in the Singing Company, and their son in the band. Les then was accepted for Teacher Training, and obtained a degree in music and education.

Les accepted a teaching post in Derby, and after about a year obtained a further post as Head of Music at a new school again in Derby. During this period he was involved with a number of bands in the North West Midlands area, just a brief spell as a player, before taking up the baton as trainer and conductor. Eventually, he was appointed Bandmaster of the South Nottinghamshire Hussars R.H.A (Royal Horse Artillery) band, as a Warrant Officer in the Territorial Army Volunteer Reserve. This was a very busy band, always with a full calendar of both military and civilian engagements. Les did write quite a lot of music, original and arrangements during this time. One of his marches was broadcast on the BBC 'Challenging Brass' program. It was written for a championship band in Burton-on-Trent. The Musical Director was Ernest Woodhouse, a then well known conductor who had encouraged Les' writing and conducting. The 'South Notts' also recorded for BBC Radio

Nottingham, occasionally playing music Les had written, in a series of brass band programs that were produced on local radio. The Band also produced an LP recording to which Les contributed some items. This was a very happy and productive period for Les, for which he was awarded the Lord Lieutenant's Certificate for 'meritorious and outstanding service' in the T.A.V.R. He acknowledged that this was due as much to a fantastically loyal group of bandsmen as it was to himself.

However, in 1980 there was quite a dramatic change for Les' family and himself. He accepted a Head of Music post in Douglas, on the Isle of Man, at the Islands' largest school. This was quite a challenging post, but it allowed him to expand his teaching and writing abilities quite exponentially, writing for orchestra, wind band, and strings in what proved to be a very busy music department. He did, for a while in the early days there, train the Isle of Man Youth Wind Band. He also wrote his single commissioned score, for the Isle of Man Youth Orchestra, an orchestral arrangemennt of *'Hava Nagila'* which the orchestra requested for a tour of the Holy Land. They linked up with the Douglas Corps, the sole Salvation Army presence on the island. However, some twenty years ago, whilst Les was still teaching (he retired in 1996), he had a visit from the Anglican Arch-deacon whilst teaching in school. He asked Les if he could assist the church of All Saints, as the organist there was having to retire because of ill-health. This was to be just a temporary arrangement. However, Les is still there.

This has been a wonderful experience. Not just playing the organ, but taking responsibility for all the music, including the hymns week by week. He has been able to write music for choir and congregational use, and introduce contemporary songs into the worship, including arranging for a small worship group. Les feels that God has, in His wisdom, found him another field to wherein to plough. He has a warm relationship with the people at All Saints, and they accepted him as a Salvationist. The attributes of service and commitment which have epitomized Salvation Army service are a part of his DNA. He still holds fast to the doctrines and principles of the Army which have been his mainstay throughout the years.

Music published by SP&S:

Songs For Male Voices. 'Let me love Thee' setting of words by Herbert Booth (circa 1960), 'We shall see the King in His beauty' arrangement of song by Sidney Cox (circa 1962), Triumph Series 1116 'Clevedon 100', a march written for the Clevedon Corps Centenary in 2002.

Musical Influences

Dr. Eric Leigh; Head of Music at Bishop Lonsdale College of Education. Who taught him the basics of organ playing, then further encouraged Les to concentrate on composition. Leslie Condon, who, when Les was a young Lieutenant, visited them at Saxmundham shortly after publication of his first song and encouraged him to write more. Ray Bowes, whom he met at Harlesden when on a Salvation Army Course, and who warmly welcomed Les in the short time he spent there, and whose music he admire. Eric Ball, whose music and immaculate scoring thrills, inspires, and moves Les. Ray Steadman-Allen; consummate craftsman, the complete composer. Kenneth Downie and Peter Graham both of whose craftsmanship Les would dearly love to emulate.

Important composition

Clevedon 100 (TS1116) 2002

HARVEY, HARRY

English by birth, Harry immigrated to Australia when on a young age and became Songster Leader of the Brunswick Corps. He was upset by the outbreak of WWII as his wedding was scheduled for two weeks time. Harry Desmond Harvey was Songster Leader at the Brunswick Corps, a suburb of Melbourne. He was also the Melbourne Central Division's Divisional Songster Leader. His occupation was listed as 'musician', and he also was known to have worked at Rackhams fish cannery. He also played cornet in the Brunswick Citadel Band under Arthur Gullidge. At the time of the commencement of World War Two on 3 September 1939, Harry was engaged to Rose Arnott, and their wedding had been arranged prior for the 16 September. The wedding proceeded on time. On 15 July 1940 Harry Harvey - aged 29 - enlisted in the Australian Imperial Force for service overseas. He joined with Arthur Gullidge and fellow Salvation Army Bandsmen to form the 2/22nd Battalion Band, which ultimately went to Rabaul on New Britain. He was captured during the Japanese invasion of the island and perished at sea when the prison ship, the Montevideo Maru was sunk by a US submarine on 1 July 1942.

Important compositions

Fellowship with Christ (TS0355) 1943, Valour (TS0236) 1936, Warriors True (TS0252) 1937

HAWKES, FREDERICK

Frederick Hawkes was born 1869 in England. He was officer of The Salvation Army. In 1891 he served as assistent to Richard Slater, on the Department of Music by the International Headquarter of The Salvation Army in London. He became bandmaster of the 'Trade Headquarter Band' (later 'International Headquarters Staff Band'). In 1899 the new 'Salvation Army Song Book' was published by Frederick Hawkes, Richard Slater and Herbert Booth, with 870 Songs and 216 Choruses. Frederick Hawkes belongs to the Salvation Army composers with the most published works. He was Promoted to Glory at the age of 90 in 1959.

In April 1891 his first song, of which he wrote the words and music, appeared in 'The Musical Salvationist' and it is evident that this and other early experiments created a favourable impression upon the music chief.

Important compositions

A Backslider's Vision (GS0363-1) 1898, Come, Sinner Wash (GS0452-2) 1904, True to Death (FS0016-2) 1924, Unfanthomed (FS0019-3) 1925, The Voyage to the Heaven (FS0025) 1926

HAWLEY, WILLIAM A.

Born in Cambellford (or Bellevill) in the province of Ontario in Canada around 1870. Already on the youthful age of eleven years he was the organist of the local Methodist church and barely five years after he became the choir leader. An unsuccessful year at the medical college led him to the Boston Conservatory of Music, and he was in later years known as Professor Hawley. Due an accident on his arm he had to relinquish his job and became a piano teacher. He became a Salvationist in Charlottetown, Prince Edward Island. Here he was active in several musical ways. He went on the soldier at the Rupert Avenue

Corps in Winnipeg for a few years which was followed by twelve years at the Calgary Citadel Corps. Besides contributing to the band journals he also wrote several Army songs and other music. William Hawley was Promoted to Glory on 9 August 1929 in Calgary, Alberta, Canada.

Important composition

From the General Down to Me (GS0354) 1898, Shall You, Shall I (GS0414) 1902

HAYDON, CLAUDE

Claude Haydon was an Australian professional musician who emigrated to New Zealand and held the position of Corps Pianist at Lower Hutt Corps from 1936 until his death 25 July 1960. Although he never became a bandsman he did write *'Army of Salvation'* FS223 in piano score. He asked Dean Goffin to score the piece for brass band because he lacked brass band orchestration knowledge. The march was played in manuscript by Lower Hutt Band under Ray Frew before submission to IMED in the 1950s.

Important composition

Army of Salvation (FS223) 1957

HAYWARD, KEVIN

Bermuda born Kevin Hayward moved to Toronto to be educated as a musician. Soon after, he joined the Canadian Staff Band on 2nd trombone and worked his way up to principal trombone and trombone soloist with an international reputation before he became the bands Deputy Bandmaster and in end he became the fourth bandmaster of the Canadian Staff Band. Health issues prevended him to stay in this position for a long time and after only four years at the helm he had to relinguish this position.

Important compositions

Joshua (Maple Leaf Brass 8)

HAZELL, TERRY

Terry Hazell was born on 9 November 1938 in London, the second son of Charles and Nellie Hazell. During World War II he was evacuated to Somerset with his mother, Nellie, and older brother, Dennis. Whilst in Somerset they lived on a farm where the family attended the local church. The Hazells went too and one day Nellie came to faith. When they returned to London in 1945 they found their way to Notting Hill Corps of the Salvation Army due to a family connection. Nellie, Dennis and Terry all became Salvationists. Terry played baritone in the Young People's Band and eventually transferred to the senior band. He also learnt the French Horn whilst at school. When he left school he first worked for Boosey and Hawkes as an instrument maker. Then he moved into music publishing. He spent 3 years playing euphonium in the Royal Army Ordinance Corps Band while on National Service. He then worked as a Salvation Army insurance agent before moving into insurance in the City of London. In 1956 he transferred to Marylebone Corps where he played Euphonium in the band. Around that time he had composition lessons with Ray Steadman-Allen. At Marylebone Corps he was the Corps Secretary and then the Songster Leader.

After his first marriage he moved to Clapton Congress Hall and then Southampton Shirley Corps where his first daughter was born. The family returned to London soon afterwards and soldiered at Harrow Corps where Terry was the Bandmaster and another daughter arrived. He then moved on to Watford Citadel. In later life, although no longer an active Salvationist, he joined the 'S. A. Historical and Philatelic Association' and was their membership secretary for 2 years. He was also a great admirer of Robert Simpson's music and was very active in the Robert Simpson Society. Despite leaving the Army in his early 30s he remained a keen supporter of it, and especially of brass band music, throughout his life and could often be found at the Royal Albert Hall at the Band Contest where he loved to meet up with other Salvationists. Over the years he conducted an eclectic assortment of groups including a banjo orchestra and a Sweet Adelines Chorus. Although he loved to keep busy and had many interests his first love was always his family to whom he gave unconditional and unstinting love and support. Terry died of cancer on 25 May 2011.

Important compositions

Marylebone Young People (US0058) 1964, Peace (TS0690) 1967, Saviour, Like a Shepherd (TS0654-2) 1964

HEATH, GEORGE A.

Was a one time bandmaster of the Knottingley Corps Band in the Yorkshire area.

No further information could be retrieved about this composer.

Important compositions

Dennis (TS0647-1) 1963, Knottingley (TS0615) 1961, Shepherd of Israel (TS0634) 1962

HEATHCOTE, AGNES PARKER (née McDOUALL)

As a daughter of Reverend James McDouall, Agnes was born on 2 April 1862. She became a Salvationist from Banff, Canada. She went to the Training College to become a Salvation Army officer, where she toured with the Salvation Songsters after only a few weeks. In 1888 she married Staff Captain Wyndham S. Heathcote, who had been a minister of the Church of England. He later moved back to the Church and served in countries as South Africa and Australia. He died in 1956 and no more information is known about Agnes after his passing.

Important compositions

I'll follow thee, of life the give (GS0145) 1891, Jesus come with peace (GS0080) 1887, Jesus is near, burdens to bear (GS0113) 1889

HEATON, WILFRED

John Wilfred Heaton was born on 2nd December 1918 in Sheffield England to Salvationist parents. His father John Heaton was Bandmaster of the Sheffield Park Citadel Band. Already at an early age Wilfred was very interested in playing the piano and cornet and composing music. He first used his musical talents in the Salvation Army and later continued composing chamber and orchestral music. Wilfred served as Deputy Bandmaster in the Corps Band where his father was the Bandmaster. As a young Salvationist he wrote music of his own and his wish was to become a composer. In his later years Wilfred had contact with Rudolf Steiner's Anthroposophical Movement. Most of his spare free time was now dedicated to a systematic exploration of the worlds of philosophy and spirituality. Wilfred's life began to take a different course. He had taken up the French horn and was working as a peripatetic brass teacher in Yorkshire. Later he was encouraged by close friends to take up his composing once again. Wilfred was Promoted to Glory in May 2000.

John Wilfred Heaton was a composer of refined sensibility and technical skill the true extent of whose creative gifts has only emerged since his death in May 2000. As his many admirers suspected the music currently in print represents just a small part of what he actually composed. Wilfred's life in music was underpinned by wide-ranging interests in the arts in philosophy and by his strong religious background and faith. Yet at times during his long life his creative impulse was often tested and questioned.

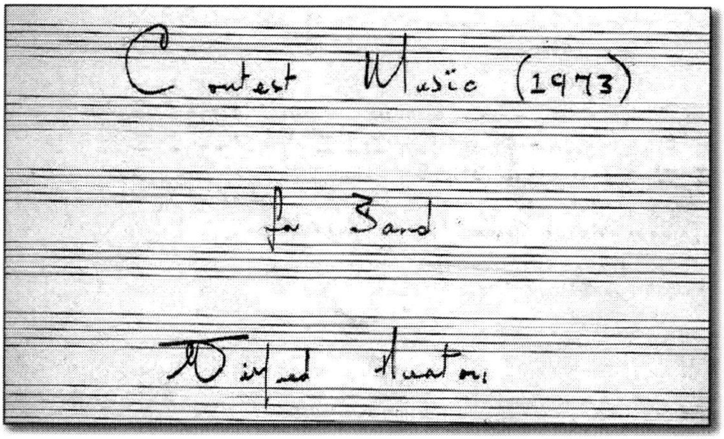

Heaton's handwriting and signature on the original 1973 full score of his denied test piece 'Contest Music' which would be the test piece of 1982 and became immensely popular later on.

Born in Sheffield to Salvationist parents Wilfred Heaton's musical talents were first nurtured through the Salvation Army. He began piano lessons at the age of 8. Soon after that he was learning the cornet and writing music of his own.

His piano teacher Salvationist songster Mrs Bennett guided him to his first musical milestone an LRAM in piano awarded when he was just 18. He left school to become an apprentice in a small brass instrument manufacturer and repair business in Sheffield. Apart from war service in the RAF he remained there for over 20 years composing whenever he could.

He noted on a manuscript page of his last work the autobiographical Variations *'I got help initially from a crippled SA musician (George Marshall) who had a very sound harmonic instinct but who stressed contrapuntal studies above all then from a local music master who initiated me into the wider world of chamber and orchestral music and finally a lot later (the 1950's) Matyas Seiber whose instruction on Bach studies was invaluable. These are three with whom I had personal contact but along with other inspiring composers of the 18th century German giants and the 20th century masters'.*

It was expected that Wilfred would dedicate his musical talents to the Salvation Army and in his own words he continued to 'do a good job' for the Army throughout his life. The technical and musical complexities of his best work whilst placing him firmly in the European classical mainstream were often thought to be too radical for Salvation Army performance. Those pieces that were published such as the March *'Praise'* and the

Meditation *'Just as I am'* have become firm Salvation Army favourites but several more were rejected. Others like *'Toccata'* eventually found their way into print many years later.

In his 20's and 30's Wilfred's musical ambitions extended beyond the brass band. There was a Suite for orchestra which later became a Piano Sonata and eventually the Partita for brass band. His Op.1 was a Rhapsody for oboe and strings - Op.2 was a suite of Three Pieces for piano. Both works received performances in London under the auspices of the Society for the Promotion of New Music. There was also a Little Suite for recorder (and flute) and piano composed in 1955 for the Sheffield based recorder virtuoso Philip Rogers. He also composed for chamber ensembles and voices.

In the late 1950's Wilfred's life began to take a different course. He had taken up the French Horn and was working as a peripatetic brass teacher a move which in 1962 took the Heaton family to Harrogate. Wilfred played in a number of teachers' orchestras and ensembles. He was a founding conductor of the Dales Sinfonia. He formed and conducted the local schools orchestra. Between 1962 and 1969 he was Musical Director of the Leeds Symphony Orchestra and in 1970 he spent several months as Musical Director of the Black Dyke Mills Band.

However as his professional activities increased his own creativity went into decline. He continued to arrange music for the performing groups with which he was involved but he composed very little. Another note on the score of Variations offers the explanation *'....all compositional ambitions were brought to a halt with my contact with Rudolf Steiner's Anthroposophical Movement. Involvement in this seemed to dry me up at a tempo. I lost the impulse to compose. Such an activity seemed unimportant compared with the spiritual impulses provided by Steiner'.* Most of his spare time was now dedicated to a systematic exploration of the worlds of philosophy and of sprituality.

From time to time he was tempted out of his creative semi-retirement most notably in 1973 when he accepted a commission to write Contest Music only for it to be rejected by the organisers as 'too advanced'. It was to be used to huge acclaim 9 years later as the test piece for the National Championships.

In his later years Wilfred was pleased but always appeared surprised at the appreciative reception his music was by then receiving. He never regained his old fluency but he was encouraged by family and close friends - notably the conductor Howard Snell - to take up his composing pen once again. After the death of his wife and his own retirement from teaching there was a welcome 'Indian summer' - two substantial concertos two marches and his final Variations.

A few weeks before he died Wilfred Heaton remarked that as a young man all he wanted to do was be a composer *'..... and I suppose that urge never really leaves you'* he added. He once said to a colleague there would be some surprises at what would emerge from his *'unregarded corner'.* He was quite right.

Both the International Staff Band, Black Dyke Band and Eikanger-Bjorsvik Musikklag has made recordings solely with the music of Wilfred Heaton.

The Wilfred Heaton Trust

Soon after the death of Wilfred Heaton in May 2000 the seemingly awesome and daunting task of sorting through his many files of manuscript music quickly turned to extreme excitement as more and more new discoveries emerged. Some had lain finished but unpublished for up to half a century whilst other newer works apart from one or two exceptions were fully sketched but only partly scored. After consulting with a number of close friends and professional admirers of Wilfred and his music, his son in law Bryan Stobart decided to set up the Wilfred Heaton Trust with a view to ensuring that the new discoveries were realised - published and exploited for wider use where considered appropriate by the trustees together with all existing compositions already in the public domain.

Objectives of the Trust

To promote - improve - develop and maintain public appreciation and education of the art and science of music relating to the late composer Wilfred Heaton in all its aspects by the presentation of his music in public concerts, broadcasts and recordings and by the publication and promotion of his works generally and such other purposes which would be exclusively charitable which the trustees may from time to time decide.

(more information on wilfredheaton.fsnet.co.uk)

Important compositions

My Master's Will (FS319-2) 1969. Oh the Blessed Lord (Toccata) (FS354) 1973, Celestial Prospect (FS481) 1990, Beulah Land (JC608) 2006

HEDGREN, VIKTOR

Amongst the very first children who would form the first Young People's Band in Denmark were no less than four future composers. This band, led by Ernst Soderstrom, father of Emil Soderstrom was active in the early 1900's. Besides Emil Soderstrom, Erik Leidzén and Kristian Fristrup, also Viktor Hedgren became internationally known as composer. After immigrating to the United States, Viktor Hedgren became a member of the Chicgao Staff Band, where he composed several pieces that saw publication within the journals of the Salvation Army. One of his compositions, a cornet solo entitled *'I know I shall be there'* (later renamed in *'Heavenly Rejoicings'*), appeared in the General Series.

Important composition

Heavenly Rejoicings (GS1148) 1938

HEDIN, ELIAS

Elias was a bandsman, songwriter and bandmaster at the Virserum Corps in Sweden. He bcame bandmaster at the early age of only fifteen, which have made him the youngest bandmaster ever appointed in Sweden. He composed the march Virserum (Svensk Festmusik 229) and the selection Love Divine (Svenska Musikserien 303) amongst others.

Important composition

Gudonlig Karlek (FM0303) 1960

HEINTZMAN, RONALD

Ronald (Ron) was born in Burlington, Ontario on February 5, 1972 to Salvation Army Officers. After stays in Burlington, St. Thomas, Toronto, and Hamilton, they ended up in Alberta where he spent most of his teen years. His father taught him how to play the cornet at the age of 7. Ron was always impressed with how his father was very proficient and had been a bandmaster himself before going to training college so he decided he'd like to be a bandmaster someday. Ron's father would take him to hear the Canadian Staff Band in the 1980's and was impressed by the band under Robert Redhead. Ron's development continued as he started taking lessons from William Dimmer of the Edmonton Symphony Orchestra and started to arrange in his late teens. Nothing was really all that good though. His older brother Brad is an incredible musician and he took a lot of formal training in composition and arranging and Ron always looked up to him and tried to learn from him. In 1988 Ron went to the National Music Camp just north of Toronto when William Broughton was the guest and learned more in that week from just sitting under him as a bandmaster than in his whole life it seemed.

In 1994 Ron moved back to Toronto and joined the North York Corps and played in the band under Robert Venables. Once again, he just sat there and learned from one of the most skillful musicians and an excellent corps bandmaster in every sense of the word. In 1997 Ron moved on to Hamilton playing in the Hamilton Temple Band. Later that year, the current bandmaster Ken Spink stepped down as bandmaster and because there literally wasn't anyone else who was willing to do the band, they gave Ron a chance. Here he was, having only been in the corps for 4 months, a 25 years old conducting one of the Salvation Army's premier Corps Bands. One of his most treasured possession is his Bandmaster's Commission signed by the Divisional Commander who at the time was Lt. Colonel Robert Redhead! One of his all time heroes in every way. Later that year he was invited to join the Canadian Staff Band on first cornet under his former bandmaster, Brian Burditt. That was another tremendous opportunity for training for him as he have always felt that Brian has the greatest 'baton skill' Ron ever saw. That obviously took his cornet playing to another level. Before too long they asked him to play soprano where he sat for a few years including an incredible tour of Australia.

The piece Ron arranged was done because they had a request to use that tune which is not in the tune book, so he did a simple little arrangement of it for the Sunday service. He had a lot of compliments on it, so they used it over the next few years in Sunday worship at Hamilton Temple (later renamed in Meadowlands). Later Ron had left the CSB again for various reasons, but they were doing a weekend at the corps and Ron's music was used again for the final two verses for the CSB's weekend at the corps. One of the most emotional moments in his life was conducting the CSB through his own arrangement and Staff Bandmaster John Lam told Ron he'd like to record it as everyone seemed to enjoy it.

Important Composition

My Jesus I Love Thee (m/s)

HERD, J.C

One of the early composers (late 1800, early 1900). Interesting detail is that 'Clydesdale' was the first piece Ray Steadman-Allen edited (or prepared for print) when he was a member oft he Music Editorial Department. The Clyde is a Scottish river near or in Glasgow. No further information could be retrieved about this person.

Important compositions

The Aberdeen March (GS0754) 1917, Clydesdale (GS1288) 1947

HERIKSTAD, EILIV

Eiliv Herikstad was born on 9th April 1942 in Fredrikstad (Norway). There he also had his first study in music by SØren GangflØt. Further studies followed at the Academy of Oslo, and University for music in Gothenburg (Sweden). During this time Eiliv served in a social institution in Motala (Sweden). He was bandmaster of The Salvation Army in Oslo Temple Citadel Band and Oslo 3 Band, in Corps Bands in Motala, Mölndal, and Moss. From 1973 until 1976 he served as National Bandmaster for The Salvaion Army in Norway. From 1977 to 1979 he was teacher for music by the 'JelØy folkehØgskole'. The period 1987 to 1991 Eiliv served on the National Headquarter of The Salvation Army as National Band Secretary for Norway, Iceland and the Faeroes Territory. On 1th January 2002 he was designated to serve on the Headquarter in Oslo as Study secretary. Eiliv's compositions and arrangements are favourites worldwide. He belongs to the first composers in the Salvation Army to compose music with a modern style. Eiliv has traveled through many countrys as Trombone soloist and guest conductor. He has been bandmaster of the Askim Salvation Army Band since 1995.

In 2008 the Norway Territorial Band recorded a full CD with his compositions, conducted by the composer himself.

Important compositions

God's Love (GS1668) 1975, On parade (FS369) 1975, A Joystrings Review (m/s), The Lily of the Valley (m/s), Schaffhausen (TS789) 1975, Teach me (TS883-2) 1983

HIMES, WILLIAM

Well known for his compositions and arrangements, William Himes has more than seventy publications to his credit. These, along with numerous manuscripts awaiting publication, are continually featured on international broadcasts and recordings. Bill Himes earned his Bachelor and Master of Music degrees from the University of Michigan. For five years he taught instrumental music in the public schools of Flint, Michigan, where he was also adjunct lecturer in low brass at the University of Michigan-Flint. Bill Himes continues to be in demand as conductor, composer, lecturer, clinician and euphonium soloist and has appeared throughout the United States, Canada, Australia, New Zealand, Sweden, Denmark, Norway and the United Kingdom. Since 1977, Bill has been music director of the Salvation Army's Central Territory, which encompasses the eleven Midwestern states. In this capacity he is also conductor of the Chicago Staff Band, an internationally recognized ensemble which has led on successful tours of Panama, Mexico, Chile, Canada, Singapore, The Philippines, Hong Kong, England and Australia. The band's 1987 tour of England included performances in the Royal Albert Hall and Buckingham Palace, where Bill was privileged to meet Her Majesty Queen Elizabeth. On July 2nd 2000 he received the Order of the Founder from General John Gowans.

By Mervyn Collins, Melbourne Australia (7/2006)

I wasn't expecting to be abused by an audience member, particularly in a well-mannered Salvation Army concert, but the voice was clear and the message unequivocal. *'Give him a go, you rotten sod!'* he said. I'd been explaining to our second horn player why he couldn't be permitted to play a solo. He was waving parts and a score in his hand, soliciting the audience's sympathies, and I was telling him that he was lucky even to be in the band – playing 2nd horn only because there were no 3rd horn parts!

'But' pleaded the horn player, *'This solo's been specially written for me' – 'By Bill Himes of America' he added as if that settled everything.'*

It was a hilarious lead in to the 'one note samba' that is Himes inspired piece of silliness *'Solo Secondo'* – a major work for 2nd horn which my veteran, ham-acting horn player always performed brilliantly.

Himes music always featured on our programs and never failed to reach the audience whether through the musical story-telling of Jericho Re-visited, the spirituality of *'To the Chief Musician'* or the joy of the pop-styled *'Celebration of Contemporary Gospel Songs'.* Himes could write it all and still does if a recent program by the Chicago Staff Band, which he has conducted since 1977, is any evidence. The accent is always on communication with the audience, so in amongst the demanding stuff from Graham, Norbury and Farr, are Himes' originals – *'Storytime',* about a whippersnapper's Very Bad Day, complete with narrator, a tableful of sound effects and a witty band backing and later, a delightful episode where some local, pint-sized beginners front the Staff Band to play simple melodies from the classics while the band does the donkey work.

Then another carefully constructed Himes program ends with *'Cause for Celebration',* a Himes paean on the doxology *'Praise God from Whom All Blessings Flow.'* Bill Himes knows how to captivate an audience. He's been around for a long time and writing for most of it. He remembers himself at 7 years of age picking out tunes under his grandmother's watchful eye and musical ear. By 11, he was creating his own piano pieces and soon trying to write them down. A year later, he was experimenting with instrumentation and at 14 wrote a new school 'fight' song, complete with lyrics, tune and full band score. At 16, Himes, though he still had had no formal tuition in composition, took his latest piece along to annual music camp. Himes is forever grateful that the Camp Musical Director that year, and for several successive years, was Eric Ball himself.

Ball recognized the young man's talent and played his piece, first at Band Faculty rehearsal and later to the whole camp. Ball mentioned the need for some counterpoint, a new concept for the self-taught composer to pursue, understand and employ. Himes, new composer, was up and running. The next camp, the young Salvationist soloist, (and pin-up girl for many an adolescent Salvo!) Carole Reinhart, now Professor of Music and Performing Arts in Vienna, featured his solo *'Nocturne'* and shortly after, an American touring band took his fresh, new Festival march, *'The Witness',* to England. Some time later, since he had never submitted it himself, Himes was surprised, but happy, to receive a note from the S.A. Music Board to say his march had 'been accepted for publication.' He was just 18. After completing his Bachelor and Master's degrees in Music Education and Performance – Himes is a fine euphonium soloist – he worked for five years as a high school music director until the Army in Chicago offered him the position of Territorial Music Director. This was the first time a layman had been entrusted with the position. The confidence was well-placed. It is difficult to see, in retrospect, how the Army could have found a more suitable, competent and dedicated person.

The appointment works, Himes says, on 'freedom and trust'; Himes is free to write and compose, administer his department and run his band without interference and trusted to produce outcomes appropriate to the Army and its mission. S.A. Officer composers such as Steadman-Allen, Redhead and Bearcroft are obliged to write only for the Army. Himes,

Albert Drury

Arthur Scotney

Arthur Goldsmith

A.E. Challinor

David Berg

Charles Skinner

Douglas Kiff

Edgar Grinsted

Bertil Anderson

Edgar Cuell

Don Morrison

Edward Dytham

Emil Soderstrom

Eric Abbott

Frank Inglis

Fred Dockerill

Philip Catelinet

Freeman Black

Eric Ball

Erik Leidzén

Victor Dimond

Richard Holz

Ernest Edwards

Harold Scotney

Harry Kirk

John Gibson

Leonard Baxter

Morley Calvert

Otto Lundahl

Paul Anefelt

Gurney Doe

Joe Bartlett

Gustaf Kjellgren

Gunnar Blomberg

George Jackson

Howard Chesham

John Allen

John Pattison

Robert McNally

Rune Froden

Sidney Hill

Soderstrom-Verkaaik

Tom Arnott

Walter Green

Wilfred Heaton

William Broughton

William Gore

William Parkins

Ernest Smith

Charles Dove

Sidney Cox

Walter Thomas

Harold Gray

Frederick Pearson

Richard Nuttall

Ray Bowes

Orville Payton

James Harris

David Thornett

Clifford Hooton

Jules VanderKam

Terry Camsey

Sidney Hubbard

John Whitehouse

Dean Goffin

Raymond Cuell

Olaf Lundgren

Lloyd Reslow

Arthur Gullidge

Bramwell Coles

Albert Jakeway

Allen Pengilly

Klaus Ostby

Leslie Condon

Percy Merritt

James Wright

James Anderson

Brian Bowen

Erik Silfverberg

Robert Redhead

Eiliv Herikstad

Norman Bearcroft

Kenneth Downie

Niels Silfverberg

Michael Clack

Ray Steadman-Allen

Roger Trigg

Nicholas Samuel

John Hynd

Dorothy Gates

Chelsea Pascoe

Martyn Thomas

Olaf Ritman

Ruben Schmidt

David Edmonds

Paul Sharman

wisely, on accepting his appointment, insisted that his 'intellectual property remained his own' allowing him to publish outside the movement.

He writes for his old S.A. friend Jim Curnow's company – they once shared a euphonium bench in a corps band – and for the respected Kjos music company. His employment with the Army means though, that he doesn't have to accept commissions merely to keep the wolf from the door; he only produces music he believes in. Consequently about 85% of his output is for the Army; some by necessity – something the Staff Band needs – some by request and some, pure inspiration. One of his best-loved works *'To the Chief Musician'* came from a request to write a piece to mark the retirement of the doyen of American S.A. music, Richard Holz. Himes says, *'Around that time I was listening to Bernstein's Mass with its texts and choirs and marching band and orchestra and I tried to incorporate some of these elements using only the band on stage.'* The concept, based on three of Holz' favourite hymn tunes, was fresh and revolutionary for Army programs. Other music Himes has written *'marks him in time,'* he says and some has come from what he described as *'a crucible of pain.'* The death of his beloved first wife, Wendy, led to a hymn of acceptance and rededication to God's will and his later marriage to Linda provided the inspiration for Procession to Covenant, a devotional outpouring based on *'O Love that will not let me go'* which he says *'completed a circle of healing'* in his life.

Himes continues to write. His own Music Deptartment produces the American Festival Series which was a welcome addition to S.A. repertoire some 20 years ago, and the Hallelujah Chorus series, contemporary backings for every conceivable instrumental grouping including full brass band. Himes strongly believes in the medium of the band and loves its inclusiveness. *'I have teenagers and grandparents, male and female in my group,'* he says. *'And what other ensemble can produce,'* he asks, *'convincing jazz, march or 'organ-like' orchestral styles in concert and give edifying support to public worship and congregational singing?'* There are many great names in American S.A. brass band history – Leidzen, of course, and Soderstrom, Broughton (father and sons), Bulla and Curnow but none has made a wider contribution to accessible and engaging band literature than William F. Himes O.F.

His output ranges from simple hymn arrangements, through bright marches and highly original, humorous program stealers to major works, in both traditional and pop and jazz idioms, and spiritual pieces which explore our inner thoughts and sacred aspirations. Long may his music continue to amuse, uplift and inspire bands and audiences throughout the world.

PROFILE - Bandmaster William Himes (b. 1949)

William Himes was born and raised in Michigan, where he attended the University of Michigan in Ann Arbor, receiving his Bachelors and Masters Degrees in Music Education and Performance. Since that time he has appeared throughout the United States and Canada, Australia, New Zealand, England, Scotland, Switzerland, Japan, Switzerland, Jamaica, Argentina, France, Norway and Sweden as soloist, clinician, and conductor.

Well known for his compositions and arrangements, Mr. Himes has more than 170 publications to his credit. These, along with numerous manuscripts awaiting publication, are continually featured on international broadcasts and recordings.

As conductor of the Chicago Staff Band of The Salvation Army since 1977, he has produced many recordings and led this outstanding 36-piece ensemble in successful international concert tours, the most recent being the June 2006 visit to the Australia. During the 1987 England tour the band performed in the Royal Albert Hall and Buckingham Palace, where Mr. Himes was privileged to meet Her Majesty Queen Elizabeth II.

Prior to assuming his present responsibilities in Chicago as The Salvation Army's Territorial Music and Gospel Arts Secretary for the eleven Midwestern states he taught instrumental music in grades 5-12 in Flint, Michigan and was an adjunct lecturer in low brass at the University of Michigan Flint campus.

Along with his wife, Linda, Bill is an active Salvationist of the Oakbrook Terrace Corps, where he served for fifteen years as corps sergeant-major and presently assists as a bandsman, songster, pianist, beginning brass teacher and worship planner. On July 2, 2000, he received The Salvation Army's highest honor, the Order of the Founder, presented by General John Gowans at the International Millennial Congress in Atlanta, Georgia.

Important compositions

New Frontier (FS365) 1975, Milestone (FS446) 1985, Jubilance for Cornet (FS507) 1994, I have decided to follow Jesus (GS1862) 1991, Rolling Along (GS1906) 1995

HILL, HENRY

Henry Hill was a Police Sergeant in Hull and had served for years in that capacity. He had also been the bandmaster of the Hull Icehouse Corps Band, and when he moved on to London, became bandmaster of the famous Clapton Congress Hall Band. He had a huge interest in the musical development within the Salvation Army, and took up a position in the Music Editorial Department, where he remained until 1888. He was one of the few men who were responsible for the Salvation Army Music. Later he left the department to become a Salvation Army officer.

HILL, EDWARD H.

Edward Hill (born in 1869) was converted in 1887. He practiced writing music on the bricks he handled in his daily job. While being Bandmaster of the Southall Citadel Band, Edward H. Hill was appointed Band Inspector for the British Territory in 1907 by the Chief of the Staff, Bramwell Booth. His tasks were to conduct special band rehearsals, which nowadays would have been called workshops, in order to instruct the bandsmen. 'Ted' Hill, as he was known, was a giant among men. For the next eighteen years, starting in 1907, he felt very responsible for the task that was given to him. Wherever he announced his coming, the bandsmen started to clean their instruments and evey bandsman was expected to attend. His daughter Rosalind was later to be married with Phil Catelinet, another noted Salvation Army composer.

A nice fact about Edward is that years after his death, when his house was being redecorated, layers of wallpaper were stripped away, to reveal a stave drawn on the walls, which he had used to teach the first bandsmen their notation. He was Promoted to Glory in 1925, age 56.

Important compositions

Scotland (FS079) 1932, Exaltation (GS932) 1925

HILL, SIDNEY. J.

One of the early composers (late 1800, early 1900). Sidney Hill was a bandmaster of the Wandsworth Corps and later of the Mordon Corps, both in the United Kingdom. No further information could be retrieved about this person.

Important compositions

Echoes from Calvary (GS0555) 1908, The Southall March (GS0506) 1905

HINGLEY, BARRIE

Barrie was born in 1938 and was awarded the OBE (Order of British Empire). He was born in Selby, Yorkshire. He attended the Salvation Army corps of Bedford Congress Hall in the early 1960's and was the principal trombone player. He made his career in the Royal Air Force, gaining the rank of Squadron Leader, conductor, composer and arranger.

The 'military band' representative in this Garland is Wing Commander Barrie Hingley OBE, recently retired as Principal Director of Music RAF, a post he assumed in 1989. He has produced many marches and arrangements for the service, also longer pieces like the Nativity ballet.

Important composition

Glorious Service (TS0660) 1964

HODSON, ALBERT E.

Albert 'Wingy' Hodson was bandmaster at Auckland. 'Wingy' being his nickname because he only had one hand. He was a former member of the 'Skeleton Army', an aggressive group with the pupose to attack the converts and people of the early Salvation Army. Instead of his hand he wore a hook, which was used to tearing uniforms from the back of Salvationists! He edited the New Zealand Band Journal and was a competent self-taught arranger and composer.

Important compositions

The good old gospel ship (GS0386) 1900, O Lord, now let the waves (GS0231) 1894, While the spark of life (GS0218) 1893

HOGG, BRIAN

Brian Hogg has been the flugelhorn player of the Melbourne Staff Band before taking up the position as Melbourne Staff Songsters Leader. He was born in Yorkshire, England, and came over to Australia in 1964 with his parents. He now considers himself as an Australian and works in the Creative Minitries Department of The Salvation Army in Melbourne. Brian has a Diploma of Music and a Bachelor of Education, and enjoys a growing reputation as a composer/conductor. Through his activity as a musician in the Salvation Army, his works for brass band have been played and recorded internationally. His compositions for concert and symphonic bands have earned him the Australian Band and Orchestra Directors' Association's Composer of the Year in both 1986 and 1989.

After gaining a Diploma of music Brian worked with a group touring around Victorian Schools presenting an interactive music educational program with Victorian Arts. Time spent as an instrumental music teacher in Government Schools led to further study for a Bachelor of Education majoring in Music Classroom & Instrumental pedagogy. Further instrumental teaching as Head of Brass Studies at a private school led to Brian taking on the role of Head of Music before he left teaching to work full time for The Salvation Army in the Creative Arts. Brian has worked throughout Australia as a guest conductor, adjudicator and clinician and has been recognised by the Australian Band and Orchestra Association (A.B.O.D.A.) for his contribution to music education. He has also received awards from A.B.O.D.A. for his compositions for the wind band repertoire.

As a Salvationist Brian has been involved in Army music making for most of his life. He currently works for The Salvation Army Eastern Victoria Division in the Southern Australia Territory as Creative Arts Director and conducts The Melbourne Staff Songsters. Brian believes that music and the creative arts can be vital components of worship services and, when utilised in God honouring ways, can be used to usher congregations into the presence of God in powerful, glorifying ways.

Important compositions

The Music of Thy Name (FS555) 2000, Star Lake III (m/s), Mr. Noah and the Fox (GS1966) 2000, From Every Stormy Wind (TS967) 1990.

HOLLIS, DANIEL GARRETT

Daniel Garrett Hollis was a member of the Melbourne Staff Band in the early 20th century. Later he served for a limited period as bandmaster of the Lismore Salvation Army Band in New South Wales and the famous Box Hill Salvation Army Band in Melbourne. He went to the First World War in 1916, was Promoted to Glory in 1971 and his wife Olive in 1951.

Brigadier and Mrs. Lonnie conducted a welcome meeting and a farewell meeting in March 1920, when Bandmaster Daniel Garrett Hollis was welcomed home after three years and eight months faithful service in the Armed Forces, and Cadet H. Thomas, who had filled the position of Young People's Sergeant Major for over six years, farewelled for the Training College. Some Local Officers were also commissioned and Mrs. Hollis, the mother of the Bandmaster received a commission as Retired Corps Treasurer, after having served over thirty years as a Local Officer in the Salvation Army.

Daniel Garrett Hollis (sometimes called Paddy) was born in Bacchus Marsh, Victoria, Australia on 7 July 1887. He was Promoted to Glory from Brighton Corps on 22 February 1971. In 1908 he attended Lismore Corps in New South Wales and became bandmaster there. 1914 saw him at Hawthorn Corps and 1916 he was at Box Hill Corps and became bandmaster. He was in the Melbourne Staff Band for 9 years c.1928 and on 21 January 1928 he married Olive Taylor at Brighton where he continued to live and serve until his Promotion to Glory. Before his marriage he went to England to study there and became friendly with a William Carey who was very dear to his heart. He was in WW1 for more than three years whilst at Box Hill Corps and his daughter says that he formed a band whilst serving overseas. He was not a bandmaster at Brighton Corps. The marches he wrote reflects the corps he attended e.g. *'Hawthorn', 'Box Hill' 'Brighton Citadel', 'Red Cliffs'* - but when it was published it was spelt *'Redcliffe'*.

He was a member of the Melbourne Staff Band (1928-1937), he was the colour sergeant and when not carrying the colours played tenor horn. In WW1 he was a sergeant and in the 4th Australian Pioneer Battalion which did have a band.

Important compositions

The Redcliffe march (GS994) 1929, The Hawthorne march (GS846) 1920

HOLMLUND, ANDREAS

Andreas, whose parents are Salvation Army officers, spent his childhood moving between different Salvation Army corps in Sweden. After a few years the family settled in Skelleftehamn, where there existed thriving Salvation Army corps with many sections of Army work. The brass band had a very high standard and Andreas learned about all the aspects of Army banding here. After finishing high school, where his studies focused on the playing, composing and understanding music. At the age of twenty he moved to Stockholm for studies at the Royal College of Music where he studied jazz and trombone. At the same time the Stockholm Vasa Band, and the corps, had the pleasure of welcoming him as a member and were able to benefit from his vast range of abilities. Andreas was the solo euphonium player as well as trombone soloist. He also formed 'Vasa Bone Unit', a trombone quintet and recorded with this group. He is an appreciated member of the staff of the Territorial Summer music school in Sweden and a great example to the students. Soon after moving to Stockholm, he was appointed Deputy Bandmaster and when the bandmaster moved from Stockhol in 2006, Andreas was appointed bandmaster.

Important compositions

I surrender all (m/s), Praise to the Lord (m/s)

HOLZ, RICHARD SR

Richard Holz was born to a Salvation Army Officer Family in Pennsylvania. He is a fourth generation Salvationist. A move to the Southwest sent Richard to school in Oklahoma City. There, following his bent, at the age of sixteen, he was conductor of the Salvation Army Corps band. He attended the University of Oklahoma, majoriting in music education. Richard came to New York in 1935, worked in the Public Relations Department at the Territorial Headquarters and at the same time continued his college studies. He become an officer of the Salvation Army. As a Captain he was appointed Territorial Music Secretary of the Eastern Section of the Salvation Army. He served as Bandmaster of the New York Staff Band from 1955 to 1963. He was written a number of musical compositions, published by The Salvation Army in USA and Great Britain. In the Eastern Territory he was often called 'Mr. Music'.

Important compositions

What a friend (FS149-2), Jamaica Citadel (AJ023), Heralds of Victory (AJ058)

HOOTON, CLIFFORD

Cliff was born on October 21st 1909 and grew up as the son of Salvation Army Officer parents, therefore he moved around with them quite a lot. Cliff's father, being rather a controlling figure, had decided that the only thing he wanted for his son was to become a Salvation Army officer and paid little attention to realizing that he was intellectually capable of so much more so did not encourage his efforts at school. But Cliff achieved many and various things in his life. He was in fact a very clever guy! He was born in Stenhousmuir in Scotland, but at the age of 10, found himself in Leeds in Yorkshire. Having previously been home-schooled in a previous appointment and passed his 11+ exam to qualify for Grammar school, TOP of the City of Leeds. But because the Divisional Commander's son failed his exam, Cliff's father would only let him go to the secondary school so as not to upset the Divisional Commander! He did eventually make it to London University where he played tennis very well, qualifying to play the Junior tournament at Wimbledon. He also qualified to become a professional football referee, and later took charge of the annual Army/Navy fixtures. But on leaving University with a degree (BA), his father insisted he go to work for the Salvation Army in the Insurance Departmen and he became an agent.

In 1932 he entered the Training College in the '*Fighters*' Session, which was the 1st intake of the new International Training College. 1933 he was posted to a place called Skinningrove in Country of Durham, a farming community so small it no longer exists! This was the time of the Great Depression, and he and his Lieutenant quickly realized they needed to do something to help the redundant and starving miners' families, so they begged for any vegetables and meats they could get and cooked up a hearty soup which they gave away from a cabin at the side of the road. They were eventually visited by the Prince of Wales (Later Edward the 6th) who had been given the remit to find out what was being done in the Country for these sad families. He was later asked to stand for Parliament, which he refused!

In 1934 Cliff was posted to the Blackpool Citadel Corps where he met his future wife Beatrice, who happened to be a Candidate too. They were married in 1935 after the commissioning but in 1936 their first child was born severely handicapped and it was too much for Cliff. His health failed, had a nervous breakdown and eventually left the Work and taking up residence in Blackpool. Cliff was also a Metropolitan (London) Policeman for about 9 months before enlisting prior to the war and played trombone in the Regent Hall Band during that time. He could play anything including all string and brass and woodwind and percussion, including the concertina, but is remembered as being very partial to the trombone. However, he mainly was seen with the baton in his hand!

In 1939 he enlisted in the RAF where he distinguished himself. He was a Prisoner Of War in Germany after having to jump out of a burning plane but there he decided that control of the prisoner's conditions was paramount. So he negotiated for more food, took over the pulpit and became their spiritual leader, and organized a decent library in the prison. He was in what was known as a transit camp where all captured allied personnel were taken to be processed, and he was one of the permanent officers on site.

Post war, he made his home in Blackpool in 1945 (with a brief 2 years in Sparkhill, Birmingham, 1946-1948) and where he worked as a commercial traveler selling industrial tape. He became Songster Leader in 1954 and later Bandmaster in 1956. He was a self-taught musician and was always writing and composing for Band and Songsters and occasionally for Singing Company. He also became a city counselor in 1957 and an Alderman in 1958 (all voluntary, by the way, unlike today) and in December 1959, emigrated to the United States. There, he set up home in Oakland California, where he became Bandmaster straight away. When he arrived, there were only six bandsmen playing, so he went round the congregation determining who had been bandsmen, and invited them to come to practice, thirty people turned up! From that he built a band that toured (they had never done anything like that before). Incidentally, the band still exists but known now as the Concord Band of the Salvation Army.

He arranged the first Band and Songster Councils in California, and invited his friend Eric Ball to lead them. Eric duly invited his friend Eric Leidzén to join him. His job there was to become one of the first salesmen to sell the new Hammond Organ which he really enjoyed, meeting many people of interest, but it was while he was out one day he bought a sandwich for lunch which turned out to be filled with Salmonella and he died within 24 hours. His funeral was amazing and included a tribute from the United States military -the flag- in acknowledgment of the American Bronze Star he was awarded for services to US personnel in WWII). Clifford Hooton was Promoted to Glory on March 22nd 1962. He was 52 years old.

Important composition

In Happy Service (GS1456) 1958

HOPKINS, DUNCAN

Duncan Hopkins is a Canadian jazz musician with roots within the Salvation Army. Originally from the United Kingdom, he resides and works in Canada, where he leads his own jazz ensemble, *The Duncan Hopkins Quartet.* Although not much music is written for the Salvation Army as such, he became known world wide when the Canadian Staff Band did a joint concert with him and his group which was also recorded. Duncan did all the arrangements for the entire album, which has proven to be a popular recording ever since.

Important composition

On the march (m/s)

HOPKINS, WILLIAM JAMES

James Hopkins was a Youth Band Leader in the East London Division and was known for having a great and good influence on many young people. Former member and Songster Leader of the Ilford Corps in London where he enjoyed his last years in the back of the hall listening to the musical sections in the corps.

Important compositions

Becontree (TS0176) 1932, Ilford Young People (TS0792) 1975

HOPKINS, JOHN

One of the early composers.

No further information could be retrieved about this person.

Important compositions

Abends (TS0695-1) 1967, The Linton March (TS0080) 1926, Steadily Onward (TS0104) 1928

HORDEN, PETER VAN DER

'The Lord has blessed me in more ways than I could ever imagine. Any talents or gifts I possess I owe to Him, and I want to use those gifts to the best of my ability to bring honour and glory to Him and bring people to a closer awareness of Him.' So says Peter van der Horden, Bandmaster of the Halifax Citadel Band of The Salvation Army for the past ten years and, until his retirement in 2001 after 37 years of military service, was Lieutenant Commander of the Maritimes Forces Stadacona Band. Peter was born in Schiedam, The Netherlands, and at six, moved to Canada with his parents and younger sister, arriving at the famous Pier 21 in the Halifax harbour. Pier 21 holds a special place in Peter's heart in that, 45 years later, he conducted the Navy Band in *'O Canada'* during opening ceremonies declaring the pier an official tourist attraction and museum. He stood, baton in hand, a few feet from where he first

stepped on Canadian soil as a lad. It was an emotional moment. The Salvation Army display in the museum includes a picture of Peter's family preparing to embark from Holland on their journey to the new world. Growing up in Ottawa, Peter's early spiritual and musical journey was shaped in his home and in both the junior and senior bands at Ottawa and Parkdale Citadels, then Woodroffe Temple, where he became Deputy Bandmaster. He declares high praise and respect for salvationist Ken Moore, one of his Bandmasters in The Salvation Army and his first Director of Music in the Air Force, which he joined in 1964.

Peter's military career is impressive. He attended the Tri Service School of Music in Victoria, B.C., and graduated into the Air Force Band in 1966, which became the National Band, then the Central Command Band, where he remained until 1983. As a Warrant Officer he was the lead trombonist and section leader. In 1983 Peter experienced a change of venue, and was selected for the Assistant Director of Music course in Victoria, B.C. He was subsequently posted to the Navy Band in Halifax, NS. He swiftly rose from Chief Petty Officer to Lieutenant (N). His star was rising. Peter graduated from officer courses in B.C., to the music staff at National Defence headquarters, to CFB Borden School of Music where he taught conducting, to Kingston as Commanding Officer and Director of Music for the Canadian Forces Vimy Band. He was eventually posted to Halifax in 1993 where he took over the leadership of the Navy band. He was then promoted to the rank of Lieutenant Commander. His roots were now firmly fixed until retirement. In retirement Peter has composed marches, solos, suites, worship choruses and hymn tune settings for Salvation Army bands, and has written several pieces for the Concert band. Several of his pieces are on file with The Salvation Army in London, England, for possible future publication. In April, 2008, he conducted the Stadacona Band of Maritime Forces Atlantic in one of his compositions which was specifically written for the band's Battle of Atlantic concert.

Important compositions

Somebody is praying for me (m/s), Vlaardingen 100th (m/s), Knowing You (m/s), Ascalon (m/s)

HORSEY, S.J.

One of the early composers (late 1800).

No further information could be retrieved about him.

Important composition

Oh, wonderful love beyond degree (GS0192) 1892

HOWARD, HENRY THOMAS

Commissionar T. Henry Howard (1849-1923) was Chief of the Staff at the time of the launch of the Festival Series in 1923; Endorsement on score of Klaus Ostby's *'Princethorpe'* (FS02). He was part of the International Headquarters board of music for a long time together with other illustrious members, and was a highly respected man.

Important composition

He was slain (GS0330) 1896

HUBBARD, SIDNEY ROBERT

Sidney Hubbard was born in London on 29 April 1889 to Salvationist parents. He became a junior soldier at the Mile End Corps after which they transferred to Limehouse Corps where he became bandmaster at the youthful age of only sixteen. His Bandmasters Commision which he received in 1920 has a handwritten comment in one corner to say that he led the Limehouse band from 1915 but would not accept the Commision until 'prevailed upon' in 1920, as he felt too young until then. In 1923 he entered the Training College and was a corps officer for the next twenty years. The Limehouse Band marched him to the Training College, then Clapton Congress Hall, playing the *'Limehouse Citadel'* march that he had composed for them. In 1947, he was appointed to the Public Relations Bureau at International Headquarters and later served for ten years in the Secretary's Department. For several years he studied music by correspondence course with bandmaster George Marshall. Sidney's first song was published when he was a cadet, but later he composed music for bands of the Salvation Army. In his retirement he trained a local school band and composed music for them to play. Sidney Hubbard was Promoted to Glory in 1984. The famous songwriter June Collins *('The Quiet Heart')* is his daughter.

Important compositions

The Limehouse March (GS1052) 1932, Meet in Bliss (TS0177) 1932, My Satisfying Portion (TS0198) 1934

HUGUENIN, WILLY

Willy Huguenin was born in 1939 in a little village in Switzerland near the French border, to a Salvationist family. He became an Officer Cadet from 1953 - 1954 in the Salvation Army School for Officers Training in Bern. In 1955 he married Lieutenant Miriam Lüthi and in the same year they received 'Marching Orders' to Africa to serve as officers in the Congo. In 1964 they returned to Switzerland as the Corps Officers of Geneva 1 Corps. From 1966 - 1976 they served in the Congo again, and returned again to Switzerland, Willy as Pincipal of the Officer Training College in Bern. From 1979 - 1987 they served again in Africa (Rep. Congo, Brazzaville), and then back to Switzerland as Territorial leaders for the Swiss Territory with the rank of Commissioner. In 1992 they served at the International Headquarters of The Salvation Army in London (IHQ) with responsibility for the Africa Zonal Department. They retired from active service in 1996.

Important compositions

All is fulfilled (TS558) 1957, Kasangulu (US0057) 1964

HURLEY, W.J.

Little is known about Bandmaster W.J. Hurley from the Tredegar Corps in the United Kingdom. Brindley Boon's book about the ISB (ISB – the story of the International Staff Band, page 32) says: *'the annual bandmasters' councils festival at Clapton the following January saw the introduction of another spate o prize winning compositions. The played the successful march 'The Cadidate' written by Bandmaster W.J. Hurley, of Tredegar' to continue 'Tredegar Corps was elated at the success of its bandmaster's march. When he arrived at the station on his return from London, town's people and railway officials joined the band and songster brigade in their march to the Salvation Army hall. One of the composer's earlier marches 'Tredegar' and the stirring Welsh tune, 'Men of Harlech', were played as the hero of the hour was carried shoulderhigh through the town. After a 'welcome home' tea, bandmaster Hurley was marched to his home, the bandsmen lining up to congrulate him with a handshake before they left.*

Important compositions

The Candidate (GS0556) 1908, The Monmouthshire March (GS0585) 1909, The Tredegar March (GS0542) 1907

HYND, JOHN

John Hynd (1929), L.T.C.L., A.B.S.M. Cert. Ed, regards himself as one who writes easy arrangements for young people according to their ability in the teaching situations. John has only had one piece published by the Salvation Army in the Unity Series, but he does have several of his arrangements for young people under review, and also two songs with words by Major Janet Arter.

1929 to 1945. Kirkby in Ashfield - Born in Kirkby in Ashfield, Nottinghamshire into an Salvation Army family and is a 3rd generation Salvationist. His interest in music began very early and John started to learn to play the cornet and piano when only eight years old. His father, was Bandmaster at Kirkby Corps for twenty six years. Left school at fourteen and worked as a locomotive fireman at Kirkby. At fifteen, he took over the Singing Company of twenty singers when Leader was 'called up'.

1945 to 1963 Rugby - John transferred by the Railway to Rugby. A new experience of a bigger Corps. For example from a band of twelve to one of thirty five. Songsters from twenty to sixty. He was overawed!!

1947 to 1949 - National Service with The Band of the 3rd King's Own Hussars in Germany. Here he played the Haydn *'Trumpet Concerto'* in a radio broadcast from Hamburg on the British Forces Network. He then returned to Rugby and began studying to become a music teacher. His friend and mentor here was Bandmaster Edwin Dytham who wrote the lovely arrangement *'Only Thee'*. The Band at Rugby toured Denmark in 1949 and 1954. For 16 years he was Deputy Bandmaster, and Songster Leader for three years. In this period he was also the principal cornet for six years and played amongst others, *'A Happy Day'* and *'Tucker'*.

1955 - In this year John married Joanne and can testify to a wonderful life together, always trying to serve God through music and the Salvation Army.

1955 to 1957 – He entered Bretton Hall Teacher Training College.

1957 to 1963 - taught Music and Religious Education in Secondary Modern Schools in Rugby.

1960 to 1961 - Seconded to William Temple College in Rugby to study Theology related to teaching.

1971 and 1972 - Produced and conducted the musicals *'Take over Bid'* and *'Hosea'* for the Birmingham Division.

1963 to 1966 Zambia – John joined Doug and June Collin at the David Livingstone Teacher Training College in Livingstone, Zambia to represent the Salvation Army at this five Denominational Christian College. Doug and June are well known Salvation Army musicians in the United Kingdom, Doug, as a Choral conductor and June as a pianist who also wrote *'The Quiet Heart'* for Songsters. June and Doug were National Music School Staff in the United Kingdom. Together, they encouraged the Salvation Army students to attend the local Corps, led morning assemblies and organised Salvation Army weekends. At the local Corps, John became Bandmaster and Doug Corps Secretary. The band consisted of students, staff and local comrades. At the college he led the Music department and decided to research Zambian folk songs and hymns suitable for teaching to school children. This was difficult as the students came from five different areas (tribes) with five different languages. With much help from African staff and students, the students returned home equipped with songs and hymns from other parts of Zambia. This initiative appealed to the President, Dr. Kaunda who said *'If you want to see One Zambia One Nation, (his slogan) go to Livingstone.'* The Zambian Schools Broadcasting Service in Lusaka asked John to broadcast these songs and games for teachers and so 'Join us and Sing' led by a student vernacular choir sent out 24 programmes to schools on Zambian Radio. The response was overwhelming with letters from teachers all over Zambia expressing interest and thanks. John still has a copy of the cassette, script and music used.

1966 to 1974 Birmingham – Here he was head of music in Birmingham Grammar Schools. Taught music up to A level, conducted school orchestras and choirs and trained and conducted several school productions e.g. *'Ruddigore'* by Gilbert and Sullivan and *'Hansel and Gretel'* by Humperdink.

1970 – 1971 - Further Studies in Music at Birmingham School of Music, now Birmingham Conservatoire of Music. Awarded L.T.C.L (Trumpet Performer). The Birmingham Citadel Band toured the Netherlands in 1967 and John played the cornet solo *'Tucker'* on the tour. Here he was Principal cornet for five years and played *'Wondrous Day'* and *'Clear Skies'*. He was also Young People's Band Leader for three years.

1974 to 1979 Norway - Head of Music at the Salvation Army Folk High School in Moss, near Oslo. The Folk High School is a boarding school unique to Scandinavia, usually around 100 members. It offers a year between formal and further education for young people to prepare for further education or to work on an interest or hobby according to the subjects offered. The Music course offered a formal music course, choir, band, individual tuition in brass, piano and singing etc. John produced and conducted a Gowans and Larssen Musical every year in which the whole School took part even though only about 25% of students and staff were Salvationists. He toured Norway, and gave performances in Sweden and Denmark over the five years he was there. John also conducted an area youth Band and was Bandmaster of the Moss Corps Band. He toured Finland and the United Kingdom (Congress) with the Oslo 3 Band.

In 1979 John returned to Birmingham. His last teaching years were as a Peripatetic Brass Teacher. This included group brass teaching and forming Bands in Junior and Secondary Schools and arranging music for each school according to range, keys and ability available. Conducting at music Centres and arranging concerts. In 1985 he toured the United States of America with the Youth Band as Assistant Conductor and the Band played in the Epcot Centre Disneyland.

1979 to 1995 Continued to play with Birmingham Citadel Band including tours to Norway, Sweden, Denmark and Germany. He was also Deputy Bandmaster for four years and Songster Leader for four years. So for the long term of 1953 to 1985 John was also Brass Instructor and later Music Director at 31 Salvation Army Divisional Music Schools in England, Zambia and Norway.

In retirement, despite a hearing loss which began in 1969, he continue to teach, play and conduct as well as travelling to several Corps in the area who have no one to teach young people to play. He wrote *'To Serve His Will'* US 233 in 1998 when his grandson, Tim Hynd (solo cornet Enfield Citadel Band), was looking for his first variation solo without double or triple tonguing and an accompaniment which the Young People's Band could manage. Therefore, range and technical difficulties were carefully considered. The words of the theme are in the Song book 867. The melody is *'Truro'* (BTB 54) which says:

He takes the brightness of my youth,
My earnest strivings after truth,
My joys, my toil, my craftsmen's skill
All have their place and serve His will.

John Hynd has tried to make this verse his aim all through his life.

Important composition

To Serve His Will (US 233) 1998

INGLIS, FRANCIS (Frank) GEORGE

Born on 18th March, 1922 at Murwillimbah, New South Wales, Australia. He was the eldest son of Lieutenant Colonels George and Eva Inglis. As an officer's child, Frank lived in various places in the states of New South Wales, Queensland and Victoria. In 1940 his parents were appointed to the command of Brunswick Corps, Melbourne. Frank was 18 years of age and his brother Gordon was a 16 year old. They both played in the band under Bandmaster Arthur Gullidge. It was here that Frank came under the spell of Arthur's wonderful music, and studied the harmony Gullidge used. Then he started to compose his own band pieces and vocal numbers.

During this time at which Australia was involved in World War II, Arthur and numbers of bandsmen joined up to become the 2/22nd Battalion Band – who tragically died at seas as prisoners of war. Frank then enlisted in the Australian Air Force as a wireless operator, serving at Darwin (Northern Territory) and on one of the South Pacific islands.

Returning to Melbourne after the War, he played in the Canterbury Corps Band and was also the Songster Leader. Then he moved to Camberwell Corps and became the Bandmaster. His health deteriorated until finally he was unable to cope. He came under the care of the Veterans Affairs Group. He was Promoted to Glory at 71 years of age.

Important compositions

The Scene of Prayer (GS1303) 1948, A Cavalcade of Choruses (GS1374) 1953, The Singing Heart (FS207) 1955, Southern Skies (TS564) 1957

INGRAM, MATTHEW J.

Studied at University of Sheffield - Lives in London, United Kingdom - From Croydon, United Kingdom - Born on August 26, 1989.

Matt began playing the euphonium aged twelve in the Croydon Citadel Young People's Band. He began lessons aged fourteen and went on to study further with former Euphonium Player of the Year, Derick Kane. During this time, Matt played Euphonium in a variety of ensembles including Croydon Citadel band, Croydon Youth Wind Orchestra and the Territorial Youth band of the Salvation Army. He moved north to Sheffield when he was nineteen to study music at University where Matt was very privileged to start lessons with the renowned international euphonium soloist Michael Dodd (Principal Euphonium with the Grimethorpe Colliery Band) and at the same time had the chance to audition for Carlton Main band.

Important composition

I love you, Lord (US0371) 2010

IRWIN, ROSS

Ross Irwin is an Australian jazz musician with his own orchestra, the Ross Irwin International All Star Big Band. He was raised within the Salvation Army and is the brother-in-law of current Melbourne Staff Band principal cornetist Garry Todd for whom he wrote several pieces of music including the one with which he became known in Salvation Army brass band circles, *'Up Yonder'* (as featured on the 2001 Melbourne Staff Band CD 'Exultation', played by Garry Todd) This jazzy flugelhorn solo *'Up Yonder'* contains the well known gospel song '*When the roll is called up yonder, I'll be there*'.

Important composition

Up Yonder (m/s)

IVES, CHARLES

Charles Edward Ives (October 20, 1874 – May 19, 1954) was an American modernist composer. He is widely regarded as one of the first American composers of international renown. Ives' music was largely ignored during his life, and many of his works went unperformed for many years. Over time, Ives came to be regarded as an 'American Original'. Ives combined the American popular and church-music traditions of his youth with European art music.

General William Booth Enters into Heaven, title poem of a volume by Vachel Lindsay, published in 1913. Intended to be sung to the music of the hymn *'The Blood of the Lamb'*, its vigorous drumbeat rhythms describe the apotheosis of the Salvation Army founder, who enters the gates of Paradise at the head of a troop of criminals and slum dwellers: Christ came gently with a robe and crown for Booth the soldier, while the throng knelt down.

Important composition

General William Booth Enters into Heaven

JACKSON, 'EBBIE'

'Ebbie' (late 1800-early 1900) was a brother of George Jackson. He was with his brother the star attraction of the then New Zealand Territorial Staff Band. Together with George composed and arranged most of the music that was played by the band. He later became the bandmaster of the Melbourne Staff Band. He became known for his splendid arrangement of '*Master, the Tempest is Raging*'.

Important compositions

Master, the Tempest is Raging

JACKSON, GEORGE GALLOWAY

George Jackson was born on 28 December 1866 in New Zealand. He was a gifted and versatile pioneer of the New Zealand Salvation Army. After his appointment as a Salvation Army Officer in 1888 he served variously as 'War Cry' editor, trade manager, financial secretary, and private secretary to Colonel Ruben Bailey, the Colonial Commander. Musically he trained the Lasses Band, was a contributor to the early issues of 'The Musical Salvationist', and was solely responsible for the early issues of the New Zealand Band Journal (NZBJ). George Jackson died of tuberculosis 27 October 1893, aged 27.

Important composition

New Zealand Band Journal

JACKSON, THOMAS

'Bandmaster Thomas Jackson, of Tyldesley, took over the Band at the age of seventeen, when it numbered only six players. Now, after five years, its membership is fourteen Bandsmen and two Recuits. The Bandmaster is an out-and-out Salvationist and a great believer on putting first things first, consequently he is greatly beloved by his Bandsmen. He is, too, a cornet soloist of no mean ability. A march from his pen, *'By and by,'* appears in the Second Series Journal just issued, No. 288'. (Musician 1939)

Important compositions

By and by (TS0288) 1939, Carlisle Young People (TS0389) 1946, The Salvation Lifeboat (GS0385) 1900

JAKEWAY, ALBERT

Albert Jakeway was born in 1893 in Aberdare in Wales. In the corps band he first played cornet and later euphonium. In 1914 he entered The Salvation Army Training College in London. In 1926 he was transfered to the Music Editorial Department. During the same time he became a member of the 'International Staff Band' (ISB). During a period of nine years he was the bandmaster of the Rosehill Band of the Salvation Army, which whom he made numerous broadcasts and recordings. Next to this he has been bandmaster of the Tottenham Citadel Band and the famous Clapton Congress Hall Band. Additionally he spent several years as instructor of the Cambridge Heath Band. Albert Jakeway was also a member of the International Staff Band for 18 years. From 1953 until 1958 he was the Head of the Music Editorial Department as successor to Bramwell Coles. In his period of office the Unity Series which enriched the repertoire of the smaller bands was started. Albert Jakeway died, 98 years old, in 1992. A part of his career was spent in the republic of Czechoslovakia, where he was the bandmaster of the Prague 1 Band.

Important compositions

Where duty calls (FS141) 1947, Gems from the great Masters (FS234) 1958, Memories of the Past (GS1147) 1938, Rosehill (GS1265) 1946, Old Campaigners (GS1197) 1941

JACOBS, BRAM A.

Both Bram's parents came from real Salvation Army families. When his father left school in the early 1900's, he went to work at the International Headquarters in London as one of William Booth's Office Boys. These were young lads, on their first job of employment, who were used to deliver messages, to and from the Founder, General Bramwell Booth and other officers before the telephone was in common use! Bram's father had two sisters, who both were officers. One of them, Brigadier Faith Jacobs, was stationed in The Netherlands in the 1930's to learn the language before being sent to work in South Africa.

Bram's playing days were spent on cornet and flugelhorn but due poor health also spent five years on percussion. His interest in musical composition started around the age of sixteen. He studied harmony and composition –by correspondence- with the veteran English Salvation Army composer, Bandmaster George Marshall. At the end of WWII, Coventry City Corps had a very strong youth group and it was for this group that Bram's earliest efforts were desgined, like brass quartets.

He was bandmaster of the Coventry City Band for fourteen years, which included a tour to The Netherlands.

Important compositions

St. Columbia (TS0562) 1957

JAMES, KEN

Ken went to be a lecturer in music teacher training in Bath. He was one of the corps pianists at the time and played solo cornet in the Gloucester Citadel Band. His piano playing for the collection was always interesting with wonderfully thought out harmonies and progressions. After several vocal contributions, his flugel solo *'Calling Today'* was his first published band piece.

Important compositions

Calling today (GS1625-2) 1971, Nearer to Thee (GS1660) 1974

JOHANSSON, FRITZ

Fritz was born in 1895 and Promoted to Glory in 1965. During the year 1913 he was a member of the Swedish Staff Band, playing Bass. Later he went to the Training College to become a Salvation Army officer, and was Corps Officer, Youth Secretary, Divisional Commander with the rank of Lieutenant Colonel.

Important compositions

Skynda till Jesus (FM0129) 1922

JOHNSON, JOHAN

Is a Salvationist at Sodertalje in Sweden. He has a degree in music from the Royal Academy in Stockholm and plays percussion. He was born in the town Mora in Dalarna in Sweden in April 1982. Nine months later they moved to the town Nässjö, at this young age he only listened to music as his mother was Songster Leader for a while at the corps and his father mostly played in the band, but for a short period he was bandmaster. In 1991 the Johnson family moved to the town of Södertälje. At the age of 10 Johan started to play cornet for bandmaster Torgny Hanson. He was a bad cornet student because he never practised so when he started playing with the Young People's Band, Torgny left the teaching to the Young People's Band Leader, which was his own son Aleander Hanson. The years passed on and soon Johan was old enough to start playing 2nd cornet in the Corps Band in Södertälje. He currently is still a member of the corps in Södertälje. At the same time that Johan started playing cornet in The Salvation Army he also started to play percussion in the public music school in Södertälje and soon joined its youth symphony orchstra and a year later became timpanist of the local symphony orchestra in Södertälje where he still plays percussion and timpani.

In junior high and in high school he always went in the class with a 'music profile' and later in his life he got accepted to the Royal College of Music in Stockholm to study to become a music teacher. Currently he works at a psychiatric ward in a retirement home.

Johan is not a high profile composer, to mark his own words but compose in a more small scale. He only has one published work and it's called *'Nåd, bara nåd'* which is an arrangement on a three verse song written by Peter Linck. The editor of Scanbrass who published it asked Johan to rescore the last verse of the song because it was considerd 'to difficult' for most bands in Scandinavia.

Important compositions

Nåd, bara nåd, Triumphant Jesus, Vi vill ge dig äran

JOHNSON, STUART

Stuart Johnson was born in Chesterton, Staffordshire, son of a coal miner, in 1935, and is still living somewhere near to Stafford. When Neville Mcfarlane (another noted composer in this book) was Bandmaster at Chesterton (1958-63) Stuart was Songster Leader and his principal trombone. He was trained as a teacher at All Saints College, Birmingham and taught in secondary schools and as a college lecturer. He left the Salvation Army in the late 1960s and has published a fair deal of music for brass and wind bands, especially for young people.

Important composition

I come to Thee (GS1575) 1967

JONES, DAVID E.

David was born into the home of Salvationist parents, Bryn and Marie Jones. The year was 1950 and the place was Swansea, South Wales. He was the eldest of 3 boys, his younger brothers were twins.

His earliest musical memories are centred at Plasmarl Corps in the Swansea Division learning the Singing Company songs of the 1950's, the excitement of blowing a trombone at the age of 6 and the fascination of hearing a guitar strummed by the Officer's wife, an Argentinean lady. The highlight of visiting his grandparents a few miles away at Troedyrhiw, Merthyr was going straight into the front room to find the 'band' – his Grandad's Eb Bass and then attempting to get a note out of it.

In 1957 David's parents were made the first Auxiliary Captains in the British Territory. His mother had previously been a single officer serving in London Corps during the blitz of the 2nd World War. Their first appointment together was to Ammanford in South Wales, a totally Welsh-speaking town, something of a culture shock to his English-speaking mother. The bandmaster at the Corps was on old friend of his dad, Howell Powell, who promptly gave him a cornet. David had a lesson on Tuesday evening, went back to his house on Saturday for a second lesson and was playing in the small corps band on Sunday. The first tune that he played on that Sunday was the 2nd cornet part of *'Deep Harmony'*, a tune that he was to feature many years later in a March called *'Century of Service'* (Triumph, November 1984) written in connection with the centenary of Nelson Corps in Lancashire.

The 'swinging sixties' heralded the arrival of The Beatles and by that time he and his brothers were playing guitars. Each Christmas they would entertain the Officers of the

Swansea Division at the annual Christmas party, Beatles wigs provided by his mother, much to the amusement of everyone gathered!

At the age of 15 David's parents were appointed to Treforest Corps, Pontypridd where he attended the grammar school. This was an appointment from heaven so far as David was concerned. The School had a wonderful reputation for music and this is where his development as a musician really started to become established. The encouragement and help that he received from the music staff at this school was to shape the rest of his life. During this time his parents arranged a meeting with Bandmaster Ivor Bosanko of Canton Corps, Cardiff to seek his advice. Ivor was the Professor of brass teaching at the Cardiff School of Music and Drama. For the next 3 years David left school early each Friday afternoon for the bus journey (plus euphonium) into Cardiff to have lessons with him at the College. His gratitude to this man, Ivor Bosanko, is unbounded. Like many other young musicians of that time, he was to play a leading role in David's development, not just musically but in many other ways. In addition to the 'playing' lessons he would also take him early attempts at composition, where his guidance and encouragement were so helpful. The memory of those Friday afternoon lessons at Cardiff Castle (the then home of the College) will live with David forever. The Salvation Army has been fortunate beyond measure in having such a supremely talented and consummate all-round musician/composer as Ivor Bosanko. The three years at Pontypridd grammar, plus the extra help from Ivor, prepared him for securing a place at Trinity College of Music, London.

Arriving in the middle of London in 1968, with the 'swinging sixties' still in full-swing, was the biggest culture-shock a lad from the Welsh valleys could ever have! David found himself getting caught up in the excitement of everything, even the daily crush on the tube train into Bond Street station. At this time, his parents organised student lodgings with an elderly Salvationist couple at Nunhead. The corps there was well-used to Salvationist students arriving to study in London. Like many others of his generation he is grateful for the welcome that they gave him, it started a very happy long-term relationship.

At Trinity College David's main interests and studies were in composition and conducting. He was extremely fortunate in winning the composition prize in his first year, which resulted in a performance at the Wigmore Hall (situated just around the corner from the college) and a cheque for £25, which in 1968 was worth having!

After graduation, newly married and living in an exorbitantly expensive London Flat, he started working as a free-lance musician, combining teaching and conducting commitments with specialist work for Transatlantic Records, transcribing many original Jazz and Blues pieces from early archive recordings. In 1973 David and his wife entered the International Training College, after 'commissioning' the next 10 years was spent as Corps Officers in the British Territory. During this period a young son, Dean Haydn arrived to complete the Jones family. For many years to come it was David's privilege to be coach and encourager to the young maestro – in recent years there has been something of a role-reversal!

Resuming a full-time career in music, his work covered a wide area ranging from education, teaching and writing, through to working in the commercial sector. It has been his privilege to be involved in a number of large recording projects at the Abbey Road studios and as a Salvationist he enjoyed working for the Pope (!) originating and editing one of the Catholic Hymn books!

Teaching, composition and arranging in the brass, wind, vocal and educational areas are the main focus of his work and David is currently involved with a number of different Publishers as a composer/arranger.

Two years ago the Jones household was blessed once again with the arrival of Finlay Haydn, Dean (David's son, and also a noted Salvation Army composer) and Emma's son. Mr. Finn is following in the steps of Dad and Grandad, strumming, blowing and banging anything in the house that resembles a musical instrument. He already conducts and sings rather better than Grandad! David and Dean are both keen golfers and hope that Grandson also follows in that particular family tradition!

Important compositions

Light and Song (GS2073) 2009, Theodora (GS1716-1) 1979

JONES, DEAN

Being asked to write about yourself is one of those tasks which on the one hand is easy but on the other, is quite daunting as you are reliant upon the reader making their own interpretation, solely upon words alone! With this in mind, I want to be able to express my thankfulness and surprise at being included in this latest book from Steef.

When I consider my own involvement in music ministry within the Salvation Army, one word above all stands out to me – privilege. Looking back at 3 decades of music making within our movement, I see the way that the army has evolved and for me personally, the way in which God has led His people in this regard. My own life has been influenced and enhanced as a result of Salvation Army music making which will be fascinating for me to consider greater as I write my thoughts in response to Steef's request.

Born into a Salvation Army officer's home, my upbringing as an only child was again one of privilege. My parents, David and Miriam never once neglected to provide opportunity through financial or personal support and development. My childhood was a very happy one and the 'dear old Army', and its music was all I knew! Even now, when I hear certain harmonic sequences, I am taken back to my childhood, growing up listening to corps music sections such as my family home corps at Diss in Norfolk. I can picture myself in the hall there and the haunting sounds of music such as Stephen Bulla's 'When we cannot see our way' seem to conjure such images immediately. I'm told that when I was an infant, I insisted on having tune books to play along with the band on my plastic Trumpet, and people would also remark that when I had my toy drum, I was able to beat along in time! I wish I was as 'gifted' now! Music played a vital role in our family home and still does today. Dad (David E Jones), who graduated from Trinity Music Collage in London and still contributes to the Army's journals to this day, would often be at the piano, writing a new song or band arrangement. One such early memory for me is Dad and I being at the piano with his short score manuscript of the hymn tune arrangement *'Theodora'* (GS1716-1). Ever the encourager, he said to me that *we* had to 'score' the piece now. 'Score' – this sounded fun…and with the quarters phone ringing, here was my chance to make an impression. So, with pencil and eraser in hand, I decided to put numbers underneath each chord. When Dad came back, he asked me what these numbers meant – *'I think this one should be a 4'* I said to a bemused and slightly amused Dad – I was 'scoring' chords which in my mind meant marking them out of 10!! I think I was 6 at the time! Another childhood memory of early 'compositions' was when, with manuscript, pencil (always a 2B, Dad insisted!) and eraser I penned a few very basic notes. Underneath was the instruction for the lower brass to 'play after this' with a big arrow pointing up to the cornet bar I'd sketched out – all very helpful stuff! It caused quite a lot of laughter from Mum and Dad which thankfully I recall being a part of!

Army music was a massive part of life for the family. My Grandad, Charles Rackham on my Mum's side was one of those wonderfully devout and inspiration army characters (from a golden generation) that simply lived for playing, singing and leading army music. He was a very decent Solo Horn player, and would clean his instrument right the way through inside and out every Saturday night, and finishing his routine by playing the tune of *French* to check all the water was out. With uniforms pristine, shoes and car clean, my Grandparents would be ready for worship the next day. Grandma (Kathleen Rackham nee Peckett) was equally as musical and a fine Alto singer who still harmonises to all congregational singing in worship! Above all, they continue (despite Grandad going to be with the Lord in October 2003) to be a huge inspiration to me as a Christian first, and as a musician second. They encouraged my Mum to play the piano – something she now teaches to children as a more of a vocation than a mere career, and to use her gifts within the Army. On Dad's side, it's always been something of a mystery where the music influence and gifting has come from. My Grandad (Aux Captain Brin Jones) used his Concertina for open air ministry and was able to vamp a bit of piano (with tonics and dominants often getting rather muddled!) and my memory of Grandma (Aux Captain Marie Jones nee Reeve) was always more of a keen supporter and listener rather than a music-maker herself. Both my Grandma's came to be at the same corps in Diss – which is ultimately how my parents met. I regard Diss corps as our family corps and my Great-Grandad (George Rackham) had one of those classic old-army conversions, where, as a drunkard, he was saved as a result of open-air ministry. The history of our family would then ultimately change, as all of Great-Grandad's children were brought up in the Army – a trend which has continued throughout the generations.

My early music-making was like most others my age. When I was 6 or 7, I remember playing the recorder at school and I'd already had a go at playing an old Euphonium when I was 4 or 5. I don't remember the exact time, but I would imagine at the age of 6 I started properly learning the Cornet. The first tune I learnt on 2nd Cornet was *Deep Harmony* and within a few weeks I was allowed in the band. At this stage, my parents had been COs at Marlow corps in Buckinghamshire set on the River Thames - a lovely town famed for its bridge and boating as well as being the neighbouring town to Bisham village, home to Bisham Abbey where the England Football team have their training base. Marlow corps was small but had some wonderful characters. In over 100 years, the corps band had only ever had 3 Bandmasters! I grew up playing 2nd Cornet within the senior band and loved every moment of those early music-making days. Over Christmas time, the band would seemingly be out 20 of the 24 nights before Christmas, to the point where by the time I was 16 I didn't even use a book - but no-one seemed to mind the huge undertaking and the atmosphere was always bright. My ambition was to be old enough to go on the Christmas Eve carolling round, where the band would go around the local pubs and clubs to play into the early hours of Christmas morning. We would make the annual pilgrimage to Temple Mill Island – a private estate with moorings onto the River Thames – and then, having been well fed and watered, the band would make their way to start the festivities. One year, I was allowed to go to the first pub...a major breakthrough! I simply loved every opportunity to get my instrument out of its case and play, especially at Christmas time. The same couldn't quite be said of my brief stage of attempting to learn the Violin and several attempts to kick-start piano lessons! I can't remember how much I practiced my Cornet as a child, but I just loved playing in the band at the Army. We had a genuine local legend as a Bandmaster. Charlie Furmston played football for the local team and had lived and worked in Marlow area his whole life. He was a decent Cornet player and could hold a melody well. Every so often at band practice we would be given a very special and unique treat; from out of the kitchen and carried proudly on a tray would be Charlie's 'world-famous' homemade bread and butter pudding! We must have been the only band in the territory to have a mid-practice break along with such a culinary delight! These were happy days for me. As Mum and Dad's officership service came to an end at Marlow, their musical gifts were used more and more as they decided to become peripatetic music teachers in the area. As a family, we went from being COs to being soldiers at the corps, which is where I stayed until I was 20. Dad was in essence, the corps Bandmaster in all but name, which, in the end and rather reluctantly, he took on a few years later. I continued to soak it all in as a youngster. The move from our quarters in Marlow to our own house in Maidenhead didn't change the fact that I loved playing my Cornet and learning more about my faith. When I was 11, I had been playing 1st Cornet in our little band for a year or so, but really had fallen in love with the Euphonium. I pestered my Dad about switching instruments with our corps CSM, who seemed to have rubber lips and could play anything. After months of nagging, Dad decided to take me up on it. So on my 12th birthday I sat proudly in the Euphonium chair at band practice. The first piece up was *'Kearny Youth'* by Stephen Bulla. I can remember that feeling of nervousness and excitement all rolled into one. And from then on, that's the instrument I have played ever since.

Our musical highlights as a very little band that reached a numerical peak of 12 in our time there, *were classics from the Unity Series such as 'Rejoice!', 'Melodies from great composers' and 'Llanfair'* but there was a little book that had recently come out that we obtained as a band and, now looking back, I feel was to capture my musical imagination in a new and exciting way. The book was called *'Play, pray and praise - 12 pieces for young bands'* (rather an irony for a band carrying several players into their 70s and 80s!!) and it came from America. Names like Stephen Bulla, Ivor Bosanko, Eiliv Heriksdad and Stanley Ditmer were now as recognizable to me as Ray-Steadman Allen, Ray Bowes, Leslie Condon and Dean Goffin. But one name more than any stood out from the rest for me, and that was William Himes. I loved the music he'd written in that little book and his march *'Effervescence'* in the Unity Series only added to that respect. His was the title piece of the book – *'Play, pray and praise'* and his incredible skill for creating 5 easy parts and making them into fun, accessible and spirit-filled pieces was ingenious. I loved the commercial sound and the expression of this kind of army music. It left a big impression on me. As a youngster, I was easily star-struck and I held people like William Himes and Ray Steadman-Allen in the same esteem as I held Ian Rush and Jan Molby who were my Liverpool FC heros! I remember my Dad would casually mention names like Norman Bearcroft, Leslie Condon and Ray Steadman-Allen and the fact he had been encouraged by them over the years, and I starred at him in disbelief! I recall seeing new names on Unity Series pieces in the late 80s and early 90s like Andrew Blyth and Martin Cordner. Little did I know I would later be friends and colleagues with such names!

That leads me neatly into my experience at West London Music School where Andrew was one of the staff members along with Gillian Pomering (nee Graham) – both who currently still serve at the Music Ministries Unit. Undoubtedly, music schools changed my life and from that first one in 1992 at Petworth School, I made friends for life and found an even greater love for army music. My faith too was greatly influenced and shaped for good which I was also very grateful for. In fact, since 1992, I don't think a year has gone by without me attending at least one music school! There were years I attended 2 if not 3 schools in a single summer – something I have since vowed never to repeat! Those early days at West London changed my all-too-narrow view of Army life, and I was able to see a bigger Salvation Army and one in which I felt I could learn from and contribute to. Trevor Davis was a tremendous influence on me as the Musical Director of our school. His leadership, encouragement and way of communicating gospel truths were second to none. I benefited greatly from having Trevor to look up to at both Divisional and Territorial Music Schools for the best part of a decade and its great to also be able to call him a friend and colleague today. In those early West London days, along with Trevor, the band was led by Bandmaster Robert Munn, Captain Mark Bearcroft and Bandmaster David Rudd. All of them brought valuable experience and musicianship to the group, and we were introduced to pieces such as *'Music Maker', 'Las Lluvias Grandes', 'Motivation', 'The king's minstrel'* and *'On Radcliffe Highway'*. Those mid 90s years were key to me in my development as a Christian and an ambitious Army musician. Influences were great and varied. Visits from legends to our Divisional school such as Colonel Norman Bearcroft and Dr Peter Graham were significant events for me and lessons were learnt that still remain with me today. Bandmaster Don Jenkins also made a huge impression on me as Bandmaster for my first Territorial Music School (TMS). Don was inspirational in front of the band and made you play with immense pride and passion. He remains one of the great characters of Salvation Army banding and is rightly respected as a wonderful Christian man with great charisma. That summer of 1994, his band played a relatively new march from Ken Downie called *'Choose Freedom'* at the midweek festival and then we focussed our rehearsals on Leslie Condon's, *'The call of the righteous'* for the Saturday night. Don's words of spiritual as well as musical wisdom remain as fresh today as they did then. The band gave an inspiring performance and it was a true testament to a group that had been so wonderfully led. Garry Lawrence, who was at the time the Bandmaster at Boscombe was part of the staff team at TMS for a good number of years in the late 90s and early 00s and I had the privilege of being his band in each of his years at the school. Garry had a wonderful way of bringing a band score to life and he had a wonderfully engaging leadership style which made him very popular. 'Garry's band' not only was a name, but also a song in his honour...most notably sung by the whole band with him sitting on the shoulders of one of the bandsman after our final rehearsal one year and paraded around the school rather like a World Cup winning captain! Our finest moment came as the band, with a rather shocked Dean Jones sitting on the end of the Euphonium section, was when we played *'Song of courage'* in the final festival of 2000. The band that year is still regarded as one of the finest 'regular' (non A band) bands of that era and I remember looking around the group on the first evening rehearsal thinking we had a great amount of experience and talent right around the stand. We almost sight-read down *'Song of courage'* that night and it left many feeling very optimistic of the week ahead. Garry also picked out the fantastically engaging *'Psalms, hymns and spiritual songs'* as our midweek festival piece and we also made some great music together and celebrating in the very truths that we were playing of. These were great days, and the visit of

Bandmaster William Himes that week also made a huge impression of me. One particular day, I nervously approached Bill and asked if he would mind taking some time to look at a song I'd written. The previous year I had had a song used in the final festival of TMS which was a wonderful moment and something of an ambition realised. I was encouraged to write another song which was the one I presented to Bill. We sat at the piano and I was utterly memorized – so much so I don't recall a single thing the great man said! I was just completely in awe and amazed that my hero was looking at my own feeble efforts of composition. What I do remember is that he was generous in his praise and also in the sensitive way he suggested any improvements. The next day I also spent half an hour with Derick Kane looking at the solo lines in *'Song of courage'* – another fantastic and slightly overwhelming experience.

In truth I have never been a great player and its something I've always had a desire to be. As I am writing this to you, I've just received an email asking me to be a soloist, and inside there is a boyish buzz of excitement…but as a 34 year old who doesn't like embarrassing himself (well, not in public anyway!) I will probably offer an alternative solution! However, I have always tried my best with my playing but never reaching the level I would have loved to have reached. As well as being Principal Euphonium at Music School bands and in the Youth Band, for a few years I was privileged to sit in that seat at Staines Band, but in truth I knew my strengths may well lie elsewhere. It took a while to discover and also accept that, mind you!

My very first composition was a very simple 3-4 tune for GCSE coursework. Dad got me started with the first bar and then I was on my own (Steef - I will attach a short score of the piece as a graphic file). I found the process easier once the first bar was negotiated for sure, and the melody seemed to come quite naturally. This lead to me scoring it out for our corps band in Unity Series format and then having to go through that horrid, yet excited anticipation of the first few notes being played. Over the years, this frightening prospect has lessened, but I think any composer would still say that there is a certain amount of tension when you hear your latest work for the first time. My apprehension was well-founded – I'd written out the wrong transposition for the Baritone part! I felt pretty dejected, but the thrill of the music being played was too big a motivation for me to ignore. The correct parts came out next week and an appreciation around the band for what I'd done felt good. My confidence was now a lot greater but the time taken for writing army music meant that until I came to the work for the Music Ministries Unit, I'd probably only written about 3 songs and a couple of simple band arrangements. My life was more about playing golf and seeing my friends at this stage of life, so writing music was too time-consuming! Also, having passed my A levels, I took a year out of education to focus on another music passion…my rock band *'Freudian Slip!'* We wrote some good material in that year, but funnily enough, I wasn't really confident enough to add anything other than the middle 8s to the groups' songs! I was the keyboard player and happy to add a few ideas, but nothing more! That said, I learned a lot about music and life in that year, and was ready to start my music degree in Kingston in the September of 1995. I'd made good friends with a crowd from Staines corps by this stage and without hesitation I went along to band practice as soon as I was able to. The corps welcomed me in and I was very proud to be 4th Euphonium in the band to DBM Andy Musgrove, Ron Young (RAF Central Band) and Steve Alcock (ISB)! I had gone from a corps band used to playing as our big piece *'Star Lake'* to a band who were tackling *'Music of thanksgiving'* by Ken Downie. What a change! But I loved every moment. So far as I was concerned, I was in Army heaven! The change of culture was something that also something I needed to learn and appreciate, but I was enjoying every bit of this new experience. I took the opportunity to have private tuition with Ron Young who was in the process of retiring from the RAF Central Band and not only did he help me change my perception of how to read and interpret even the simplest of lines, but also his life influence was a great lesson to me. His old sparring partner from RAF days, Dave Cooper, was again a great enthusiast for all things Army and his encouragement to me was vast. Bandmaster Tim Parker already was something of a hero to me. He knew how to bring out the best in the band and his technical advice and fine detail work was always superb. I learnt so much from Tim and we struck up a great friendship which remains to this day. On my very first full Sunday at Staines the band played *'Reflections in nature'* in the evening meeting and Ron and I were on Euphonium together. I remember Ron turning subtly to me at the end and putting a hand on the shoulder, whispering 'Well done'! Those that know, will recall that the Euphonium part in that piece is pretty straight-forward, but such was Ron's nature, he wanted to assure me. The corps band in those days was right up there with the best in the territory; a front row that was as good as any and a group packed with musical ability and enthusiasm. What always struck me was the sincerity in which Staines Band always ministered. Tim was in innovator in communicating with a brass band. He asked if I could work with him on a whole section of music we used in the 2nd half of Saturday programmes which was about the life of Christ. My task was to write musical links between various band and vocal works and along with narration, the whole presentation was both creative and powerful. I learnt a great deal about not only how a good corps band works and presents itself musically and physically, but most importantly, the art of communicating gospel truths in an attractive way. I was privileged to soldier at Staines for 10 years before meeting my wife, Emma and settling into a new area and corps at Reading Lower Earley where we have now served for 4 years. Tim has always encouraged my writing and as well as some arrangements over the years, I was delighted to pen an idea he had for an Easter piece in 2008 called *'The wondrous cross'*.

In the spring of 2001 I was called by a good friend of mine regarding a possible job that may wasn't ideal for him but may be of interest to me. I had been doing some fairly routine sales jobs since my graduation in 1998, and so this came as a great boost. The job was as a sub editor for the Army's Music department and so it needed no further explanation or time to apply. I wanted that job more than anything! I immediately called THQ to get an application form posted and made every effort to be efficient and organised. I was delighted to be offered an interview and went to THQ knowing I had to make a great impression. On arriving into the interview room I was excited at the opportunity I knew was there and wanted to prove how much I wanted the job. I was asked if I knew each of the people in the room by Joy Fisher from Personnel. *'I know Steve (Cobb) and Andrew (Blyth), but I don't know…'* and as soon as the words came out my mouth, out came an outstretched hand from the gentleman next to me… *'Dr Peter Graham'*, came the accompanying words! Oh dear! Having not seen him since his visit to music school a few years previous, failing to recognise the modern-day giant of the brass band world wasn't quite the first impression I was hoping for! Still, I couldn't have done too bad as the news came to me that I was offered the job to work for the Music Ministries Unit. I actually had missed the call from THQ that same afternoon because I was on the phone telling everyone how the interview had gone! Eventually I managed to find out after a series of phone calls, and I started work on September 10th 2001 – the day before that fateful chain of events in New York and

Washington. What has evolved for me ever since joint the department is a series of privileges and opportunities for which I will forever be grateful. Those first few days, weeks and months were extraordinary. I felt almost overwhelmed with excitement but knew I needed to prove my worth and work hard to justify my place. I had been to the Gospel Arts Festival that year as a member of the audience, and suddenly, here I was on my first day with a proof copy of the CD to listen to. Having been here now 9 years, I wryly smile at my own star-struck boyish bewilderment at my new employment – but the passion for music ministry cuts as deep today as ever…maybe even more so having grown with experience. I was encouraged to write for the department which was an incredible honour and something I immediately worked on. My first band arrangement was based on *'Faithful God'* (TS1111) and hearing the ISB play it through in practice was an incredible privilege. Within my role as a Sub Editor, I was also the project manager for the 'Sing to the Lord Mixed Voices' journal. Andrew encouraged me to write a bright song for the journal which I was really excited to put my mind to. I put together a gospel style song and penned my own rather limited words and called the song 'We'll praise Jesus' which was my first published song by the Army. Many of my compositions have been under the watchful eye and ear of Dr Kenneth Downie who I will go on to mention in more detail. Going to the ISB bandroom to have Ken look at my rather humble composition efforts in those early days in particular was a mix of excitement and panic! He would make my very simple ideas sound incredibly grand with his own fantastic harmonies at the piano (Ken can stretch a 10th which is a strong contributing factor to the rich low brass writing he produces). I would use it as an opportunity to ask him about his own new work and he would play extracts of numerous pieces that also he is inspired by. As I still do now, I felt I was in the presence of deity! Ken has an extemporary gift for harmony and it's a feature of his inspirational work. Within the first year of being the department, I was greatly inspired to write 15 works for the Army and I'm privileged that 11 of them were subsequently published by the department. I could be satisfied with my start certainly in terms of my writing output. By 2003, I had been privileged enough to have a piece of music published in almost every journal, including Male and Female Voices. The tough nut to crack was the high-end brass journals – the General and Festival Series'. My first piece to make that particular grade was *'Glorifico Aeternum'* which was written for the A band at Yorkshire Music School (YSCA) in 2003. It still to this day amazes me at the journey that piece has taken and the many kind messages and congratulations that have been offered over the years. As writers, our aim is to bring people in to a presence of God and give them a new insight into His love. To hear someone has been moved by your music and brought closer to the Lord as a result is without a doubt the biggest privilege of all. It provides sincere, spirit-filled fulfilment which makes every note worth writing. The song, *'Somebody prayed for me'* seemed to have resonated with many people at the time and so it was an honour for me to arrange it for songsters as well as use the song for the middle section of *'Glorifico'*. The piece has been used in concert halls around the world by the best brass bands around – and to me the best thing about this is the message of that middle movement to non-Christians as well as those who claim a faith: 'Somebody went to the throne of heaven, somebody lifted my name, bringing me into his holy presence, saying what I could not say, Somebody showed me the face of his mercy when darkness was all I could see, Somebody pleaded the blood of Jesus, somebody prayed for me.' I can safely say that that piece and that song were real yardsticks in my life and not just within my music. The truths and also the confidence that the music of those two works gave me were greatly significant. *'Glorifico'* was first played publicly at the final festival of the

2003 Territorial Music School. As he still is today, Stephen Cobb was a massive encourager to me – and enabled his band that year to play the piece. Having played at the midweek festival, I felt Thursday morning was a sensible time to politely ask Steve is the band could play through my new piece, which incidentally wasn't totally finished at this stage! By the time it came to Friday lunchtime, the decision had been taken for the band to premiere the piece at the final festival. I was both shocked and extremely excited at the prospect! My Dad drove up to Sheffield to hear the piece and we exchanged excited views and emotional hugs after the festival finished. I couldn't have felt more humbled at the almost constant encouragement that was coming my way from people. I don't think I'm being overly sentimental by suggesting that that night and that piece was life-changing for me. The piece was played by the ISB at the 2004 Gospel Arts Festival which was a tremendous honour for me on a night when Major Joy Webb was given the Order of the Founder. I owe a great deal to Steve for all of these experiences and continue to appreciate his on-going encouragement to me as a writer and colleague.

Growing up, being a music leader was an extremely attractive proposition to me. I've always been able to express myself and loved the prospect of one day standing in front of a group. My first ever opportunity for this came at Marlow where at 17 I was encouraged to lead our singing group through Joy Webb's song *'It is Jesus'*. Later in life, as part of my degree, I opted for the conducting module and was able to be assessed leading a brass group of friends at Staines corps. After that, the next opportunity was to lead a piece through at Divisional Music School with the band. As it turned out, I conducted the band's accompaniment to the timbrel item, *'Keep me praising'* by Andrew Mackereth. I was 23 years old, so felt I'd bided my time well…but was still extremely grateful for the opportunity. A couple of weeks later back at the corps at Staines, I conducted the composite Sunday morning band in worship for the Harvest Sunday. This was all new to me but I was really enjoying the responsibility. On a regular basis around this time, Tim Parker would come over to me during open air ministry and pass the baton for me to conduct the band in a tune or two. I would love this opportunity and am still thankful to Tim for it. Soon enough, I was the Assistant YP Bandleader to Allan Martin, who again was a great encourager and friend to me. Allan had served as a Bandsman in the Scots Guards and was an excellent brass teacher. He was superbly organised and gave 110% to every task he had as Bandleader. He was excellent with beginners and brought on many very good young players. With Allan's expertise, I was beginning to find my feet and learn on-the-job. I was learning practical lessons such as how to deal with people as much as I was learning how to conduct and communicate within the band. I gained some valuable experience and felt I was beginning to find my way as a young leader. Around the same time, I was approached to be the Deputy Bandmaster for the Divisional Youth Band which I readily accepted and enjoyed leading a full band on a regular basis for the first time. In 2002, the opportunity arose for me to assist Lesley Nicholson with the girls' chorus and SATB elective at the Yorkshire Music School (YSCA) which was a fantastic opportunity I instantly took up. I was privileged to be part of the staff team in both 2002 and 2003 and felt humbled and honoured to work alongside such great people as Brian Johnson, David and Leslie Nicholson, Sue Blyth and Stuart Bate. Above all though, the inspiring ministry of Mark and Andrea Sawyer left a lasting impression on me and I am so pleased to still work alongside them here today at THQ. I met some fantastic people in those two schools - but one more than any other stood out to me. Emma and I became close friends and she became a really confidante for me at a time when I lost two Grandparents. By the summer time our relationship had grown to the point that Emma moved from Selby in North Yorkshire to lodge in Bracknell near where I lived in Wokingham. Our relationship strengthened, sometimes through testing and sad circumstances, and we got married in July 2007. Then, in February 2009, our first child, Finlay Haydn was born – an incredible time for us!As a family we feel richly blessed and fulfilled, serving at our corps in the suburb where we live in Lower Earley. In meeting Emma, my life had been enormously enriched as a result of music ministry and my own early efforts at writing, and this was something that I have always been amazed by at God's leading and goodness to me.

From 2004 to 2010, Emma and I were privileged to be part of a great staff team at the South Western Summer School. There was a wonderfully unique atmosphere at those schools and we were blessed by the friendliness of the students not only to us, but to each other. It seemed that it was one big and very happy family, which was a wonderful way for us to spend a spirit-filled week together in Taunton School, Somerset. So for six successive summers, I was fortunate enough to lead the band and put my creative ideas into action. This was a unique opportunity for me and it proved to be an ideal place for me to develop my leadership skills in a very friendly and accommodating environment. Emma and I have made friends for life from the school there – again, our lives being enriched as a result of us being willing to give of ourselves…which was never a hard task as we loved the school so much. In September 2007, the South Western Division was without a Youth Band leader and so the opportunity came to lead the group in a temporary capacity. I was very happy to accept the responsibility and enjoyed 3 seasons with the group. The journeys down from Berkshire down to Somerset every 2nd Friday of the month were made all the more enjoyable with my good friend Jason Wells and his son, Jordan - and in the early days, before Finlay arrived, Emma frequently joined us too. Suddenly I had a divisional group to look after and as well as the monthly rehearsals, I thrived on the responsibility of putting a full festival programme together – something I'd never done before. The band had some great players and great characters! We would always stick to pieces within our grasp, I always felt more comfortable and in control erring on the side of caution rather than risk the band being stretched. The wonderfully warm people of the South West were always so supportive and appreciative; it made the big effort of travelling to rehearsals and festivals well worthwhile. My conducting and leadership skills were now being used on a frequent basis both within brass and vocal, as I was appointed Songster Leader at our corps also in 2007. Although my experience was far greater in brass, I felt very comfortable leading a vocal group having observed leaders such as Susan Turner and Andrew Blyth. There is a definite cultural difference between the two groups; something I've grown to enjoy and appreciate, and can honestly say I enjoy leading both equally. I have much to learn and have always looked for advice from people such as Muriel Yendal as to how to go about bringing the best out of music sections. I still regard myself in my infancy as a leader, but feel it's something I can keep developing. In teaching and leading the music, I feel strongly that it has to be conveyed with a purpose and so I will always take the time to bring the presence of God firmly into our musical expression. I feel strongly that the very God we are singing and playing about must be a vibrant and active part of all we do. One man who is able to seemingly do this as well as produce some of the finest and inspiring music the Army has ever had is Dr Kenneth Downie. Ken continues to be a tower of strength to me as a friend, and colleague and composition mentor. He is the finest of Christian gentlemen and a wonderful example of a music leader and composer. In 2008, Ken asked me if I could put together a group for the 130th corps anniversary at Salisbury. I'd been involved in a fabulous group, flamboyantly led by Julian Bright, called *'Festival Brass'* so here was a brand new opportunity to create something along those lines but with my own stamp on it. Having contacted a few good friends, who were within an hour or two of Salisbury, we met in the afternoon to rehearse. The foundation of the band was very much routed around staff and students from the South West Summer School as well as local Salvationist friends. The band were in good company – along with Ken and his wife Patricia as guests for the evening festival, Yvonne and Ian Field were the weekend leaders – so good musicianship was certainly called for. I led the group in the only way I knew and that was to engage with them and to bring a strong sense of ministry to our contributions. Once we had reached the interval, the band was asked by 3 separate corps if we would go and visit them in 2009. The idea I had had was very much 'one night only' but again, God seemed to prompt other ideas and opportunities. What has evolved is a group we have called 'Salvation Brass' and the group has now been fully functioning as a composite band for 2 years. For me, it has represented a fantastic vehicle upon which to use music in a creative way along with audio visual technology and 19 other committed people. We have been blessed beyond measure at the way in which the group have been received – the more us and the corps have contributed, the greater the blessings have been...all very scriptural in every sense. The band has had an incredible time and we are booked until 2013. There has been much to learn in many ways in the management and leadership of the group, but I feel able to draw upon experience now in handling all manner of details – both musical and non-musical. Being able to draw upon like-minded friends who are willing to serve and put themselves out for the sake of God's blessing is a unique and wonderfully fulfilling prospect. Our time spent together has resulted in many wonderful outpourings of God's spirit, and we have felt humbled at such moments. I have been able to bring to the group brand new pieces from composers such as Ian Feltwell, David Leak and Kevin Ponsford as well as some of the most precious pieces in the Army's repertoire; all of which has been an extraordinary joy.

People often ask of my favourite piece and composer. I'd rather take the opportunity to explore this as something of a study case. For me, there the way in which Army bands' serve has evolved. For instance, with 'Salvation Brass', I only use fairly short to medium length pieces. This also is connected to the amount of rehearsal time we have, but largely it's dictated by my own judgement of what people are looking for at a modern-day Army festival. So here is a list of pieces that have inspired and blessed me when I have used them with 'Salvation Brass' as well as the Youth Band and other times I have been privileged to work with Army groups:

'The light of the world', 'Just as I am', 'My comfort and strength', 'From that sacred hill', 'Above All', 'We saw love', 'Praise Party', 'Shekinah', 'Mid all the traffic', 'Thanksgiving' (mov II from *'Splendour of Youth'*), *'Amazing Race', 'Blessing and honour', 'Since Jesus', 'Who is He? ', 'To the chief musician'* (mov I and II used separately), *'The power of the cross', 'The Name', 'The Lord is gracious'*; from the 'outside' publications – *'I'll walk with God', 'God, and God alone'* & *'Vitae Lux'*. I could go on and on, but I'll leave it at those! I am passionate about strong harmony and lyrical melodies as well as exciting, uplifting sounds which can lift the congregation. The use of good visual images and videos is also something I use within presentations as I feel they can be a great compliment to the music. Sometimes I use videos on their own – other times to accompany a piece. Adding creativity to our music I believe not only engages people into the heart of what we are doing as a group, but also maximises our own gifting as God's communicators.

The Salvation Army has been blessed with some amazing and innovative composers. I have found true blessing and inspiration from the work of many gifted people and I give thanks to God for each of them. From the lush chordal work of Kenneth Downie, Leslie Condon and Ray Steadman-Allen to the exciting sounds of Bruce Broughton, Andrew Mackereth and Martin Cordner; the innovation of William Himes, Peter Graham, James Curnow and Wilfred Heaton, I have been truly brought into God's presence by these great composers. My friend and colleague, Paul Sharman is writing fabulous pieces and I much also mention again Stephen Bulla whose craftsmanship is so revered. My own father, David E Jones has provided a range of works for the Army for 4 decades and his own skill of harmony and innovation is something I have always looked to aspire towards. Along with Ken, my Dad is my composition mentor which is something we enjoy sharing together as Father and Son.

Of course, there are larger scale works that have meant a great deal to me over the years as a listener and player. William Himes works, *'Aspects of praise'* and *'To the chief musician'* completely caught my imagination as a youngster. I loved the innovation of both rhythm and harmony but also the fantastic Vocal section as featured in *'To the chief musician'*. Leslie Condon's *'Present Age'* is for many the most revered piece in our repertoire and for me it has always had a very special place in my heart. The imagery of the story-line was highly innovative and the wonderful section featuring 'It is well with my soul' is pure gold. Another immensely inspiring piece for me is *'Shine as the light'* by Dr Peter Graham. He set a new compositional template for a more modern-day selection which, along with other writers, I have personally tried to imitate. *'The kingdom triumphant'* by Eric Ball is another classic Army piece which has brought great blessing to me on countless occasions. The great American sound of pieces such as *'Psalm of praise'*, *'Psalms, hymns and spiritual songs'*, *'The good old way'* and *'Covenant'* have been massively influential on me with their rich and exciting sounds. Vocally, there are some wonderful songs that continue to move and inspire me…far too many to even start mentioning! Both within the army and in the larger Christian world, we are indebted to gifted writers of music and poetry who have provided many God-inspiring moments where His presence has been tangible. The creativity that has gone into the music we use reflects the very nature of our Creator God. I am thankful for so many wonderful writers who have given of their gifts freely for so many years. Their passion, as well as their talent, is equally remarkable.

It's always fantastic to see how people are so passionate about Army music and I am fortunate to have been able to encourage emerging composers such as Ian Feltwell and David Leak to name but two with their skills. I consider it an honour to listen to new work and asked to give some helpful advice. As Ken (Downie) often says to me and I in turn say to others, we are all in the business of learning and developing and I am glad to see there is a genuine sense of encouragement between many Salvation Army composers of all ages and experience levels. What many people don't always appreciate is that when composers create something new, they really are putting their heart and soul up for public consumption. Criticism is something we all have to face and understand as composers and there are expectations that need careful handling. I've been privileged to write music for a good number of Army sections of all levels and have learnt to gain as much input as possible from them so that the result is worthwhile. I've had my fair share of disappointments and knocks, but over the last few years, these have been far outweighed by people's encouragement and belief in my gift. Music writing can be a patient business - my 2nd major work, *'Lord of all'* took a number of revisions until it was ready to be performed and eventually recorded by the Melbourne Staff Band. In fact, there aren't many pieces I've written that have been completed and left untouched – almost every one has had some follow-up revision work done to make it more to be the finished article. I've always rather seen a piece reach its peak than leave it under-achieving as the time taken to reach that point merits the music to reach its potential. Undoubtedly, the advent of modern technology and in particular the music software writing programme, Sibelius has made composition work far more accessible to many potential writers. Over the last 10 years or so, I've written in excess of 100 pieces of music and it is largely due to Sibelius that this has been made possible. Writing larger works in particular really does take a lot out of you as a person. You find it hard to detach away from the music and find yourself regularly visualising the next section or even material already written that needs improving. Any piece takes time and patience, but larger works, for obvious reasons, mean more attention and of course, more time. Add to that, the weight of expectation as well as trying to do everything in your day-to-day life (and Salvationists know how busy the week can get!) then it's something of a minor miracle when you reach that final chord! Since the birth of our son, I can certainly vouch for finding it harder than ever to write big pieces. The relief I found when I finalized both *'Vista'* and more recently, *'Validus Deus',* was vast! Writing for all manner of situations and groups has been rewarding. Just now I have completed a quintet piece for a friends' wedding – these are great privileges that writing music provides. Some of the most satisfying music I've written has been 4 or 5 part material; the need to create harmonic as well as rhythmic and of course melodic interest is a challenge I really enjoy. Writing for a small amount of parts is rather like a footballer refining his skills in a 5-a-side match! There is a greater speed of progress due to the smaller amount of parts, but there has to be a sharp and fundamental approach. Writing for the Unity Series and 'First things first' journal has provided this stimulus and also a satisfying reward. One of the hardest dilemmas of writing is when you hear your piece played with wrong notes – something that more simple music usually evades! When I have experienced hearing groups attempt something I've written for the first time, it is quite awkward as your hope is that 'The Musician's won't judge the music despite it not being accurate at this early stage. Your hope is that there is enough in there to convince them to take it further and bring the music to a satisfying level. Having been blessed enough to have had a greater impact with *'Glorifico'* than I could have very imagined, I have tried hard to make my following work at least as strong. *'Supremacy',* which was a lot shorter work seemed to make a positive impact but only took a short amount of time to write. *'Lord of all'* and *'Vista'* were both works that took a lot longer to create and I have had to have patience and understanding over both of these pieces. Not even the greatest composers have hit the mark with every new work so I have learnt to handle my own expectations accordingly. Both *'Lord of all'* and *'Vista'* were used at the TYB festival of 2007 and 2010 respectively and I remember being very nervous as I prepared to listen to both. Even the greats like Ken Downie still get nervous when they hear their latest pieces, so I feel in good company in that respect! *'Vista'* in particular was something of a 'comeback' piece for me personally and I was relieved and encouraged at the response it was given.

Being involved in Salvation Army music has certainly been instrumental to my life. I have been afforded wonderful opportunities and privileges – playing as part of an ensemble in 2008 for Christmas Carols at 10 Downing Street with the then Prime Minister Gordon Brown and an assembled gathering, springing immediately to mind. Other honours such as mine and Emma's visit to the Texas Music Conservatory in 2008, singing with the

Territorial Youth Choir at the Royal Albert Hall and playing carols on live television have been incredible experiences. The influences upon my dedication to Army music have been rich and vast and have broadened my horizons greatly. To have grown in confidence and feel as if I have a peer group of writers to 'bounce' ideas and encouragement with such as Andrew Mackereth, Paul Sharman, Martin Cordner and Stephen Ponsford is a great privilege for someone like me. Others from overseas also such as Gavin Whitehouse, Olaf Ritman and Lorne Barry are inspiring writers of a similar age and experience to me too and worthy of adding to that list of names. Within my work at the Music Ministries Unit, I have been fortunate enough to be alongside people like the evergreen Lieut-Colonel Ray Steadman-Allen (OF), Bandmaster Don Jenkins and Dr Peter Graham along with my current colleagues such as Dr Stephen Cobb, Andrew Blyth, Paul Sharman, Derick Kane and of course Dr Kenneth Downie. In fact the entire current team with the Unit are incredibly gifted in their own area of expertise and together our passion and belief in music as a tool for good within the Army is without equal. I have always been brought up to give of myself in the best way I can and to make time for others as many have done for me. I've always enjoyed teaching young brass players and currently I have two very promising students who are keen to progress their skills and express themselves. I feel it is important to encourage others in all their endeavours and find it inspiring to see people using their gifts to their God-given potential – whatever avenue of service that may be. My prayer is to see this more and more for people within our movement – that they recognize the gifts God has given them and use them without reserve according to His will. Maximising our God-given potential will see our halls filled with people and it's something I strive towards. I want my own son to have the same kind of experiences for himself that I have had within the Army and see it flourish and be a great beacon of hope to others. Music has a vital role to play within that process and I believe whole-heartedly in using it as a strong tool for worship and evangelism. Good corps sections can help drive a corps forward and so I feel strongly that I must do all I can to enable this. I feel truly blessed and honoured to have had so many incredible experiences and adventures through the medium of Salvation Army music. God has used a mustard-seed of talent to enable me to bring people closer to Him in various ways. There can be no greater reward in this lifetime than that and I thank God for this very special privilege and pray for many more to come according to his will.

Important compositions

Glorifico Eaternum (FS595) 2005, Supremacy (JC622) 2007, Written in Red (GS2083) 2009

JONES, IAN

Ian Jones was born 1943 in Middlesbrough, UK. Son of SA Officer parents grew up in London, but most of his formative years was spent at Upper Norwood corps where his banding was influenced by Bernard Adams, Jos Walford and Leslie Condon. He was also the Young People's Bandleader for a number of years during which time he undertook the IHQ's Bandmaster's Course. Migrating to Australia in 1973 Ian soldiered at the Camberwell corps, playing euphonium under the baton of Brian Davies. He keenly led the YP band for 3 years. Ian joined the MSB in 1983, serving in the band for 19 years. During this time Ian commenced writing and arranging with primarily the MSB in mind, and has had a number of pieces published both within and outside the Salvation Army. Ian was bandmaster at Hawthorn Citadel for a number of years, and also at Waverley Temple corps from 1986 to

2001. Ian is a member of the Melbourne Veterans Band and continues to write and arrange. He is currently the contracted arranger/composer for the Silver Threads Band in Perth.

Important compositions

Greensleeves (TS1067) 1998, Lullaby of Angels (TS1170) 2007

JONES, MARLON

Marlon Jones is a young Salvationist residing in Phoenix Arizona. He works as the South West Divisional Media Specialist at The Salvation Army in the United States. Marlon studied at Edna Manley College for Visual and Performing Arts. He originates from Kingston, Jamaica.

Important composition

My Tribute (US0343) 2008

JONES, NOEL

Noel Jones was born in Australia on the 31st of January 1941. As a child he was taught to play the piano. Later he studied music and earned a A.Mus.A qualification for piano performance. Noel Jones worked as a piano teacher. In 1983 he became leader of the Music Department of the Salvation Army Australian South Territory. He was Bandmaster and Songster Leader from Ringwood corps in Melbourne and is known as an excellent composer. His motivation is to spread the good news as found in the Bible through music.

Bandmaster Noel Jones has been a Bandmaster and YP Bandleader for well over forty years and up until a few years ago was Bandmaster of the Ringwood Salvation Army Band. He gained his major in piano (A.Mus.A) at a youthful age and is well known and much traveled throughout the Salvation Army world as a composer of note and an arranger of brass compositions. He is an accomplished keyboard player and conductor whose musical skills and leadership are greatly appreciated by the band and its wider audience. Noel served as the Terrirorial Music Director of the Australian Southern Territory for the period, 1982 - 1996. He is in demand as a session conductor and in tutoring at music workshops and music camps.

Noel wrires: I was in my mid thirties before I took hold of the opportunity to write band music for the Salvation Army. My first area of employment was in the National Bank of Australasia and the Investment Services Department involved many hours of overtime, particularly during the mining boom. The second area of employment was in teaching instrumental music at secondary schools for a period of five years.

During these years I found more spare time to write music. I was fortunate to be given the opportunity to have piano lessons at an early age and gained my Associate for Piano Teaching at the age of seventeen years. My parents gave faithful service as Salvation Army officers for many years and provided a wonderful opportunity for us four boys to see the Army throughout the Southern Territory of Australia. Learning to play a brass instrument at an early age was the accepted thing. I salute the musical leaders in the various corps we attented who not only gave of their time in teaching but more importantly encouraged us in the Christian way of life. I recall a visiting Divisional Commander who stayed at our home and asked me to play the piano for a 7.30 am kneedrill prayer meeting. I practiced the tune 'I surrender all' for a couple of hours. I was only eight years old. The Divisional Commander listened to me playing this tune prior to the prayer meeting and then asked me to play it without looking at the tune book. From that moment on I found that I developed the ability to play by ear. Even at that tender age I knew that the Lord was preparing me for musical service within the Salvation Army. Even today I reflect back on those early years and gain inspiration when writing a new piece. I have no doubt that the Lord has a time and place set aside for me to write a piece which may be used for the extension of His Kingdom. I never worry as to what type of band piece I should write next. It is always in His hands.

General Eva Burrows who was appointed Territorial Commander of our Territory in 1982 invited me to become the first Territorial Music Director. This necessitated in me finishing teaching with the Education Department. This opened up many wonderful opportunities of service. I was Young People's Bandleader at Ringwood Corps and naturally had a strong leaning towards encouraging our young musicians. I feel that my forte in musical leadership in those days was developing a Young People's band. As a composer I felt the need to write for smaller groups particularly Unity Series and Triumph Series. My preference in scoring is to write music for use in meetings. The Founder often referred to 'Soul Saving Music' as the best music for service in the Salvation Army. I always invited parents who could play an instrument to accompany their children to Young People's Band rehearsals. We developed a very fine band. I recall with fondness a safari which we undertook. Our guest campaign leader for this safari was the late Brigadier Horrie Wishart. We needed funds to hire two busses to transport our players, their dads and equipment. Two weeks prior to our trip I received a nudge from the Lord to phone a fruitener and hopefully get my dear Mary and other mums to make fruit salad. This unnamed popular Melbourne fruitener gave so much fruit that I could not fit it in my station wagon! This gracious gift meant that we sold fruit to the Ringwood Corps folks for the next two Sundays. All expenses were covered as a result of this fundraising project. A few months later our Young People's Band played at a Congress Festival. What an honour to be on the same platform as the Melbourne Staff Band! I introduced the band to the packed congregation and said that if the band played well I would cancel the rehearsal for next week and take them to the Ringwood Pizza Hut instead. After we had finished playing and following a prolonged applause, Commissioner Eva Burrows announced that she would pay the account. My only embarrassment was that some of the youngsters brought their mates along to the Pizza Hut. Commissioner Eva Burrows insisted on paying the full bill anyway!

I always offer a word of Prayer before I commence writing a piece. One other item helps me too. Mary, my wife, provides me with a block of Cadburys chocolate! I find Mary to be a very helpful judge on any piece I write. Recently I was preparing a piece of music and trying a few fancy ideas which I thought were good. I ran through it with The Veterans Band and felt embarrassed. When I got home I asked Mary to listen to the computer playback and lovingly informed me it was a bit off. I graciously thanked her and back to the drawing board. It does not pay to rush the completion of a piece. Avoid complications; keep it simple and appealing. Warm harmonies enhance particularly devotional settings however it is important that the melody is not overshadowed. It is satisfying when a piece of music is learnt in a short time frame. I have been in some rehearsals where a leader talks too much and all the music is far beyond the bands capability.

I have always informed Music Ministries Unit in London, England, that I am never offended if a piece is not considered suitable for publication. They do an amazing job with the preparation of the vocal and brass journals.

Both Mary and I thank the Lord for the opportunities we have had in visiting many countires through the medium of Salvation Army music making and always have our songbook as a supplement to our daily Bible devotions.

Important compositions

No one ever cared for me like Jesus (TS980) 1991, MSB 100 (GS1917) 1996, Keep in Step (TS868) 1982, At Thy feet (AJ166) 1995

JONES, RALPH

Written by Ralph Jones:

The Salvation Army began in Adelaide, Australia in 1880, in the same city that I was born and began my life as a Salvation Army musician. I was born in 1953 and at the age of 7, my father started teaching me to play a baritone, after becoming a Junior Soldier, I joined the Young People's band at the Prospect Corps, in Adelaide. At the age of 14 I was enrolled as a senior soldier and joined the senior corps band, and played euphonium. After leaving school I wanted to further my talent and love of music, so I enlisted into the Royal Australian Navy, where I spent my first 12 months at the Navy's School of Music. I graduated by passing 7th grade A.ME.B. (performance) for trombone and euphonium. For the next five years I was fortunate to visit several countries in the Pacific Ocean region, such as New Zealand, Fiji, New Guinea, Singapore and Hawaii – including Los Angeles and San Francisco on the west coast of the USA. I was stationed on an air-craft carrier (H.M.A.S. Melbourne) as a musician of the RAN Fleet Band.

Wherever possible, I would make contact with a Salvation Army corps at each of the countries and cities that I visited. I was always invited to play in the local corps bands either for their Sunday meetings or for band practice. I have experienced first-hand that as a Salvation Army musician you are made welcome whenever you visit another corps, and find a Salvation Army band. After 6 years as a Navy musician I decided to transfer to the Australian Military to continue my career as a musician. For the next 14 years I served in a military band in my home city of Adelaide. During my time in that band I played euphonium, tenor and bass trombone. Throughout the world, many Salvation Army musicians have served in military bands in their country - including Australia, during those years of world wars and in peacetime. I have met several Salvation Army (Military) musicians from the UK and USA who visited Australia, performing at Military Tattoo's and other concerts.

I met and married my wife (1979) and in that same year I passed The Salvation Army Band Training Course from the UK Territory. In 1981 my wife and I, along with a small number of other Salvationists were pioneers at a new outpost. I was commissioned as the bandmaster and then in 1984 as the corps Bandmaster. It was in those early days with a small corps band that I started to arrange brass band music, mainly to suit the needs of my own band. Those were the days when you had to write on manuscript and no computer software to help you! Since then, I have written and arranged a lot of music of which some have now been either published or approved by the Australian Southern Territory Music Board.

In 1991, I left the Military but continued leading my corps band. My wife and I have 2 adopted children from South Korea and it was with that link that I was able to take my corps band on an overseas tour to Singapore and South Korea in September 1992. Then in

1996 I was invited to lead a Territorial Music Camp in Zambia (Africa) with 8 other Salvationist musicians. Whilst there, we were also involved in outdoor meetings. We then travelled to Johannesburg and Pretoria (South Africa) taking part in concert, meetings and open-air meetings. Whilst in Zambia, I was asked if I would return to take up a new appointment of Territorial Music Secretary, with other duties as Trade Manager, Public Relations and as the Bandmaster of the Territorial Band.

May 1997, began a new era in my music life, having to relocate to a new country on another continent with my wife and 2 young children. For the next 3 years, I was privileged to help teach the Zambian bandsmen and to establish 4 new corps bands. With financial assistance from the Norwegian Government, I was able to take 25 bandsmen from the Territorial Band to a Summer Music Camp in Oslo, Norway. Bandmasters' Eiliv Herikstad and Phillip Hanevik were on hand to give of their vast experience in band training. There is no shortage of young people eager to learn to play but there is never enough instruments to go around, due mainly to insufficient funds to purchase instruments. Zambia, like many other countries on the African continent rely on donated second hand instruments. As on previous occasions, I have been able to continue to keep in contact with fellow S.A. musicians such as Eiliv and Phillip in Norway.

In 2000 our family returned to Australia and our home corps, where I resumed as the bandmaster. Soon after I purchased the Sibelius music software and continued to arrange music for my corps band. Since our return, I have only made one trip back to Zambia, but will treasure the many fond memories I experienced in Africa. In 2008, I was able to travel to several countries visiting Officers and soldiers whom I served with in Zambia, before arriving in London to attend the Bandmaster/Songster Leader Councils. This included a visit to a rehearsal by the International Staff Band, a concert at the Royal Albert Hall and Sunday meetings at the Training College. I was fortunate to arrive at the Askim corps in Norway for their Band weekend lead by Eiliv Herikstad, who invited me to play bass trombone – which I had not played for more than ten years!!!

I have always wanted to return to Zambia, but that has not happened. My next venture happened in March 2010, when I was invited to go to Taiwan, where The Salvation Army have home for delinquent boys. Taiwan has only 5 corps and it is at the Puli corps where the boys are cared for. I was asked to run a music program to encourage some of the boys to learn to play a musical instrument. There are about 25 boys who are learning in various grades. The better players make up the band for the Sunday meeting. I am now teaching some of the young soldiers of the corps to learn – as the boys eventually return home, it is a vision of the Corps Officers to have a regular corps band. I returned home at the end of the year with plans to take a group of bandsmen from my home Territory in July 2011.

Whilst in Taiwan, the brass group will assist me with teaching the learners (the now established music program) and we will also take part in Sunday meetings, Concerts and Open-air witness. When the group return home, I will stay for a further 2 months and possibly return to Taiwan towards the end of this year!

In my spare time, I collect and paint miniature model bands (from 6mm to 90mm in size) of which I have about 1,000 figures. For a few years I lead a Trombone ensemble called 'Slides from the Soul' consisting of 6 x trombones and 3 x rhythm section, similar to the USA group 'Spiritual to the Bone.'

At this stage in my life I am still open to where and whenever the Lord may lead to use my musical talents for his glory. Currently Ralph is Bandmaster of the Noarlunga Corps, South Australia

Important composition

Into Your Presence Lord (Noel Jones Series NJS1002)

JONES, SIDNEY

Definitly not the same person as the one with the same name (James Sidney Jones, 1861 - 1946) who was a famous English conductor and composer. The Sidney mentioned here was an active member of the Maesteg Salvation Army Corps in Wales until his Promotion to Glory, around 1999. None of his relatives are in contact with the Salvation Army as such and therefore any other information is not available.

Important composition

Maesteg Young People (US0157) 1992

JORDAN, DEREK

Derek was born in Bedford on the 30th of December 1927 where his father was the Bandmaster of the Bedford Congress Hall band and where his mother was the Young People's Sergeant Major. Most of his education was in Sudbury, Suffolk during WW2. He returned to Bedford when he was 16 years old to be trained as a chartered electrical engineer. Derek joined the Bedford Congress Hall Band on 1st Cornet and was soon promoted to play Eb Soprano Cornet. They were led by Kenneth Elloway (another noted Salvation Army composer) who was the Bandmaster of the 'Bed's and Hert's Military Band' and a composer in his own right. Some years later Derek was appointed to be Deputy Bandmaster and gained plenty of experience in 'Stick-Wagging'. In 1964 his career as an electrical engineer took him to Lincoln to supervise the building of a Power Station and to marry his wife Diana. In 1957 they moved to Banbury in Oxfordshire as a Research Engineer in Aluminium Cables whilst becoming involved in the local Corps and eventually being made Bandmaster in 1960.

Derek began to start making arrangements of music for the band at this stage although in a rather amateur fashion. In 1964 his career brought him to East Sussex and the village of Hartfield where they still live. Hartfield is renowned as the home of 'Winnie the Pooh' where the Author A.A.Milne lived with his son Christopher Robin. Derek worked at the Grid Control Centre of the Central Electricity Generating Board in East Grinstead. He joined the corps band on Soprano Cornet at nearby Tunbridge Wells in Kent. He decided that he would improve his musical education in the study of harmony and take a course with the London College of Music and is now 'Associate in Music' at 'London College of Music'. He began writing for brass band and in 1969 his first selection in the Triumph Series was published called *'In Concert Sing'*. This was to be the first of many pieces in the Triumph Series format and in the Unity Series. The latest piece, *'Were you there?'* was published in 2010. All this music was hand-written and Derek began to get requests to copy music for non Salvation Army publishers of the band world who were looking for economical means of production in the years before computers took over. He even wrote the score and parts for Eric Ball's test pieces *'Peniel'* and *'Cornish Festival Overture'*. Being a life-long admirer of Eric this was really inspirational for him. So here we are in 2011, he is still writing but with the aid of the computer and the Sibelius Music System. No hand-written parts anymore!!

Important compositions

A Shrine of Quietness (GS1649) 1973, Where you there (TS1208) 2010

JOY, EDWARD HENRY

The composer of the piece *'Wanderer, come home'* was probably Edward Joy. The last name is certain. Edward Joy (16 November 1871) became a Salvationist in Canterbury though moved to Folkestone where he was a bandsman before becoming an officer in 1894. Besides several corps appointments he also worked at International Heardquarters. In 1919 he accompanied Commissioner T. Henry on an international tour that included the United States, Canada, New Zealand, Australia and India. After this he served in Canada as Immigration Secretary and in South Africa as Editor in Chief. He retired as a Colonel in 1938 and moved back to the United Kingdom. He died on 16 February 1949.

Important composition

Wanderer, come home (GS0342) 1897

KANE, DERICK

Derick Kane, principal euphonium player of the International Staff Band (ISB), has been named the 1991 Euphonium Player of the Year by The British Bandsman. Joining the ISB in 1976, Derick has given many important premier performances, including that of Norman Bearcroft's solo *'Better World'*. Derick hails from Hamilton, Scotland, but has been based in the south of England for more than 35 years, and is now bandmaster at Bexleyheath, a suburb of London. In addition to his duties with the International Staff Band, he has studied for a BMus degree at Goldsmith's College in London.

Important composition

I've Got Joy (GS2091) 2010

KEELER, ROBERT H.

The only information that was found says: *'A fifteen year-old Robert Keeler formed a band in Wilson, Ontario Canada, in 1881'*. Whether or not this is the same person is not totally clear but likely. He became eventually an officer with the rank of Staff-Captain. Staff Captain Robert H. Keeler was the father of Sallie Chesham who was the wife of the Chicago Staff Band tenor horn wizard, Howard Chesham, for whom Erik Leidzén wrote *'The Old Rustic Bridge'*. The Keelers and Cheshams were beloved by all who knew them. Keeler's son and Sallie's brother was the first National 'War Cry' Editor -In-Chief in the USA and a legendary euphonium player in the Chicago Staff Band, Lt.-Colonel R. Lewis Keeler. He was a very accomplished artist (painting/drawing) as well. He was a big barrel-chested guy who lifted weights and would hold his arm straight out to his side and his boys, would grab hold of it and do 'chin-ups' and he'd say 'let me know when you're on!'

Important composition

Melody (TS0232) 1936

KELLEY, STAN

Stanly Kelly is a first generation Salvationist. He came to the Salvation Army through the music program in St. Paul, Minnesota at the Temple Corps. His father was friends with the Army bandmaster who became also his first teacher when he started on cornet. Stan made friends at the Army and soon was hooked both on brass playing and the Army. He entered the senior band when he turned 16 and became a Soldier, making the decision to join The Salvation Army. His parents were members of another denomination so it was a considerable step. The band was a group of 35 players who could play General Series routinely and the occasional Festival Series piece for a concert. The band marched, played open air meetings in front of the building, and played at the local prison twice a year. They played at several public events annually including Easter and Christmas as well as playing at the cemetery each Memorial Day. The corps also had a competent Songster Brigade and band and songsters would make a trip into the division to support the smaller corps and occasional trips to Canada. Stan was also a member of the Songsters.

His corps was a Scandinavian corps and many members spoke Swedish. A number of meetings were held in Swedish each year. Emil Soderstrom visited the corps on occasion when passing through as did Colonel Ernest Rance who had family members living in the area. Several friends and he started a Joystrings-type group at the corps in the mid-to-late1960s in which he played guitar and bass guitar.

His interest in music was very strong and eventually he took his B.A. degree in music and is qualified to teach music K-12. He was lead trumpet in his University's jazz band and concert band. He just completed an M.A. in public administration.

Stanley moved to Chicago to work for the Salvation Army in the public relations department in 1977, the year William Himes took over the leadership of the Chicago Staff Band. He applied to be admitted and was appointed to the solo cornet section of the Chicago Staff Band. However, the flugel player simply did not show up for the first few rehearsals under Bill and Stanley volunteered to take that spot. A 'claim to fame' is that Bill Himes wrote the flugel solo, *'So Glad'* for him. He had been playing beautifully arranged but slow hymn tune arrangements Sunday mornings on 'out weekends' with the Chicago Staff Band but he asked Bill Himes if he couldn't write something just a little peppier. *'So Glad'* was the result. It was an honor for Stanley to record *'So Glad'* with the Chicago Staff Band. It was released on CD in the late 1970s and in 2007 it was re-released for 'Pleasure in His Service,' a 2 disk set of solo performances released in conjunction with the 100th Anniversary of the Chicago Staff Band. The eight staff bands played it again during ISB120 in June 2011 in London. The Chicago Staff Band played William's new arrangement for four soloists at the Festival of Gospel Song and Commissioning weekend in Chicago some weeks later and Stanley was privileged to be one of the four soloists. It was great fun for him and an honor to premier the piece (at least in the U.S.) a second time!

At the Festival to which was just alluded, two of Stanley's compositions were played. A march called *'Peru Cien'* written in January 2010 for the 100th anniversary of the Peru Division in the South America West Territory and a choral item entitled, 'Perfect Faithfulness' for SATB and piano just completed in April 2011. His wife Jan was the lyricist and provided the melody. Stanley did the choral arrangement and the piano accompaniment.

His primary musical influence was William Himes. Stanley was in the Chicago Staff Band for 16 years. Over that time, of course, the band premiered nearly every piece William

Himes wrote – something the band continues to do. Favorite Himes items for band include, *'Message of Christmas'*, *'Amazing Grace'*, the four movement suite *'To the Chief Musician'* and, of course, *'So Glad'*. On the vocal side, *'All that I am'* and *'Isaiah 40'* are favorites.

Other influences include James Curnow and Mark Freeh. James' brass and vocal work was contemporary while also containing timeless truths. From that time in his life he remember particularly the songster piece, *'Christ's Part'* and later the flugel solo, *'Have Thine Own Way Lord'* which he played many times with the Chicago Staff Band. Mark Freeh's cornet solo with band of *'What a Friend We Have In Jesus'* played by Philip Smith and recorded with the New York Staff Band was incredible. Finally, more on the contemporary side, there is Major Leonard Ballentine who has written not only successful traditional brass band type items but many 'pop' or 'commercial' sounding items for both band and vocal ensembles.

Stanley retired from the staff band in 2007. His final 3 years in the Chicago Staff Band were on solo cornet. He presently play solo cornet in the Chicago, Illinois Norridge Citadel band and his wife and he sing in the songsters. One of Bill Himes' axioms is, *'If you can't sing it, you can't play it'* and he continues to believe sight singing and ear training are very important to young students.

His music leadership roles have included being bandmaster, and later songster leader, for the Oakbrook Terrace Corps in suburban Chicago. He was also the divisional bandmaster for the Intermountain Division in Denver, Colorado when they lived there and was the bandmaster of its divisional band. His leadership activity started when he was appointed deputy bandmaster and Young People's songster leader at his home corps in Minnesota when he was a relatively young man. Those were great opportunities for him to develop as a conductor and as a leader.

Most of his arranging has been occasional music – something for a specific occasion and with no particular use beyond that application. Some examples include a music camp theme song written for band and voice for a divisional camp and a brass band arrangement of the Bahamian National Anthem when he took the Intermountain Divisional Band to Nassau on a band trip. He did not start any serious composing and arranging until he purchased his first copy of the music notation program *'Finale'* in 2008. William Himes offers a Central Territory composers' forum every other year and on alternate years there is a North American Composers' Forum at Asbury University sponsored by the 4 United States territories and the Canada and Bermuda territory. While they are primarily for young composers, Stanley has been privileged to attend each twice and found them extremely helpful. To sit at the piano with Bill Himes, James Curnow, Len Ballentine, Lt.-Col. Robert Redhead, Dr. Harold Burgmayer, Dr. Ronald Holz, Dr. Beatrice Holz and others to review his music with them is helpful and encouraging.

There have been many helpful people along the way, far too many to mention, but Stanley must give credit to his first bandmaster and first brass teacher, Albert Swedeen for not giving up on him even though he gave him ample opportunities and good reasons to do so. Also, after he completed his undergraduate work and moved to Chicago, he played solo cornet in the Norridge Citadel Band (then Chicago Mont Clare Citadel) with Phil Smith and Peggy Thomas in the section. They set the bar very high both in terms of performance and in terms of commitment to Christ. He has been privileged to meet many other notable Salvationist composers, musicians and conductors who have provided impetus and encouragement along the way. Also thanks to his wife Janet who has always provided encouragement and recently provided lyrics, melodies and who endured many weekends home alone while he was out with the staff band. Stanley lives with his wife of 33 years, Janet, in Wauwatosa, Wisconsin, a suburb of Milwaukee just 90 miles from Chicago. They have two grown sons one of whom lives in Milwaukee and the other in Denver, Colorado. The Salvation Army published one of his most recent arrangements in 2010. It is *'Standing,'* a solo for flugel (or cornet) with band accompaniment based on the tune, *'Standing on the Promises'.* It is #1099 in the Triumph Series.

Important compositions

Standing (TS1199) 2010, Peru Cien

KELLNER, PAUL

Paul Kellner, born on 9 January 1935, is an officer of the Salvation Army in America, and was director of Adult Ministries at the Territorial Headquarters (in the Southern Territory), and the executive producer of 'Wonderful Words of Life' the radio voice of the The Salvation Army. Paul's son, Steve, is also a composer.

Having completed 38 years and 4 months as active officers, Commissioners Kellner concluded active Salvation Army officership service on September 30, 2000. Both of the Kellners are products of the Tampa, Florida Corps. Commissioner Paul Kellner graduated from Florida State University in 1960 with a degree in Music Education, and prior to entering the School for Officers Training was a school music teacher. Paul served as Divisional Youth Leader in the National Capital and Virginias Division, and worked in the Viet Nam refugee program in the Arkansas-Oklahoma Division. While serving on the Training staff they were invited to conduct music and Corps Cadet camps in Haiti and later felt called of God to serve in that country. Returning to the Southern Territory in 1980, they served on the Maryland and Northern West Virginia Divisional Headquarters. His last appointment in the Southern Territory was as the Territorial Secretary for Adult Ministries and Evangelism.

The Salvation Army has benefitted greatly from the musical skills of Commissioner Kellner. While serving at the School for Officers training, Captain Kellner wrote several commissioning musicals, and the Kellners together have written and produced a number of musical dramas down through the years. Further contributions have included new settings of familiair words as well as contemporary songs and melodies.

Important compositions

Infinite Grace, The Risen Savior

KELLNER, STEVE

The son of Salvation Army officer parents, Steve received nearly all of his early music training in SA bands and vocal groups. He first joined the National Capital Band as a teenager in 1974 and has served several stints with the band in the 1980s and 90s, playing on many of the band's recordings. He has also served with several other SA bands, including the Atlanta Temple Band and Southern Territorial Band, and was bandmaster of the Prince George's Corps Band from 1988 to 1991. Steve retired in 2004 after a 25 year career in military bands, including eleven years as principal euphonium of the U.S. Marine Band in Washington, D.C. In addition to hundreds of performances with the band at the White House and in support of the President, he was a featured soloist on several of the band's national concert tours, summer and chamber concerts, and served as principal euphonium on the band's tours of Norway, England, the Soviet Union, and Switzerland. He also played on more than fifteen Marine Band recordings and was a featured soloist on the band's recording Charles Ives's 'America'. In addition to being an active free-lance musician, Steve teaches at the University of Maryland, College Park, the Peabody Conservatory, and the Washington Bible College. He is also music director of Dominion Brass, a Christian professional brass ensemble that performs in the Washington metro area. Steve received his bachelor's degree in trombone performance from the University of Maryland, and his Master's and Doctoral degrees from the Catholic University of America. He resides in Bowie, Maryland

Important compositions

Be Thou My Vision, Breathe, Variations on 'O Worship the King'

KENDRICK, WESLEY

Wesley learned to play, and gained much of his musical experience in The Salvation Army, later studying at Birmingham Conservatoire under Denis Masters and Stephen Daw. During this time he was he became bandmaster of the Birmingham Citadel Band for a while. He has had an interest in arranging and composing from an early age, and The Salvation Army have published a number of his works. He has also written for educational groups at all levels. In 1997 he joined The Staffordshire Band and became their Arranger in Residence in 1999.

Important compositions

Life, Peace and Joy (TS1086) 2000

KENYON, MICHAEL

Michael born in 1932 as a son of Salvation Army officers. After his school time he started to work at the Music Editorial Department of the Salvation Army. Later he became a music teacher. He also was, for some time, a member of the International Staff Band. Michael was bandmaster of Hadleigh Temple Band, Southampton Citadel Band, Sholing Citadel Band and from 1974 onwards, Southsea Citadel Band. He traveled to places such as Switzerland, Canada, USA and Australia as guest conductor and leader of seminars. Until his death in 1992 he was the Divisional bandmaster in the Southampton und Channel Isles Division.

Important compositions

Hold Thou My Hand (GS1792) 1985, Endless Song (FS394) 1978

KETTERINGHAM, KEITH

Born to Salvation Army officer partents in 1932 Keith was immersed in music at an early age - his father was both bandmaster and songster leader at a country corps in East Anglia UK. At the age of eight he was already in the senior band. World War II was taking their young folk into the armed forces. Considered by many to be a competent player as he grew up, Keith never thought much about composing until he was in his thirties. His family moved to the London area in 1950.

He was the Young People's Band Leader at the time (1968) when he needed a simple march that their Young People's Band could handle so he thought he would try to lay out something that could be useful. The result surprised Keith. People liked it. It was later recorded by the Salvation Army Metro Toronto Reservist Band on their CD (Something Old - Something New) recorded 1992 under the title *'Yorkminster Youth'*.

Along the way he had been a member of the Rosehill Band under Colonel Albert Jakeway. In 1969 Keith crossed the Atlantic with a wife and five children and no job. They settled in Cambridge, Ontario. Within three months or so Major (later Colonel) Norman Bearcroft asked him to join the Canadian Staff Band on trombone. He listened to a presentation given by Norman and picked up a few hints concerning composition. The result was that he started putting together a few band songs and other items. He now has eight marches to his name and the peak was winning a second prize in a writing contest in North America. The specs asked for a contest march. He named his entry *'Castlefrank'*.

Most of the music Keith has produced over the last few years has gone to bands outside the Salvation Army and have been written by request. Weston Silver Band has adopted another march called *'Weston Express'* as their signature march. A school band asked for a march in Concert Band Format and also Brass Band Format and *'Speed River'* was born. Keith enjoys his little hobby and hopes to be around for a few more years to listen to good music of his choice. He now plays in the Heritage Brass (Salvation Army Reservist Band) as a 'spare part' in the lower end of the band.

KETTERINGHAM, KENNETH

Kenneth's first banding experience was at a small country town called March in Cambridgeshire where his father was the bandmaster of the local Salvation Army band. In 1950 the whole family moved to London. Shortly after arriving in London he became responsible for the Hanwell Salvation Army Band (West London). The band at Hanwell was quite small with limited ability and presented him with a real musical challenge.

Whilst living at March Kenneth had taken lessons in harmony and on moving to London was fortunate to be accepted as a private pupil of the late Dr. Denis Wright. Dr. Wright had 800 published compositions to his name and was a leading figure in the brass band world and he will always be grateful to him for all his encouragement. At this time Eric Ball was attending the Salvation Army at Hanwell and for some ten years he was a great help to Kenneth. Both Denis and Eric conducted rehearsals for him with the Hanwell Citadel Band.

Around this time Kenneth was a member of the Association of Brass Band Conductors whose membership included people like Phil Catelinet, and Harry Mortimer, these were great times during which he was fortunate to win a hymn tune composing competition. At this time Hanwell Silver band was in the championship section under its professional conductor Eric Bravington and rehearsed some 500 meters down the road from the Salvation Army hall. Kenneth and Eric became good friends and after they had built the Salvation Army band up to the necessary standard they were able to share a concert platform with them.

The years Kenneth spent building up the band at Hanwell were most rewarding. They decided to adopt an approach similar to that taken by contesting bands. He became the conductor, his younger brother Kelvin was the Bandmaster with Allan Cooper as the secretary and Charles Kirk as band Sergeant.

This management approach was necessary as his business commitments took him all over the world which left the team to run the band in his absence. Together they were able to attract enough players in order to gain the reputation as being one of the best bands in the London area. Kelvin went on to become the Bandmaster at Reading Central Salvation Army Corps where he built up a fine band. Allan Cooper became the band secretary at Enfield.

Kenneth's first published piece was a March *'Marching Onward'* Triumph Series No.572. He has the original manuscript score with the late George Marshall's hand written notes on it. Over the years he has contributed a number of pieces to the journals with the last being a March *'Neath the Banner'*, General Series No.1921. His latest march *'Metropolis'* has recently been recorded by the Norwich Citadel band on their latest CD.

Important composition

Neath the Banner (GS1921) 1996

KEY, JACK VICTOR

Jack Victor Key (born on 21 March 1921, Promoted to Glory on 20 October 2007) was born and brought up in the Salvation Army at Shoeburyness. Firstly a junior soldier and then moving into senior soldiership and was a very active member of the corps. At the age of just 17 he was made bandleader and took over as bandmaster in 1947. In 1948 Jack married Ivy and they remained in Shoeburyness until in May 1953 they left to join the Salvation Army Assurance in Luton, after several moves in the next decade including homes in Crouchend, Northampton, Lincoln and Dartford they finally settled in Bexleyheath in 1963 becoming bandmaster in 1964, a position he was to hold faithfully for the next 26 years. His life has been music with several pieces he wrote being published by the Salvation Army for band and songsters. Along with Major Malcoln Westwood 8 full musicals have been written with Jack providing the music and Malcoln providing the scripts. Jack his tireless work was welcomed in the division where he was divisional bandmaster between 1991 and 1994 but in all spent some 10 years traveling around the division helping out at Lewisham playing for the songsters and taking band practice to allow the bandmaster the opertunity to play his cornet. It was only in recent years that struggling with ill health he became less active in turns of travelling but it did not stop him writing and playing music at any opertunity that came his way including supporting corps worship on Sundays. It should be noted much of Jack's work in recent years has been unseen but even up to the week before entering hospital he was finishing off a piece of music which he recorded on CD.

Dave Harrison about Jack:

Jack was a very close friend of mine, for over 40 years, I was his Band Secretary for a good number of years, and we were very close. It was a sad day for many when Jack was Promoted to Glory, but not for Jack as he knew where he was going. We are still very close to Ivy, his widow. Also Major Malcolm Westwood, and Jack wrote a number of Salvation Army musicals, Jack composing the music and Malcolm compiling the words. Two main Festival pieces Jack wrote were *'Happy Saved and Free'*, which the Amsterdam Staff band made a record of, which Ivy gave to me when Jack died, and I have had the record sleeve framed and is hanging on my wall. The other piece is *'Days of Rejoicing'*, and I have a recording of the Melbourne Staff Band playing that.When Norman Bearcroft had the Canadian Staff Band, they were playing *'Happy Saved and Free'*, and Norman was so impressed by it, that he wrote to Jack to see if any more were in the pipe line, at about the time he was writing *'Days of Rejoicing'*, so Jack finished it and sent it to Norman, which the Canadian Staff Band played that as well.

Major Malcolm Westwood about Jack:

Jack was originally Bandmaster at Shoeburyness in Essex. He moved to Luton in Befordshire to work for The Salvation Army Assurance Society as an agent (my father was his boss!) He was Young People's Bandleader at Luton Citadel. He was promoted to District Superintendent as an Auxiliary Captain and appointed to Lincoln where he was also YP Band Leader at Lincoln Citadel. When the Wesley And General Assurance Company took over The Salvation Army Assurance Society, Jack became an agent for the W & G in Bexleyheath where he became Bandmaster and eventually Divisional Bandmaster. Jack and I wrote about 8 musicals together and he had songs published with various lyricists. Personally, I knew him for 60 years and can say that he was a fine Christian. I never heard him say a bad word about anyone. He was a true Christian gentleman and a wonderful composer, pianist and band trainer.

Rowland Little about Jack:

I knew of and played Jack's music for many years but only met him about 5 years before he died. I took music lessons-mainly composition and harmony- from Jack and travelled every week to and from his and Ivy's home. Jack was becoming increasingly frail throughout this time and only able to leave his home infrequently but he would always be waiting, smiling, to greet me at the front door. He would say that our meeting each week when we talked about music was a highlight for him-it certainly was *the highlight* of the week for me- and I cannot think of a time when I did not leave his home feeling better and spiritually uplifted. He really was a true Christian gentlemen, a gifted pianist and musician and a very humble man. It is often the case that the greater a man's gifts, the humbler he is. (Eric Ball comes to mind.) This was certainly true in Jack's case and a more gracious man would be hard to find.

I would take my elementary attempts at composition to Jack and he would send me his own latest ideas and so we always had plenty to discuss so that our two and a half hours always passed very quickly. His mind was still very active and he would always produce scraps of manuscript on which he had jotted down the latest ideas that had come to mind. Ivy always had Jack's dinner on the table at 12.30 precisely and most weeks our lesson overran much to Ivy's consternation! Ivy was devoted to Jack and looked after him so well. She would always pop her head round the door to see that he had inished the tea and biscuit that she brought in to us half way through the lesson.

Jack had a great gift for looking at a score and spotting its weaknesses and suggesting how it might be improved. But he was always encouraging and would say *'This is good but what do you think if we used this chord instead?'* and Jack would play my piece but inserting his chord. It was always the chord I had been searching for without success! Jack had a thorough schooling in and knowledge of harmony and would say *'It's alright to break the rules but only when you have mastered them'*. Sound advice, as indeed was everything Jack said.

Jack composed at the piano and used Sibelius software which he had mastered to a very high level despite him being well into his 80's. His piano was connected to the computer so everything he played was instantly recorded on the staves. He had a great love of the masters, Chopin and Bach particularly. I remember taking him a transcription I had made for band and piano of the 2nd movement of Beethoven's 5th Piano Concerto (the *'Emperor'*). Jack loved Beethoven so we spent a lot of time working on it and how best to put the orchestral writing on the band. Jack said how much he would have loved to have played the piano part with a band but his deteriorating health meant that this was never to happen.

Jack still practiced every day and was still working on new compositions until quite near the end. One of these was a new tune to *'The Old Rugged Cross'*. Jack told me he was working on it and asked me what I thought about the idea. I replied that it was a brave man who would try to write a new tune to such a well known and loved song. But Jack pulled it off and his arrangement has been used to good effect in concerts by the South London Fellowship Band under Major George Whittingham. I suggested to Jack that he send it in to the Army for publication but Jack's humility and modesty meant that he declined to do this. (Maybe I should send it in, now he is no longer with us and cannot say 'no' any more).

When we studied band scores together, I will never forget his advice which was always: *'Never stand in front of a band until you have mastered the score both horizontally and vertically'*. He said that you must be able to hear the music *before* the band played it so that any incorrect notes or imbalanced chords etc could be picked up immediately. I cannot think of any better advice for budding conductors and oh that all conductors would follow his words of wisdom!!!

Jack was an admirer of the great classical masters and Salvation Army music, both band and choral. His published works were relatively few but invariably of great quality, good to play, rhythmic, and always popular with congregations. I think Jack liked honest, sincere music, nothing ostentatious or too fancy or designed to show off how clever the composer was. (I wish some of our modern day composers for band would heed Jack's views!) He always wanted his music to have a message. It was surprising to me to find that his interest in bands was confined to the Salvation Army and did not extend to the wider brass band scene of contesting bands and contest music. I have been a 'pondasher' (a follower of Black Dyke) for over 50 years so I would take my CD recordings of the Dyke, Grimethorpe etc and the scores of the latest test pieces to try and 'convert' Jack to this higher level of brass playing than existed anywhere in the Army as well as to the intricacies of the writing of the leading brass band composers of modern times.

Jack was surprised to find the demands made on secondary parts compared to Salvation Army scoring- he would often say in our lesson *'This is fine but are you sure you have a band that can play all the parts'*. He was particularly conscious of the limitations of the secondary parts in many Salvation Army bands and would often recommend 'doubling up'. I remember showing him the Howard Snell arrangement of Wagner's *'Procession to the Minster'* and his amazement to find the *second* cornets being asked to play top Bb's and even a top Eb. I was studying conducting under Ray Farr at the time and this involved going through several test pieceseach with Ray, then discussing them at length with the composer, and finally conducting each piece with a championship band. Jack was always interested in what the next piece was and I recall showing Jack the score for John McCabe's *'Cloudcatcher Fells'* and listening with him to the Dyke playing it. Jack of course was hugely impressed with both the playing and the quality of the music but I knew that this was not for him and that his heart would always be in Salvation Army music.

Important compositions

Happy, Saved and Free (FS338) 1971, Days of Rejoicing (FS436) 1984

KIFF, DOUGLASS – by Retired Colonel Mrs. Jean Kiff

Douglas Kiff was born on 3 May 1925 in Market Drayton, Shropshire, England, the only child of Salvation Army Officers. I first met him when he was about twelve years old as he played cornet in the Junior Band and accompanied the Singing Company on a harmonium in Salisbury, Wiltshire. He sang in his grammar school choir and also had a few private singing lessons after his voice had broken. When he was a teenager, his first love was a Soprani Piano Accordion which lasted him many years and was invaluable throughout his vocation as a Salvation Army Officer.

We were married in 1953 in Singapore, and on honeymoon Douglas wrote a song as a gift to the parents in England, and with a change of lyrics this became Number 1 in the Song Book, Happiness and Harmony. A list of his vocal music is available, but there was much of his work that was widely used, though unpublished. Appointed to Bombay, Western India Territory, in 1964, he arranged music and trained a group of nine singers, accompanying them with the accordion or harmonium. They sang in a very small studio and in spite of the intense humidity an attractive medley of gospel songs was heard over the airwaves each Sunday evening through the Far Eastern Broadcasting Corporation.

From the time when he was a cadet in the 'Peacemakers Session', his accordion was put to good use, especially when he preached in the open air with no other musical support.

In latter years, when the accordion was too heavy for his weakened state, when requested Douglas gave piano solos. One of his favourites was an adaptation of *'Amsterdam Congress'*, and by this time he had been blessed by a Dutch daughter-in-law.

During the ISB120 celebrations, three composers were present at Upper Norwood where the Fellowship Band played Terry Camsey's suite *'Happiness and Harmony'*. They were Terry Camsey, Norman Bearcroft and Brian Bowen. Many memories were stirred as this selection of music was based on three songs written by Douglas and myself.

The brass band journal, Unity Series of 1998, number 7, is a selection *'Smile!'*, Douglas Kiff arr. Leonard Ballentine. There may have been more of his instrumental compositions of which I am unaware. One of his songs, *'I reckon on You'*, was written to the accompaniment of the creaking of the ship's timbers when he was sailing to the East to take up his first appointment in India. This was adapted for trombone. You might find out more from the International Music Board.

When, in 1964, Douglas was appointed to Western India Territory as the Finance and Property Secretary, the Territorial Commander also expected him to be Bandmaster of the Byculla Central Corps Band. Regular band practices were held and Indian Salvationists, including the first woman, and others from overseas, reached a high standard. In fact, a visitor from USA was so impressed that he provided the finance for a completely new set of instruments which were purchased locally. Police permission was obtained so that the Band could march the streets and hold open air meetings in a nearby park where people crowded round and listened to the gospel message, each in his own language. Early on Easter Sundays the Band marched the streets playing *'Christ the Lord has risen today'*. Hallelujah!

His appointment to the International Audit Department took Douglas to many parts of the world where he was happy to share in the music of the country. His ability to play almost any instrument presented to him was quite remarkable.

For eight years, in his retirement, he enjoyed the Bandmastership of the Salisbury City Corps Band, revelling in the open air ministry and fulfilling many engagements in Salisbury and the surrounding district. He always professed only his best was good enough in the service of his Lord Jesus Christ.

Important composition

God's Servants (TS0805) 1977

KIMBERLEY, NICOLAS

Nicholas Swan Kimberley was born on 23 April 1925 when his parents, Adjutant & Mrs Henry Kimberley were the Corps Officers at Gateshead, near Newcastle upon Tyne. From the start there was music in the family because mother had her own piano which moved with them to each new appointment. At an early age Nicholas was attracted to the 'Boys' Band', as it used to be known, but his parents explained that members needed to reach the age of 7, and must be saved. So at Camborne Fortress Corps he asked Jesus to help him, and he signed the Junior Soldier's Pledge. He was then allowed to attend the young people's band learners' class where he was delighted to be assigned the triangle - the sole player of the instrument. All went well until he moved with his parents and baby sister Marjorie to Devonport Morice Town - where to his chagrin he found himself fourth man down in the triangle section!

By 1935 the family was at Pentre, in South Wales and Nicholas was playing tenor horn. The Young People's Band was doing well and were preparing for a specialling engagement at a corps where they were to be billeted overnight. Nicholas and two friends - all away from home for the first time - were to share a bedroom. While their hosts prepared supper they allowed the boys to explore the house, which they noticed had several clocks in every room. So they did their hosts a favour by winding them all up! With the result that at frequent intervals during the night the household was awakened by clock chimes or the sound an alarm going off.

In 1936 the Kimberleys were appointed to London corps, first to Kilburn, then in 1937 to Willesden Green. It was here that mother decided to send Nicholas for piano lessons. He welcomed the idea until he discovered that his was to involve daily practice of some 30 minutes. After a couple of sessions, he hit upon a plan. Half way through the appointed time mother noticed that the notes had stopped. Going in to inquire she was directed to the clock on the mantelpiece which had received some attention from the reluctant player! In years to come, when he began composing, he was to find his piano playing a great help, and was glad that his mother had encouraged him to persevere. In 1938 the family moved to Burton upon Trent in Staffordshire. By this time they had acquired a gramophone, and Nicholas used his pocket money to buy Salvation Army Band recordings, under the Regal Zonaphone label, which he played every day.

By 1939 Great Britain was at war with Germany, and at the age of 18 Nicholas was conscripted into the Royal Navy. Within six months he became a Midshipman prior to being commissioned as a Sub Lieutenant. He served in a convoy protection unit until the war ended, and during that time he made 17 visits to St Johns, Newfoundland where he was warmly welcomed into the corps band and into the homes of Major and Mrs Genery and Major and Mrs Pedler who arranged a wonderful celebration for his 21st birthday.

Home from wartime service, Nicholas enrolled for training as part of a Government scheme. He qualified as a member of the Institute of Cost and Management Accountants and as a member of the Institute of Chartered Secretaries and Administrators. In 1949 he married Marguerite Blagg, and in 1955 they moved to Rugeley in Staffordshire and settled at nearby Hednesford Corps.

Nicholas had music going round in his head all the time. The family always knew where he was in the home or garden because he whistled. Just as his mother had been known to prepare her sermons in her head, so he composed while mowing the grass, or just walking down the road. First you would recognise a well known tune from the Salvation Army tune book, and then would come a set of variations for solo cornet, or some jazzy harmonies for the trombone section, he was playing trombone by that time which he greatly enjoyed. Then the variations would get more difficult, and the harmonies more spine tingling. When his three little girls were in bed and the tasks of the day were done, Nicholas would bring out the manuscript paper while Marguerite sat with her knitting. This routine lasted for fifty years and the arrival of the Sibelius program made his life as a composer much easier.

Nicholas was a great encourager, particularly of young people in the corps. When a member of the Young People's Band moved into the senior band he would arrange a tune from the Tune Book especially for the youngster to play at his commissioning to the senior section. The arrangement would be well within the youngster's ability and Nicholas would rehearse him in it.

In the late 1960's, Nicholas and Marguerite took their teenage daughters to a performance of *'Takeover Bid'* and when their young friends at the corps heard about the wonderful songs, they went to the nearest presentation. They too were hooked! As soon as they managed to obtain words and music they would meet for a sing-a-long after the Sunday evening meeting with Nicholas at the piano - how fortunate that he persevered with the dreaded scales in his boyhood. Then the youngsters demanded that this small corps should put on the musical. Most people in the corps were involved in the production as well as members of local churches and Nicholas conducted and organized the presentation. On the opening night, the young Captain John Larsson was there to cheer. Three more of the musicals were presented by Hednesford, and these activities had a tremendous influence on the corps. It is interesting to note that now, in 2011, three officers serving in the United Kingdom Territory with the Republic of Ireland were involved in those productions, namely Carol Evans, John Martin and Jane Kimberley.

For 49 years Nicholas submitted a new composition every year to the International Music Editorial Board – or its equivalent. Each time the manuscript would be returned to him, usually with some helpful comments. Throughout this time he was profoundly influenced by Colonel Albert Jakeway and Colonel Ray Steadman-Allen and learned a good deal from their notes and suggestions. Then in the fiftieth year of his annual submissions to the Board his manuscript was accepted for publication and shortly afterwards a second manuscript was accepted. I do not know which came first - the arrangement of the *'Horn Concerto'* or the march *'SA'*.

Nicholas undertook a correspondence course in music with Huddersfield College during which he was required to introduce a project of his own choosing. He was aware that many professional musicians had received their early training in The Salvation Army, although they might no longer be involved with the Salvation Army. Retired Songster Leader Maisie Wiggins and her husband Ray helped to compile a list of such musicians well known in the professional world - Maisie herself having held the post of principal trombone in the Halle Orchestra for many years. Nicholas wrote to some sixty of these asking them to complete a questionnaire in which they were asked about SA influences in their personal lives and work. He received a very large number of replies, many with photographs. He was highly satisfied with the results, and completed this study and included it with other papers for his correspondence course.

For about 14 years until 2007 Nicholas regularly attended the adult music school held every year at Sunbury Court in the week following Easter, in fact this event was a highlight of his year. As well as enjoying the company of friends known over many years, he always found time to encourage anyone who appeared to be struggling with the demands of the music set before them.

Nicholas was corps treasurer for 30 years and enjoyed fund-raising for special Salvation Army projects. In 1986 a £3 million Scheme was launched to improve the accommodation for cadets at what was then known as The International Training College at Denmark Hill. He felt he should give a worthwhile sum, but how? Then he remembered his best-loved toys from boyhood - his lead soldiers equipped as Salvation Army Bandsmen complete with instruments, flag carriers and three women in uniform carrying tambourines and The 'War Cry'. The international auctioneers Phillips were known to run specialist sales in London solely of lead soldiers and they readily agreed to include the SA group in their next catalogue with a note that they were being sold on behalf of the SA. Phillips would forego their usual charges and commission. Salvationists in uniform attended the sale and were delighted hear the topmost bid of £2470. Nicholas was Promoted to Glory on 17 February 2008.

Important composition

S.A. (US0243) 1999

KING, H

A former member of the first Household Troops Band who toured Canada, and after a further period of service as bandsman at Watford, eventually holding the positon of Bandmaster, he moved on to Canada.

Important composition

Haste Away (TS0076) 1926

KIPPAX, MILTON

Was an officer of the Salvation Army. He was born on December 17, 1902 and died in May, 1974. He retired to Rhinebeck, in New York, where he died. He was a skilled euphonium player and was also one of the soloists of the New York Staff Band, where he was the principal euphonium in the 1950's. He played an old front-bell euphonium and was very reluctant to give up this instrument for an upright one. His most well known composition is the march *'Golden Jubilee'* although it is believed that this march was first re-arranged by Erik Leidzén before publication.

He was the soloist who played the euphonium solo *'The Song of The Brother'* immediately after Staff Bandmaster George Granger died of a heart attack in Ocean Grove during a New York Staff Band festival in 1945. Deputy Bandmaster William Bearchell (himself a noted composer) got up to lead the band after George Granger was carried out and checked out by the medics, while Milton Kippax played the solo. It was announced after this performance that George Granger had passed away. The show went on.

A letter, dated 11 July 1950 stated: *'Major Milton Kippax, euphonium soloist of the Eastern Territorial Staff Band, was stationed at the Army's Brooklyn Men's Social Service Center. He has been a bandsman since 1916 and joined the Staff Band in 1939. The major has travelled extensively in the United States and Canada with the Staff Band, which uses many of his arrangements of cornet and euphonium solos. For many years he was band leader for the Newark West Side Corps Band and later led the Bushwick Corps Band which made numerous trips throughout the Eastern Territory. Major Kippax is an experienced instructor and has been for many years a trained bandsman in various Corps in the New York area. Since 1940 he has been an instructor at the Band Camp at Star Lake and was in charge of the Metropolitan Band Camp in 1946'.*

Brigadier Kippax entered the school for Officers Training from the Newark, NJ #1 Corps in 1925. Following his commissioning he was appointed as Prob. Lt. to assist at Irvington, NJ. In 1927 he was appointed as commanding officer at Hoboken and a little later to Jersey City. He was married to Captain Anna Ernst on October 12, 1927. Soon after they assumed command of the Nyack, NY Corps. Other appointments included Clearfield, Milton, Stroudsburg, Tamaqua, Mount Carmel and Plymouth in Pennsylvania. In 1939 they were transferred to the Men's Social Service Department where they have served well for the last 28 years. In addition to the outstanding service given this department, Brigadier Kippax was noted as an outstanding brass instrumentalist. Tens of thousands of persons have been thrilled by his outstanding solos on the Euphonium. He loved playing with brass bands and was featured as one of the Army's outstanding musicians. He was with the New York Staff Band for 16 years. In addition to this, Brigadier Kippax was a well known composer of music. His march *'Golden Jubilee'* is played around the world while his solo number *'I love to tell the story'* has been a featured item on many occasions. Brigadir Milton Kippax was Promoted to Glory in 1974.

A letter that Staff Bandmaster Vernon Post wrote to him on January 11, 1968 says:

'Dear Kippie,

The Salvation Musicians of the Eastern Territory salute you as you enter into honored retirement after many years of contribution to the music program. There are not many now active as Staff Bandsmen who had the privilege of playing in the New York Staff Band with you. Even before this privilege was mine, I would listen to the Staff Band on every occasion possible and thrill to you euphonium playing. We thank you for all of the extra hours of discipline and lonely practice which you devotedly gave to your chosen instrument in order to be such an outstanding artist. As a Star Lake Music camp Staff Member you inspired and enlarged the horizons of some of the finest youth of our territory, and many parents of young men and women admire you for what you are and give you thanks.

Your compositions have always been good music, written in the finest of traditions but with the imprint of your personality that has proven your work practical and inspiring. Such numbers as your meditation on 'Covenant', your euphonium solos 'Love of the Lord' and 'I love to tell the Story' and others, seem to frame your testimony in sound. Your march 'Golden Jubilee' is the item most played and recorded by the New York Staff Band. It is the favorite of the Army's Nationally televised Rose Bowl Parade Bands until it has become the Army's unofficial theme song at Pasadena. There is hardly a Salvation Army Band in this country and beyond that has not played it. What a tribute! We wish you well as you leave active service. We pary that God will continue to bless you with good health and the memories of a life well-lived in partnership with Christ. And as we continue to play your music, and listen to your compositions, we will recall the many pleasant hours spent together as friends.

God Bless you.

Vernon Post

Captain

Territorial Music Director

Bandmaster New York Staff Band'

Important compositions

Golden Jubilee (ABJ13) 1950, Song Arrangement: Bullinger (TS577 - 2) 1958, Meditation: Covenant (FS186) 1952, Euphonium Solo; I Love to Tell the Story (ABJ39) 1958, March; Joyful Faith (GS1526) 1963

KIRK, HARRY

Harry Kirk's career as an Army musician commenced at the age of eleven, when his uncle, Band-Reservist Charles Whiting, gave him a tenor horn, a few scales, and some instruction on how to produce the notes. After several weeks of struggling with the C scale, and trying unsuccessfully to hit the right notes to start the G and F scales, young Harry gave up in despair and neglected practicing for a while. This rather disappointed his uncle, who exclaimed somewhat crossly, *'Oh, you're a dummy, you'll never learn! '* When his uncle had gone from the house, Harry, with tears in his eyes, said to his mother, *'I'll show uncle whether I'm a dummy or not*', and he started again to practice with a courage born of desperation. This incident proved to be a turning point, and very soon the boy had made progress enough to enable him to play in the Meetings. He remembered his first Sunday out, and how he was afraid in case any of his school-mates should see him with The Salvation Army, and perhaps he had cause to be, for they were only three musicians in number, a cornet, tenor horn, and Eb bass player. That was the beginning of the Band at Leeds Burley, of which Harry Kirk has been the Bandmaster for more than twenty-six years. However, having made progress numerically, the Band required an euphonium player, and he was given this part. *'How I gloried in the semiquaver runs!'* he says, *'the more there were, the better I liked it!'* Then came that wonderful first Music Competition, which produced those famous marches *'Melbourne', 'Southall', 'Christchurch',* and *'The Cadet'.* As he listened to these being played, there burned within him the ambition to write a march. Young Kirk then discovered that he could make up simple tunes quite easily, but not knowing much about harmony, etc., he purchased a copy of Lieut.-Colonel Slater's 'First Lessons in Harmony'. After studying this little textbook, and trying to worry things out for himself, and inadvertently getting more and more befogged, he was fortunate enough to come into touch with an organist who was also a professor of music. For a considerable time he studied harmony and counterpoint under this man's guidance. Then, in 1910, he entered the *'Leeds'* march in the International Music Competition, and gained third prize. At the engineering works here he was employed he was known as 'Young Boothie', but after the event of the *'Leeds'* march his workmates rechristened him 'Young Sousa'! Since then several other marches have appeared from his pen, and have been well received. In 1926 he wrote the selection, *'Songs of Happiness'*, which was awarded second prize in the International Music Competition. One of Bandmaster Kirk's greatest moments was when he was presented to H.R.H. the Duke of York, later to be His Majesty King George VI, at the big Composer's Festival at the Clapton Congress Hall, some years ago. The Bandmaster has a window-cleaning business. *'I hope to continue to write music for The Army'*, says the Bandmaster, *'and if my efforts bless people, and turn their thoughts to God, I shall feel that all the hours of study and work have been worth while'.* ('The Musician' 27-8-1938)

Colonel Peter Wood was the Bandmaster of the corps band at Leeds Burley. In fact he took over after a period of about 10 years when they didn't have a Bandmaster. His predecessor was Bandmaster Harry Kirk. Harry's story is a classic story of Salvation Army musical history. This little man was a window cleaner. Amazingly against all the odds he became, in Salvation Army circles, a highly respected composer. A former generation of course, but there were days when Harry Kirk's music was always a part of the major festivals. When Harry's wife died he was deeply affected by her passing. He was living alone, struggling to cope with his grief, still writing his music. One day the Corps Officer called to Harry's little terrace house near to the infamous Armley Jail, in Leeds, to find Harry, sitting in front of his small coal fireplace, in the depths of despair and depression. As he went in the Corps Officer could see there was a problem. *'What is it Harry?'* he asked gently. *'Oh, what's the use?'* Harry said in a strained voice. *'What's the point?'* he went on, picking up a manuscript and shaking it in the face of the Brigadier. *'All this, all this... it's not worth it'*, and he threw the manuscript at the fire. But when Bandmaster Harry Kirk went to throw the manuscript into the fire the alert Corps Officer grabbed his arm, and stopped him, saying, *'No, don't do it Harry, God understands your feelings, he knows your grief, hold on, hold on, it is worth it'.* And the manuscript for one of Harry Kirk's most loved devotional works, *'The Penitent'*, was saved from destruction. It is a beautiful meditation based on the song *'Nothing but Thy blood can save me'*, and verse 2 is especially poignant:

Bandmaster Harry Kirk conducts the Dutch National Band in 1951 (forerunners of the Amsterdam Staff Band) in his daily window cleaners cloths.

See my heart, Lord, torn with grief,
Nothing but Thy blood can save me;
Me unpardoned do not leave,
Nothing but Thy blood can save me.

For many years there was a black and white photograph pinned to the wall of the Leeds Burley Corps Band room. It was taken by a local newspaper photographer in 1951. The Dutch National Band (fore runners of the Amsterdam Staff Band) were visiting England after the Second World War, and were presenting an open air concert outside the Leeds Town Hall. It just so happened that Harry Kirk was on his window cleaning rounds in the city at that time. Hearing the band he, naturally, came over to listen. When it was discovered that this window-cleaner listener was none other than Harry Kirk, a well-known Army composer, the Bandmaster of National Band, Bernard Verkaaik, was quick to invite Harry to conduct the Band in one of his own pieces. And that was the photograph – Harry in his window-cleaning work clothes, standing in the middle of the circle, conducting the Dutch National Band.

Colonel Brindley Boon remembers Harry Kirk

Oldest in a family of ten children, Harry Kirk, born in Leeds on 17 February 1889, became a hero to his brothers and sisters. Early in his boyhood it became clear that he had been blest with musical gifts and was not only able to 'think out tunes in his head' but, after receiving instruction in the elementary theory of music, also succeeded in expressing those thoughts on paper. His mother's pride in her first born's achievements led to her mentioning him to a professor of music at whose home she carried out domestic duties. Her assessment that *'my Harry is clever with music'* resulted in the professor agreeing to see the boy. He was impressed, and asked Harry to let him see some of his compositions and passed on some helpful direction for serious study. Such interest and application bore rewarding fruit when the acquired knowledge was put to good use in the construction of his melodious marches, attractive selections and singable songs. World wide recognition came to 21 year old Deputy Bandmaster Kirk of Leeds IV (later renamed Leeds Burley) when his composition *'Leeds'* gained third place in the Army's international march competition of 1910. Other marches from his inventive mind and concise pen included *'Happy Warrior'*, *'Comradeship'*, *'the Scout Leader'*, *'The Sunshine Way'*, and *'Glorious Freedom'*, all of them extremely popular.

In 1928 Bandmaster Kirk, who had been entrusted with the leadership of his corps band in 1911, was one of a handful of composers selected to conduct their works at the Composers' Festival at Clapton Congress Hall in the presence of the Duke and Duchess of York (later King george VI and Queen Elisabeth). It was a slightly-built, shy, nervous Harry Kirk, with no more than fourteen players in his band at Burley, who conducted Clapton Congress Hall Band through his selection *'Songs of Happiness'*, which had earned him second prize in the international competition of 1926. It was always a source of wonderment to him how he had reached such heights if international 'fame', how his humble efforts at composition were played, and received with such acceptance, in all parts of the world. He need not have wondered. Here was a man who, conscious of his humble beginnings, and of his early struggles without adequate financial support to develop his musical gifts, was ever mindful of God's hand upon his life and upon his service in the ranks of his beloved Army. He walked humbly with the Lord. Never seeking the bright lights, he was content to fill the little space provided for him in the district of the industrial city where he was born and spent practically all his life. The musical efficiency of his little band was a credit to his ability to teach and to train. The spiritual tone of his lads likewise was a reflection of his own Christian attitude to all aspects of life. By trade he was a window cleaner, greatly in demand not only for the careful and conscientious attention he gave to the task of removing grime which so rapidly accumulated on the limited daylight-providing apertures of the phalanx of back-to-back houses which crowded the district, but also as 'Mr. Salvation Army', who could be relied upon to offer a word of good advice when it was sought or to pray with his customers at times of personal sorrow or other domestic crises.

Harry Kirk was a 'bread-and-butter' composer who, with skill and loving care, met the functional needs of Army bands and left the 'jam and treacle', harking back to his frugal upbringing, to the 'bright boys' of a later generation. There was no need for him to apologise. The diet he recommended in his creations was always varied, well-balanced and tasteful. At the time of Bandmaster Kirk's Promotion to Glory, 27 august 1972 at the age of 83, Colonel Albert Jakeway wrote; *'he was not a prolific composer, but his manuscripts were so academically and impeccably correct that very little, if any, editorial attention was considered necessary.'* This quiet, unassuming, dedicated Salvationist musician wrote many marches which, because of their melodious attraction and technical accuracy, will live on. He made one considerable contribution to the Festival Series Band Journal, the air varie *'Stands like the Brave'*. His most permanent memorial, however, could prove to be the meditation *'The penitent'*, based so effectively and convincingly on Richard Slater's song *'nothing but thy Blood can save me'*. That simple testimony was the immovable foundation of Harry Kirk's humble consistent faith.

(source: The Salvationist, 18 February 1989)

Important compositions

Stand like the brave (FS133) 1939, Joy of the Soldier (FS287) 1965, The Dawn of Victory (FS333) 1971, The Penitent (GS1404) 1954

KIRK, MICHAEL

Michael was born on 9th May 1949 in Watford where he started to learn to play the cornet, like so many other youngsters. His parents moved the family to Letchworth when he was seven or eight, and that is where he progressed through the Young People's Band, Singing Company, Senior Band and Songsters. He started to attend summer Music Schools, as they were then called, which widened his musical view. He started arranging in his early teens, and was much encouraged in those days by Leslie Condon (a distant relation of his mother). Later in his teens Ray Steadman-Allen was a great influence and mentor, taking much time to explain in detail a number of SP&S rejections of Michael's attempts at arranging (and a few acceptances as well). Definitely a great and influential man.

In his twenties and thirties Michael was privileged to lead a number of music schools in the United Kingdom and Moscow, and that is where he started to compose songs, mostly for use as school theme songs. This was most helpful to him, as it involved examining Bible studies and trying to capture the message in both words and music. It is where his composing output has been most prolific. The normal life experience of marriage and children was a blessing that musically resulted in solos for two of his boys.

He was a trombonist but more latterly transferred to the Baritone. For some time he also was the bandmaster of the East Midlands Divisonal Youth Band. The opportunity to join the International Staff Band –on Baritone- was quickly grabbed. Michael served under Ray Bowes as bandmaster, and enjoyed trips to USA, Scotland and Ireland, as well as many United Kingdom Salvation Army centers. This enabled him to use his pianist skills (limited though they are, Michael recalls) and raised his brass band composing ambitions, although these were soon to be found wanting. This period taught him to appreciate quality brass banding. By this time he was soldiering at Wood Green, where he was Deputy Songster Leader to another legend and influence; Robert Redhead. This was also the era of musical parties (i.e. small groups leading away weekends), and that too provided arranging opportunities.

A work move to Peterborough resulted in some piano recordings under the title 'And So Worship' where again arranging was required. Finally a move to the Bourne corps in Lincolnshire with its contemporary worship style, provided an opportunity to write worship songs for both group and congregational use.

Important compositions

Histon (TS1009) 1994, Redeemed (TS1047) 1997

KIRK, PETER

This is Deputy Bandmaster Peter Kirk, the younger brother of Bandmaster Harry Kirk, both of Leeds Burley Corps. *'Fighting On'* was the only piece of Peter published by the Salvation Army. He played in the Band when Peter Wood was the Bandmaster - by that time getting on in years, but still doing well on second cornet. Naturally, he lived in the shadow of his illustrious elder brother, Harry.

Important composition

Fighting On (TS0180) 1932

KIRKLAND, CAMP

Although not a Salvationist, Camp's music is often used as source for arrangements used within the Salvation Army. Over the past three decades, Camp Kirkland has emerged as one of the premier Church musicians in the nation. He is recognized as the pioneer in establishing instrumental music as a viable medium in the life of the church music program. In 1971, he began the instrumental music program at First Baptist Church of Jacksonville, Florida. This program is still a model of excellence in music and effectiveness in ministry. Students and associates of Mr. Kirkland lead many of the great church orchestras around the country. In addition to being a highly skilled and recognized educator, clinician and spokesman, Camp Kirkland has enjoyed a brilliant career as an arranger and orchestrator. He has over a thousand publications in his catalog and is an important contributor to the leading publishers of church music today. He has the reputation of being a consummate professional both in the creative process, in the recording studio, and in working with church music programs around the country. Camp's love for Christ is evident in every phase of his art. Church musicians around the world have been blessed not only by his music but also by his testimony to the faithfulness of God. Camp Kirkland continues his music ministry, assisted by his wife Fran, through Camp Kirkland Productions, located in Nashville, Tennessee.

(source: campkirkland.com)

KITCHING, WILFRED

Wilfred Kitching was born in the United Kingdom on 22nd August 1893. He become an officer of the Salvation Army 1914. He would serve over 30 years in corps, divisional and National Headquarters appointments, and the British Territory. He and Adjutant Kathleen Bristow were married in 1929. In 1946, he was to serve in Australia South as Chief Secretary. He was sent to Sweden to serve as Territorial Commander in 1948. In 1951, he became British Commissioner. The Commissioner was elected General of The Salvation Army by the High Council in 1954. During his years as an officer, he wrote many songs in The Salvation Army song book. He also wrote two books, *'Soldiers of Salvation'*, which came out in 1963, and his autobiography, entitled *'A Goodly Heritage'*, which came out in 1967. General Kitching retired November 22, 1963. This day is remembered for the assossination of the President of the United States John F. Kennedy. General Kitching was the 7th General of The Salvation Army. He was Promoted to Glory at the age of 84 on December 15, 1977.

'The Musician' 12-2-1938: Eldest son of the late Commissioner T.H. Kitching, Wilfred Kitching was a Junior Soldier at a small North London Corps, New Barnet. He received piano lessons at the age of eight, and was taught a brass instrument at nine years of age. During the week that he took his place in the Band, a Regulation was made placing an embargo on boys playing in Senior Bands until they were fourteen. Much to the distress of the young musician, he had to immediately step out! He has always stood for strict adherence to Regulations, and considers it did him good to have 'the shoe pinch' him in early life. Wilfred Kitching formed the first Young People's Band at New Barnet when he was sixteen years of age, and was commissioned as its Leader when his mother was the Young People's Sergeant-Major. He was made Deputy Bandmaster at eighteen years of age. His first effort at composition was made when he was fifteen, he wrote two melodies to verses written by his Quaker grandmother, which songs were almost at once printed in 'The 'Musical Salvationist''. They were to be the forerunners of many other published compositions. A number of his pieces had already appeared in 'The Musical Salvationist' when his first march, *'North London'*, was published. This was written when he was nineteen years of age. The Brigadier gives generous tribute to the kindly encouragement and help he received in those days from Lieut.-Colonel Slater, then in charge of the Music Editorial Department. In 1915 Captain Kitching was appointed to his first Corps, Devizes, with the Editor of 'The Musician' as his Lieutenant. He spent ten years as a Corps Officer, and though time did not permit of much creative work, had marches and songs published from time to time. After a short term on Divisional work he was appointed National Secretary for Bands at almost the same time as the announcement was made of his winning First Place in the 1926 International Music Competition for the selection *'My Jesus'*, which has become a universal favourite. In this same competition the Brigadier also took Third Place with his selection, *'Gethsemane'*. During his nearly five years as National Secretary for Bands he travelled extensively throughout the United Kingdom, meeting Bandsmen in small and large groups in Council, and seeking to do all possible for their spiritual and musical advancement. At this position he was also a member of the National Music Board and the Song Book Council, which was responsible for the collection of songs now in use. During his term of office he introduced the first National Songster Festival and Sunday Councils, and also conceived the idea of the Associated Headquarters Festival, which is now an established institution and held each year at Clapton Congress Hall in connection with the Self-Denial Effort. The establishment of the Bandmasters' Correspondence Course and its workings was also his, and for the first three years of its institution he was responsible for examining the papers of some 250 students. As a composer-conductor he took part in the first Composers' Festival held at Clapton Congress Hall, conducting the International Staff Band through his manuscript selection, *'Warriors of the Cross'*. He has acted as commentator at numerous Festivals, including National Band and Songster Festivals. In collaboration with Major Wiggins, he took First Place with *'Happy am I!'* in the first International Vocal Solo Competition. Brigadier Kitching has strong convictions regarding the place of music and song in Salvation Army life, and has no interest in either unless they are a type to bring men and women to Christ. He seeks to stress the fact that saints are not made by diligent musical studies or skill in performance, but only by more and more diligent study of the Word of God, and by prayer. He considers that unless the services of Bandsmen and Songsters tend to make better saints, and bring about the conversion of sinners, their talent and time are wasted. He is not slow to suggest, either, that a little more thought and time spent in the choice of pieces used would bring about better spiritual results, and sees tremendous danger in playing merely for entertainment's sake. He even goes so far as to state his conviction that there is danger in applause. Indeed, he would like to hear more pieces rendered by Bands and Songsters in Festivals without any applause, so that the blessing and benediction of the music might be enhanced. After his National Headquarters experience the Brigadier was appointed a Divisional Commander, and now considers it a great honour to be in charge of the East London Division, the 'Galilee' of the Salvation Army. Of recent years he has been ably supported and encouraged by his wife who, before her marriage, was known as Adjutant Kathleen Bristow. She was for many years in the alto section of Penge Songster Brigade.

Important composition

Warriors of the Cross (FS41) 1921

KJELLGREN, GUNNAR

Gunnar (3 April 1909) was bandmaster of the Göteborg II Corps Band in Sweden during the 1930's. He left his position in advantage for his cousin Gustaf Kjellgren who was a very talented young musician. The march that Gunnar composed – *'Göteborg II'* - was played at his wedding. As a theme in his march and often sung in those days was:

'I am happy, I am happy,
Sunday, Monday, Tuesday, Wednesday, Thursday, Friday, Saturday.
I am happy o so happy,
for Jesus is my best of friends.'

Gunnar Kjellgren was Promoted to Glory on 5 January1975

Important composition

Göteborg II (FM0218)

KJELLGREN, GUSTAV

Gustav Kjellgren was born in Sweden on 1919. With eighteen he became bandmaster of the Göteborg II Citadel Band. Gustav was a composer and arranger. He wrote music for Brass Bands, Songsters and String Bands. He also had share with the revise of the Swedish Song Book of the Salvation Army. Gustav Kjellgren had a good connection with the 'Vetenskapliga institutionen i Göteborg' (scientific institute of Gothenburg). This was a good help to Gustav and the Salvation Army. He also often worked together with the

Department of Music of The Salvation Army in Stockholm. As a testimony in one of his songs (Frälsningstoner No. 137) he wrote: *'To follow Jesus is my greatest fortune, His love to me is every morning new'.* Gustav Kjellgren was Promoted to Glory on 26 June 2006.

Important compositions

My light and song (FS228) 1957, Begone, vain World (GS1493) 1960

KNIGHT, ALEC F.

Alec Knight grew up in the East End of London, spending his time in bird fighting, boxing, betting, drink and public-house songs, a leader in any group he joined. Confronted by open-air meetings, he organized a Skeleton Army and attacked. He was gravely disturbed when, after hitting a Salvationist, he was told, *'God bless you, my brother!'* Converted, he became a mighty antagonist for God. He wrote the following *'Fight Song',* which is not included in the Song Book today, and also wrote the band version of it:

The Light of the World is Jesus

I once was very worldly, the same as many more; But since I've been to Jesus He's saved me I am sure; And if you're only willing to give up all your sin, My Savior now is waiting, I'm sure, to take you in.

The light of the world is Jesus; The light of the world is Jesus; And if you come to Him, He'll cleanse your soul from sin; The light of the world is Jesus.

Important composition

The Light of the World is Jesus (GS0065) 1887

KNIGHT, LEONARD CLARENCE

Born on 22 December 1911, Promoted to Glory on 23 October 1995, Leonard Knight was born in Maidenhead, United Kingdom, and settled in Stratford, Ontarion, Canada with his family in 1919. He took an active part in the local Salvation Army and through diligent practice became proficient on the piano, trombone, mandolin and concertina.

Leonard entered the Salvation Army Training College from the West Toronto Corps and following his commissioning in 1934, was appointed to the training college staff as sergeant of the men cadets. In 1942, he married Captain Jean Bunton of the Women's Social Service Department and shortly thereafter, they joined the Canadian War Services Department in London, England.

After the war, Leonard and Jean were appointed in Ottawa and to the Territorial Young People's Department wher Leonard was privileged to oversee a contingent of Boy Scouts and leaders who attended the first Salvation Army International Boy Scout Jamboree in The Netherlands (Motondo). In retirement Lieutenant Colonel Leonard Knight played trombone in the Reservist Band and offered concertina solos.

Important composition

The Good Shepherd (CM0008) 1955

KRINJAK, KAREN

Karen Krinjak (October 9, 1950) is a native of Manchester, CT, USA, and a 4th generation soldier of the Manchester Corps where she serves as Songster Leader. She was born in Manchester, CT into a Salvationist family. She grew up in the corps, sang in the singing company and played in the junior band and all the other things that Army kids do. She received her undergraduate music training at the Boston Conservatory of Music, and a graduate degree at the University of Connecticut. In both programs she was a music education major and a piano minor. She taught in the Connecticut public schools for 35 years and retired in June of 2010. She continues to teach band part-time at a Christian school in Manchester. Karen is also employed by the USA Eastern Territorial Headquarters as the pianist in the special events/arts ministries department, and travel widely with Carol Jaudes (singer, actress) as she presents her one-woman plays and Broadway programs.

Karen has been the Songster leader at the Manchester Citadel Corps for 30 years, where they have a brigade of about 26. It is always challenging to find appropriate music, especially for the Holiness Meeting. She has been writing new tunes to old words for many years - knowing one's group makes it much easier to tailor the difficulty/range to the singers. Some of the frequently-used compostitions are *'Tis So Sweet to Trust in Jesus.' 'Jesus, the Very Thought of Thee,' 'He Lifted Me'* and *'Breathe Upon Me.'*

Karen has also written quite a bit for piano solo...Here *'At The Cross,' 'Just As I Am'* and *'Send the Fire'* are some of those. Many years ago USA East published a volume of the American Soloists' Album containing six of her compositions/arrangements for Bb soloist and piano.accompaniment. A big influences on her writing has been Ivor Bosanko, who has produced some of the most beautiful melodies ever written. Karen has also always been completely awed by the compositional genius of Dean Goffin.

Important composition

Little David (TS1059) 1998

KROMMENHOEK, DICK

Dick Krommenhoek was born in Amsterdam, the Netherlands, in 1952, of Salvation Army officer parents. Already at the age of 14, Dick began composing music, and his large number of compositions are widely used throughout the Salvation Army world. In 1974 Dick graduated as a chemical analyst, after which he continued his studies for seven years at the Amsterdam Conservatory, receiving a Masters Degree as a professional orchestral and choir conductor in 1981. In 1974, Dick met his Danish wife to be, Vibeke Schou Larsen, during an international student camp in The Netherland. Dick and Vibeke were married in 1978. In 1981 Dick and Vibeke Krommenhoek entered the International Training College for Officers in London. When commissioned, they were appointed as corps officers to Hoogeveen in the Netherlands. Both of their chidren, Daniël (1983) and Solvej (1985) were born in Hoogeveen.

Their next appointment was to Territorial Headquarters in the Netherlands where Dick became the National Music Secretary. Among his duties was the conducting of both the Amsterdam Staff Band and the Amsterdam Staff Songsters. Dick was appointed as Divisional Commander of the Southern Division of the Netherlands in September 1991. In March 1995 he returned to territorial headquarters as Editor-in-Chief/Literary secretary. At the same time he was re-appointed as National Music Secretary, conductor of the Amsterdam Staff Band and the Amsterdam Staff Songsters. In 1990 Dick became a full member of the International Music Council, the International Literary Council and the International Communication Council of The Salvation Army. In the summer of 1997, the Krommenhoeks moved to Denmark where Dick was appointed as Financial and Property

Secretary. From 1 September 2000, Dick was appointed as Chief Secretary of the Denmark territory, where soon after he was appointed as the Territorial Commander. After having fulfilled their responsibilities for almost four years, Dick and Vibeke Krommenhoek moved to France where now, Colonel Dick Krommenhoek was appointed as the Territorial Commander.

On 1st November 2006, he was appointed the General's Representative for Global Evangelisation. In this responsibility the colonel was given the task to visit countries in which the Army is not present and to evaluate the possibility to commence the mission of The Salvation Army. For this purpose, Colonel Dick Krommenhoek has visited and researched the countries of Namibia, Greece, Burundi, Mali, Kuwait, Benin, the United Arab Emirates, Sierra Leone, Vietnam and Nepal. From 1 October 2008 Colonel Dick Krommenhoek was appointed as the Territorial Commander of the Finland and Estonia territory. The General decided to promote Colonel Dick Krommenhoek to the rank of Commissioner on 30 May 2009.

Important compositions

From that Sacred Hill (GS2027) 2005, Celebration and Praise (m/s), Potton Centenary (m/s)

KROMMENHOEK, DIRK

Although he has lived in Canada for the past 50 years or so, Major Dirk Krommenhoek, who is not related to Dick Krommenhoek, originated from Schiedam, but emigrated in the 1950s. His first published composition was a vocal song *'To Save Sinners like me'* and became popular with Songster Brigades nationwide. His brass compositions include the march *'Listowel'* named after the band for which it was written (Listowel Citadel Band). He also wrote *'Slane'* and *'Quaker Variants'* amongst others. Probably his best known composition is the march *'Schiedam 90'*.

Dirk was born in Schiedam, the Netherlands, in 1928. His mother and father were Promoted to Glory in 1966 and 1964 respectively. He had a brother who is no longer living and two sisters and his father was a baker in a bread factory. Dirk was a 'Blood and Fire' child, growing up in the Salvation Army.

Dirk's musical pursuits began early in life. His father was quite musical and introduced him to the mouth organ and the recorder. He graduated to a clarinet which, unfortunately, he found too difficult to master. Then it was on to the alto saxophone which he played in a Christian band during the Second World War until the invading Germans confiscated the instruments in order to melt them down to make bullets.

In order that Dirk's musical pursuits should not be frustrated, his father arrived home one day with a pump organ. The family could not afford music lessons but a friend of his father gave Dirk some pointers on theory, harmony and fingering, then left him to his own devices. This was the only thing close to tutoring that he ever received. Moving into the sphere of brass banding, Dirk made a start and shaped his embouchure by playing second horn in the Young People's Band. He would eventually play every instrument in the Band including the G trombone, complete with handle. In 1943, as a teenager, he moved to the flugel horn, cornet and BBb bass, in that order, saying that he 'filled in where needed' until he immigrated to Ottawa, Canada, in 1959. In Ottawa he played horn and baritone in the Ottawa Citadel Band and was the commissioned Deputy Songster Leader.

After completing his high school diploma in Schiedam, Dirk was employed as a clerk/bookkeeper and office manager until he was conscripted into the Marines where he served as a Corporal for eighteen months. One of his tasks was to act as the bugler, riding his bicycle around the camp waking the troops. Of 2,000 troops being trained and prepared to go to Indonesia, two were eventually chosen and Dirk was one of the two. Fortunately, that mission was cancelled at the last minute. After his stint in the Marines, Dirk worked in a couple of office jobs until a disagreement with an unsympathetic superior cost him his job. Shortly after he was visiting a pair of Salvation Army Officer couples and sharing a cup of tea on a Sunday evening. He listened as they talked 'shop', recounting their many difficulties with local officers and soldiers. A small flame of desire for that kind of commitment in his own life was pretty well doused, as he began to think, *'If that's what officership is all about I want no part of it.'*

On a bus the next day he was reflecting on the same theme when the bus seemed to fill with a strange light and he heard a voice as if the Lord was speaking directly to him, *'This is where I want you.'* In spite of his fears and shortcomings he made a full surrender at the Holiness Table of his Corps the following Sunday. Subsequently, Dirk made contact with the Candidates Secretary and became a 'working' candidate, serving first in men's social work in The Hague and then in the Army's Boys Home where he was responsible for some 20 young teenagers 'around the clock'. Dirk entered the Training College in Amstelveen, outside Amsterdam, as a member of the 'Intercessors Session' where he was Cadet Sergeant. Commissioned a Lieutenant in 1953, he was promoted to Captain in 1957, resigning his officership for health reasons the same year and was re-instated in Canada in 1962. He was promoted to Major in 1975.

In Holland, Dirk served in four Corps: Aalsmeer, Hoensbroek, Gorin-chem and Klazienaveen. Between Aalsmeer and Hoesbroek he served for five summer months on the ship the 'Febe', travelling the canals, stopping here and there and setting up tents to accommodate some 300 curious and interested citizens. Such impromptu meetings were very well-attended and profitable results for the Kingdom were noted. Following re-instatement in Canada, he and Ida served in six Corps: Notre Dame West in Montreal Quebec, Lippincott, Toronto, Ontario, Fenelon Falls, Ontario, Point St., Charles, Montreal, Quebec, Charlottetown, Prince Edward Island, and Listowel, Ontario. In 1972, Dirk was appointed to the Property Department at Territorial Headquarters where he served for four years. In 1977, he was appointed to the Finance Department. In 1992, he retired from active service in the position of Assistant Financial Secretary.

During his 20 years on the staff at Territorial Headquarters, he was twice appointed to the Canadian Staff Band, playing under Colonel Robert Redhead and later Brian Burditt. He was the Band Colour Sergeant and the 'Assistant Principal Second Horn', as he amusingly termed it. One can only imagine that William Himes may have written *'Solo Secondo'* ('a major work for Second Horn and [brass] Band') for the likes of Dirk Krommenhoek.

Dirk can't remember when he originally began to compose music but the march *'Listowel'* was written in 1972 and was the first of his compositions to be published in the General Series. Lt. Colonel Norman Bearcroft had used this march in manuscript form with the Canadian Staff Band in an anniversary festival. After a few suggested alterations by Norman, he was encouraged to send it in to the Music Editorial Department at International Headquarters.

Other publications in the General Series were '*Variations on Lord of the Dance*' and the hymn tune arrangement '*Slane*'. Some other, unpublished, arrangements of Christmas music were written for the Guelph, Ontario, Citadel Band. 'The Musical Salvationist' has published one of his songs, an arrangement of '*To save a poor sinner*'. Now, at a time in his life where there are increasing health challenges, Dirk often contemplates those very basic human 'Why' questions - Why me? Why this? Why now? In these times he always reflects on songs and in his heart, falls back on words found in John's Gospel, Chapter 1, verse 12: '*Yet to all who received Him, to those who believed on His name, He gave the right to become children of God*'. (NIV)

When asked about a musical highlight in his life, without hesitation, he refers to the two tours he made with the Canadian Staff Band. One trip covered Holland, Germany, Switzerland and Italy. The second, a shorter tour, was to Holland, Switzerland and Norway. Of the first trip, he recalls that they had a Dutch-speaking coach driver, English-speaking Bandsmen and French, German, Swiss and English congregations, indoors and outdoors. Could not the United Nations learn something from such ventures? During the second trip he was thrilled to be asked to lead and speak in two locations, Vlaardingen and Apeldoorn.

'Everything for Jesus' has been Dirk Krommenhoek's life's passion.

Important compositions

Listowel (TS823) 1978, Schiedam 90 (US186) 1994

LAKEN, ALAN D.

Alan D Laken (1947 - 2002) was born in Ilford, Essex on 31st March 1947. When Alan was seven he started piano lessons and when he was eight he began learning a brass instrument at the Salvation Army. In 1961 at the age of 14 he auditioned on trombone and piano for the Royal Marines Band Service. Having passed the entrance examination, Alan was taught flute and piano at the Royal Marines School of Music at Deal, Kent. Aged 17 in 1964, he was awarded the Cassels Prize for best overall student. In November 1971 Alan came out of the Band Service to begin his teaching career.

Alan became a peripatetic woodwind teacher for various London Education Authorities before gaining full time employment for the London Borough of Redbridge. He gained a teaching diploma from the Royal Academy of Muisc in 1974 and a Certificate in Education in 1981 before being appointed as Head of Woodwind for Redbridge in 1982. During his career at Redbridge Alan composed/arranged extensively for wind band, voice, orchestra, brass band, wind quintet and massed woodwind groups. He was also commissioned by Chappels/IMP to arrange five flute and seven recorder books, some of which are still in publication.

The Salvation Army remained a large part of Alan's musical life and has published several songs and brass band compositions. In 1994 Alan became one of the founders of the Salvation Army Symphonic Wind Ensemble and has composed a large part of their particular repertoire. In December 2000, Alan and his wife, Jenny moved down to Dorset in the south of England where he died in September 2002.

Important composition

To Him belong (GS1978) 2001

LAMPLOUGH, GAVIN

Raised in the corps of Chesterton Citadel in the United Kingdom, Gavin, altogether with his family moved to Birmingham Citadel where he also became a member of the Birmingham Citadel Band, occupying the principal solo cornet chair since 2007. On leaving the Royal Northern College of Music and completing his studies in 2000, Gavin returned to the Midlands to work as a Free-Lance trumpet player. His Orchestral experience includes work with orchestras such as the C.B.S.O. and the Royal Liverpool Philharmonic Orchestra, and work in theatres around the country both in musical theatre and more 'classical' theatre such as the Royal Shakespeare Company.

He also enjoys playing in chamber groups and is a member of Sennet Brass Quintet and the Salvation Army ensemble Vision Brass. He was Principal Cornet of the Birmingham Citadel Salvation Army Band recording solos on CD recordings and playing as cornet soloist throughout the UK and abroad, until he was appointed Bandmaster in 2011. He has also played with Bands such as Enfield Citadel, The Household Troops Band, Brighouse and Rastrick and The Black Dyke Band. He has an interest in Big Band Jazz, in which medium he has performed with British stars such as Kenny Baker and Mark Nightingale. Gavin also fulfils a number of solo engagements throughout the year and has recently performed Trumpet Concertos, as well as more varied recitals at venues such as Birmingham's Symphony Hall, Manchester's Bridgewater Hall and the Sage in Gateshead. Gavin has featured on numerous CD recordings, including several as a trumpet or cornet soloist.

As well as performing, Gavin is also in demand as a teacher. He was, until recently, on the teaching staff at Birmingham Conservatoire Junior School and in 2008 took up the post of Director of Music at Stafford Independent Grammar School. Gavin enjoys conducting ensembles from various musical genres but particularly enjoys his work with Brass Bands. As a composer and arranger Gavin is in increasing demand. Having had music performed at major concert halls in the UK his interest in composition is giving him further opportunities in the music world. Besides playing in the Birmingham Citadel Band he is also a founder member and one of the current two cornets of Vision Brass, a Salvation Army brass ensemble located in Birmingham.

Important composition

Venite Adoremus Dominum (m/s)

LANGLEY, F.C.

One of the early composers (late 1800).

No further information could be retrieved about him.

Important composition

Gathered home at last (GS0327) 1896

LANGWORTY, BERT

Bert Langworthy was the bandmaster at Birmingham Citadel in the 1950's, he was also the bandmaster at Sparkhill corps (also in the Birmingham area). As well as *'Heavenly Gales'* he wrote 2 marches, *'Birmingham Citadel'* and *'Sparkhill'*. The eventual commissioning in 1946 of Bert Tregoning Langworthy as Bandmaster of the Birmingham Citadel Band was a significant landmark in the band's history. BTL, who came from Penzance, Cornwall, was the first recipient of the LRAM for cornet playing in his country and he also made a broadcast as a cornet soloist from the BBC Midlands studios in 1923. Known as a strict disciplinarian and excellent band trainer, he was also a composer of some repute, but perhaps best remembered for his marches *'Birmingham Citadel'* and *'Regeneration'* as well as his cornet solo *'Heavenly Gales'*.

Important compositions

Regeneration (FS052) 1929, Heavenly Gales (FS168) 1950

LAURIE, ANDREW C.

Andrew Laurie was born in Scotland and became a member of the Drum and Fife Band at Parkhead (Glasgow). Eventually he became the solo cornet player in the Senior Band. When he and his family left for Canada he joined the Band at Montreal 1, and before reaching his seventeenth birthday, he had taken temporary hold of the Songster Brigade. In 1910 he entered the Toronto Training College, and seventeen years later, after commanding such Corps as Halifax 1 and Earlscourt, was transferred to New York, where he became the Staff Band's xylophone soloist. At the height of the depression days the Major was appointed Manager of the Gold Dust Lodge, which for a long period housed 2000 men nightly. The Major was a contributor to both 'The Musical Salvationist' and the Band Journals, his first published piece being the march 'Friendship' Second Series No. 193. Major Laurie had retired and was living in St. Petersburg, Florida, where he was Promoted to Glory following a heart attack.

Important composition

Friendship (TS0193) 1933

LARSSON, JOHN

John Larsson was born on 2nd April 1938 in Stockholm to a Salvation Army officer family. He started to study music in Denmark, and continued it in Chile, Argentina and England. He was awarded with the 'Bachelor of Divinity' (London). He become an officer of The Salvation Army 1957, and served in England, Scotland, Chile, New Zealand and Sweden. John wrote many musicals* together with John Gowans. John Larsson composed the music, and John Gowans wrote the text. John Larsson was the 17th General of The Salvation Army (2002 - 2006), following General John Gowans.

Even his grandparents were officers in The Salvation Army, and his grandfather on his father's side, Commissioner Karl Larsson, is known in the Army's history as the one who 'opened fire' in Russia the first time (1914). John Larsson became an officer in 1957 from the Upper Norwood Corps, London, England. He graduated from the University of London with a BD degree. After a year as a corps officer in the north of England, he served on the staff of the International Training College in London for seven years before returning to corps appointments. He and Captain Freda Turner were married in 1969 while John was stationed at the corps in Ealing. They have two sons, Karl Larsson and Kevin Larsson (see LARSSON, KEVIN), who are both members of The Salvation Army.

John Larsson and his wife were appointed to the South America West Territory in 1980, he as chief secretary and she as Territorial Home League secretary. In 1984, they were appointed to the International Training College as principal and librarian, respectively. They were appointed to International Headquarters in London in 1988. John Larsson, as assistant to the chief of the staff for United Kingdom administrative planning, was given the task of researching and planning for the separation of the international and national administrations. Freda Larsson served as coordinator for married women officers. The Larssons were then appointed territorial commander and territorial president of Women's Organisations for the United Kingdom Territory with the Republic of Ireland in 1990. In 1993, they were appointed territorial leaders for the New Zealand, Fiji and Tonga Territory; and in 1996, they received similar appointments for the Sweden and Latvia Territory.

John Larsson is the author of *'Doctrine Without Tears'*, *'The Man Perfectly Filled with the Spirit,'* *'Spiritual Breakthrough'* and *'How Your Corps Can Grow'*. He is also the author of *'1929'*, a history of the events that took place that year in The Salvation Army.

He is also a composer and, together with John Gowans, co-authored ten full-length stage musicals, *'Take-Over Bid'* (1967), *'Hosea'* (1969), *'Jesus Folk'* (1972), *'Spirit'* (1973), *'Glory'* (1975), *'White Rose'* (1977), *'The Blood Of The Lamb'* (1978), *'Son Of Man'* (1983), *'Man Mark II'* (1985), and *'The Meeting'* (1990).

In 1999, Commissioner John Larsson became chief of the staff, second in command of The Salvation Army worldwide. His wife, Commissioner Freda Larsson, became World Secretary for Women's Organisations (later Women's Ministries).

Larsson was elected General on September 6, 2002, and assumed the office following the retirement of his predecessor, General John Gowans. Shaw Clifton succeeded to the office of general when Larsson retired at midnight on April 1, 2006.

Important composition

It's New (TS833) 1979

LARSSON, KEVIN

Kevin is the son of General John Larsson (R) and hails from the United Kingdom, where he has played with the Household Troops Band of the Salvation Army.

Kevin Larsson is the Southern California Divisional Music Ministries Director and April 1st, 2011 marked the ten year anniversary of Kevin's leadership within the Division. Kevin was brought up in The Salvation Army with Officer Parents and had to opportunity to live in various countries while growing up, including a 4 year stay in Chile. In 1996 he graduated with a BA Honors Degree in Music. Kevin is a published composer and has had the opportunity to travel around the world representing The Salvation Army and Music Ministry. Kevin has been married to Jacqui for 10 years and has two lovely boys, Ethan (6) & Aidan (4).

He was born in May 1973 when his parents were Corps Officers at the Bromley Corps. He still considers Bromley as his home Corps even though it has been many years since he soldiered there.

His first music education came when he moved to Chile and began learning both the Cornet and Piano. Kevin looks back on those years with a great deal of pleasure and has since had the opportunity to return for various musical events which has been very special. Many of the young people that he grew up with are now in leadership positions within the South America West Territory which is down to the leaders like Max Espejo and Major Ed Ringle who played such a prominent and important role in our musical growth.

After 4 years they returned to Bromley Temple where he was very fortunate enough to be able to soldier for nine years. There were many young people and they all grew to become very close, much of which was based around the junior band. Their leader was Robert Mitchel and he instilled into them a discipline that has kept him in good stead to this day. With the natural progression to the Band and then the Songsters Kevin didn't think twice about spending five or six nights a week at the Army! It was during this time that he first dabbled with composition. The Corps officer at the time, Major Shaw Clifton encouraged him to write a little theme song for a summer kids club that they put on. He still remembers it now although he does hope that no copies are left floating around as it is certainly not his most accomplished work.

At this point he didn't take composition too seriously until he went to University at the Colchester Institute. Kevin decided to major in Composition and was hugely influenced by Michael Clack, head of brass and performance, and also Bandmaster of his new corps Chalk Farm. He opened Kevin's eyes to a whole new world, especially at Chalk Farm where he had the opportunity to play some of the great Salvation Army Brass Band repertoire from composers like Eric Ball, Leslie Condon, Dean Goffin and Kenneth Downie. But for Kevin, the one composer who moved him more than any other is Ray Steadman-Allen, with *'The Lord is King'* possibly being his favorite work. His composition tutor, Allan Bullard who also had a huge respect for RS-A, also played a huge role in his musical education, pushing him out of my comfort zone and allowing him to experiment with ideas that he had never previously considered.

A few months after university Kevin moved to the United States of America and worked as the Music Director for the Torrance Corps before moving to the Divisional Headquarters as the multimedia specialist. After the untimely death of bandmaster Chris Mallett in 2000, he took over as the Divisional Music Director. The three names that immediately come to mind, as people who have helped him in his journey are Chris Mallett, a great leader and encourager with a real heart for young people: Ivor Bosanko, an incredible musician and composer and William Gordon, who helped him explore and develop some of the more contemporary music. All hugely talented. With the nature of his job there have been plenty of opportunities for composition since moving to America and he enjoys the huge variety that is asked of him.

Throughout all his life his biggest inspiration is without a doubt his father, General John Larsson. His music has touched so many people, including Kevin and it will live on for generations. Growing up surrounded by the musicals left a huge impression on him. It is something he has always wanted to try and now he is finally going to get the opportunity. Working with his brother Karl Larsson who is writing the script and Malcolm Westwood, the lyrics they are starting work on a full length musical that will be the continuation of *'Spirit'* which will be performed in 2012.

Important composition

Just like Juan! (Judd Street Collection)

LARSSON, KARL EDVIN

Born in 1884 and Promoted to Glory in 1954. He was a member of the Swedish Staff Band between 1910 and 1913 playing Eb Cornet, Bb Cornet and Bass. He was a music instructor at Uppsala and Vasa (Finland) and Bandmaster of the Borlänge Corps Band. He was the owner of a music shop.

Important composition

Borlänge march (Swedish Festival music no 116)

LARSSON, NILS-PETTER

Nils-Petter was born in 1877 and Promoted to Glory in 1918. He played in the Swedish Staff Band from 1907-1910 in which he also was their Executive Leader. In 1901 he when to the Training College to become a Salvation Army officer and worked in the Trade Department from 1910 to 1918 with the responsibility of the music instruments.

Important composition

Gävle (FM0209)

LAW, W.H.

One of the early composers (first half of 19th century).

No further information could be retrieved about him.

Important composition

Fighting on (GS0762) 1917

LAWSON, EDWARD

Not much is known about Edward Lawson. He is a former Bandmaster of the Mansfield Salvation Army corps band.

Important composition

Jesus' praise (TS0560) 1957

LE BUTT, EDWIN GEORGE

Edwin (1866) became a Salvationist from the Folkestone Corps (1890). An excellent cornet player and vocal soloist, Edwin served in the ISB and was one of it's earlier leaders. He also served as private secretary to William and Bramwell Booth. He resigned with the rank of Colonel. His wife Charlotte, passed away on December 27, 1915, the following year he married Eva Ellen Hudson, a Salvationist employee at IHQ. They were visiting Michigan, USA, when that country entered World War I, and decided to stay rather than risk the Atlantic recrossing in wartime. While in the USA, Edwin played with several bands. He was Promoted to Glory at age 93 on May 10, 1959. His daughter Agnes was married with Bramwell Coles. They were together for fifty-one years.

Important composition

The Y.P.L. March (GS0334-2) 1897

LEAK, DAVID

Born in November 1988, and originally from Hereford Citadel, David is currently studying at Bristol University and is in his final year of an MEng in Civil Engineering. While at university he has joined Bristol Easton Band playing solo cornet, and has recently joined the Household Troops Band on solo cornet, as well as playing with Salvation Brass, another composite band within the ranks of the Salvation Army. He has had music performed by Salvation Brass and at divisional congress, and is mentored by Dean Jones of the Music Ministries Unit in London.

LEGG, F.A(drian?)

One of the early composers (first half of 19th century).

No further information could be retrieved about him.

Important compositions

The best Friend (TS0036) 1923, Cymro (TS0020) 1922

LEGG, H.F.

One of the early composers (first half of 19th century).

No further information could be retrieved about him.

Important composition

White Robes (TS0124) 1929

LEGGETT, EDWIN GEORGE

Eddie, as he was known was born on 11 July 1914 and was a third generation Salvationist who was dedicated at Southsea II Corps where his father was the Bandmaster for about five years, but the family returned to Portsmouth Citadel after World War I. He was a Junior Soldier and joined the Young People's Band aged seven and firstly played cymbals. He, with three friends, transferred to the senior band when he was seventeen as they had to wait! They called themselves 'The Big Four'. His instrument was mostly Tenor Horn but often played Euphonium which was the case in 1955 when the Portsmouth Citadel Band toured Germany. In the 1930s he was the Chums (Cub Scout) Leader at Portsmouth Citadel. He was Young People's Band Leader at Portsmouth Citadel in the 1940s and again in the 1980s. He was the Torchbearer Youth Club Leader in the 1950s and was Bandmaster at Sholing, Southampton for two periods of time between the 1960s and 1980s after which again he returned to Portsmouth Citadel.

He was self-taught having bought a book on harmony in a second-hand shop. His main study for the Bandmaster's correspondence course was in a cafe out of the city away from the bombing of World War II. He kept buying cups of tea to warrant his being there as he could not afford anything else! Eddie passed the Intermediate Course with Honours in 1942 and the Advanced Course with Merit in 1943, a month before his daughter was born. His published pieces of music are; *'Pull for the Shore'*, *'Our Rising Army'*, *'Steadfast* and *'Liberated'* mainly written in the 1940s. He wrote *'Glens Falls'* at the request of a former Sholing bandsman living in Glens Falls, USA. There is also an unpublished march called *'Calcutta'* which he wrote to commemorate the Calcutta Red Shield Band of which his brother was a member. Other pieces were written and submitted but not published. In the late 1950s he became a peripatetic brass/music instructor for the Local Education Authority and also taught brass and music in two private Catholic Schools. The Principal of the Portsmouth Teacher Training College requested he taught brass there and he was approached about teaching in Her Majesty's Prison Kingston where he then taught for 25 years.

All of the inmates were serving life sentences and two became Salvationist. He formed a brass band and or ensemble in each school scouring second-hand shops for instruments, as finances were very tight in the schools. The first was an all girls' brass band, three members became active Salvationists because of his influence, one now serves in Melbourne, one at Portsmouth, the third was at Portsmouth but was Promoted to Glory a few years ago. Each of the School bands was in great demand making appearances at both school and church Fetes, at carnivals, on T.V. for special celebrations and for the launching of local ships. One band even played for the whole journey from Portsmouth to Cherbourg at the launch of the P & O service. The girls' band visited and played at a residential school for the deaf and this was the first music these children had ever experienced! They felt the vibrations by putting their arms around the instruments. It was wonderful to see the joy on their faces. Eddie was the conductor of the Portsmouth Youth Band which won the London and Southern Counties Regional Champions of the Butlin's Championship of Great Britain 17th March 1974. As well as the published marches he wrote and arranged innumerable pieces for his various brass groups and bands. In fact he was always writing music! He taught up until just after his eighty first birthday and loved every minute of it. Edwin George Leggett was Promoted to Glory on 6 January 1996

Important compositions

Glens Falls (TS0877) 1983, Liberated (GS1332) 1950

LEIDZEN, ERIK

William Gustav Erik Leidzén was born on 25th March 1894 to Salvation Army Officer parents in Stockholm. As a child he learned to play cornet, flute and violin. In November of 1893 his father Staff-Captain Erik Leonard Leidzén became ill and died after a swift, virulent sickness. His son, Erik, was born several months later on Easter Sunday morning. March 25th, at 11:00 a.m. In 1899 he moved with his family to Copenhagen, Denmark, where his mother served as National Youth Secretary for Denmark. Erik played cornet in the 'Danish Staff Band' of the Salvation Army. In 1908 he finished school and becomes cashier at Copenhagen Headquarter. Later he moved back to Sweden. In 1912 he studied music on the 'Royal Conservatory of Music' in Stockholm, with headbranch Brass Performance (Cornet). One year later Organ and Contrapoint. Erik started to play Cornet in the Swedish Staff Band and traveled with this group throughout Sweden, Finland and Norway. In 1915 he left Sweden, via Denmark to America. On 9th February he arrived in New York and worked at the Salvation Army and served as bandsman and later as bandmaster in Corps 2 (49th Street). Erik Leidzén was one of the greatest composers in the Salvation Army World.

A SERVANT NOT ASHAMED

By David Appleby

'Even a child is known by his doing.'

Young Erik never saw his father. While traveling throughout the Division of which he, at twenty-eight, was Youth Secretary, Captain Erik Leidzén Sr., had died of pneumonia four months before his son was born. Captain Mrs. Leidzén, nee Elinor Kelly, chose to remain in service as an Officer of The Salvation Army, and after various further assignments in Sweden, she was appointed to the Training College in Copenhagen. Erik was five when the family, which included two older sisters, Carin and Margaret, moved to Denmark. At an age when most youngsters are learning to hold a pencil, Erik was writing poems and displaying an amazing aptitude for the cornet. As the youngest and at times the best musician in various Bands in which he played, including the Danish Staff Band, it was not unusual for Erik to be offered the baton, which explains his conducting the massed Bands in Congress at Copenhagen when he was only nine. A piano album donated to The Salvation Army (already in those days!) gave young Erik the impetus to learn to play the piano. He discovered and solved, unaided, the riddle of the bass clef, and after two days played for his mother *'Home, sweet home'* (both hands).

In his boyhood, as a throughout life, his eyes and ears were open to discovering the elements of beauty around him, and his mind alert to developing the skills involved in reproducing this beauty.

The germs of 'music' in his 'inner ear' found expression, and he became ever more skilful in handling the self-discovered rules of order pertaining to harmony, motion, and rhythm. His musicianship became more and more evident at the piano and on the cornet. In addition, his poetry began taking form, and his sketches and paintings from school were sent on exhibition. And tenderness, of which he remained an open disciple throughout his life, developed and grew within him.

At sixteen Erik turned his back on the advantages and shelteredness of his existence to undertake the life of a seaman, which unregretted experience lasted six months. Finally, at the insistence of relatives, he applied for admission to the Royal Conservatory of Music in Stockholm. Accepted and granted a stipend, he regularly earned awards for his achievement during his study there. His mother too was now in Sweden, having been placed in command of an Army Home just outside of Stockholm. So Erik was able to enjoy friendship of home life and beauty of the countryside while going to school and, later, between trips through Sweden and Finland with the Swedish Staff Band. But his eyes were now fixed upon America.

'What doth the Lord require of these?'

Erik arrived in America in 1915. His early years here during and following the war were not pleasant. Music seldom affords an easy means of livelihood. And in a new land among strange people, Erik's task of making his way and providing for his wife and daughter was further complicated by his wife's fatal illness. His poetry from this period, some of which was already finding its expression in English, reveals not only the weight and desperation of his sorrow, *'Who among men can understand Thy law, Thou Ruler great and stern… (Song of Noah, 1921)'* but simplicity and gratitude with which he was able to recognize and accept hope, kindness, and friendship when such appeared. Erik returned with his wife to Sweden in 1922, at her wish to live her last days and be buried in her native land. Salvationists will be interested in learning that the beseeching hymn, *'With my sin and with my sorrow, Lord, I come to Thee!'* dates from this crossing.

Upon the death of his wife, he returned to America and to his daughter, Lisa. In August 1923 he married one who had won Lisa's heart and his, Maria. She had proved as able to refresh and encourage as, in Erik's words, *'A Raindrop,'* and together they shared *'each other's friendship'* through the times which followed. These were the days of the famed New England Staff Band, formed at Colonel William McIntyre's request and conducted by Erik for three years. As was his custom, Erik accepted the tasks and assignments given him with a freshness and determination that belied the personal struggles he was facing. Despite the magnitude of these struggles, he refused to submit to hopelessness. Indicative of his perspectives is this affirmation of confidence in his acknowledged Maker and Master contained in the concluding lines of a poem he wrote at that time: *'The clouds of my life, whether smaller or vaster, must, pierced by Thy sunshine, be light and then break.'*

His troubled and tormented life in his new land had not embittered his outlook. Rather it had served to fashion his childhood concepts into precepts and principles capable of satisfying his adult quest for the meaning of life with its knowns and unknowns. In an extensive and penetrating allegory, *'A Dream'* (1928), we witness his renunciation of the pursuit of self-ful ambition and his unqualified confidence in a simple, age-old, and succinct definition of man's calling: *'He hath showed thee, O man, what is good forever. And what doth the Lord require of thee, but to do what is just, not merely clever, Love mercy well and despite it never, and humbly walk with thy God. These three Commandments, if only thou wouldst endeavour to keep them, are all that is needful to see'.*

Back in New York, Erik assumed direction of the Metropolitan Ensemble and, in co-operation with Colonel Alexander Ebbs, formed the Temple Chorus to inaugurate the weekly 'Friday Evening at the Temple' services (which have continued functioning to the present day). Among the many Army classics which Erik wrote during these New England and New York years were *'The Call,' 'The Saviour's Name,' 'On the way home,'* and *'At the Cross where I first saw the light.'* In one of his *'Sonnets of a Musician'* (1928) he had written (perhaps with music boards in mind) *'What matter if my songs are never sung? Take heart, my soul, take heart and tune Thy lyre, Not as expecting ever to be heard, But keep on singing for the sake of singing'.*

Nevertheless, his music was written with a greater sense of urgency than merely that of adding to the sound already loose upon earth. In another of his *'Sonnets of a Musician'* he wrote: *'These streams of music in my inner ear I must not dam them up within me. Vain endeavor! For if I did, I know they would be sinking from me, the violator of my trust, and leave their empty channels dry forever'.*

And in another poem of the same year he added: *'From every ownership and right I'm driven, my sacred stewardship remains alone'.* His works in those years demonstrated the uncompromising qualities to which he was by them firmly dedicated, but not everyone accepted those standards or approved his methods. He formulated clear and poignant statements concerning the function of music in the worship of the Almighty, but too few listened. He demonstrated the beauty and simplicity of praising God, but too few got the point. He was patient and understanding with his colleagues, both those whom he directed and this from whom he graciously accepted direction, but he refused to condone slovenliness of attitude in giving service to the Eternal. Erik was eventually relieved of his Salvation Army duties, but a guest who was present on that occasion offered a helping hand, warmly and eagerly. Thus began, in 1933, a life-long friendship with Dr. Edwin Franko Goldman.

'My times are in Thy hands.'

During the following year, Erik, with Maria and Lisa, journeyed to Europe. A translation he made while in England of a poem he had originally written in Swedish may serve to indicate the simplicity and implicitness, regardless of the circumstances in which he found himself, of Erik's determination:

My path is dark, I cannot see,
And hidden dangers threaten me,
But God Almighty is my guide.
Day by day we journey side by side.

Upon his return to America, he undertook his first assignment with Dr. Goldman, transcribing works of Bach for band. More assignments followed. In addition he undertook freelance work for a growing number of publishers, and private pupils, studying piano, harmony, and composition, continued to seek him out. Work also continued on his *'Irish Symphony,'* which now began to near completion after what eventually proved to be twenty years of work. (Erik strove to develop and refine all ideas he engendered, since he believed that the first idea was never the best and less than his best did not satisfy him). Later, with the beginning of his association with Ernest Williams and the William School of Music, Erik was involved on more extensive writing among other works, an opera and arranging, as well as teaching. But he always managed to share a good portion of his time with Maria. Their long walks together remained daily high-points for both. A tribute to Maria's quiet contribution may be found on many of Erik's sonnets, including this one written for their Crystal Wedding Anniversary in 1938: *'In secret places, hidden well from view, As time goes on a substance crystallizes'.*

War returned and to it Erik committed his energy and artistic values, by conducting choral groups in war plants, by helping to reorganize military bands and provide better and more serviceable music for them, by working one summer with young people at Interlocken. Erik felt an obligation to use his time fruitfully, and though many activities found their way into his full schedule, he felt no pressures about either time or his schedule, no frantic illusions about time's shortness. On their twentieth anniversary, as he himself approached his fiftieth year, and with their daughter grown, educated, and married, he wrote to Maria:

Though now behind us lie the mountain ranges,
Not stagnant, but in purifying motion
We glide towards the level of the sea.
Oh, may we still be one, whatever changes,
When rainbow-spanned at last we reach the ocean
And meet the tidal wave Eternity.

At the end of the war Erik found himself suddenly famous in band circles across the country. Musicians returning from the service, many of them to teaching positions in public schools and colleges, began demanding music from the composers and arrangers whose music had proved itself to them during their military band careers and Erik's name seemed to lead all the rest. His workmanship, to him his sacred stewardship, had become recognized. For several summers at the end of the war, Erik accepted invitations from Dr. William Revelli to serve on the faculty of the summer sessions of the University of Michigan. From one of his Michigan summers this tribute to Maria, part of an anniversary sonnet, was sent:

And chief among the verities you stress
These three have most impressed my mind and soul
And added much to my felicity:
That solitude does not mean loneliness,
That sweet fulfillment dwells in self-control,
And regal riches in simplicity.

At Michigan Erik found his environment and many friendships both stimulating and enjoyable, and hiscolleagues, on the other hand, were often gratified to find that they had a thinker as well as a musician on their hands. Once, when asked whom he considered the greatest of mankind's philosophers, Erik answered, *'Jesus of Nazareth, who followed the philosophy of the straight line!'*

Amid all the attention and the increase number of requests for his work that came following the war was a request from Captain Richard E. Holz of the Salvation Army to edit several prize-winning compositions from a recently sponsored contest. Impressed with the Captain's evident sincerity and premises for working, premises for which Erik had stood all his life, he agreed. The result was the 'Band Music for Evangelism' journal, which is now expanded from the original twelve to some fifty numbers, with many of the subsequent inclusions his own. Erik's service on behalf of Salvation Army music during the next decade and a half, in addition to the aforementioned journal, found expression in a variety of ways. He edited and composed numbers for the journal of 'First Marches and Selections for Brass Bands,' the 'Brass Ensemble (Quartet) Journal,' and the 'American Soloists Album.' He also made choral arrangements for various combinations of male voices, mixed chorus, and young people's choral groups. In addition he compiled and edited (in Erik W. G. Leidzén collaboration with Maria) the new hymnal for Men's Social Service Centers. Salvationists recall with affection the enthusiastic participation of Mr. Leidzén in various music congresses, in the band and choral conducting courses he organized and taught in over a dozen cities, in the classes he taught at the School for Officers' Training, in the various music camps in all four territories from New England to California and Hawaii (including twelve summers at Star Lake).

But his work with The Salvation Army constituted only 'spare time' activity. He maintained his association with Dr. Goldman, whom he honored as 'a friendly gentleman, a gentle friend,' and continued teaching, both privately and in classes at New York University, Potsdam and other schools. He served as evaluator and consultant for the armed forces music program, and guest-conducted the premiere of his *'Irish Symphony'* with the Air Force Orchestra in 1951. He made numerous guest appearances, conducting district and state festivals of high school and college musicians, and served as sage, lecturer, and adjudicator at countless clinics, demonstrations, and contests throughout the country. In addition Erik's services as composer and arranger remained in constant demand from several publishing houses.

In 1955 Erik and Maria took a 'sabbatical' for themselves in the form of a trip to Europe. There were places to visit and scenes to revisit, friends to meet and honored friendships to renew. And this they took time to do. Erik thought of himself as a minstrel, and what a minstrel he was! He had a song, and he was determined to share it. One of his great joys in life was the communication possible between kindred minds, the empathy and sympathetic vibrancy between one heart and another. And so Erik sang. Perhaps this directness and uncomplicatedness of motive is the reason his songs are such a joy, both to the performer who re-sounds them and to the hearer who receives them, be that hearer but a *'little old lady in the third row.'*

Erik's outlook was positive. With both his eye and his ear he searched for and dwelled upon the beautiful, the good, the pure. Songs, therefore, passed between his lips, but sneers never did. He was one who refused to submit to the commonplace. Early in his career he summed up this aspect of his credo in these words:

Look for the higher things, look for the purest!
Grope not like moles in the dust of the earth.

Perhaps Erik's affirmation of life was most dramatically expressed in his gentleness, for he believed that:

Fondness can fill the heart,
Fond hearts can tremble with love;
Love Heaven's counterpart
Make earth like heaven above.

For just such a gentle servant of the Most High must the text of the *'Elegischer Gesang,'* which Beethoven set for chorus and string ensemble, have been intended:

Sanft wie du lebest
Hastdu vollendet,
Zu heilig für den Schmerz!
Kein auge wein'
Ob des himmlischen Geistes Heimkehr.

Two Tributes

I cannot accept that Erik is dead, I know he is not, and I hope he will approve of anything I write about him and his music! He will know that I admire his work tremendously and have done so ever since I read the proofs of his music when first it began to appear regularly in British Salvation Army publications many years ago. The great march *'Fling Wide the Gates'* thrilled me, as did *'The Saviour's Name'* and *'The Cross.'* I conducted these con amore many times in the years before 1940, and in more recent times I have found same delight on directing performances of *'Where Flowers Never Fade,'* the *'Concertine for Band and Trombone,'* and other works. His poetry and songs also have brought me much pleasure, although few enough soloists or choirs sing them. One day perhaps some of these will be 'discovered' as having more real value than much of the light-weight songs popular, even in religious circles, today. There was a choir-piece, *'Immortality,'* which struck deep chords for me. Erik and I corresponded irregularly and met all too rarely, but the scene of friendship was natural and free. We understood each other, I think, although I felt his knowledge of so many things towered above mine. Now he is nearer than ever to the Eternal Wisdom. There are many memories. One of a lighter nature comes to mind. In our home in London our ladies, Maria and Olive, sat quietly amused as Erik and I talked at great length about a modern composition, both of us spurred on by our own oratory as we decided that this sort of writing was negative and purposeless. Then dear Maria broke in with a few quiet words. What these were I cannot remember, but Erik's response was immediate: *'There you are! We talk and talk, then Maria says a word or two and puts the whole question into perspective, and we suddenly see we are talking about nothing!'* The fact was, we had neither of us heard the composition in question, but had been enjoying our own spate of words! And how brilliantly his conversation always flowed: grave, gay, humorous, penetrating! What we must not do, in writing or speaking of him, is to sentimentalise, seeking for the pious phrase about the 'dear departed.' He was a thorough professional, doing his work well, as many professionals do, he would except no particular praise for that. That which I most cherish is the remembrance of a rich personality, through whom, in times of closest communion, shone the Light of Christ.

We shall meet again.

Eric Ball

The death of Erik Leidzén last December deprived all who knew him not only of a valued colleagues but of an inspiring example of personal conduct and devotion to an ideal of the good life. Erik's accomplishments as a musician, and especially in his chosen field of the band, need no recounting.

His fine compositions and splendid arrangements will keep his memory alive for years and years to come. But perhaps even more important, in these difficult times, is the memory of Erik as a person who radiated health, confidence, and serenity. One knew immediately, on first meeting him, that this was a man of great inner strength, of deep conviction, at peace with himself and with the world. And this sense of goodness communicated itself to all with whom he came in contact, his pupils, his colleagues, his friends. And it is this that will live along with his music.

Richard Franko Goldman

LIGHT OF MY LIFE

By Grace C.J. Ross

'My husband is acclaimed by many people throughout the world as a great musician, but I claim no credit whatsoever for his achievements. His so called 'success' is entirely his own. He is Erik Leidzén, which should be answer enough for any who may think that I had a part in it.' ('The Musician', April 1, 1961) This is typical of Maria Leidzén's modesty and humility. It would be impossible to change her mind about the impact she has had on Mr. Leidzén's life, although from the evidence of his poetry it is obvious that she was the inspiration and object of scores of his finest verses. In 1928 Erik wrote:

Thou art the source, the 'only true begetter'
Of these attempts of mine, weak though they be;
And that they may be somewhat worthy thee,
I weigh and scan each syllable and letter.
Thy quick approving glance repays me better,
Than if great multitudes did fawn on me.
Thy smile and simple 'thank you' leave me free
Where worldly praise might prove a golden fetter.
Let others then condemn or laud at will;
Their firefly-flashes show no proper goal,
Indifferent to me is their opinion.
Be it thy task to check or cheer me still;
Be thou my guiding-star and o'er my soul
Unchallenged hold forever your dominion.

Maria came into Erik Leidzén's life at a crucial time. The tenderness and understanding she brought to him made the struggling young man's way easier at a time when life showed its dismal side. In his poem *'Rain-drop'* he expressed this thought:

Rain-drop, Rain-drop, you fell on my heart
Cool and refreshing with innocent art.
You are a tear that fell from the eye
Of God the most holy, of God the most high,
His power of healing you are revealing.
Now I can live, or at least I can try.

In the thirty-nine years of their married life Maria Leidzén has studiously fulfilled her role as a helpmate, but her avoidance of the limelight has possibly obscured her own accomplishments and the effect she has had on Erik's life. She came to the United States from Dalarna, Sweden, as a young girl. Within a day of her arrival she enrolled in an English course at a school in New York City and soon developed a remarkable command of English. She worked and lived with a family in Springfield, Massachusetts, where she met Erik. After their marriage, the Leidzéns read together regularly and avidly. Such were their reading habits that their daughter, Lisa, was never assigned an English literary work in all her years in school which she had not already read at home with Mamma and Pappa.

But Maria did not content herself with a thorough acquaintance with Scandinavian and English literature. With Erik's help she learned German and Italian. Up at the crack of dawn, she was drilled thoroughly each day in the formal aspects of the language she was working on at the time. In keeping with the Leidzéns whole approach to literature, they have not spent their time reading 'books about books,' but have approached the authors directly and without preconceived notions, accepting what a writer has to say 'in search of nourishment for the soul.' Maria's favorite German authors are Theodor Storm and Friedrich von Schiller. The Leidzéns have read the whole of Dante's 'Divina Commedia' in the original fourteenth-century Italian. An appreciation of nature was furthered by the many walks they took together, and what a pace to keep up with! Some of us would be more inclined to call it hiking. At Star Lake, Maria conducted early morning classes in calisthenics; she is obviously an authority on how to keep trim. Order and precision are apparent in all she does. She proudly speaks of herself as a 'housewife' and has kept her home a warm and comfortable haven. Even here her creativity is evident, both in her vegetarian cooking and in the many dainty and fine pieces of needlework. On one occasion she presented Erik with a pair of socks she had knitted, along with this verse:

Ah knits and knits and knits,
And you supply the wits,
We laugh a silly jokes
And seem to many folks
A pair of old Nit-wits.
However that may be,
These are from me to thee,
May you in health them wear
(Do with my rhyming bear!)
At Christmas fifty-two
With love from me to you.

It is difficult to think of Maria without Erik, but then, it is difficult to think of either of them without the other. The 'marriage of true minds' has been an inspiration and a model of wholesome living to all who have known them. Few will ever know the extent to which Maria has affected the Erik Leidzén that we know and love. Our debt to Erik Leidzén is great and, in some ways, easily perceived, but our debt to Maria Leidzén in incalculable, both for what she meant to Erik and for what she continues to mean to those of us who know and love her. Perhaps we should allow Erik to speak for us in the sonnet which he wrote for her on their twenty-sixth wedding anniversary in 1949:

Had but my pen the point-blank power and skill
To write your true biography, my dear,
Your winsome way would wondrously appear.
Noblesse and charm and cheerfulness, until
The reading of the book would be a thrill.
Your merry laugh, your sympathetic ear,
Your sayings, wise and witty, kind and clear,
I would record and thus the chapters fill.
Most likely all except a chosen few
Would but accept as idealistic fiction
The factual truths the volume should unfold;
But still, my heroine, because of you
All readers would pronounce it with conviction
The most enchanting story ever told.

(source: The Enthusuast , 1963 by Mark D. Freeh and R.E. Richardson, copied with permission)

Erik Leidzén conducting his own composition 'On The Way Home', played by the New York Staff Band.

Book - '**Erik Leidzén Band Arranger and Composer**' by Dr. Ronald W. Holz.

Book - **Stories from the Life of Erik Leidzén, an American Salvationist Musician** - by Leslie Fossey

Erik Leidzen's fine compositions and splendid arrangements will keep his memory alive for years. He was a man of great inner strength, of deep conviction, at peace with himself and the world. This sense of goodness communicated itself to all with whom he came in contact: his pupils, colleagues and his friends.

Important compositions

Tucker (FS84) 1933, The Cross (FS121) 1938, Song of the Brother (FS136) 1939, The Children's Friend (FS242) 1959, Songs in the Heart (FS266) 1962, Concertino for Trombone and Band (FS211) 1955, In the King's Service (GS1213) 1942, The Call (GS1357) 1952, The Invincible Army (GS1510) 1962, Secret Prayer (GS1463-2) 1958.

LICHTENBERG, WIM (VAN)

Wim van Lichtenberg was born on 23 April 1934. During the 1960s, for a short time between 1965 and 1967, there was a Netherlands Series of musical journals published by the Salvation Army, for the same instrumentation as the current Unity Series. Besides very well-known composers like Ray Bowes, Eric Ball and Leslie Condon, the Dutchman Wim van Ligtenberg contributed to this journal with at least two compositions. During this time, Wim was Bandmaster of the Arnhem Salvation Army Corps Band and by profession a teacher at the local conservatoire. His compositions were in the style of Bernard Verkaaik and Wilfred Heaton. He moved to the north of Holland where he became a member of the Leeuwarden Corps Band, on baritone.

Important composition

Like the tendril to the Vine (Netherlands Series 4a), Come All Ye Thirsty (Netherlands Series 4b)

LIDDLE, R

Former Bandsman. One of the early composers (first half of 19th century).

No further information could be retrieved about him.

Important composition

Starry Crown (TS0192) 1933

LIECHTI, WALTER

Born in 1951, Walter Liechti grew up in a family of Salvationists. Together with his brothers and colleagues from the Salvation Army Corps he got his first instrument when he was twelve years old. First on flugelhorn, then it became tenor horn and baritone. In a music camp of the Salvation Army, he then discovered the trombone. At 18 he started to work with the junior band as Deputy Bandmaster and arranged the first pieces of varying occupations and so made the first attempt as an arranger.

Chopin and the piano, Bach and the organ at that time were his first discoveries of classical music.

He completed the military service as a trombonist and met some excellent musicians. In 1973 he was together with 16 other enthusiasts for a music camp in Adelboden (Switzerland) and became a founding member of 'Brass of Praise' the National Salvation Army Band where he stayed for a total of 17 years, playing first trombone. In 1977 he wanted to know how to play trombone properly and applied for an apprenticeship with Branimir Slokar, who was then known by his revolutionary soft virtuosity and trombone playing. With him Walter received some educational years of teaching.

After that, Walter wrote for Brass of Praise many arrangements (including for trumpeter Carol Reinhart) and had in 1984 a great success with his first march *'Glad I Am'*. Walter enrolled at the Conservatory in Neuchatel in a harmony class at Samuel Ducommun. He was the only student. So he enjoyed during 5 years of private lessons in harmony and composition with a gifted composer and musician and wonderful human being. With him he learned the three B's: Bach, Brahms and Bruckner, who were the focus of the teaching.

With his compositions and arrangements, Walter was only interested supporting the Salvation Army. After his resignation of 'Brass of Praise' Walter gave up playing and composing for almost ten years and only around the year 2000 he started again with his musical activities. A music publisher in Switzerland has published several of his works. Nowadays Walter plays again in a wind sextet, for which he does most of editing, as well as taking on engagements as guest conductor in and outside the Salvation Army.

Important composition

This is the Moment

LODGE, EDMOND J.

Edmond Lodge, a Salvation Army officer, only published one piece, which is *'The Glory of the Cross'*, which appeared in the first release of the USA East American Band Journal, the famous 'Yellow Book' collection containing winning compositions in a 1948 Contest. At the time of the publication of this piece Edmond was a bandsman and assistant corps officer of the Binghampton Corps Band in New York. From Binghampton Citadel Corps he was commissioned to Seneca Falls Corps as Commanding Officer.

Important composition

The Glory of the Cross (AJ0006) 1948

LOVATT-COOPER, PAUL

Paul was born and raised in the Salvation Army with his parents who were Officers. He was quickly introduced into music by all of his family members who were all keen musicians. He started his musical career by playing the drums at school at the age of twelve. He joined the school band shortly after, which led to an invitation to play for former British Open Champions Kennedy's Swinton Band. The invitation came from his music teacher and conductor of the band Kevin Bolton. He has been percussion player with the world famous Black Dyke Band, and is their 'Composer in Residence'. Some pieces used often within the Salvation Army are shown below, with *'Fire in the Blood'* especially written in 2011 for the International Staff Band's anniversary celebrations.

Important compositions

Vitae Eaternum, Where Eagles Sing, Fire in the Blood

LOWCOCK, EDWARD

Edward Lowcock (1919-1977) was born in St. Helens, England on April 17, 1919. He was a glassblower at Pilkingtons in St. Helens. He was an active musician, both in the community and The Salvation Army. The family was active in the local Corps in St. Helens. In 1922, the family emigrated to the United States, first relocating to New Kensington, Pennsylvania, and then on to Buffalo, New York. Under the influence of his father, Edward's musical education blossomed early. While in high school, he was national trumpet champion in 1936, and 1937. His High School trumpet trio was national champion at the same time. During his high school years, he would make the journey weekly to Rochester, New York, to study at the Eastman School of Music; undertaking studies in keyboard harmony, composition and, of course, trumpet. At the age of 16, he also became the Deputy bandmaster of the Buffalo Citadel Band.

Following graduation, and after a brief family relocation to Los Angeles and back, Edward Lowcock moved to New York City, working at Territorial Headquarters. During that time he began his tenure as Cornet soloist with the New York Staff Band, which would continue until the transition from Edward to Derek Smith in the early 1950s. While working at THQ, he studied with Eric Leidzen; making weekly trips to the Leidzen home, being well fed by Maria (Erik's wife), and well challenged by Erik. During this time, he submitted a number of works to the music department.

In 1939, he entered the training College in New York. At the time, he continued his membership in the New York Staff Band, being the only Cadet at that time to have a key to the front door, so he could get into the building when returning from band trip weekends. He also arranged both brass and vocal music for the Training College weekly radio broadcasts. Following training, he was appointed to Ossening NY, and then following marriage to his fiancee, Tarrytown NY and Stapleton, Staten Island. All during this time he continued his ministry with the New York Staff Band.

In 1944, Edward Lowcock and his wife were appointed to THQ, and began soldiering at the Brooklyn Citadel Corps. Shortly thereafter, he became Bandmaster of the Brooklyn Citadel Band (1944 – 1952). In subsequent years, as the family relocated, he became the Bandmaster at Paterson, New Jersey (1952-1960, 1964-1969), Inglewood, California (1969-1972), and Mont Clare, (now Norridge Citadel, Chicago) Illinois (1973-1977). He was also Deputy Bandmaster of the New Jersey Youth Band (1962-1967), and Bandmaster of the Northern Illinois Youth Band (1973-1977). It was during his time at the Paterson Corps that Edward resigned from Officership. But their commitment to God and the Army never changed or wavered. The only thing that changed from one week to the next was the trim on their uniforms.

It was at Mont Clare, as the band was preparing to represent the USA Central Territory at the 1978 International Congress, Edward was Promoted to Glory following the inaugural rehearsal of Jim Curnow's *'Psalm 100 – A Psalm of Praise'* that he had asked James to write for the band's trip to the Congress.

While Edward Lowcock was well known as a cornet soloist with the New York Staff Band and as guest at many USA East, USA Central and Canadian Territory Corps, and to a lesser degree as a composer and arranger, he is best remembered for his leadership of Corps music sections. No matter what the Corps, it's history and tradition, he was always ready to point out the priority of the spiritual ministry of the band; that it's primary duty was to enhance the worship and witness of the Corps, and the necessity of the band members maintaining their high standard of Christian witness and lifestyle.

LUNDAHL, OTTO

Otto Lundahl was born in Kristiansand, Sweden on the 9th of March, 1867. He was a musician in the miltary, became converted and joined the Salvation Army in 1888 and became an officer. The Swedish Music Department of the Salvation Army was founded in 1988 in Stockholm. The first Leader of this department was Otto Lundahl. Otto Lundahl was a newly converted militairy bandsman and was promoted to Captain of the Salvation Army and charged with the organization of the Territorial Music Department for the

Sweden Territory, which didn`t exist at that time. He was only 21 years of age. He had to divide his time between office work, composing, arranging and the energetic extra task as bandmaster for the Swedish Staff Band. His primairy task was to develop the department and to train Salvation Army musicians to be able to start a 'staff band'. He also received an order to arrange tunes, to enable bands to accompany the singing during the meetings of the Salvation Army. The first arrangements were printed on single sheets of paper. In 1906 the first tune book containing 420 hymn tune arrangements was published. The Swedish Staff Band, established in 1988 had the instrumentation of an English Brass Band and had Otto Lundahl as Bandmaster from 1890 until 1894. He was pensioned in 1904 because of health issues and died in 1918.

Important composition

Swedish March (GS0419) 1902

LUNDGREN, OLOF

Olof Lundgren was born in Huskvarna, Sweden, on 10 December 1907, to Salvationists Oskar and Anna Lundgren. He became a soldier and attended the Huskvarna corps until he moved with his family to the United States in 1928. He heard God's call to officership at the 1929 Scandinavian Summer Congress in Worcester, Mass. He entered the School for Officer Training in New York City from the Jamestown, New York #2 Corps in 1930, and was commissioned the following year as a member of the Climbers Session.

Lundgren served in tent campaign ministry and at corps in New York and Pennsylvania before marrying Lieutenant Karin Carlson in 1936. Together the couple served in Scandinavian corps in New York, Massachusetts, Rhode Island, and Connecticut. In 1944 he became Young People's Secretary for the USA Eastern Territory's Scandinavian Department and the New York Metropolitan Division, and also served as divisional secretary for the Western New York and Scandinavian Divisions. In 1960 he transferred to Territorial Headquarters, serving in a number of roles. He also served in the New York Staff Band for 30 years, playing solo cornet and Eb soprano cornet. He joined the cornet section in 1951, performing both instrumental and vocal solos. His final appointment as an active officer was as assistant field secretary for special services. The Lundgrens retired from active service in 1975; Karin Lundgren preceded her husband to Glory in 1996. In 1971 the King of Sweden bestowed on him the Swedish order of Knighthood, the Royal Order of Vasa First Class, in recognition of his long and devoted service to Swedish-Americans in the United States. He was Promoted to Glory on September 17, 2005.

Important compositions

Over me (TS0531) 1955

LUNDHOLM, LENNART

Bandsman of the Landskrona Corps in Sweden. Of particular interest is that the tune he used in his cornet solo *'Er du rett av hjertet glad' ('Happy in the Heart')* was written by Erik Leidzén.

Lennart Lundholm was born in 1938 in the city of Halmstad. His parents were Salvationists, and Lennart was Bandmaster at the Corps for a few years in the early 1960s. Later he moved to Landskrona, where he continued his Bandmaster career in the latter parts of the decade. He is a music teacher by profession. He has written several songs, but also a few brass band pieces, some of which have been published in Norway. His songs have also been published, for example in 'Sång och Spel', the Swedish sheet music series for Songsters.

Important composition

Er du rett av hjertet glad (NM0026) 1979

LUNDKVIST, KRISTER

Currently a well known Swedish composer, arranger, musician and producer, he was born in 1958 and raised within the ranks of the Salvation Army. He studied trumpet, piano and composition on the Conservatory in Sweden en was Rector of the Stockholm Conservatory fom 2001 to 2003.

His arrangement of *'This is my story'* is his only published arrangement in the journals of the Salvation Army although very well know the world over.

Important composition

This is My Story (GS1926) 1996

LYNNE, A.S

In the history book of the International Staff Band a 'Brother' (Jabez) Lyne (although with one 'n') is mentioned as bandmaster of the (predecessor of the) International Staff Band together with other executive leaders. The announcement that he would become the bandmaster was signed by W. Bramwell Booth in 1893. It is not likely the same person but no further information could be retrieved about him.

Important composition

The Lowly one (GS0208) 1892

LYONS, ALAN

Retired music educator in Glastonbury, Connecticut, public schools and a graduate of the University of Connecticut. At the time his one piece appeared in the ABJ he was serving as Young People's Bandleader and Solo Euphonium of the Manchester (CT) Citadel Band, as well as with the SONED Youth Band.

Born on April 7, 1940 in the United States of America, Alan is a retired public school music teacher after 45 years. He grew up within the ranks of the Salvation Army, where is father was a famous cornet soloist and deputy bandmaster of the Manchester Citadel Band in Connecticut. He played with great enthusiasm in the band until 1967 when a difficult situation caused him to leave. Since that time Alan has never lost his love of and enthusiasm for Salvation Army band music. He finds it a great inspiration and blessing. He has but one piece published in the Army's band journals which is *'A Christmas Trilogy'* and is published by the Army's Eastern Territorial Music Department in a journal called 'Band Music for Evangelism'. It is a relatively short piece starting with a purposely dreary arrangement of *'God Rest Ye Merry Gentlemen'*. The contradiction of the title and the setting is supposed to depict the irony that the world was not a merry place. The second tune is a setting of *'Away in a Manger'*, indicating Christ's birth and the third is *'Joy to the World'* the joy that we can all now experience. He has had no other music published although he did make several arrangements for both the Salvation Army and his school band. This published piece was written for a composers' contest in 1963 and awarded honorable mention. Alan presently lives in Vernon, Connecticut with his wife, Carol with two grown up children, Jennifer and Gordon.

Important composition

A Christmas Trilogy (AJ0076) 1967

MACDONALD, TOM

Londonderry is the second Irish Corps of The Salvation Army, and was founded in 1880. The Londonderry Corps Band was founded in 1891, and the first bandmaster was William Macdonald - he and his wife were saintly people whose legacy lives on in the corps. The story goes that his brother Tom Macdonald was a professional musician at the turn of the century. He played in the old style music halls, composing his own pieces of music and arranging others. However, Tom got saved, came to the Salvation Army, and after a short period of time, he became Bandmaster: his brother William (who was the first corps bandmaster of Londonderry, and died in 1897 at the age of 28) humbly stepping aside believing his brother had more musical talent than him which would help the development of the music side of ministry. Tom held the role during the first decade of the 1900s with a total of nine years. The Macdonald family attended the corps up until the 1980s when William's three children (none of whom married) were separately PtG within a few years. The corps only had five commissioned bandmasters.

Important composition

Pray, Sinner, Pray (GS0252) 1894

MACGEORGE (first name unknown)

One of the early composers (first half of 19th century).

No further information could be retrieved about him.

Important composition

Wonder of Wonders (GS0445) 1903

MACMAHON (first name unknown)

One of the early composers (late 1800, early 1900). Was a bandmaster.

No further information could be retrieved about this person.

Important composition

Glory in the Highest (GS0359-1) 1898

MACK, THOMAS

Thomas Mack was born to a Salvation Army officer family in Boston USA. The major's formal educational background includes music theory and harmony studies at the Hartt School of Music, Hartford University, Hartford, CT; liberal arts studies at Bronx Community College NYC: Adelphi University, Garden City, NY and Pace University, NYC; a diploma in paralegal studies from New York University, and a bachelor of science degree in organizational management for Nyack College, Nyack, NY. In September 1961 he entered The Salvation Army School For Officer Training in New York City. 1963, he has held the following appointments in The Salvation Army: Assistant corps officer in

Williamspor and Wilkes-Barre, Pa.; field training officer at the school for officer training, NYC; corps officer in Providence, R.I., Hartford (Temple) CT, Stamford, CT; and finance officer at USA Eastern territorial headquarters. He has also seved as USA Eastern territorial music department director (1974-1981), and assistant legal secretary (1981-1985). Since 1985 his appointment has been that of legal secretary for the USA Eastern territory. In April of 2001 he was designated chairman of The Salvation Army National Legal Commission. Thomas played solo euphonium in various Salvation Army bands. He was the euphonium soloist of The Salvation Army New York Staff Band from 1970 through 1990, the band's male chorus leader from 1975 to 1990, and deputy bandmaster during the 1990 season. He continued in the band, playing 1st baritone and serving as band chorus leader and assistant executive officer. Major Mack was also the bandmaster of The Salvation Army Hempstead Citadel Corps Band from 1981 to 1990, has been the corps songster-leader since 1993, and has been a member of The Salvation Army USA Eastern territotial music council since 1974.

Important composition

By His Hand (AJ261) 2008

MACKERETH, ANDREW

Andrew Mackereth was born in England in 1965. A fourth generation Salvationist, he first attended a meeting aged barely a week old. The son of Salvation Army Officer parents, he has lived in many places including 4 years in Zambia and nine years in Kingston-upon-Hull. It was here that he began his earlist musical training. In 1982, he returned to his native North-East to enrol on the Certificate in Brass Band Studies Course at Newcastle College of Arts & Technology, studing trombone, euphonium and tuba. In 1984, Andrew gained a place at the Birmingham School of Music to study Trombone and Composition, later studying Percussion and Conducting also. In his fourth year, he won the Bernhard Brown Memorial Composition Prize. At the completion of his studies he entered the teaching profession first in Nuneaton before moving to Birmingham to become Head of Music in the largest UK school. Currently he is working as a Headteacher at the Heart of England School, Solihull. Andrew is a very well known and popular Composer in and outside the Salvation Army. In September of 2000 he was named 'Composer-in-Residence' to the Coventry City Salvation Army Band and in January 2001 he was named 'Composer-in-Residence' for the Melbourne Staff Band (MSB), tour of Great Britain. Numerous commission include *'Standard Bearers'* for the International Staff Band (ISB), *'Hymnus'* for Wilhelmina Easterein (Netherlands) and 'Exaltation' for the Melbourne Staff Band (MSB). Recent collaborations include Bristol Easten Citadel Band, Canadian Staff Band (CSB), Amsterdam Staff Band (ASB) and Songsters and the renowned Douglas Yeo who recorded his trombone solo: *'Swing Low'* in February 2004. Andrew lives in Nuneaton with his wife Stella and two children, Eleanor and Joshua. They all attend Nuneaton Citadel where Andrew serves as Bandmaster.

Important compositions

Millennium Flourishes (FS564) 2001, Trailblazers (JC656) 2010, Keep me praising (GS1957) 1999

MAGNUSSON, TOBIAS

Tobias Magnusson was born in 1887 and Promoted to Glory in 1973. Although the exact date is unknown, Tobias Magnusson played in the Swedish Staff Band around 1910. He was a well respectable non-commissioned officer at the Jönköping Corps, and Leader of the Freedom Choir (Male voice choir). He was a member of the Jönköping City Council. Director in the business trade of butchers.

Important composition

Jubileumsmarsch, Jönköping (FM0249-1) 1960

MAIN, HECTOR

Hector Main was born in Dumfries, Scotland in 1911. His mother was widowed whilst pregnant, and life was hard. Although gifted academically, at age 14 he left school, abandoning hopes of becoming a doctor and instead serving an apprenticeship as a cabinet maker.

Life in The Salvation Army was a hugely formative influence - and filled all of his spare time, with activities every week night as well as on Sundays. In Dumfries Corps he learnt to play the concertina, and took his place in the concertina band alongside his mother. He also gained a reputation as a solo concertina player, playing a wide range of music - some not usually heard on the concertina!

Hector responded to God's call to become an officer and was a cadet and then a sergeant in the 'Awakeners Session', being commissioned in 1934 as a junior officer to Nottingham. During the war he was in charge of the first of the Salvation Army Red Shield mobile canteens, ostensibly serving tea and refreshments, but in reality providing spiritual and moral support and counselling. This was during the blitz in Clydebank, Scotland. Marriage to Margaret McNab in 1944 also saw a change of direction to becoming Corps Officers, first in the north-east of England, then east London, then back up to the north, before resigning as an officer and settling in Kent. Both here, and later after moving to Bournemouth, Hector was active in Corps life, being Songster Leader at Dartford and Boscombe.

As a young man Hector took lessons in composition by correspondence course from Bandmaster George Marshall. Colonel Charles Skinner, later of the Music Editorial Department was in the Training College at the same time as Hector, and was also a musical influence and support. Most of his music was vocal at first, and remained a great love, culminating in a beautiful setting of *'If I Forget Thee'*, words by General Albert Orsborn. However, he also wrote music for brass bands, including the *'Whitley Bay March'*, written while Corps Officer at Whitley Bay.

Hector Main's life was cut tragically short when he was drowned whilst on holiday in 1965 - a loss to his family, friends, and Salvation Army musicians.

Important composition

Dumfries Citadel (GS1304) 1948

MAJOR, WILLIAM

A former bandmaster of the Coventry City Corps in the United Kingdom, his most successful period with the band was around the mid 30's of the previous century. He was a somewhat special character in this that he always wanted to play 'forbidden' music (unpublished). His own compositions were send to the Music Editorial Department but were never published which might have caused some frustration to him. Possibly due to these frustrations and the restrictions on bandmasters, William Major resigned in 1939 from his position, followed within four days by 29 bandsmen. William's successor as bandmaster was James Greig, brother of composer Alex Greig.

Important compositions

Three Spires (m/s)

MALLETT, CHRIS

Born on April 26, 1947 in Newport, South Wales, Chris Mallet, a fourth generation Salvationist, commenced his musical training at an early age at the Abersychan Corps, where both his parents were leaders of the musical forces. When he moved to Cardiff to study music, he became a member of the Cardiff Canton Band, where, after some time he became the Deputy Bandmaster. While studying under the mentorhood of Ivor Bosanko, he obtained L.R.A.M. and L.T.C.L. for trumpet playing and L.C.C.M for trumpet and piano. When moving to the Euphonium, Ivor Bosanko wrote the challenging solo *'Glorious Liberation'* for him. In 1972 Chris Mallett moved to Bristol, and became Bandmaster of the Bristol Staple Hill Corps Band for the next three years. During this time he also managed to get his F.T.C.L for euphonium playing. A next move saw him going to the Bristol Easton Corps where he became first their Singing Company Leader and later their Songster Leader. With his group of songsters he toured the Western Territory of California, which was during Easter 1986. Almost immediately after tour he immigrated to the United States to become the Divisional Music Director for the Southern California Division. Ever since he has featured as a Euphonium soloist throughout the Salvation Army world. He was a mentor of Aaron vanderWeele, who would later become the famous Euphonium soloist with the New York Staff Band. Amongst his output he wrote the march *'Tournament of Roses 2000'*, which has been used for many years at the Tournament of Roses Parade, which is held every 1st of January. Chris Mallet was very unexpectedly Promoted to Glory on June 18, 2000.

Important compositions

Travelling Along (FS611) 2006, Great Things (TS977) 1991

MALM, AXEL

Axel Malm was born in 1898, though the date of his passing is unknown. He went to Traning College to become a Salvation Army Officer in 1919, and became Bandmaster of the Swedish Staff Band in 1920, a position he held until 1923. He resigned as an officer in 1928, but became the bandmaster of the Stockholm 1 Corps Band from 1928 to 1934. He composed the march *'Solskenssånger' ('Sunshine')* amongst others. He also was Divisional Bandmaster of the Stockholm Division.

Important composition

Solskenssånger (FM0121)

MALPASS, LESLIE F.

Born on 16 May 1922. He grew up in the Salvation Army and studied at the Cincinnati Conservatory. He pursued a career in higher education administration, including presidencies at several universities. When at Western Illinois University he hosted the International Youth Congress of The Salvation Army in the mid-1980s. He was a trombone player and a very interesting, well liked, dynamic, intelligent person, according people who surrounded him.

Important composition

Nearer home (TS0515) 1954, On the Cross (AJ0007) 1948

MALPASS, TOM W.

Captain Tom W. Malpass, was an officer of the Salvation Army in the United States. He was the uncle of the previous composer Leslie Mallpass. No information other than what he has composed was found.

Important composition

The U.S.A. (GS632) 1911

MANN, ??

One of the early composers (late 1800s, early 1900s). One of the early Salvation Army officers, Mann (first name not known) was an Ensign at the time of the publications of his compositions. No further information could be retrieved about him.

Important compositions

The All-atoning Blood (GS0390) 1900, Are all the Children in? (GS0403-1) 1900

MANNERS, KEITH

Born on 3 May 1958, Keith's interest in music began at the age of seven when he learned to play the Euphonium with the Salvation Army. As well as studying Cello and Organ, he progressed through the Youth Band to become principal Euphonium and Soloist with the Southend Citadel Band and at the age of seventeen was appointed conductor of the Youth Band.

For over eleven years Keith conducted brass bands at summer music schools in Anglia, Coventry, Kent and Essex where he was responsible for the training of young people in brass playing. In 1984 Keith relinquished his position as Principle Euphonium with the Southend Citadel Band to 'take up the baton' as Bandmaster.

Membership of brass bands includes five years as a member of the Salvation Army Household Troops Band and ten years as a member of the International Staff Band, the Salvation Army's premier brass band. During this time he visited many countries including the USA and many in Europe. Concert work in this country has included annual festivals at the Royal Albert Hall, Royal Festival Hall and two memorable occasions when he was privileged to meet the Queen at Buckingham Palace. In 2003, Keith was appointed as Musical Director of the Essex Police Band in January 2003.

Keith has a number of of compositions and arrangements published by The Salvation Army and The Music Company (UK) Ltd

Important compositions

Songs of Harvest (GS2051) 2007, Power Divine (TS1110) 2002

MARSHALL, GEORGE

George Marshall was born in England 1887. When he was a young man of thirty, a Salvation Army bandmaster and already making his mark as a composer, his back was broken when a portion of roof collapsed at a coal face three miles under the North Sea. The remainder of his life become an epic of courage in disability. Although confined to a wheelchair, the lower part of his body being paralysed. George obtained a position at The Salvation Army Music Department in London and in 1915 he became bandmaster of the South Shields 1 Citadel Band. In 1928 he conducted one of his own compositions during the Composers–Festival of the Salvation Army and became acquainted with the guests of honour, King George VI and Queen Elizabeth. In 1951, General Albert Orsborn admitted Bandmaster George Marshall to the Order of the Founder. George Marshall O.F. was Promoted to Glory in January 1956. Amongst all his brilliant pieces, he also wrote a march for and played by the Czechoslovakia Territorial Staff Band entitled *'Armada Spasy' ('Salvation Army')*.

Book - **Triumph of Faith** - by Arch R. Wiggins

An early book (1958) about the life and work of one of the most profilic writers in Salvation Army history, George Marshall, who became known within the wider audience because of his mining accident which left him paralysed for the rest of his life.

Important compositions

Horbury (FS62) 1930, Visions (FS45) 1928, Army of the Brave (FS06) 1923, The Citadel March (GS655) 1912, Soldiers of Christ (GS667) 1912, The Emblematic Flag (GS923) 1924

MARSHALL, THOMAS CHARLES

Born as the son of Thomas D. Marshall on 7th September 1854. He went to the United States of America in 1873 and lived for five years in Illinois, Kansas and Missouri, before going to China where he was a proofreader for the Imperial Maritime Customs Service in Shanghai. In 1882 he returned to the United Kingdom and became a Salvationist at Regent Hall. One oyear later he joined the staff of The 'War Cry'. He served as an officer until 1898 both in the United Kingdom as well as in the United States of America. He started to write songs and music at the suggestion of William Booth and did so until only a few days before he died on 7 October 1942.

Important compositions

He Called me out of Darkness (GS0155) 1891, We're the Army that Shall Conquer (GS0073) 1887

MARTI, PAUL

Paul Marti was born in Switzerland on the 21st of November 1934, as the son of Salvation Army Officers. He entered the International Training College in London and was commissioned a Salvation Army officer in 1958. Following Corps appointments in Switzerland, he served as the Music Secretary for the Swiss Territory. During this time he was the Bandmaster of the Swiss Officer's Band and was also the very talented and popular Conductor of several Swiss Military Bands. In his service as a Salvation Army Officer he spent two periods of service in Norway, the homeland of his wife Åse. During one period in Norway he served as the Territorial Music Secretary in Oslo. He served as the Territorial Commander for the Denmark and the Germany Territories before being appointed with rank of Commissioner as the Territorial Commander for the Switzerland Territory. Paul was an accomplished musician and has a number of band compositions to his credit. He was Promoted to Glory in January 1999, a short time before his retirement.

Important compositions

O Return unto God (TS0743) 1971, St. Gallen (TS0765) 1973, Summertime (TS0729) 1970

MARTIN, DIANE

One of Erik Leidzén's students in the early sixties. She was the first woman composer world wide to publish in a Salvation Army Journal. *'Friendship with Jesus'*, Quartet Series, published in the sixties. *'Jesus, Lily of the Valley'*, a baritone solo written for Bob McNally, was accepted by the New York Music Department for publication but then the score was lost.

No further information could be retreived about Diane Martin. She still lives in the United States of America.

Important compositions

Friendship with Jesus, Jesus, Lily of the Valley

MARTIN, WILLIAM

A former bandsman of the Regent Hall Band in London, and who later moved south to become, for a short time, a member of the Eastbourne Citadel Band. Prior to his Regent Hall and Eastbourne period he was a member of the Tottenham Citadel Band where he played baritone and euphonium. Also a former member of the Rosehill Band of the Salvation Army.

An interesting detail is that William Martin can be heard on a Tottenham brass quartet on Regal Zonpahone 78 rpm in Eric Ball's *'Jewels'* and *'Love Eternal'*. This was in the late 50's. This disc was made in a great haste as SP&S had a breakdown. Hence a quartet! It also includes James Williams, the long time bandmaster of the Tottenham/Enfield Citadel Band and Deryck Diffey, the famous soloist with the Tottenham Citadel Band and later Canadian Staff Band.

Deryck Diffey wrote about William Martin:

'Bill, as we knew him was in the Rosehill Band and was a very good arranger with the awesome skill of writing vocal arrangements that were able to throw the challenge out to the congregations. Sunday meetings were never the same when Bill's arrangements were sung. He was also playing in the prize bands. He played Euphonium, Baritone, and Trombone equally well'.

Important compositions

Front Rankers (GS1728-1) 1980, Jesus is calling (TS0928) 1987

MASSARELLA, J.E.

One of the early composers (first half of 20th century).

No further information could be retrieved about this person.

Important compositions

Fellowship (GS0943) 1926, On joyful wing (TS0100) 1927, The Weymouth March (GS0864) 1921

MASTIN, GEORGE

One of the early composers (first half of 20th century).

No further information could be retrieved about this composer.

Important compositions

Dauntless (TS0050) 1924, My deliverer (TS0096) 1927, Our Conquering Band (GS0930) 1925, The Pathway (TS0012) 1922

McFARLANE, NEVILLE WILLIAM

Was born on 19 May 1934 in Brighton, Sussex. He was married in 1957 to Christina, daughter of Lieut.-Colonels Arthur and Jeannie Gray. He was educated on the Varndean Grammar School, Brighton (1945-1953), Balliol College Oxford (1953-1957) and Nettleship Open Scholarship in Music, MA (Joint Honours) in French and German with a Diploma in Education. He has a Licentiate of the Royal Academy of Music (1969).

Neville learned the piano from age seven, and as his parents were Salvationists it was not surprising that he also quickly learned the cornet and joined Brighton Congress Hall Young People's Band, where he was also Singing Company pianist until leaving for College. At age eighteen he moved into the Senior Band. At Oxford he was Principal Trumpet in the University Orchestra under Professor Jack Westrup as well as playing with the Corps Band. Moving to Staffordshire Neville became Deputy (1957) and Bandmaster (1958) of the Chesterton Corps Band. When he came to Sleaford he was made Bandmaster and formed a small band, over the years it has always been a small combination but effective in the Corps situation. Since 1994 he has also been Divisional Bandmaster for Lincolnshire in the East Midlands Division. In the 1960s and 1970s Neville directed a number of Music Summer Schools for the Salvation Army and for five years in the 1990s he was a member of the Territorial Advisory Council. In 1998 with a colleague he made a CD 'From a Distance' to raise money for the Salvation Army's work in Russia where his Corps Officer had been appointed. He was Musical Director of Sleaford Choral Society (1975-2001) and conducted Sleaford Schools Orchestra (1974-1980).

Neville had no formal training, although composition and form formed part of his basic school music education and the examination for his Oxford Scholarship involved a combination of harmony, counterpoint, recital performance and the requirement to submit a number of original compositions. He had begun writing tunes as a boy and took his first band effort (a selection) to Hadleigh Music Camp in 1949 where he received some helpful advice from the late Captain Hector Main. His first published song *('Walking with Jesus')* and band piece *('Faith Alway')* came out in 1952 and these were followed by several more.

Brigadier Charles Skinner encouraged him to write, and a number of pieces were accepted for publication by the International Music Council, but there was always a frustrating delay of several years before they made it to print, and after leaving Chesterton he had no opportunity of hearing what he had written. Neville gained first place for a trombone quartet in the Centenary Competition and was commissioned to write a march for the visit of Oxford Band to Germany and the Netherlands around 1970, which he accompanied as guest pianist. With increasing professional and family commitments on his time, he took the decision that it was not good stewardship and perhaps self-indulgent to spend a lot of time on things which would not see the light of day for a long time if ever. Therefore for some years he stopped writing music except for immediate use for school and Choral Society purposes. Over time most of his earlier manuscripts at SP&S were lost, a number of them in the Judd Street fire, and of course they were single copies as all this early work was done without benefit of photo-copier or computer. However somewhere in the 1990s he came to the decision that he really should be practising the gift he had been given, regardless of eventual use, and began writing again, both songs and instrumental music. A little of this has found its way into print and more has been used in a number of less official ways. He know that his harmonic and rhythmic styles may not be 21st century – more Coles than Krommenhoek, but many people seem to appreciate his efforts and have asked for copies.

Neville enjoy the challenge of making ad hoc arrangements for special occasions, and looking back he is also aware that a number of pieces were born of reaction to specific spiritual influence and occasions, this would certainly be true of *'Faith Alway'*, *'Live Thy Life in Me'* and *'The Secret Place'* among others.

O Live Thy Life in Me (written by Neville McFarlane)

This was written when I was about 21. In those days Salvationists had a very restricted concept of vocation: you could be 'called' only to be an officer; anything else was second-rate. Many well meaning people tried to convince me that I should be an officer; however, the Lord and I both knew that He had not chosen this path for me. Nevertheless, I found it frustrating that I wanted my life to committed to His will and purpose, but was limited to second best. Candidates Sunday in 1955, when my two friends, the other University students in the Corps, were both heading for officership, was a difficult day for me. I backed out of the usual Sunday evening supper at the Band Sergeant's house and went back to my College room where, with no access to a keyboard, I worked well into the night writing *'O Live Thy Life in Me'* in short score.

In the next few days I quickly wrote it up in full score, but made no other changes to what I had written that night, and then sent it to Colonel Jakeway. Soon after, he wrote to inform me that it had been passed for publication. Nearly a decade later when it was printed the then Major Ray Steadman-Allen, reviewing new publications in 'The Musician', wrote of the *'inspired reference to My All Is On the Altar'* at letter D. This puzzled me; I hurried to consult the score and discovered that indeed the second half of the verse does give way to 'My All Is On the Altar'. I had no idea; I had not intentionally included that quotation, and though it was my hand that had written it instructed by my mind, I am convinced that it was literally 'inspired' in that it was the Holy Spirit guiding me to write something without my knowledge.

Important compositions

I Live Thy life in Me (GS1607) 1970, Rejoicing Every Day (GS1576) 1967, Room in My Heart (FS0250) 1960, The Secret Place (GS1648) 1973

McLAUGHLIN, GEORGE

Initially active as a Salvation Army officer, including one appointment as Divisional Music Director in Western Pennsylvania in the late 1950s, he resigned from officership and became a professional musician and educator, first in Kentucky, including faculty responsibilities at Asbury University (then College). He moved to Florida in the 1970s and there directed a number of fine community choirs and orchestras, in addition to other teaching responsibilities.

Important composition

Northern New England (ABJ5, no.26) 1954

McANALLY, ROBERT

Robert origins are from Sydney, Australia and he became an officer in 1903. He played cornet with several corps bands and worked a various times for the Music Department in Melbourne. He had the strange habit of putting down his baton, picking up his cornet and playing the cadenza's in his own compositions. In 1920 McAnally became Deputy Bandmaster for the Melbourne Staff Band and became staff bandmaster in 1923.

Captain Robert McAnally

The winner of the prize march. The Name of the Australian Officer who this week forms the subject of our character sketch is familiar throughout The Army world as the winner of the Prize March, 1907. He is a fine specimen of The Army musician, 'born and bred' a Salvationist, coming up from the Juniors, finding his talents a stepping-stone to Army service, and gladly dedicating them in their entirety to the glory of God and the saving of souls. One who knows him well writes: *'He has 'musician' written in every line of his strong countenance. You cannot look at him without seeing that he is a musical enthusiast.'* Best of all, his countenance also bears the happy expression of a Salvation Army Officer rejoicing in his appointed work. Our comrade was born in Sydney, the capital city of New South Wales, and as a Junior was attached to the Leichardt Corps. Sydney is a very musical city, and there are all sorts of associations for furthering its study amongst those who desire to take it seriously. Undoubtedly, also, there are many temptations in Sydney for a young fellow whose talents enable him to minister to the pleasure of others. Situated on the shores of the most beautiful bay in the world, where rhododendrons bloom down to the water's edge, and the soft winds rustle amongst waving palms. Sydney, in spite of all its go-ahead character, is also a pleasure-loving place. The soft, luxurious climate encourages open-air festivals, dances kept up far into the night, and a lover of the lighter side of life. With all these things music has much to do, and it would have been quite easy for young McAnally to have 'done well for himself' from a worldly point of view by throwing his talents into the service of the gaiety of his native city. But The Army had inspired him with a higher ideal of life, and a better sense of responsibility to God for the right use of the talents entrusted to him. At a very early age he had been acquired a mastery of music, but he was also a consistent, right living, God-honoring Soldier of the Corps, and his great desire was to see the Band as good as instruction could make it. Outside, he gave lessons in music where he could do it consistently with his Salvationism, but presently the call to the Work grew so clear, and the way was so opened to our comrade, that he gave himself to The Army. His talents were so obviously musical, that he has since been engaged in developing the musical side of our Australian Work, all of course to one end, viz., the glorification of God and the spread of the Kingdom. Given the rank of Captain, our comrade became leader of the Australian travelling Band, which improved rapidly under his able tuition. At present he is on the Musical Staff at Headquarters, and this angers well for the future of our Bands in Australia. Captain McAnally will spare no pains to help bring them to that state of efficiency which has done so much to make The Salvation Army Bands at home the power they are 'for God and souls.' That he should have written a Prize March is perhaps a great surprise to his friends. In Australia it was thought his genius lay more particularly in the direction of selections. He has shown, however, that in both these branches of Army music he is a competent writer. Captain McAnally is a thorough Salvationist, and from a religious standpoint knows little of anything else but The Army in which he was brought up. He is married, and his wife is a clever pianist. A descriptive analysis of the Prize March was given in No.1 of 'The Bandsman and Songster.' The march is a brilliant, showy piece, and will tax the soprano, solo, and first cornet, as well as the baritone and euphonium players of our best Bands.

(Source: The Bandsman and Songster, May 4, 1907)

Captain Robert McAnally.

Captain Robert McAnally, the composer of the winning prize march in the 1906 competition, only had one day at his disposal for arranging the piece. The march was therefore composed, scored, all necessary parts written out, and posted from Melbourne in that one day!

(Source: The Bandsman and Songster, June 1, 1907)

Important compositions

Gems from Great Masters No.1, The Jubilee No.1, Victory with Honour

MATTHEWS, CLIFF

Cliff Matthews (born 9 December 1950) is an accomplished pianist and accompanist, accompanying the Songsters at The Salvation Army each week. He is a highly regarded musician within the Salvation Army, having held the position of Bandmaster at Gloucester for over 25 years, and spent two years singing with The International Staff Songsters.

Important compositions

The meeting of the carol singers (US0300) 2004. On the Lord's side (GS2014) 2004

MEAKIN. ARTHUR

A former Bandmaster of the Ilkeston Citadel Band in the United Kingdom.

Important compositions

Ilkeston Citadel (TS0496) 1953, Stepping Heavenward (TS0752) 1972

MEHLING, CHARLES

A former member of the New York Staff Band, Charles was born on 22 May 1889 and was converted in 1905, which was followed by becoming a bandsman. He became an officer from the Philadelphia II Corps and after his commissioning in 1911 served in the Eastern Territory in several functions. He retired in 1952 as a Lt. Colonel. Playing the trombone was one of his joys to do and he performed many duets with his wife. In retirement he lived at Asbury Park, New Jersey. He died on 11 January 1969.

MELLINS, ?? (Mrs.)

One of the early composers (late 1800). It was, certainly in the early period of the Salvation Army, a rare occasion that woman composers got the chance to write music that not only was played, but even more, was used for the Army's publication. About Mrs. Mellins herself is nothing known. No further information could be retrieved about her.

Important compositions

Near to the Lord (GS0149) 1891, Oh, the Love of Christ my Lord (GS0273) 1895

MEREDITH, JOHN

John Meredith was born in Bournemouth, Dorset (Hampshire at that time) in 1944 into a non Salvation Army family. It wasn't until he was 12-13 years old that he had his first contact with the Salvation Army and the Corps at Boscombe. A family living near to his home suggested attendance at Sunday School with their son David Wilkinson who is the current Bass Trombone player of the Corps band.

And so a life long dedication to the Army began. It was in those early years that because of the Sunday School attendance, John had his first encounter with live music listening to the Corps band under the baton of bandmaster Courtney Bosanko and this live sound was to have a profound effect upon his life and music making within the Army. Writing music at this stage was very far from his mind. In fact, as the list of his writings show, most of his Army music making was as a Tuba player and soloist rather than a writer. This was to come much later in his life. As he developed as a player, first in the Young People's band on cornet, then euphonium it was at this stage he was asked to take the solo chair of his school band and during this time he appeared on BBC Music services as a euphonium soloist. At the age of 15+ the desire to transfer to the senior corps band required him to attend rehearsals as a non playing attendee until made a Senior Soldier. This he did with a very deep sense of awe and respect for the men whom he had come to regard first as upstanding Christians and as first rate music makers. In the very early days of attending rehearsals he would sit well back in the body of the hall away from the platform where these music makers produced such exciting sounds. His future as the principal Tuba of the band was far from his assessment of his own ability. Having eventually been commissioned a Boscombe bandsman on the 9th April 1961 one of his first poignant memories was of the first weekend campaign away. This was as 4th euphonium when the band travelled to Ipswich Citadel and the late retired General Albert Orsborn, who soldiered at Boscombe Corps and travelled with the band, led the meetings for the weekend. What a baptism of Army banding!

Very soon after his commissioning John was asked to take a seat on the Tuba section as number 4 EEb. A place he took with some sadness at the time having enjoyed the euphonium playing days but also with relish to be part of this great Salvation Army Corps band. The desire to play at another level - that of being a professional tuba player - was realised when he joined the Royal Air Force Music Services and served in a number of RAF bands; RAF Uxbridge; Locking and Akrotiri in Cyprus. In 1971 he returned to his home corps of Boscombe where he took the principal's chair on the Tuba section and where he remains to the present time.

Composition was still some way away for John as he concentrated on his performance as a tuba player although an early arrangement of June Collin's song *'The Quiet Heart'* was completed in these earlier days. Three conservatoire performance diplomas followed over the next few years; John became a Licentiate of the Trinity College of Music London; a Fellow of the Trinity College of Music London and an Associate of the Royal College of Music. In addition to his banding commitments with his corps band John has completed a number of engagements with the International Staff Band. It wasn't until the early nineties that he began writing - first with arranging and, up to the present, original compositions. Of the number of arrangements and original compositions there have been recordings made of his writings:-

1. Arrangements of Fantasia de Concerto - subtitled Sounds from the Riviera(Boccalari) played by Steven Mead with The Fairey Band conducted by Howard Snell. CD Polyphonic label Number QPRL 209D.
2. Vladimir Cosma Euphonium Concerto. Steven Mead with The Fairey Band conducted by Howard Snell. CD Polyphonic label Number QPRL 217D.
3. Finalé Giocoso from the Cosma Euphonium Concerto. David Childs with The Cory Band conducted by Robert Childs. CD SP&S/Doyen label Number DOY CD262.
4. The Quiet Heart -June Collin. Boscombe Salvation Army Band conducted by Howard Evans. CD SP&S label Number SPS 283 CD.

In addition to these recordings John has recently signed publishing contracts with Kirklees Music for two of his original works: *'Sonata for Tuba and Piano'* which, it is anticipated, will be included in the syllabus of the ABRSM Tuba examinations. The other, original piece for contesting bands *'The Well of Eternity'*, a set of variations on the hymn tune *'Abbot's Leigh'* - will be presented into the European contesting arena.

As can be observed from a list of his work, it is only comparatively recently that writing has become more and more of an earnest pursuit of music making in composition as much as performing and it was in 2007 that John gained his Master of Arts degree in composition from Salford University under the tutelage of Professor Peter Graham and in 2010 the degree of Doctor of Philosophy also from Salford University with composition as his discipline.

MERRITT, HENRI

Henry Merritt is one of nine children on a typical Salvation Army immigrant family. His father James was a 46-year-old shepherd, when he with his wife and nine children immigranted to Canada. Originally Methodists, James and Annie Merritt joined the Salvation Army in 1881. James played cornet in the Petersfield Corps Band (England) for 26 years before bringing his family to Winnipeg in 1907. James and his five sons, James Jr., Benjamin, Henry, William and Percy, all became bandmasters, made outstanding contributions to Salvation Army banding as instrumentalists and composers. James and Benjamin also became Salvation Army officers. James and Annie Merritt's legacy is now in its 13th decade and fifth generation of Salvationist musicians.

Important composition

Ever Near (GS1160) 1939

MERRITT, JAMES

James Merritt was the brother of Henri (above).

Important compositions

Christmas Reverie (FS087) 1933, The Canadian (FS76) 1932

MERRITT, PERCY

Percy was the brother of Henri and James (above).

While visiting Cariboo Hill Temple, probably better known as Vancouver Citadel, in British Columbia, Canada with the Canadian Staff Band, I met their Bandmaster, Dave Michel, who is also the author of the book 'Symphony in Brass, the History of the Cariboo Hill Temple Band', which was released just prior to his emigration to Indonesia to be headmaster of a school. It was through his book that I discovered something about another musical hero, the composer Percy Merritt, whose son is the trombone virtuoso, Robert Merritt, long-time Principal Trombone with the Canadian Staff Band, under Norman Bearcroft and Robert Redhead (and also, for a short time, under Brian Burditt). The music of Percy Merritt has always fascinated me. Although his output was not immense, his works have been invaluable to me. In Dave Michel's book, I learnt that Dave was married to a grand-daughter of Henry Merritt, one of the five very musical Merritt brothers. They all originated from Winnipeg, where they were part of the famous and illustrious Winnipeg Citadel Band, early in the previous century. The five Merritt brothers started their Canadian experiences in Winnipeg. The five were: James Merritt – composer, amongst other works, of the well-known festival march *'The Canadian',* he became a Salvation Army Officer and was stationed in Vancouver. He was actually Bandmaster at Vancouver Citadel for one year. William and Percy Merritt eventually settled in Toronto. Benjamin Merritt moved to the USA where he became a member of the Chicago Staff Band. Henry Merritt became Bandmaster of the Winnipeg Citadel Band which was arguably the finest SA band in North America during the 1930s. Henry's youngest son was William Merritt, who became an SA Officer and is the father-in-law of Bandmaster Dave Michel.

As I said, for a very long time I have been impressed by the music of Percy Merritt. Although his brother, James, is probably better known, mainly because of *'The Canadian',* it was Percy who took my attention. He is probably mainly known for his march *'Sword and Shield',* but it is through the Canadian Staff Band's recording of his brilliant march 'The Golden West' that he got my utmost interest.

Percy F. Merritt was born January 25, 1899, in Petersfield, England, and emigrated to Canada in 1911. One of nine children, Percy and his family augmented the large musical forces of the so-called 'Mother Corps of the West' - Winnipeg Citadel, one of the most legendary Corps in Canadian Salvation Army history. As one of its earliest Young People's Band Members, he was soon called into the Senior Band because of the serious depletion caused by the First World War. He developed as a euphonium soloist along with his musical brothers, Colonel James, Henry, William (Bill) and Captain Ben, who all assumed leadership in Army circles in Canada and the USA. In 1922, Percy met Jean Armstrong, a Girl Guard, Songster and Sunday School teacher at the Corps. They were married in 1924. In August of that year, Percy visited Toronto as euphonium soloist with the Winnipeg Citadel Band. They were to be the only Salvation Army band to participate in the official opening of the annual Canadian National Exhibition.

Later, while touring Canada and the US, Percy helped produce one of the Salvation Army's first classic band recordings in Canada. During these years Percy also achieved fame as composer and arranger of many popular marches and selections, including *'Winnipeg Citadel,' 'The Golden West,' 'Dovercourt Citadel,' 'Sword and Shield'* and the fantasia *'Sunshine.'* As Songster Leader, his male-voice arrangements of *'The Lord's Prayer'* and *'Onward, Christian Soldiers'* still remain in the repertoire, mainly because of his expertise in vocal writing. During the following decades he undertook many periods of leadership in the first Music Camps in both Western and Eastern Canada. Moving to Toronto in 1939, Percy became a member of

Dovercourt Citadel Band, serving in similar leadership capacities until becoming the Territorial Band Inspector. In this appointment he gave unstintingly of his talent in building up post-war banding throughout the territory. This was followed by a period of leadership in the composite band formed for the production of the then Major Arnold Brown's renowned radio series 'This Is My Story.'

'Perce' Merritt, as he was affectionately known, built up an outstanding record of service for God and the Salvation Army that will be gratefully remembered by the Army's whole musical world. Although he officially retired in 1961, he maintained his interest and involvement in Salvation Army music at the new Etobicoke Temple Corps, where he eventually retired as Deputy Bandmaster. He also assisted in the Toronto Public Relations Department. Deputy Bandmaster Percy Frederick Merritt (by then retired as active bandsman) was Promoted to Glory on August 29, 1974 at the age of 75.

From 'Play the Music, Play!' by Colonel Brindley Boon (Campfield Press, St. Albans, 1966), p. 58-*59 'The Merritt family is unique in Canadian musical history. Colonel James Merritt is remembered for such compositions as 'The Canadian.' 'A Christmas Reverie' and 'Lift Up the Banner.' Bandmaster Henry Merritt served with distinction at Winnipeg Citadel for many years until his promotion to Glory in 1946. Deputy Bandmaster Percy Merritt of Winnipeg Citadel and Dovercourt Citadel, Toronto, is the writer of several band pieces, including the marches named after the two Canadian Corps mentioned above. William was Bandmaster at Dovercourt for some time, following Colonel Bramwell Coles in that appointment, and Benjamin was a senior-captain and a member of the Chicago Staff Band at the time of his passing in 1958.'*

Important compositions

The Golden West (GS1117) 1936, Sword and Shield (TS0112) 1928, Dovercourt Citadel (GS1229) 1943, Winnipeg Citadel (GS1008) 1929

MEYER, DONALD

This brief introduction provides what is quite probably the best and most appropriate segue into a much appreciated (albeit frankly humbling) invitation to contribute to your biographical anthology in which the life and work (such as there is) of musician/composer Donald Meyer (July 9, 1950) may perhaps be (though of dubious merit) graciously included.

Fact is, the most remarkable quality of Don's compositional efforts is the non-existence of virtually any work of significance! This is of particular import with regard to not only his many compositions finished or un-finished, abandoned or neglected (whether by himself or by those for whom they were [to have been] penned, but those as yet un-begun (or, not 'actualized'). And it is precisely the impetus and essential substance of this ostensibly negative attribute that lends credibility to his ['applied'] musicianship and/or [absence of] accomplished productivity.

Chronologically speaking: From his precocious childhood E-Flat Alto Horn playing at age 7 in his [Aurora, IL USA] Corps Senior Band and Central Territorial Music Congress solo debut (age 10) through his joining the Chicago Staff Band as Principal Euphonium [and accomplished soloist]; and his local experience as a professional Bass Trombonist in the Metropolitan Chicago area, he was primarily self-taught. That is, with the exception of his truncated college education (The American Conservatory of Music--Irwin Fischer [a pupil of Bela Bartok, Zoltan Kodaly and Nadia Boulanger; Chicago Symphony Organist for 22 years] his music theory mentor) and private study with Chicago Symphony brass section members Edward Kleinhammer [Bass Trombone]; Arnold Jacobs [Tuba]; Frank Crisafulli [2nd Trombone]; Charles Geyer [Assistant Principal Trumpet]; Norman Schweikert [3rd Horn]; Dale Clevenger [Principal Horn]; Ray Still [Principal Oboe]; and Jay Friedman [Principal Trombone].

While briefly in Boston, Mass., Don also had some lessons with John Coffey [former Principal Trombone, BSO]. His compositional instruction (likewise self-initiated) had included occasional coaching sessions with Irwin Fischer, Bruce VanderValk, William Ferris and Art Lauer.

However, Donald's predictably inevitable frustration and disillusionment with his short-lived musical 'career' developed, not for a deficit of any inherent self-confidence, abject discouragement, nor even his justifiable disgust of 'politics' and similarly rational repulse-driven contempt for institutionalized anti-individuality, but rather was, and is to this day, attributable to his ingrained evangelical Christian orientation and family-Salvation Army/upbringing-influence: '*That which you love, live and are -- per se -- are all worthless; it is only [in] the afterlife that [where] when eternal meaning and genuine purpose exist.*' (See Phil.1:21)

Important compositions

Grateful Joy, Herald of Christ, Earnest Hope, Heavenly Eden, Anchor Brigade

METCALF, KEVIN

Major Kevin Metcalf (6 December 1953, Sault Ste. Marie, Ontario, Canada) joined MAGA in 2007 as the 'Secretary for Music and Gospel Arts'. Kevin brings a long history of music ministry and degrees in theological studies. He has been a member of the Canadian Staff Band for a considerable time, and still is one of the band's cornet soloists.

He grew up attending the Steelton Corps in Sault Ste. Marie. His father was the Sergeant-Major and Kevin would go with him to the Sunday evening open-air meetings and stand beside the cornet players. He couldn't wait for his chance to join the Young People's Band. Then, at the age of seven, Kevin finally got his chance, and it has been a great journey ever since. Banding has taken him to places like Holland, Germany, Switzerland, Italy, United Kingdom, United States, Brazil, Australia and New Zealand. He started writing arrangements after he became a corps officer. His Young People's Band didn't have any appropriate music to play so he began writing things for them. Like most Salvation Army writers he usually only write something when he has to, when he has been asked to do it, or when there is a need for something that doesn't already exist. He never had time to sit down and write a big epic for some imaginary 'ideal' band. So in this way Kevin has written a lot of music for beginners and for Young People's Bands, a lot of congregational song accompaniments, some cornet solos for himself to play, as well as a few marches and selections.

Important compositions

The Power of your Love (m/s), Mary, did you know? (m/s)

MILLARD, ARTHUR WILLIAM

Arthur William Millard was born on 18th December 1888 in Invergargill as youngest son of pioneer Invercargill Salvationist, Bob. He only attended primary school because father Bob was killed in a saw mill accident. Arthur became a bandsman at Dundedin North Corps at fifteen. He was trained as a boot repairer, a trade which he returned to and retired at seventy six. He also worked as a pastry cook and tram driver. Worked for store W. Harris and Son, managing the Dundedin store and other during WWII. He moved to Palmerston North in 1944 because his childern had married and moved to the North Island.

Musically Millard was self-taught: 'Ebenezer Prout's Harmony' and 'Analytical Key to Harmony' were important volumes. He led a family orchestra (days before radio/tv) of 3 violins, viola, 'cello, saxophone, cornet and piano. He was a fan of of the music and scores of Haydn, Mozart and Beethoven. Some unpublished songs bear a resemblance to Schubert. He wrote much vocal music with wide-ranging texts, including those by his wife, Janet Rose. Millard was a competant organist and would compose at the keyboard. Before his move to Palmerston North he was Bandmaster of Dunedin Citadel Band for 20 years.

He wrote much music for the band and was encouraged by Wellington South Band (bandmaster Dean Goffin) and Palmerston North Band (bandmaster Harrison Millard [son]). Much of Millard's music was unpublished. It was written for special occasions or tours, especially tableaux at the Dunedin corps. In 1953 he was awarded £3 second prize for a march in a competition to celebrate the Salvation Army's 70th New Zealand anniversary (the first prize went to Herbert Rive's *'Spirit of Joy'* which became General Series 1441). He was appointed Divisional Bandmaster and encouraged band music making in small corps in the southern North Island. Millard was familar with and wrote to Henry and Dean Goffin, and Tom Rive. He was a quiet and unassuming man who accepted criticism and would have held no grudge concerning the 'editing' of scores sent to IMED. For example, on 12 October 1956 Millard's selection *'Pardoning Grace'* was approved for publication by IMED but on 31 October Albert Jakeway wrote to Millard expressing the desire to delete the last 10 bars because he felt the composition was too long.

By February 1960 the piece had not been published and Millard wrote to the new IMED head, Charles Skinner, wanting to know what the delay was and Skinner replied apologising for the delay and expressing doubts as to whether it would now be published. The piece was not published by IMED but it was performed on at least 2 occasions in manuscript in New Zealand. Millard had submitted a number of pieces to IMED during the 1940s, none of which were published (*'Dunedin Citadel', 'Beautiful Stream', Maori Farewell Songs'*). The Salvation Army's IMED did publish 5 pieces by Millard, and the New Zealand Brass Band Journal a further 2. Millard had a song, *'Hark, tis the Master's Call',* transcribed by Col. Fred Hawkes for brass.

Millard's first piece was the Festival Series meditation *'Hursley'*. It's the first to have the instruction restricting Festival Series music to festivals, not normal meetings. Top shelf piece first up for the boot repairer.

Millard did not use a 'formula' to write his music. It has a rich harmonic palette and his scoring combinations are not 'safe'. Although he employed the standard forms he composed into them contrapuntal and harmonic complexities which made his music stand apart from that of his contemporaries, Scotney and H Goffin. He was Promoted to Glory on 26th December 1965 in Palmerston North in New Zealand.

Important composition

Hursley (FS27) 1926, The Timaru March (GS1025) 1931, Palmerston North (GS1446) 1957

MILLER, ANDREW STEWART

Commissioner Andrew Stewart Miller, was a former National Commander of the Salvation Army in the United States of America. He was born on October 14, 1923 and his parents were Ralph and Martha Miller in Roselle Park, N.J. Andy, as he was known, was a fourth generation Salvationist. His great-grandfather heard William Booth, the Founder of the Salvation Army preaching at an open air meeting in London and wanted to join the Army. As a young boy, Andy displayed his gift of persuasion and sales. His corps officer asked young Andy to go out and find someone to bring to Sunday school. So he went out and found a friend, Petie. Because of Andy, Petie became a Salvationist until he was Promoted to Glory. On February 20, 1941, only seventeen years old, Andy gave his life to Christ. While attending Asbury College, he felt called to officership and in 1942, Andy entered the New York Training College as a member of the Valiant session from the Newark, N.J. Corps. He married Lieutenant Joan Hackworth in 1946 and together they served at various corps, divisional and territorial appointments in the USA Eastern, Central and Southern Territories, including Territorial Commender of USA South and eventually National Commander in 1986. Commissioner Andrew Stewart Miller was Promoted to Glory on January 19, 2011.

Important composition

Create in me a Clean heart (AE200522) 2005, Fanfare Prelude – To God be the Glory (AE200431) 2004

MILLS, DAVID

David Mills was born in Vancouver's Grace Hospital in 1965. His father was an avid Salvation Army bandsman (cornet) and bandmaster, and his mother was a talented vocalist and pianist (her father was Commissioner Leslie Pindred). He comes from a long line of Salvationists (5th generation). David's father taught him to play the cornet at seven, and his mother taught him piano at five. He continued with formal lessons for many years and recall writing his first song at 10 years old. After graduation, he started writing secular music, and played in many rock bands which did this professionally for a time, touring and playing around western Canada. David has been a member of the Cariboo Hill Temple Band for many years, including being their principal cornet. His music is recorded by several bands, including his own corps band, as well as the Canadian Staff Band of the Salvation Army. In 2005 the Canadian Staff Band visited Cariboo Hill Temple as part of their '2005 Western Tour'. During one of their concerts here David got the opportunity to play with this famous band, which had several of his compositions on the repertoire.

In the 1990's, David played in the Christian rock band 'Erasmus'. They made several recordings, and performed at many events across Canada and up and down the west coast (from Alaska to Los Angeles), mostly at youth events, including these by the Salvation Army. In his mid-20's, he went to University to get his Bachelor of Music (Major in trumpet performance, minor in theatre tech) and then his Bachelor of Education.

He then began his teaching career (1997). David has taught in the public and private school systems, and havs taught band, choir, and jazz courses as well. He now has a very successful school music program, and has won several awards in the past few years. Since acquiring a teaching partner 3 years ago, he now specializes in concert bands and jazz bands (at present, 6 concert bands and 3 jazz bands).

David's musical influences were first his parents and family, and then his church (the Salvation Army Vancouver Temple, now Cariboo Hill Temple). *'I can't remember a time when music was not a big factor and influence in my life'* he says. He also recalls playing cornet in the Young People's Band, and then moving up to the senior band when he was 14. In his early 20's he started to really listen to the music he was playing, and started to study scores, and then began writing, or more accurately - arranging.

He has done several transcriptions for brass band (i.e. *'Jupiter'* [from Holst's The Planets], the entire *'Nutcracker Suite'* (still unplayed by any bands!). But many of his arrangements have been new (and old) praise & worship songs. He tries to keep most of his works playable for bands of 'average abilities' and always strive to give every section of the band a moment to shine in everything he write.

He is also a lover of the percussion section, and will continue to write music that keeps percussions (and audiences) engaged. His output contains an average of about 4-6 works per year, sometimes more, sometime less. David has always been a very busy person within the Salvation Army in Vancouver, with responsibility for a diversity of musical groups, including leading the junior and senior bands, and a 10 year deputy bandmastership.

From a professional point of view David works as a Music Director at R.E. Mountain Secondary. The music program is under his direction, and has seen tremendous growth under his leadership. There are currently 4 concert bands, 3 jazz bands, and 5 choirs. There is also a part-time percussion ensemble, woodwind choir, and a brass band!

Since David's arrival at the school in 2003, R.E. Mountain's music program has been very active performing many concerts both in the community and across British Columbia. They regularly attend numerous music festivals, with many of the groups receiving gold & superior awards. The senior ensembles have also been invited to take part at *'Musicfest Canada'*. The Senior Jazz Band recently was a finalist at Surrey's Envision Jazz Festival and performed in the showcase concert. Most of these members also perform in the Senior Concert Band.

David Mills is the director of bands and head of the Fine Arts Department at R.E. Mountain Secondary. He earned his Bachelor of Education and his Bachelor of Music at the University of British Columbia, specializing in trumpet performance. Coming from a long family line of conductors, David Mills has taught bands of all levels for over 22 years, and has performed and recorded with a variety of bands over the years as a trumpet soloist. As a composer and arranger of band music, his compositions (and numerous commissions) have been recorded and performed by many fine bands around the world. In 2002 David was chosen to attend a composer's symposium in Asbury, Kentucky, where he worked with James Curnow, William Himes, and Ron Holz (all three noted Salvationist composers).

Important composition

A Quiet Place (m/s), Victory in Jesus (m/s), Western Fantasy (Maple Leaf Brass 9)

MILLWARD, CLIFFORD

A fine cornet soloist, Millward studied trumpet at the Cincinnati Conservatory. While serving as cornet soloist with the West Point Academy Band he also played with the New York Staff Band under Richard Holz. At that same time he studied composition with Erik Leidzén, his one publication in Salvation Army journals the result of that study. After military service, he settled in the Salt Lake City area as a music teacher in the public schools. In retirement he is still active as a composer, and until recently led a fine community wind band in Salt Lake City, Utah.

Important compositions

March - Land of Promise (AJ0049) 1960

MITCHELL, CHARLES HERBERT

Commissioner Charles Herbert Mitchell, born on 10 March 1893, was converted as a boy in a memorial service for Queen Victoria at Wood Green. Entering the work from Clapton Congress Hall in 1915, he served at Poplar and Leyton Citadel Corps, and in 1917 he was appointed to the International Training Garrison. Fifteen months later he was transferred to International Headquarters to work for General Bramwell Booth in the Secretary's Department and later served in the Accountant's Department. Realizing a call to missionary service, he sailed for India in 1920. He served there for 27 years in financial assignments of increasing responsibility and importance. To this was added the Editorship of the monthly English-language 'War Cry'. In 1934 he was appointed International Auditor in Poona, entailing travel throughout India, Burma and Ceylon, conducting audits and inspections and engaged in soul-saving campaigns. Whilst serving in Lahore, he then Adjutant Mitchell married Ensign Klara Muskaug in 1927. She had become an officer from Mysen Corps in Norway in 1919. In 1947 the Commissioner returned to London to be the Assistant Finance Secretary at International Headquarters and took up assignments as Chief Accountant (1951) and Finance Secretary (1952). In 1956 he became the Chancellor of the Exchequer and from this appointment he retired with his wife, from active service in 1961.

Charles Herbert Mitchell's interest and talents have extended to music and he has more than thirty-five published compositions, both vocal and instrumental, to his credit. His last composition was published in the July 1979 issue of 'The Musical Salvationist'. He was Promoted to Glory only a few months later on 4 September 1979.

In celebration of his work and stay in India he wrote a march called *'Poona'* found in the Second Series Band Journal No.401, published in April 1947.

Important compositions

Melodies from India (TS0379) 1945, Our Flag (US0028) 1960

MITCHELL, HUBERT

Hubert (born in 1914) wrote a new melody for *'He Giveth More Grace'*, in the 1960s, which was later used by James Curnow in the American Festival Series publication. He was not a Salvationist but as his melody is so well known within the use of churches and the Salvation Army he is significant enough to include here.

Hubert was conducting meetings in a church and was in the pastor's study. He saw the poem pinned to a bulletin board. He took it down and started humming a tune to the poem as he walked through the empty sanctuary. He than put it on paper and the rest is history as the say. He also spent a great deal of his life in India.

Important composition

He Giveth More Grace

MORGAN, DAVID

With a family background in The Salvation Army, brass banding is well and truly in David's blood. Born in Kidderminster, Worcestershire in 1982, David has played euphonium, trombone and percussion with Worcestershire Youth Brass Band, Stourport on Severn Brass Band, and The Staffordshire Band.

Important composition

Joshua! (US0228) 1998

MORGAN, J. HAROLD

Harold was bandmaster of the Sydney Congress Hall. He was born in the United Kingdom and immigrated in 1924 to Australia. Prior to his bandmastership of the Sydney Congress Hall Band he was bandmaster of the Lambton Corps Band in New South Wales, Australia. He had to honours of taking the SCHB over from colleague composer Harold Scotney, this happened in 1941 and eleven years later he took the band on their first overseas tour to New Zealand. He became Eastern Territorial Bandmaster in 1956 and held this position until 1967. He awarded with the Order of the Founder in 1981.

Important compositions

Joyful Praise (GS1037) 1931, Liberty (GS1416) 1955, Under the Flag (TS0265) 1938

MORRISON, DON(ALD)

Don Morrison was a contemporary of Derek Smith, noted cornet soloist and former Bandmaster of the New York Staff Band and of course father of world renowned trumpeter Philip Smith. They were both in the Young People's Band at Hendon, England. Towards the end of the 1930's a Young People's Band had developed and was being recognised as a youth group capable of playing the best-published Army music of the day. Sidney Smith (father of former New York Staff Bandmaster Derek Smith) was the greatly respected leader and his group of young people included more than one embryo 'name' in Brass Banding terms both within and outside the Salvation Army. Sidney's son Derek, Roland and John Cobb, the Morrison brothers, Don and Stuart, were amongst them. Don played the Euphonium in the Young People's Band and occasionally the accordion. The outstanding leadership of Bandmaster Fred H. Cobb continued until his retirement in 1950 when he handed over responsibility to Don Morrison who led the band on a number of tours to Europe with the band playing at a high standard. Don Morrison was a former member of the Internernational Staff Band (around 1938 he joined the ISB), next to his duties with the Hendon Citadel Band. In the ISB he held the position of second horn for a while but also soloed on the piano-accordeon. Don unfortunately then left Hendon Citadel Band and took over the John Laing (Hendon) town band which became a popular concert band on platform as well as Radio and TV, often playing his own arrangements. In later times Don retired to Eastbourne Citadel Corps on the South Coast, where he used his piano playing to the enjoyment of retired people and visitors at the Eastbourne Corps. Don passed away in Eastbourne around the turn of the millennium.

Donald Morrison of Hendon, this talented piano-accordionist of but fourteen years of age, owes much of his success to 'tips' received from the late Bandmaster John Dockray. He holds five certificates for pianoforte and two for theory of music from the Royal College of Music, and plays solo euphonium in Hendon Young People's Band. Amongst the many visits he has paid to Corps, both in and out of London, are those to Clapton Congress Hall, Regent Hall, Battersea (United Festival in Town Hall), Barking, Luton Citadel, Wood Green Citadel, Penge, Ilford, Balham, Hastings Citadel, and Wellingborough. He has also played to the Spanish refugee children. ('The Musician' 1-1-1938)

Important compositions

Consecration (GS1919) 1996, The Day of the Cross (GS1880) 1992

MOTT, CHARLES BERTRAM

Charles Mott was born in 1904 and died in 1976. He was a musical prodigy as a child and composed music for the Salvation Army and for contesting bands throughout his life. He became the Bandmaster at Cambridge Citadel Corps at the age of 18 and continued for about 25 years in that capacity. He wrote everything by hand and often in 'Indian ink', so that the manuscripts could be used outdoors.

The most famous story about him that is remembered is that he went to the Band Contest at Crystal Palace on a Saturday, heard the tune *'Silver Hill'* played there that evening (this was prior to it's publication in the tune book) and was so taken with the tune that he arrived home at about 11.30 pm, sat down and arranged the tune for full band and took it to the open-air meeting the following morning and the Cambridge Citadel Band played it! His father, Charles Mott often wrote poetry to his son's manuscripts and some of these songs were also published by the the Salvation Army in the 1920's. The heritage of Charles Bertram exists in his three sons, two of whom were band conductors, a grandson who is also a band conductor, and a great grandson who plays cornet in the Coldstream Guards Band

C.B. stands for Charles Bertram, his christian names and in fact the name Charles has been carried by the first-born male child for 7 generations.

It is known that he wrote a march called *'En Avant' ('Forward')* in tribute to the French Salvation Army. He submitted it to the Salvation Army, they turned it down, and so he sent it to R. Smith & Co. who did publish it.

He also conducted the City of Cambridge Brass Band for a number of years after retiring from the Salvation Army band. His music was all-important to him, everything else in his life was sacrificed to that. I dare to say his work, his family and everything else beside. He gained the A.L.C.M. diploma for pianoforte at the age of 18 and remained a great pianist till his death and was able to play extempore on any given tune.

'Regrettably he did not live to see me (Major John Mott) as the National Bandmaster nor as the Bandmaster of the Household Troops Band....I think that even he might have shared a little pride in that'.

Important compositions

Blessedly saved (GS0958) 1926, Cambridge Citadel (GS1632) 1972

MOUNTAIN, HERBERT ARTHUR

Nearly forty-eight years ago four year old Herbert Arthur Mountain was brought with his brother James, by their parents, George and Mary Mountain (Mary was once Lieutenant Mary Brice), from Keighley, Herbert's birthplace, to Sheffield, where George had secured a job in a steel works. All linked up with the Citadel Corps. Herbert loved The Army and he loved music. When his father brought home a cornet and a baritone, both the worse for wear, he was delighted. Soon he was playing the baritone, while James played the cornet (James Mountain has continued to play the cornet throughout his life. He became the Young People's Band Leader at Sheffield Citadel and has instructed scores of boys in the musical art). Soon too, Herbert found that 'making parts fit' came naturally to him and he was arranging music for himself, his brother and other boys to play. When his family's stay in Sheffield was broken by two years' residence in Royton, Lancs. Herbert, then twelve, and his brother played in the Senior Band and the Band played tunes arranged by Herbert. The young lad even sent an original tune to the Army's Music Editorial Department, but it was returned.

Back at Sheffield, young Herbert made rapid progress as a trombonist in the Sheffield Citadel Band. He made progress in another direction too. In the Corps was a bonnie, golden-haired girl who was always ready for a bit of fun. Jessie Gilberthorpe had, moreover, a natural gift for verse. If the girls in the millinery workrooms where she earned her daily bread grew tired of the songs given by sea-side Pierrots wintering inland, she supply fresh words for them to sing. After her conversion she realized that her talent could be put to a better use. She wrote verses inviting sinners to Jesus and gave them to Herbert Mountain, who set the words to music. The young couple sent the song to the Army's Music Editorial Department and it appeared in 'The Musical Salvationist' for June, 1919 under the title *'Come and be Saved'.* It seemed appropriate that the two who could so complement each other's gifts should share the loveliest things of life and, in August 1920, Herbert and Jessie were married. Herbert was by this time the Deputy Bandmaster of the Sheffield Citadel Band.

Two and a half years later a baby girl arrived to enrich the young couple's home and increase their happiness. In December 1921, Herbert was made Bandmaster of the Sheffield Citadel Band, on Jessie's birthday! Herbert Mountain was now living a full and interesting life. His first band march, *'Faithful Warriors',* had been published when the Second Series Journal was introduced in 1922 and his composing gave him a satisfying form of self-expression. His home was not only a happy retreat for himself but a social centre. Never a Sunday passed without at least one Salvationist friend coming to tea. It is not surprising that later he built an air varié on the tune *'Love at Home'.* Further, his Band gave him a contact with men whose company he enjoyed and an avenue of service for God which taxed his fighting faith to the utmost. *'Any one has to have a fighting faith to be a Bandmaster for twenty-five years',* he said. Herbert Mountain had high standards for Army banding. The Sheffield Bandsmen were required to give, and gave, a minimum service of outdoor and indoor Meetings on Saturday night, three indoor and outdoor Meetings on Sunday, outdoor and indoor Meetings on Monday night (in full uniform) and band practice. Their music was their hobby. They had no time for the cinema and the football field lost its attractions.

Herbert had a secret for maintaining the fighting faith of his men, so that the exacting service was the natural outflow of their love to God. He instructed and conducted his Band from a box some nine inches high. That box often became a Mercy Seat. If the bandmaster knew that any bandsman was in spiritual difficulty –and he usually knew- he would say, quietly and simply, as the practice was closing; *'is there anyone who would care to kneel at the box?'* Oftentimes there was a response and Herbert has seen men crowding around the box to renew their dedications to God.

But the life of the Mountains has not all been sunshine. Clouds of adversity and sorrow sometimes darkened their sky. They needed the fighting faith that ran through their lives like a golden cord. Walking home with his wife from one of the Monday night Meetings, Herbert was not exactly gay at heart. Always he had had to struggle for his living. As a boy of twelve he had started work in a cotton mill. At one time he had followed the calling of William Booth as a pawnbroker's assistant. Now the carpet planning trade, to which he had been apprenticed, was, like others, hard hit by depression. That week for the first time in his life Herbert Mountain had stood in the queue at the Employment Exchange and drawn the 'dole'. Suddenly, as they walked, a man stopped them and respectfully requested a word with 'Mr. Mountain'. *'I am the secretary of the Sheffield Transport Band'*, he explained, *'it was unanimously agreed at our last band meeting that you should be asked to become our bandmaster. It will mean a good job in the Transport Offices. Will you entertain the offer?'* Herbert hesitated only a moment. *'If I were less happy than I am in the Salvation Army I might consider it'*, he replied in his soft Yorkshire brogue. Fighting faith had won. About this time too, Freda, always a frail child, became seriously ill. As Jessie watched through the long nights, waiting for the dawn to bring relief, she meditated on the promises of God which she had proved true in her life. Lines began to jostle rhythmically in her brain; *'Weeping may last till the night-time is past, But with the morning comes joy'*. She made a note of the lines as they came to her. Later Herbert set the words to music and *'Wonderful Promises'* – which won the first price in The Army's Music Competition in 1931- was the result. Incidentally, the Mountains' *'The Clarion Call'* won the second place in the competition, though one competitor was not allowed to carry off two prizes in the same section. Concern over Freda's health on a second occasion led to the creation of another popular vocal selection. This time Freda was down with diphtheria. Her life was in danger. Fighting faith not only saw the anxious parents through the crisis, but inspired Jessie to write the words of *'The Lord will provide'*, which begins *'The Lord will provide for the needs of His people.'* Freda recovered and has not looked back since, Jessie said.

Meanwhile, Herbert Mountain was turning out contributions to the Second Series Journal as he had time and opportunity. He judged the simple music of this Series to be within the scope of a self-taught composer whose only expenditure on lessons had been 12s. 6d. paid for evening classes to assure the already established composer that he was on the right lines. Then bandmaster and Mrs. George Marshall, of South Shields, visited Sheffield for the weekend and were guests of the Mountains. *'When are you going to give us a piece for the Festival Series?'* asked Marshall of Mountain. Herbert laughed. The Festival Series seemed to him right out of his league. Marshall must be joking! But the Shield's composer was not. He assured Herbert that it was as easy to write for the Festival Series as for the Second Series, and Herbert took his words to heart. Shortly afterward *'Hardy Norseman'* appeared in the Festival Series. It became immediately popular. *'Little Ship, 'Echoes from the Hills', 'Love at Home', 'Army on Parade'* and *'Coming to Christ'* all followed.

War, which in 1916 had snatched Herbert away from Jessie's side, struck him a further blow in 1941. Air raids on Sheffield affected Jessie's nerves. It became necessary to leave the area. Herbert said farewell to his band with a heavy heart. The door of his greatest opportunity for service to God seemed closed to him. He secured a job in Blackpool and took his family there. He was at once asked to become Band Instructor to the Blackpool Citadel Band and shortly afterward became the Bandmaster. Blackpool teemed with Air Force men. Hundreds of Salvationist-musicians were among them, and Herbert shared the concern of other Blackpool Citadel Salvationists for their welfare and sought to aid them. The band became a focal point for the men. Of the thousand of Salvationists who must have passed through the band during the war years, Herbert Mountain has the names of six hundred and fifty of them. A hundred of the men visited his home. He will not talk to you of what he did for them, but he will declare what a great inspiration the boys were to him. He was anxious that as many of them as possible should 'have a blow'. At the conclusion of one of the Service, men comprising the band that night would give up their instruments to bandsmen in the audience who had not been able to play. At once every man in the band rose to his feet. Keeping the half-dozen Blackpool bandsmen on key instruments, Herbert invited Salvationist-musicians in the audience to come forward. Sufficient volunteers were forthcoming to reconstitute almost complete the band. Only the G-tromboninst could not be duplicated, so Eddie Scotton resumed his seat. It would be difficult to say who enjoyed *'Witnesses for Jesus'* (one of Herbert's own selections) most, the conductor, the players or the congregation.

In 1945 the firm for which Herbert worked in Blackpool sold the business. Herbert had again to move. This time Boscombe benefitted by the family's transfer. They took with them not only their love of the Army, their delight in music and song, but a little son, Ian, born in Blackpool. Herbert Mountain, as bandmaster of Boscombe Citadel Band, is still demonstrating in his quiet way the effectiveness of his fighting faith.

'As far as can be ascertained, the first Salvation Army trombonist to broadcast a solo was Bandmaster Herbert A. Mountain of Sheffield, England, in December 1923'

(Source: 'The Musician', April 12, 1947)

Boscombe Band were indeed fortunate in securing as its new bandmaster, one of the Army's leading musicians. When commissioned on 22nd July, 1945, Herbert Mountain had already served 23 years in this capacity, firstly with the Sheffield Citadel Band, and then with the Blackpool Citadel Band. He bid a reluctant farewell to Blackpool in 1945 when the firm for whom he worked ceased trading, but he soon established himself in the house furnishing business at Bournemouth, partnering Retired Bandmaster E. Broughton of Salisbury. Born into a Salvationist family in Sheffield, Herbert Mountain had soon grown to love the Army and its music. At an early age he realized his ability to 'make parts fit' and before he was twelve had already arranged music. He made rapid progress as a trombone player, though later confessing that he seldom practiced. And in December 1923 became the first Salvation Army bandsman to broadcast a trombone solo. Upon his commissioning as Boscombe Bandmaster he was warmly received by the bandsmen, who greatly respected his reputation. Herbert Mountain had high standards for Army banding, music had to be the hobby that took over from all other. Regular attendances at all indoor and outdoor meetings was mandatory, a very good explanation had to be given for any absence. This well intentioned enthusiasm for putting the band first sometimes proved detrimental to the corps, bandsmen were not encouraged to join the songsters, and all but the Young People's Band Leader were forbidden to teach in Sunday school. It was also considered unworthy for a bandsman to stay at home with the children, this was the wife's responsibility.

Great things were expected of the band after his appointment and 'The Musician' reports of 1946, the National Secretary for Bands conducted a musical and spiritual weekend at Boscombe in February: *'The band (Mountain) numbering about 35 is in excellent form, and gave me some of the best playing I have heard since before the war. It has cultivated a very pleasing 'singing' tone and its future seems assured. The Band, practically at pre-war strength, has been revolutionized under bandmaster/ composer Herbert Mountain. It is reaching a standard of technique that will place it as one of the best in the South of England. The bandmaster seldom uses a score, even in the most intricate scoring, and it was a thrill to hear the correct interpretation'.*

A score was never used in public by Herbert Mountain, who apparently had difficulty in interpreting music directly from it. He preferred instead to take the score home and commit it to memory by playing it through on the piano 3 or 4 times.

MOUNTAIN, JESSIE (née GILBERTHORPE)

As a child, Jessie Gilberthorpe was a member of the junior singing brigade and young people's legion in Sheffield, and later became leader of a Bible class and founder member of the Sheffield Citadel Songsters. In 1920 she married Herbert Mountain, and later visited several corps with his musical party 'The Melody Makers'. In 1940 they moved to Blackpool Citadel. During the years 1945-1950 they lived in Boscombe before returning to Blackpool. She wrote a number of poems and songs, many of which were published in 'The Musical Salvationist', with music by her husband.

Important compositions

Indomitable (GS1344) 1951, Armee du Salut (FS145) 1947, Sheffield Citadel (GS1180) 1940, Stories of Galilee (FS0194) 1953

MOWAT, CHRISTOPHER

Former Salvationist from Chelmsford in the United Kingdom who was the son of an Anglican Clergyman. During the period 2000-2005 Christopher was Head of Brass and Percussion at RWCMD and before that Professor of Trombone at the Royal College of Music of the Trinity College in London. Christopher (MA (Cantab) LRAM) studied at Emmanuel College Cambridge and won second price in the Concours International d'Execution Musicale de Geneve. He has been principal trombone with some of the leading orchestras in the United Kingdom including the Halle Orchestra. He was a member of the world renowned brass ensemble of Philip Jones (the famous 'PJBE') for whom he also did many of the arrangements. When the PJBE was disbanded he became a member of its successor, the London Brass. Christopher was made an 'Honorary Fellow of the Royal Welsh College of Music & Drama' in 2008.

Important composition

Pastorale (FS332) 1970

MÜLLER, HANS

Hans Müller, was born in Basel and became a Bandsman of the Basel 1 Band of The Salvation Army. He served as Deputy Bandmaster under Bandmaster Paul Schiffmann. 1948 -1949 and graduated in conducting from the 'Konservatorium Basel'. He emigrated to Spain and was Promoted to Glory 2005.

Important compositions

Basle (TS0337) 1942, Grace (GS1324) 1949

MUNDAY, A

Bandmaster A. Munday, who has recently taken charge of Islington Citadel Band, is an old and experienced Army Bandsman. At one time he was Bandmaster at King's Cross, and was also for some years attached to Hastings 1 Corps. (The 'Bandsman and Songster', April 20, 1907)

Important compositions

Comrades, Arouse to the Call (GS0418) 1902, Possess My Soul (GS0410) 1901

MUNN, JONATHAN

Jonathan (23 June 1992) started composing at the age of 18 when he brought out a Christmas piece in 2010 called *'Christmas Spirituals'*. It was played at his Corps Young People's Band Open Christmas Concert and it went down very well. The reviews of the piece were so encouraging that Jonathan carried on writing. Jonathan, since writing *'Christmas Spirituals'* has composed around ten other works. Some of which are small ensemble works. One of the pieces he has written is a little piece called *'Redeeming Grace'*. This was written as a prayer for the people of Japan following the earthquake and devastating tsunami in March 2011. To him, this piece expresses that God, even through that difficult time, will always be there and that he will always love us.

Jonathan has been very lucky to have sat down with the likes of Kenneth Downie and Andrew Blyth to look through his works and to get some very encouraging tips and critisims. At such a young age, Jonathan has some very exciting times ahead with a couple of big pieces of music being worked on. He plays Euphonium with the Salvation Army Maidstone Citadel Band, as well as with the Union Brass which is comprised of five youngsters from the Maidstone Citadel Band.

Important compositions

Christmas Spirituals (m/s), In the Footsteps of Pilgrims (m/s)

MYLECHREEST, EDWARD

Edward Mylechreest was born 28th December 1991, in Ipswich in the United Kingdom to officer parents. As such he has been to corps all over the place, including Felixstowe, Nungead, Blackpool (UK), Camberwell (Melbourne, Australia), and Bournemouth (UK). He currently attends Birmingham Citadel (UK) whilst he is studying towards a music degree at the University of Birmingham. He started out, as all Young People's Band members do, on the Cornet, before moving onto trombone when he was twelve which he has stayed on ever since. Edward used to have Piano lessons when he was much younger, so had some basic keyboard skills too. His parents were a great musical influence to him, with Army and classical musical always being on in the house. He always loved film music, in particular that of John Williams. On a practical level, Young People's Band leaders, Bandmasters and music teachers along the way have all been great influences. Kenneth Downie and Andrew Blyth in particular have been incredibly helpful in terms of Edward's own compositional development, always happy to help look over some of the music he send in to Music Ministries Unit, and offering advice on how to improve. In terms of Salvation Army compositional inspiration, Edward loves the music of Leslie Condon and Ray Steadman-Allen, whilst the new compositions coming from Paul Sharman, Dean Jones, Steve Ponsford and Roger Trigg are all composers he takes a lot of inspiration from. Edward started composing in secondary school, as part of doing music as a subject, and at the same time he began writing music for the Young People's Band and the band at Boscombe

Citadel. He has written all sorts of pieces, from Unity series right up to General series, as a way of expressing his own faith and belief through music.

Important composition

Easter Jubilation (US392) 2012

NEEDHAM, PHIL

Achieved the rank of Commissioner in the Salvation Army, retiring as Territorial Commander in the USA South. Better known as a theologian and writer (graduate degrees from Princeton Theological Seminary, and Emory University), he was an excellent alto hornist in various Salvation Army bands. He has only one brass composition published, which took honours in the 1965 USA National Composition Contest.

Important composition

Selection - A Seeker's Prayer (AJ0070) 1966

NEVARD, E

One of the early composers (late 1800).

No further information could be retrieved about him.

Important composition

Jesus the conqueror (GS0278) 1895

NEWBIGGING, JOHN L.

Bandsman John L. Newbigging was the Euphonium player in the Leeds Burley Band in the same era as Harry Kirk and Peter Kirk. The Leeds Burley Corps was really only a small Corps, but it had some fine musicians. John was also an accomplished pianist and had a very musical family, with his wife, and two daughters who were each fine singers in their own right. The family often did 'specialling' together. His *'Joy'* composition did secure a place in the 1939 Band Music Competition.

Important composition

Joy (TS0323) 1941

NIEUWLAND, COR

He was Bandmaster of the Amsterdam Staff Band, before and after Major Maurice Cooper's tenure of the position, and former Head of the Music Department. However, little is known about the compositions of Brigadier Cor Nieuwland. It is well-known, however, that he compiled the last 'NB', the *Nederlandse Muziek Boek* or Dutch Music Book, the equivalent of the Band Tune Book but containing mainly Dutch songs. However, he also wrote at least a march called *'Blijdschap' ('Happiness')*. Furthermore, he wrote an Intrada on the *'Battle Hymn of the Republic'*, that saw its first performance at the Jaarsbeurshallen in Utrecht, in central Holland during a National Youth Congress of the Salvation Army. The 'Senior Band' of the Music Camp became the National Youth Band for this occasion. He is the uncle of current Amsterdam Staff Band Secretary Jan Nieuwland. Cor Nieuwland now lives in retirement in Leeuwarden, in the north of Holland.

Important compositions

March – Happiness (m/s), Intrada on 'Battle Hymn of the Republic' (m/s)

NOBLE, ANDREW FLETCHER

Andrew Noble was Deputy Bandmaster of the Sunderland Monkwearmouth Band of the Salvation Army and in charge of the band during the First World War. When leading the band during this time he wrote his best known work, the *'Wearmouth March'*. The odd item in this march is that the bass drum has a very unusual 'off the beat' line in the bass solo.

'The Musician' of 1939 says:

Bandsman Andrew Fletcher Noble, of Monkwearmouth, Sunderland, was first attracted to The Salvation Army as a young man, and consequently has given forty-one year's service as a Bandsman. His wife and family are also devoted Salvationists. His son, Robert, is the Deputy-Bandmaster, and is well known as a cornetist, he having for a time been the soloist in the Salvationist Publishing and Supplies Band. Bandsman Noble owes a big dept of gratitude to Divisional Bandmaster L. Halcrow, of South Shields, who gave him his first instrument to learn when he was Instructor to Monkwearmouth Band, and also to the late Jack Stobart, who was Bandmaster at that time. Young Andrew made such good progress that within a short time he was put on solo euphonium, which instrument he has played with credit until quite recently. He is now doing good service in the Band's splendid Bass section. During the war period he began to take a serious interest in composition which resluted in *'The Wearmouth March.'* He was also Bandmaster and Songster Leader in the days of the war.

When the Young People's Band was formed, our comrade was asked to write an easy march for it, thus the Second Series march *'Always Cheerful,'* came into existence. The trio was the first tune the boys learned to play. For about eighteen years Andrew Noble was Deputy to Bandmaster MacBeth, and whilst holding this position he played a great part in training a number of young men, some of whom have gained distinction as soloists.

Important compositions

Serve to save (TS0082) 1926, The Wearmouth March (GS0890) 1922

NOBLITT, TOM L.

American Tom Noblitt was Deputy Bandmaster of the Dallas Temple Band in Texas, United States of America. He is a graduate of the Southern Methodist University in Dallas where he was studying for his music degree. The son of officer parents, he has always had only small corps brass to associate with. He, however, has been largely influenced by the various Music Camps, both as a student and latterly as an instructor. The march *'Dallas Temple'* was his first to be published the Salvation Army.

Tom Noblitt went on to complete his PhD and became a noted American musicologist, especially in 16th-century, Renaissance period. He taught for years at the prestigious Indiana University School of Music.

The *'Fairest Lord Jesus'* hymn tune arrangement in the Salvation Army 'General Series' is a very interesting one as it shows Tom's interest in contrapuntal technique.

While Tom did not continue as a soldier, he did serve terms on the Advisory Board in Bloomington, IN. Tom would visit Atlanta Temple once or twice a year throughout the 1980's and 90's to see his father, Brigadier Tom Noblitt, who was a faithful soldier at

Atlanta Temple. The folk in Atlanta would see Tom at the corps during those visits and he expressed strong interest in the work of the music department, especially their publications and TMI.

Important compositions

Dalles Temple (TS0543) 1956, Fairest Lord Jesus (GS1455-1) 1958

NORBURY, KEVIN

Kevin Norbury was born on 17th July 1956 in England. He studied music at different universities, ending up with the qulifications of B.Mus, A.R.C.M., A.R.C.O., L.T.C.L. and P.G.C.E. He was a member of Chalk Farm Corps and served there as a bandsman and Corps pianist. Kevin was instructor at various schools of music of the Salvation Army in England. He mainly composes music for Brass Bands and Songsters and sometimes also arranges orchestral music. He plays piano, organ and every Brass instrument. Kevin emigrated to the United States of America and became a member of the New York Staff Band and their music department. After several years in the United States he moved on to Canada, where he still lives.

Important compositiosn

The Ransomed Army (FS456) 1987, Orwell Park (GS1788) 1985, Partita on 'St. Theodulph' (FS540) 1998, Variations on 'Maccabeus' (FS532) 1997.

NORDIN, HANS

Hans Nordin was born in Sweden. His parents were Salvation Army Officers. He played euphonium in the Stockholm 1 Citadel Band. After the consolidation of the Stockholm 2 and Stockholm 5 Corps, Hans became deputy Bandmaster of the new Vasa Corps, under Bandmaster Per Ohlsson. His music is published in the Swedish series of the Salvation Army. He was Promoted to Glory on 28th June 2007.

Important composition

Rhapsody on Swedish Folk Songs

NORRIS, F

A former Bandsman from Sydney, Australia. The piece *'The Army Spirit'* was his first published work.

Important composition

The Army Spirit (TS0317) 1941

NTOYA, KAPELA

Major Kapela Ntoya is a Salvation Army officer from the Democratic Republic of Congo. After completing his officer training he served as a corps officer, at Territorial Headquarters as Private Secretary to the Territorial Commander and later as Assistant Extension Training Officer. In 1996 he received an international appointment to be Assistant Principal of SALT College of Africa in Zimbabwe. After nearly six years in that appointment he returned to his home territory to serve as a university chaplain and then, three years later as Territorial Music and Creative Arts Secretary. He is currently Principal of SALT College of Africa in Zimbabwe. Married with four children he is in internationally published composer and has a BA degree in French and African Linguistics as well as a diploma in Theology (ThA). He is a member of the Salvation Army's International Doctrine Council.

Important compositions

A People of Power (TS1060) 1998, Kinshasa IV (TS1076) 1999

NUNN, GEOFFREY

One of the early composers (first half of 19th century).

No further information could be retrieved about him.

Important composition

Full Salvation Offered (GS0401) 1900

NUTTALL, RICHARD

Son of Richard Nuttal Sr, who was a butcher and Sarah Nuttall. Richard Jr, was born on 2nd April 1891 in Blackpool where his parents were Salvationists. Here he learnt to play the piano, euphonium and cornet. Richard had to spend the afternoon at the corps because it was too long a walk to go home between the morning and afternoon meeting, thus their mother brought along a meat pie and they ate at church each week. He became a bandsman in 1911 and later would become bandmaster of the Blackpool Citadel Band. During the First World War he served in France where he conducted the band at the hostel for service men in Rouen. After the war he became a Salvation Army officer and went to India in 1923 where he became known as 'the Happy Servant'. In India and Ceylon he was Divisional Commander, training officer, finance and property secretary. He was also an organist and and was taught by organist of St John's church in Blackpool. Richard has three tunes in the Band Tune Book – *'Nuttall'*, *'Sunshine'* and *'Love Divine'*. Also *'Wonderful Peace'*, *'I Gave my Life' and 'Love Slave' were of his hand.* One week before his death, the General, High Council and International Staff Band played *'Nuttall'* for the High Council at Royal Albert Hall. Brigadier Richard Nuttal was Promoted to Glory in Madras, India on 2 May 1946.

Important compositions

Blackpool No.II (GS0805) 1919, Consecrated Service (GS0858) 1920, Peep into India (2nd Series 956) 1926

NUTTALL, THOMAS AMBROSE

Thomas Ambrose Nuttall was born in Blackpool, on the 30th of April, 1886 and was Promoted to Glory on the 7th of June 1910. He was the eldest of seven children, born to Richard Sr and Sarah Nuttall and hence the older brother of Richard Jr, also described in this book. There were six boys and one girl. Both Thomas and William also played in the Blackpool Citadel Band and wrote Salvation Army music. Thomas was known as a great cornetist, he was, just like Richard, also an artist and had some fame for his pen and ink drawings. There was also a third brother, William Nuttall, who also wrote music, but which wasn't published within the Salvation Army band journals.

Important composition

The Blackpool March (GS0621) 1910

OGG, RAY

Bandmaster Ray Ogg was born of Salvationist parents, attended public schools in Illinois and received his early musical training in the corps of Peoria. In his late teens he moved to Chicago to become a member of the Chicago Staff Band where he spent sixteen years as trombone soloist, Deputy Bandmaster and eventually Bandmaster, which lasted only one year (1939-1940). For eight years he was on the faculty of the Central Music Institute, a development of the Territorial Music Camp of the Salvation Army in Chicago. He has composed numerous vocal and instrumental numbers, some of which have been published by The Salvation Army in the United States and Great Britain. Ray Ogg has been the Bandmaster of the Los Angeles Tabernacle Band (now Pasadena Tabernacle Band), and has seen its rise to a position of one of the most distinguished Salvation Army bands in the United States. He became known in wider circles for his famous march *'Rousseau'.*

Important compositions

Rousseau (GS1172), Chicago Temple

OKPEBHOLO, SHAWN

Born on March 28, 1981, Shawn began private composition study at age fourteen with James Curnow. He received a B.A. in music composition and musicology from Asbury College where he continued to study composition with James Curnow and Ronald Holz.

In 2010, Shawn joined the faculty of Wheaton College-Conservatory of Music as Assistant Professor of Theory and Composition. He previously taught at Union University, Northern Kentucky University and the University of Cincinnati, College-Conservatory of Music.

The music of Shawn E. Okpebholo has been performed all across the United States of America, and in Canada, Africa, Europe, and Asia. Shawn's musical education began at age eight at The Salvation Army in Lexington, Kentucky, where he and his family attended church. The free music lessons he received at The Salvation Army would spark his strong penchant for creating music—which would ultimately become his career. He received his B.A. in composition and music history from Asbury College and his M.M. and D.M.A. in composition and theory from the University of Cincinnati, College-Conservatory of Music—with additional study in film scoring at New York University. His primary teachers were James Curnow, Joel Hoffman, Ronald Holz, and Michael Fiday.

Shawn has received numerous commissions from noted soloists, universities and organizations since 2004. He was also one of eighteen featured composers in Volume IV of the book series, 'Composer's on Composing for Band,' edited by Mark Camphouse. In 2010, Dr. Shawn Okpebholo joined the faculty of Wheaton College-Conservatory of Music as Assistant Professor of Theory and Composition. He previously taught at Union University, Northern Kentucky University and the University of Cincinnati, College-Conservatory of Music. He currently lives in Wheaton, Illinois with his wife, Dorthy (a violist) and daughter Eva.

Important compositions

Ye Banks and Braes, Sovereign Pageantry

OLIPHANT, CELESTINE

Celestine Oliphant, born on April 25, 1863 in the Netherlands, died on April 13, 1941 in Italy. She was a song writer and composer, Commander of the Salvation Army, sister of Cornelia Booth and married in 1888 with Commander William Elwin Oliphant.

Her father was an aide in the Dutch army and later became Major in the Salvation Army. During a trip to England was Celestine in contact with the Salvation Army and she began working in the slums in different parts. Together with her husband, she was leader of the Salvation Army in Belgium and the Netherlands. Before the 1896-1901 was the leader of the Salvation Army in Sweden. They later became the leader of the Salvation Army in Germany, Switzerland and Italy. After retirement they settled in Italy.

Important compositions

All the waters of the Sea (GS0250) 1894, Oh, far whiter than the snow (GS0104) 1889

OLSSON, BERTIL

Bertil was born in 1949. He was a bandmaster of the Stockholm Vasa Band from 1974-1976. He took the music directors exam at the Royal College of Music in Stockholm where he also studied counterpoint with Valdemar Söderholm and conducting with Stig Westerberg and Siegfried Naumann.

Important composition

Sköna advent

OSBORNE, S.J.

One of the early composers (first half of 19th century).

No further information could be retrieved about him.

Important compositions

The Dartford March (GS0820) 1919

OSGOOD, DONALD

Donald Osgood was born 1931 to Salvation Army Officer parents in Wellington, Somerset England. He was a member of SP&S Band (Salvationist Publishing & Supplies) under Bandmaster Eric Ball. In 1949 he became the Bandmaster of the Southall Citadel Band and 1960 the Songster leader of the Southall Songsters. Donald Osgood served as Professor for Brass Band Orchestration of the Guildhall School of Music. As a talented composer and trombonist he had good authority in the Brass Band scene in and outside of The Salvation Army. He has got orders as Contestjuror and has served as Instructor and Leader in different Music-Schools and Music-Camps of The Salvation Army. He was Promoted to Glory 1981.

Important compositions

Balm in Gilead (FS389) 1978, Motondo (GS1481) 1959, Mountain Camp (TS782) 1975

OTWAY, HARRY T

American Harry Otway was a composer who gained recognition as composer in the beginning of the 20th century, around 1905, when he participated in International music competitions. In 1910 Lieutenant Harry Otway wrote one of the winning compositions entitled *'The Crown of Victory'*.

In 1942 the now Colonel Harry Otway, of The Salvation Army, came to The American Conservatory to study composition with Irwin. Harry Otway was Musical Director for the eleven Central States in the United States for the Salvation Army and in charge of their top music camp – The Central Music Institute (CMI) – at Wonderland Camp, Camp Lake, Wisconsin. For a short period (1926) he was also the bandmaster of the Chicago Staff Band.

Important composition

The Crowns of Glory (GS629) 1911

ÖSTBY, KLAUS

In 1904, a Norwegian officer, Klaus Östby, was summoned to take charge of the Music Department in Stockholm. This was a courageous decision by the Salvation Army at a time when serious political tension had brought Sweden and Norway to the brink of war; the controversy, however, was brought to a peaceful solution in the following year. Klaus Östby became a great success in his new homeland, where he remained until his retirement in 1930. Klaus Östby had also been a military musician. He was born in 1865 at Fredrikshald near the Swedish border in Southern Norway where he jouined the local regimental band. He was sent to Oslo, then called Christiana, to continue his musical training and was a pupil of such highly respected musicians as F.A. Reissiger and Ole Olsen. His studies aroused his interest in the works of the great masters, a fascination he retained for the rest of his life. During his stay in the Norwegian capital, Klaus Östby met the Salvation Army in 1890. Through the devoted interest of the officers of the Christiana 1 Corps (now Oslo Temple) he was guided to a personal Christian conviction and was soon engaged as a clarinet player in the corps band. After a short period at the primitive Training Garrison, he was commissioned as an officer and shortly afterwards became head of the new Music Department and Bandmaster of the newly established Norwegian Staff Band.

Very soon Klaus Östby began composing and arranging. On one of the Staff Band's tours in northern Norway's icy and stormy waters he wrote his famed Kabelvag March, claimed to be the first march composed in the Salvation Army. From the very outset, he made it a habit to start each day by composing a tune, just as a practice. Most of them never survived his critical scrutiny, while some were revised several times before being published. On his arrival in Sweden, Klaus Östby immediately took up the work began by Otto Landahl, his predecessor. One of his first tasks was to produce a standardized band journal. He worked fast. In only a few months he arranged 429 songs for six part band. He read all the proofs himself and had it all printed in a durable leather-bound volume, which was released in early 1906. Klaus Östby's band journal was welcomed with open arms and provided song accompaniment during half a century. Some arrangements have become classics and are still being used. Klaus Östby introduced several features that charmed bandsman and listeners alike, such as counter melodies, and embellishments, particularly in Bb valve trombone/euphonium part, and optional bass-solos in martial tunes.

Very early, Klaus Östby initiated a series of Festival music, 'Svensk Festmusik', containing marches, selections and song arrangements. Some of it was re-arranged from London produced series, but most of it was local material, the chief contributor being Klaus Östby himself. Next followed the arranging of songbook tunes for piano/organ harmonium or four part choir; it was published in 1907. Then came Favoritsanger, the Swedish counterpart of 'The Musical Salvationist' (a periodical publishing vocal music for choirs etc). He also produced and arranged material for the Staff Band and the Staff Songsters. His other duties included; extensive travelling to visit corps bands and string bands, arranging educational and inspirational councils for bandsmen and musical leaders, organizing musical activities and producing music for the annual congresses, and conducting choirs and bands at special meetings. Klaus Östby accomplished all this alone. He had no assistant and very little help with the deskwork. He **was** the Music Department!

While Klaus Östby was a profilic contributor to Svensk Festmusik and other publications, a number of his pieces were also published in international editions, including the *'Kabelvag March'* (GS1109), *'The Joly Salvationist'* (GS717), *'To the Land of Glory'* (FS12), and *'Princethorpe'* (FS2), one of the first meditations composed in the Salvation Army. His style was truly Nordic and his music was very much different from anything else published by the SalvationistPublishing & Supplies in London, England. Klaus Östby was a close friend of Richard Slater, the 'Father of Salvation Army music'. Both were Wagner enthusiastic and exchanged views on this and various aspects of life and Army music through an extensive exchange of letters and personal contact. Klaus Östby visited London several times, often staying in Slater's home. At the International Congress in 1914, he conducted the Swedish Silver Band, a combination of 35 specially recruited members wearing tunics in the Swedish colours, blue and yellow. The band aroused much enthusiasm, partly because of its playing, partly because of the Sweden-produced instruments, which had a different sound compared to the British made ones.

When Klaus Östby retired in 1930, he moved back to his native Norway, but he continued his musical activities and studies to the end of his life. In the 1930's he acted as musical adviser to the Territorial Headquarters in Oslo. When his country was invaded by foreign troops in April 1940, he quitly escaped back to Sweden. He spent his final years at the Army residence for retired officers, being the only male among 14 lady officers. Klaus Östby was Promoted to Glory on 27th April 1945, in The Residence for retired Officers in Sweden just less than two weeks before his beloved Norway was liberated. His funeral took place in Stockholm with full battle honours in the presence of virtually all the bandsmen in the region, but his ashes rest in Norwegian soil.

Among not published band compositions are two major pieces, the overture in classical sonata form *'Feast in the Salvation Army'* (1926) and *'Passacaglia'* (1910). These two compositions together with 'To the Land of Glory' and 'Princethorpe' must be considered as some of the very first real compositions for band in the Salvation Army literature.

When Torgny Hanson in 1978 visited Eric Ball in his home, they had a discussion about Östby, especially his *'Passacaglia'*. He (Ball) admired Östby highly and said: *'Östby was 50 years ahead of the rest of us and instead of him sending his music to London for 'approving' we should have sent our music to him!'* According to Ray Steadman-Allen the *'Passacaglia'* has twice been on the table of the international music board but been considered to advanced and not useful for SA purposes!

Important compositions

The Jolly Salvationist (GS717) 1915, Princethorpe (FS02) 1923

OWEN, EDWARD

Very little is known about Edward Owen. He was born in the United Kingdom around 1890, and was a member of the Maesteg Citadel Corps.

Important compositions

The Kingly Crown (TS0722) 1970, Maesteg Citadel (GS1356) 1951

OXLEY, J

One of the early composers (late 1800).

No further information could be retrieved about him.

Important composition

Fully trusting in the battle's fray (GS0053-1) 1886, I'm happy day by day (GS0053-2) 1886, Sad and weary with thy sin (GS0100-2) 1888, When in the Darkness (GS0284) 1895

OZANNE, MAURICE

Born in the Salvation Army Mothers Hospital in East London on 7th June 1933 to serving Salvation Army officers who were stationed in Willesden Green at the time. Maurice had two elder brothers and later a sister and two younger brothers. (A third generation Salvationist). His first fifteen years were spent in and around London, so experienced the war first-hand, but his whole family came through safely.

His education started whilst a member of the Salvation Army at Upper Norwood, but much time was spent in air raid shelters, they moved to Sutton in Surrey and attended the Secondary School, but somehow managed to pass the exam for the County School. When living in Nunhead, South London, he attended Alleyn's School Dulwich, and finally Eastbourne Grammar School. Alleyn's School provided an introduction to non-Salvation Army music, sang in a Gilbert & Sullivan Opera produced at the school and had violin lessons, later moving on to Viola, which was the main instrument until leaving school.

All this time Salvation Army banding was ticking over, at Sutton, Nunhead, and Eastbourne. During National Service, Maurice was drafted into the regiment of the 4/7th Dragoon Guards and joined the band, becoming their cornet soloist.

In 1954 he entered the William Booth Memorial Training College, where again he was the end man in the Cadets band, before being appointed to several Corps. Altogether served about seven years as a Corps Officer and eight years in the International Music Editorial Department. As a late starter he had tried to write some band music, and must thank Brian Bowen for his encouragement, but it was as a member of the department, with Ray Steadman-Allen, Ray Bowes and Leslie Condon that some facility was gained.

In 1976 he gained a Trumpet Teaching Diploma with Guildhall School of music, gaining the highest marks, in honours, throughout the British Isles, gaining the Silver Medal, the highest given to and external student. Later, whilst a member of the department. He gained a conducting diploma with Trinity College London. (with a big thank you to the Regent Hall Band!).

During a long period outside the work Maurice had a somewhat chequered career, but enjoyed periods of peripatetic teaching with Berkshire and Hampshire County Councils, and at the latter was the conductor of the Southampton Brass Youth Band. More recently he was conductor of the Littlehampton Concert Band, for whom quite a bit of music was arranged, that resides in the filing cabinet together with many other arrangements made for specific occasions. Recently he wrote a march for a local British Legion band, which was accepted by a publisher in Switzerland. There are so many really talented composers around there is a reluctance to submit music that may not compare but writing music is something that is satisfying in itself. He is working on six short Christmas Crackers, and has a few ideas that may reach fruition one day. When time allows intend to look at some of the wind band arrangements and may transcribe for brass band. Recently he wrote a short march for Eastbourne Citadel 121st Anniversary, which after further edits may be suitable for publication.

Important composition

You know I love you (GS1803-1) 1968

PAINE, ANNIE

One of the early composers (late 1800). No further information could be retrieved about her. It is however quite significant that, especially in this era (19th Century), women composers had the power to come as far as their work becaming published.

Important composition

I Will Be Thine, Dear Lord (GS0355) 1898

PAINE, W

One of the early composers (late 1800).

No further information could be retrieved about him.

Important composition

Bleeding, Crying, Groaning, Dying (GS0187) 1892, Touch Me Again (GS0346) 1897

PALM, RUBY

Ruby Palm was born in Hannaford, north Dakota on January 14, 1922. From the moment her family moved to Anacondan, Montana and joined the Salvation Army, Ruby, aged five, attended the corps and participated in corps activities. Ruby entered the Training College out of Wenatchee, Washington. From the day of her commissioning as a member of the 'Steadfasts Session', June 1, 1942, the young probationary lieutenant's musical skills made her a valued asset to the Salvation Army. Her musical influence spread far beyond her corps appointments in Redlands, San Pedro, San Francisco Citadel and other corps. In 1950, after five years on the Southern California Divisional Headquarters staff, Captain Ruby Palm was married to Leonard Adams, an officer out of Penge Corps in London, England. In 1968 Ruby and her husband were assigned to duty in Vietnam for five months. On their return, Ruby assumed responsibility for the banding and music program of the Training School. A year later they became Divisional Leaders of the Alaska Division and in October 1970 they were appointed to Hong Kong, where Ruby became a member of the Hong Kong Staff Band. Another noted band she played in was the Los Angeles Congress Hall Band (eventually becoming the Pasadena Tabernacle Band). She was at home on the trombone and accordion. In 1976 Ruby was appointed head of the Music Department at Territorial Headquarters.

On 29 January 1977, she was featured in the edition of 'The Musician', published at International Headquarters, Mrs. Lt. Colonel Adam's musical contributions to the world-wide Army were highlighted as indicated in the lead paragraphs of the article; '*In naming Mrs. Lt.Colonel Rudy Adams as Music Secretary for the USA Western Territory, Commissioner Richard E. Holz, the Territorial Commander, has added another 'first' to the list of honors afforded this talented Salvationist-musician, whose accomplishments include those of conductor (vocal and instrumental groups), composer (band and vocal), keyboard artist, accompanist, instrumentalist and music teacher'*. Even

Colonel Brindley Boon wrote about here in his 'Play, the music Play!' Ruby was of special musical significance during here work not only in the United States but also in the Far East, Hawaii, Japan and Hong Kong. Mrs. Lt. Colonel Ruby Adams Palm was Promoted to Glory on 2 March 1982.

Important composition

Colne

PALMER-BARNES, RAYMOND C.

An officer who served in the West Indies. Possibly a 'Second' series composition prize-winner pre-War. Was Promoted to Glory around 1946.

Important composition

Come to the Cross (TS0338) 1942, Fellowship (TS0302) 1940, Forward March (TS0201) 1934

PARKINS, WILLIAM

Known as Billy Parkins - he was the cornet soloist with New York Staff Band under William Darby (approximately around 1930). Later he became the Commissioner and the Western Territorial Commander located in Los Angeles, California.

By Eric Ball: 'The Musician' 4-6-1938

Whether he realizes it or not, his fame seems to be almost legendary. I travelled eighteen thousand miles before I heard him play a solo, and nearly everywhere I was told of his prowess. In New York they told me Erik Leidzén had written *'Tucker'* and *'A Happy Day'* especially for him. Well, I heard him play *'A Happy Day'*, and it was excellent, very fast, beautifully clear, no 'wangling' of difficult phrases, and a clear, almost crisp, tone that sounded fresh and youthful. His style and expression were fine, and added to all this he has a platform presence that shows him to be at ease with his instrument, and quite at home with a large audience. He told me his Divisional Work at Cincinatti has taken more of his attention than is good for cornet playing, and Major Grainer told me that when the Adjutant was with the Staff Band he was never known to miss or 'fluff' a note.

Important composition

Lover of the Lord (AJ0015) 1950

PARR, ERNEST HENRY

Ernie Parr, born on 19 may 1909, a young lad from Govan, Glasgow in Scotland discovered the Salvation Army and quickly became involved in its activities by becoming a member of the Govan Junior . He commenced his Christian Pilgrimage as one of group of boys who had been led to Christ through the understanding and patience of a godly bandleader. As a senior bandsman and songster he was actively engaged in the corps life. He was also a clerk in the Glasgow Branch of the Salvation Army Emigration and Travel Department Service and the Govan Band was his whole life. He particularly remembered traveling to the Chrystal Palace and Regent Hall in Lonond, where he met outstanding personalities of Salvation Army Music. His prowess as a soprano cornet player supreme was recognized.

In 1928 while touring with the International Staff Band to Southend-on-Sea he met Bandmaster Henry Merritt who was visiting from Winnipeg in Manitoba, Canada. The invitation was extended to him to become a member of the Winnipeg Citadel Band and a year later this was accomplished. During his six year stay in Winnipeg Ernie played in the Citadel Band and became Young People's Bandleader and was employed in the Finance Department at Territorial Headquarters. There he met the inspriration of his life in the person of Eva Snowden, whose radiant personality and Christian example brought rich blessing through his lifetime. In the year 1937 Eva and Ernie were married while members of the Dovercourt Citadel Corps and in 1938 the entered Training College in Toronto. They were commissioned by General Eva Booth and appointed to the Gravenburst Corps. Following appointments were Territorial Headquarters in the Printing, Trade and Youth Departments in the Toronto and Hamilton Divisions as Divisional Youth Secretaries, Chancellor of the Toronto Division, appointed to Bermuda as Divisional Commanders, Principal of the College for Officers in Toronto, Territorial Headquarters as Staff Secretary and retiring in the year 1975 as a Lt. Colonel.

For many years Ernie Parr travelled through Canada and the United States to participate in congress meetings and festivals with his soprano cornet and in a special manner was grateful for the privilege of the ministry of music. In his prime as a soprano cornet soloist he was guest soloist with the New York Staff Band, the Chicago Staff Band and later as Executive Officer of the Canadian Staff Band. He considered it as a 'plus' to be so closely associated with banding throughout his entire career. On August 2, 1982, his wife Eva was Promoted to Glory from Toronto.

Ernie Parr was Promoted to Glory from Toronto, Ontario on June 20, 1999

Important compositions

Camp Selkirk (CM0027) 1958, The Canadian Standard (CM0003) 1955

PASCOE, CHELSEA

Chelsea Pascoe – 14 June 1990 was born in Northern Ireland, attends Sydenham Corps in Belfast and has grown up through the ranks of junior sections and activities and is currently the Singing Company Leader and assistant Corps Pianist as well as an active soloist and member of the Senior Band and Songster Brigade. She is also a member of the Divisional Youth Band and Chorus in Ireland.

Currently (2011) in the final year of a BA Honours Music Degree at the famous Queen's University of Belfast Chelsea will also undertake a Masters Degree in Composition at Queens commencing late 2011. She is also Principal Horn for the inaugural Queens University Brass Band

Chelsea has composed for all genres of Salvation Army musical sections including works for Young People and Senior Bands as well as Vocal works. Her setting of *'Prayer Gently Lifts Me'* is being released on the latest CD by Enfield Citadel Band (*The Enfield Connection*) and was premiered by the same Band at the 2010 Pre-Contest Festival in London. Chelsea has written a number of pianoforte solos for devotional use. Her overall musical style reflects her obvious love of Jesus and her desire to see others come to know Him as Saviour.

In terms of musical influences Chelsea is a great admirer of Dr Kenneth Downie and Eric Ball as well as many of the classical greats such as Beethoven and Wagner. Chelsea is a fan of musical theatre and film music, with George Gershwin and John Williams listed as favourites.

Important compositions

King of all Kings (m/s), Sydenham (m/s), Prayer Gently lifts me (m/s), How Great (m/s)

PATTISON, JOHN

For many years John (Jackie) Pattison was the bandmaster of the Seaham Harbour Corps Band in the North East of England. He mainly wrote marches and was a prize winner in the Army's International Music Competition in 1947. John Pattison, converted as a lad in the Young People's Corps at Seaham Harbour, was soon sought after by Bandmaster J. Swinney, and taught a few scales. Within the course of a few weeks he appeared in public as a fully-fledged Bandsman. At the age of seventeen John commenced to learn the principles of harmony, using Ebenezer Prout's famous work as the basis of his study. Soon afterward he had composed his first march, entered his effort in an International Music Competition, and gained fourth place. This was in the same year, 1909, that Brigadier Bramwell Coles won the first prize with the *'Chalk Farm'* march. By strange coincidence, Bandmaster Pattison's march, *'The World for Jesus'*, which appears in the Second Series Journal, No. 261, was commented upon in 'The Musician' of April 12th, 1938, by Brigadier Coles. *'Thus, twenty-nine years after that memorable evening in 1909, when amid tense excitement at the Clapton Congress Hall, Commissioner Carleton rose to announce the prize-winners of the competition, the names of these two musicians were again united. After this achievement the budding composer was encouraged to write more extensively, and burnt much midnight oil in the pursuit of musical perfection'*. More march compositions followed including *'Recuit'* (B.J. 593), *'Seaham Harbour'* (B.J. 838), and *'Emancipation'* (B.J. 891). On one occasion, Brother John Cockles, a dark-skinned Salvationist, visited Seaham Harbour Corps, and so impressed by the youthful musician with an address about the emancipation of slaves that he was inspired to write his march of that name. The spirit of a freed people can be traced in every lilting bar, and an air of liberty is admirably expressed in musical form. The *'One by One'* Campaign, which swept the British Field years ago, provided John with another inspiration and theme for a new march, which he named *'One by One'* (B.J. 915) and what would became his most well known work. An interesting letter regarding the popularity of this march in Canada appeared in an issue of 'The Musician'.

Important compositions

One by One (GS915) 1924, What a Saviour! (TS0519) 1954

PAYTON, ORVILLE

Orville's father, Herbert Payton, was born in Peterborough, Ontario, Canada. He played cornet in the Peterborough Corps band. Orville's mother, Ivy, was born in Catford, England. She played violin in the Queen's own Orchestra in London, England. They first met in Catford, England when Herbert, as a Canadian Soldier, visited the Catford Corps. They both attended the Salvation Army's Training Collage in Toronto, Canada. As new officers their first appointment was to Hamilton, Ontario where Orville was born on May 1st 1923.

His earliest music training was through his parents where he learned to play the cornet, the trombone, and the piano. His music abilities were developed at Salvation Army music camps in Chicago's Wonderland Camp, Kansas City, Missouri Camp and Detroit, Michigan Camp during his teen years.

His first attempt at composing included writing the words and music for the Port Huron High School 'Fight song' in his senior year. It is still being used at every school sporting event for the past seventy years. The second composed selection was his class song that was played and sung at Orville's class graduation ceremony in June 1941.

Under the guidance and leadership of Bandmaster Herb Little at the Port Huron Citadel Corps in Port Huron, Michigan, Orville began to receive instructions on the fundamentals of leading a band. At the age of thirty-one he became the Bandmaster of the Port Huron Citadel Band and held that position for eleven years.

In 1976 Orville moved from Michigan to Mesa, Arizona and began attending the Corps there. At the time Mesa Citadel Corps was a small relatively new Corps that did not have a band or songster group so he proceeded to start both. Orville held that position of band and songster leader for fourteen years at which time he retired but continued to play in the band. For over fifty years Orville served as Bandmaster and Songster leader for either Port Huron Citadel Corps or Mesa Citadel Corps. He has composed several Marches, over a dozen Selections, and a Christmas Cantata and vocal selections for Songsters.

He also played and directed The 'Bluewater Sextet' in the United States and Canada. He wrote a special 'Mimic' arrangement of LeRoy Anderson's trio called *'Buglers Holiday'* and named it *'Heavenly Herolds'*. Orville never submitted any of his music to the Salvation Army Headquarters for publishing as he preferred keeping his writing exclusive for the Corps he was attending. At 87 years of age Orville composed a march entitled *'God's Grace'* and had the honor of being ask to lead it at Mesa Citadel's annual concert last year. He was Promoted to Glory on 8th of February 2012.

Important composition

Cornet trio – Heavenly Heralds

PEARCE, RALPH

Born in a Salvation Army nursing home in Glasgow, Scotland to officer parents Ralph Pearce can claim with some justification and no embarrassment to 'bleed Yellow Red and Blue'. His earliest musical education was at various Salvation Army Corps where his parents served as Corps Officers. Early musical talent was revealed as a boy soprano. Whilst at the George Dixon School in Birmingham he became involved in that establishment's Anglican-style choir singing services five days a week. Ear problems led to his being medically forbidden to play a brass instrument for life an order he has consistently ignored culminating in much professional playing and being involved as a charter member of the USA Western Territorial Band – as a trombonist – the only instrument that matters! Ralph returned to Scotland to study musicology at the University of Glasgow with further studies in composition at University College Cardiff. Whilst studying in Cardiff he returned to his father's home Corps, Abercarn, where he reformed the Songster Brigade bringing to a highly regarded standard of singing. For around a year he had the double privilege of also conducting the band at Risca as well. (The Abercarn Corps having merged with

Pontymister to form this new Corps). It was whilst in Wales that the first music began to appear.

The Festival March *'The Caledonian'* was his first essay for the Army – a march featured by the ISB, recorded by the Amsterdam Staff Band and Norwich Citadel Band was in fact written for the Springburn Young People's Band for a tour of Northern Scotland. (Ralph had soldiered there whilst studying at University – as well as receiving his degree he also gained his wife of 36 years – Isobel). Teaching at the Tredegar gave other opportunities to write for that school's band and where he taught a number of student who are now involved on the contesting band world.

Invited to move to Phoenix AZ, USA to develop the Music Department for the Southwest Division the Pearce family arrived in the USA in 1990. Musical standards in the Division have risen considerably since he and Isobel have headed up the music program there. A quarter of the Western Territoial Band hail from the Southwest and their daughter Fiona has been a member of the New York Staff Band's cornet section and now plays Flugel in the Montclair Citadel Band. After arriving in Phoenix Ralph conducted the Salt River Brass for ten years. This brought him into contact with British Brass Band luminaries such as Russell Gray, Sandy Smith and Roger Webster for whom he has written extensively.

Feeling that his music was not wanted by the Army after a serious of personal slights, a chance remark made in Toronto by Bandmaster Ron Waiksnoris concerning *'The Threefold Glory'* led to him to begin again. Waiksnoris has been behind the trombone feature *'There is a Redeemer'* and the overture 'The Cry of the Warriors' as well as recording a number of pieces with the New York Staff Band. Since the year 2000 Ralph has been one of the Army's most widely published contributors. He has also forms a solo writing relationship with many of the contesting world's most prominent players. *'In writing I strive for musical integrity without ever losing sight of the important requirement that Army band music must be 'music with a message. I use a symphonic approach in terms of thematic development often finding a small motif in the theme tune itself or a counter to that main theme which can be the unifying idea that holds the whole piece together. Although this is of use to me as a writer the listener need not know this – the only desire is that the heart is touched and led towards God. There is much more to be written and I trust that it will be of use to the kingdom.'*

Important compositions

A Suite of Thanksgiving (TS1200) 2010, Dutch Variations (m/s)

PEARSON, FREDERICK HENRY

Fred was just a farm worker's son and yet he held such potential in his hands. He was born on October 19th 1901 to Charlotte and John Pearson in the small market town of Sudbury Suffolk. He was the youngest in a family of eight and grew as boys do and at 15 years old was captured by the music of the recently formed Salvation Army. He went along and became saved in his first week night meeting. The following Sunday he was interviewed by the Bandmaster and was given a cornet, tied up with string in places, but no scale sheet and with encouraging words was told to 'do his best'! He quickly became proficient and was taken under the wing of Young People's Sergeant Major Mary Ambrose, little realising that in a few short years he would fall in love and marry her daughter! The YPSM was the first uniformed Salvationist at Sudbury. Fred was not just a musician, he was a keen sportsman and enjoyed playing cricket and football. But the First World War came and he joined up aged 16 years old and became a military bandsman with the 2nd Battalion Suffolk Regiment. He was found a place in a regimental band and there came under the personal tuition of bandmaster H.E. Adkins, Mus Bac, L.R.A.M., A.R.C.M. where he learned about theory and musical interpretation. Then came his appointment as Bandmaster at Kneller Hall and two years later he was discharged from the forces. He found work through the 'Bandsman & Songster' and was appointed bandmaster of the Coalville Corps Band in Leicestershire. This post he held for three years. After their wedding Fred and Ivy moved to Ipswich and there became members of Ipswich Citadel Corps. Fred was an extremely talented soprano cornet player and he would bike home from work every lunch time to get in some practice. In 1927 their only son, Raymond Frederick was born. Many is the night that he went to sleep with the sound of his Father's playing ringing in his ears. It was whilst Fred was in Coalville that he met and was befriended with Bandmaster George Marshall and his wife Jenny. Fred was instantly plunged into a world that he loved, music making! He wrote most of his music during this time and found in George Marshall a man who was an encourager and teacher. He bought many books to help with composition and became an avid student. Fred sayd about George Marshall: *'I got in touch with bandmaster George Marshall and under his direction took up the study of harmony. He encouraged me in my musical career, but his letters, without exception contained some real spiritual blessing and help'.*('The Musician' 17 September 1938). His first march published was called *'Our loving redeemer'* and was printed in the Triumph Series, No 239 and was closely followed in 1938 by *'Fighting to Conquer'* No 270.

Whilst in the Midlands Fred had affiliated himself with Nottingham Memorial Halls Corps and wrote a march for them but when it went to print it was refused by the Editorial Board for having such a long name! This march was later to become *'Ipswich Citadel'*. This was published in General Series in 1947, No1312. Fred used the chorus that George Marshall had used in Army of the Brave. *'Let us stand our ground tho' all Hell surround'*. He had asked George for permission to include this as a mark of respect for the friendship, care and teaching he had been shown by the great man. In 1942 Fred wrote the march *'Sudbury Citadel'*, no 1169 as he remembered his happy grounding at that small corps. In 1942 *'Fare Thee Well'* was published. In the meantime, his son Ray, had become an accomplished pianist and so now Fred was able to listen to the chording and harmonies and change anything that he did not like accordingly. Previous to this he had played every part separately on each instrument before committing it to paper. He became Deputy Songster Leader and then Deputy Bandmaster of the Ipswich Citadel band and then for a brief period of about a year their Bandmaster. His Deputy Bandmaster was his son, Ray. It was whilst Fred was Deputy Bandmaster that his work was published. His son Ray, became the bandmaster after him and then Fred was his trusty and talented soprano player. He would often be heard to say that a soprano would either make or break a band and that it should be an embellishment to the playing. If it were not so, then do without!!

Fred's granddaughter well remember visiting her Grandad and his first question would always be had she practised her instrument and what scales she was learning! He was relentless in his passion for music and told her that scales were the backbone of good playing and that without them she would never succeed. Not what a small girl wanted to hear. But how those words have rung in her brain since then and how right he was! He also wrote some songster music. In 1937, in 'The Musical Salvationist' there is a song called *'Refresh our souls'* with the words by Songster organist E Ward. In his day to day life Fred became a senior cashier for the Ipswich Malting Company, a job which he relished and was very proud of. In his job, as in his Salvation Army soldiership he was meticulous. His legacy lived on in his son Ray, who was an accomplished pianist and accompanist. He was Bandmaster of Ipswich Citadel and Stowmarket bands and the Songster Leader of Ipswich Citadel songster brigade. The legacy carries on his Granddaughter Lindsey Moye who teaches Class Music for Suffolk County Music Service. He was very proud of his two Great Grandson's, Robert Moye who is an accomplished pianist, tuba player and an International Staff Songster and Keith has a Music degree and is principal cornet player in Stowmarket Salvation Army Band. Frederick Henry Pearson was Promoted to Glory on June 30th 1992.

Important compositions

Fare-thee-well! (GS1205) 1942, Fighting to Conquer (TS0270) 1938, Ipswich Citadel (GS1312) 1949

PEARSON, LEONARD

Leonard Pearson was born on 13 January 1914 and was Promoted to Glory on 24 June 2001. He was appointed Songster Leader at Sittingbourne in 1955 and held the position for 19 years. His first published vocal contribution was in 1953 in 'The Musical Salvationist' and in the end 40 songs were published by the Salvation Army between 1953 and 1990. So he was foremost more a vocal composer rather than a brass composer. Of particular interest is that he wrote arrangements for his adopted soprano daughter; *'Dearest name of names'* and *'O happy day'*.

'A Sittingbourne man has won an International competition organized by the Salvation Army to compose music for a gospel song. He is Mr. Leonard Pearson of Poulsen Court, who is choirmaster with the local Salvation Army Corps. Mr. Pearson, who plays the piano and organ, has composed over ten different pieces of music. The Competition was organized by the Harrow Corps of the Salvation Army in November, and was open to entrants from all over the world. The competitors had to provide music to words written by the late general Albert Orsborn, of the Salvation Army. Mr. Pearson, who received a certificate for his entry, is expecting to have another composition published by the Salvation Army this month'.

(source: The East Kent Gazette – Thursday 4 January 1965)

Important compositions

Happy Service (US0195) 1995, Hosanna (US0246) 1999

PEARSON, WILLIAM

William Pearson (born in 1832, died on 19 October 1892) was an early Salvationist in the United Kingdom and was the composer of the song *'Joy! Joy! Joy! There is joy in the Salvation Army'*. William joined The Christion Mission in 1874, and was evangelist in Bradford in 1878 when The Christian Mission became The Salvation Army. He was well known for his ministry of faith healing. For a number of years he wrote a new song each week, contributing to The 'War Cry' and sometimes to 'The Musical Salvationist'.

PENBERTHY, ALBERT

It was the playing of a Salvation Army band in the street that to Albert, seated in the church, had sounded out God's call to service in the ranks of the Salvation Army. Soon after he became a member of the Salvation Army, he went to the training college to become an officer. In between corps appointments there had been experience as a Divisional Young People Secretary in Bendigo and Tasmania, and in 1932 he was again appointed to this work, at the Metropolitan Division. Three years later he received his first Divisional Command, and for the next seven years he was in charce of the Northern Victoria, Western Australia, and Eastern Victoria Divisions. A change of work in 1942 brought an opportunity, which the Brigadier used most successfully, as a Prison Chaplain, and it was from this position that he retired in 1946. Versatile and original in thought and action, he was an impressive speaker. To these talents there was linked outstanding musical ability, his fame as a concertina player being widely known throughout the territory. Another achievement was the winning of a 2nd prize in the Australian Salvation Army Brass Band Compositions in 1913.

Important composition

Bendigo March - #311 in the Brass Band Journal published in Melbourne Australia

PENGILLY, ALLEN

Retired Corps Secretary Allen Pengilly of the Morley Corps was born on May 16th 1913 and Promoted to Glory on December 27th 1982. A grandson of 'grandma Pengilly', one of the early Salvationists in Australia. Allen Pengilly became a well known Australian Salvationist. He began his Salvation Army music activities as a Young People's Band member at Adelaide Congress Hall in 1926 and in 1929 moved with his parents to Perth, where he took his place in the Perth Fortress Young People's Band until his transfer to the senior band in 1932. As a lad he provided piano accompaniment for the Songster Brigade and he was commissioned as Songster Pianist in 1935. He held this position for five years before becoming the Songster Leader and apart from service with the RAAF in World War II he continued in this position until December 1959 when he transferred to the Maylands Corps (now Morland Corps). Here he took his place as bandsman, played the organ for the Songsters and was Male Voice Party Leader for a short period.

Allen Pengilly was known for his regular contact with the Music Department in London. He even kept the written letters to and from it by means of proof. Except for one composition, all his further output was solely for the Triumph Series. *'Room for Jesus'* was his first contribution to be published in 'The Musical Salvationist', appearing in 1954. Over a dozen songs have since been published with many more being written for special occasions. Songs such as *'In the mansions above'* and *'Let us sing unto the Lord'* were based on Scripture, whilst words for other songs came from the pen of well known Army writers.

His first published march *'Westralia'* was in October 1956 and titles for his other marches similarly express his love for his adapted State. Two of his published marches *'Dandenong Citadel'* and *'Alice Springs'* were associated with appointments held by his officer daughter. Sickness curtailed his activities and brought about his early retirement. During his years of retirement, his passion for music, also reviving an earlier interest in painting and friends from around the world are pleased to have received one his paintings.

Important compositions

Balga Citadel (TS852) 1980, Morley Citadel (GS1753) 1982.

PETERSON, STURE

Sture Petersson was born into a Salvation Army family on 13th December 1930 in Jönköping Sweden. His father was bandmaster of the Jönköping Citadel Band. After he finished his studies in Jököping 1949, he continued and finished a military education as an officer in the Swedish Army. 1951 to 1953 he was educated as a teacher at the Jönköping Seminary. 1953 Sture had an examination as organist in Gothenburg and studied until 1957 music at the 'Royal Academy of Music' in Stockholm and became Director of Music. 1956 to 1958 he served as teacher and bandmaster at the 'High School of Music' in Lidingö and was also conductor of the 'Lidingö Orchestra Society' 1959 to 1963 he made further studies in conducting by professor Tor Mann at the 'Royal Academy of Music' in Stockholm. 1957 to 1975 Sture was bandmaster of the Temple Corps Band of The Salvation Army (Stockholm 1). Since 1958 he worked part time for the 'National Music Department' of the Salvation Army in Stockholm and part time as music teacher at the Stockholm seminary. 1963 to 1995 he was lector in music at the Stockholm University. From 1984 to his retirement 1995, Sture served as the National Music Secretary at the Headquarter of the Salvation Army in Sweden.

Important compositions

Din Spira, Jesus, Strackes ut (SF0002) 1961, Evigt Liv (FM0310) 1961, Till Fralsningens Saliga Brunnar (FM0313-1) 1962

PETHYBRIDGE, MATTHEW

Matthew currently works for the Salvation Army's Creative Ministries Department in New Zealand as the Unit's Director. He studied at the University of New South Wales. He wrote in particular music for the Staff Songsters of New Zealand, 'Spiritsong' and for the National Youth Band of New Zealand.

Important composition

Once in Royal David's City

PHILLIPS, RICHARD

Richard Phillips was born 1962 in England. He played his first notes on a cornet when he was four and began his first piano lesson at age seven. On leaving school he attended the Royal College of Music where he gained the ARCM and Dip. RCM. Since then he has directed many musicals, has arranged for such luminaries as Moira Anderson, Marilyn Baker, Wendy Craig, George Hamilton IV and Howard Keel, and was the Senior Editor in the Salvation Army Music Editorial Department. Richard was Bandmaster of the Chatham Citadel Band, Enfield Citadel Band and now Kettering Citadel Band. He was pianist for the Salvation Army's Premier Vocal Group, The International Staff Songsters (ISS). Richard Phillips produced as pianist four solo CD's, *'Love's Song'* (1991) and *'There is Music everywhere'* (1993), *'Christmas Precence'* (2002) and *'Inspirations'* (2008) and is currently (2011) busy with his fifth solo recording to be released later in the year.

Important compositions

Joyous Song (FS534) 1997, Metamorphosis (FS587) 2004, In Christ Alone (JC642) 2009, Joy, Peace and Happiness (GS1872) 1992, New Life (TS996) 1992, Lord, with my all I part (TS1031) 1995

PILLEY, MICHAEL

Michael was born on 24 March 1983. He studied at Melbourne University gaining his Bachelor of Music, majoring in trombone performance. For seven years, 2002-2009, he was a member of the Melbourne Staff Band and for 3 years, 2008-2010, he was bandmaster of the Preston Citadel Band in Melbourne. Currently he is establishing a Music Academy at the Camberwell Citadel Corps. In 2005 Michael attended Star Lake Music Camp in the USA, under the Richard Holz scholarship programme. When composing, he is exploring contemporary Christian music, jazz and popular style idioms, and looking at new sounds for brass. He is published by the Australia Southern Territory with *'I'll Fight'* and *'You Are Good'*. Michael is currently conducting the Engineering Music Society Concert Band (Melbourne University) and the MoJo (Monash University Jazz Orchestra). He worked as typesetter and transcriber for All Music Publishing & Distribution.

Important composition

I'll Fight (Arthur Gullidge Series AGS1002)

PITCHER, GRANT

Grant Pitcher (1969) was born in Napier New Zealand. From an early age Grant learnt about Jesus through attending Sunday school at a local Presbyterian Church that he and his family attended for a short time. From a young age Grant was involved in music. One of his first musical memories comes from a time when he was a beginner bugler in the Boys Brigade. At eleven Grant joined the Napier City brass band and at fourteen he attended a New Zealand Army Band concert. He was so mesmerized by the upbeat brass and rhythm sounds that he decided that Military music was the future occupation for him. Under the guidance of his then tutor Cecil Fitzwater, who was a Salvationist and exceptional band trainer, Grant worked tirelessly on his playing and at the age of seventeen after a successful audition joined the Military as a bandsman in the New Zealand Army Band.

As an eighteen year-old, Grant made his first attempt at writing music when he transcribed an orchestral piece for brass band which was consequently approved for performance by the then Director of Music. Many more band arrangements and transcriptions followed.

His career as full time in military musician expanded over twenty one years.

1987 – 1992 & 1994 - 1997: New Zealand Army Band

1997 – 2005: Royal New Zealand Air Force Bandmaster (RNZAF Base Woodbourne)

2005 – 2009: Royal New Zealand Air Force Deputy Director of Music (Wellington)

In 1989 Grant met Lynda who was a Senior Solder in the Salvation Army, fell in love and as a result they were married in 1994. Through Lynda Grant was introduced to the Salvation Army, recommitted his life to Jesus and in 2000 was enrolled as a Senior Soldier.

In 1998 Grant experienced devastation when his first son Timaeus passed away unexpectedly and in tribute to his sons very short life he wrote his first composition *'Highly Prized'* (Performed on 2007 Wellington Citadel band Lightbringer CD).

(Words by Tracy Boon)

Verse I

Here in my arms you sleep with such peace
your dreams soft and light your life just be gun.
Sent to this world your days all prepared
a child yet a teacher leads me back to Christ.

Verse II

My heart bursts with love my soul full of joy
and thanks to our Christ for this gift so pure
and as you sleep I'll make you this covenant
to love you as God loves me Christ's highly prized gift to me.

Aside from his band training Grant had minimal formal musical schooling either as an arranger or composer, he says. *'I've pretty much taught myself music theory by working through Royal School theory books, basic harmony books and studying brass band scores'.* Years later, someone suggested he needed credentials, so he took some Trinity College London examinations (in New Zealand). As a result of those exams, Grant became a fellow of Trinity College.

After nation auditions Grant was elated to be chosen for the 2003 National Band of New Zealand, which was another childhood ambition of his.

Grant was a member of the prestigious Wellington Citadel Band (WCB) that toured Japan in 2007. A highlight was to perform the Euphonium solo *'The Great Adventure'* during the tour concert series (Performed on 2007 WCB Lightbringer CD). In 2008 Grant was appointed as bandmaster of the New Zealand Salvation Army National Youth Band which is a position he still holds. In 2009 this group produced a CD entitled *'Glorify'.*

Philosophy

He believes in the creativity and giftedness of individuals and am committed to utilising his own talents, life skills and gifts in ministry to optimize, draw-out and nurture the talents, skills, passions and giftedness of other people. Grant highly values the opportunities which he has had (and self created) in life and believe that through God's love and leadership he can enhance, inspire and encourage people. He firmly believes that God has the power to change lives forever. He is committed to the sentiments of the late Sir Dean Goffin when he said *'I will not be content with mediocrity,'* in respect to his pursuit of excellence in the service of his Lord.

Important composition

Highly Prized, The Lord's Prayer, People Need the Lord, Superstar Melody

PITTEWAY, CHARLOTTE

Charlotte Pitteway (wife of composer and International Staff Bandsman Paul Sharman). Charlotte Louise Sharman was born on June 18th 1980. She grew up in Harrow (North West London) with her parents and brother and sister. She has attended the Regent Hall Corps of the Salvation Army all her life. She was in the singing company and played horn in the Young People's Band. She then became a senior soldier in 1997 and soon after joined the senior band on horn. The band has taken part in some tours overseas which she has been able to take part in. She has travelled to California in 1998, Norway and Guernsey. Charlotte met Paul, her husband, at Regent Hall and they were married in July 2004. They now have two young children, Anna and George, and still attend Regent Hall corps.

'The Power of Your Love' was the first band piece she has attempted to arrange. It is a tune that means a lot to her. She hopes to write some more music in the future when time allowes. She also enjoys writing lyrics, and Paul and Charlotte have been able to write some songs together. This is something she hopes to continue doing as she enjoy expressing her faith in God through songs.

Important composition

The Power of your love (US0294) 2003

PITTOCK, DALE

Originally from Woodstock, Ontario in Canada, Dale was born in 1952 into a Salvation Army family and is a 3rd generation Salvationist. He started playing cornet at age 5 and moved on to low brass exclusively by 1980. In 1965 the Woodstock Citadel Band the first Salvation Army band to visit Jamaica. Dale's father, 4 brothers and he were in the band, they even had their own quintet (2 cornets, horn, euphonium, BBb bass) with his father playing bass drum! When he was 21 he relocated to Southern California (United States of America) where he played in corps bands at Inglewood, Long Beach Temple, Santa Ana (now Tustin Ranch). He was for a time the deputy bandmaster at Inglewood, followed by a bandmastership with the Long Beach Temple Band. Dale and his wife were commissioned as Salvation Army officers in 1982 and their career as such included three corps appointments and six divisional headquarters appointments (financial and business secretary). During 16 years of being an officer Dale played in corps bands at Torrance (Southern California), Denver Citadel (Colorado), Oakland Citadel (now Concord Corps – Northern California), Pasadena Tabernacle (Southern California), Phoenix Citadel (Arizona) and for a short time the Salt River Brass in Phoenix.

Often called upon to play in numerous ensembles for Salvation Army musicals, Commissioning and Congress events his highlight of his Salvation Army career was 21 years of playing in the annual New Years Day Tournament of Roses Parade in Pasadena, California. In 1998 Dale and his wife resigned from officership and moved to other fields of endeavor in the Tri-Cities area of southeastern Washington State. After not playing for nearly 5 years, in 2002 he was asked to play in a small orchestra for a church Christmas pageant. A contact there resulted in an invitation to audition for the Mid-Columbia Symphony Orchestra (Richland, Washington). In January 2003 he was appointed bass trombone for the Mid-Columbia Symphony and shortly after the Oregon East Symphony in Pendleton, Oregon. He played in the Oregon East Symphony from 2003 to 2006 and continues still with the Mid-Columbia Symphony. Since 2003 Dale has 'played in the pit' for the Richland Light Opera Company performing such productions as *'Carousel'*, *'1776'*, *'My Fair Lady'*, *'Miss Saigon'*, *'South Pacific'* and *'The Gondoliers'*.

Dale also played in full orchestras for Mendelssohn's Oratorio *'Elijah'*, Mozart's *'Requiem'*, Brahms' *'Eine Deutsches Requiem'* and Vaughan Williams' *'Dona Nobis Pacem'* and *'Five Mystical Songs'*. Between 1973 and 1980 he completed numerous short pieces whilst at Inglewood and Santa Ana Salvation Army Corps. He composed music for Western Territory SFOT session song in 1982 and arranged musical segments for SFOT special production. Dale recommenced active arranging in 2004 to reconnect with Salvation Army music-making, although it is a challenge to get pieces into the hands of Salvation Army bands since he is not pro-active in the Army as the nearest Salvation Army Corps (band) is over 4 hours away!

Playing and composing is certainly a part-time endeavor, but it gives a sense of accomplishment to use God-given talents and abilities developed early on in The Salvation Army. Dale's usual back-stage warm-up routine (apart from long notes and flexibility figures) is to play one or more ballad-like Salvation Army melodies in the low register. Although he has not enjoyed any what he would call a mentor, his arranging has been influenced by Erik Leidzen, Bruce Broughton, and his playing influenced by George Roberts and Chris Mallett.

Important compositions

The Invitation, All that I am, The Great Physician

PITTOCK, JON R.

Jon R, Pittock was born in Ingersoll, Ontario in Canada on May 13, 1947. From there he moved on to Woodstock when nine years of age. He developed his musical skills while taught by James M. Gordon and soon found himself in the Senior Band of the corps, when only eleven years of age. One of the musical highlights in his life was to be on tour in 1965 with the corps band, which included his four brothers and his father. In 1970 Jon moved to London (Ontario) where he became the Young People's Band Leader. Under his leadership the Youth Band, which included his son Erik and daughter Cherie, became very active, including a tour to Southern California. After nearly two decades at London Citadel he moved to Westminster Park Corps where he became the bandmaster.

Important composition

Jesus loves me and you, Endless Day, The Day Thou Gavest, Love is When, Sarnia Citadel, Suncoast Citadel, Great Lakes Senior Band, Tribute To Fallen Soldiers

POIRIER, ANDREW

Born in Lewisporte, Newfoundand, Canada on December 13, 1980, Andrew grew up in the Lewisporte Citadel Corps, where he became a member of the corps band, but also was a member of the Divisional Youth Band there. For nine consecutive years he went to the Salvation Army's National School of Music, held in Jackson's Point, some 30 miles outside Toronto. He has a Bachelor of Music degree from the University of British Columbia, a Master of Music degree from the San Francisco Conservatory and is currently a professional Trombonist in the Vancouver area in British Columbia, Canada. He is a former member of the Vancouver Symphony Orchestra and is now in demand as trombone soloist in Salvation Army Bands in North America and Europe including performances with the Canadian Staff Band of which he was a member, and Amsterdam Staff Band. Currently is the Bandmaster of the Southmount Citadel Band in British Columbia.

Andrew Poirier sees himself preferably not as a composer but rather as an arranger and transcriber. Some of his works has been performed and are recorded by notable bands such as the Canadian Staff Band and the North York Temple Band. Other bands that have recognised his music are the New York Staff Band and the London Citadel Band.

Important arrangements

Joy to the World, Chiming Bells, Good King Wenceslas, Jingle Bells, Lux Aramque

PONSFORD, KEVIN

Kevin Ponsford was born on 5 January 1980 in Plymouth, and is the older brother of Steven (below). His father was the Bandmaster when he was growing up so there was always music in the house. Although Kevin is the least published composer of the two Ponsford brothers, his contribution to the band journals is certainly of significant meaning, as it has been, and still is, a popular composition and has appeared frequently on many recordings.

Important composition

Glorify Your Name (TS1143) 2005

PONSFORD, STEVEN

Steven Ponsford, (born on 1 February 1983) hails from Plymouth, where he still lives. He is what you could call a self-taught composer and arranger. His father was the Bandmaster when he was growing up so there was always music in the house, and often music scores which he found fascinating. Steven would often find himself studying scores to try and work out how a composer puts a piece of music together. He would sit at the piano and try to find the same chords as used in some great band scores. He was a cornet player from the age of 7 but also played percussion where needed. Steven received top class advice and help from the likes of Kenneth Downie, and top encouragement and support from Dr. Stephen Cobb, International Staff Bandmaster. He is thrilled with how many pieces of music he had published already and hope there is a lot more to come. Steven aims to write in many different styles, and try not to hold back, and not get caught up in tradition but to experiment and push the boundaries. Every music writer would probably agree that it can be a very lonely hobby, but it's amazing to think that something you've worked hard with can eventually be heard and enjoyed by many people, all over the world in some cases.

Important compositions

Kergygma (JC619) 2007, Turris Fortissima (JC647) 2009, Christo Redentor (JC633) 2008

POST, VERNON

Vernon Post was born of Salvationist parents on March 14, 1927 in Elizabeth, New Jersey.

At the farewell festival for General-Elect Evangeline Booth at the Brooklyn Academy of Music in 1934, a seven-year-old Vernon Post sat entranced as bands and songsters from all corners of the territory played and sang their praises. But he wondered, *'Why does the music of some groups make you want to march, dance, cry or clap your hands, while other efforts are disappointing?'* He has spent his life finding out what makes music effective.

In high school, he received a scholarship to study cornet with the renowned Dr. Frank Simon. He was an award-winning student at the Cincinnati Conservatory of Music where he received a Bachelor of Music degree in composition. Later he was awarded a Master of Arts from Trenton State College.

As a Salvation Army officer, he was appointed to the Eastern Territory Music Department where he continued composition and arranging studies with Erik Leidzèn. He served in the New York Staff Band as principal cornet, deputy bandmaster from 1954-63 and bandmaster from 1963-72. He led the Staff Band Male Chorus for eighteen years and the Temple Chorus for nine years. His arrangements have been played and sung around the Army world. For seventeen years he also served as program or camp director for the famed Star Lake Musicamp. Vernon's arrangements for band, chorus and orchestra were featured throughout his twenty-four-year tenure as a music educator in the Summit, NJ public schools. For twenty-two seasons he was music director for 'Broadway Shows' such as *'Music Man', 'Fiddler on the Roof'* and Bernstein's *'West Side Story'*, all performed by students. His orchestras featured the simpler symphonies of Schubert and Haydn. Post was chosen as conductor for the New Jersey All-State High School Opera concert presentation of Verdi's Aida.

(source: music.use-salvationarmy.org)

Important compositions

(arr) Hummel Trumpet Concerto (FS0330) 1970, Rejoice Ye Pure In Heart (ABJ19-81) 1973

POULTON, GEOFFREY

Born on 9 February 1947 in West Hartlepool, County Durham (now Cleveland). When a few months old, moved to Blackburn, Lancashire, where he grew up. He was taught the baritone, followed by trombone by grandfather Tom Poulton. He attended Birmingham Citadel Corps.

Geoffrey Poulton is a professional trombonist, composer and audio engineer, with over forty years of professional playing experience encompassing a wide variety of styles from big band jazz and dance orchestra, to symphony orchestra and recital work, with numerous orchestras and ensembles, in concert halls, theatres, hotels and recording studios. Much of his time as a professional arranger has been spent in writing for musical theatre. As a composer he has written for orchestra, brass band, and for voices.

PRESS, GREAME

When Graeme and his wife Neryl returned from Atlanta in the United States of America, where they had worked for a number of years, Graeme took up the appointment of Territorial Director for Music & Creative Arts. In this role he also took on the newly re-formed Sydney Staff Songsters and has remained the leader since. Under his direction the group has toured nationally and internationally, recorded several albums and even had a number of television appearances. Graeme's reputation as a choir director, arranger and visionary extends across the globe, leading to many invitations for himself and the SSS to lead vocal workshops or worship sessions both within the Salvation Army and into the wider Christian Church.

Important compositions

As the Deer (AJ0159) 1995, Saviour, Like a Shepherd Lead us (US0225) 1998

PRESTAGE, ??

One of the early composers (late 1800, early 1900).

No further information could be retrieved about this person.

Important composition

Jesus Calls (GS0417) 1902

PRIEST, CHRISTOPHER W.

Christopher Priest immigrated to Atlanta over nineteen years ago with his wife and daughter from London, England. He has completed over 25 years service as an employee of The Salvation Army. On arrival in Atlanta he quickly introduced and established worldwide marketing and distribution of Salvation Army music publications and recordings. This included the 'Spiritual to the Bone' series where he is one of the players on three of the four recordings. In 1998 he became Program Coordinator for the International Millennial Congress, held in Atlanta, Georgia. This included the coordination of 28 international music & gospel arts groups, and the programming of each of the Congress events. Following the Congress, he joined the Community Relations & Development Department and is now Territorial Director of Communications. Under his direction, the Communications Bureau has direct emphasis on Communications, the Internet, and New Media.

Christopher Priest is an accomplished composer, and arranger, with many choral and instrumental works published by The Salvation Army, and other publishers. In the non Salvation Army music world he has been commissioned to write for HM Coldstream Guards, and also had a song recorded by the world famous King's Singers. During the 1980's he was the bass trombonist of the International Staff Band, and has traveled extensively around the world as guest conductor/clinician. He is the founder of the USA Southern Territorial songsters having been its leader for eleven years. Chris has served as an active music leader for over 30 years. This has included Songster Leader, then Bandmaster of the London based Staines Band; Bandmaster, the Songster Leader of the Atlanta Temple Corps. He has a long association with Salvation Army summer music camps having attended, served on staff, and been the guest leader in many parts of the world. He has a number of notable achievements with The Salvation Army; the responsibility for the first Salvation Army CD recording; first DVD recording; and the first Podcast. Chris has been married for 40 years to Heather. They became U.S. Citizens in October 2006. They have one daughter, Emma, and one grandson, Tristan Daniel.

Important compositions

Echo Grove (TS1052) 1997, Foundations (US0189) 1995, A Marvellous Wonder (US0295) 2004

PULLIN, STUART

Stuart Pullin, born in Great Britain, began brass lessons at the age of 7, joining the Eccleston Junior Band on Cornet and later changing to Tenor Horn. He commenced studies at the University of Salford in 1992, graduating with a BA (Horns) music degree in 1995. During his time at the university he has won two major composition awards and, as a postgraduate student, completed an MA in Composition with distinction. As a performer on the Tenor Horn, Stuart played with some of the finest bands in Northwest of England, including Wingates and Marple. He was a member of the famous Yorkshire Building Society Band, winning multiple European and British Open Championships. Moving on to Eb Bass, he also changed Bands again, to take up the position of Principal Eb Bass of the Marple Band. Stuart played also the Euphonium 'just for fun'. He passed away at the age of 32 on 5 September 2007 but leaves a wonderful legacy of compositions. It was his wish that his version of Deep Harmony (S.A.T.B.16) be donated to The Salvation Army and Territorial Music Director and Bandmaster of the International Staff Band Dr Stephen Cobb, cared for publication.

Important composition

Deep Harmony (JC0641) 2009

RAIKES, STAN ARTHUR.

Stan Raikes was the deputy bandmaster of the Norland Castle Corps and became known by the fact that he was also the bandmaster of the British Military Service Band during World War 2 in Cairo, Egypt. This also made him write one of the best well known marches ever written in the Salvation Army banding history; '*Cairo Red Shield*'. He was also the bandmaster of Cairo Red Shield Band for a little while during the war [WW II]. He then was the deputy Bandmaster at Hammersmith under Roy Burton for a number of years and then was the bandmaster at Harrow for a little while. He was a Salvation Army insurance collector for his day job.

Important compositions

Cairo Red Shield (GS1260) 1945, Harrow Citadel (GS1478) 1959

RANCE, ERNEST

Ernest Edward Rance, was born in Gloucester in 1896. He went to the training college in 1919, and prior to this he was the corps secretary at Gillingham. After corps and training college appointments he worked for twenty years at the Men's Social Work Headquarters and was, although for a short while, the bandmaster of the Men's Social Work Headquarters Band. He also conducted the East London Chorus. During and after the War he worked in various appointments as an Officer, and became National Secretary for Bands and Songster Brigades from 1950 to 1960. Lieutenant-Colonel Ernest Rance succeeded Adjutant Edward Saywell in this role. He remained to be here for the next ten years after which he was succeeded by another composer, Major Dean Goffin. He composed band music as well as songs and was equally at home on the concertina, piano, organ and trombone. He died on 3 February 1988 in Orpington, Kent.

Important compositions

Divine compensation (FS182) 1952, Symbols of Service (FS206) 1955

RAWLIN, GEORGE

Born in Warsaw Indiana and the only son of Salvation Army Officers who were both cornet players. George graduated from The Great Cass Tech in Detroit in 1965 and was a student of Dr. Harry Begian. At the age of thirteen hewas on the stage of the great Chicago 'Orchestra Hall' and presented a cornet solo to a full house and was 'hooked'. At the age of seventeen he toured Great Britain and Scotland with a fine Salvation Army band as soloist. On that same tour he had the dream of his life and sat in with the International Staff Band in rehearsal.

In 1965 George attended the Asbury College and then left for the road with the famous Christian Musical group 'the Spurrlows band and singers'. Later he moved to Atlanta and began a career as sideman, lead player, teacher, and Church Instrumental Minister.

Important compositions

Channels of Blessing (GS1452) 1957, Coming to the Cross (GS1512-1) 1962, Give to Jesus Glory (FS0289) 1965, Lord above all (FS0269) 1963, Love's Offering (GS1492) 1960, Ring the Bells (GS1732-2) 1980, Thy Dwelling Place (GS1585) 1968

RAWLINS, KENNETH

Kenneth Rawlins, a retired Salvation Army officer has been responsible for the musical affairs in Canada since 1955 and became Music Secretary for the Terrory in 1959. He was the first to hold such an appointment.

Born in Toronto, Canada in 1916. Entered the Salvation Army Training College, Toronto, as a member of the 'Dauntless Evangelists Session', 1938. Commissioned as a Lieutenant by General Evangeline Booth, 1939. After a short period as a Commanding Officer, served with the Salvation Army Red Shield Services, 1940 – 1946: 1940-43 Canada, 1943-1946 Overseas, England and Germany. Following the war returned to Canada and became Private Secretary to three Territorial Commanders: Commissioners Baugh, Dalziel and Booth 1947 – 1954. He served as Bandmaster of the Toronto Temple Band for some of that period.

In 1954 was appointed as Territorial Music Secretary for the Canada and Bermuda Territory. He held this position for 14 years, until June 1968. During this period he was given instruction in Brass Band Music composition by his mentor, Colonel Bramwell Coles who had recently retired as the International Music Secretary.

His first composition was published in the General Series and was entitled *'Channels of Blessing.'* This Sunday morning devotional piece was well received and became a favorite among the bands in our Territory, and the writer had the privilege of hearing many renditions as he travelled across the Territory in his role as Music Secretary. Many bands used the timing of his visit to prepare this selection for use in the Sunday morning meeting. He recounts saying to himself on more than one occasion – *'oh no, not again!'*

In addition to a March featuring the tune *'And Can it Be'* subsequent publications in the International Music Department General Series and Festival Series included *'Lord Above All'* and *'Give to Jesus Glory.'* The latter piece was written at the request of Colonel Jakeway, the International Music Secretary of the day, and was performed by the massed bands in Royal Albert Hall at the International Congress, 1965.

During his tenure as Territorial Music Secretary, Colonel Rawlins instituted publication of The Canadian Band Journal which featured selections by Canadian writers and was written so that it could serve as a resource for smaller bands in the Territory. This was a successful venture and continued until a new Music Secretary was appointed and the idea was dropped. Colonel Bram Coles and Emil Soderstrom were two of the editors and the music was painstakingly hand written by Fenwick Watkin, a prominent Canadian musician at that time.

Following his time as Territorial Music Secretary Colonel Rawlins served as Divisional Commander in Alberta and Toronto. He then became Field Secretary for the Canada Bermuda Territory, and concluded his Salvation Army career serving for four years as the Chief Secretary for this Territory. He has been retired for 30 years.

Important compositions

Crown of Victory (CM0019) 1958, Bullinger (CM0024) 1958

RAYMENT, PHIL

Bandmaster Philip Rayment (October 17, 1970) received his earliest musical training through The Salvation Army. As a young person, he was also privileged to perform as a member of such wide-ranging musical groups as the Hamilton All-Star Jazz Band, the Ontario Youth Concert Band and the Canadian Forces Band of the Ceremonial Guard. He holds Bachelor degrees in Music and Education from McMaster University and the

University of Western Ontario respectively. Phil's full time occupation is teaching instrumental music in the public school system to students aged 11 to 13.

As a performer, Phil spent four years as the bass trombonist for the New York Staff Band, where he had the privilege of performing with artists such as Elton John, The Canadian Brass and members of the New York Philharmonic. Shortly after moving back to Canada, he joined the Canadian Staff Band and held the position first of second trombone and then bass trombonist. His arrangements have also be performed and recorded by these bands. Phil has enjoyed serving on the faculty of several music camps, including the renowned Star Lake Music camp in New Jersey.

He was appointed the third bandmaster of the Mountain Citadel Band in October, 2000. During his time as bandmaster, the group recording three CD's entitled *'A Christmas Collage'*, *'Above All'* and *'Salvation's Song'*. Phil has always had a strong belief that our talents and gifts should be used to help others, especially young people. Under his direction the band was involved in many charitable endeavors including an ongoing initiative to raise money that would help send young bandsmen to music camp. Another annual concert called Backpacks for Kids saw the coordination of three public school bands and the Mountain Citadel Band performing together to raise money for school supplies for children in our community who could not afford to purchase them otherwise.

Important compositions

Winter's Snow (GS2064) 2008, The Outriders (m/s), Duke Street Intrada (m/s), Feierlicher Einzug (m/s)

RAYNER, IAIN

Iain was born in Northampton in the East Midlands and brought up in the Salvation Army where he started playing the cornet. He later moved to Bedford and changed instrument to euphonium in the Army band. Here he progressed to play in Bedfordshire County Youth Concert and Brass Bands and also in the Salvation Army's East Midlands divisional youth band. On gaining his 'A' levels and leaving school he joined the band of Her Majesty's Life Guards in the Household Cavalry. Here he took part in many prestigious events including Trooping the Colour and the Lord Mayor's Show. After leaving the Army Iain joined the Salvation Army's renowned Kettering Citadel Band where he became Deputy Bandmaster. Iain began writing music for Salvation Army bands and in 1996 and 1997, he enjoyed success when two of his arrangements was played at the Royal Albert Hall by the Army's International Staff Band. He later began writing for the wider brass band world and in 2000 won the NABBC composer's competition with his original concert work *'Tsunami'*. Iain has since had a number of works published for brass bands and was a prize winner in the final of the 2002 European Young Composer's Competition with his work *'Eclipse'*. In 2003, he completed his BA honours degree in Brass Band Studies at Sheffield University studying with Richard Evans, Arthur Butterworth and Darrol Barry. Here he was awarded both the composition and conducting prizes. Iain has enjoyed success writing for some of the top players in the brass band field including David Daws, cornet soloist, Melvyn Bathgate, principal horn of Brighouse & Rastrick band, Donna Lewis, principal horn of the Leyland Band and Gary Fountain, soprano soloist with the GUS Band. He also conducts and is resident conductor and composer for Salvo Brass in the Midlands. At the time of writing, Iain is Bandmaster of Northampton East Salvation Army Corps, having previously served as songster leader and he continues to write music both for and outside the Salvation Army.

Iain is married to Jan and they have two girls, Peta and Gemma, and he currently works as a Primary School teacher.

Important composition

His Glory Proclaim (FS550) 1999, In the Light (GS1934) 1997

REDHEAD, ROBERT

Robert Redhead was born in Manchester in 1940. He had no formal music education except that which he learned through the Salvation Army. At the age of 12 he was invited to play piano duets with his Young People's Band Leader and besides playing the classics, transposed many Salvation Army Band pieces for four hands. Thus he was learning band instrumentation and scoring without realising it, and began writing band music in his teens. He married Gwenyth in 1965 when he was already serving as an officer in the Salvation Army. They pastored a congregation in the East End of London, before they were appointed to the International Training College where Robert, among other responsibilities, directed the music programmes. There were approximately 270 Cadets and 90 Officers, so every public event was a large one, and, for five years, he wrote the music for and conducted the annual Commissioning pageants performed in the Royal Albert Hall. Quite a few of the songs were eventually published in 'The Musical Salvationist'. His following appointment was to the International Music Editorial Department, and in 1971 he joined the bass section of the International Staff Band (ISB). In 1976 Robert and Gwenyth were appointed to Canada with Robert as the Director of the Music Department and Bandmaster of the Canadian Staff Band. With that band he toured throughout North America, Europe (1979), Britain (1983) and New Zealand/Australia (1985). However, as Robert and Gwenyth wanted to develop further pastoral ministry they where apointed Corps Officers at the Southmount Corps in Vancouver, British Columbia. He returned to London in 1990 when he became Head of the Music Editorial Department and Bandmaster of the International Staff Band, and at the forming of the United Kingdom Territory, became head of all the Music and Gospel Arts Departments. This new territorial design enabled some major changes to be made, probably the most significant of which were the re-aligning of the relationship between the Salvation Army and the non- Salvation Army Band World enabling Salvation Army Band personnel to share in the larger world of banding and for Salvation Army band music to be available to the larger banding world. During his time at the Music Editorial Department and Head of the Music Department in Canada, Robert got the chance to develop his compositions and editorial skills, which resulted in many compositions, which are still very popular. Gwenyth and Robert were also very busy developing the further use of music and drama for evangelistical purposes and wrote and produced musicals as a result. In the mid 90's the Redheads moved back to Canada and held executive roles, and in 1998 were appointed to New Zealand. They returned to Canada four years later and in 2003 were appointed by General John Larsson to be his International Representatives for the Development of Worship, Music and other Creative Ministries, which resulted in visiting 31 territories, many of which were in the developing world. They retired from active service in 2005. In his retirement Robert was also asked to take over the Melbourne Staff Band for half a year due circumstances, which he did! Currently the Redhead's continue to travel the world encouraging and facilitating creative and innovative styles of worship.

Important compositions

Isaiah 40 (JC616) 2007, A Pastoral Symphony (FS485) 1991, Quintessence (JC602) 2006, Life Abundant (m/s) 1979, Euphony (m/s) 1979, He Gave Me Joy (m/s) 1980

REID, WILLIAM

Born on 8 January 1935, Portland, Maine, United States of America. His parents moved to Hartford, Connecticut later that same year.

William Reid grew up in the Hartford, Connecticut, Citadel Corps in the late 1940s and 1950s. He learned to play cornet at age eight and mostly struggling with the tune, *'Duke Street'*, like so many others. As a teenager he became the bandmaster of the Young People's Band and eventually the bandmaster of the senior band in the late 1950s into the 1960s.

Around 1963 the Salvation Army in the United States, Eastern Territorial Music Department under Richard Holz and Vernon Post held a composers' contest. William entered a piece in the 'Selection' category and was fortunate enough to win first prize. This selection being entitled, *'How Sweet the Name'*, which is number 66 in the New York Band Journal.

His banding experience includes being a member of the Southern New England Divisional Band and youth band and various brass ensembles. In the mid 1960's he transferred to the Manchester, Connecticut, corps where he played solo horn in the band and conducted the male chorus. While attending the University of Connecticut he also had played French horn in the university concert band.

In the late 1960s he joined the Methodist church in Manchester, Connecticut. of which he is still a member. His musical endeavors include a stint as the bell choir director as well as being a choir member. William continues to arrange anthems for the choir and also does conducting. He leads and arrange music for a small ensemble called The Wesley Brothers Vocal Ensemble, a male quartet. He also has been a vocalist with the Hartford (CT.) Symphony Chorale, the Manchester Symphony Chorale, and presently sings with the Vernon (CT.) Chorale, a topflight vocal group in the central Connecticut area. Bandmaster Reid was a Science Teacher in the Public School System by profession.

Important composition

Selection - How Sweet the Name (AJ0066) 1966

REILLEY, J

One of the early composers (late 1800).

No further information could be retrieved about him.

Important composition

The Children's Friend (GS0334-1) 1897

RESLOW, LLOYD

Lloyd Reslow was born April 7, 1922 in Pawtucket, Rhode Island (USA). His mother Selma (Anderson) Reslow was a Salvationist from Sweden who came to the United States as a young woman. Lloyd's father, John Frederick Reslow, was born in the United States but was brought up in Sweden, returning to the United States when he was 19. He sought out the Swedish American Salvation Army in Providence where he met his wife, and played cornet and led the band.

Lloyd took four years of cornet/trumpet lessons as a youth. He had great musical aptitude and by his high school years was not only performing but writing music. Early pieces, such as his trumpet trio *'Endeavor'* were performed by his high school symphonic band. Around the time of his graduation, a young Captain, Olof Lundgren and Lloyd formed the 'Boys Band' at the Providence Temple Corps, with Lloyd as the Bandmaster. This group of young men would later all head off to the armed services in WW II, but while they were together Lloyd wrote music for them, including marches such as *'Black Out'*, and cornet solos and duets that he and his friend Carl Johansson would play. Most of these pieces remain unpublished.

After graduating from high school in 1940, Lloyd enrolled in an apprenticeship program at Brown and Sharpe Mfg, then one of the leading Machine Tool and Instruments manufacturers in the US, but he felt the call to serve in the armed forces. Lloyd joined the US Coast Guard in 1941. After boot camp, Lloyd auditioned for, and was selected to the Philadelphia Coast Guard Band, as tubist! He played for a season in the band doing war bond fund raisers, radio shows and parades. During this time he wrote some melodies, one of which became the opening theme to *'The Wanderer'*, but at the time he called it *'Rain in Norfolk'* written as a solo piece for his friend Bob Cole (eventual flautist in the Philadelphia Symphony). Eventually, he felt the call to active duty and resigned from the band to train for fire control (artillery), and finished the war aboard ship.

Upon his return to civilian life in 1946, Lloyd resumed is apprenticeship at Brown and Sharpe, and became active writing music for the Scandinavian Division/Territory of the Salvation Army in the Northeast US. Two of his pieces were award winners in the 1946 contest which was the start of the American Band Journal in the US. Both pieces, *'The Name Above All Other Names'*, and *'The Wanderer'* contained Scandinavian themes. The latter of the two was perhaps his best known work. As Steve Bulla once mentioned to me, it was the piece that started it all (among SA composers in the US), meaning that it was not merely an arrangement of one or more hymn tunes, but more of a symphonic, and at times impressionist work. Leidzen became interested in the work and tinkered with it more that Lloyd would have liked.

Lloyd and his wife May Britt got to know Leidzen, who was the editor for Salvation Army music in New York for the pending SA American Journal to be published in 1948. Leidzen once asked Lloyd when he did his writing (composition). He replied that he would write evenings when his wife went to Home League, at which point Leidzen turned to May Britt and told her she should be very faithful to the Home League!

1946 - 1956 were very productive years writing for the Scandinavian Congresses in Worcester MA and New York. He wrote marches, *'En Kjampande Skara'*, the 1947 and 1957 *'Jubilee Marches'*, and various other works. In terms of composition, Lloyd Reslow was largely self taught. He wrote what 'sounded good'. He did some outside reading of books like 'Harmony' by Walter Piston, and took the Bandmasters course with Erik Leidzen.

In the early 1960's, Lloyd submitted entries for the 2nd Eastern Territory contest and again won awards, this time for his March *'Constant Companion'* and a Selection *'Joyful Voices'*. These were pieces specifically written for the contest.

Published works (Salvation Army):

'The Wanderer' (1946), 'The Name Above All Other Names' (1946), 'March-Rhode Island - All of My Life' (1950), 'Joyful Voices' (1964), 'Constant Companion' (1964).

In the late 60's and early 70's Lloyd wrote and arranged music for the Salvation Army Providence Corps band. It was a smaller band, often made up of the officers stationed at the corps and at the ARC in Providence. Pieces written/ arranged at this time included *'Enslingen vid Zithran'*, an Overture of *'Hosea'* scored for smaller band and a series of arrangements of music by the Spurlows. He also wrote a solo piece, *'The Gift'* for the dedication of his first grandson in 1976.

In the 80's Lloyd continued writing for music for special occasions. His *'March Rhode Island – 100'* was written to commemorate the 100th anniversary of the Salvation Army in Rhode Island. He also wrote for the Alaska music camp, the *'March Anchorage'*.

In the 90's he began arranging Salvation Army Choruses for brass ensemble. In performance, Lloyd had crystal clear tone and clean articulation on cornet, but never had the kind of endurance that others enjoyed on the instrument. He always felt he was best suited to Tuba. Still he performed cornet solos and duets well into his seventies. Lloyd was a self taught pianist, and would accompany his wife and daughter Christine in vocal solos as well as playing for congregational singing, choruses, etc. He played guitar and was a part of Swedish String Bands, ultimately leading the New England Stringband Association. He wrote 5 and 6 part brass accompaniments for this music, which are both interesting and challenging to play (a lot of sharps!). In younger years, Lloyd and May Britt were in demand for musical programs around the Scandinavian Corps in the Northeast with the entire family performing. However, the most requested performances were by Lloyd on his ocarina on which he would perform theme and variation cornet solos, and last but not least, the musical glasses, which were played by touch. The glass music was unique, and accompanied by May Britt, Lloyd would play to rapt audiences especially at Christmas concerts. They performed together well into their early 80's.

Little of Lloyd's music has been recorded, but there are several notable recordings out there. One is a recording of *'Constant Companion'*, by the National Capital Band (Salvation Army) under Steve Bulla. Another is a recording of *'The Wanderer'* by the Brass Band Flaacht (Switzerland), which they released first on an LP and then rereleased on CD. Finally, there is the recording of his March Rhode Island 100 by the New England Brass Band, which was a part of their award winning *'Be Glad Then America'* CD. The NEBB performed this piece throughout their 2006 – 2007 season including performances at Boston's Symphony Hall.

Dr Ron Holtz in his critical review of the CD offered the following; *'Our winner disc opens and closes with two scintillating items that symbolize the vitality Yeo and Everson have given to the NEBB these past years--the famous Williams Liberty Fanfare, and the closing march, Rhode Island, by Lloyd Reslow. This man is an unsung hero in Salvation Army music, having played a vital role in New England band and Scandinavian Salvation Army gatherings for many years'*

Lloyd's continuous service in Salvation Army music is remarkable. While he has enjoyed performing, and hearing his music played, one is struck by his faithfulness in providing music and support to his local corps. He probably could have, and should have published more music, but his main focus has been in support of worship at the corps and Scandinavian Events. Lloyd received the order of the Great Commission 2007 for his faithful service.

Lloyd has enjoyed a long and fruitful retirement from Engineering at Brown and Sharpe in 1986. His activities included Habitat for Humanity where he was Volunteer of the Year in 1997 and recognized again for lifetime achievement in 2006. Lloyd was also faithful in League of Mercy visitation, bringing his electric keyboard and playing hymns and other songs on request at assisted living and nursing homes. Lloyd was also an Advisory Board Member to the Scandinavian Home for the Aged.

As recently as summer 2009 Lloyd arranged for, and performed with the Greenwich Bay Brass during which several of his unpublished pieces were featured. He and May Britt live in their home in East Greenwich, Rhode Island.

Important compositions

Meditation - The Name Above All Other Names, Meditation - Joyful Voices, March – Rhode Island

RICHARDSON, RENNIE

Bandsman Rennie Richardson was too young to remember his first contact with The Army. His earliest recollections are of his father lifting him from his knees while he stood to give his testimony in the Holiness Meetings. He received his first red Guernsey when he was seven years of age, and almost immediately took his place in the Drum and Fife Band to play the triangle. His first promotion came when he was admitted to the Senior Band at twelve years of age, for, after playing 2nd cornet for two weeks, he was moved up to 1st cornet. The first 'high spot' he can recollect was, when he was fourteen, making an all-night journey of 230 miles to play with the Band on the Central Transept of the Crystal Palace on the occasion of the International Congress of 1904, and returning home the same night. At seventeen years of age he was promoted Songster Leader, and in the following year his first composition appeared in 'The Musical Salvationist'. About the same time he submitted the score of a march to Lieut.-Colonel Slater which was, however, turned down*! 'I thought',* he says, *'when I saw the red ink splashes all over my cherished score that the Colonel was too severe a critic, but now I wonder how I had the audacity to submit what must have been a very unworthy and elementary venture'.* A few years later he was commissioned Young People's Band Leader, and had the pleasure of building up a Combination of more than thirty members, with all instruments and music paid for by their own efforts. Then came the Great War, during which he served in the R.A.M.C. for four years at Reading, assisting in off-duty time as Bandmaster of Reading West. *'My Heavenly Pilot',* and one or two other compositions which later appeared in 'The Musical Salvationist', were written during quiet periods in the wards of Reading War Hospital. On his return home he took charge of Nelson Band for six months, owing to the illness of Bandmaster Cooper, and on his return was appointed Deputy-Bandmaster. Later he had a term of active service as Bandmaster at the adjoining Corps of Brierfield. It was while acting in this capacity that the *'Bierfield'* march was written and published in the Second Series Band Journal.

Rennie has contributed in 'The Musical Salvationist' since 1907 and has other compositions published in the 'Second Series' (now renamed as Triumph Series) such as the march *'Pakefield',* the *'Brierfield March'* and the anthem *'Make a joyful noise'.* The period covered where in he contributed to the journals of Salvation Army spans more than 30 years. He originated from Nelson. He has had the pleasure of writing Salvation Army music for more than thirty years, his first song appearing in 'The Musical Salvationist' in May 1907. Since that time a fair number have followed in the same periodical, and also in 'The International

Demonstrator', and on all but two occasions he has been privileged to supply both words and music. Two compositions have found their way into the Second Series Band Journal. If Rennie is not mistaken, his musical monologue *'If'*, set a precedent insomuch that it was the first to be published by The Salvation Army. This was in The International Demonstrator, No. 7.

Important compositions

Pakefield (GS1157) 1939, The Brierfield March (TS136) 1930

RICHARDSON, ROBERT

Dr. Robert Edward Richardson Jr. (1936-2011), Co-founder (with composer Mark Freeh) of *'The Enthusiast'* (a brass band news magazine), and former bandmaster of the Manchester Citadel Band in Connecticut, United States of America. Richard graduated from the Princeton University, and was Head of English department at Trinity College (Connecticut). He has a perfect pitch, a photographic mememory, and his instruments are piano, bass trombone and BBb Bass. He recorded the Ray Steadman-Allen piano solo *'Christ is the Answer'* with the New Jersey Youth Band on their 1964 Scandinavian tour recording.

Robert Richardson died on Sunday (October 16, 2011) at his home in Pembroke, ME, after a long and valiant struggle with several forms of cancer. He was 75 years old. Dr. Richardson was born and educated in Manchester, CT. He was the son of the late Robert E. Richardson Sr. and Lucy (Addy) Richardson. He graduated from Trinity College in 1957, and entered the US Marine Corps achieving the rank of 1st Lieutenant. He received his PhD from Princeton University. He taught at Westminster College in PA, American International College in Springfield, MA, and was a Professor for 28 years at Manchester Community College where he was known simply as 'Doc'. In addition to his career in higher education, Dr. Richardson was a gifted musician. He began his studies at age eight with Frederick Werner. For many years he attended the Manchester Citadel Corps of The Salvation Army and was the youth, and later, senior bandmaster. He was self taught on every brass instrument in the band. He performed as the piano soloist with the New Jersey Youth Band of The Salvation Army at Nobel Hall in Stockholm, Sweden, and Philharmonic Hall at Lincoln Center in New York City.

Important composition

My Humble Cry (ABJ64) 1964

RIDENOUR, MARK

Mark Ridenour (6 June 1959) is assistant principal trumpet of the Chicago Symphony Orchestra. He was appointed to this position by Daniel Barenboim in 1994. Mark began his professional career when he was appointed third trumpet in the Lexington (Kentucky) Philharmonic while a senior in college. Mark has appeared as soloist with the Chicago Symphony Orchestra, the Florida Orchestra, Highland Park Strings, and Roosevelt University Orchestra as well as brass bands in the United States and Canada, including the Canadian Staff Band of the Salvation Army. Mark began playing the trumpet at age ten and played trumpet, baritone, and tuba in the band through high school. His first private lesson came when he enrolled at Asbury College, where he earned a Bachelor of Arts degree. He earned a Master of Music degree at the University of Cincinnati College-Conservatory of

Music and completed two years of doctoral studies. *[copied with permission cso.org]*. Mark attends the Des Plaines, Illinois Corps and is the Bandmaster of the corps band.

Important compositions

Two Heavens Declare, Voluntary - Old Hundredth

RINGLE, EDWARD

Edward Ringle was born on September 18, 1928, in Loma Linda, California, USA and grew up in nearby Riverside. When Edward was eight years old, music began to take a central role in his life when he accompanied his sister, Della, to a Young People's Band practice. Although Ringle was too young to join the band, the Young People's Bandleader handed him an instrument which was not in use at that moment and from that moment on he was in the spell of it.

In 1946, Ringle entered The Salvation Army School for Officer Training (SFOT) and was commissioned as a probationary lieutenant with the 'Warriors Session' in 1947. After serving several years in the Cascade Division, he met Ruth Bass, another officer, whom he married in 1952.

The Ringles served together for 38 years in various appointments that included the Cascade, Northwest, Alaska, Southern California, and Intermountain Divisions. Additionally, they served in British Honduras -now Belize- Bolivia, and Chile. After 22 years of missionary service, they returned to the SFOT to develop a new Spanish track. Even though Edward Ringle retired in 1990, he still devoted much of his time to The Salvation Army. And his love for music continued. He would purchase instruments in thrift stores to fix up and give to youth both in the USA and overseas. He also taught Spanish and music in Colorado. Retired General John Larsson wrote a tribute about Ringle. *'Since we first met, I have been one of his great admirers. His creativity, capacity for hard and detailed work, and his total and sacrificial dedication to the task were astounding.'* Major Edward Ringle was Promoted to Glory on 2 February 2011 from his home in Escondido, California, USA.

Important compositions

Suplemento Sudamericano (South American Supplement) is a tune book supplement published in the 1980s in Santiago, Chile (South America West Territory). The arrangements are all written by Major Edward Ringle

RITMAN, OLAF

Olaf was born in the city of Schiedam, The Netherlands (nearby Rotterdam) in 1977. At the age of fourteen he and his family moved to Apeldoorn, in the centre of The Netherlands, where he graduated in Business Informatics in 1999. In 2003 he married Marleen with whom he has a son and a daughter: Julian (2006) and Meike (2009). Olaf's main interest is music: Brass Band, Classical and some genres of Pop and Jazz. He learned playing the cornet and piano at the school of music from the age of ten and started playing in the Schiedam Corps Band of The Salvation Army at the age of eleven. He also played 2nd Cornet in Amsterdam Brass during his father's last two (of over 25) years in the band (Bass Trombone). From the age of 14 Olaf started writing music (first ensemble works later for larger bands) that resulted in some published and recorded pieces.

Ever since he was a child his parents took him to the Salvation Army where he became a fourth generation salvationist. Olaf attends the Ede Corps where he is the Bandmaster and plays the piano for both the choir and the congregation. At the age of seventeen Olaf became a member of the Amsterdam Staff Songsters where he sung 2nd bass. In his last two years with this choir he also fullfilled the task of assistent songster leader. In 2000 Olaf was asked to join the Amsterdam Staff Band on solo cornet where he also was appointed as the Deputy Bandmaster with the change of conductors (2006). Between 2000 and 2003 Olaf was a member of both the Staff Songsters and Band. In a short period of two and a half years Olaf was the bandmaster of the Regional Youth Band in the North-East of The Netherlands. This Salvation Army band that consists of mainly young people gathers once a month to rehearse and give concerts. With the birth of Julian, Olaf decided to resign from this duty. In 2009 Olaf was appointed Bandmaster of the Amsterdam Staff Band which makes him fully responsible for all artistic aspects of that band.

Important compositions

Before His Throne (GS2084) 2010, The Lord is Gracious (2047-2) 2006, When I survey (GS2059) 2007, The Lord bless you and keep you (m/s) Copenhagen 125 (m/s).

RIVE, HERBERT

A cousin to Dr. Thomas Rive, Herbert contributed much less music to the Salvation Army journals and ended with only but two (but two great nevertheless!) compositions published for the Salvation Army. Herbert Rive won an international competition with his March Spirit of Joy which was published in 1957. He served as Songster Leader of the Dunedin Fortress Corps. Herbert Rive was Promoted to Glory in 1968.

Important compositions

The King's Command (FS323) 1969, Spirit of Joy (GS1441) 1957

RIVE, THOMAS

Dr Thomas N. Rive (1920-1978) was born into a Salvationist family in Waimate in the South Island in 1920, Tom Rive very early on showed distinctive musical ability. At 16 years of age he was the bandmaster at Waimate, and after shifting to Wellington in the late 1930's he was Dean Goffin's deputy bandmaster at Wellington South for a period, before moving to Auckland to study at Auckland University. He completed the B.Music degree in 1943 and was appointed to the lecturing staff in 1945. In 1945, Thomas Rive was appointed to the Auckland University as a lecturer, where he gained the distinction of being Senior Lecturer in Music. Honours came his way again in 1964 when he earned his Doctorate of Philosophy in Music. For this thesis, he studied the life and music of a Spanish composer, Luis De Victoria. Continuing his interest in this man, Tom Rive translated into English a biography written by a Spanish Roman Catholic priest. This book was accepted for publication by a leading Bristish publisher. In 1949 he was awarded a New Zealand Government Bursary which enabled him to undertake post-graduate study in composition at the University of Oxford. He was the first graduate to be awarded a Ph.D in music by Auckland University and in 1974 was awarded the rare distinction of a personal chair. His special interest in Roman Catholic liturgical music of the Counter-Reformation, led to his recognition as the leading world authority on the 16th century Spanish composer Thomas Luis de Victoria. For 18 years Tom trained and conducted the University Madrigal Choir, and served a term as President of the Guild of New Zealand composers.

Dr. Rive's achievements within the context of the Salvation Army were as distinguished as his outstanding academic career. His contributions to Auckland Congress Hall as bandmaster, songster-leader and Corps Sergeant Major were in the finest traditions of local officer leadership, and in the final phase of his life he was a greatly loved bandmaster at the Newton Corps. Throughout these years of Salvation Army service he was blessed by the devoted and loyal support of his wife, the former Audrey Skellon, whom he married in 1943.

Dr. Rive's two Festival Series selections for brass band *'I know a Fount'* and *'Pilgrim Song'* brought him world renown. The former symphonic variations were once described by a very well known Army conductor as *'the Army's most profound published music thus far'.* Certainly, Thomas Rive, through the years fulfilled many engagements throughout Australasia, North America, and Europe as guest conductor, lecturer, and preacher. His Promotion to Glory at the comparatively early age of 57 on February 10, 1978, was a significant loss to both the Salvation Army and academia.

An news paper article of roughly eighty years ago already shows the great future Tom Rive had, as one of his first compositions was featured while only eleven years old!

Boy composer

Ashburton, this day.

One of the features of the music at Ashburton Salvation Army Bands' Sunday festival was the presentation for the first time of 'Blantyre March', an intricate piece composed by Master Tom Rive, of Waimate, who is eleven years of age.

(Evening Post, volume CXIII, Issue 126, 30 May 1932) .

His life is encapsulated in his obituary:

Thomas Norman Rive - *2-12-1920 ~ 10-2-1978*

Professor Thomas Rive, born at Waimate in the South Island of New Zealand in 1920, was in his youth doubly fortunate, not only receiving Christian teaching from his parents, ardent Salvationists, but seeing their faith in action in their lives. Nevertheless, his own acceptance of Jesus Christ as Lord and Saviour was, as it always must be, a personal matter, and there was nothing secondhand about the faith to which he testified in the contribution which followed. Apart from graduate study at Oxford and independent research in England, Italy and Spain, he was educated wholly within New Zealand (B.Mus, N.Z.; Ph.D., Auck). His field of special interest was the ecclesiastical polyphony of the late 16th century, and his sphere of work within his beloved Salvation Army was with its choirs and bands. His service as a local officer began at the age of 16 when he was commissioned Bandmaster of Waimate Corps. Subsequent responsibilities included Deputy Bandmaster Wellington South, Corps Sergeant Major, Bandmaster and Songsterleader Acukland Congress Hall and Bandmaster Newton Citadel. His guest appearances with the International Staff Band, London, and at summer music camps in England, North America and Australia, widened his sphere of influence. In the University he was active in administration as well as in teaching and research and was concurrently Acting Head of Department and Dean of the Faculty of Music.

Important compositions

A Pilgrim Song (FS309) 1968, Valiant in Fight (FS279) 1964, Auckland COngress Hall (GS1336) 1950 Colne (GS1733-2) 1980, Free Grace (GS1604-1) 1969, I Know a Fount (FS0238) 1959, Redeeming Love (GS1495) 1961

RIVERS, PATRICK CHARLES

Patrick Rivers started his musical career within the ranks of the Salvation Army as pianist, horn player and bandmaster. He was awarded a Batchelor of Music degree in composition and went into Military Band service as a euphonium player, pianist and arranger.

He wrote for many publishers notably 'Off The Cuff' and 'Portrait of Brunel'. He has directed In-Service courses for teachers in school band training, correspondence courses in composing and arranging, and conducted a number of school bands. He has also been elected to the Advisory Council of the NSBBA, been a reader for Hinrischen Edition, and is a writer-member of the Performing Rights Society.

Having retired from his 50-year teaching career he was for a time principal euphonium and Associate Conductor of the Bourne Concert Band.

Important compositions

Keep Singing (GS1406) 1954, Letchworth (TS0495) 1953

ROBERTS, J

A former bandmaster of the Chester Corps Band. No more information could be retrieved about J. Roberts.

Important compositions

Fellowship with Jesus (TS0111) 1928, Our Flag (GS0990) 1928, St. Agnus (TS0147) 1930

ROBINSON, G.P

One of the early composers (late 1800). It is believed he might have been a member of the first Household Troops Band. No further information could be retrieved about him.

Important composition

Jesus has redeemed me (GS0068-2) 1887

ROBINSON, GRAHAM

A former bandsman and later bandmaster of the Andover, Southampton Corps, Channel Isles Division, in the United Kingdom.

Important composition

Holy Spirit come o come (TS0807) 1977

ROBINSON, IAN

Written by Ian Robinson

My earliest indication of interest in brass banding was at Govan Citadel Corps where my parents were involved in the music sections. Mom was Songster organist and Dad played solo horn, but at the age of two I developed a fascination with the trombone section! They were my idols, my heroes, and so I was given a small plastic trombone to emulate them. Naturally, when I joined the YP Band I wanted to play trombone but all of us had first to learn a valve instrument, which turned out to be very useful in later years. Eventually I achieved my ambition and joined the trombone section. My first influences as a composer came from listening to the senior band. From an early age I was attracted to American composers like Erik Leidzen and Emil Soderstrom, because of their unusual chords, voicing and progressions.

We moved to Ayr when I was twelve, to a much smaller band with a complete trombone section. I was redirected onto euphonium which soon became my second love. Four of us got together to form an informal quartet because our band didn't, or couldn't play the kind of music we liked. We had fun on Saturday afternoons blowing through pieces like Praise, Treasures from Tchaikowsky and so on. Not ideal quartet music, but we managed to cover the missing parts and somehow get through! I began to dabble in writing for the group at this time.

Then came 1965 and a major breakthrough in brass band music. I was in the Royal Albert Hall for the Army's Centenary celebration and heard the premiere performance of Ray Steadman-Allen's *'The Holy War'*. I was enraptured. I had never heard anything like the dissonance he produced in that epic piece and when I returned to Ayr I started attending Govan's band practices to enjoy playing more exciting music like Eric Ball's Resurgam and Leslie Condon's *'Call of the Righteous'*, composers who also were great influences on me.

But the call of the world won the day and at age twenty I left The Salvation Army to enjoy the dubious pleasures of alcohol and drugs and wandered for fourteen years in a spiritual and musical wilderness. I played bass guitar and keyboards in a folk rock group and again dabbled in writing songs but the passion was not there. Fast forward to 1983 in Southern California. At the bottom of my spiritual decline I started reading the Bible and found Jesus in the Gospel of John, just as my wife had a few days earlier. We decided to go to the nearest Salvation Army Corps at Santa Ana and my love for brass bands was reborn. Within weeks I was in the band and since the only opening was Bb Bass that's where I went! Suddenly I was introduced to a new breed of composers who made their mark on me – Stephen Bulla, Jim Curnow, Bill Himes and Bill Gordon were remarkable influences. I got to meet some of them too! Bill Gordon pushed me into composing both vocal and band music and steadily encouraged me. Barrie Gott was another encourager around that time. Pretty soon I found a gift for writing and Morning Star was my first published composition. Swing was my forte for a while with *'Gentlemen's Carol'* and *'Soon and Very Soon'* both being widely received. I broke out of that mold with *'To a God Like This'* however! Both the Santa Ana Band and Songsters used the stuff I wrote – some of it quite bad – and Bandmaster Ed Freeman encouraged me to write more. Some of my composition are direct results of his suggestion. Songster Leader Al Stickland loved *'He is Exalted'* which became our first published vocal work.

Of course, many composers outside of The Salvation Army have also influenced me. I love the music of Aaron Copland, Leonard Bernstein and Charles Ives. I enjoy listening to most of the classical composers from Bach on and still retain a healthy interest in rock, folk and pop music. Vocally, John Rutter has probably played the most important part in my development.

Some of you may remember Malcolm and Connie High. They were Corps Officers at Ayr during my teenage years and I recently had contact with Malcolm because of our move to Sheringham. That's his home town and our new appointment. As I reminisced about those distant days I began to recall just what a rotten and troublesome teenage Salvationist I was!

Yet, more than forty years on, I am now a Major and soon-to-be Corps Officer at Sheringham. How did that happen? That's the story of my life journey and there is a certain irony to it. In fact that's a good way to explain it; I-R-O-N-Y!

Insensitive. It began with my insensitivity to my parents, Corps leaders, and most of all to God's Holy Spirit. I must have sat through countless sermons, hours of Bible study at Corps Cadet Class, umpteen altar calls and yet all I thought about was me! I just wanted to live life my way; Romans 2:8 describes it perfectly – *'Other people are selfish and reject what is right in order to follow what is wrong'* (Good News Bible).

Rebellious. My insensitivity quickly led to rebellion against my parents, my leaders and God. I was trapped in a spiral of ever-increasing sinfulness. The Bible says that rebellion is as bad as witchcraft, and arrogance as sinful as idolatry (1 Samuel 15:23). My sin and arrogance were dragging me away from God, as well as the godly influence of The Salvation Army, and closer to Hell.

Open. I thank God for spiritual people who never gave up praying and encouraging me. It was the incredible witness of Isobel's changed life that led me to read God's word again. Suddenly all those old Corps Cadet classes with Malcolm and Connie came flooding back and began to make sense. Finally, I opened my heart to Christ and my journey took an amazing u-turn.

New life. With new life came a new direction. I couldn't keep going down the old road – God was showing me a different way. I had grand ideas of how to find a new church, but Isobel's pragmatism cut through all that and led us to the Santa Ana Corps of The Salvation Army where good officers and new friends helped me to grow into my new life. I learned again how to study the Word, pray and to worship. What a difference it was to know Christ and not just to know about Him!

Yielded. Now that God had my attention, He began working other miracles in me as I yielded myself completely to his will. Not easy but necessary. Paul says, *'Offer yourselves as a living sacrifice to God, dedicated to His service and pleasing to Him'* (Romans 12:1). Having committed to follow Him wherever He led, I began to go along with His wonderful plan for my life.

An even greater irony is that all the effort I poured into rebelling against God is now being used to serve Him! Paul says, *'At one time you surrendered yourselves entirely as slaves to impurity and wickedness for wicked purposes. In the same way you must now surrender yourselves entirely as slaves of righteousness for holy purposes'* (Romans 6:19).

Surrendering to Him has taken me on a journey I could never have imagined, as well as to places and to people I will never forget.

The letter 'S' has played a critical role in our journey. We left Ayr in 1977 to live in Surrey, and five years later immigrated to the USA with our two girls. We had a simple plan – open an English pub to sell British drinks and food to Americans at extortionate prices, then retire to a Greek Island where we would write books in the Mediterranean sun! But as Burns once wrote, *'The best laid plans of mice and men …'*

After eighteen months in our California paradise our relationship was in trouble and our Catholic faith was failing to meet our spiritual needs. The dream was crumbling until one of Isobel's nursing friends suggested we read the Bible. Trial and error led us to the Living

Bible and when she read the Gospel of John she was utterly convicted by the Holy Spirit and surrendered her will to God. Seeing a dramatic change in her I did the same. We then knew that we needed to find a church where we could develop this new relationship with God, so I made a list of churches in the area and suggested we visit one each week until we found one we liked. Isobel, ever the pragmatist, looked over the list and, seeing The Salvation Army at the bottom, said, *'We'll just go there!'* So I returned to the Army and we went to the Santa Ana Corps. Within six weeks I was in uniform and playing in the band. The girls loved Sunday school and we made many new and lasting friendships. Most importantly, we grew spiritually and our family bond was strengthened because of our relationship with Jesus Christ.

Our journey was very pleasant and comfortable. We had a wonderful church home, a nice house, good jobs and a growing family. I played piano at the Corps and began writing music. We taught an adult Sunday school class, started a home Bible study and were increasing our understanding of God's will and purpose for our lives. Then I was made redundant and spent several months trying unsuccessfully to find a new job. I was told by more than one company president that I was the one they wanted then never heard from them again! It didn't make any sense until one day Isobel came down to breakfast and asked if I had been talking to God about Salvation Army officership.

'Don't be so absurd!' I said, utterly shocked.

'Well,' she said, *'I've just been arguing with God upstairs and He told me I was stopping you from becoming an officer!'*

She had been praying and asking God why her talented and intelligent husband – her words, not mine – could not find a job. God answered that it was because she was stopping me. At first she was confused, and then she realized what He was saying. *'You don't mean THAT job?'* she asked incredulously. And God said, *'Yes, that job!'*

Isobel never wanted to be an officer so that avenue of service appeared closed. Now it suddenly opened up and within a few months we were appointed as Auxiliary Captains to Santa Barbara on the Pacific coast about ninety miles north of Los Angeles. After seven and a half years we were moved to Santa Rosa, forty-five minutes north of San Francisco in the Northern Californian wine country. Then in 2004, two and a half years later, the Army sent us to Singapore where we served for four and a half wonderful years before reluctantly returning to California. Now, following a few months at THQ we are ready to leave for Sheringham, the sixth 'S' in our journey.

We never achieved our dream but received something infinitely greater and more valuable. Instead of serving alcoholic drinks we have helped people overcome their addiction to alcohol. Instead of serving British food we have given out the bread of life to those who need it most. Instead of making a lot of money we have stored up for ourselves treasures in heaven. And instead of retiring to a Greek island we will spend eternity in heaven with our Lord and Saviour, Jesus Christ! We have riches beyond our wildest imagination and the journey's not over yet!

Life's journey takes many twists and turns. Over the years since I left Ayr God has taken me to some incredible places and introduced me to many delightful friends along the way. Here are just a few:

- Santa Barbara – We spent seven and a half years in this beautiful Mediterranean-style community about one hundred miles north of Los Angeles. It was our first Corps appointment and we grew to love this wonderful city with the Pacific Ocean breaking on its shore and the mountains standing tall behind. We grew from rookies to seasoned officers here. In January 1999 we were commissioned as 'full' Captains in the Corps with the Regent Hall Band led by Stephen Hanover accompanying us – they were in California for the Rose Parade!

- Singapore – Part of our hearts will always be there. It is a magical, enchanting island with everything ancient and modern. In just a few square miles you can be in England, or China, or India, or Malaysia, or Indonesia, or even the USA! We loved the people, the food, the pulsating, driving lifestyle, the convenience for traveling throughout Asia, and the ministry that God gave us among the people.

- Asfirrudin – He was a fourteen year old Malay Muslim boy with a brain tumor who was admitted to Peacehaven, the nursing home we ran in Singapore. When he came in he was not expected to live more than a few weeks. He could not move or do anything for himself – he was literally in a vegetative state. But the constant care and love that was showered on him by our staff saw him begin to respond, first with slight movements of his eyes, then with his hands. Soon he was sitting up and quite aware of his surroundings. I visited him often and was always surprised at the progress he was making. Our chaplain, Jimi, also visited him and kept telling him about the love of Jesus. One day, more than a year after his arrival, Jimi asked him in Malay if he wanted to accept Jesus into his heart. He told him to squeeze his hand once for *'Yes'* and twice for *'No.'* Asfirrudin squeezed his hand once and accepted Christ as his Saviour while Jimi prayed. He went to heaven a few weeks later. His doctors said that the quality of life he enjoyed was far greater than anything they expected. He was my special friend and I still miss him.

- Mui Lang – She was the cause of some of our greatest headaches in Singapore, but became one of our best friends! As the Assistant Executive Director for Nursing in Peacehaven she really ran the place. We called her 'the matron' since that was her role. It was also her attitude. But we recognized her leadership and potential to help us achieve our goal of making Peacehaven truly a Salvation Army ministry. Over the years we saw her move from adversary to friend. She began attending the Corps, then became a soldier, and finally we commissioned her as our Corps Sergeant-Major! What a woman! A five foot nothing bundle of nuclear energy, she kept us running from morning till night. When we left Singapore, we proudly and confidently handed over the reins of Peacehaven to her, and she still calls us every week with an update!

- Kolok – Captain Tan Guat Hai, or Kolok as he is known, is the Corps Officer in Bintulu, East Malaysia, on the island of Borneo. I visited Kolok several times and was always impressed by his energy and compassion. One day, while conducting the Corps Review we were interrupted by a phone call. A longhouse belonging to an Iban family had burned to the ground. Kolok told me we needed to deal with this so the review was put on hold and we loaded his van with food, clothing and other supplies. Then we set off on a two-hour trip into the jungle where we found the family living in a makeshift tent alongside the ashes of their former home. We gave them the supplies and spent some time listening to their story. It was only later that I discovered that the Iban people used to be headhunters! Many still have the little shrunken heads hanging on their doorposts to ward away evil spirits. But this young officer and his Chinese Hong Kong wife bravely and regularly carry the compassion of his Christian faith into the heart of Borneo, because they love Jesus.

- Myles and Debbie – These two are among our newest friends. While we were attending our 'home' Corps in California (Tustin Ranch), we met Myles and Debbie after a Sunday morning service. Myles was going through a very difficult work-related trial and although he was a Buddhist, he was looking anywhere to find some peace and help. They were Japanese-Americans from Hawaii who both worked as pharmacists. Isobel talked to them and quickly realized they needed Jesus in their lives. Led by the Holy Spirit, she asked if they wanted a relationship with Christ and to know His peace. They blurted out, 'Yes!' and we led them into a small room where they both invited Jesus Christ into their hearts. We only had a few weeks with them before we left for the UK, but saw tremendous growth in their faith, and great joy and peace come into their lives. They now attend the Corps regularly, and we look forward to seeing them in a few weeks.

Throughout this journey Isobel has been my constant companion. She is my best friend, my inspiration, and my soul-mate. Without her I would have been lost. Of course, the same is true of Jesus Christ, who brought us together and has kept us in His love. Together we travel through all the twists and turns and eventually will be united for all eternity. What a wonderful hope! Jesus says, *'Whoever follows me will never walk in darkness, but will have the light of life'* (John 8:12). And so we journey on singing the words of Fanny Crosby:

I must have the Saviour with me,
For I dare not walk alone;
I must feel his presence near me,
And his arm around me thrown.

Then my soul shall fear no ill;
Let him lead me where he will,
I will go without a murmur,
And his footsteps follow still.

Important compositions

Gentlemen's Carol (GS1897) 1994, Morning Star (TS962) 1990, Beyond the Blue (GS2057) 2007

ROS, CORNELIS T.J.

Cor Ros is versatile musician who has played trombone in Rotterdam Congress Hall Band, cornet in Amsterdam Congress Hall Band, as well as in several secular bands. However he became known as trombone player with the Amsterdam Staff Band. After moving away from the Netherlands he started a life in Portugal where he soon was involved in corps activites including the band. It was only a matter of time before he became bandmaster of the São Brás de Alportel Corps Band. Next to this task he joined the Command Band of the *Exército de Salvação* as the Salvation Army is called in Portugal, and later became the National Band Instructor. He has written many pieces and is a published composers for Lake Music.

Important composition

Trial and Error, From Paul to Saul, Amsterdam March

ROSS, DONALD

A former student of Erik Leidzén, and probably one of his closest friends, Don went to New York University, studied Spanish and did graduate work at the University of Madrid in Spain. He speaks about eight languages, and later played euphonium in the New York Staff Band. He was on the 1960 tour to England with this band. By profession he was the head council (lawyer) for General Electric Corporation, and was Bandmaster of the Schenectady corps band in upstate New York.

ROWLANDS, ??

This could have been Ron Rowland (though note the missing S at the end of his name), an officer who also played in the Chicago Staff Band, although this is not confirmed.

Important composition

Hymn Setting - Blaenwern

ROWSELL, DAVID JON

David Rowsell is an established composer with many pieces published by the Salvation Army. These include the American Band Journal (New York), the Maple Leaf Brass (Toronto, Canada) and the Unity and Triumph Series (United Kingdom). He holds the degrees of B. Mus. and B. Mus. Ed. He is a retired music teacher with 26 years experience as a Band Director of Elementary and Middle School Bands. He has composed and arranged many pieces while teaching in the school system. He also taught Brass and Woodwind privately for 20 years. He is presently Bandmaster of the Salvation Army St. John's Temple in Canada, a position he has held for 27 years. As a retired music teacher, he now composes and arranges music full time.

Important compositions

Glory Days (TS1168) 2007, Introit On An Easter Hymn (TS1186) 2008

ROWSELL, JONATHAN

Jonathan Rowsell is a relatively new Salvation Army composer. His first piece was published in October 2010 in the Unity Series (United Kingdom) with his second composition set to be released in the same series in June 2011. He holds a B. Mus. degree and has completed his M. Mus degree in 2011. Throughout his studies, he has written pieces for a variety brass instrumentation, including brass band, brass choir, brass quintet, and brass trio. He was Young People's Bandmaster at the Salvation Army St. John's Temple in Canada, as well as a member of the senior band and songster brigade. As a developing composer, he intends to regularly submit new music to the Salvation Army's many brass band journals. He currently resides in London, Ontario, and is a member of the London Citadel Band and Canadian Staff Band.

Important composition

Franconia (US337-1) 2010

SAGGERS, HERBERT

Approximately born in 1910 and Promoted to Glory around 1930 at the young age of twenty. A former bandsman and Songster Leader of the Bexley Heath Corps in London. The 'Bexley Heath March' was his first composition for band, and it was hoped and expected he would write much more, but he was suddenly Promoted to Glory. He had two brothers who were Salvation Army officers.

Important composition

Bexley Heath (TS0144) 1930

SALT, NIGEL

Nigel was born in Sale, United Kingdom on 27 January 1953. He loved to sit at the piano playing and commenced having lessons at six years of age. He was playing in eisteddfods (*festival of literature, music and performance*) from seven years age and first learnt to play a brass instrument about when he was ten. He was playing piano musical accompaniments for Gilbert & Sullivan musicals at High School from age twelve. After his immigration to Australia he became well known for playing piano duets with his father, Derek (who passed away in 1988, six years prior to Nigel's death).

Nigel wrote a vocal trio for his wife's younger twin sisters and his sister to sing at his wedding in 1977. He was Bandmaster at Parramatta Corps in the early nineties but retired from that due to ill health. However, he continued as songster accompanist until only a couple of weeks prior to his death. He loved music and expressing through music and was always giving time to support others, e.g. music arrangements and accompaniments etc. Nigel Salt was Promoted to Glory in September 1994, aged 41years.

Important compositions

Jesus Stand Among Us, Variations on St Phillip

SAMUEL, NICHOLAS JAMES

Nicholas James Samuel was born on 26th July 1980 in Billinge, Lancashire, England, to Salvationist parents, Clive and Marjorie Samuel. Born into a very musical family, Nicholas grew up being very active within the Warrington Corps, becoming a junior solder at the age of seven, joining the Young People's Band and Singing Company, and later becoming a senior soldier at the age of fifteen, then joining the senior band and songsters. After finishing high school and sixth form college, Nicholas studied music at the University of Salford, with final electives in conducting and arranging under such great tutors as Professor David King, Professor Peter Graham and the late Dr Roy Newsome. This led him to study further for a Post-Graduate Diploma in Performance, specialising in brass band conducting at the university. Graduating in 2001, Nicholas applied for a job as a Sub-editor in the Music Ministries Unit at The Salvation Army's Territorial Headquarters in London, and here began a great journey of musical and spiritual growth.

Upon moving to London to begin work, Nicholas soldiered at Hendon Corps whilst lodging with friends of the family, but following a house move and regularly playing for Enfield Citadel Band whilst they were a percussionist short, it seemed to make sense to transfer to the Enfield Corps only a few months later. It was then that Nicholas had the privilege of playing alongside Simon Jenkins under the leadership of Bandmaster James Williams MBE, both of whom were a great source of encouragement and inspiration. During his time there, the band visited The Netherlands twice, toured part of the United States of America, and travelled the UK extensively. At Enfield Corps, Nicholas served as a bandsman, the songster pianist and for three years as the Young People's Bandleader. Shortly before leaving the corps to go to the training college, the Young People's Band made its first recording entitled *'More than a song'*, which marked not only the end of Nicholas' leadership of the group, but the achievements of a significant number of the young people involved who had made the transition from the Young People's Band to the senior band in that short time.

The year after commencing work at THQ, Nicholas applied for the vacant position in the percussion section of the International Staff Band, and spent six very enjoyable years of ministry in the band as both a percussionist and as the band's pianist. It was on his first overseas tour with the band to the United States of America and Canada in 2004, that mutual friends introduced Nicholas to cadet Heather Richardson. They were married in April 2008.

In September 2008, Nicholas responded to God's call on his life to become a Salvation Army Officer, and entered the William Booth College in London as a member of the 'Prayer Warriors Session' of cadets, and Heather was appointed as the Associate Officer to Upper Norwood Corps. During his second year at the training college, Nicholas was appointed as the college bandmaster. In July 2010, Nicholas was commissioned as a Lieutenant and appointed with Heather to the Thurso Corps on the north coast of Scotland. Shortly before their move to Thurso, their son Philip was born.

Nicholas Samuel's interest in composing and arranging began at an early age when he was taught music theory by his grandfather, James Lovatt, who was a prominent music teacher, conductor and adjudicator in the local region. At an early age he was taught to harmonise a hymn tune in four parts, and transpose and score it for brass ensemble (the Young People's Band Leader at Warrington was very gracious in allowing him to try these out every once in a while!). His first published vocal composition was a song written for the Divisional Junior Soldier Camp in 1995, with lyrics by Rob Little, entitled *'Jesus Understands'*, and was published in the 'Sing to the Lord Children's Voices' Series. His first published band arrangement was a setting of *'Who is he?'*, which had been an arranging assignment at university but with the encouragement of his tutor, was submitted for publication to 'North Music' Holland. His first band piece published by The Salvation Army was the Festival March *'Grounded Firm'*, published in the 'Unity Series Band Journal'.

Asked about significant compositions, Nicholas would say that writing *'Gift of love'* (General Series Band Journal, August 2004) was a piece that marked a new phase in his writing as he attempted to transcribe his testimony into music. *'The Warrior Covenant'* (unpublished) was written in 2010 for the commissioning of his session, and played in the evening celebration by the International Staff Band. This work also forms a testimony in music as the songs seek to echo the Officer's Covenant. Published shortly after Commissioning was the sessional march, *'Prayer Warriors'* (General Series Band Journal, February 2011), featuring songs appropriate to the session and references to the national anthem of each country represented by members of the session. As a Salvationist musician, Nicholas's passion is creating music that communicates the Gospel of Jesus Christ, clearly and simply, to both the players/singers and the listeners.

Important composition

Banners Aflame (US0319) 2006, Everlasting Praise (JC0624) 2008, Gift of Love (GS2019) 2004, Grounded Firm (US0286) 2003, Sweet, sweet sound (US0332) 2007, More than a song (m/s)

SAMUELSSON, OTTO

A member of the Swedish Staff Band for a somewhat longer period than the other Swedish composers mentioned in this book. Otto was a Staff Bandsman from 1900 to 1912, and was a member of the Trombone section. He composed the *'March for the Emigrants'* (svensk Festmusik 37), 'Across the Ocean' (svensk Festmusik 28) and 'Motala March' (svensk Festmusik 37). He later immigrated to the United States and became a valued member of the New York Staff Band.

Important compositions

Motala (FM0037) 1906, Across the Ocean (FM0028-1) 1906

SANDBERG, AMANDA

The only known female brass composer from Sweden, Amanda Sandberg was born in 1873 and Promoted to Glory in 1961. She went to the Training College in 1897, and was except a brass composer, also a song writer and instructor for the famous String Bands in Sweden during 1923 until 1928. She composed the march *'The Front is calling'* (Svensk Festmusik 221).

Important composition

Fronten Kaller! (FM0221)

SA(U)NDERS, MARK

One of the early composers (late 1800). He was West Indian and a pioneer early song writer in the Salvation Army. Envoy Mark Saunders (also called Saunderson) was know as 'Blind Mark' in his early days. He was an organist and entertainer in an English Pub when the Salvation Army held a street meeting in front of the building. As a result, he became converted and was used by the founder, General William Booth, as organist in his campaigns and travels. In the 1880's he was sent to open the work among his native people in the Bristish West Indies. Among the operations he established there was work among the blind. He was a fine teacher of Braille. Blind Mark went to Salt Lake City, Utah, USA, in 1928 and was a faithful soldier of The Salvation Army Corps until his death in 1941. He wrote *'Never Quit the Field'* and *'Let Us Stand Our Ground.'*

Important composition

He Loved Me, I Cannot Tell Why (GS0367) 1898, Keep Me Unspotted (GS0091-2) 1888, Take Me Home Again (GS0328) 1896, Will You Quit the Field? (GS0101) 1888

SAYWELL, EDWARD V.

After eighteen years in the position as Band Inspector, Edward 'Ted' Hill, was succeeded by fellow composer Edward Saywell. Edward started in this function in December 1925. He, like Edward, was respected and loved around the British Territory. He remained in this role until 1941, when he became National Secretary for Bands and Songster Brigades. In total he was a member of the Bands Department for thirty-four years, and even in retirement he continued to serve the Army by serving the interests of the Army musicians. He was Promoted to Glory in March 1959.

Important compositions

The Challenge (GS1017) 1930, Resignation (GS1119) 1936, Unmeasured Love (GS0917) 1924

SCHEIBNER, THOMAS

Thomas Scheibner has served as Songster Leader at Montclair Citadel (The Salvation Army USA Eastern Territory) since September 1995. He obtained his B.A. in Music Education from Drew University in Madison, NJ and has undertaken additional studies in Music Education at New York University and Boston University. Tom is a member of the staff of The Salvation Army's USA Eastern Territory Music Department, where he has worked for 28 years and currently is the Assistant Territorial Music Secretary. He has attended Star Lake Music camp every year since 1969, first as a camper, then as a program staff member and now serves as the musicamp program director. Tom is also a member of the New York Staff Band and has served for 33 years in the band.

Prior to working for The Salvation Army, Tom taught music in public schools in the Boston area for a period of 3 years. In addition to his duties in the Music Department, Tom serves as an adjunct instructor at The Salvation Army School for Officer Training in Suffern, NY. As part of his job responsibilities in the Territorial Music Department, he helps to organize and administer a program each year called Star Search Talent Display. This soloist/ensemble competition has taken place each year within the USA Eastern Territory for over 25 years and now includes Gospel Arts categories such as drama and sacred dance in addition to categories relating to musical performance. Tom has served as a guest instructor at Salvation Army music camps in North and South America. He also is a percussionist in the Montclair Citadel Band. Tom and his wife Charlene are the parents of three daughters, all of whom are active Salvationists.

Important composition

The Blessing (AJ0114) 1981

SCHMIDT, RUBEN

Ruben Alexander Schmidt was born on the 25th of November 1984. He was born into a Salvation Army family in Solingen. His father, Heinrich Schmidt, is bandmaster at the local corps and also bandmaster of the German Staff Band. In the Corps he had his first lessons on the cornet, later he changed to tenor horn.

Most influences came from his father, who teached him in the Junior Band and later in the Senior Band. He is also Ruben's Bandmaster in the German Staff Band. He also enjoyed the times abroad, for example the time he spend in international music schools like Star Lake and the Territorial Music School in Canada. There he took his first composing lessons with Dr. Howard Evans, at that time bandmaster of the Amsterdam Staff Band and currently bandmaster of the Boscombe Citadel Band in the United Kingdom. But all the time the fellowship especially in the Band in Solingen was most important for Ruben. There he is playing with people he knows his whole life and who always gave him strength. Especially his family, his father, mother, and brother, who is now a professional percussion player, his sister and his uncles.

When Ruben was 14 years old he also started playing the French Horn, which brought him in contact with the Orchestral world. With the Western German Youth Orchestra he toured through Germany, but also through the Netherlands, Luxembourg, Belgium,

Poland, the Baltic States, Russia and Finland. These expierences made him even more interested in music. So after school he started studying music padagogy, French Horn and music theory at the university for music in Cologne.

Ruben was always interested in how music works. That's why he always looked at it more carefully and that's why he started doing his own little compositions. First just for his small Corps Band, which is just a small band of around 8 players, than later for the territorial music schools, the Divisonal bands and now for the German Staff Band. His music was also featured by non-army bands like the Cologne Concert Brass Band in their yearly concerts and competitions and the West German Youth Brass Band.

Important compositions

This is My Father's World (m/s), Lobe den Herren (m/s), Come Thou Fount (US393) 2012

SCHRAMM, ROBERT C.

Robert C. Schramm, was a professional musician with 23 years in the United States Air Force Band, was Deputy Bandmaster and principal euphonium of the National Capital Band for 37 years, and has had compositions published by the Salvation Army in New York and London.

Robert Carman Schramm was born on 21 October 1940 in Carlisle, Pennsylvania, where his parents, Dwight and Winifred Schramm, were stationed as the corps officers. Musical talent was prevalent in the Schramm family; Robert's father was a noted vocal soloist, and two of his uncles, Roland and Charles Schramm, were long-time members of the New York Staff Band. His early musical education was in Salvation Army music programs in the USA Eastern Territory.

When in his teenage years, Robert attended Star Lake Music Camp and other Salvation Army music camps. At a divisional music camp in the Southwest Ohio/Northeast Kentucky (SWONEKY) Division, where his parents were serving at Divisional Headquarters, he met the composer Emil Soderstrom, who became an early influence on his composition and brass arranging. At the age of seventeen, he was appointed Bandmaster of the SWONEKY Divisional Youth Band. In addition to his Salvation Army music service, he was also a key member of his high school music program and studied euphonium with Betty Glover, the bass trombonist with the Cincinnati Symphony from the Cincinnati College Conservatory.

In 1959, Robert was accepted at the Eastman School of Music in Rochester, New York, one of the premier music conservatories in the United States. After studying at Eastman for three years, he auditioned for the United States Air Force Band on euphonium, and was accepted into that group, which is one of the top US military bands. In July, 1961, he arrived in Washington, DC to take up his duties in the USAF Band.

At the beginning of the 1961-1962 season, Robert became principal euphonium and deputy bandmaster of the National Capital Divisional Band of the Salvation Army (now known as the National Capital Band). He remained a member of this ensemble for 37 years, serving as deputy bandmaster for his entire term of service. From 1965, he was also a key member of the Prince George's Corps Band, serving as Bandmaster for several different terms.

In March 1962, Robert married Naomi Heinz of Philadelphia, Pennsylvania. They have two children, Robert (born May 1963) and Karen (born June 1965). Eventually, Robert transitioned from a playing role in the USAF Band to a position in the Manuscript Music Section, where he worked as a copyist preparing parts for the custom arrangements used by the band. Manuscript preparation in the days before computer typesetting was a skilled occupation which was critical to the operation of a premier military band.

In 1977, he was appointed as Divisional Music Director of the National Capital and Virginia Division. The concept of having music directors at the divisional level was a new one in the USA Southern Territory at that time, and the position was part-time. During his six-year term, he upgraded the level of instruction at the summer music camp, supported corps music programs in remote parts of the division by personally traveling to teach there on weekends, and created a Divisional Youth Band. His tenure set a firm foundation for the current strong and vibrant music program in this division.

As a composer, his most prolific period was the 1970s, when he wrote many pieces for the National Capital Band and the Prince George's Corps Band. His most well-known work, the festival arrangement *'The Children's Song'*, based upon two melodies associated with the song *'All things bright and beautiful'*, was written to challenge a student band at a music camp, and is scored with all sections having parts of the melodies at various times. After his retirement from the United States Air Force in 1984, his musical output slowed, mainly because of a career change which led him to become a skilled computer professional.

In addition to his compositional ability, Robert also was a poet, and wrote several songs. One notable project, unfortunately never published, was a collaboration with Stephen Bulla on a Christmas cantata entitled *'Christmas Vision'*, where Robert supplied the book and lyrics and Stephen the music, consisting entirely of original songs.

Robert retired from the National Capital Band at the end of the 1997-1998 season, but continued to be active in the Prince George's Corps music programs until he moved out of the Washington area in 2003. Now fully retired, he resides with his wife in Dover, Delaware.

Important compositions

The Children's Song (FS367) 1975, At the Foot of the Cross (GS1680) 1976

SCOTNEY, ARTHUR

One of the eight older brothers of Harold Scotney. His story is similar to Harold's until Arthur starts teaching brass at Hamilton Corps. Arthur's only musical appointment was bandmaster at Hastings where in the 1920s he wrote the march *'Hastings'* NZBBJ 17. Arthur did not find composition easy and it is possible this was his only attempt to write something. It does not contain a referential hymn tune. He died in Rotorua. Those who attended the funeral, said Arthur was such a tall man and the Rotorua hall entrance so small that the coffin had to be tilted almost upright to get it in and out for the service.

'The Scotney family is one of the best known Salvationist families in New Zealand. Over twenty five years ago they came to this country, and within a short time after settling had all got converted in The Salvation Army at Dannevirke, and became hardworking Salvationists. The Atjutant and Commandant (Tom and Albert) want to the Australian Training Home some twenty years ago, and were kept in that Commonwealth as Field Officers, commanding many of the leading corps. Later, Albert returned to New Zealand, and is now in charge of the Boy's Home, Eltham. Tom is still an Australian Officer, having seen service in almost every part of the Commonwealth. The last two years he has been on service overseas with the

A.I.F. The other three boys, Secretary Herbert, Bandmaster Arthur and Deputy Bandmaster Harold, hold commissions at Dannevirke, Hastings, and Wellington City Corps respectively, while the mother has also held many local commissions in the Dannevirke Corps. Truly our sister is receiving a reward in the sight and full stretch for the Kingdom. Losing her husband when the youngest son was but ten months old, her battle can be imagined, but she has fought through, giving glory to God and thanking Him for the gift and help of her five sons. The total length of Salvation service punt in by the whole family reaches 135 years, and average of 22½ years service. They all met together recently in Wellington for the first time in twenty years, and took active part in the weekend meetings. It was a fine sight to see the proud mother with her sons, all fighting hard for God and finding full satisfaction in the ranks of the Salvation Army'.

(source: New Zealand 'War Cry' of 1918)

Arthur Scotney, son number five of the Scotney family, was born on 1 May 1880 and Promotoed to Glory in 1968.

Important composition

Hastings (NZBBJ 17)

c1918 – The five Scotney brothers – Herbert (18.2.1878 - 22.12.1966), Arthur (1.5.1880 - ?.?.1968), Tom (19.8.1870 - 18.3.1939), Harold (26.12.1888 - 19.1.1973), Albert (6.12.1876 - 10.11.1943)

SCOTNEY, HAROLD

Harold Scotney (Born in Treeton, Yorkshire 26 December 1888). He was the youngest of nine sons, and his father passed away in 1890. They immigrated to New Zealand in 1898 with mother and five brothers. They settled in Dannevirke where his elder brother Tom became associated with local Skeleton Army before his conversion. The Scotney boys learned brass music from Arthur Pearce, an early Salvation Army musician. Harold started on cornet around 1900. Brigadier W.H.Gore, formerly of the Melbourne Staff Band was Corps Officer at Dannevirke and taught Harold rudiments and encouraged him to compose.

Scotney became Bandmaster at Dannevirke in 1904 in his sxteenth year, the youngest bandmaster in New Zealand at the time. Harold Scotney had no secondary education because his mother was a widow and he was working by twelve. He collected music texts and was largely self-taught. He entered the Australian brass competition and *'Ruahine'* appeared in 1910 as Australian BJ 299 and 'Dannevirke March' as AuBJ 308. He moved to Feiding [note the 'incorrect' spelling here] in 1912 where he became organist and deputy bandmaster in 1914. He became a painter and paper hanger working for Starford's and Sons, Feilding. Much unpublished music was written for the Feiling band, including *'Congress 1915'*. The Drum and Fife Band went to the 1916 Congress (in Wellington). In 1915 he became Songster Leader but moved to Wellington in 1916 where he worked as a staff member of the Trade Department at Territorial Headquarters. He joined the Wellington Citadel Band and became deputy bandmaster to Harry Goffin [these must have been wonderful times!]. Harold Scotney became bandmaster in 1919 because Goffin (an officer) has upset THQ once too many times and was transferred to Foxton (even now, a dot on the map). Upon Goffin's return from exile Scotney relinquished the bandmastership. Scotney did not write to order but presented whatever he was working on as a 'new' piece (although GS 1567 *'Herald of Australia'* was written for the 1959 Melbourne Staff Band tour to New Zealand but not published until 1966). Scotney resumed bandmaster of Wellington Citadel when Goffin was appointed to oversee the opening of the new Congress Hall in Auckland in 1929. The band made a number of radio broadcasts and toured during this period. Because of ill health he immigrated to Sydney in 1934.

Still popular are Scotney's marches *'Wellington Citadel'*, *'The Wellingtonian'* and *'New Zealand Warriors'*. The trio in *'New Zealand Warriors'* is a tune written by Harold Cutts, also a Yorkshireman. He immigrated to New Zealand sponsored by the Salvation Army and was a cornetist. He was a market gardner and wrote the occasional song or chorus.

While working at the Salvation Army Trade Department in Sydney, Scotney was bandmaster of the Sydney Congress Hall Band for 7 years after which he became Territorial Band Inspector. In his late 60's he undertook oral, written, composition and conducting exams with the British College of Music and graduated from there as Bandmaster.

He retired to Collaroy and helped out with the music camps held there. He died 19 January 1973 from Collaroy.

His cousin Len Scotney recalls:

'I have fond memories of my uncle Harold, (actually my great uncle) and I played under him is some special events in composite bands. He was strong on all the old traditional priorities like deportment, punctuality, and he heard everything! He would stop at the end of a section and detail all the 'mistakes', like the 2nd baritone played Bb on a quaver instead of B natural, he could remember all the little slips, and list them at the end of the piece!'

Harold had publications in the Australian Band Journal, New Zealand Band Journal, in the English Ordinairy Band Journal, the Festival Series, Second Series and 'The Musical Salvationist'.

Important compositions

The Wellingtonian (GS934) 1925, Wellington Citadel (GS887) 1922

SCOTT, LLOYD W.

Lloyd (October 23, 1923 – October 19, 2003) was born in Lynn, Massachusetts, to corps officers James and Minni Scott. In 1947 he married fellow soldier Marion E. Russell, left his roles as corps songster leader and deputy bandmaster, and with Marion, entered the King's Messengers session at the New York training college. At his 1948 commissioning in Carnegie Hall, Lloyd conducted the New York Staff Band during the session song, music written by him. He commanded corps in Barre, Vermont, Rockland and Augusta, Maine, and Portsmouth, New Hampshire, before briefly serving at Portland, Maine DHQ in 1960. During the next 14 years he served in finance positions with a brief interlude in 1964 in the Eastern Territorial Music Bureau. After retiring in 1987, he was a faithful soldier of the Old Orchard Beach, Maine corps and the Clearwater, Florida Corps. Major Scott lived his testimony of sincere Godly faith. Much of who he was can be seen in the expression of his God-given musical abilities. One of his many published instrumental and vocal compositions, which wed his beautiful music with Albert Orsborn's lyrics *'I have no claim on grace'*, has special meaning to Salvationists around the world.

Living his own life in a low-key manner, without fanfare, and holding a special place to the Army in his heart, he wrote music that could be played and sung by the average Salvationist musician in the corps setting. A Bandmaster of the Paris corps in France was so blessed by it that he named his son 'Lloyd' in Major Scott's honour. Recognizing God's voice in music presentation, Major Lloyd Scott said of his nine years as a baritone player in the New York Staff Band, *'the inspiration came when we played a deeply devotional item and I sensed that God was speaking to each member of the band'*. A faithful Salvationist, he was an active soldier during all of his non corps appointments, often serving as corps songster leader or bandmaster. He also led the Temple Chorus for several years, the Swonkey Youth Band and the Old Orchard Beach Camp Meeting Band.

Important composition

The Solid Rock (TS1023-1) 1995, Commitment (AJ238) 2005, Endless Day (GS1672) 1975

SHARMAN, PAUL

Paul was born in Rotherham (near Sheffield) before moving to Birmingham when he was 8 years old. His first music lessons (cornet and piano) were given to him by his father (a music teacher) from about the age of 6. Having been a member of the YP Band, Paul joined the senior band at Birmingham Citadel in 1988. And in 1990, he was awarded a scholarship to study Trumpet Performance at the Royal College of Music in London. He studied with Michael Laird and Malcolm Smith and while he was there won the First Year Trumpet Prize, the Ernest Hall Prize for Orchestral Trumpet Playing and the Senior Brass Prize. There followed a period of playing the Trumpet as a freelance musician with various orchestras and ensembles, and also in shows in the West End. When moving to London in 1990, he joined the Regent Hall Band and has been principal cornet for the past 13 years and deputy bandmaster for the past 6 years (before that he served 10 years as Young People's Bandleader). In addition, he has been a member of the International Staff Band for nearly 17 years, playing Solo Cornet and Soprano. Paul Sharman's composition/arranging started back when he was at school and used to arrange pieces for him, his brother and his father to play. This went on to arranging pieces for quintets and ten-piece while at college and also for the Young People's Band. Since starting work as a Music Editor in the Music Ministries Unit (UK THQ) he has developed this further into writing larger scale works for brass band and also some songs. His experience in many and varied styles of music, he feel, has helped this. Paul has been lucky to have been encouraged by such well-known brass band composers as Dr. Kenneth Downie and Lt. Colonel (Dr) Ray Steadman-Allen. He has been priveleged to be asked to write for the International Staff Band, Territorial Youth Band and Philip Cobb amongst others. He currently lives in Hertfordshire with his wife Charlotte and children, George and Anna.

Important compositions

Flourish (JC646) 2009, Psalm of Thanks (JC655) 2010, The Power of the Cross (GS2082) 2009

SHAW, DARREN

Darren was born in 1974 to a Salvationist family, growing up at Southampton Sholing Corps. Music has been a central thread in his life, his earliest hero being his Grandfather who always played and sang with heart and passion. Darren first picked up a brass instrument at around seven years old, joining the Young People's Band which his father was leading at the time. Darren wanted to be a cornet player like him, but was most at home playing tenor horn which he has played ever since. Not long after, he started experimenting with piano and keyboards, discovering over time a sound and technique that suited him. While he later had more formal training, these early years of exploration formed the roots of all his later writing. Darren must have started writing at about 12-13 years of age, improvising and refining as he went. It became a necessity for him as he would come home from school and play, letting his thoughts and feelings flow through his fingers. He stuck to keyboards at first, then moved into songwriting which was to become his main focus over the years. Gradually, more of his songs were being used at the Corps and taking on lives of their own, although Darren was reluctant to submit any for publication. He began arranging for small groups and then finally gave a full brass score a go for his GCSE composing. It was great to be in a fellowship that valued and encouraged his creativity, the singing company and band particularly willing to try his latest creations, but he didn't feel as if he knew what he was doing with band scoring and didn't know where to go for help, so early experiments with that were abandoned.

Darren grew up appreciating the Army greats like Goffin, Condon and Heaton, and really enjoyed the swagger of a Bramwell Coles march. He found himself absorbing the wide range of vocal music that was being produced during the eighties and early nineties, particularly loving the new directions taken by writers such as Len Ballantine. Then, through music schools and moving into the Senior band, there was the rich harmony of Kenneth Downie, the cool rhythms of Barrie Gott and the contemporary creativity of William Himes. All this was playing to a backdrop of Michael W. Smith on his Walkman, alongside a number of other music styles. Darren particularly loved the pianistic brilliance of Chopin, the shear beauty and emotion of Debussy, and the originality and texture of Sibelius. Much of what he was writing didn't 'fit' in the established Army journals, but that didn't deter Darren and some of his work was published elsewhere, some has been used at Music Schools and for one off performances. Some songs, he later discovered, managed to make it round the world entirely on their own! He has always written for groups and people wherever he is, enjoying a particularly rich time when, as a student, joined Wood Green Corps. It was there that he wrote *'Guardian of My Soul'* (based on a melody he had written aged 13) which is probably one of his best known and widely used songs. Darren and his wife were commissioned as Salvation Army Officers and also became parents in 1999 and composition had to take a back seat, but, after moving to Southsea in 2011, he has been inspired to pick up the composer's pen once more, writing for band, piano and working on a long backlog of unfinished songs.

Important compositions

Guardian of My Soul (m/s), That Will be Glory (m/s)

SHELDON, W.H

One of the early composers (first half of 19th century).

No further information could be retrieved about him.

Important compositions

Our invincible Army (TS0204) 1934, Triumphant (TS0052) 1924

SHERRIFF, CHAT. A

Chat Sherriff was bandmaster of the Balham Corps Band. He was a well known figure in the London band circles where his musical activities in various parts of the metropolis has brought him in touch with many bandmasters and bandsmen. Before his first published band piece, *'The Balham March'*, he was not unknown as a composer, as several of his songs had previously appeared in 'The Musical Salvationist'.

Important compositions

The Balham March (GS0938) 1925, Travelling on (TS0084) 1926

SHIELS. JAMES Jr.

James was born on 27th February 1960. James is a third generation Salvationist and son of Salvation Army Officer parents Majors James and Nellie Shiels. His wife Susan and James were Salvation Army Officers for thirteen years until God led them to St. Louis and the Gateway Corps because of family medical reasons. Since 1999 he has followed a career path in Development & Fund Raising and as a semi-professional musician. Recently he has moved from St Louis, Mo to Richmond, Virginia to work with Child Fund International. Musically James has had the opportunity to play with some great groups and to be part of some wonderful music programs. As a trombone player and vocalist he has been privileged to play with many bands, groups and soloists. As a Salvationist he has been part of many wonderful Corps Songster Brigades and Bands and has served on the staff of the Central Music Institute, Star Lake Music Camp and Divisional Music camps throughout the Central Territory. James feels very privileged over the years to serve as Assistant Divisional Bandmaster for the Heartland Division, the Director of the Divisional Worship Team in the Northern Division and Bandmaster of the Gateway Citadel Corps in St Louis. He currently is serving as Bandmaster of the Richmond Citadel Corps in Richmond Virginia and playing BBb Bass in the National Capital Band in Washington D.C. James feels very honoured to have had the opportunity to arrange and compose music for many groups and individuals throughout the United States, but is blessed to have publications in the Salvation Army's Triumph Series, Sing to the Lord and Hallelujah Choruses series. He was educated at the Webster University and has a Masters in Music theory and Composition and a Master in International Business which he got from the St Louis University. He also was a delegate at North American Composers Forum held by the Salvation Army.

Important composition

Anchor (TS1037) 1996

SCHOLES, WILLIAM

William Scholes was converted at Rushden Citadel when eleven years old. As his parents were not Salvationists or musically inclined, he had as a youth largely to make his own way both musically and spiritually. He learnt to play the cornet soon after his conversion in 1917 and made rapid strides. In 1921 the budding instrumentalist became the Young People's Singing Company Leader, a position he held for four years. Of this appointment William wrote: *'I pay tribute to the assistance and opportunity given me by Retired Bandmaster H. Giles, who put the baton into my hands'*. Since that day the baton has seldom been out of his hands, for this hundred percent Salvationist has been Songster Leader for thirteen years, for eleven of which he has also held the responsibility of the Deputy Bandmastership. He later played euphonium. On January 26, 1935, the Songster-Leader's Brigade provided a solo item at the National Songster Festival held at the Clapton Congress Hall.

William has studied musical harmony and theory under Bandmaster George Marshall and Mr. John Baldwin, L.G.S.M., B.B.C.M., and holds a first and honours certificate for harmony from the London Trinity College of Music. He has also taken a course of voice production under Professor B. Tomkin, and as a tenor vocalist has visited all parts of the United Kingdom. Three of the Songster-Leader's vocal compositions have been published in 'The Musical Salvationist'. They are, *'Why not tonight?'*, *'Compassionate Healer'*, and *'My Grace is Suffient'*. The *'Rushden Citadel'* march, *'Captain and Lieutenant'* cornet duet, and *'The Conquest'* trombone solo are also published pieces from his pen. Songster-Leader Scholes pays a glowing tribute to his present Bandmaster, W. Giles. He wrote of him; *'His sterling Salvationism and example prove that character counts more that cleverness'*. Our comrade is married to the Bandmaster's sister (née Winifred Giles), and is a brother-in-law of Bandmaster Tom Giles, of Upper Norwood, a product of Rushden.

Important compositions

Captain and Lieutenant (GS1140) 1938, Rushden Citadel (GS1064) 1933

SHOULTS, GERRY

Gerry is the oldest son of Commissioner and Mrs. Harold Shoults (retired). When he was seven years old, his parents bought an old upright piano and he started taking piano lessons and so this was his first introduction to music making. His father was a euphonium soloist in the Chicago Staff Band at that time, and he developed a great interest in music during those early years, listening to CSB records and reel-to-reel tapes. He also enjoyed hearing the Chicago Austin Corps Band each week, as his mother and father played in this band. At eleven, Gerry learned to play baritone at the Kansas City Blue Valley corps in a class taught by his father. His father also personally taught him music theory and harmony lessons during this time. His family moved to Chicago when he was fourteen and they were soldiers at the Mont Clare Corps (later to be renamed into Norridge Citadel). Gerry was also privileged to be the songster pianist at Mont Clare for eight years which greatly enhanced his sight-reading skills at the keyboard. There were many people at Mont Clare corps that influenced his decision to follow Christ at age fifteen, and many who encouraged him to become a composer and arranger such as Cliff Monk, Howard Cox, Ed Lowcock, Art Shoults, Jack Thomas, Walt Winters, and many others.

Gerry began playing 1st Baritone in the Chicago Staff Band when he was fifteen years old, the youngest member of the band. Bandmaster Ernie Miller also encouraged him to write music, so he began writing brass quartets, SATB vocal settings, and band compositions. Some of those early compositions were good learning experiences for him, but admittedly not the best music. Bandmaster Miller was gracious to try these out at CSB rehearsals and he always gave positive encouragement. Gerry's goal was to make each new composition his best effort and to continually improve his skills. In those early years, he used paper and ink to write music. It was very time consuming and error prone, compared to the tools we have today with PC music publishing software.

He was strongly influenced by attending Central Music Institute (CMI), a summer camp where he got to know William Himes and James Curnow who were both beginning to expand Salvation Army music horizons, not just in the USA Central Territory, but all over the world. They both had a huge influence on Gerry and inspired him to continue to write and arrange music. He spent one summer during his college years traveling in a small contemporary music evangelism group led by William Himes. This is when he got to know William more personally, and he played in a brass quartet at his wedding to Wendy at the end of that summer. Within the next year or two, William and Wendy moved to Chicago and William become bandmaster of the CSB. Gerry served as bandmaster of the Oakbrook Terrace corps band for several years and played in CSB for just over 20 years before moving to Dallas, Texas where he served as songster leader for a short time.

Gerry graduated from Northwestern University with a BS and MS in Computer Science. At Northwestern, in addition to engineering school, he studied music composition for one year with composer David Noon, along with other classes in the school of music. By trade, he has been an engineering manager for Texas Instruments the past 35 years, but music has continued to be his life's passion.

Over the past 40 years, he has been writing music, sometimes commissioned, and other times to commemorate a special occasion or people in his life. Two pieces were recorded by Chicago Staff Band, *'Freedom Rhapsody'* commemorating the USA bicentennial year, and a three-movement suite *'Wonderful Story'*. He wrote several marches including *'Hallelujah'* (often played by CSB), and *'Oakbrook Terrace Anniversary'*. CSB also performed his suite *'Pathway'* written for his parent's retirement service, along with several pieces designed for congregational singing, essentially medleys of well-known songs and choruses.

He composed the processional and recessional for his own wedding, which included brass choir, organ, and hand bells. For his wife, Gerry has written three piano pieces all based on the original *'Kathie's Tune'*. As each of his three children were learning to play euphonium, he wrote solos for them: *'Ballade for Euphonium'*, *'Variants on Rachie'*, and *'Greenwood Air and Variations'*. He also wrote a baby dedication song for each of his children: *'In His Image'*, *'Greater Love'*, and *'We Adore Thee'*. In the past five years, he wrote processionals and recessionals for all three of his hildren's weddings, which was a very special honour for him.

He has been a regular contributor to the USA Central Territory worship series 'Hallelujah Choruses', with 14 published arrangements to date, including one original song *'My Desire'* written in memory of his aunt Sherry Cox. The USA South also published his vocal arrangement of *'I Know Whom I Have Believed'*. The USA East published a euphonium solo arrangement of *'All That I Am'* (words and music by Bill Himes), and this was recorded as a cornet solo by David Daws. He also wrote a cornet solo *'Because He Lives'* for Josh Olsen, and an Eb Bass solo *'Praise to the Everlasting King'*.

His current project is a set of variations for band based on *'Slane'* (Be Thou My Vision). This was written for the recent CSB UK tour, but has not been performed to date. He is still working on some enhancements and modifications to this suite based on Bandmaster Himes' feedback. Gerry view music composition as a lifetime learning experience and a key part of his Christian stewardship, using the time and talents he possesses to bring glory and honour to God. He was born to worship Him and He deserves all of his praise and Gerry never regretted devoting his life to serving Him. His best music is yet to come.

Important composition

All That I Am

SHOTTON, RAY

Born in late 1923 in Chester-le Street in the North of England in the county of Durham. Ray was born out of Salvation Army parents. His early days included taking piano lessons at ten years of age and soon he became involved as songster accompanist, both on the organ and piano. When Ray started to play brass instruments, he had the advantage of the background of earlier involvement as a pianist in playing for vocal soloists and intrumentalists. This became a life long activity as Ray married a Songster who was already a vocal soloist in her own capacity. Ray played various instruments in the Sunderland Millfield Band and moved round the band when asked to and even had two years on the G-Bass Trombone as few bandsmen knew bass cleff in those days. He had early lessons in harmony and scoring for brass bands from Bandmaster George Marshall of South Shields, although his intentions were not to be a composer. However, he was successful in having a brass band march and other (vocal) pieces published by the Salvation Army. By profession he was a lifelong clerk in an office, which was part of the British Coal Industry.

Important composition

The Joyful Sound (GS1620) 1971

SIDDLE, M

One of the early composers (first half of 19th century).

No further information could be retrieved about him.

Important composition

The Bentinck March (TS0010) 1922

SILFVERBERG, ERIK

Erik Silfverberg was born on 1th October 1934 in Copenhagen. After finishing College, Erik studied Chemistry and has a degree as Civic Engineer in Chemistry. He worked for many years as lecturer and provice chancellor at 'The Danish College of Graphic Arts' (Den Grafiske Højskole). Erik grew up in the Gartnergade Corps in Central Copenhagen, becoming Y.P. Band Leader when he was only 17, holding that position for more than 30 years. Erik has for many years been involved with musical development in the Army in Denmark, and has been guest conductor at Star Lake, Jacksons Point, New York, Detroit, Hong Kong, Buenos Aires, and London to name but a few places. He was Bandmaster for the Copenhagen Youth Band, which took part in the 1978 International Congress. In 1989 Erik became Bandmaster at the Valby Corps (formerly Gartnergade Corps), having been the bands principal cornetist for many years. In 1956 he had his first piece - *'The Awaited Welcome'*, published by The Salvation Army. He has since then had over 100 pieces published by The Salvation Army in London, New York, Stockholm and Oslo. He took initiative for the ScanBrass Series of The Salvation Army in Scandinavian, of which he is also the editor. Erik has also written music for many songs, where his wife Anne-Lise has written the lyrics.

Important compositions

Miracles (GS1690) 1977, Joy in my soul (GS1952) 1998, Joshua (FS552) 1999, Rotterdam Kralingen (m/s)

SILFVERBERG, NIELS

Niels Silfverberg was born on 11th February 1962 in Copenhagen to a Salvation Army Familiy. He studied music and mathematic at the Highschool. Further he made studys in Management, Manager, Jurisprudence, Psychology and a Bachelor in Social Science and took his Master in Education Development. He is now an Educational Developer at the Institute for Research and Development at the Metropolitan University College in Copenhagen. His love of Salvation Army Music descended from his Father. Niels has played Soprano Cornet since he was 13, and has been sitting in different bands as such. He was for some years principal cornetist with the Valby Corps Band, but is back now as the bands Soprano cornetist. Niels took over the Young People's Band at Valby Corps from his father - Erik Silfverberg, keeping that position for 12 years. He is a popular Guest-Conductor and Instructor on Music-Camps of the Salvation Army. Niels writes music for Brass Bands of The Salvation Army in a amusing style. He is married to Dinah, who plays Percussion in the Valby Corps Band, and they have a son Marcus, who is playing Solo Cornet in the band.

Important compositions

I Will Enter His Gates (GS1891) 1993, True Colours (GS2052) 2007

SIMMONS-SMITH, NICK

Is a 5th generation Salvationist from Chelmsford, Essex (UK). He was heavily involved in the Chelmsford Citadel Corps participating in 4 musical sections and Corps Cadets. He became a Senior Soldier at age 16 (1991) and became principal trombone of the corps band, and string bass accompanist for the songsters and singing company. His first opportunity as a leader came when he was 17, appointed as Assistant Young People's Band Leader.

Nick studied music at Colchester Music Institute under Professor Michael Clack (former Chalk Farm Corps Bandmaster) majoring in trombone performance and music composition. Most of his influences came through the corps, however, and he started arranging for various groups while in his first year at Music college. Nick was heavily influence by corps music leaders including Young People's Bandleader David Hayward, Bandmasters Eric Hayward and Dr. Simon Schultz, as well as Songster leader Joanne Schultz. These individuals shaped him as a leader, as well as Professor Clack.

Upon graduating from college he looked for work in the publishing business, but did not find anything permanent. Nick then applied for an advertized job in The Salvationist looking for someone to move to Dallas, Texas to join the Divisional Music Department with Bandmaster James Anderson. He spent four years in Dallas, and continued to develop his arranging skills – often writing pieces for specific groups. He tended to write music that young people would enjoy, including many in a swing style, or March medleys specific to the players in the group. In 2003 he returned to the United Kingdom to teach in high school and ran a private weekly music school. In 2004 he returned to Dallas to commence work on a Salvation Army Performing Arts School in the region. In 2008 Nick moved with his wife to Atlanta, where he became responsible for the musical publications of the Southern Territory (American Instrumental Ensemble Series, Sing Praise, Children's Praise, and Piano Offerings). Upon Dr. Richard Holz's retirement as Territorial Music Secretary in February 2009, he assumed the role of Territorial Music Secretary and Southern Territorial Bandmaster. Nick has continued to write sporadically, mostly by request, with compositions published by the UK, USA East, USA South, & USA West Territories.

Important composition

In Dulci Jubilo (ABJ63-272) 2009

SKINNER, CHARLES

Lieutenant-Colonel Charles Skinner (1911) was appointed to succeed Colonel Albert Jakeway in 1958, after he had became a member of the Music Editorial Department in 1945. Charles had made a considerable impression with the efficient workmanship in what few compositions he had written, among them being several prize-winning entries in the 1939 International Music Competition. As a brass instrumentalis, Charles Skinner made his mark as a soprano cornet player with the Men's Social Headquarters Band. Later on he became a member of the International Staff Band where he played cornet and flugelhorn. He left the band in 1946 but returned in 1955 when he became the band's Deputy Bandmaster.

September 28th, 1911 – February 24th, 1978. Born into a family whose roots were deeply grounded in the soil of the early Salvationism of 'Broken Earthenware' Norland Castle, Charles Skinner grew up in the corps at Bishop's Stortford, where his parents were respected local officers. Upon leaving school at the age of fourteen, Charles, in 1925, commenced work as a junior on the old International Headquarters, thus beginning an association with the Army's centre which lasted until his Promotion to Glory, In retirement he continued to serve the cause that has been his life's work. The promise of musical brilliance showed in his personality from a tender age, and whilst still in his teens he earned a name as an outstanding soprano cornet soloist with the Men's Social Headquarters Band.

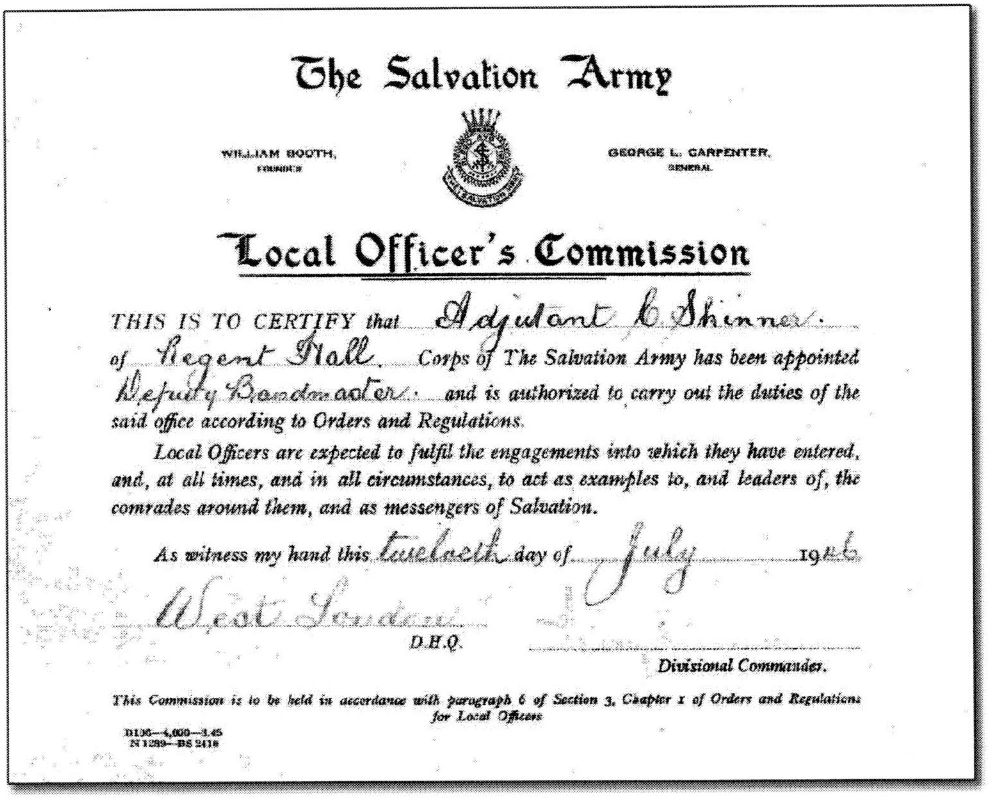

The Salvation Army

WILLIAM BOOTH, FOUNDER

GEORGE L. CARPENTER, GENERAL

Local Officer's Commission

THIS IS TO CERTIFY that Adjutant C Skinner *of* Regent Hall *Corps of The Salvation Army has been appointed* Deputy Bandmaster *and is authorized to carry out the duties of the said office according to Orders and Regulations.*

Local Officers are expected to fulfil the engagements into which they have entered, and, at all times, and in all circumstances, to act as examples to, and leaders of, the comrades around them, and as messengers of Salvation.

As witness my hand this twelveth *day of* July *1946*

West London *D.H.Q.*

Divisional Commander.

This Commission is to be held in accordance with paragraph 6 of Section 3, Chapter 1 of Orders and Regulations for Local Officers

Certificate of Charles Skinner's appointment as Deputy Bandmaster of the Regent Hall Band, July 1946

From his earliest days, Charles Skinner was nurtured in the Salvation Army being a third generation Salvationist. On leaving school at fourteen, he started work at International Headquarters in the Staff Department, and was later transferred to Men's Social Headquarters Accounts Departement where, under the influence of Colonel Arthur Goldsmith, his love of music was encouraged. On his long train rides from Bishop's Stortford, Charles studied accounting and then music to get his degrees in both. He became the Soprano Cornet player in the Men's Social Works Band and the thought of giving up his banding was quite a problem when he felt called to officership, a needless anxiety as it transpired. His combined talents for accountancy and music were used to good affect throughout the years. He entered the International Training College in 1935 and was made Cadet Sergeant Major, having the distinction of attaining the highest marks of any previous cadet during his 2 years at the College. After one year on the United Kingdom Field, he returned to the International Training College for 5 years, most of which time he was Private Secretary to the Training Principal, Commissioner. S. Hurren and various others. Following the ITC, he was appointed to Ineternational Headquarters Accounts Department. He married Lieutenant Lily Cossar in 1943 and two years later he was appointed to the Music Editorial Department where he served for 22 years, eight and a half of this time as Head of the Department. His analytical mind and attention to detail were ideal qualities to bring to this new task. He was always grateful for the many opportunities he had for travel both through his work and with the International Staff Band in which he served for 27 years. He will be remembered not only for his music which has enriched the Army repertoire, but also for his kindness and practical caring and dedication to the task in hand. While of a reserved and rather conservative nature himself, he nevertheless always tried to provide for all the Army musicians and kept in mind 'the little corps down yonder' as well as the more advanced and sophisticated band epics. In 1967 when he was transferred to National Headquarters as Financial Secretary, these same qualities of judgement, complete sincerity and integrity were evident in his ceaseless work for Corps Officers and later in detailed preparation for the Annual Appeal – whatever the cost to himself physically, only the best would do. He was very self-critical of his own efforts, whether musical or his platform ministry, yet so kind and encouraging in his dealings with others. A modest man, he was just as willing to lead the local Singing Company or play the drum on the march for the Young People's Band, as to lead 1000 voice choir in the Royal Albert Hall.

He loved his home and family. When problems arose at work or at home, the motto was *'Let Nothing Disturb Thee'*. His interests were many and always had to be studied in great depth be it art, history, current affairs but especially detailed information about any country to which he travelled. He retired in 1976 having spent two and a half years is International Finance Secretary. He continued to serve until the day before he died when, to his great joy, he had completed his accounts. He was greatly respected by all who came in contact with him as being a true Christian gentleman – one who had *'studied to show himself approved unto God – a workman that needed not to be ashamed'* (in Paul's words). As more than one has written – a true Hero of the Faith.

An article which appeared in 'The Musician' of 16 July 1938 tells: Captain Charles Skinner, Assistant Intelligence Officer, William Booth Memorial Training College, Denmark Hill, London. Former Bandsman and Songster at Bishop's Strotford. His father and two sisters have also given efficient service in the Band and Songster Brigade. Charlie first learnt to play a cornet at the age of seven, his father, who was then the Bandmaster of Bishop's Strotford, being his first teacher. Within a short time he became a player of unusual merit, and as such was well known on International Headquarters, where he was employed in the Staff Department. In consequence, he later had the opportunity of assisting such Combinations as the International Staff Band, Upper Norwood Band, Cambridge Heath Band, and Tottenham Citadel Band, with which last-named he toured Sweden. On transferring to the Men's Social Headquarters he came under the direction of Colonel Goldsmith, who gave him advice regarding the soprano cornet, and also on the composition of music. He played his soprano cornet in the Men's Social Headquarters Band when it recorded *'Rockingham'* and *'Freedom from sin'*. Captain Skinner's study of theory, counterpoint, etc., was mostly done in the train, whilst travelling the thirty-one miles from his home to the office. His persistent study was rewarded eventually by being appointed in charge of the Men's Social Headquarters Vocal Party and Band singing in addition to feature as a soprano soloist, transposition of Bb cornet solos being necessary. In March 1934, he soloed *'A Happy Day'*, with Band Accompaniment, at the Associated Headquarters Festival. In addition, the Captain is also a pianist, organist, and an exponent of the concertina and piano-accordion. He is one of our promising composers, and the music of the following pieces written by him has been published in 'The Musical Salvationist': *'I love the Lord'* (which won the Second Prize in Section 1 of the 1934 International Vocal Music Competition), *'Toward Sunrising'* (June, 1935), which was popularized by Major Eva Fouracre and featured by Songster Majorie Hughes at the Queen's Hall Festival in 1936, *'What Manner of Love'* (April, 1936), *'Crown the Savior'* (March, 1937), *'Thousand Threads in the Web'* (September, 1935), and *'Joyful Tidings'* (July, 1938). His published musical efforts commenced with his arrangement of a carol in the 1933 Christmas number of The 'War Cry', when he harmonized *'Rejoice and Sing',* the words and air of which were composed by Songster-Leader A.H. Vickery. In 1935 Charlie Skinner entered the Training College, where he secured distinction in that he lost only one mark in all the examinations. He became solo cornet player of the 'Liberators' Cadets Band. In the following year he was appointed Cadet Sergeant-Major, and formed the Sergeants into a Vocal Party, which featured some of his own compositions at the Central Holiness Meetings and Cadets' Festivals held at Camberwell. His last Corps command was Sevenoaks, from which he farewelled recently in order to take up the leadership of the Cadets Band and singing.

Important compositions

Heroes of the Faith (FS170) 1950, Amsterdam Congress (GS1343) 1951

SKOOG, BJÖRN

See Skoog, Jens.

Important composition

King of Glory (SB2004-01) 2004

SKOOG, JENS (Jens Ståhlmanke)

Jens was born in 1971 in the Swedish town Nässjö where he still lives. He has however studied and lived 400 km north as well as 350 km south of Nässjö but always seems to return to Nässjö as he likes the friends and Salvation Army corps there. Both his parents are, and grandparents were, Salvationists. He started to play the cornet and piano when he was only six years of age and never played anything else, by decision. As from his early teens he has written music which included some attempts for brass band, however the main part was for brass quintet until 2002 when his first composition for brass band *'King of Glory',* which he wrote together with his brother Bjorn (1968), was published at ScanBrass, the Salvation Army's brass band publications in Norway. *'King of Glory'* won first prize at the Salvation Army's Song and Brass Contest in 2002. By profession Jens he has been a warehouse worker, making kitchen interiors in industry, piano tuner, computer teacher, music teacher in elementary school, checking and selling tickets on trains and currently works as a personal care assistant. As a musician Jens consider himself a piano player rather than a cornet player although he has been the principal cornet of the Nässjö Templet Band for a long time.

Important composition

King of Glory (SB2004-01) 2004

SKYVULSTAD, LEIF

One of the lesser known composers, even in Norway, is Leif Skyvulstad, who was born on 10 October 1905 out of Salvationist parents. He was for years a bandsman in the Sarpsborg Corps Band in Norway, where he played cornet. However his musical skills also covered the accordion, the violin and the mandolin. By profession he was an industrial mechanic and worked as a foreman. It is unknown if he wrote more music than only the published march *'Sarpsborg'.* Leif Skyvulstad was Promoted to Glory on 22 May 1956.

Important composition

Sarpsborg (FM0220)

SLACK, JAMES

One of the early composers (late 1800). While being a captain of the Salvation Army, he was appointed to South Africa in 1885 where he served for the following six years latterly with the rank as major. No further information could be retrieved about him.

Important compositions

Only Jesus I Will Know (GS0188) 1892, Steadily Forward March (GS0078) 1887

SLATER, RICHARD

In September 1882 a very talented young musician by the name of Richard Slater (1854-1939) was converted at Regent Hall Corps, London. He became a soldier in 1883 and at that time wrote a song, the chorus of which expresses his consecration:

Ever Thine, Thine alone,
Henceforth, Savior, I will be;
This my hope, my life's ambition:
Day by day to grow like thee.

Slater was to be the head of the Music Department for 30 years, relinquishing his responsibilities in 1913. In 1923 at the age of 69, he was recalled to take temporary charge of the department and on August 25th, 1923, General Bramwell Booth accorded Richard Slater the Army's highest honor by appointing him a member of the Order of the Founder.

The citation read:

'Whereas it has been reported to me that Richard Slater, a Lt-Colonel of The Salvation Army, rendered invaluable service in the Army's ministry of music, as a composer, also for many years as director of the musical publications issued by International Headquarters, and whereas it seems to me that the service of the said Richard Slater as above recorded was in itself and in its spirit and purpose such as would have especially commended him to the attention and approval of our beloved Founder, now I hereby appoint the said Richard Slater a member of the Order of he Founder and direct that his name be inscribed on the roll of the Order'.

As a songwriter Lieut-Colonel Slater must have first place in our history. Sixty-five years after his death his considerable output has not been surpassed, nor is it likely to be. Of his published songs he wrote the words of 127, the music of 166 and the words and music of 294. Another 264 were in manuscript at the time of his passing, making a grand total of 851.

His incredible contribution to the annals of Salvation Army music during this formative time earned Slater the title of 'Father of Salvation Army Music'.

Book 1 - **Father of Salvation Army Music** - by Arch R. Wiggins

'Father of Salvation Music' was General Bramwell Booth's description of Richard Slater, O.F. whose story, together with much of the early history of Salvation Army music is given in this book. Slater was foremost among the many music makers of a Movement whose playing has encircled the globe.

Book 2 - **'The Musical Salvationist' – The World of Richard Slater** – by Gordon Cox

'The Musical Salvationist' – The World of Richard Slater' frames the musical history of the Salvation Army through the life story of Richard Slater, popularly known as the 'Father of Salvation Army Music'. This book focuses upon the significant contribution of the Salvation Army to British musical life from the late Victorian era until the outbreak of the Second World War in 1939. It demonstrates links between the Army's music-making and working class popular culture, education and religion.

Of particular interest is the fact that Richard Slater wrote a solo, one of the very few, for the Monstre Bass (Great Salvation, Great Redemption! GS0519-2).

Important compositions

To difficult to mention any particular titles here as Richard Slater probably provided the largest amount of compositions of all composers to the musical library of the Salvation Army. Literally hundreds if not thousands.

SLATER, WILLIAM

William Slater was the New York Staff Bandmaster (1951-1955) after William Bearchell and just before Richard E. Holz. Not much is known about him other than that he was Staff Bandmaster. Not many compositions are known these days written by him, but probably one of the most well known is his *'Missionary'*. Although he wrote several compositions, he was more a musician rather than a composer.

Important composition

Missionary (m/s)

SLETTHOLM, YNGVE

Is a Salvationist in Norway, and has been the bandmaster of the Oslo Temple Band at various times. He holds a Doctors degree in music and has been headmaster at the Royal Academy of Music in Oslo. He has also held high government positions in Norway as a Secretary of Culture in the Department of Church and Culture.

Yngve Slettholm (born 28 December 1955) is the Executive Director of Kopinor, composer, politician and member of the Salvation Army. Slettholm took his diploma exams at the Norges Musikkhøgskole (the Norwegian Academy of Music) in 1980 and began his composing career in contemporary music. In the period 1982–1986 he was the President of the national organisation Ny Musikk – New Music (Norwegian Section of ISCM). After this, he travelled to the USA and studied under Morton Feldman (1986–88) while he worked towards his doctorate. Slettholm has won many prizes for his work, as well as many study and work grants. Despite his wide recognition, not everyone likes or understands his brand of contemporary music. To those people, Slettholm said: *'It would be terrible if the only thing that would survive from our time would be something that everyone agreed on!'*

Slettholm has comprehensive teaching practice, running from instructor and conductor workshops in musical ensembles via school work as an Associate Professor in composing and music theory at Norges musikkhøgskole (the Norwegian Academy of Music).

Important composition

Templett 119 (SB2008-05) 2008

SMITH, ANTHONY R.

Anthony Smith (Bristol, United Kindom) is Young People's Band Leader in his corps, principal euphonium of the renowned Bristol Easton Salvation Army Band as well as a member of the International Staff Band (Baritone). He is a medical student. One of the younger nowadays composers, he was the first within the Salvation Army world wide to bring in a harp as additional instrument to a brass band. His composition is a small work for string orchestra based on the well-known folk tune of the same title. The melody is named after the parable which Jesus told, recorded in the Gospel of Luke (Luke 16:19-31).

Important compositions

Dives and Lazarus (US377-2) 2010

SMITH, BERNARD

The legendary Bernard Smith was the founder of The Salvation Army's (USA) Central Music Institute (CMI) in 1935. As as teenager he was the National Champion Cornet Soloist in the USA for two year in a row. Also at age eighteen he was made Bandmaster of the famous Flint Citadel Band (Michigan) when it was at its best (guessing that is in time for the 1930 congress wherein the band participated in New York, and Sousa was present to lead the massed bands in his *'Salvation Army'* march). Bernard Smith had total-recall and had every piece of Salvation Army band music memorized and seldom used a score, even when he came back to CMI as a guest at the 25th anniversary in 1958 (an incorrect year).

John Philip Sousa was interested in hiring Bernard Smith for his band when Bernard was in his teens. Bernard Smith wrote the cornet solo *'Glorious Fountain'* and an alto horn solo for Howard Chesham *'Robes of White'* (among many other things) - the latter was for the first CMI. Richard Holz (commissioner) wrote a different last variation for *'Glorious Fountain'* for Derek Smith, of which Bernard Smith eventually was informed and approved. He was a kindly gentleman of the first order, a deep Christian, and most profoundly humble man of good spirit. He was a Captain, Territorial Music Director and Chicago Staff Bandmaster. Many feel he was the best bandmaster ever to conduct that band - he was profoundly musical. He resigned as a Salvation Army Officer in the early 1950's. Upon resigning he became Professor of Brass and Related Subjects at Baylor University in Waco, Texas (a top rated Christian university). He died of cancer in the 1970's.

'The Musician' of March 28, 1942 tells us;

Bandmaster Bernard A. Smith, is one of the three sons of Corps Sergeant-Major and Mrs. Fred Smith, of Flint Citadel, Michigan, USA. His parents transferred from Canada about twenty-seven years ago, after having left England a few years previously. Bernard was born in Canada thirty-one years ago. His two brothers and three brother-in-law are members of the Band. A Bachelor of Philosophy, the Bandmaster took music as his major subject. At present he is director of instrumental music at the Northern High School in Flint. *'We have band and orchestra training as part of our education system in most of our schools'*, he says. *'You would be amazed at the proficiency of the better of these groups. They play all the best music literature and make a good job at it'.* Appointed Bandmaster when he was seventeen years of age, Bernard Smith remained as such until he went away to college.

Following the completion of his studies he was for three years Bandmaster of the Chicago Staff Band. Six years ago he returned to Flint and resumed the Bandmastership of the Flint Citadel Band.

Bernard Smith receiving his BM Commission at Flint Citadel, Michigan at age 18 - 2nd from the right. This is a very rare picture of Bernard Smith.

Important compositions

Cornet solo - The Glorious Fountain, Tone Poem – Finlandia, Horn Solo - A Robe of White

SMITH, C

One of the early composers (first half of 19th century).

No further information could be retrieved about him.

Important composition

Love's great sea (GS0421) 1902

SMITH, ERNEST ALFRED MAFEKIN LAMBERT

Ernest Smith (born on 18 May 1900, Promoted to Glory 4 June 1987) was known by two names. To all who knew him he was Ernie and as a Salvation Army Composer he was E. A. Smith. Ernie started attending the Swindon Old Town Corps from the age of eight and transferred to the Swindon Gorse Hill Corps when he was sixteen years old. He was commissioned a bandsman on 28th January 1916.

Ernie worked for the Great Western Railway for fifty-one years and worked in the Mileage Office processing times and payments of train drivers and firemen, retiring on 18th May 1965. Swindon was well known as a railway town since the time of Isambard Kingdom Brunel and the 'railway' was the major employer in the town employing, in its heyday, some

14,000 men and women and seventy five per cent of the local workforce at the time of Ernie's birth.

On 'call up' to the military he joined the Band of the 15th Gloucestershire Regiment in 1915 and attended Lowestoft Citadel Corps when the band moved to Lowestoft.

E.A. Smith always considered himself fortunate to have studied musical composition with Bandmaster George Marshall for five years. He won three prizes over the years in the Salvation Army International Band Music Competition – a First and two Seconds. His composition was always text book correct and had a unique style, with many pieces containing a legato unison passage from the bass end. His first piece of music was a meditation on the tune *'Nottingham'* and was published in the Second Series Band Journal in June 1926. He went on to write some ninety four pieces of music, with forty five of these being published. Incidentally, Ernie would relate that Colonel Hawkes had at some point informed him that he would do well to have a publishing rate of one in three, so almost one in two must have been quite an achievement. Some were published many years after Ernie submitted them to the Music Editorial Department. (MED)! His last published piece of music, a General Series March entitled *'Stand Like the Brave'*, was published in December 1979 although his last piece of music, a solo item, *'Be Glad In The Lord'*, was sent to the MED in August 1985. He had therefore been writing Army music for fifty nine years! He was meticulous and kept a little book detailing dates of when a composition was sent to MED and publication.

Ernie held positions in Swindon Gorse Hill Corps as Band Sergeant, Deputy Bandmaster (1945) and Bandmaster on three occasions (prior to World War 2, during the War years and again from 1951 – 56). He retired as a bandsman on 16th September 1976 and Lieutenant Colonel Ray Steadman-Allen attended a Programme of Tribute to Ernie on 14th October 1978 and paid tribute to his contribution to Army music.

Ernie was a prolific Army composer of very playable, good quality music including marches, selections, meditations, air varies and solos for Triumph, General and Festival Series as well as vocal music for 'The Musical Salvationist'. Tributes from both Cliff Parker (Bandmaster) and David Bird (Songster Leader) at his funeral and thanksgiving service on 15th June 1987 spoke of the quality of the man and his faith in the Lord he loved and served so well and consistently as a Salvationist for all of his long life. Cliff Parker's personal favourite composition was the selection *'My All in All'* written from the heart of E.A. Smith, for whom Christ was so evidently *'All in All'*.

Important compositions

Above the rest (GS1055) 1932, Belmont (TS0347) 1943, A Call to prayer (TS0770) 1974, Christ the King (TS0290) 1939, Complete Surrender (GS1385) 1953, Conquerors (GS1078) 1934, Everlasting Joy (TS0309) 1941, Faithful Service (TS0756) 1972, Fidelity (GS1426) 1956

SMITH, G.S.

One of the early composers (late 1800, early 1900).

No further information could be retrieved about this person.

Important composition

Thou Art a Mighty Saviour (GS0075) 1887

SMITH, JEREMY

Jeremy Smith (March 31st, 1991) is currently in his third year at the University of Toronto's Faculty of Music in the Concurrent Teacher Education Program. He is also very active with the Salvation Army and plays in numerous Salvation Army bands including the Canadian Staff Band. Jeremy also has his Grade 10 in piano and euphonium with the Royal Conservatory of Music and is an active composer, having had works performed by various levels of Salvation Army bands. His future goals are to become a high school music teacher while continuing a high level of performance and composition. For more information, please visit his website: musicsmith.ca

Most of the groups that have performed his works are in the Salvation Army including several Junior/Youth Bands across the country. He wrote the massed band piece for the Young People's music festival in the Toronto division, entitled *'Praise and Glory'*.

Also one piece in particular, Jeremy submitted for publishing, has been performed by at several Divisional (regional) Youth Bands in Ontario. It is called *'Still'*, and is an arrangement of the modern song by Reuben Morgan with that same title. He has also been commissioned to write an arrangement of the popular song, Jabulani Africa for the PENDEL Brass (a Divisional youth band in the PENDEL division in the U.S.A. East Territory) and their trip to South Africa this summer.

Jeremy Smith is the son of composer Kenneth Smith.

Important compositions

Praise and Glory, Still, Jabulani Africa, Euphonium Concerto

SMITH, KENNETH

Commissioned as a Salvation Army officer in 1986, Major Kenneth (Ken) Smith has served in corps appointments in Calgary, Alberta and St. Thomas, Ontario, and on the training college staff in St. John's, Newfoundland and Wellington, New Zealand. Following two years as overseas personnel officer at Canada and Bermuda Territorial Headquarters, he was transferred to the editorial department, where he is currently the associate editor of The 'War Cry'. An avid musician, Ken is actively involved at his home corps of North Toronto Community Church where he serves as worship co-ordinator, bandsman and corps pianist. He is a skilled soloist and accompanist, a published composer of Salvation Army music and a member of the Canadian Staff Band. Ken's wife, Major (Dr.) Beverley Smith, works full-time as a medical practitioner at Salvation Army hospitals in Toronto.

Important compositions

Britannia (FS454) 1986, Songs of the Pioneers (GS2093)2010, The Call to Service (GS1973) 2000

SMITH, STEPHAN

Steve was born in Portland, Oregon (USA) on January 23, 1958 to a Salvationist family. His father was the long-time corps bandmaster and his mother was the Young People's Sergeant Major. So, he grew up around music and became interested in playing the cornet at a young age. His father owned his own business selling and repairing sewing machines but his real passion was music. He was primarily a self-taught musician but did take some college courses to learn how to compose music. Steve remembers as a young person playing several of his marches.

When he was a young teen he became interested in composing himself and wrote his first march when he was 14. Steve proudly presented the march to his music camp guest - Bandmaster Terry Camsey, who stayed up all night to make the piece presentable for the advanced band the next day. It sounded great, but for that Steve has to thank Terry.

Not too long after this he wrote another march and promptly sent it to London for publication. The response back was less than favorable and the writer (who shall go unnamed) suggested strongly that Steve get some instruction before attempted any further compositions. Eventually, this is what he did.

In 1976, Steve moved to Los Angeles to attend college and play cornet in the Hollywood Tabernacle Band. During this time he was exposed to composers such as Bruce and Bill Broughton and William Gordon. These three, and especially Bruce, became primary influences on his writing.

In about 1981 he met a wonderful Salvationist gentleman at a music retreat named Erik Silfverberg. They got to know each other quite well during this short event and in the end Erik asked him to write a piece of music for the Norwegian Junior Series. The result was his first published piece, the march – *'Cascade 82'*, named after Steve's home division. While in college he also wrote for wind band, brass choir, jazz ensemble and choir as well. Ultimately, he ended with the BA in Music Performance from Portland State University and went to work as the Divisional Music Director for the Cascade Division, headquartered in Portland, Oregon. Later, he served in a similar capacity in the Northwest Division in Seattle, WA before his wife Marcia and he decided that God was calling them to be officers and in 1986 they entered the SFOT in Rancho Palos Verdes, CA.

Throughout his officership, he has continued to write music and participate in camps and when possible in a local corps band. In 2003 after deciding to study composition on a deeper level, he was awarded a Master's in Music Composition from Long Beach State University. For his thesis he wrote a composition for Wind Symphony based on Eclesiates 2. This served as quite a witness to his fellow students and hopefully to the faculty as well.

In 2006 his arrangement of the chorus 'King of Kings' was published in the General series. This was first written for the Torrance Band, California Corps while he was stationed in the Southern California Division. Steve feels that God has given him a passion to write music, even though his duties as a Divisional Commander take up much time, he hopes to continue to pursue this passion in the near future.

Important compositions

King of Kings (GS2041) 2006 , Cascade 82 (NM0037) 1982

SMITH, ORRIN C

Orrin C. Smith (1920-1997) has one published piece of music, a cornet duet *'Lift Up the Banner'* written for the old Western Territory (USA) Band Journal in the early 1950's. Orrin was known regionally in the Western United States as a composer and bandmaster. For over 35 years he was the bandmaster of the Portland, Oregon Corps. While he only has one published piece of music, he was quite prolific, writing many special arrangements, selections and marches for many of the bands in the region. Perhaps his best composition is the March - *'Sunshine Mountain'* written in 1955 for a trip by the Portland Corps Band to Oakland, California. Orrin also spent many years at Salvation Army Music Camps encouraging young people to develop their skills in order to serve the Lord through music.

Important composition

Lift Up the Banner (*The Western Territory Band Book #4. It was published in 1948. Orrin's composition is #10 in the book.*)

SNELL, MALCOLM

Malcolm Snell is a Welshman and was born on the 25th of Januari 1928. After working for a railway company he became a Salvation Army Officer. He became quite well known as a pianist at the Salvation Army Holiday and Fellowship weeks. His last appointment was Territorial Secretary for Over Sixty Clubs. It was not until after his retirement that he took up composing seriously. This resulted in a few published pieces and numerous others which are played by the small bands he composed them for. He is a cousin to former International Staff Bandsman Bernard Snell and former Canadian Staff Bandsman Ivor Snell.

Important compositions

The Flag Still Flies (US0250) 2000, UK Melodies (US0236) 1999, Day by Day (US0352) 2008, Catford Citadel (TS1093) 2001

SNELSON, ROBERT

Robert Snelson is the Territorial Music Education Director for The Salvation Army's Southern Territory. In this position, he provides direction to music education programs of The Salvation Army throughout the fifteen southern states and coordinates the annual music publications of the Southern Territory, including collections of instrumental (American Instrumental Ensemble Series and American Instrumental Solo Series) and vocal music (Sing Praise and Children's Praise).

Robert has been the Bandmaster of the Atlanta Temple Corps Band since 2004 and led the band at the School for Officer Training from 2005 to 2009. As a Salvationist music leader, he has had the opportunity to lead various corps and divisional ensembles throughout the territory and has been a guest at territorial music camps in Argentina, Brazil, and Jamaica.

Robert has played and sung in a variety of band and choral ensembles. He has been a member of the Southern Territorial Band since 1998 and the Songsters from 1998 - 2001. While in Texas, he participated in the Texas Divisional Band, Texas Brass, and the Dallas Temple Corps Band and Songsters and has traveled with these ensembles to Costa Rica, Mexico, Bolivia, Panama, Guatemala, Canada, and Cuba. He was part of the Asbury College Salvation Army Student Fellowship (SASF) Band and Songsters for several years. In addition to playing in many school ensembles during his time in Kentucky, he was also a member of the Lexington Brass Band and Saxton's Cornet Band.

Robert graduated from Asbury College in 1999 with a Bachelor of Arts degree in Music with emphasis in trumpet performance. He also spent two years studying music at the University of Louisville (1995-97). Robert studied trumpet under several teachers including, Terry Everson, Dr. Ronald Holz, Dr. Mike Tunnell, and Vince DiMartino. While at Asbury College, he studied composition/arranging with James Curnow.

As a composer and arranger, Robert has had several arrangements published by The Salvation Army's Southern Territory in the American Instrumental Ensemble Series, Sing Praise, and Children's Praise.

Important compositions

He keeps me singing (AE200834) 2008, Holy is the Lord (AE200312) 2003, I Surrender all (AE200724) 2007, I will enter his gates (AE200532) 2005

SPENCER, WILLIAM

Born at Lyme Regis in Dorset 8th May 1888, and Promoted to Glory 29th February 1960. William Spencer was one of a family of five children who early in life showed a keen aptitude for music and quickly learned to play the violin. Coming from a sea faring tradition his father; the master of a coastal steamer; moved to Goole from where he sailed with his crew to the continent. After leaving school William became an apprentice hairdresser and eventually had his own business in Goole. At the turn of the century he met and married Lily Dixon, a native of Barnsley, and a Salvationist whose parents were members in the very early days of the Salvation Army and who were involved in the early day riots in Barnsley. The father of five children also worked as a lead violinist in the local theatre orchestra doubling as required on trumpet and saxophone. He was also a fine pianist.

In the late 1920's the family moved to Goldthorpe where he took up again as a hairdresser. His two sons, both accomplished brass instrumentalists, played in local orchestras and colliery bands.

After his conversion he very quickly took over leadership of the Goldthorpe Citadel Band, whose membership was over forty players and even in those early days the band had a very full programme of engagements including an Easter weekend in Belfast, an engagement in 1929 that was rather venturesome.

His aptitude for music led him to compose several pieces for the Salvation Army including the cornet solos *'Jesus is Strong to Deliver'* and *'Loves Glad song'*. After writing *'Jesus is strong to deliver'* he was invited to feature this at an annual Salvation Army Festival in London as the cornet soloist. Other music from his pen included *'Two Friends'*, a cornet duet and a very difficult pianoforte solo *'Conferences'* (which incidentally he could not play) as well as a march, *'The Army Standard'* and the selection *'My Saviour'*. At his funeral there was a very large assembled band of Salvationists from the South Yorkshire division who met to pay tribute to a very fine Salvation Army Bandmaster.

William Spencer is the father-in-law of (composer) Frederick Cooper and grandfather of (composer) Lt. Colonel Maurice Cooper.

Important compositions

The Army Standard (GS1076) 1934, Jesus is strong to deliver (FS0034-2) 1927, Love's glad song (GS1027) 1931, Thy Saviour (GS1003) 1929, Two friends (GS1372) 1952

SPICER, RICHARD JOHN

Bandmaster Richard J. Spicer, L.G.S.H., A.B.S.M., Dip.Ed, was born in Brighton, England in 1945. He had a successful and varied career as a professional musician, graduating from the Birmingham Conservatory in England with degrees in Trombone, Piano and Conducting. He played bass trombone with the East of England Orchestra and the Midland

Brass Quintet and taught widely in schools and colleges. He played with several of the (Salvation) Army's top brass bands and was the conductor of the Birmingham Sparkhill and Nottingham Memorial Halls Songster groups. Richard met his wife, Yvonne in Clacton at a Salvation Army Holiday Camp in 1968 and were both very active in the Salvation Army.

In 1985, Richard moved with his wife and two children to the United States to take a job offer as the Divisional Music Director in the Empire State Division of the Salvation Army. As Divisional Music Director in New York, he formed and developed the Empire Brass Youth Band and Chorus. This band went on to be known as one of the eastern territories finest youth bands and were very active in divisional and territorial events during the time period of 1985 - 1990. Richard led that group on a successful and wide ranging tour of the British Isles and also recorded two albums, the first was named *'To the Chief Musician'* and the second, *'Empire to Empire'* which was recorded in England while on tour, hence the title name.

Moving to the West Coast in 1990, he expanded his activities as Music Director for the Del Oro Division and the Oakland Citadel Corps and tirelessly continued to encourage the formation and growth of new brass and vocal groups. Notably he is responsible for the San Francisco Bay Area Band and the Acapella Plus singing group which he led on a tour of Hawaii, Malaysia and the Philippines in 1994. As Bandmaster of the Oakland Citadel Band, they recorded a CD in 1992 titled *'Our God Reigns'*. This 14 track album contained two compositions by Richard, one of which is a suite named Colours and the other a Trombone Ensemble named Strong and Mighty, featuring trombonists Mike McKaigg, Harold Solvang, Merle Miller, Victor Leslie, Kevin Thomas, and Dale Pittock. Colours was written to feature three songs about the Army flag: *'There's Only One Flag for Me'*, *'I Cannot Leave the Dear Old Flag'*, and *'Yellow Star, and Red, and Blue'*. The Oakland Citadel Corps eventually moved 20 miles east to the town of Concord, where they continued their ministry. It was then, in 1995, that the former Oakland Citadel Band, now Concord Band recorded a CD and titled it *'New Pastures'* to mark their move to Concord, a vibrant, growing community nestled at the base of Mount Diablo. The CD *'New Pastures'* features a march *'Concord'* written by Richard, and it reflects the vibrancy and bustle of a city at the nexus of major commuter routes. Timeless classics such as Mozart's *'The Marriage of Figaro'*, Saint-Saens' sound portrait of *'The Swan'*, themes from Mendelssohn's *'Italian Symphony'* and Cappuzzi's *'Concerto for Bass'* are also part of this CD. Two more tracks from the CD are compositions of Richards, a joyous salute to fellow Salvationists in the Caribbean named *'A Caribbean Overture'*, originally written for the Oakland Citadel Band's tour of the Eastern United States and the Caribbean in 1993, and a Carol Arrangement *'Still, Still, Still'*.

The year 1996 would bring about the recording of a third CD with Richard as the Bandmaster, titled *'Synchronization'*. The title track showcases the talents of one of Richard's sons, Darren Spicer, for whom it was written. Each movement is a variation on part of the Salvation Army song *'Keep in Step All the Time'*. Richard also included a work which he wrote especially for young people, and the young at heart, titled *'David and Goliath'*, an epic musical story of the legendary courageous boy who defeats a giant.

Only months after the tour in March of 1997, God decided that it was time to call Richard back home, and Richard died in September of '97 at the early age of 52. Yvonne and their son, Darren, now live back in England where Yvonne attends the Stotfold Corps. Their other son, Stephen, still attends the Concord Corps in California where he is still a bandsman.

Important compositions

Strong and Mighty, Colours, Concord

SODERSTROM, EMIL

Emil Otto Edward Soderstrom was born in Copenhagen, Denmark on May 31st, 1900 to Salvation Army officers. He became a member of 'The Danish Staff Band of The Salvation Army' in Copenhagen where his father, Lt.-Colonel Ernst Soderstrom was the bandmaster. He graduated from the 'Royal Academy of Music' in Copenhagen, in 1918. Emil then studied privately in France, Germany and Norway before immigrating to the USA in April 1923. He became bandmaster in the Danish Corps of Chicago, later on a member of the 'Western Territorial Staff Band' in San Francisco and then becoming bandmaster of the 'Chicago Staff Band'. With the Chicago Staff Band Emil tried out almost all of his new manuscripts. In 1926 he won the 1st price in a composer competition of the Salvation Army with the march *'Fighting for the Lord'*. Emil Soderstrom worked 25 years as an arranger for the 'National Broadcasting Company' (NBC) in Chicago. He wrote music for Brass Bands and Songsters. Emil Soderstrom was Promoted to Glory on August 14th 1972 in Santa Monica, California, USA.

A 1954 American newspaper gave a nice impression of what happened with Emil Soderstrom outside musical circles:

Resident of Sweden Fined for Speeding

It was all a misunderstanding about licenses but no one denied that 70 miles sn hour was illegal on Hamilton St Emfrid Berglund. 30, Norrkoping, Sweden, pleaded guilty to speeding and operating a motor vehicle without a license. He paid a 320 fine on the first count and sentence was suspended by Judge Thomas A. Kane on the other. Charge of permitting an unlicensed driver to operate his vehicle was dismissed against Emil Soderstrom of Chicago. He was the owner of the car involved. Both men are connected with the Swedish Salvation Army band, now on tour of the United States, The group was on its way from Buffalo to Utica for an engagement The band, some of whom came by bus, had dinner at the Salvation Army citadel here. Berglund told Judge Kane he had a Swedish license to drive. He said he had seen Informed miss license made him eligible to drive in this country.

Book - '**Aspriration… anecdotal snapshots of Genius**' - by Robert Getz

The life and music of Dr. Emil Soderstrom'. Historic manuscripts & rare music and music illustrations. This is a treasury of little-known facts and insights into Soderstrom's inner thoughts often given in his own words. There are excerpts from hundreds of letters. This all reveals the uniqueness of the man and his music.

Important compositions

March of the Hours (FS315) 1986, Song of Israel (FS267) 1962, Low in the Grave he lay (FS283) 1964

SOUSA, JOHN PHILIP

John Philip Sousa (1854-1932) was not a composer or even a member of The Salvation Army, but he wrote two marches for The Salvation Army, one has been re-arranged for Brass Band by Lieut-Colonel Ray Steadman-Allen, and published by the Swedisch Music

Department in Stockholm in 1960 (*'March-The Salvation Army'*, No. 315) and *'The Revival March'* (Manuscript). He had a good relationship with Salvation Army Officers and composers. William Booth and John Philip Sousa met upon several occasions.

John Philip Sousa was born on November 6th 1854 in Washington D.C. as the 3rd of 10 children. He was an excellent Bandmaster and composer, and world-wide known as 'The March King'. In the 1890s he developed a type of bass tuba now known as the Sousa-phone The first sousaphone was made by C.G. Conn in 1899 expressly for Sousa's Band. His patriotic march *'The Stars and Stripes Forever'* composed 1897, is today something of a second national anthem of the USA. During The Salvation Army's Golden Jubilee Congress in New York City in May 1930, John Philip Sousa was present. It marked the Army's 50th anniversary in the United States. With 700 bandsmen parading down New York's Fifth Avenue, and such contemporary Army composers as Emil Söderström, Kristian Fristrup, Harry Orway, Harold Turkington, Divisional Bandmaster Erik Leidzén and Adjudant-Bandmaster William Broughton in attendance, the congress is still regarded as the high-light for Salvation Army music-making in the United States. On Saturday, 8000 people filled New York's 71st Street Regiment Armory for the festival of music where Sousa's march *'The Salvation Army'*, which included William Booth's universal anthem, *'O boundless Salvation'* was presented by 15 massed Salvation Army bands. John Philip Sousa wrote: *'Nothing brings us closer to God than beautiful music. If you want to know one of the very good reasons why the world needs bands just ask one of the Salvation Army bandsmen and let him tell of the Army's of men that have been turned toward a better life by first hearing the sound of a Salvation Army band. The next time you hear a Salvation Army band, no matter how humble, take off your hat'*. Sousa died at the age of 77 on March 6th 1932, after conducting a rehearsal of the Ringgold Band in Reading, Pennsylvania. The last piece he conducted was *'The Stars and Stripes Forever'*.

Important composition

The Salvation Army (1960)

STAINES. (first name not known)

One of the early composers (late 1800).

No further information could be retrieved about him.

Important compositions

Is there a pardon (GS0333) 1897, The questions of a sinner (GS0368) 1898

STANYON, EDWIN ALDINE SHERWIN

Edwin was born on 10 January 1907 and Promoted to Glory on 3 February 2003 in Atlanta. Edwin Aldine Sherwin Stanyon was born to Salvation Army Officer parents in Marion, Indiana. He converted at an early age during a meeting conducted by Commissioner Samuel Logan Brengle. Edwin entered training college in New York and was commissioned as an officer on 25 June 1928, and directly appointed to the officer training staff. A year later Edwin was promoted to the rank of Captain and appointed to the Finance Department at the USA Eastern Territorial Headquarters. In 1931 he transferred to the USA Southern Territorial Headquarters and served here in the Finance Department, Trade Department and Atlanta Transient Department. In 1933 he married Captain Ruth Gethin and together they served in Florida, Tennessee, Arkansas and Kentucky. Stanyon enlisted in the armed forces from 1943 to 1945, while Ruth continued her Salvation Army service at the North-

South Caroline Divisional Headquarters. Following his tour of duty, they served together in divisional staff appointments until 1968, when they returned to THQ. They retired of active service on 12 January 1972 and Ruth was Promoted to Glory the year after. Edwin married Major Pauline Dudding in 1974. His officer service was paralleled by an equally significant career as a musician. Since his early days as a cadet in New York, he served as pianist, conductor and composer for divisional and territorial music camps.

Important compositions

Atlanta Temple (GS1676) 1975, The Golden Crown (GS1589) 1968

STAVIK, MORGAN JUEL

Morgan Juel Stavik (born May 27, 1980 in Askim, Oestfold, Norway.) A versatile composer, with a production comprising works for choir, brass band, wind ensemble, songs, piano music, string quartet. el viola and flute. Studied composition at The Grieg Academy (Bergen, Norway). His teacher was Morten Eide Pedersen and Stavik followed masterclasses with Hans Abrahamsen, Kaija Saariaho Seminars; Kaija Saariaho, Bent Sørensen, Henrik Ødegaard, Christian Eggen, Anna Lindahl, Henrik Hellstenius, Karen Tanaka, Georg Friedrich Haas and Nuria Schoenberg. Stavik's earliest compositions were written for Salvation Army brass bands and he has continued to write music for the organization. His serious music is often referred to as melancholic, eerie and transparent, some jazz influence is also evident. Drawing his earliest influences from his friend and mentor Eiliv Herikstad. He studied choir conducting with Professor Magnar Mangersnes and completed his exam with highest distinction.

Important composition

Nearer, My God to Thee (TS1201) 2010

STEADMAN-ALLEN, RAY

Ray Steadman-Allen (RSA) is one of the greatest composers in the Salvation Army. He was born in September 1922 in Bath (England) as the son of Salvation Army Officers. During his moves with his parents from corps to corps and town to town his love for Salvation Army music developed continually. He started his musical career with the age of eleven in the Young People's Band at Barnsley Corps. At the age of 18, RSA started composing music and experimented with great fantasy and skill. His first published work was the march 'Gladsome Morn'. He became a bandsman of the Battersea Citadel Band and later of the Harlesden Citadel Band. Then he served as Band Instructor and Bandmaster of the Harrow Citadel Band. In 1949 he entered the Officers Training College in London. As an Officer he became Bandmaster of the Tottenham Citadel Band (later Enfield Citadel Band) and Songster Leader at Hendon Corps. Ray Steadman-Allen also played Bass Trombone for two years in the International Staff Band (ISB). From 1967 to 1980 he was head of the International Department for Music in London. Today more then 400 compositions by Ray Steadman-Allen have been published by the Salvation Army.

He also composed and arranged many songs for Songster Brigades. Many manuscripts are still waiting to be published. The new revised Tune Books (BTB 1 and BTB 2) are also Ray's work. He also wrote several books about music. His compositions are a spiritual message promoted through Brass Bands. Countless bands, inside as well as outside the Salvation Army has recorded his music, and on nearly every cassette tape, LP and CD you can find his compositions. People like Professor David King is a true lover of RSA's compositions hence the fact that even the world famous Yorkshire Building Society Band recorded a CD with his music called *'Alpha and Omega'.*

Important compositions

Logos (FS397) 1979, The King's Minstrel (FS313) 1968, The Warriors Psalm (FS358) 1974, Romans 8 – A Brass Celebration (FS455) 1986, Daystar (JC640) 2009, On Ratcliffe Highway (JC601) 2006, In Quiet Pastures (GS1330) 1950, Silver Star (GS1513) 1962, Here at the Cross (GS1697) 1977

STEVENSON, WILLIAM

The cornet solo *'I Love Him Better Every Day'* which is probably one of William Stevenson's best known works was the first published by the Salvation Army which was in the form of an *air varie* in which a known melody is given a showy way with several variations. This solo was published in 1922. William Stevenson emigrated from the United Kingdom to the United States of America in the late 1920's of the 20th century. In America he played for a while solo cornet in the Chicago Staff Band and for a short term served as their bandmaster.

Important compositions

Chicago Temple (GS1149) 1938, The Goldthorpe March (GS0886) 1922, I love Him better every day (FS0016-1) 1924

STONE, MARK

Corps Bandmaster in New Zealand; assisted with Territorial Music School early 1980s, appointed Territorial Contemporary Music Director mid 1980s. Established 'God's Army Band' and produced brass tutor with cassette 'Blow your heart out for Jesus'. A notable example of this was the instrumental series 'New Direction' produced by Mark Stone.

Important composition

Blessed Assurance

STOREY, ABRAHAM

The 'Story of the International Staff Band' (Brindley Boon, 1985) tells us that Adjutant Abraham Storey was an elderly officer who led the band (one of the predecessors of the ISB), consisted in the main of a few middle aged instrumentalists augmented by one or two office boys possessed of the right aptitude and enthusiasm.

Important composition

God's harvest home (GS0194) 1892

STOREY, T.H

One of the early composers (first half of 19th century). It is likely that this person is the same as Captain George Storey, a Salvation Army officer who had led an unofficial Headquarters Band around the time that the International Staff Band was set up (1890) but this can not be confirmed. George Storey later moved to the United States and worked there as a Salvation Army Officer. He died with the rank as major when he was on a high age of over eighty.

Important composition

The daring Salvationist (GS0770) 1917

STORM, HELGE

Almost nothing is known or could be found about Helge Storm. Helge composed the cornet solo *'Gå fram!'*, meaning *'Walk on!'*(Svensk Festmusik 252). Helge Storm (1904-1973) was a bandsman and deputy bandmaster of the Sandviken Temple Band. He left the Salvation Army and joined the Swedish Covenant Chuch in Sandviken where he was Songster Leader for many years. He was from Sweden.

Important composition

Gå Fram! (FM0252) 1963

STREETON, W.L

One of the early composers (first half of 19th century).

No further information could be retrieved about him.

Important compositions

Songs of Ireland (GS0707) 1913, Songs of Testimoney No.1 (GS0738) 1916

STREHLE, KENNETH Jr

Son of stalwart music leader Bandmaster Kenneth Strehle, Ken, Jr., had just one piece published in Salvation Army brass journals. He was by profession a medical doctor, and in his youth known as a fine euphonium soloist. He was bandmaster of the Eastern Pennsylvania Youth Band and bandsman of the Phildelphia Citadel Band.

Important composition

Meditation - Neath the Cross (AJ0075) 1967

STROMBECK, GEORGE

Was born in Moline, Illinois in 1939. He became acquainted with the Salvation Army at age 18, when school friends from the Moline, IL Salvation Army Corps invited him to play his baritone horn at the 'Farewell Service' for Major Gunnar and Esther Erickson, who were being transferred to the Rockford, IL Temple Corps. In 1957 George traveled with a brass quartet, sponsored by 'Youth For Christ, to Copenhagen, Denmark, for a 2 week crusade. He wrote all of the arrangements, and played cornet in the quartet. He continued to play in the Moline Salvation Army Band, until attending the University of Iowa. After graduation he married Dorothy Olson, who he met at the Moline Salvation Army Corps!

In 1963 he was invited to travel with the Rockford Temple Corps Band on their trip to Sweden. The invitation came from Major Gunnar Erickson! George was very impressed with Salvation Army band music, especially the use of hymn tunes and Gospel songs. His first attempt at arranging for the Salvation Army was a selection called *'The Good Shepherd'* - a medley of hymns about Christ the Shepherd *('Savior, Like A Shepherd Lead Us' 'Follow, I Will Follow Thee'* and *'He Leadeth Me').*

He taught in public schools in Iowa (2 years) and his hometown of Moline, IL (for 3 years), and finishied a 'Master Of Music' degree from the University of Illinois. In 1968 he was appointed the 'Director Of Instrumental Music' at Trinity College, the Evangelical Free

Church School in Deerfield, IL, where he served for 18 years. During those years he wrote several 'full concert band' arrangements, to be used for our concert tours. These were full instrumentation 'military band' settings, including woodwinds as well as brass and percussion parts. In the 1970's George also established, and directed an orchestra (with string instruments). He resigned from Trinity in 1984, to move to Michigan to work with David E. Smith, publisher of Christian Instrumental Music.

In 1980 he was invited to be a guest teacher and performer at the Salvation Army Silver Lake Band Camp, near Minneapolis, MN. Here he had the privilege to meet William Broughton, and Bill Himes! Over the years he continued to write full (military style) band arrangements - about 40 in all. He also became very involved with the 'Christian Instrumental Directors Association' serving as president and other office positions, hosting many conferences. Through CIDA he had opportunity to meet Mr. Jim Curnow, who has been very much an encouragement to him.

George has taught at all levels, including beginning band, middle school band, high school band, and at college for 18 years. In Michigan he directed a community band, performing summer concerts, and parade participation. He is currently the director of the 'Rockford Christian Fellowship Band.'

In 2000 they retired to Rockford, IL, to babysit their grandchildren. Shortly after moving here, Bandmaster Steve Sjogren invited him to join the Rockford Temple Corps Band, playing the 1st Baritone part! It has been a joy for George to perform with this wonderful brass band during the past 10 years!

Last fall he revised one of my brass arrangements (originally written for a tour at Trinity in 1972) to Salvation Army full brass instrumentation, to be played by the Rockford Temple Corps Band. It is titled *'Day Of Pentecost'* and portrays musically the events of Acts Chapter 2, using appropriate hymns to depict the coming of the Holy Spirit. It was featured on their tour to Toronto, Canada last November (2010), and was well received. Most of his writing has been for the full concert (military) band, but he now look forward to doing special Christian arrangements for the Salvation Army instrumentation.

George became a Christian at the age of 9 (at a church camp), and have been pleased to use his talent for the Lord with instrumental music all these years. He look forward to someday being part of the exciting music we have been promised that will be used as we give praise to Jesus in Heaven!

Important composition

Euphonium solo – The Stormy Sea

SUZUKI, HAJIME

Hajime Suzuki improved his music skills through the lessons by Mr. Fujio Nakayama who was a famous trumpeter and a professor of brass instruments at Tokyo University of the Arts (Tokyo Geijutsu Daigaku). Suzuki encountered the music of The Salvation Army and discovered the spiritual realm behind it. This experience led him to the way to be a Christian. Since the conversion, he has been working in the music field of the Salvation Army, as a member of Japan Staff Band for the first, and as the principal cornet player, then a Deputy-Bandmaster. Finally, he was appointed as the bandmaster in April, 1984. Currently, he is also in the position of Territorial Music Secretary. His career in Salvation

Army since 1974 raised his leadership potential and he has been busy using the limited resources of Japan's small Salvation Army. As one of local Salvationists, he has been in Kiyose Corps and serving as Corps Bandmaster since 1976. He also has academic connections in Japanese brassband world as a Director of the Japan Trumpeters' Association and as a Member of the Academic Society of Japan for Winds Percussion and Band. Many of his compositions were played and several were recorded by the Japan Staff Band.

Important compositions

How Much More (m/s), The Little Lost Lamb (m/s)

SWANSBURY, JOHN G

Born on 2 September 1951, John was commissioned in 1977 as bandmaster of the Nunhead Corps Band in South London, having been both Corps Sergeant Major and acting bandmaster for a year following the departure of Carl Stephens. John held that post until 1986 when Duncan Cameron took over and he became Corps Secretary. Most of that time, the band numbered 12-15 players, being a mixture of regular attenders and of varyingly occasional helpers from the staff of the William Booth Training College.

Some music sections use a seasonal repertoire of well-rehearsed and frequently-played items; this never appealed to John . He preferred to keep interest by having a quick turnover of music, and tried never to repeat within a year a contribution to a Sunday evening meeting. He soon found that this approach quickly exhausted the suitable music in the Salvation Army's published band journals. It perplexed him that the Triumph Series, designed for small bands, devoted half of its output to marches, which small bands can least use on the march. Of course, a good march can be played in a Sunday evening meeting, but something more reflective was usually preferred. This lack prompted him to make his own arrangements of songs and choruses that were popular in the Corps, and the band very kindly tried out whatever John produced. Indeed, Nunhead band was very good at sight-reading new music.

John had a previous interest in the theory of music and had gained an Associateship diploma of the London College of Music (A.Mus.L.C.M) as an external student. He had also attended evening classes in composition at Morley College, London, by Hugh Wood and Melanie Daiken, and had produced some modern pieces there using tone rows, etc. However, this type of music was never going to suit a Sunday Salvationist congregation. He was no infant musical prodigy: it wasn't until John was eleven, after five years in Kenya with his officer-parents, that he started having piano, theory, and cornet lessons. These came to an end when he left for university, but the interest in theory of music persisted. It was back at his home Corps (Leek, in Staffordshire), a few years later, that he had his first arrangement played, a setting that combined St Clements with *'A little star peeps o'er the hill'*.

John has written a few pieces for larger bands, such as *'Old Bones'* by request of his uncle, Ron Burr, for the Salvation Army Bournemouth Area Fellowship Band. However, there seems to be more than enough music written for the big bands in the UK, much of it extended and excellent, but really rather little for the average band that has slender resources. That's where John's focus lies: accessible, varied arrangements for small groups, with interest for the inner parts, not too tiring for the cornets, and written with the listener in mind, not just the player. In recent years, most of his band output has been for the ensemble at Carshalton Corps, which has only 5-6 players. In addition, he has brought together and arranged music for a choir every Christmas for over twenty years at the Royal Marsden Hospital, where he works as a clinical scientist. And very recently the songsters at his current Corps, Croydon, have kindly used some of his music.

It is always more of a stimulus to write music for a specific group of players, tailored to their strengths and abilities, than to write for a standard ensemble. For this reason, John has offered little to the Army's Music Editorial Department.

Important compositions

Blessed Assurance (TS1007) 1993, Quem Pastores Lauda Vere (TS1092) 2000, Three Czech Carols (US0086) 1979

SWANSON, (first name not known)

One of the early composers (first half of 19th century).

No further information could be retrieved about him.

Important compositions

My Homeward Journey (FS0039) 1927, The Seattle March (GS0910) 1923

SQUIBB, RICHARD

Richard was born in Devonport, Tasmania (a small Island at the bottom of Australia) and attended the local Salvation Army. He had piano lessons when he was eight years old and started playing a Brass instrument when he was twelve. He then started on Tenor Horn before moving to Euphonium. One of the biggest influences on his life was the then bandmaster of the Devonport Corps, Bruce Hammond. He got him practicing and unlocked the world of Salvation Army music. At the age of fourteen, Richard's family then moved to the Launceston Corps, in Northern Tasmania. This corps had a large band and a rich history of Salvation Army music making. While living in Launceston he completed a Bachelor of Performing Arts, with a major in conducting. When Richard was twenty he moved to Melbourne where he joined the Melbourne Staff Band playing first Baritone. He attended the Box Hill Corps and played in the band under Bandmaster Lawrence Clarke. He then moved to the Brunswick Corps in inner Melbourne where he was the Bandmaster for four years. During this time he got married and they transferred to the Camberwell Corps. Here Richard became Bandmaster one year later. In 2006 he left the MSB due to work commitments and two years later resigned as Bandmaster, as his wife and he were having their first child.

Richard was a member of the Melbourne Staff Band for eleven years, and went on a number of overseas tours to the United Kingdom, United States of America, Canada and New Zealand. During this time he also completed a postgraduate diploma in Education and began teaching music at a number of schools. He is now currently the Director of Music at Presbyterian Ladies College, a large Independent Girls School, and has been teaching at the College for thirteen years. During his time teaching and as a member of the MSB he had many opportunities to compose and arrange music for school orchestras, wind bands and brass band. The MSB have recorded a number of his arrangements, such as Percy Grainger's *'Shepherds Hey'*, Fanfare & Prelude on Westminster Abbey and Touching the Wave. More recently he has been writing choral music, as he is currently the leader of the

Gospel Choir at the Camberwell Salvation Army, where his wife and he attend with their two children, Fletcher and Jemimah.

Important compositions

Touching the Wave, Fanfare & Prelude on Westminster Abbey

TALBOT, J.

One of the early composers (first half of 19th century).

No further information could be retrieved about him.

Important compositions

The Garston (TS0088) 1927, My Desire (TS0155) 1931

TAYLOR, ALASTAIR

Was born on 5th March 1967 in Manchester, the first of four children. At the age of two he was brought to Scotland by his parents and they settled in a small village in West Lothian called Fauldhouse. Even though he was born in England, he thinks of himself as Scottish, as all his parents and grand parents were from West Lothian. His parents were Salvationists and they attended Fauldhouse Corps until September 1981 when they moved to Hamilton. During the time they spent at Fauldhouse, Alastair was encouraged to play both the piano and a brass instrument and joined the Singing Company and played along with the Senior Band. The Band was not particularly large but averaged 10 to 15 players. He started off playing a baritone at the age of about 8 but was quickly moved on to euphonium soon after. This is where he formed a great interest in both brass and piano. At the age 10, he occasionally played for the Singing Company rather than singing which he preferred.

During this time, he regularly played piano solos and accompanied the family on occasions when they sang and his father would allow him to play for the congregation now and again. His main interest at the time was playing football with his younger brother and many of their friends from The Salvation Army. There was a good youth fellowship as well which kept them busy.

At the age of 14 they moved to Hamilton due to work commitments of his father. Here things were very different as the Corps was much larger with bigger sections. When he arrived, the Corps assumed that he was a Senior Soldier and he was promptly asked in to the Senior Band. Again, he played another instrument but was soon placed on to his first love, the euphonium which he was so pleased to do. The family felt after a few years that they should return to Fauldhouse, their first home. However, Alastair was a young man by this time and felt that he should stay with Hamilton Corps as there were more opportunities there. The Songster Leader and his wife took 'pity' on a young lad and fed him every Sunday. At the age of 15 he was asked to play for the Singing Company and then a year later or so he was asked to play for the Songsters leading to him becoming the Corps pianist. At this time, he was also asked to play for the Glasgow Divisional Youth Chorus which he did for approximately 15 years. During this time, Alastair started writing a number of vocal compositions that the Youth Chorus used on a regular basis. The highlight for him with the Youth Chorus was them singing some of my compositions at the European Youth Congress in Holland 1993. One the pieces *'Wonder Working Power'* has been recorded even though this has not been published to date. Commissioner Keith Banks saw his talent and asked him to play at Corps Cadet Camps which were held at Balvonie Conference Centre which is now sadly closed. Alastair then played for the Territorial Congress which was regularly held in Scotland as Scotland was then a Territory on its own right. Commissioner Banks always comments that he was the one who 'discovered' him. He went on to write an arrangement for one of Keith's songs 'A new world' which was published in 'The Musical Salvationist' in 1985 written for the International Youth Year which also appeared later on in 'Happiness & Harmony'.

From the age of 16 he attended the Music School in Scotland not as you would think as a student but he was invited on to staff and played for all the rehearsing and festivals attached to this. This accounts for approximately 14 years. Alastair was always prepared with some compositions to take to Music School each year. Another influence through this time was Ivor Bosanko who he met at the Music School. He would sometimes arrive at the School with only the vocal part written and would play the accompaniments to him expecting Alastair to play these back which he took great delight in trying to do. As a result of their friendship and Ivor's influence, he eventually invited him to the USA to play piano in a small orchestra for a musical which he wrote called *'True Blue'* that had been prepared for their congress. Alastair had never flown before and never travelled on his own so you can imagine how big this was for him. On the Sunday of the congress, his song *'I Need Thee'* was performed whilst the then General Eva Burrows was in attendance.

One of the vocal directors of the Music School, Songster Leader George Bell also had a great influence in Alastair's life and would always give him words of encouragement. This influence was to last all his life until George was taken from them to be with his Master. In 1988 Alastair wrote *'I Need Thee'* for the Music School for female voices and later decided to re-arrange it for SATB and send it to SP&S to see what reaction he would get and if it was likely to be published. To his surprise, *'I Need Thee'* was published some 3 years later in 'The Musical Salvationist'. To this day, people still come up to Alastair and tell him how special this piece has been for them.

Other pieces published included *'A Gift From Me'*. Again, having written this in 1990 for the Music School and rearranging, Alastair sent this to London and did not hear anything until the then Captain Peter Ayling contacted him to inform him he had found the music in a cupboard at THQ and would like to use it for the International Staff Songters. This was published in 'Sing To the Lord' 2001 and recorded by the International Staff Songsters as was *'I Need Thee'* during Major Leonard Ballantine's reign as Leader. *'Splendour Of His Service'* was originally written for Clydebank Singing Company and published in 2000 in the 'Sing To Lord Female Voice Series'. During Peter's time as Leader, Alastair was honoured to be asked to audition for the pianist post with the ISS. However, he felt that a move to London was not for him. On that visit, he was given the honour of accompanying the ISS at rehearsal as they sang *'A Gift From Me'*.

In more recent years, he has written *'Prayer of Our Time'* which incorporates the Lord's Prayer and has been sung by Birmingham Citadel Songsters and is currently used by The Glasgow Phoenix Choir. Alastair has also written a number of solos for his wife, Julie who is a soloist with the Choir. He would reckon that in his cupboard there are still many pieces that he has written that have neither been published nor performed on a regular basis.

As for brass composition, Alastair has only one claim to fame which again revolves around *'I Need Thee'* and was a solo for Bb instrument published in the American Soloist Album No6. Michael Kenyon saw fit to arrange *'I Need Thee'* for brass and this was published in

1995 in the General Series. Alastair has ventured less in writing brass however he has written marches such as *'Fauldhouse Centenary'*, *'Hamilton 100'* and *'Marching To The Future'* which was written for the opening of the new hall and played by the International Staff Band. Other pieces include *'Variations on St Clements'* & *'Chorale & Prelude – Beethoven'*. His arrangement of *'Give Thanks'* was recorded by Boscombe Band. Whilst at Hamilton, he wrote a few pieces which include a *'Musical Moments from Scotland'* for the Young People's Band and a Christmas Suite entitled *'The Lord has Come'* for the Senior Band. Many of these pieces were written during his twenties. Alastair has also done other song arrangements for congregational use.

He can honestly say that his greatest achievement was *'I Need Thee'* which was the title of his CD which was used to raise funds for the new Community Programme at Hamilton. He has however had a number of highlights throughout his life. This would include being the Euphonium Soloist for Hamilton Corps Band and also given the opportunity to play alongside Derick Kane on a number of occasions when he came back to his home Corps of Hamilton. The highlight of these times was playing the duet *'Pearl Fishers'* with him. He has had the privilege of playing in Germany with another musician, Alan McDonald where apart from accompanying Alan, Alastair conducted and played with the German Staff Band. He was for a number of years the Deputy Bandmaster at Hamilton Corps and although sadly he no longer is in a position like this, he still continue to serve the Lord through music at Corps as a guest pianist and accompanist most of the time with my wife.

Alastair currently finds himself, doing a small amount of teaching piano and he is involved with St Patrick's Operatic Society in Shotts where he plays at their annual show every year. He has in the past accompanied a number of Scottish Celebrities including Bill McCue and Moira Anderson. Whilst at Earnock High School in Hamilton he won the award for Best Composition for the whole of Scotland. He also played with the school wind band and recorded with them and also played with the Glasgow Parks Orchestra which sadly disbanded after a year due to lack of sponsorship.

Alastair currently still lives in Hamilton with his wife, Julie and have been grateful for those who have encouraged and influenced him during his lifetime. He can see along his pathway, the people that the Lord has put in place to do just that. He does not profess to be anything special as a composer or musician and do what he does so people may enjoy it. Alastair does it because music means so much to him and to this day he still feel that God can use him and his music as a blessing to those who listen.

Footnote from Julie Taylor (Alastair's wife):

My husband has blessed me with his music all the time that I have known him. However, his sense of humour is also musically influenced. Mention a word and there is sure to be a tune comes out of the piano relating to it!!! Eg. 'We now have the bones of the bio'. What does he play? Dem bones, dem bones, dem dry bones!

Important composition

I Need Thee

TAYLOR, DENNIS J.

Dennis was born in South Norwood, Borough of Croydon, South London on September 4th 1925. His early years were eventful in that his father was a heavy drinker, which meant that they moved around a great deal. However, July 22nd 1933 his father was challenged by the presence of the local Salvation Army Band while they were holding an Open-Air Service on this particular Saturday night. So, there was a great change in his family, because both his father and mother accepted Jesus as their Saviour.

Dennis' brother and he went along with their parents to the local Salvation Army Corps the Balham Congress Hall, South London. At the age of seven he commenced learning the cornet and soon took his place in the Young People's Band. In 1934 at the age of eight, Dennis was accepted as a pupil at the Trinity College of Music, London, where he received a Junior Exhibition Scholarship which took place on a Saturday morning. This involved the teaching of the theory of music, instrumental tuition, and pianoforte lessons. He was able to attend the college right up to the age of thirteen. But, his parents moved away from Balham which meant that it was not possible for him to attend any more. By now they were attending the Sutton Corps which is in the South London area, where he took his place in the Young People's Band on the solo cornet bench. However, within a couple of years in 1939, the Second World War had commenced, and within a very short time there were changes. There were a large number of the bandsmen called up into the armed forces, and Dennis with a number of the boys at the age of fourteen were transferred into the senior band. He had the privilege of sitting in the principal cornet position. At the age of seventeen Dennis joined the Royal Navy and served his country from 1942 to 1947.

After the war he returned home to Staines where his parents had moved, owing to the fact that their house had been damaged in a bombing raid. He took his place in the Staines Citadel Band, again having the privilege of sitting as the principal cornet. Also within a very short time he was appointed as the Young People's Band Leader, and in 1950 he was appointed as Deputy Bandmaster. During this period he was invited to join the National Brass band Conductors Association, and he now has the honour of being a Vice Chairman of the Association. 1952-1960, his wife and he served as Salvation Army Officers. During that period he had the privilege of being the Bandmaster of the Officers Band at the Annual Councils, also the Bandmaster of the South Yorks division Officer's band, with his friend Norman Bearcroft playing trombone in the band.

In 1960 he and his wife resigned from their service as Salvation Army Officers, and he qualified as a teacher, because he had already passed his teaching diploma from Trinity College (LTCL) in 1956, later in 1965 he gained the Fellowship of the College (FTCL). His service as a Bandmaster commenced at Dudley Corps in the Birmingham Division, 1966-1970, then he moved to a new teaching appointment in Harlow, Essex, where I was appointed Bandmaster at Woodgreen Corps, North London, 1971- 1973. Dennis moved up to Sunderland in the North East of England, and was appointed Bandmaster at Sunderland Millfield Corps 1974 – 1976. Unfortunately, they had a family problem so he had to move to the South of England again.

His wife and he ceased attending the Salvation Army at this time and joined a Baptist Church, but he did not sever his ties from the Salvation Army because if it had not been for the Salvation Army, he would not be where he is today; he has much to thank the Lord for as far as the Salvation Army is concerned. His Teaching career covered a period of 30 years from 1960-1990 when he retired. During this time Dennis was a Musical Director of a number of bands in Essex and the Birmingham area. In all of his schools where he was Head of the Music Department, he formed brass bands, and they were very successful. In one case at the Stourport Comprehensive School, Worcestershire, the band entered a number of Youth contests, and was always placed in the top three. Another school in Loughton, Essex, Lucton Boys School became the Youth Champions of the London and Home Counties National Contest for two years in succession. They also did a tour of Germany in 1978, and the band made a couple of recordings.

Later the school was joined with the Girls School and became know as Epping Forest High School. Unfortunately, he had to change direction and the band became a Wind band, because of the number of clarinets and flutes that were being played by the girls, but the band became as successful as the brass band. They toured Italy three times and entered a Youth Contest which took place in Valkenburg, Holland, and received a Golden Award, Highly Commended, in October 1988. The next year Dennis was invited back to adjudicate at the same concert of 1989. As far as adjudicating is concerned he did a number of assignments 1966-2003. In the year of his retirement he had completed a B.Mus. course at London University, and gained the degree in the year of 1990. They moved up to Sunderland to be near their youngest daughter in that same year, and he decided that he wanted to do further studies, so he was accepted as a Post-Graduate at Durham University to do a four year course for a Master's degree.

Dennis gained his M.Mus degree in 1994 for research, and he submitted a thesis on the Life and Music of Eric Ball. He still was not satisfied and wanted to do something about improving his composing, so as a Post-Graduate he enrolled at Newcastle University to do a Master's degree in Composition. Dennis was successful and received an M.Mus. degree (Composition), 1999.

In 2001 he was made an Honorary Fellow attached to the Music Department, of Durham University, and researched into the Brass Band Movement, and the result being two books have been published; *'The Heritage of the North East Brass Band Movement'* published in cooperation with the Brass Band Aid charity. The second book is more academic and has been published by Canbridge Scholars Publishing, the title being *'English Brass Bands and their Music 1860-1930'*. His fellowship comes to an end on July 5th this year. Dennis did not send music for publication during his teaching career, simply because he did not have time to do serious composing, it was not until he retired that he was able to send material with the aim of publication. Although, he did have four vocals published by Salvationist & Supplies, Ltd in the 1950s and 60s.

Music published by S.P&S.Ltd.

1) *Within this Temple Abide*, Musical Salvationist, September-October, 1955
2) *In the Home League*, Songs for Home League Singers
3) *Remember 'Tis Christmas Day*, Musical Salvationist, December,1958
4) *The Orchestra*, Songs for Young People
5) *Gospel Bells*, Festive arrangement, Unity Series, February,1994

Secular music published by Mostyn Music, Stayley Bridge, Cheshire, about 20 works.

Sacred music published by Musikhaus Ruh, Thayngen, Switzerland, just 2 works.

Here are a few titles. Mostyn Music:

1) *Wearside Suite* a work of three movements commissioned for Vaux Samson Band in 1994.
2) *Spirit of South Bank*, March, commissioned for the South Bank Band 1996.
3) *Calypso* for String Orchestra, 1999
4) *Finnish Folk Songs*, Rhapsody, 2000
5) *Saffron Walden High*, March, 1990
6) *Shari's Tune*: Violin solo for the young daughter of our friends in Holland

Sacred work for Musikhaus Ruh:

Gettes Liebi isch wie d'Sunne, 1996

Important composition

Gospel Bells (US0176) 1994

TAYLOR, E.W

One of the early composers (first half of 19th century). This might have been one of the early International Staff Bandsmen. No further information could be retrieved about him.

Important composition

The Company Guard (TS0038) 1924

TEBB, G

One of the early composers (first half of 19th century).

No further information could be retrieved about him.

Important composition

Shipley (GS0582) 1909

THOMAS, MARTYN

Martyn Thomas' roots are in the Salvation Army. Grampy (Walter Thomas) actually worked for the Salvation Army's Musical Editorial Department as long ago as 1918 with such luminaries as Albert Jakeway, Henry Hall and Eric Ball. Walter had several compositions published and went on to become Bandmaster of the Southsea Citadel band. Martyn's father, Stanley Thomas, was appointed to the position of Bandmaster in 1961, succeeding his father, Walter. Stan, as he is affectionately known, in addition to directing The Joybells Singing Group, was also involved for many years instructing at Salvation Army Summer Schools of Music. Martyn's uncle (Derek Thomas) and brother (Melvyn Thomas) were also Salvation Army bandmasters.

Martyn Thomas started playing the piano 'by ear' at the age of 2, learning the cornet at age 7 and the guitar at age 8. In addition to playing in Salvation Army Bands, he was often involved singing and playing in various groups, his preference being rock, blues and jazz. In 1978 he was the top student at the Welsh School of Music winning the coveted HB Award. Other additions to his CV include being an instructor at the world famous Star Lake Music Camp in the United States of America in 1995 and 1996 and being awarded the degree of Doctor of Music by the Canterbury University in 2005. His first published work for brass band was the march *'South Coast'*. This march was subsequently included in the journal

'Favourite Marches of the Salvation Army'. His last stint of playing in a brass band was when he was principal cornet with the Portsmouth Citadel Band, from January 1992 until October 1996. Since then he has continued to write for and play with various bands and groups. The year 2007 saw the commencement of his music being recorded and published in The Netherlands by Brass Band De Waldsang and Lake Music respectively.

Important compositions

Comforth and Joy (GS1937) 1997, Portsmouth Citadel (GS1913) 1995

THOMAS, MARTYN SCOTT

Martyn Scott Thomas, or Marty as he is affectionally known is currently playing 1st Cornet in the Chicago Staff Band after playing Flugelhorn for 10 years. He also plays Solo Cornet in the Norridge Citadel Band, but has also played 1st Baritone and Percussion in that group. In addition, he leads the corps youth band.

Martyn was born in Buffalo, New York in August of 1965. His father, Herbert Thomas, was the corps bandmaster at Buffalo Citadel and his grandfather, Eugene Thomas was the bandmaster before him. Martyn started playing cornet when he was eight years old and soon joined the junior band.

In 1977, his father went to the School for Officer Training in Suffern, New York. After two years as a cadet, his first appointment was in Washington, Pennsylvania where the corps band consisted of his dad, his brother, his sister, Martyn and one other. Fortunately, the high school had an excellent music program. His brother and he were also able to play in a pretty good divisional youth band. He also attended Star Lake Music camp in the summers.

Martyn was really drawn to music in many forms and decided to attend college to become a high school band director. He attended West Liberty State College (now West Liberty University), a small school outside of Wheeling, West Virginia (very near to Washington, PA). And while there, he became more and more interested in school music programs and was only connected to the Salvation Army through summer camps. In 1986, just before his final year of college, he once again attended Star Lake Music Camp. Barrie Gott was the special guest and the music they played got him hooked on Salvation Army music again. Upon graduation in 1987, he worked at Camp Allegheny in Western PA as a lifeguard and while there, interviewed for the vacant Divisional Music Director's position. He was hired in September, with responsibilities for corps music programs, summer music camp and the divisional youth band.

After four years in that position, he moved to Chicago to take over as the Divisional Music Director for the Metropolitan Division with similar responsibilities. He was also involved with a divisional Gospel choir and started a Steel Band program (Pans of Thunder) at the Chicago Midwest Corps.

In January 1999, Martyn started working in the Territorial Music and Gospel Arts Department as the production specialist, with responsibilities for music typesetting, drama writing and editing, and other production support. In September 2000, he joined the Chicago Staff Band.

His composing and arranging has developed out of a need (i.e., writing arrangements for the youth bands, etc.). Favourite composers and influences include: James Curnow, Bill Himes, Stephen Bulla and Robert Redhead.

Important composition

Island Dreams (AJ0222) 2003

THOMAS, PERCY

Born in Aberystwyth in Wales. He played in the Aberystwyth Municipal Orchestra. He probably moved to Rugby for work but the date of this is not known. He conducted the Rugby Town Band (non Salvation Army Band) for several years. He was appointed Deputy Bandmaster of the Rugby Salvation Army Band in 1944, probably at the same time as (composr) Edward Dytham was appointed as Bandmaster. It was also during this time that he wrote the march that made him famous; *'Rugby Citadel'*. During Band weekend visits to other Corps he often recited on the Festival programmes and was a very able and sincere leader of spiritual meetings. In 1948-1949 he was acting Songster Leader for a short time but no record could be found of him being commissioned. In 1949 he composed *'The Burton March'* for the retirement from the band of Retired Bandmaster John Burton who had served the band for 62 years. A record was presented to Bandmaster Burton with this march on one side and *'The Wealdstone March'* on the reverse side composed by Edward Cuell who later became Songster Leader. In the same festival, Percy Thomas recited *'Ode to a Grand Old Man'* and the Songsters sang a special song written for the occasion by Percy called *'How Wonderful'*. He was Deputy Bandmaster when the band toured Denmark in 1949 and was a very able euphonium player. In 1951 he retired as Deputy Bandmaster.

Important composition

Rugby Citadel (TS0388) 1945

THOMAS, WALTER J.

Walter Thomas (1900 - 1974) was Bandmaster of the Southsea Citadel Band from 1943 to 1961. His first publication was in 1920: *'The Whosoever March'*. This March was considered years ahead of it's time and technical demands meant that only a handful of bands could play it! Stanley Thomas, his son, succeeded Walter in 1961 and continued as Bandmaster until 1973.

An excerpt from Southsea 1 band brochure in September 1924 signed by Bramwell Booth: *'The music played by all Salvation Army Bands is composed, or arranged, and published by The Army's Musical Department, and it is a noteworthy fact that two of the marches published for Salvation Army Bands (viz, 'Southsea 1' and 'Whosoever') were composed by a member of the Southsea 1 Band--Bandsman W.Thomas. This young man, who served during the war in the Mercantile Marine, was born in The Army and came up through the Young People's Work.*

Bandmaster Walter J. Thomas was an accomplished musician and for two years worked in the Army's International Music Editorial Department. This was in the Hawkes/Goldsmith era and Walt prized very highly the privilege of having worked with these men who so influenced Salvation Army music. His was the difficult task of re-building the Band in the post-war years, and how well he did it can be judged from the fact during his period as Bandmaster the Band twice toured abroad, in France and Norway. He retired in 1961 through ill-health and was succeeded by his son Stanley.

Bandmaster Stanley Thomas was appointed Bandmaster in October 1961 following many years working with young people locally and at music schools around the country. Stan was ever determined that the Band's ministry would be appreciated by a wider audience and so his programmes were well balanced with 'crowd' appeal. He also encouraged the use of 'The Mercy Beats' consisting of five young bandsmen, proving not only a lively addition to the programmes but also an effective evangelistic tool. During his period as Bandmaster, the Band conducted tours of Germany and Holland, and Scotland, as well as visits throughout the UK'.

Important compositions

Southsea 1 March (GS0871) 1921, The Whosoever March (GS0898) 1923, The Holly March

THORNETT, DAVID B.

Son of Brigadier Bramwell Thornett, who was well-known in the United Kingdom Salvation Army circles as a concertina player. David was one-time principal trombone of the BBC Concert Orchestra.

His entry into this world happened on the 31st October 1932 at 2.39 pm. in the Salvation Army Mothers Hospital, East London. Interestingly Ray Steadman Allen was also born there ten years previously. David was born to Salvation Army officer parents who were both musical. His father, Bramwell, was a virtuoso concertina player with a vast repertoire of classical music. His mother, Jessie, was blessed with a beautiful voice. There was much music making in their home and at a very young age he was familiar with a fair amount of music. When he was about twelve years old he was introduced to the treble clef, and was presented with an old brass cornet which was to become his friend ! David's teacher, Jim Mountain (the composer Herbert Mountain's brother) a great chap, was the Young People's Bandleader at Sheffield Citadel, and David was soon a band member. He started piano lessons at about the same time. Soon he was attempting to compose and was encouraged and helped in his first efforts by Albert Jakeway, Wilfred Heaton, and at the first Salvation Army music camp, by Ray Steadman-Allen.

It was that music camp experience that inspired him to write *'Youth Undaunted'* which was published in 1950. Some years later, Eric Ball kindly and favourably commented on his song *'Take all my sins away'* which was subsequently published in the 'Musical Salvationist' and is also included in 'Gems for Songsters' No.6, 1960. His setting of *'Take my life and let it be'*, under the title *'Consecration'* is in 'Vocal Solos' No. 2. (for some reason he has never heard this performed.). David's first accepted composition was *'Childrens' Praises.'* with words by his mother. A later song, also with words by his mother, was *'God's Voice'*. Apart from another march, *'Glorious Liberty'*, he has only a few more published compositions (songs.). After leaving school he was due for military service.

David decided to join a military band where he taught himself to play the trombone and widened his musical experience. He was with them for five years. After a year in civilian life he enrolled as a full time student at the Royal College of Music in London studying trombone and composition. He left college prematurely without finishing his graduate course, when he was successful in an audition for a vacancy in the London Philharmonic Orchestra. Sadly his association with them did not last and he was thrust into the hostile freelance world. This was a very lean period. He was out of work for eighteen months with no money coming in. Eventually the phone rang and he was offered a tour with the Royal Ballet. After that came some theatre work, a couple of West End shows, and a tour with the Ballet Rambert. On 1st May David auditioned for the post of Principal Trombone with the BBC Concert Orchestra. He was successful and held that job down for thirty years! Now in his retirement he plays the piano in a hospital in Romford. This is very worthwhile. He goes several times a week and play each time for two or three hours a wide selection of music (mostly improvised and some of his own arrangements of George Gershwin, Cole Porter, Jerome Kern, Irving Berlin); some jazz, religious music, hymns, Salvation Army songs etc. David is a great believer in the healing power of music and has seen it working so many times when he plays. He left the Salvation Army many years ago but still has a place in his heart for it and a love for its vast treasury of music.

Important compositions

Glorious Liberty (GS1595) 1969, Youth Undaunted (GS1364) 1952

TIBERG, WIKTOR

Wiktor Tiberg, born in 1900 and Promoted to Glory in 1939. He was a bandman and Deputy Bandmaster during 1920 - 1924 of the Stockholm 1 Temple Band. He composed the May-march (Svensk Festmusik 49). Wiktor studied at the Stockholm art-industrial school. Later, he was employed at The Salvation Army Headquarters Property Department as architect during the 1932-1939 period. He was a skilful violinist and Erik Leidzéns Suite for violon and piano is composed for Wiktor and his wife Gunhild Tiberg. Apart from being a bandsman and violinist he was quite a famous artist. He painted many paintings, covers for the 'War Cry', books and all kinds of things. He was a soldier at the Temple corps in Stockholm.

Important composition

Maj-Marsch (FM0049-1) 1906

TITSHALL, BRIAN

Deputy Bandmaster at Edmonton and a former Songster Leader at Tottenham Citadel around 1958. He was a tremendous pianist and musician and taught piano to the daughters of Ray Steadman-Allen. After a Sunday afternoon concert with Emil Söderström the Songsters sang a difficult piece by him. Afterwards Brian left the hall and they never saw or heard from him again. He just vanished from the scene.

Important composition

Hanover (GS1388-2) 1953

TOFT, JOSEF

Josef was a Swedish-American who lived in New York City. He grew up with Erik Leidzén and were boyhood friends. He wrote many orchestral works for brass band which are still in the New York Staff Band music files. Joe Toft was a kindly old gentleman and ran the Post Office Department at Territorial Headquarters.

Joesf was also violinist, and with whom Leidzén used to present chamber music recitals when they were both active performers, including several in the Carnegie Hall Recital Hall during the 1920s. He formed a boys' band at an orphanage sponsored by the Salvation Army, writing various pieces for them, and training a generation of players, while also serving on various music camp staffs. Leidzén's famous First Swedish Rhapsody in its initial form was composed for this young band, the work dedicated to Toft. Leidzén later rewrote it for the famed professional wind band, The Goldman Band.

TOVEY, BRAMWELL

Bram Tovey was born in 1953 in the United Kingdom. He was raised within the Salvation Army where his father was the bandmaster of the Coventry Citadel Band. He is a well known as conductor of orchestras but has also great experience in the brass band world, in particular as musical director with the Fodens Band. He has been the music director of the Vancouver Symphony Orchestra since September 2000. He has written several works for brass band, but one that was a real eye opener, also in Salvation Army circles was his *'Coventry Variations'*, as recorded by the Canadian Staff Band and London Citadel Band.

Important composition

Coventry Variations

TREMAIN, RONALD

Although very little is known about Ronald Tremain and his activities within the Salvation Army as such, there are only a few compositions known by his hand, which were all arranged later, to be published in the Army journals. Despite of this, he is of significant importance, at least for his *'How Sweet The Name'*.

Ronald Tremain was born in 1923 in Feilding, New Zealand, and died in 1998 in Niagara on the Lake, Canada. He was a composer and teacher. Initially studying piano, he gained Trinity College Diplomas before gaining his first degree in music at the University of Canterbury. After war service he taught at Feilding High School and attended Cambridge Summer Music Schools in the late 40's. He continued his studies at the Royal College of Music in London, gaining diplomas in piano performance and a doctorate in 1953. After some years working free-lance in London as a teacher, composer, and examiner he returned to New Zealand, where he spent ten years as a lecturer at the University of Auckland. In 1970 he moved to Canada where, until his retirement in 1989, he was Professor of Music at Brock University. He was made a Professor Emeritus in 1991.

Important compositions

How Sweet the Name (French) (GS1491-2) (arr. Donald Osgood) 1960, Praise (FS263) (arr. Ray Steadman-Allen) 1962, Three Song Transcriptions (GS1592) (arr. Donald Osgood) 1968

TRIGG, ROGER

Roger Trigg was born in Melbourne, Australia in 1971. Gaining his early musical experience in The Salvation Army in Melbourne and Perth, he went on to study at The Victorian College of the Arts, Melbourne, gaining a B.Mus. (Performance). This included studio tuition from Ken McClimont (Associate Principal Trombone, Melbourne Symphony Orchestra). In 1996, he continued his studies completing a Graduate Diploma in Secondary Education with the Australian Catholic University. As a trombonist, Roger has been a member of The Salvation Army's Melbourne Staff Band (1993-1997) and the New York Staff Band (1997-2001). Whilst in New York, Roger worked at The Salvation Army Headquarters as Assistant Divisional Music Director.

In 2001, he returned to Melbourne and commenced work as Director of the Creative Ministries Department for The Salvation Army Melbourne Central Division. During this tenure, Roger directed Gospel Choirs, Contemporary Music Groups, Choirs and Brass Bands. Roger has accepted commissions from various groups and has had numerous works, recorded and published in the USA, Australia and the UK. Roger was Bandmaster of the

Preston Citadel Band, Melbourne (2002-2005) and is currently a member of the Sydenham Salvation Army Band, Belfast. He works for the Council for the Curriculum, Examinations and Assessment (CCEA) as an Education Manager with responsibilities for GCSE and GCE Music and Drama. Roger also keeps busy in both his role as part time tutor at the City of Belfast School of Music and as an occasional freelance trombonist. Roger lives in Belfast, Northern Ireland with his wife Cheryl and son Jacob, born in December 2008.

Important compositions

Rejoice, Worthy is the Lamb, The Father's Love, Christmas Prelude (AJ0270) 2009, I Saw three ships (US0359) 2009, Once, in royal David's City (US0348) 2008

TUCKER, THOMAS

One of the early International Staff Bandsman, Adjutant Thomas Tucker became a member of this band in the mid-twenties of the previous century. He was for a time the Editor of 'The Bandsman and Songster'. No further information could be retrieved about him.

Important compositions

Climbing up the golden stair (GS0295) 1895, I'll follow Jesus (GS0425) 1902, Power Divine (GS0216) 1893, Tucker (in memoriam) (GS0308) 1896

TURKINGTON, WILLIAM

William Turkington was born in 1926 and was Promoted to Glory on May 12, 2006. Although written when only sixteen year-old in the 1940's, William's *'Able'* has never lost its dazzle and energy as it features the well-known hymn, 'Are ye able'.

There is not much known about the composer, although his *'Able'* became very popular when William Himes did a 'revised' scoring of this great festival march. Turkington was a soldier at the Tampa Corps in Florida, United States of America.

Important compositions

Able (AF0001) 1988, American Commander

TURNER, EDMUND

Was a Salvation Army officer in the United Kingdom and heavenly involved in the musical activities there. *'Sun of my soul'* was actually a transcription done by Albert Jakeway. The piece is based on Keble's famous tune.

Important composition

Sun of my soul (GS1274) 1946

TURNER, GORDON

John Kissack (currently in Cambridge, Canada) wrote the following about Gordon Turner:

'With regards to the info required, Gordon Turner, was my military bandmaster, when I served from 1959 to 1961 in the band of the 15/19th King's Royal Hussars. We were stationed at Barnard Castle in County Durham in England. At that time I believe he was the youngest bandmaster in the British Army. At that time he was in his twenties. I was told that he passed the Kneller Hall three year bandmaster's course in two years. His home corps was Willenhall, near Birmingham. I was always amazed, at how fast he could transpose. After I left the military, I lost contact.'

Important composition

Happy Evermore (GS1418) 1955

TURRIN, JOSEPH

He was born on January 4, 1947, in Clifton, New Jersey, United States of America. Joseph Turrin is a composer of contemporary American music and is a composer, arranger and pianist. He studied composition at the Eastman School of Music and the Manhattan School of Music. Although a Catholic he joined the New Jersey Youth Band on solo horn for their tour of England. His first brass band piece was *'Concertino for Tuba'* which was premiered by Harvey Phillips and the New York Staff Band.

His name became known in brass band circles when New York Philharmonic Trumpeter Philip Smith recorded his *'Escapade'* on piccolo trumpet with the Rigid Containers Group Band (better known as the GUS Band) in 1989. Although not a Salvationist or a direct relation with the organization, in 1997 he wrote his big break through when making a name is concerned when he came with what would become a favourite amongst brass bands world wide, both in the Salvation Army as well as in secular circles, with *'Hymn for Diana'*, a beautiful piece of music that he wrote in memory of the Royal Princes of the United Kingdom after her untimely passing. This piece was published by the Salvation Army in New York and was recorded by (amongst others) the New York Staff Band and the Yorkshire Building Society Band.

Important compositions

Hymn for Diana, Arabesque, My Song of Songs, Escapade.

TWITCHEN, GEORGE

George Twitchen was born in 1927, in High Wycombe, Buckinghamshire. His first interest in music was at 4 years of age when he was given a toy glockenspiel for Christmas. He was brought up as a member of the Church of England and sang in the choir. Although he only had a few music lessons when he was young, he did manage to know enough to play the church organ for Sunday services. But he didn't study music seriously until later in life. His part-time musical studies included, Piano at Leeds College of Music; Brass Band arranging and orchestration at the London Guildhall School of Music; and Orchestral conducting at the Morley College, London. These latter lessons were given by a former student of the Romanian conductor, Sergui Celibidache.

The Salvation Army allowed George to go to Paris, where he met Celibidache and was invited to attend his orchestral rehearsals with the French National Orchestra; and later, when he came to England, to attend the rehearsals with the London Symphony Orchestra; which was a great musical experience. In his late teens, whilst doing his National Service in the Fleet Air Arm, his off duty periods saw him playing Tenor Saxophone in the Ship's dance band. During his time in the Forces his widowed mother had remarried; so, after he was demobbed he went to live with his Grandparents, who were enthusiastic Salvationists. Very soon he became a Salvationist himself, and responding to the call to Officership he entered the International Training College in 1950, the 'Ambassadors Session'. His close friend at that time was Major Leslie Condon and they not only shared a musical interest, but also company in the Trombone section of the 30 strong Cadets Band.

He was commissioned in 1951 and served as a Corps Officer in 13 appointment throughout the United Kingdom. During this time he married Captain Joan Taylor, and they had three children. (Their daughter Pauline was the Flautist in Major Joy Webb's Joyfolk). Then followed 9 years as a Regional Public Relations Officer, in East Anglia, Ireland, and the West of England. In 1984 he served in the International Music Editorial Department, working with Lt. Col. Trevor Davis on the music for the then new song book. When this was completed he was appointed to International Headquarters as the Asst. Under Secretary for Public Relations.

His wife was Promoted to Glory in 1987 following a long illness with cancer. In December 1990 he married Major Olive Candler, Asst Chief Secretary, I.H.Q. and they retired in 1995 and now live in Norwich, Norfolk. Amongst his published vocal compositions are; *'Just Like Him'*, (for which he is also wrote a band arrangement –Triumph Series, July 1989): a setting to *'The Lord's my Shepherd'*, *'Wise Men Seeking Jesus'* and *'Loved with everlasting love'*, a transcription of Wilfred Heaton's classic hymn tune arrangement, *'Martyn'*. He has also completed an abridged version of Handel's *'Messiah'*. Some of his unpublished brass band arrangements include, Brahms, *'Academic Festival Overture'* (Norwich Citadel Band recorded this on CD): Ravel's, *'Alborada del Gracioso'*: *'Easter Prelude'*, which is an excerpt from Rachmaninoff's, *'Prelude in C sharp Minor'*, linked with, *'Low in the grave He lay'*: Also, John Rutter's, *'For the beauty of the earth'*. During his officership he has been the pianist at many Divisional, and I.H.Q. meetings; but has always felt most 'at home' just playing quietly during a prayer meeting. During his retirement he has been invited to play at many non Salvation Army venues in and around London, including three times in Switzerland. Now in his 80's he still plays regularly at the Norwich Mile Cross Corps.

Important composition

Just like Him (TS0956) 1989

TWITCHIN, HERBERT

Herbert Twitchin (Bert) was born on 21 September 1878 in England. Present with his parents at the opening of the Regent Hall was young Bert Twitchin, not then eight years of age. The family linked up with the corps, the father becoming one of the first sergeants and Bert began to play the cornet. He played variation solos years before they were popular in the Army and rendered his first compositions *'Silver Threads'* and *'Wondrous Love'* to the International Music Board of The Salvation Army in 1926. After serving for 25 years as Deputy Bandmaster, Bert became Bandmaster of the Regent Hall Citadel Band in 1909. He served with distinction in that capacity for 37 years. He was admitted to the Order of the Founder by General Evangeline Booth in 1939, and in 1946 was awarded the MBE for 64 years' voluntary work with The Salvation Army. Bandmaster Herbert Twitchin was presented to King George V and Queen Mary, with whom were their grand-daughters, Princess (later Queen) Elizabeth and Princess Margaret. Bandmaster Herbert Twitchin was Promoted to Glory on October 21, 1954, just a month after his eightieth birthday.

Book - **Always in Step** - by John Atkinson

A really small and thin booklet, that was published by Salvationist Publishing and Supplies in 1956 as part of the 'Liberty Booklets' series about several significant Army people. This writing is about probably the most famous Salvationist and Bandmaster the Regent Hall Corps, in the heart of London, has ever seen.

Important compositions

Silver Threads (FS0043) 1928, Wondrous Love (FS0088) 1933

VANDERKAM, JULES FRANCOIS

The Salvation Army opened fire in Belgium in May 1889. The work began in Mechelen, under impulsion of the Dutch Headquarters of the Salvation Army. The first Corps in Belgium were Ledeberg-lez-Gand (now a district of the city of Genth) (Jan. 1890), Genth (Feb. 1890), Jumet (Sept. 1890) and Dampremy (also Sept. 1890). Jumet and Dampremy are now two districts of the city of Charleroi. The last two corps are the first French language corps in Belgium.

The family Vanderkam had a protestant background. They came into contact with Dampremy Corps. At that time, the protestant Church was praying for a revival. Many Protestants rallied the Salvation Army. They saw the Salvation Army as a mean chosen by God. Salvationists used to sing in the streets, sell a newspaper ('War Cry'), and invite people to the meetings. A meeting was held almost every evening and many persons became converted.

The family of Jules Vanderkam.

His father, François Vanderkam, was born in Dampremy, on 22th March 1845. He became a Soldier of Dampremy Corps in 1890 and was Promoted to Glory in 1935. He was an underground worker in a coalmine. Later on he became a foreman. But at that time it was difficult to receive the responsibilities he could have had because he was a Salvationist. However, a long time later, because of his testimony, he acceded to the position of director of the mines. Jules' mother, Marie-Philippine Sacré, was born in Court-Saint-Etienne, on 8th September 1842 and was Promoted to Glory in 1916. She was a housewife.

They got married in Dampremy on 15th June 1867 and seven children were born:

1. Henriette, born in Dampremy on 28th March 1868.
2. Elisa Eudoxie, born in Dampremy on 19th January 1870.
3. Rosa, born in Dampremy on 1st May 1872. She was a Salvation Army officer (1891-1899).
4. **Jules François**, born in Dampremy on 12th July 1874. He was Promoted to Glory on 17th August 1958.
5. Fernand François, born in Mont-Sainte-Aldegonde on 12th September 1877.
6. Georges, born in Montignies-sur-Sambre on 9th January 1880. He was a Salvation Army officer in the period 1906 – 1946. Lieut-Colonel Georges Vanderkam was the Territorial Commander in Belgium from 1942 to 1946. He was Promoted to Glory on 4th February 1962.

His son, Samuel Vanderkam served as a Salvation Army officer from 1949 to 1986. He served for a long time in Belgium as the General Secretary, and then finished his career at the Territorial Headquarters in Paris (France).

7. Léa Julia, born in Montignies-sur-Sambre on 10th July 1882. She was a Salvation Army officer (1903-1939) and was Promoted to Glory on 23rd October 1980.

Jules grew up in a protestant structure. His education was strict. After primary school, at 12, he started to work and met many persons who mocked God. He was daily in contact with vulgar adults and bad company. World attractiveness made a deep impression on him. But because he wanted to resist to that pressure, and to stay in a religious environment, he signed a commitment of abstinence at the 'Blue Cross', and he became a member of the Young People's Christian Union. Jules worked in a glass-making company but he registered for courses at the Industrial School, in order to climb the social ladder. During the week, he worked from 5.45am to 5.45pm. Three times a week, he took a course at school from 7pm to 9pm, and on Sunday from 10am to 12am. During several years he couldn't attend the Sunday morning Service because of this. It was also very difficult for him to attend the meetings during the week. At the end of his studies, he competed in front of a Board of Examiners. The subjects were; *accountability*, *commercial geography* and *industrial economy*. He graduated 'Cum Laude'. It was very rare to see a so young person finishing his studies.

A rare picture of the Jumet Corps Band (Belgium) in 1928-1929.

Jules VanderKam; second row, third from the right.

His conversion and beginnings with the Salvation Army

Jules' sisters, Elisa (20) and Rosa (18), where the firsts of the Vanderkam family who attended the meetings of the Salvation Army in Dampremy. Rosa was the first who became converted. Later Jules attended the meetings and also became converted. He wrote:

'Lieutenant Mrs Anet came to me at the end of a meeting and she asked 'Young man, are you saved? Don't you desire to abandon you to God tonight? Despite my conviction to do so, I tried to quibble and to make that officer believe that I didn't need to go to the penitent-form. I told her that I was the Vice-president of the young section of the Blue Cross (Section Cadette de la Croix Bleue) and of the Young's People Union (Union des Jeunes Gens)'. She said then 'I don't ask you that. I ask you if you are saved'.

She urged me to decide now between God and the world. I couldn't resist anymore. I went with her to the penitent-form'.

Jules became a Salvationist on 2nd December 1890. He was sixteen. An anecdote must be mentioned; He was sick the day of his enrolment, and his sister Rosa brought him the S's at home. At that time, it was difficult to buy a uniform and a cap. Wages were too low. Then, as many of the Belgium Salvationists, he wore a red jersey to actively serve the Lord in his Corps. He wrote;

'I attend the meetings as often as possible. I am the doorkeeper. I give my testimony and I pray. I go out on Sunday to sell the 'War Cry' (5 cents each). We form a brigade of 6 to 8 comrades. We are happy when we have sold about 100 'War Cry''s after we have walked in the streets for 2 or 3 hours. And then I learn how to play the cornet'.

Jules lived the early beginnings of the Salvation Army in the 'Black Land' (le Pays Noir). This name was given to the area of Charleroi, principal city of that area, because of the important presence there of coalmines, and iron and steel industries. Early 1892, when Jules was nearly eighteen, Dampremy Corps was transferred to Gilly, a neighbour town. The Salvation Army hall was located in a dangerous area, surrounded by many odd pubs. Many fights broke out in that place so that the police had to intervene. Jules wrote; *'It was the right place for the Salvation Army, which could do her work of regeneration among these persons who were fallen so low'.* In that region, Salvationists had to face the worst persecutions. Indoor and open air meetings were very disrupted. When they came back from an open air meeting, officers were on the front of the cortège, after them came the women, older people and children. At the end of the cortège, the rearguard was formed by soldiers and the young people, who received the knocks and blows. But persecutions gradually became less and less violent because a number of the worst delinquents became converted. As they came from a low position (low class), their testimony was powerful for people of their ancient sphere. At that time, a band was more an orchestra with some mandolins, a guitar and a accordion. That instrumental ensemble was used to accompany the Salvationists who were selling the 'War Cry', in the streets and in the pubs.

On 15th September 1899, Jules married Emily Tuck. She was English, from Cambridge, and had been an officer. They settled down in Lodelinsart and became members of the Corps of that town. Jules wrote;

'Meetings are not well attended (few people). Except of some devoted and loyal comrades, other are really cold. We don't see them during usual meetings, they only come for great occasions. Some weeks, we are only three of four persons at the meeting. But for us, we have taken the good decision. My wife is to attend the meeting of holiness on Sunday morning, while I will be preparing the soup. In the afternoon, I will leave at about 2pm for selling the 'War Cry', or in order to go to a meeting in an outpost. In the evening, we will go to the meeting. During the week, we will organize so that at least one of us can attend the meeting. Doing so, we will strengthen our faith'.

Jules VanderKam and Emily Tuck had four children; Nelly, born in 1900. She was an officer from 1922 to 1960, in Belgium and in France. She passed away on 9th June 1966. Alfred, born on 1904. He worked on business, associated with his father (selling of glass and chemical products). Paula, born in 1907. She was a midwife, settled abroad in Washington D.C, and got married to a Salvationist. Ruth, born in 1908. She was a nurse and worked in Brussels. She rejoined her sister in the USA. She also got married with a Salvationist. In April 1919, Jules was appointed commercial director of a glass-making company. The couple was comfortably off. But his wife did not take advantage of that situation, she was Promoted to Glory in august 1919, after 20 years of common life. Some months later, Jules wrote;

'According to my wife's desire she expressed when she was still living, and giving in to my father's entreaties who was giving me plausible reasons to do so, I remarried with Eléonore Michaux'.

In 1923, the new glass-making company of his employer settled down in Roux. Jules became a member of the Salvation Army Corps of that town. He wrote about this;

'We've got a good and well-balanced string orchestra of more than 20 musicians, specially mandolins, with brass instruments, piano, organ. Meetings are well attended. Every Sunday evening, 60 to 80 persons attend the meeting'.

It is for this band that Jules composed a selection *'Veille & prie' ('Keep awake and pray').*

In 1931, Jules Vanderkam faced what he called the 'great tribulations of his life'. He became independent and made a good business. But at that time a Union between all the glass-making companies in Belgium was created. He finally had a stock of products he could not sell. He was adjudicated bankrupt. All he possessed in the bank was seized and his house was sold. Jules was ruined. Moreover, the couple knew adversity and Jules was abandoned by his wife. He wrote: *'It was a terrible shock for my spiritual live. Satan persuaded me that henceforth anything I could do as a Salvationist would have no value. There is no longer any need for my testimony during a meeting, as the thought which would have cross listener's mind, would have been that God himself had abandoned me so that I am arrived to that personal extreme situation'.* He received encouragements from certain Salvationists, but others were cold towards him. For eight years, Jules did not go to the Salvation Army. He, above all himself, made a spiritual self-criticism and he did not let himself have a public Christian life. At the end of 1939, encouraged by his brother Fernand and several Salvationists, Jules and his new wife were invited to the Jumet corps. Of this he wrote; *'Contrary to what I feared, my ancient comrades showed a lot of friendship and sympathy towards us'.* Several months later, on 3rd October 1940, encouraged by the officers and comrades of the Corps, Jules went back to his former position as a Salvationist, young soldiers instructor and bandmaster. It is unknown which music training Jules has followed, but he was an exceptional autodidact. This makes believe that he found his skills and musical inspiration in his Saviour.

Jules wrote in 1948 at the age of 74, in his diary;

'During summer months, I do some gardening in the morning. Then I am during a half-day at the office, with my son Alfred. We still have our business with glass-making and chemical products. Otherwise I have some activities with the Salvation Army. I am a young people teacher and am the bandmaster. I regularly attend two meetings during the week, and be there the entire day on Sundays. I continue to compose music. Recently, I composed half a dozen of selections which sound lovely. This was told by my musicians who rarely make a compliment. Good for me because otherwise I could become an arrogant or proud person. Music and choir rehearsals are very absorbing. As far as the partitions are concerned, I have to make handwritten copies of each instrumental part. I could often be discouraged if I let my feelings overcome me, especially with the young people I am teaching presently, but I look higher and to the future. I can say that I have had a really well full life. I am happy with that. As long as I can, I must work without respite to serve the Lord, and I find there a great blessing'.

Jules Vanderkam was Promoted to Glory on 17th August 1958, he was 84 years old.

In 1946 Colonel Thomas E. Dennis went to Prague to conduct congresses, which were the first for nearly ten years. A special congress band was formed for this occasion and Vanderkam's march *'Czechoslovakia'* was played here. This was also played many times during the war although for safety purposes renamed for the time being into '*We still live*'.

An excerpt of a Salvation Army newspaper of 1928 says:

'The Composers' Festival held at Clapton Congress Hall in February 1928 was attended by the then Duke and Duchess of York. 'The Musician's who conducted their own works were Lieut-Colonels Fred Hawkes and Arthur Goldsmith, Captain Eric Ball and Bandmasters Jules Vanderkam (from Belgium). Bandmaster Vanderkam recalled years later that he was nervous, but the duchess immediately put him at ease by speaking to him in French'.

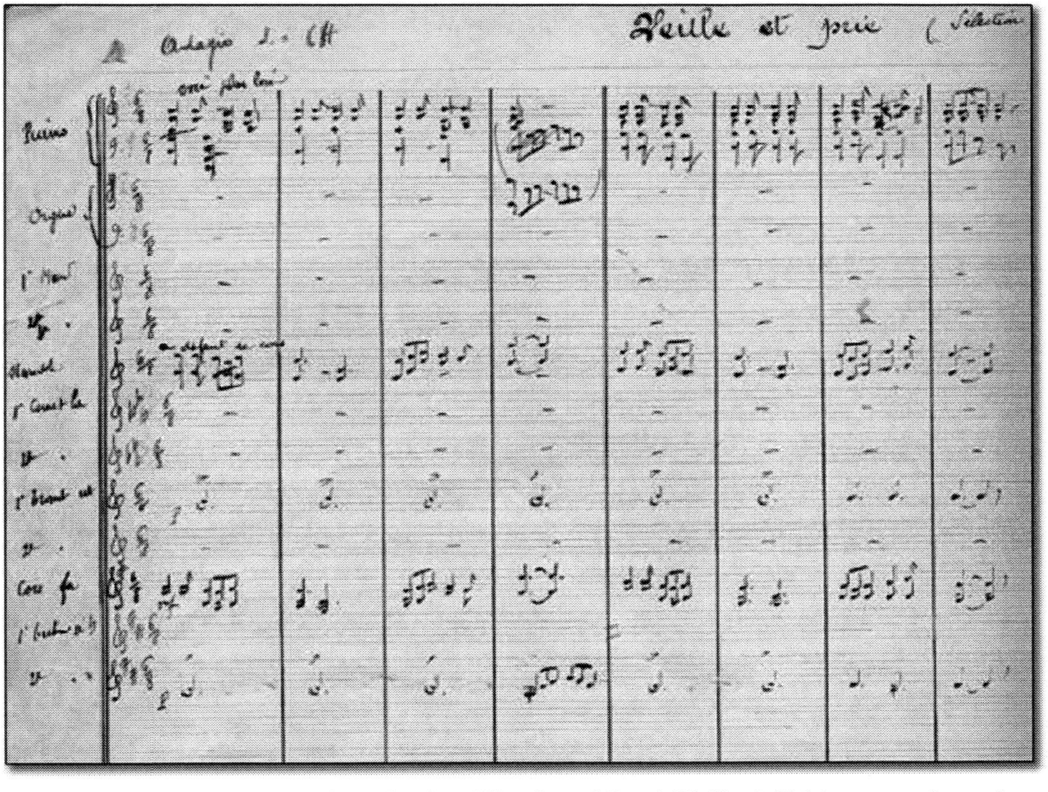

For a musical he composed a selection 'Watch and Pray' (Veille & Prie), a page from the original manuscript full score, 15 June 1927. This piece has not been published.

Important compositions

The Wanderer (FS023) 1925, Joy and Triumph (GS814-1) 1919, The Danish March (GS814-2) 1919, Czechoslovakia (TS0042) 1924

Important non-published compositions

Avec toi (With you) - 20th March 1921, Combats (Fight) - 30th October 1922, Veille et prie (Keep Awake and Pray) - Selection 15th June 1927, Semailles et Moissons (Sowing and Harvest) - 25th August 1943, Ruth Marche, Paula Marche, Nelly Marche, Alfred Marche,

François Marche, En avant, soldats (Onward Soldiers), Notre œuvre (Our works), Mon Sauveur (My Saviour), Souvenir du 15 Août (Souvenir of 15th August)

VAUGHAN WILLIAMS, RALPH

Ralph Vaughan Williams (Down Ampney, Gloucestershire, 12 oktober 1872 - Londen, 26 augustus 1958) was an English composer of symphonies, chamber music, opera, choral music, and film scores. He was also a collector of English folk music and song which influenced his editorial approach to the English Hymnal, beginning in 1904, containing many folk song arrangements set as hymn tunes, in addition to several original compositions.

In April 1953, Dr. Ralph Vaughan Williams presided over a festival given by the International Staff Band at Dorking. Adressing himself to '*these musicians who play so finely*' (RVW was not a fan of brass band music!), he expressed pleasure at the '*sincere, healthy music*' they played and added; '*I have heard many bands, but never a band with so fine a sense of style, a real classical style*'. This encounter resulted in the great composers' expressing a desire to write something for the International Staff Band. The outcome was '*Prelude on Three Welsh Hymn Tunes*'.

Important compositions

Prelude on Three Welsh Hymn Tunes (FS0209) 1955, English Folk Song Suite, Variations for Brass Band

VENABLES, MARCUS

Marcus Venables was born on February 28th 1991 in Toronto, Canada. He joined the North York Temple Band of the Salvation Army at the age of 13 (2004) on 1st chair first Cornet and moved up the ranks very quickly, and presently holds the Soprano Cornet position. Marcus joined the Ontario Central East Divisional Youth Band at the age of 14 (2005) on Solo Cornet 2 (below his brother Brindley). He is currently playing Soprano in the OCE-DYB.

He joined Intrada Brass at 15 (2006) on Flugel horn and at 17 became their Soprano player. He has also played Principal Horn, Trombone, and Eb Tuba at various times.

He commenced writing Music at 13, and because of his banding experience, Marcus grew in knowledge of scoring, range, technique, and harmony. Marcus' first big break as a composer was when the Hannaford Street Silver Band performed his '*Motondo*' in 2007. And since then has had many world premiers by many brass bands and wind ensembles. Marcus was home-schooled and is currently writing/arranging full time until he goes to university. Marcus has had brief sit downs with composer greats such as Kevin Norbury, William Himes, James Curnow, Bramwell Tovey and Robert Redhead. His favourite composer is Kenneth Downie (Rejoice the Lord is King).

Together with two of his brothers he has formed the Vena Mills Band: The Vena Mills Band is a full Multi Track Brass Band. The band was formed in July 2008 to make recordings. After a few test runs, the band recorded the album 'TRINITY' The Music of Marcus Venables for Maverick Music. Vena Mills Band has another recording date in the summer of 09 also featuring the music of Marcus Venables.'

Important compositions

Amazing Grace (m/s), The Gathering (m/s)

VENABLES, ROBERT

Robert Venables (April 20, 1958), principal cornet of the North York Temple Band (bandmaster Glenn Barlow) is a professional freelance trumpeter, performing with a wide range of ensembles including the True North Brass, Hannaford Street Silver Band, Intrada Brass, Hamilton Philharmonic, Toronto Philharmonia, and The Canadian Opera Company. As a soloist he has travelled throughout North America, Europe, and England performing with such bands as The International Staff Band, Canadian Staff Band, Southern Territory Band, Earlscourt Citadel, and most many corps bands in Canada. His solo recording (Exaltation) with the Brighouse & Rastrick Band is perhaps a highlight of his musical career, but without question his true joy is the fact that five of his children are serving in the North York Temple Band, and that they all love the Lord. Robert is also the Young People's Band Leader and Songster Leader at North York Temple. His best known composition is the Festival March *'The General'* which was also recorded by the Canadian Staff Band.

Important composition

The General (m/s)

VERKAAIK, BERNARD

Bandmaster Bernard Verkaaik was born in Holland on April 1918 and Promoted to Glory on 10 July 1988 in Redondo Beach, USA. At the age of forty, has achieved considerable status as a conductor, composer and pianist, but was also equally at home on a variety of brass instruments. He was a member of the Royal Dutch Musicians Association, completed his formal study at the Amsterdam Conservatorium, and received accreditation for teaching, composition, and performance at the States Conservatosium at the Hague. Many of his band and choral works have been published by The Salvation Army. He was editor of music publications for Leger des Heils (The Salvation Army) in Amsterdam. He was bandmaster of the Dutch National Band of the Salvation Army and led this great band, who was known for their great sound, on a significant four week tour to the United States of America and Canada. Back home Bernard Verkaaik soon was approached by the Americans who were very impressed by him, to emigrate to the USA to become the Divisional Music Director of the Salvation Army in the state of California, which he did. In the USA he conducted many Salvation Army bands.

When the National Band of the Salvation Army, the predecessor of the ASB, was active in the 1950s, their Bandmaster, Bernard Verkaaik, was the best known Dutch composer. In fact, he became their first Bandmaster when the band was inaugurated on 22 April 1948, for a short period after the Second World War.

THE NETHERLANDS NATIONAL BAND

In 1945 several letters were written to Ensign Gerrit Claeys, who was at that moment of time responsible for the development of music in the Salvation Army in the Netherlands.

In one letter the suggestion was made that there should be a National Band in the Netherlands, and described in detail how this band could function. The writer was Bernard Verkaaik, then living in Zwolle because of the lack of food in Amsterdam where he originated from. In a meeting which followed the foundation was laid for the Netherlands

National Band, with its instructor Bernard Verkaaik. The band started to practise in the beginning of 1948 and the installation meeting was on the 22nd of April in the same year. *'Heroes of the Combat'* was the first march which as played.

In the first years many Corps in the Dutch territory where visited. With eager anticipation people were looking forward to the band visiting their area. Every year the band was featured during Bandsmen's Councils Festivals. Several of those festivals were in the famous Concert building in Amsterdam. The press spoke about the wonderful sound of the band, the technical capability of soloists and the beautiful singing. Of course there were some critical reviews as well.

Soon the band was invited to visit other countries. The first tour was made to Great Britain in 1951, with another visit in 1957. Other countries visited were Belgium in 1952 and 1957, and Denmark and Sweden in 1953. Towards the end of its existence in 1959 the band toured the USA and Canada. The music of the Netherlands National Band of Amsterdam has often been compared by the European press with the best symphonic efforts. Organized in 1947 from the leading players of Holland's fifty-six Salvation Army Brass Bands, this elite group has enjoyed remarkable success under the skilful baton of its brilliant bandmaster Bernard Verkaaik.

Leading music critics, evidently inspired and surprised by the gallant Hollanders have reflected their impressions of the Band with lofty phrases such as: *'absolute dedication'; 'fantastic, radiant, and sonorous sound'; 'a sublime example'; 'impeccable technique'; 'pure and won-derful balance'; 'the conductor is a connoisseur as well as an artist'; 'a high standard of repertoire'; 'the velvet sound of a symphony orchestra'; 'this proud possession of all musical Holland'.*

The band is a symbol of the courage and fortitude of the Dutch people in their rapid rebuilding and recovery from the unparalleled destruction and ravages of the World War 2. In less than twelve years it has progressed from the humblest of beginnings to an instrument of musical maturity. It is used to demonstrate the best in service and musicianship to the growing brass band movement in the Netherlands, and exemplifies the highest standards of Salvation Army Bands.

For important civic occasions the National Band is frequently called upon to provide noble music. When the city of Alkmaar celebrated its 700th anniversary with a festival in its great cathedral, it required the conducting of Bernard Verkaaik. Such an idea was projected many years ago by George Bernard Shaw who claimed that Handel's oratorios would have been immeasurably enriched if the instrumentation of one of the great Salvation Army Bands had been available to him.

While the band is touring North America for the first time, its musical ministry has been by no means confined to the Netherlands. England heard them in 1951 and 1956, Belgium in 1952 and 1957, Denmark and Sweden in 1953, and Scotland and Ireland in 1956. In addition the band broadcasts regularly on several Dutch radio stations and has been featured by BBC and Radio Stockholm. The band is featured each year in Amsterdam's famed 'Concertgebouw'.

True to its descriptive by-line, 'A Symphony in Brass', the Netherlands National Band has developed a broad repertoire of traditional symphonic material but specializes in playing modern classics and pioneering works. That the band also trains and performs as an excellent MALE CHORUS is considered an important clue to its excellent intonation and ensemble work. A leading Rotterdam journalist (G. Michels of the 'Vrije Volk' newspaper) departing from the usual music critic's viewpoint revealed the secret of the deeply moving playing of the NNB when he wrote: *'These men, giving their lives to sublime thoughts and works of the Salvation Army not only gave us a lesson in music, but also an example of absolute dedication and surrender to their spiritual convictions, from which they draw their inspiration'.*

One of the programmes of the Netherlands National Band said:

'Bandmaster Bernard Verkaaik, at the age of forty, has achieved consi-derable status as a conductor, composer and pianist. He is a member of the Royal Dutch Musicians' Association, completed his formal study at the Amsterdam Conservatorium, and received accreditation for teaching, composition, and performance at the State Conservatorium at the Hague.'

Verkaaik's compositions reached far beyond the Dutch borders and he had several compositions published in Salvation Army journals. His musical output included not only hymn tune arrangements but also extensive marches and major works like tone poems. Most of his output was unfortunately never published and has probably been lost. I have to mention at least his march *'Je Maintiendrai'*, which means *'I will Maintain'*, and on the sleeve notes of the 1959 tour to the USA recording we read:

'The march is the staunch motto found on the coat of arms of the Nether-lands. Bandmaster Bernard Verkaaik projects the virile character of his countrymen in this composition which introduces the melodies 'Holland's flag, you are my glory' and the militant 'Keep strong' '.

Two other well-known compositions of his are the march *'Resolute Soldiers'* and the tone poem *'Victory in the Light'*.

Tone Poem – *'Victory of the Light'* - Duration: 9.23 min

This exciting contemporary music was commissioned for a special film documentary on The Salvation Army's great social work in the Netherlands. It requires the utmost in technique and musicianship from the players as evidenced by this brilliant reading.

March *'Resolute Soldiers'* (General Series 1410) - duration 2.46. This was the first composition by Bandmaster Verkaaik to be published in The Salvation Army International Band Journal. It is a favourite throughout the world.

In spite of these fine compositions, probably the best known work by Bernard Verkaaik is a male chorus based on a Dutch folk song and used not only during the tour to the USA in 1959, but also during the tour to Canada in 1974 with great success. The song is called *'De Zilvervloot'* (The Silver-fleet) and it became unbelievably popular amongst audiences. In particular, Dutch people living in the USA and Canada were touched by this brilliant song, as it reminded them instantly of their own childhood when they had sung this song at school. There are two recordings of this song, one performed by the Dutch National Band on their 1959 tour LP and the other by the Amsterdam Staff Band on their 1974 LP, recorded live in Canada.

When the National Band did a tour of the UK in 1951, the great Harry Mortimer went to see them. After the concert, Bernard Verkaaik had the opportunity to speak to this great figure of the brass band world. They spoke about the band's sound, and how to improve it, although the National Band was actually known for its great brass band sound.

During the 1950's, 'The Musician', the musical newspaper of the Salvation Army in the UK, did a series about 'Outstanding Musical Leaders' and Part One of this was all about Bandmaster Verkaaik. The article read as follows:

* Outstanding Overseas Bandmasters *

At the invitation of 'The Musician' some overseas Territorial Commanders have provided interesting details concerning a few of their outstanding musical leaders.

1. Bandmaster Bernard Verkaaik of the National Band

Bernard Verkaaik, the thirty two year old Bandmaster of the Dutch Na-tional Band – which will be campaigning in the British Territory next spring- had his first contact with the banding at eight years of age when he became a member of the Groningen II Young People's Band. Later on, at Rotterdam I, he benefited considerably under the tutorship of Young People's Band Leader van Dalen (now Senior-Major and Training Principal). The Bandmaster quickly displayed considerable versatility by playing trombone at Amsterdam I, euphonium at Leiden, soprano cornet at Groningen II, and solo cornet at Dordrecht. Upon the Promotion to Glory, at the latter Corps, of Bandmaster Stam, seventeen year old Verkaaik was appointed Band Instructor. Later he became principal solo cornet player at Amsterdam Congress Hall and formed an instrumental combination of two cornets and three trombones which visited many Corps. In 1946 he was commissioned bandmaster. For some time the bandmaster accompanied Brigadier C. Claeijs to many Corps in Holland, playing cornet solos and assisting the Brigadier in piano duets. At big Army occasions he has played the famous organ in the Amsterdam Concertgebouw. Following musical studies, the bandmaster obtained the L.O and M.O (theoretical) diplomas for piano teaching, harmony, history and performance at the States Conservatorium at The Hague (equivalent to L.R.A.M.). He is a member of the Royal Dutch Musicians Association. Since 1947 he has been occupied at the Territorial Headquarters Music Department and is now Secretary of the Music Board, assisting the Music Secretary (Senior-Captain D.J. Rolls.), who speaks highly of his work in furthering the interest of the territory's music sections.

A brother – a fine solo horn player- is Songster Leader at Middelburg Corps (Zeeland) and another brother is Deputy Bandmaster at The Hague Congress Hall.

The National Bandmaster has several links with the British Territory. He has happy recollections of accompanying Banmaster Will Overton, Senior-Captain Lyndon and other British instrumentalists. In 1948 he attended the Bandmasters' Councils in London. He is endeavouring to model the National Band on the pattern of the best British Territory Bands, but realizes that he has much to do. His motto in all things is *'The Best for God'*. The Bandmaster's parents are in charge at the Zeist Corps, and for a number of years his father (Bernard Verkaaik Sr.) was a member of the Dutch National Band, playing Eb Bass when the combination under the leadership of the late Lt. Colonel Rawie, visited England in 1914 for the International Congress.

Note the amount of different instruments Bernard Verkaaik mastered.

'...The Bandmaster displayed considerable versatility by playing:

- trombone at Amsterdam I Corps,
- euphonium at Leiden Corps
- soprano cornet at Groningen II Corps

- solo cornet at Dordrecht Corps. '

Besides all these brass instruments, he was equally at home at the grand organ and piano, but became known more than anything as Salvation Army composer and Bandmaster of the Dutch National Band. He was an incredibly gifted man.

Bandsmaster Robert Getz (USA), himself a noted composer, writes of Bernard Verkaaik - *'I only briefly met Bernard on the American tour, but was very taken by the clean and smooth sound of the band, and especially the male chorus. His music caught my attention by its well-crafted beauty - this before I realized it was written by him! His arrangement of, and performance of, 'We Gather Together' remains my favorite of all male chorus treatments that I have heard. His March 'I Will Maintain' is one of the most determined and mascu-line/militant/driven of any I know of. It has an almost grinding strength. This seems appropriate if we are at 'war' with sin. His music, though available to me only on a recording over fifty years old, still draws me through its convincing competence. I truly wish I had gotten to know him, as we have a lot in common. When he was in the states, travel was not as easy as now, and California is about 3,000 miles from here. So, it was apparently not meant to be. That Soderstrom thought so highly of him is the real test... Sodie knew his stuff and was not generally given to flattery!'*

The Dutch National Band made four official recordings. However they accompanied congregational singing on several others. The two most outstanding recordings are by far the following two, *'Tour of Canada and the US'* and *'A Festival of Music'*. The first was made for their tour to the US in 1959, and the second was recorded in New York on 8, 9 and 10 May 1959, live at the Centennial Memorial Temple during their tour. Note the inclusion of rare compositions by Emil Soderstrom and, of course, the music of Bernard Verkaaik.

As a result of the Dutch National Band's tour of the US, Bernard Ver-kaaik was invited by the Salvation Army to immigrate to California, to the Los Angeles area, where he became Divisional Bandmaster, and was responsible for the education of bandmasters, and leading the Divisional Band made up of the best players in the area.

An official statement tells us that:

'Salvation Army greets new Music Head. - Dr. Bernard Verkaaik arrived yesterday with his family from Amsterdam to become the new musical director for the Southern California Division of the Salvation Army. Lt.Colonel William J. Parkins, Division Com-mander, said that Dr. Verkaaik will assist in supervising and training approximately 50 Salvation Army music aggregations, with a personnel of more than 1,000 in an all-age range. One of the first of the Bandmas-ter's public appearances will be as conductor of the Salvation Army Tournament of Roses 100-piece band in Long Beach Municipal Audito-rium August 27th at 20.00 hour. Prior to the band's first concert appear-ance, at which General Wilfred Kitching of London will preside, Ver-kaaik will conduct several practice sessions, Parkins added. The Hollan-der was a national music director in his country for 14 years. He holds a master's degree from The Hague Conservatory of Music. 'The Musician' with his wife and three children will make their home in Redondo Beach at 125 W. Beryl St.'

Important compositions

Resolute Soldiers (GS1410) 1955, Victory of the Light (m/s), There is Peace (m/s)

VERHELST, STEVEN

Bass trombone player Steven Verhelst (30 September, 1981) studied at the Rotterdam Conservatory with Ben van Dijk, Jörgen van Rijen and Pierre Volders. He has performed with most Belgian and Dutch orchestras such as the Rotterdam Philharmonic Orchestra, the Metropole Orchestra and the Radio Philharmonic Orchestra. In 2005 he was a member of the World Youth Orchestra's Summer tour. He is also a performer with ensembles such as World Brass, NBE, het Belgisch Koper Offensief and many others. Along with his bass trombone studies in Rotterdam, Steven Verhelst also attended lessons and master classes with trombonists from the orchestras of Berlin, Vienna and Chicago, with the Swedish trombone soloist Christian Lindberg and the French soloist Michel Becquet. As a composer and arranger, Steven has written several pieces for Ben van Dijk, Henrik-Jan Renes, Fritz Damrow, the New Trombone Collective, and the Rotterdam Philharmonic. His compositions has started to appear within the Salvation Army repertoire as well and for the 2011 recording of the Amsterdam Staff Band for which he wrote a 12 minute long bass trombone solo with Ben van Dijk as soloist entitled *'World Concerto'*.

Important compositions

World Concerto (m/s), Intrada (scored for two tenor trombones, nine bass trombones and one contrabass trombone), Oblivion

VERMIJ, RUUD

On a certain Sunday evening around 1973, Mrs.Vermeij was strolling through the Kromhout (Dordrecht) and heard nice singing coming out of a building. She went in and came into a Salvation Army meeting. She must have felt at home, because not long after that time the whole Vermeij family was attending the meetings.

Ruud (31st May 1965) and his two little sisters were loyal attendees of the Sunday school meetings (they even got a 'diploma' for that!) Once, the Young People's Band was playing before the Sunday school meeting would start. It was noticed by the band leader, Ton Kruidhof, that Ruud stood listening to them, and he asked whether he was interested in joining the band. The first years of his musical career on the cornet Ruud counted for nothing, not knowing the meaning of those flats and sharps, etcetera. But after some years, this changed enormously; especially when Olaf Kruidhof (Ton's cousin) leaded the Young People's Band and tutored Ruud privately. (Olaf is now the principal Euphonium player of the well know Brassband Rijnmond). This was at about 1979, when Ruud also entered the Senior Band, lead by Bert Kruidhof (Olaf's dad).

In his teens Ruud became very active in the Dordrecht corps as a songster, and later on as Songster Leader and other tasks. At this time he also started entrusting his musical thoughts to music sheets. He attended the national youth music camps in 1981, 1982 and 1983 and followed the Salvation Army music courses in Lunteren in 1986-1987 (led by the music professionals Mr. and Mrs. Van Mourik). He also took piano lessons from 1987 - 1991.

Around that time Ruud felt a call to become Salvation Army officer and entered the training college in 1991. During the study in Almere at the National Headquarters, there were good contacts with the leader of the music department, Peter Ayling. Once (apparently it was clean-your-desk-day) a manuscript of a song called *'Psalm 100'* was found at the music department. It was decided to publish it. During a 'spiritual day' (which the cadets had from time to time) by surprise the framed manuscript of the song was handed over to the composer cadet by the head of the music department, Peter Ayling. Ruud served as Corps Officer at the Meppel and Terneuzen Corps, but after a thorough rethinking of his capabilities and a period of illness he decided to resign from this responsibility.

Now a period of spiritual search started and Ruud ended up in an evangelical church, though the link with the Salvation Army always more or less remained. But when a borrowed trombone entered the house, slowly the brass band blood began to flow again. One day a used euphonium was offered at 'Dal Segno' (a music store owned by Peter Groenewegen, Bandmaster of the Dordrecht Corps Band). After a few days of thought, the decision was made to buy the instrument, which turned out to be a very good choice.

Evangelical churches and (mellow) brass instruments don't match very well, and Ruud also underwent some spiritual development. He already had started playing at the rehearsals of the Dordrecht band and went along on special occasions to support the band, though on Sunday mornings he went to his own church. However in August 2008 the decision was made to join the Salvation Army again, where he became a Salvationist in 2010.

In June 2005 Ruud began a period of composing and arranging tutoring via e-mail by the British brass band composer Nigel Horne. In this period he was working on the brass band piece *'Precious Stones'*, for which Nigel gave some valuable hints and tips. In September 2005 the contact with Olaf Kruidhof was renewed. An appointment was made to play *'Precious Stones'* at a Brassband Rijnmond rehearsal. Their conductor, Erik Janssen, was also artistic director of a Dutch publisher. Although Erik liked the piece, in the end they decided not to publish it.

Around the same time Ruud posted a message on a brass forum titled 'How to get published'. There was also a weblog at *brassbandmusic.com* where the piece was presented. On 22 December 2006 these actions lead to a Devilish Publishing e-mail saying that they would be pleased to publish the piece. On 19 February 2007 *'Precious Stones'* was published by this British publisher. In 2010 *'Precious Stones'* was used in the Devilish Publishing Online Brass Band contest, which was won by Brassband Rijnmond. (Their performance is available as download from the publisher's website.)

Other Works of Ruud, *'Joy to the World'*, *'Clair de Lune'* and the four movement piece *'Variations on Merck toch hoe Sterck'* are available at Prisma Music. Another piece has provoked a lot of enthusiastic reactions from professional musicians, but it has not been performed or published yet. This piece, *'Colourful Trinity'*, also consisting of four movements, makes use of mode 3 of Olivier Messiaen, a Twentieth Century French composer.

Important compositions

Precious Stones, Colourful Trinity, Joy to the World

WAINWRIGHT, ANDREW

Written by: Andrew Wainwright – my life as a Salvationist musician/composer.

'I was fortunate to spend the early years of my life in Africa, namely Kenya and Zimbabwe. The Salvation Army is a thriving presence in both countries, and being the child of officer parents I was immersed in Salvation Army music making from a young age. My first memories of Salvation Army banding were of sitting, as a toddler, for endless hours in Sunday meetings at Nairobi Central Corps. My father, John, was at the time Bandmaster of the corps band, and, quite unusually for a Salvation Army band, the bass section included a sousaphone. I was fascinated by this instrument and most of the meetings were spent sat in the front row as close to the band as possible, with reels of paper drawing this curiously shaped contraption.

However, Sunday meetings would never be the same again as one weekend, the band embarked on a trip to a corps some distance away. As is customary in that part of the world, the instruments were tied somewhat precariously to the top of the band bus, most without cases. As the band arrived at their destination some hours later it was discovered, to the sousaphone player's alarm, that the bell had come unscrewed from the body of the instrument and somewhere along the way had parted company with the bus! Unconfirmed rumours were that it was found in a ditch and someone was using it as a flowerpot! Needless to say, I was as distressed by the situation as the sousaphone player himself!

After four years in Kenya, a move to Zimbabwe followed, and it was here that my interest in Salvation Army music making really began to develop. I attended Harare City Corps along with my family, but at the time to my disappointment there was no young people's band, and so I made the suggestion that one be started. Within a few months a group of beginners were meeting weekly, and soon there was a YP Band of around ten to call our own. It was during these years in Zimbabwe that I commenced cornet lessons with an English Salvationist, Gordon Howard, who had been in Zimbabwe a number of years and was working at The Salvation Army's Athol Evans Hospital. Gordon ensured that discipline was instilled in me from a young age, and whilst I didn't perhaps appreciate it at the time, as I look back I am eternally grateful for his tuition. In fact, on leaving Zimbabwe in 1992, Gordon was kind enough to give me a cornet to take back to England. In 2011 I sadly learned that Gordon had passed away.

I remember vividly the first time the YP Band played in public, and we presented a less than recognisable version of the hymn tune *'South Shields'*. It is amazing to think that many of that band are now spread around the world, as far afield as Democratic Republic of Congo, South Africa, Switzerland, New Zealand, the USA, and of course the UK.

It was during my time in Zimbabwe that I developed an interest in composition, and my first few scribbles coming on holiday in the Eastern Highlands area, a splendid setting not unlike the Highlands of Scotland. I set about writing my first piece of music, an arrangement of *'I'll go in the strength of the Lord'*. The piece was never played (it probably only included the solo cornet line!) but it taught me some lessons in how to write music down. It's funny how one remembers certain places by the piece of music they were listening to at the time, and I have vivid memories of those trips to the Eastern Highlands of *'The Blue Bells of Scotland'*, played by trombone soloist Clarence White with the Canadian Staff Band, Ken Downie's wonderful *'Princethorpe Variations'* and *'He can break every fetter'* and the cornet solo *'Jubilance'* by William Himes. It was music like this that first inspired me to start writing.

It was in 1990 that The Salvation Army centenary celebrations in Zimbabwe took place, and a week-long series of meetings unfolded across the capital city of Harare. General Eva Burrows was the esteemed guest, along with the Zaire Territorial Band. At the time, they were the best band I had ever heard live, and despite the battered instruments were able to play seemingly anything that was put in front of them! As is customary in Africa, songs are repeated over and over with no apparent end in sight, and the band would busk their way through song after song. Several new songs were borne out of the congress, and it as a result of this that I came up with the idea of having a march written to celebrate the occasion. My father, who was in contact with Norman Bearcroft at the time as he had been out to lead a music school in Zimbabwe, enquired as to whether he would be willing to compose the march. He duly obliged, and the march *'Zimbabwe Centenary'* was soon on music stands around the Territory. It has proved to be a popular item, although as I have always said to people, it needs to be played in true African style (with musical freedom!)

In 1992 I returned to England and, living in south London, began attending Bromley Temple Corps with my family. I soon became a member of the YP Band cornet bench and continued to pursue my interest in composition. I wasn't in England long before I composed my first piece that was ever played in public, a hymn tune called *'Great Peter Street'* for The Salvation Army's rehabilitation centre in Westminster, which had just been refurbished.

During my first few years back in England my father worked at Judd Street, and one of his colleagues in the finance department happened to be Ray Bowes. Ray was one of the composers who I most looked up to in my early years, and so for a young aspiring Salvationist composer such as myself to meet him was something of an honour. So when my father set up a meeting with him I was over the moon! I had just finished writing my first march, aged 12, and took it along to show him. My immediate anxiety of meeting such a great man was soon quelled by Ray's warmth and unassuming manner, and he soon made me feel at ease. I still remember his advice – adding the euphonium to the bass tune (I was oblivious to the fact that I was starting something of a trend by leaving the euphonium out!), adding timpani to accentuate the bass line and thinking about music in terms of lines (I recall I had written an entry on one instrument of a single note which Ray described as a 'hiccup'!) - all useful advice that I have taken on board.

It was not so long after that that I was given the opportunity to visit Robert Redhead at International Headquarters, who at the time was serving as head of the music department. I went to see him in his office, which was next to The International Staff Band's bandroom in those days, of whom Robert was of course the Bandmaster at the time. This time I had brought with me a new arrangement of 'Shine Jesus Shine', for brass ensemble and piano. Aside from the technical advice Robert gave me, such as devices including contrary motion (when the top line goes up, the bass line should go in the opposite direction), I remember him talking about what a rewarding experience composition could be, and to keep going with what I was doing.

I started attending music schools aged 13, and my first was South London Divisional as it was known back then. Those music schools were always inspiring, both spiritually and musically. I was also starting to get more of my pieces played by the senior band at Bromley, and always found the bandmaster at the time, Don Oliver, to be encouraging in that respect. He would often ask what I was writing and would offer to run them down with the band. He must have been a patient man because some of the music I was churning out was less than pleasing to the ears!

It was in 1997 that I heard of a competition being run by Performance The Arts' Channel. They were looking to showcase young composing talent and were inviting entrants for a 'Young Composer of the Year' contest. I had just finished writing a Christmas march and decided to send it in as I had nothing to lose. I never expected a response, but was delighted when I received a letter informing me that I had made it through to the final of the competition, which was to be televised. The day soon came along, and I went, along with family and friends to the concert in Covent Garden. I asked Bromley Temple Band if they would play the piece for the programme, and they were happy to oblige and gave a fine performance. In the end the judges decided to award me the runner-up prize, but in fairness I was happy just to be there given that I had never expected to make the final.

In 1999 I was informed that my parents had been appointed to the London Central Division, and that we would be moving to North London. Our nearest corps was to be Hendon, where we would stay for the next six years. I joined the band on 1st horn, before later moving to 1st baritone, my first engagement being Hendon Highlights at the Queen Elizabeth Hall. There were close to 50 in the band and it was an honour to be able to play under the baton of Stephen Cobb, although it took a while to adjust to the level of discipline required to play in such an outfit!

It was while I was at Hendon that I got my first composition published, an arrangement of the tune *'Take my life'* coincidentally entitled *'Hendon'*. It was also during my time at Hendon that I started attending the UK's Territorial Music School, and was privileged to meet and play under such luminaries as William Himes and Brian Burditt. Both have a gift for music ministry and both were huge inspirations to me.

One of the wonderful things about the Salvation Army is its internationalism. One can go anywhere in the world and meet like-minded people, and immediately you will share a common bond. There could be no better demonstration of this than the International Congress in Atlanta, USA. With well over 20,000 Salvationists from all over the world gathering together, anyone fortunate to have been present would attest to the fact that it was the most awe-inspiring of events. Hendon Band had been invited to participate at the event, and I recall the opening ceremony, which was more akin to an Olympic opening ceremony and a packed Phillips Arena crowd took in the occasion. Afterwards an informal dinner was held for all the bands involved in the event, and it was good to rub shoulders with members of the New York, Southern Territorial, Canadian and Chicago Staff Bands. The memory that most stays in my mind however was the final congregational song at the closing meeting, an arrangement of the Founder's song which William Himes had penned especially for the occasion. Joined by the voices of 20,000-plus Salvationists, it would have taken a hardened soul to not be moved by this exhilarating rendition.

During my time at Hendon, the renowned cornet player David Daws transferred to the corps and David was a real source of encouragement to me, both as a player and composer. David asked me whether I would consider writing a solo for his up-and-coming CD, 'The Sound of David Daws' which of course I was delighted to do, and I went on to write several more solos for him.

During my time at Hendon I commenced a music degree at Middlesex University, after three years of studying graphic design. The degree at Middlesex helped me to open my eyes to the wider world of music, and I began experimenting in techniques I had not used before. Many were ideas that I would not use in my music if I chose to, but I was able to diversify my approach and find my compositional voice.

In my third year I was required to do a proposition module, which was basically anything I wanted it to be. I had been listening to a work by Karl Jenkins, *'The Armed Man – A Mass for Peace'* which is quite simply an inspirational piece of music. One of my colleagues at university, Duncan Gibbs, had also been listening to the piece and wondered about organising a small-scale performance of the hour-long work. Knowing my brass background, he asked whether I could provide a small backing group. After listening to the piece again, I thought *'well why don't we go full scale and arrange the whole work for brass band?'* Having heard a couple of works with brass band and organ before, I thought the added colour and mass of sound an organ would provide would be the perfect combination to emulate the sound of the orchestra. Duncan agreed, and so we embarked on arranging the work – Duncan the organ part and myself the brass. Within three or four months we'd completed the arrangement and soon it was approved by Karl Jenkins and Boosey and Hawkes we set about organising a concert to premiere the work.

It turned out to be a mammoth task, as we had to get a choir together that was big enough to compete with the volume of a full brass band. We would also need a brass band for the occasion, and so I invited various players from across the UK to come together and form a composite band. We also invited Karl Jenkins himself to the concert and were quite taken aback when he agreed not only to attend but also give what I believe was his first public interview. It wasn't until the day of the concert that we actually heard the arrangement for the first time. Fortunately everything went to plan and the evening turned out to be a great success. I was able to speak to Karl Jenkins briefly during the interval and after the concert, and he seemed pleased with the arrangement.

After six years at Hendon Corps my parents were appointed to THQ, and with that came a move back to South London and a return to Bromley Temple Corps. There had been talk in the immediate aftermath of the *'Armed Man'* concert about repeating the event, and after the problems we had had finding a choir to perform the work, asking Bromley Songsters seemed the obvious solution. They were more than happy to participate, and a follow-up concert was duly scheduled for the following May (2006), a year after the original concert. It turned out to be a wonderful opportunity for ministry because it meant a number of singers from other choirs came along to songster practice who wouldn't have otherwise. After around 14 weeks of rehearsals, the songsters and additional singers were ready to perform at the event, and again a composite band was brought together for what was to be entitled *'A Time for Peace – A Musical Spectacular'*.

The band presented a programme in the first half, along with guest soloists Chris Turner, Owen Farr, Katrina Marzella and David Childs. The second half comprised of *'The Armed Man'*, and the Musician's performed admirably. The evening was all in aid of a relatively new charity, Brass Band Aid, which was helping to raise money to build a school in Ethiopia. Having read about this fantastic initiative, and given my links with Africa, it seemed like a most appropriate cause to support.

After the concert, a few of The Musician's suggested the idea of producing a studio recording of the arrangement. This project came to fruition a year later, in 2007, and this time the Brass Band Aid Celebrity Band, an all-star band featuring many of the top players from around the UK, came together for the recording. In order to enhance some of the tracks, I spoke to Dorothy Nancekievill, Leader of The International Staff Songsters, and she was more than happy to lend a helping hand. The ISS obliged and recorded several tracks, which certainly bolstered the recording. All proceeds from the sale of the recording were to go towards the good work of Brass Band Aid.

It was just a few months before the recording that I found out my company, Salvationist Publishing & Supplies, were moving to Wellingborough from London. The move of course meant moving corps again, and so Kettering Citadel became my home. I duly joined the band on euphonium, later moving to baritone. After a year or so at the corps I also took on the responsibility of Assistant YP Band Leader, which would give me the opportunity to work with a great group of youngsters.

Not long after my arrival at Kettering Corps, the Corps Officer, Major David Radford, touching on my links with Africa and the fact my parents were now serving in Zambia as Territorial Commanders, suggested the possibility of organising a trip to that part of the world. The idea was to give people from the corps an experience of a third world country, but not only that, to support many of the people and projects that The Salvation Army was involved with there. Having already been to two music schools there in the past year, I also suggested that we try and support the music school, which was to be held during Easter 2010.

There was a great deal of interest when the potential trip was announced, and although not everyone who originally expressed an interest was able to go, a group of eight committed themselves to the trip. We would of course have to raise a fair amount of money to make the trip happen, as well as money to support some of the projects we were going to see. Having previously invited the Brass Band Aid Celebrity Band to feature on the *'Armed Man'* recording, I thought it would be wonderful to get them together for a live concert, and so set about organising an event which was to be called 'Brass for Africa – A Musical Spectacular'. I made a list of who I considered to be the best brass and percussion players in the country and was both delighted and surprised when nearly all the players I asked to come and play were able and willing to give of their time. In order to appeal to those in the audience who were not so brass-minded, I also invited young singing sensation Charlie Green, a young Salvationist from Droitwich Spa Corps who had shot to fame on ITV's 'Britain's Got Talent'. Charlie turned out to be the perfect foil for the band, and he raised the roof with his performance in what was a fantastic evening. A sequel was planned some 18 months later, which again was a terrific success and raised money for two projects which I had identified as having the greatest need - Chikankata Hospital and John Laing School and Clinic in Zambia.

I touched on The Salvation Army's internationalism earlier, and the trip to Zambia further enhanced in my mind the fantastic diversity that is found in the SA world. During the first week of the trip we visited a number of projects in and around the Chikankata area, and for the second week we attended the Territorial Music School and helped in whatever way we could. In a way it was like coming full circle, because having begun my musical experience in southern Africa, I was now giving back what The Salvation Army had given me during that time. I had the privilege of conducting the 'A' Band, as I had done in my two previous years at the music school. The first music school I had been involved in, in 2008, was actually the first for many years, and had heralded something of a renaissance in terms of music making in Zambia. It was good to see the progress that had been made since then and one could not help but be inspired by the sheer enthusiasm of the staff and delegates. The trip turned out to be everything I'd hoped it would be and more, and it was indeed life changing for all who participated.

In June 2011 I took on the role of Editor of SA Bandsman, a new publication that was launched to cater for the Salvation Army banding world. It launched at the ISB120 event, which I, like many, will remember for years to come as one of the greatest SA events of all time. It was simply a privilege to have been there as a spectator, and showcased all that is good about SA music making. The event was one of the first main features in SA

Bandsman, and since then it has given me the opportunity to connect with banding colleagues from across the world. The magazine is still in its infancy, but I hope it will continue to grow and give me the chance to further develop my links with Salvationist banding colleagues across the world.

I thank God for all the opportunities that have come my way as a Salvationist musician, many of which I simply never could have imagined. I am indebted to The Salvation Army for what it has provided me – far more than I could ever give in return, although as I always say, it's not about what The Salvation Army can give me but rather what I can give The Salvation Army, and ultimately of course, God.

Important compositions

The Armed Man - A Mass for Peace (arranged), Stabat Mater (arranged), A Christmas Fantasia, Spanish Dance, Distant Land (arranged), Fill the World with Glory, The Candlelight Carol GS2042-2 (2006), Hendon

WALLTENG, GUSTAF

Was born in 1889 in Uppsala, and died in 1935. He was an officer (Major) of the Salvation Army as well as song writer and composer. Gustaf Wallteng became a Salvation Army officer in 1909 and after having been '*pastern*' (which was then called Commanding Officer) of a number of corps around Sweden, he became an employee of the 'battle cry' at the end of the 1920s. He was head of the Salvation Army's music department from 1931 until his death in 1935. He had also taken an organist diploma.

Important compositions

Rönninge-Marsch (FM0131) 1922, Församlingssånger (FM0194) 1936

WALKDEN, WILLIAM

William Walkden was Songster Leader of the Tottenham Citadel Songsters in London. His composition 'St. Clemens' was his first piece in the Band Journals of the Salvation Army.

Important compositions

St. Clemens (GS1322) 1949

WALKER, ALAN

Alan Walker, FRSC (born 6 April 1930) is an English-Canadian musicologist and university professor best known as a biographer and scholar of composer Franz Liszt. He's a world authority on the Hungarian composer Liszt. Lives in Canada but originates from England. He lived as a lodger with Ray Steadman-Allen when he first moved down to London many years ago, then became a Salvationist. He came from the Scunthorpe Citadel Corps and worked briefly in the Salvation Army Music Editorial Department possibly while a student at Guildhall School of Music.

Important compositions

The Challenge of the Fight (FS0224) 1957, Triumph (FS0240) 1959

WALKER, T. HAROLD

One of the early composers (late 1800, early 1900). Harold Walker was a brilliant cornet soloist, from the Boscombe Citadel Corps. He often featured at national Salvation Army festivals such as in the Queen's Hall and the Christal Palace. He was an exceptional cornet player, and refused an invitation by Sir Dan Godfrey to join the Bournemouth Symphony Orchestra. His family lived in Wales before moving to Boscombe where his father William became Bandmaster. He was succeded by his son-in-law Sylvester Henning, who sadly was killed in the war.

Important composition

The Hull March (GS0729) 1915

WALLACE, W.V.

No real information about W. Wallace could be found, however it is of interest that *'The Bellringer'*, the only known published band piece by him, was actually arranged (for publication) by Edward Saywell (See: SAYWELL, EDWARD)

Important composition

The Bellringer (GS1283-1) 1947

WARD, KEN A.

Ken Ward was born in Ashton-under-Lyne in 1924. His interest in music was encouraged by his father, Songster Leader William Ward, who later became the local secretary of the Victoria College of Music. Ken began learning the piano aged eight and made rapid progress, gaining his first diploma when only thirteen years old. He also enjoyed considerable success in local musical festivals. In 1944 Ken was called up and joined the RAF as a wireless operator eventually being stationed in Singapore. After the War he returned to Ashton where he was appointed Bandmaster, a position he held for about five years before moving to Blackpool in 1955. In 1961 he became bandmaster of the Blackpool Citadel Band. During Ken's years as bandmaster the band enjoyed considerable success conducting many weekends at corps throughout the United Kingdom as well as taking the band to Switzerland twice, in 1977 and 1988 and to Canada in 1993. The band was also invited to take part in the Bandmasters' Councils Festival in the Royal Albert Hall in 1976. Ken eventually retired as Bandmaster in 1996, after thirty-five years of service in this capacity. Over the years Ken has made a number of arrangements of hymn tunes or classical pieces for the band but has not had anything published in the Army journals. These include *'Be Still'* ('for the presence of the Lord'), *'Beautiful Zion'*, *'His Provision'* (cornet solo), *'Precious Jesus'* (Flugelhorn Solo), *'All that I am'* (Euphonium Solo), *'A New Creation'* and a band arrangement of Ivor Bosanko's *'The Lord Bless Thee and Keep Thee'*, which was recorded by the Household Troops Band. An abridged version of *'Be Still'* was included in the first edition of the worship songs published by the Salvation Army. Now (2012) aged 87 Ken is still an active Soldier at Blackpool Citadel. He is the Corps and Songster pianist and continues to bring much blessing to people through his playing in the services.

Young People's Bandmember Kenneth A. Ward, of Ashton-under-Lyne, who is only twelve years of age, has passed the Victoria College of Music examination in pianoforte playing, which entitles him to place A.V.C.M. after his name. He has also won a bronze medal and three book prizes for the highest number of marks in other exams, and four first class certificates and six 'thirds' for music. Kenneth is the pianist for the Young People's Singing Company and a Life-Saving Chum. He is the son of Bandmaster and Mrs. W. Ward, and the nephew of Major and Mrs. Bamford, now stationed in Great Yarmouth.

('The Musician' 29-1-1938)

Important compositions

The Lord Bless Thee and Keep Thee (m/s), Peace like a river (m/s), Precious Jesus (m/s)

WATSON, TY

Ty Watson (B.Mus.Ed, B.Ed) was born in Portage La Prairie Manitoba, Canada in 1968 and received his early musical training in the Salvation Army. His formal training was completed at the University of Toronto where he graduated with a degree in music education.

Ty spent 7 years playing euphonium with the world renowned Canadian Staff Band and also served as euphonium soloist and Deputy Bandmaster of the Mississauga Temple Band. Ty has written music for some of the Salvation Army's finest bands and has also had his compositions performed by European Championship Section Bands. He has been published by Bernaerts Music (Belgium), Eighth Note Publications (Toronto) and the Salvation Army in both Brass Band and Concert Band Mediums. Ty was selected as a finalist in the Canadian wide march composition contest sponsored by the Hannaford Silver Band in 2001 for his composition *'Strength and Honour'*. In 2002 two of Ty's compositions were featured on a CD featuring Doug Yeo of the Boston Symphony Orchestra and Nick Hudson Of the William's Fairey Band. At present Ty teaches music at Heart Lake Secondary School in Brampton, Ontario where he is the Head of the Arts Department. In the summers Ty has been a guest conductor at music camps throughout North America.

Important compositions

Swing Hosanna (TS1041) 1996, Czardas (Eb bass solo), Eyes upon Jesus (horn solo) Joyful Song (cornet solo, written for his wife Melody), Now (trombone solo), The Standard (cornet solo), Mississauga Spirit (march) and Vigilant (bass trombone solo) *[all m/s]*

WATSON, STUART

Stuart is a member of The Salvation Army at Kirkcaldy Corps in the East Scotland Division. He graduated as a Tuba player from the Royal Northern College of Music, Manchester, and later gained a Masters in Biblical Studies from the University of St Andrews. He subsequently worked in education, based first of all at The Salvation Army's William Booth College, School for Officer Training, in London, and then in Los Angeles. He returned home in 2009 to resume working as a freelance musician. A number of his songs, compositions and arrangements have been published in the UK Territory's brass band journals and in the choral series, Sing to the Lord. The International Staff Band have regularly featured his composition *'Psalm 91'* in their repertoire, and the International Staff Songsters have recorded the songs, *'Three Love Letters'* and *'Introit: From Psalm 24'*, both of which are collaborations with Rob Little. Stuart is also a regular contributor to the American Instrumental Ensemble Series and Sing Praise, both published by The Salvation Army in the United States.

Important composition

Psalm 91 (TS1188) 2009

WAY, WILLIAM

William (Bill) holds a Master of Music performance degree from Indiana University in Trombone. He has had the privilege of accompanying many wonderful soloists both instrumental and vocal over the years. William is active in the Salvation Army as both a Bandmaster (Agincourt Temple Band) and Church Organist/Pianist. William also serves as Principal Trombone with the Oshawa Durham Symphony Orchestra. For several years he was a member of the trombone section with the Canadian Staff Band and got world wide recognition as pianist of Douglas Chaulk's musical ensemble for the 'Masterpiece' CD recording.

Important compositions

At the Well, Wonderful love

WEBB, JOY

Joy Webb is an officer of The Salvation Army in England. She was the founder of the famous popgroup 'The Joystrings' with whom she had many successes not only within the Salvation Army but also outside the Salvation Army. They were the first Salvation Army pop group achieving chart success with *'It's An Open Secret'* and *'On A Starry Night'*. The main members through the years were Joy Webb, Peter and Sylvia Dalziel, Bill Davidson and Wycliffe Noble. The group had a number of other singers who changed, due to them consisting of cadets originating from The Salvation Army's training college in London. Joy Webb was a pioneer for use of modern music in the Salvation Army, to proclaim the Gospel. Many of her written songs are used by Salvation Army composers in arragements for Brass Band with *'Share my Yoke'* as probably the best well known. In 2004 Major Joy Webb received the Order of the Founder (O.F).

Important compositions

Share my Yoke (GS1831-1) 1988, There Will Be God (GS1641-1 [RSA] and GS1967 [Richard Phillips])

WEBBER, SAMUEL

Prior of joining the Salvation Army he was bandleader of the Inniskinning Dragoon Guards. He was the Conductor of the 2nd Household Troops Band in 1890, formed at the London Headquarters. Webber was also the bandmaster of the Headquarter's Junior Staff Band when they played to welcome the first Household Troops Band back from their tour to the United States.

Important compositions

Always the same is Jesus (GS0331-1) 1897, But is the story true (GS0366-1) 1898, Farewell to thee (GS0405-2) 1901, Let it roll over me (GS0405-1) 1901, A Wonderful story (GS0344) 1897

WEIGLE, C.F.

No information about this composer is available.

Important composition

No One Ever Cared For Me Like Jesus

WELCH, GLENN MATTHEW

Glenn Welch was born in Ludington, Michigan, USA on March 16, 1962. Born to Salvation Army officers, he was the youngest of five children. When Glenn was two years old, the Army transferred his parents to Indiana where they held appointments in Mishawaka, South Bend, Fort Wayne, and Indianapolis over the next twelve years. For this reason, Glenn considers himself a 'Hoosier' (a native of Indiana). At a tender age, Glenn gave his heart to the Lord – so tender in fact, he cannot recall a time he didn't believe in God or know that Jesus died to save his soul. At age four or five, when his Bible School class went up to the altar en masse, Glenn simply told his teacher he didn't need to go up and he alone stayed behind, confident that he already belonged to God.

Music came naturally to Glenn, growing up in a Salvationist household where all seven members loved to play instruments and sing. In addition, Glenn's father, Major Jeffery Welch, collected Salvation Army recordings and hosted Salvation Army radio shows that featured brass band and songster music in a number of cities the family lived. Jeff's long-play record albums had an enduring impact on Glenn. Groups especially close to his young heart were the Cambridge Citadel Band, the Chicago Staff Band, the London Singers – and the band featured on whatever new record his dad happened to bring home. Meanwhile, his older three brothers and sister were heavily into the pop music of the late 1960's and early 1970's so in addition to Army bands, Glenn was fed a solid diet of Tijuana Brass, Chicago, Chase, The Guess Who, and a myriad of other secular bands. The Jesus Movement soon opened up a whole new dimension to Glenn's musical world. By attending Christian rock concerts and coffeehouses, Glenn discovered music that spoke to him in a more real way than ever, and from age 9 to 13 he lived in a hub of early Christian rock, Fort Wayne, Indiana. Glenn attended The Adam's Apple, the home of Petra and Honeytree, where Phil Keaggy, 2nd Chapter of Acts, The Salvation Air Force, and others came to play in an intimate setting. This was before Christian rock became commercialized. During this time, Larry Norman emerged as Glenn's lifelong favorite Christian artist.

Glenn's own music performing began on the bass drum at age five or six, with the Mishawaka Corps Band. After successfully keeping time in rehearsal, on Sunday morning a very anxious Glenn aggressively pounded the bass drum in his debut, only to see his father make frantic gestures for him to quiet down – the band was accompanying a prayerful song – and Glenn received his first lesson in dynamics. By age eight Glenn had switched to trombone and learned a few tunes by ear. His proud father took him around to show people how good his son could glissando on '*Aloomp went the Little Green Frog*', though it's quite improbable his arm was even long enough to be in tune on some notes. Though Glenn memorized well, the discipline of learning to read music didn't come very easy. While attending Indiana Music Institute at age nine, Glenn merely imitated the slide positions of the girl trombonist sitting next to him, and soon he was singled out to play his part alone. Tears gushed from embarrassment, and the kindhearted Major George Hogg took Glenn aside to calm him down and encourage him. Even so, Glenn decided then and there he didn't want to play trombone anymore. After camp ended, Glenn took up the baritone on Dad's condition that he would remain in the basement until he could successfully play the C Scale. When it looked like he would be there all night, his dad compromised by allowing Glenn to pass the test by simply memorizing all the fingerings of the scale. Fort Wayne had a small youth band and a decent senior band and Glenn soon got 'over the hump' learning to read notation. From that point, he advanced quickly, joining the senior band by age 10, mastering many of the marches and selections from the Green Book

(Favourite Triumph Series Band Journals No. 2), and moving up the baritone line. He won solo contests at camp at the 'C' and 'B' Band level, and at age 12 he arrived back at camp fully intending to make the 'A' Band and win the 'A' Band solo contest with '*Jesus is Strong to Deliver*'. He had practiced so hard during the previous year, he memorized the solo. But first there came tryouts. Major Jeff Welch was assigning the euphonium and baritone players to bands and Glenn hadn't a worry in the world. His dad knew very well how good Glenn had gotten. When Glenn's dad instructed him to play the C Scale and counted off the tempo, Glenn ripped right up and down the scale effortlessly. Dad was not impressed. He said, 'Incorrect'. Glenn panicked – the thought that his hope of playing in the 'A' Band could be dashed by his own dad – who knew his ability – was inconceivable. But all ended well – Glenn merely got set straight about following a given tempo and not rushing off to the races, after which the tryout continued successfully and he joined the 'A' Band. One more dramatic moment at the same camp came during the solo contest. Glenn was one of four 'A' Band finalists who performed for the evening program in front of the entire student body. Confident, and with no music, Glenn went through the theme and first variation; then began the third variation while his pianist played the accompaniment for the second variation. Glenn had accidently skipped the second! They stopped and tried it again. Glenn again played the third variation while the pianist played the second! Neither performer figured out the problem, but by now, Glenn was convinced his pianist was somehow responsible. He jumped off the stage and ran straight down the center aisle and out of the building in tears. Fourth Place. That unfinished performance so affected Glenn, he uncharacteristically refused to prepare and play a solo the following year.

Still, Indiana's Camp Elm was very dear to Glenn's heart – the closest spot to Heaven it seemed. He had his favorite climbing trees and would balance himself while walking across Indian Creek on a footbridge's handrail. He also admired Brigadier Herbert Hill from a distance. This was Indiana's 'Mr. Music', former ISB cornetist, son of the Salvation Army's first Band Inspector Ted Hill, and namesake of Indiana Music Institute's highest honor. Glenn's trumpet-playing brother Steve had received the Brigadier Herbert Hill Award in 1971 and went on to get a music degree from Indiana University. Around this time in Glenn's life, Major Jeff Welch brought the Flint Citadel Band to Fort Wayne and the boy enjoyed listening to this great band. As an officer's kid behind the scenes, he got to see his dad rub shoulders with Bandmaster James Curnow and the band's euphonium players Dallas Raby and Bill Himes. Thanks to his dad's records, Glenn recognized some of the pieces the band played, like the '*Wonders Begin*' trombone feature, and it was thrilling to hear it 'live'. Upon entering Junior High School, Glenn was encouraged and pushed by his band director Dave Showalter. Glenn worked on his bass clef reading and played tuba in the 7th Grade Band and valve trombone in the Jazz Band. His tuba was a brand new Yamaha – and that was a good selling point to convince him to play tuba. Imagine that – a motorcycle company that made tubas – or so he thought. Glenn was also one of a handful of students picked to be a member of the school's Dixieland Band. The Jazz Band met before school started, but the Dixieland Band rehearsed before the Jazz Band – and before sunrise – at 6:30 a.m! Glenn religiously rode his bike two miles to school in the dark to take his place in the group of otherwise 9th-graders.

After a year in Indianapolis, Glenn's folks resigned from officership and Glenn's dad took a position as an administrator of a medical care facility back in Ludington, Michigan, Glenn's birthplace. Glenn went from playing euphonium in a good Indianapolis Central Band to playing duets with his dad in the front pew of a very small corps. This experience taught him things he wouldn't necessarily learn at a big corps. His dad showed him by example that one should simply make himself available and regularly use the gifts God has given. If there's only one brass player in the congregation, he should still play for the meetings, plain and simple. Glenn came to the conclusion that, of the three T's of stewardship, time is so much more important than talents and treasure. Glenn's dad would often sit at home and play meaningful tunes by ear on his baritone, including *'All my days and all my hours'*. Glenn saw that one's ability didn't matter much without his availability. With little ensemble opportunity at the Ludington corps, Glenn was relieved to find he could join the Western Michigan Northern Indiana Divisional Youth Band, led by John Hamilton. This was a better band than any he had been in up until that time. In 1977 the Youth Band took a bus to Hamilton, Ontario and played concerts at Argyle Citadel and Hamilton Temple corps. Glenn played Eb Horn, a little out of his comfort zone, but it was what was needed and it further expanded his experience.

Glenn spent his entire high school career in Ludington and his parents attended every one of his concerts, dad with battery-powered cassette recorder in hand. Glenn received superior ratings all three years of soloing on euphonium at the Michigan district and state levels, playing Salvation Army solos such as *'Jubilate'* and *'Song of the Brother'*. His high school band director, Howard Hornung, transcribed brass band accompaniments into wind band accompaniments for those two solos and Glenn performed them at his school's Spring concerts in his Junior and Senior year. He also received his school's top sophomore and junior band awards and the John Phillip Sousa Award as a senior. He was named Band Captain as a senior, and with it came the honor of directing the High School Pep Band. This not only gave him experience choosing and conducting music, he began writing short charts for the Pep Band: The old Olympic Theme, *'Babe'* (by *Styx*), the *'Gong Show'* theme, and *'Gene, Gene, Dancing Machine.'* Not masterpieces, the tunes were at least recognizable and the harmony worked.

Glenn's love for rock music continued as well, throughout his teen years. His brother Jonathan showed him the basics of playing guitar and brought home a drum set, and the two often spent hours jamming in the basement of the Welch home. Glenn developed his talents on both the guitar and drums, learning and playing the guitar more often when alone, and playing drums when his brother was around - and adding some background vocals to Jon's high-range lead, sometimes supplemented by their sister Val, or brothers Keith and Steve, when they visited from out of state. Glenn's mother, Shirlee, was a singer and pianist, and there was a piano in the dining room which Glenn took advantage of as well. He began to love playing so many types of instruments; he didn't know which one to concentrate most of his energy on. In the meantime he began to write songs. Over the course of the next thirty years he would write over 500 songs, most of which were written for personal use, though others would be evangelistic in nature or attempts to communicate spiritual truth and lessons learned. His favorite subjects were God and girls, and many songs were therapeutic in nature as he matured, the musical staff serving as a form of journal or diary. Glenn was a dreamer, a romantic, and he was never interested in growing up. He had too much fun as a child and didn't see the desirability of facing the challenges of life. Why should he do the driving and be faced with all those decisions when he was content to be a tag-along and ride in the family car? He had a sweet childhood, but even with that, there were certain unpredictable disadvantages. Every happy puppy needs to grow up someday.

In many ways, Glenn led the typical life of an American Salvationist teen. His first job was ringing bells at the Christmas kettle and he worked at summer camps starting at age 16. He was viewed by the kids at school differently than he viewed himself. He was surprised to learn he was voted quietest boy in student mock elections. Quietest?? He, of course, had hoped he would win 'most musical' but that was given to a friend who was an accomplished guitar player, and who happened to have been a 'baritone brother' who had sat next to Glenn back in 9th grade Cadet Band. Though Glenn felt special, he began to sense that he was seen as common. Someone once told him that there was certainly nothing about the way he carried himself that would impress anyone, but yet there was something a little deeper, when you got to know him, that was genuine and good. He felt that assessment was very acceptable. He didn't have to be 'Mr. Personality' to enjoy life. As Glenn grew older, he didn't shake the image of I Corinthians 13, *'spoke like a child…'* There was a sense in which he never *'became a man'*, nor *'put away childish things'* until much later in life, around the time he got married. He wasn't particularly afraid to talk; often he could talk too much, but with all the practice, he never became eloquent with words. This was apparent even in many of his songs where he purposefully wrote in slang and used bad grammar and sometimes the content was brutally candid. Remember, his songs functioned as a diary.

The one area he did become polished was euphonium performance. He especially looked forward to performing solos, not as an ego trip, but to share what God had given him. This was something he was blessed to be able to do well, so it only made sense that he should do it. Something that perhaps made less sense was his drive to compose serious music. Though Glenn had a lively imagination, he was limited in his ability to craft compositions and only slowly improved after years of education and practice. Still, there was something in him that kept telling him to write. At age 17 he entered his first composition contest, a Salvation Army contest in connection with the American SA Centennial in 1980. He wrote a hymn *'Rend Your Heart'* and a euphonium solo with full band accompaniment called *'Gipsy Smith'*. Adolescent hopes were high but for naught. Still, he kept writing.

He longed for his Indiana home. He dreamed of attending Indiana University, majoring in music, but he won a State of Michigan scholarship for good grades in High School, and was a resident of Michigan, making it much more affordable to stay in-state, so he chose Western Michigan University in Kalamazoo. After a successful audition he received music scholarship assistance as well. He declared a double major: euphonium performance and composition. The former was chosen because of his strengths, the latter, in spite of his weaknesses, because his heart wanted it. At some point he concluded that a bad composer is still a composer, and Glenn had the heart of a composer so that's what he was, whether good or bad. But for now, he wouldn't dwell on his deficiencies. He had hope. God would inspire him and College would teach him.

Although Glenn had received plenty of euphonium instruction courtesy The Salvation Army in group settings, he hadn't experienced his first private music lesson until he was a freshman in college. Professor Bob Whaley, tubist with the Kalamazoo Symphony Orchestra, was Glenn's coach for four years and his instruction was profoundly enlightening. Up until that point, Glenn hadn't thought much about pedagogy. He thought the various characteristics in playing were merely natural and personal; nothing really to question or dissect, but Mr. Whaley taught Glenn to be analytical about his playing. While giving Glenn a better idea of the mechanics of playing, Mr. Whaley also opened wider the interpretive and expressive side of playing. He was a master teacher who tried to squeeze the last drop of meaning out of music. He may have followed Harvey Phillips' philosophy better than the famed Harvey himself, who said, *'two things; make sure you pick a good tune, then go out and make love to your audience.'* Glenn grew immeasurably under Mr. Whaley's wing. Whaley taught Glenn that one should never brainlessly play music, but must be an intelligent player – know the composer, the period, the instrument of the original version, the message behind the music and the feelings behind the message. Then know the mechanics – the appropriate way to interpret the music, how to imitate the original instrument, the articulation, dynamics, shape, phrasing, ornamentation, use of vibrato – it all had to be thoughtfully considered. But after all was said and done, Mr. Whaley inspired Glenn and his other students most of all by the way he relished each musical moment itself. Making music enlivened Mr. Whaley; it energized him, and his excitement was contagious. Glenn heard the tuba played like he never heard it played before – as a gorgeously lyrical solo instrument. He learned much from Mr. Whaley through imitation and taking his lessons to heart, and Whaley impacted Glenn in his solo performance career more than anyone else had before or has since.

On Glenn's first Sunday upon arriving at college, he attended the Kalamazoo Salvation Army and was welcomed to sit in with the twenty-piece uniformed band led by Scottish Bandmaster Andrew Stewart. Glenn immediately sensed the warm fraternity of the players and pleasant spirit of the corps and had no doubt where he would be attending church for the next four years. When he missed band rehearsal that first week following, Bandmaster Stewart called him that very night and asked where he had been. Glenn apologized and said he'd love to come but he didn't have a car, so the Bandmaster arranged transportation for him every Wednesday and Sunday. Andrew Stewart was a tenderhearted old man with a sweet smile and long baton, but he wouldn't give the shirt off his back. Actually, he'd buy you a brand new one. That's what he did for Glenn, almost reducing the college freshman to tears. Glenn, the fifth of five kids, was more than familiar with hand-me-down clothes. Many times he'd received used white shirts by good-intentioned family members, but this was his first white shirt in many years that he received without a yellow collar.

The camaraderie at the Kalamazoo corps was second to none, and the band, steeped in tradition, was the core of the corps. Salvation meetings usually had good attendances, but on football's Super Bowl Sunday evening, a congregation of very few would look up to a full platform of bandsmen! Glenn learned valuable lessons about the benefits of traditions while at Kalamazoo. The corps calendar was full of activities, annual events, special guests and special events; band reunions, trips, park services, marches at the mall, and Community Christmas Sing-alongs. Glenn was so impressed, he did the same when he later became music director of various corps. He recognized the advantages of setting goals before bands, preparing to reach those goals, and realizing a meaningful outcome that was good for here and for eternity.

On campus, Glenn attended weekly convocations, required concerts for music majors, to expose them to a wide variety of musical experiences. As a freshman, he had almost no prior exposure to atonal or 'twentieth century' music, and during a Bartok string quartet performance, he and a few other disinterested students near the back were goofing off and just waiting for the end of the seemingly pointless program. At the conclusion of the performance, the crowd applauded politely and as the clapping quickly died down, one set of hands kept violently clapping from behind. With a smile, Glenn turned around to see what smart-aleck was being so silly, but to his amazement, he found that the noisy lone clapper was Donald Para, resident composer – on his feet and with tears streaming down his face, profoundly moved by the music he had just heard! Immediately Glenn sobered up. He thought to himself, 'I totally missed it. I want what he's got!' By the time Glenn graduated, he had learned to listen and allow music to speak to him. He could make a list of modern composers and he knew their music, but although he still would not particularly enjoy most of it, he did respect it – and he happened to thoroughly enjoy Bartok.

It was unclear to Glenn where God would lead him after college. He wasn't motivated to get a higher education only to be able to land a high-paying job. In fact, he had little ambition to make money. He simply loved music and thought it made sense to follow where he felt driven in his heart to go.

Professor Whaley tried to help Glenn set some career goals and made clear the limited options for a euphonium major. There were next to no symphony gigs. The only serious performance career opportunity in the U.S. was in the military bands. He suggested that Glenn consider going into music education and when Glenn expressed no interest, Mr. Whaley said he could become a university professor and teach euphonium majors. This had a little more appeal as an occupation, but still seemed undesirable to Glenn for philosophical reasons. He felt the primary focus of a musician should be performing, not teaching, and he definitely didn't want what amounted to teaching future euphonium teachers, to teach more teachers, and keeping this specialized teaching occupation alive for its own sake – maybe an unfair assessment, but that's how Glenn looked at it. Mr. Whaley seemed to have more of a purpose as a teacher; his tuba students had ample performance opportunities as he himself had plenty of gigs as a tuba player. But could one convincingly justify being a euphonium professor? Beyond this question, the bottom line was: Glenn wasn't an educator at heart. If he only knew what was in store for him! He spent a career teaching music within The Salvation Army, took some students on the side, and had a few stints helping out in schools and universities, while most of the time still wishing he was in a little room writing music or playing a gig.

Glenn took 'forms' class, learning the basics of musical forms and having his first opportunity to write short composition assignments. He was proud of one piece in particular that received a 'C' grade and a lot of red ink because he used parallel fifths, a 'no-no' for the class. The professor wrote on his paper, 'Why the onslaught of rock-type parallels?!' Glenn saw that word 'rock' and he felt good, like a rock-n-roll rebel! Maybe he didn't follow the conventional rules, but he could apparently write rock music. Glenn spent three and a half years in college as a composition major but during his fourth year, found he would have to come back for a fifth year if he wanted to receive both a composition and an applied (euphonium performance) degree. Meanwhile his composition class was now getting into atonal music heavily and he studied under Ray Zupko, definitely not a traditional composer. The thrust of the required class was way out of Glenn's comfort zone and he simply could not find the inspiration to write a twelve-tone piece. Finally, after much struggle, and when nearing a deadline, he called Mr. Zupko, explained his feelings of being incapable. He stated that he had decided to drop the composition major and go ahead and graduate in 1984. Then Glenn asked if Mr. Zupko was willing to change his composition assignment so he could come up with something other than nonsense. He relented and Glenn passed the class after cranking out an old-fashioned piano ragtime piece called RayZ Rag. Just for fun, Glenn wrote a few more rags during college and afterwards, and declared there was no musical genre more enjoyable to write in. His pleasure in writing rags was as great as was torturous that twelve-tone assignment – the difference between heaven and hell to him.

Starting in 1980 Glenn attended a few campus ministries and became a weekly regular at 'Campus Action', an Assembly of God group. There he was introduced to the newly developing praise-and-worship movement. He was already very knowledgeable about Jesus Rock, but this was different. This was not Christian entertainment. These were simple, repetitive choruses that were specifically addressed to God; a form of informal modern worship that was unheard of by Salvation Army congregations in the U.S. in general until a few years later. Glenn enjoyed the worship experience and the new choruses, but he gave no thought to trying to push it on the Army crowd. To him that wouldn't have been a good idea. He loved the traditional Army meetings and music, and he loved the informal get-togethers at Campus Action – equally but separately, as two different aspects of his spiritual walk. Maybe it just wasn't time yet.

In 1981 Glenn attended Central Music Institute at Camp Lake, Wisconsin for his sixth time. Through the years he had worked up to the Wonderland Band, and now he was Principal Euphonium. He won the Wonderland Solo Contest playing, 'Song of the Brother' and was accompanied by the Faculty Band in performing before the entire camp and guests. One morning, he and some other students were heading out the door of their cabin, on the way to their first class when their counselor said someone needed to sweep up a quadrant of the cabin. Glenn decided to stay and do the chore even though it wasn't his bunkroom; it just seemed like the Christian thing to do. He ran down the hill to class but got there late and was greeted in a strange manner by his Bible instructor. *'Some of you are up for the Ben Merritt Award and it's not wise to come to class late – you can ruin your chances with a careless move like that.'* Glenn didn't know how to respond. He felt hurt and a little upset that someone would think he would or should try to keep his nose clean – or to brown-nose, just to win an award. His motivations for wanting to give his best were spiritual, not self-serving ambition. He just mumbled something like, *'I'm not worried about winning awards.'* He wasn't disappointed. He was content to receive third place, Wonderland Band.

He came back the next summer, won first place in the Wonderland Solo Contest again, this time playing 'Carnival of Venice', won the Irwin Fischer Composition Award, and won the Ben Merritt (top student) Award. Though grateful for the honor, as he looked at his trophy, he said, 'Well, it's not the Herb.' He had never won the Herbert Hill Award at Indiana Music Institute, and while most would argue the territorial award was more prestigious, Glenn realized then how much the smaller camp had meant to him. 'The Ben' came with an automatic scholarship to return to CMI the following year; basically an easy-ride freebie – one is not eligible for any more awards and often the winner would switch instruments or go vocal. So Glenn decided to play trombone in 1983. His jaw dropped when he found out he was selected to be Principal Trombone in the Wonderland Band. He knew he was unworthy of the position – it must have been a down year for trombone players, but he gave it his best shot, paranoid of his intonation and struggling to get the edge he needed when it was called for. Bernard Adams was merciful as Glenn tried to give him what he wanted in '*Treasures for Tchaikovsky*'. Always wanting to take advantage of opportunities to perform solos, Glenn played a gorgeous euphonium tone solo, the second movement,

'Serenade' of a Tuba Sonatine by Jacques Casterede. He purposely avoided playing a technical solo – his point was to make music, not show off, and he reminded the judges before playing, that he wasn't eligible for any awards – he just wanted to share his music with the little crowd that was present. Either there was a waiver or Glenn misunderstood the camp policy, because he was awarded second place in the Wonderland Solo Contest – on a lyrical tone solo!

In total, Glenn attended fourteen CMI's; eight as a student and eight as a faculty member. As a faculty band member he played euphonium next to Karl Strand. He also taught composition, euphonium technique class, contemporary brass ensemble, guitar and recorder electives. Another year, when the theme was the 1950's, Glenn came up with probably his most clever idea. He challenged Special Guest Barrie Gott, a percussionist, to compete with Chicago Staff Band percussionist Dick Vander Wheel, in doing a drum solo for the song, 'Wipeout'. The catch was, they were to play it on their bellies with their hands. Both contestants were not thin men, and when they lifted up their shirts to perform bare-bellied, the dining hall erupted in cheers and laughter. The following day, Barrie Gott showed Glenn where he had welts on his belly.

On the final day of one CMI, Glenn characteristically was down to the last of his money (he would be bumming a ride back to Indiana with some friends). He found fifteen cents in his pocket and decided he would go ahead and put it in the offering plate during the Holiness Meeting at camp. On his way to the Amphitheater, a kid said he needed some money and without a thought Glenn gave him his fifteen cents. To Glenn's great disappointment, he watched the kid use it to get a pop (soda) out of a machine. Not only was this offensive in that, during Glenn's growing-up days, there was a strict taboo on buying pop from the corps machine on Sundays, Glenn suddenly remembered this was his church money. Well, during the meeting, Glenn was sitting in the faculty band, next to Karl Strand, and as the plate began to make its way around the band, Glenn felt like he'd let God down. Clueless to Glenn's feelings, Karl reached over and put some change in Glenn's hand so he'd have something to put in the plate. Guess what. Fifteen cents! Glenn hadn't mentioned what had happened to anyone, yet Karl had happened to give Glenn money for the plate, and the exact amount. It may have been a pittance, but to Glenn it was like a million bucks – and like the smile of a gracious and tenderhearted God. Little is much when God is in it.

As a euphonium player Glenn was very active and successful during his college days. He was the member of three brass quintets, was principal euphonium of the Symphonic Band, principal trombone of the Concert Band and played trombone in the University Symphony Orchestra, played in an opera pit orchestra, was a member of the tuba ensemble, and jumped in the pep band a few times. He was on his instruments up to five hours a day and performed a half-recital his sophomore year, and full recitals his junior and senior years. He and a few other students were chosen to perform with the prestigious Western Brass Quintet for a Christmas Renaissance concert and he played euphonium with the Kalamazoo Symphony Orchestra on '*The Pines of Rome*'. He was a Senior Concerto Competition winner, which earned him a solo performance with the University Orchestra, playing Lars-Erik Larsson's Trombone Concerto. He was also soloist with the Symphonic Band in his senior year, performing '*Symphonic Variants for Euphonium and Band*', by Salvationist Jim Curnow. urnow won the coveted American Bandmaster's Association Composition Award with this solo and he was to receive the award and listen to the solo's performance in Arizona but Curnow was already booked that evening – at Western

Michigan University's annual Spring Conference. That evening he was instead treated to a performance of his *'Symphonic Variants'* played by Glenn Welch and the WMU Symphonic Band, to which the composer and performer both received a warm reception at 3,000-seat Miller Auditorium.

At WMU, Glenn studied conducting under Mel Ivey and Richard Suddendorf and picked up some tips from Bob Whaley. He also gained conducting skills and insight from annual guests he sat under at Central Music Institute, including Eric Ball, Bernard Adams, Per Ohlson, Dudley Bright, Jim Curnow, and Vernon Post, to name a few. Glenn also had ample opportunity to sit under some excellent conductors who were relatively local: Bill Himes, Peggy Thomas, Max Wood, and Victor Danielson.

At the end of summer 1984, the opportunity of a lifetime presented itself when a position to play euphonium In the Washington D.C. U.S. Air Force Band opened up. The winner of the auditions would be honored to sit next to Brian Bowman, considered among the best euphonium players in the world. Glenn practiced up as best he could during the summer, and playfully tested himself against other Salvation Army players, getting humiliated every time! He was outplayed by his brother Steve on a duet that Glenn himself had written – and Steve was sight-reading. Then Robert Schramm Sr. politely kept Glenn in his place in the euphonium section of the TMI Band. Lastly, David Chaulk, who was also at TMI, was...well, he was being David Chaulk. Glenn had been friends with Dave, a Canadian, for years and Dave had lived in Indianapolis for a time and had taught Glenn composing and euphonium techniques at CMI. Glenn had the ultimate respect for Dave as a performer – Glenn felt Dave was the best euphonium player, period. And he left Glenn in the dust when they worked on getting Glenn ready for the Air Force audition. Glenn's Dad, always his ultimate supporter, drove Glenn to Washington D.C. where they spent the night in a sleazy hotel and drove to the Air Force Base in the morning. There he met Brian Bowman and played his audition. He soon found out that out of the sixty players who were auditioning, Glenn didn't even make the first cut. He was done for the day and it was maybe ten o'clock in the morning. Talk about a bubble bursting. Glenn had just came off of a successful college career, but what he realized at that moment, was that, in Ludington he had been a big fish in a little pond, at WMU he had been a big fish in a medium-sized pond, but he wasn't in the same league with the big fish in the big pond. He had to let that sink in for a while. But first, he and his dad took a quick tour of the nation's capital city, and at the foot of the Washington Monument Glenn offered, *'You know, I figured out what I want to be in life.'* Dad said, *'What?'* Glenn said, *'A tourist.'*

Up until that point Glenn wanted to think of himself as one of the best euphonium players compared to others. After the Air Force audition, he learned that he shouldn't judge himself against others. He should just be himself and do his absolute best. It didn't matter if there were a hundred – or two hundred other euphonium players better than him in the country. Good for them! He recalled Zig Ziglar's words, *'Comparison kills contentment'* and the Bible's words, 'The gift is acceptable according to what one has, not according to what he does not have.' He could live with himself. It was okay – and the older he got, the more comfortable he settled in with that perspective. He auditioned a few more times during his career, and one day he received a letter stating he had been chosen out of thousands to be hired at Busch Gardens. He was to play euphonium in a tuba quartet. His initial excitement faded as he realized he would be playing in a beer tent, and to top that off, his work week included Sundays. He declined the position.

Sometimes key people come together at a point in time and special things happen. When Glenn arrived at the southern Indiana hill-country, back-woods town of Bloomington, a few other Salvationist musicians were converging as well. Although the corps family was small and met in a tiny chapel, six or eight members were good musicians, a number of who attended Indiana University and who would later play in the Chicago Staff Band. Glenn was biting at the bit to write music for this group, and they became guinea pigs for his new compositions. First there was the Bloomington Brass Quartet, and soon it became Bloomington Brass, an octet. The group made a studio recording, played at Territorial Music Congress, and locally for open airs and at the corps for Sunday services and special events, like the performance of the national anthem at an Indiana University basketball game when Bob Knight coached the team. Glenn was commissioned as Bloomington's Bandmaster and his band members were also key players in the Indiana Divisional Band, led by Lt. Colonel Victor Danielson, former Chicago Staff Bandmaster. These were glory days for both the divisional band and corps band.

Glenn had the privilege of playing in some pretty good bands down through the years, usually as a ringer (substitute player). He performed with the Chicago Staff Band, National Capitol Band, Agincourt Temple Band, CMI Faculty Band, Wonderland Band, St. Louis Carondelet Band, Salvation Armt bands in Cleveland, Louisville, Dallas, and Grand Rapids, as well as a number of community bands. But the most memorable concert Glenn felt he had ever participated in was the Indiana Divisional Band Thanksgiving Festival of 1984. It was not the most perfectly played concert, although the band was in top form. But several things came together to make it uniquely special. The band was led by Lt. Colonel Victor Danielson and was made up of some wonderful bandsmen and friends, like Tom Howard on euphonium, Al Reasoner on Soprano, Carolyn DeWitt and Todd Herndon on Solo Cornet, Brian Swan on Bass, and Jessica Velazquez on Percussion. It was a tribute concert to Leslie Condon and Dean Goffin, both of whom had recently been Promoted to Glory – so the repertoire was tops. The band played '*Call of the Righteous*', '*The Crusaders*', '*O Boundless Salvation*', '*Compassionate Christ*', and '*Peace of Heart*'. Most importantly, God spoke. During the beautiful meditation '*Compassionate Christ*', Glenn was deeply moved, and then the realization hit him that although these composers were no longer walking the earth, God still spoke to hearts through them. They were still being used of God, witnessing to his love, and He could take what they had done while on earth, and continue multiplying it like the loaves and fishes after they were gone. Glenn felt an overwhelming desire in his heart to be used of God in like manner. Though he knew there would be other aspects to life, he now truly felt called to be a composer. He recognized the divine purpose. He could never be a Condon or a Goffin though, or a Heaton or a Ball. But he could be a Glenn Welch. He knew his limitations and his unique makeup – and found a different niche in writing.

Glenn became the Divisional Music Director for the Western Michigan Northern Indiana Division in January 1986, but there was a catch. He also had to agree to be the Service Extension Director, a public relations job that came with committee meetings, budgets, suits and wing-tip shoes. Up until this point, Glenn had been a long-haired, bearded, blue-jeaned, tennis-shoed musician. He had to transform his image, and even the simple change from all white socks to brown was traumatic. The salary for his new job came from the Service Extension budget and to get the positions, he faced two interviews. The Divisional Secretary interviewed him for the Music Position and this went well. Unfortunately, the Development Director who gave the Service Extension interview was also the Bandmaster of Grand Rapids Centennial Temple Corps, and that interview became all about music as well! No attention was given to the Service Extension side of things, and Glenn soon floundered. He could foresee the Army losing money and support with him in that position. After six months of growing guilt, he resigned.

He had managed to have success in his short stint as a DMD though, organizing a Youth Councils Pep Band, leading the Divisional Band and taking them to Territorial Congress and to Michigan City for concerts, conducting a Divisional Music Day, directing the Music Camp, and booking a hall and guest for an upcoming Thanksgiving Festival. He greatly disappointed some at the 'Headquarters' corps when he decided to attend a smaller corps in Grand Rapids. Though it wasn't in the print, he was hired with the assumption he would play in the Centennial Temple Band. The problem was, Temple had five pianists and a big band, and the Burton Heights Corps had zero music. Glenn, not an impressive pianist, none-the-less felt it was his duty to support Burton Heights. Although his Sundays belonged to Burton Heights, he did show great support to Temple by attending its Wednesday night rehearsals faithfully, played with the band, and sang with the songsters for their big events. Upon resigning his headquarters position, he moved back to Bloomington, Indiana.

Around this time he had a couple of job prospects from outside of Indiana. One was in Chicago, a Youth Band Leader at a good-sized corps, with the prospect of playing in the Chicago Staff Band. One would think this was very appealing, but a few things prevented Glenn from accepting. He thought it was more desirable to stay in Bloomington – he loved the area, and he was a Senior Bandmaster already. He didn't want to accept any job primarily for an unrelated benefit – that he could play in the CSB – and he knew deep down that this would be his primary motivation if he were to accept; it wouldn't be fair to his new boss. Thirdly, he was becoming so attached to the state of Indiana, he eventually concluded he would never live outside the Hoosier State unless he had a 'kick in the pants' from God to leave it. So he probably passed up an opportunity that would've changed the course of his life, all because he had the simple conviction that someone had to take care of Indiana.

At the annual Indiana Divisional Music Day in 1987, one title listed in the written program would draw no attention. It simply said, *'Torchbearers'* by Eric Ball. This was deceptive though, because Glenn had transformed the march into a swing piece, and after the first measure was played exactly as the original march was written, the drum set entered with a crash-boom-bang, and the little Bloomington band surprised the audience with the brand new swing version. Bill Himes happened to be the guest of the day and was making recorded comments for each group as they participated in the concert. His first reaction was a laugh; then an on-the-spot suggestion that Glenn might consider changing the name to something like Torch…swingers. He also suggested that Glenn rescore it for full band. Little did either of them know what would result from giving this devious little arrangement a longer life.

Glenn was more comfortable writing for small ensembles but did as Bill suggested and rescored and renamed his arrangement of Torchbearers. Eric Ball was still alive at the time and Bill Himes called him to get his feelings about Glenn turning *'Torchbearers'* into a swing piece, and he might have asked whether Ball would be open to Chicago actually publishing it. Ball raised no objection. Meanwhile, Norridge Citadel Band (Chicago) planned a trip to California and Bandmaster Peggy Thomas pulled out *'Torchswingers'* to rehearse for the trip.

Some members of the band became uptight and objected to the notion of performing the piece so it was shelved, and Bill Himes waited over a decade before including it in the American Festival Series (#28). In the meantime, somehow the sextet-plus-drums version wound up as the theme on someone's website without Glenn's knowledge. Thanks to a Chicago Staff Band tour of Australia in early 1990s which included performances of *'Torchswingers'*, people began to talk about it – both pro and con. Bandsmen around the Army world became curious when they heard that someone had 'desecrated' Eric Ball's music, and opinions began flying. Norridge Citadel Band performed and recorded it and Norridge took the piece on its British tour in 1999. Then after it was published in 2001, an Ontario Youth Band recorded it and many other bands have since performed it, including bands from Eric Ball's own England. *'Torchswingers'* became Glenn's signature arrangement. Many writers seemed cursed with the 'one-hit wonder' label, but Glenn appreciated that his music was at least getting used. When Glenn first met composer Jim Anderson, he introduced himself by saying, *'Hello, Goldcrest, I'm Torchswingers.'*

Glenn continued writing for his Bloomington group during the late 1980's and completed sixty 4-part brass accompaniments to Sunday School choruses, with some contemporary praise and worship choruses thrown into the mix. He would start by writing a short introduction, then present the tune and sometimes add a tag at the end. At CMI he mentioned to Bill Himes what he was doing and later on Bill got back with him and encouraged him to expand on the idea, develop the arrangements more and send him some charts. Glenn never got around to it, feeling his purpose in writing the music worked fine as the simple one-time-through tunes that they were. He didn't catch Bill's vision, but Bill had something on his mind and he and Peggy Thomas ultimately came up with the 'Hallelujah Choruses' series, now 200 arrangements strong. Glenn always wondered if he might have contributed the germ that got the process started, or was at least one of the momentum-builders. Glenn was approached again, once the Hallelujah Choruses series was all planned out. This time he submitted an arrangement but it wasn't accepted. Then years went by – and Glenn was approached a third time. Third time's a charm. Glenn arranged two choruses for Chicago in 1998 and these were published – Glenn's first published pieces of music, even before *'Torchswingers'*. These were *'Fan the Flame'* and *'I'm Gonna Praise the Lord'*. Both were successful, and *'Fan the Flame'* was used at Atlanta's Millennium Congress in 2000.

He continued writing one or two Hallelujah Choruses annually for the next dozen years – the longest continuous stint of any writer for the series outside of Himes himself. By 2010 Glenn had 17 pieces published by The Salvation Army – *'Torchswingers'* and sixteen *'Hallelujah Choruses'*. Some commented that various Welch concoctions were their favorite *'Hallelujah Choruses'* arrangements. His arrangement of Donna Peterson's *'Blessed Assurance'* was a big hit, and other popular Welch titles were *'Cry of My Heart'*, *'Shine on Us'*, *'How Great is Our God'*, *'Sing for Joy'*, *'Open the Eyes of My Heart'*, *'Every Move I Make'*, and *'Take My Life'*, *'I am Yours'*. It seemed Glenn had found his groove. After a few years in, Bill told Glenn that some of the bigger name composers didn't have a knack for writing in that format, but that Glenn was good at it. At last, after over twenty years of struggling at the piano with pencil in hand, Glenn received affirmation – by Bill Himes himself – that he could indeed write, and more importantly, God could use his music to reach people throughout the world. This brought Glenn a great sense of fulfillment.

Having grown up in the American Midwest, Glenn felt blessed to have had the opportunity to become a lifelong friend of Bill Himes. Many stories could be told of Bill's support and encouragement through the years. Over twenty years ago, the busy Territorial Music Secretary spent the better part of one day with Glenn, the two taking the subway in Chicago to Fischer Publishing, checking out music, lunching, and preparing Glenn for his upcoming responsibilities as a faculty member at CMI. After Glenn's dad had died, Bill was on the phone with Glenn, not making a rush call out of a sense of duty, but taking the time to be there for him, almost like an older brother. When Bill was having a difficult time At CMI because of his wife Wendy's failing health, the faculty had a prayer time and offered their support. Glenn, not really a hugger, none-the-less felt that Bill needed one, so brother to brother he shared in Bill's grief in this way.

Once, when Glenn was thinking about the fact that he and Bill hadn't talked on the phone for a long time, he considered how busy Bill was, how many people must demand his time, and what a vast responsibility was his – Glenn knew Bill had to be strategic with his time. Then he thought back and realized that it was during Glenn's most difficult days that he would get the call. Bill would take whatever time was needed, to connect with Glenn, offer guidance and keep him going. These phone calls weren't part of the job description, but they revealed the concern and the wisdom of a great man. And Glenn felt that every time Bill published one of Glenn's charts, more than anyone else had, Bill Himes had given him a sense of dignity.

Glenn received second place in the USA Central Territory's 2011 composition contest for a songster arrangement called *'Under the Blood'*, the first time he'd placed in a composition contest after six tries. He appeared as a euphonium soloist across twelve states and performed the twenty-minute Brahms Cello Sonata on euphonium at the 2003 International Tuba Euphonium Association Regional Conference at Ball State University. He has been a member of the semi-professional Kokomo Park Band for eleven years and has been featured as the band's soloist six times. In addition to writing 520 songs, he's written over 100 short works for brass, 25 for piano, and four children's musicals. He's received a number of commissions to compose. Most notably, he wrote a trumpet solo for Broadway (and Salvationist) trumpeter Chris Jaudes. He has been a guest conductor at music camps in eight divisions. Three times he was honored to be a delegate at The Salvation Army North American Composers Forum, in 2002, 2003, and 2006. He also authored articles published in The 'War Cry' (USA), Young Salvationist, The Officer, Central Connection, Priority!, and the ITEA Journal. Glenn and his family live on 2 ½ acres on the outskirts of town where he continues to compose, work on the property, and enjoy the wonderful life God has blessed him with.

Important composition

Torchswingers (ABJ28) 2001

WELCH, J

One of the early composers (first half of 19th century).

No further information could be retrieved about him.

Important composition

The Westgate March (GS0926) 1924

WELLS, DAVID GEORGE

Born on 29 September 1942 in Balham, London, United Kingdom, where his parents were Salvation Army officers. They moved around England in different appointments then when David's father was Corps Officer of the Regent Hall Corps in London, he learned to play the cornet in the Junior band. When he was eleven years old they moved to Edinburgh in Scotland and then to Paisley where he became the Young People's Bandleader. David tried to write a bit of music then but not very sucessfully. When his parents moved back to Territorial Headquarters in London they went to Croydon Citadel Corps where he played in the Bass section and met his wife-to-be; Kathryn Goffin, eldest daughter of Dean Goffin. Dean gave David some helpful advice when he wrote some pieces for the Trumph Series and he had one or two of them played at the Tylney Hall Music School, so David could hear them. After David and Kathryn's marriage, they went to Zambia and then came to New Zealand for officer training. They went back to Zambia as officers and David wrote one or two more pieces while at Chikankata Salvation Army mission. While there he developed a strong interest in indigenous Zambian music and through the school choir was able to introduce genuine local music into the Salvation Army songbook. They resigned from officership in 1983 and settled in New Zealand where they were ministers in the Baptist Church and then David taught at an Apostolic Bible College. Now he is back working for the Salvation Army. They attend a local Christian Church of New Zealand congregation but have been senior tutor at the officer training college Booth College of Mission in Upper Hutt in Wellington for the past twelve years teaching Bible, preaching, etc. David Wells is also the conductor of a community brass band called Kapiti Brass.

Important compositions

Answered Prayer (TS0677) 1966, Armour of God (GS1738) 1981, Buckland (TS0699-1) 1968, Caribbean Congress (TS0776) 1974

WELLS, JOHN F.

Born in Bedford, United Kingdom in 1903, John Wells entered the Salvation Army International Training College from Bedford and was commissioned as an officer in 1923. He served for two years a Corps Officer before being transferred in 1925 to China for missionary work. These first years were colourful, and included a period of teaching and preaching on the gospel boat which plied up and down Chinese rivers. Later he was constantly on a bicycle, riding narrow wheelbarrow-paths to visit outlying village corps. On November 12, 1931, John married Captain Grace Hoddinott in Peking. She was also a missionary in China, and came from Victoria, British Columbia in Canada.

In 1948 they returned to Canada and became corps officers of Danforth Citadel and Earslcourt Citadel in Toronto. Two years as men's side officer in the Toronto training college followed before they were appointed to New Zealand as Training Principal and more than six years were spent in this country. In 1964 they returned again to Canada and became Training Principal in Toronto.

In 1926 young Lieutenant John Wells submitted his first composition to the International Music Board for publication in 'The Musical Salvationist', and the editor's footnote read '*A very praiseworthy initial effort in song writing*'. Since that time numerous –mainly- songs, have been written by him.

Lt. Colonel John Wells was Promoted to Glory on 7 October 1978.

Important compositions

Advance (CM0005) 1955, The Seeking Saviour (CM0014) 1955

WERRY, R.S

One of the early composers (late 1800).

No further information could be retrieved about him.

Important composition

Oh, I'll Take Another Look (GS0105) 1889

WHITEHOUSE, GAVIN

Gavin (October 26, 1976) is actually from Sydney in Australia but his wife and he have lived in New York since July 2005. His parents are Salvation Army officers and so he moved around a lot as a child. After high school he studied music education at the Sydney Conservatorium of Music. His main instrument was piano but he also did a lot of singing as well. During Gavin's first year at the conservatorium he was at the Gosford Salvation Army Corps just north of Sydney. The next year his family moved to Blacktown Corps in western Sydney. This became his home corps from 1996 - 2005. In 1997 Gavin became the songster leader at the corps and played bass trombone in the band, apart from a brief time on 1st trombone.

Gavin also for some time was the leader of the corps contemporary worship team. In 1997 he also joined the Sydney Staff Songsters and was in the group until moving to the United States of America, and was deputy songster leader for the last 6 months of that time. He moved to the US and took up the position of Assistant Music Ddirector (piano and vocal) in the Greater New York in July 2005. One of his first responsibilities was to form the Greater New York youth chorus.

He also plays bass trombone in the Greater New York youth band, lead by New York Staff Band principal cornetist Gordon Ward. Gavin is also currently the pianist for the Eastern Territorial Songsters. He has been composing since he was in high school. He enjoys writing band and vocal music. His first published composition was in 2006 in Psalms Hymns and Spiritual Songs which was soon followed by a band piece *'Forever you will be'* in the American Band Journal. He has been married to Jennifer since 2002 and they attend the Times Square corps where he is the corps cadets counsellor, running a youth music program and lead worship on Sunday's.

Important composition

Open Our Eyes (ABJ268) 2009

WHITEHOUSE, ALLAN STANLEY

Born in Alexandria, Sydney in February 1905 and married to Ruby Lillian Whitlock on June 18th 1927. Lillian passed away in January 1952. They had three children; Raymond Allan, (who was Promoted to Glory in July 1983), Allaine Lillian and John David. His father John Whitehouse was a Master Builder and his mother, a German by birth was Maria Beneke. Allan was the youngest child of the family and had an older brother, John and a sister, Grace. He was still quite young when his mother passed away and his sister filled the role of 'mother'. He became apprenticed to his father on leaving school but unlike his brother John did not take to the building trade so gave this up and for a time looked for work that was meaningful and satisfying. He studied accountancy at night time and at the time of his death was a member of the executive staff of Clifford Love where he worked as Grain Buyer and Payroll Manager.

Allan was self taught, and his only formal training was the Bandmaster's course provided by International Headquarters. He began arranging at a young age. His daughter Allaine remembers pupils for both brass and the piano coming to the house for lessons. His wife came from a very musical family and she was a great encouragement to him, making sure that he had quietness to compose and arrange and that he attended practises and engagements even when she was quite ill and really needed his help at home and with the family. Music was his recreation and his solace during his wife's long illness and subsequent death. Allan's four brothers-in-law formed a Male quartet and for some time had a weekly radio broadcast on a Sydney radio station and Allan did the arranging for them and provided the piano accompaniments as and when required.

In 1934 he became Bandmaster at Rockdale Corps, Brother John was Bandmaster of the Campsie Corps Band (following a short term as Bandmaster at Hurstville Corps) and Father John was Bandmaster at Waterloo Corps. Both his father and his older brother were his mentors. Upon transferring to Sydney Congress Hall, he became Songster Leader and held this position for quite a long time. He played Eb Bass and Baritone in the Sydney Congress Hall Band but didn't claim to be any more than an average player and whilst he sang in tune did not claim to be a singer either.

Commissioner Allistair Cairns recalls Allan as a born leader, an humble and self effacing man, but one who fiercely stood up for what today would be called '*the Songster's rights*'. The Commissioner recalled that during his term as Corps Officer of Sydney Congress Hall Corps three momentous events occurred in which Allan was involved. The Sydney Congress Hall Band undertook its first overseas tour to New Zealand in 1952, the Songster Brigade undertook its first inter territorial visit to Box Hill Corps in Melbourne and in conjunction with Songster Leader (later Major) Elwyn Sandercock (whom Allan had mentored) the combined Songster Brigades of Sydney Congress Hall and Rockdale presented the first ever performance by a Salvation Army Songster Brigade in Australia Eastern Territory (and probably of Australia as a whole) of Handel's *'Messiah'* – Allan's son Ray being the Bass soloist, and the Commissioner with some pride said *'and I sang in The Messiah!'*

Whilst he composed for bands, Allan's real love was vocal music and he arranged and composed for Male Voices and soloists alike and there are still copies of unpublished work around. In the later years of his life he joined forces with the late Major John Irwin OF in Prison Ministry and together with his second wife, Mary and the late Major Reg Turnbull and, on occasion, his younger son John, he organised music support for Chapel services in various penal institutions in Sydney and surrounds. Allan Stanley Whitehouse was Promoted to Glory in Brighton-Le-Sands in Sydney in April 1961.

Important compositions

My Desire (GS1459-1), 1958, Security (TS0333) 1942, Tidings of Joy (GS1192) 1941

WHITEHOUSE, JOHN

There were two unrelated Whitehouse families in Campsie corps in the 1920s. Charlie Whitehouse, Recruiting Sergeant in 1929 was not related to John Whitehouse, who was Bandmaster from late 1926 to at least 1931. Just to confuse the issue because they both had sons called Stan Whitehouse! Bandmaster John Whitehouse composed the *'Campsie Citadel'* march especially for the opening of the grand, new Campsie Citadel Corps building in 1929. Campsie Corps grew dramatically in the 1920s and the small citadel built in 1913 was quite inadequate.

An undated obituary for *'Brother John Whitehouse'* describes him as *'A leading Sydney Salvationist musician'*. It also says *'at the age of seventeen he succeeded his father as bandmaster of Waterloo Corps. Later John was Bandmaster at Newtown, Newcastle, Hurstville and Campsie'*. As well as composing music, Bandmaster John Whitehouse was also a frequent contributor to the 'Local Officer and Bandsman' magazine published by the Salvation Army. Bandmaster John Whitehouse had a brother Allan in the Sydney Congress Hall corps who was also a noted musician and composer in that era. He was married to Amie Jarret, a well known name in Campsie Corps.

The obituary of John does state that *'Allan Whitehouse of Sydney Congress Hall is a brother to the departed comrade'* and that 'Bandsman Stan Whitehouse, cornet soloist of Dulwich Hill Band is a son'. The 1926 Souvenir issued to commemorate the 13th anniversary of Campsie Silver Band as they called themselves in those days says that Deputy Bandmaster John Whitehouse had been a bandmaster for 14 years. Now if he was first bandmaster at 17 years of age, that would give a birth date of 1895. The Souvenir says *'One of the latest marches the band has been rendering (Joyful Echoes) is one of his composition. He is also a good pianist, and renders valuable assistance in this direction. Plays 1st Baritone in the band'*

When a new officer had come in at Camspie Corps during John's tenure as Bandmaster, he decommissioned existing leaders and appointed others. John Whitehouse and his son (also called John but everyone called him by his second name, Stan) went over to play in an 'elite' Savation Army band under the leadership of Harry Berry. John didn't really do much banding after leaving Campsie until his death on a relatively young age. With Bandmaster John Whitehouse at Campsie, brother Allan Whitehouse at Sydney Congress Hall and their father, also called John as long time bandmaster at Waterloo corps, they were certainly a musical family.

Important compositions

Campsie Citadel (GS1048) 1932, True to the colours (GS1161) 1939

WIDMER, WERNER

Werner Widmer is the son of Salvation Army Officers. He started his music career in the Young People's Band at Zurich Central, where his parents were the Corps Officers. Later when they transfered to Basel as Divisional Commanders, Werner became a bandsman of the Basel 1 Band. During that time he served in the Music Department in Bern as the National Bands Secretary for Switzerland and as Bandmaster of the National Band of Switzerland 'Brass of Praise'. He studied music at the 'Konservatorium' in Bern. His compositions were published by the Norwegian Music Department of the Salvation Army. Many of his compositions are played as manuscripts by Corps Bands of the Salvation Army in Switzerland.

Wener was born in 1953. His parents were Salvation Army officers. He was a member of the Basel 1 Corps Band from 1969 until 1990. He studied music theory at the Conservatory of Berne (1974-1978) and was working part time as Territorial Music Secretary at Territorial Headquarter from 1978 until 1985. In 1974 they founded the National Band 'Brass of Praise', which he conducted from 1980 to 1985. Werner wrote some lyrics for songs, composed some songs and music for Brass Band.

From 1980 to 1984 he studied ecomomics at the University of Basel, followed by further studies as assistant and a Doctorate in management (1989). His professional career continued in the health care system. Among other jobs he was director of the university hospital Zürich. Since 2002 he is the CEO of a foundation with homes for elderly people and a hospital at Zollikerberg/Zürich.

Important composition

This Is Why I Love Jesus (NM0039) 1982

WIGGINS. (first name not known)

One of the early composers (late 1800).

No further information could be retrieved about him.

Important composition

Swing Those Gates Ajar (GS0107) 1889

WIGGINS, ARCHIBALD RAYMOND

Although not a brass composer as such, because he was more a vocal composer, Archibald Raymond Wiggins is of huge significance to anyone interested in the history of Salvation Army bands and banding as he is the author of some important books.

Born in 1893 in Kensal Green, Middlesex in the United Kingdom. Archi, as he was effectionately known, attended a Church of England Sunday-school and later became a Salvationist at Harlesden where he was a member of the Harlesden Songsters, which were formed in 1911. In 1914 he entered the Training College located at Clapton. After various appointments as a Salvation Army officer, he joined the editorial department in 1922 and was serving as editor for amongst others, 'The Bandsman and Songster' and 'The Musician'. For some time he was a member of the International Staff Band and moved in 1947 to Australia as Editor-in-Chief to return some four years later. In 1957 he became the Personal Literary Secretary to the General. Archi Wiggins retired as a commissioner in 1959. He wrote over 250 songs and contributed for more than half a century to 'The Musical Salvationist'. He was the author of volumes four and five of The History of the Salvation Army and wrote biographies of Richard Slater 'Father of Salvation Army Music' in 1945, and of Bandmaster George Marshall 'Triumph of Faith' in 1958. He died on 20 November 1976 in Christchurch, Dorset, United Kingdom.

WILBY, PHILIP

Philip Wilby is born in 1949 and became a violinist by profession. He is not a Salvation Army composers, nor is he a Salvationist. However besides his grant output as a composer for various instrumentations, including those for brass bands, are many pieces with a spiritual character, like his '*Revelation, Psalms and Alleluias*' and '*The new Jerusalem*' just to name but three pieces. It was when he wrote his gorgeous piece '*Wondrous Cross*' that also

Salvation Army bands started to use his music. Philip is a much recorded composer and was '*Composer in Residence*' with the world famous Black Dyke Band. '*Wondrous Cross*' was recently (2011) recorded by the Enfield Citadel Band.

Important compositions

Wondrous Cross, Revelation, Red Priest, Paganini Variations, Flight

WILKINSON, A

One of the early composers (first half of 19th century). It is believed that the composer was a member of the Nelson Corps Band although this could not be confirmed. No further information could be retrieved about him.

Important composition

The Nelson March (GS0763) 1917

WILKINSON (DR) KEITH M.

Already in 1965 a young Keith took his first appointment, as Deputy Songster Leader at Great Horton (Bradford Salvation Army Corps). He was still in High School when he took this appointment and this lasted until 1969. In between -1966- he became 'top student' at Territorial Music School, run by the Salvation Army. The first few years of the seventies, Keith was bandmaster of the Ashton-Under-Lyne Citadel Band and at the same time a post-graduate student at the University of Manchester. When leaving Ashton-Under-Lyne he became bandmaster of the Derby Central Corps Band with whom he also recorded a LP. His bandmastership here was until 1976 when he became the Musical Director of the Teversal Colliery Band after which he became Assistant Musical Director of the famous GUS Band with full responsibility as Musical Director in 1978. With the GUS Band he recorded ten commercial recordings. This lasted until 1985 when he went on to the William Davis Construction Group Band as Musical Director. With this band he did several overseas tours, as well as six commercial recordings.

During this time, from 1976-1995 he was a Salvationist at Stapleford Citadel where he sang in the songsters and played in the band. Here he was also the (acting) bandmaster for some time. In 1996 Keith and his family moved to the United States of America to become the Divisional Music Director of the Northeast Ohio Division of The Salvation Army, as well as becoming bandmaster of the Cleveland Temple Band, when in 2000 he changed this function and became the Army's Music Coordinator. He founded the Central Ohio Youth Band and became their bandmaster. In his spare time Keith was also Musical Director of the Brass Band of the Western Reserve which he still conducts as today. With this band he recorded seven CD recordings, which included numerous Salvation Army compositions. During the period 2000-2002 he was principal guest conductor of the St. Louis Brass Band and next to his already impressive list he became Musical Director of the Chapel Brass, which he still conducts today. Furthermore, within the Salvation Army he became the bandmaster of the Chapel At Worthington Woods Corps Band in 2002, which he also still conducts. Keith Wilkinson is a valued arranger since 1972 of brass band music and has nearly hundred published titles with publishers in the United Kingdom, United States of America and Switzerland. He has formed his own publishing company 'Alum Creek Music' in order to make his arrangements available more quickly.

In 2008, Keith was presented the God And Country Music Award by The Salvation Army and Brass Band of Columbus for 'his outstanding contributions to brass banding in USA, Britain and Europe'.

Important compositions

March from First Suite in Eb (Holst), Winter (from Vivaldi) – Allegro non molto, largo and allegro

WILLERING, ALFRED

Alfred Willering started with music at an early age. His father was a bass player and organplayer and received his first organ tuition from him. While still at a young age he was taught at the music school at Hardenberg in the Netherlands, first on organ, later on flugelhorn. Having played the flugelhorn for several years he moved onwards to euphonium and eventually ended on bass tuba. While only eighteen years of age, Alfred became conductor of the youth orchestra 'De Eendracht' in Hardenberg. This experiences made him decide to follow an education to become a full time musician. He then followed a study at the ArtEZ Conservatory in Zwolle, in the east of Holland where he studied basstuba and conducting. He graduated in 2001. Willering is currently basstuba player for militairy band '*Garde Grenadiers en Jagers*'. Next to this he conducts several amateur orchestras as well as being the organ player at the Reformed Church in Hardenberg. His free time is mainly devoted for compositions for windband and brass band.

At the request of Salvationist –and at that time Amsterdam Staff Bandmaster Thijs Musch- Alfred composed a few significant works for the Amsterdam Staff Band, whereas the major piece 'In Primus' even was the title track of the bands 2007 recording.

Important compositions

In Primis (m/s), Onward (m/s)

WILLIAMS, (first name not known)

One of the early composers (late 1800).

No further information could be retrieved about him.

Important compositions

What Will You Say to Jesus? (GS0135) 1890

WILLSON, MEREDITH ROBERT

Robert Meredith Willson (May 18, 1902 – June 15, 1984) was an American composer, songwriter, conductor and playwright best known for writing the book, music and lyrics for the hit Broadway musical *The Music Man*, which won the Tony Award for Best Musical in 1958. Meredith was no Salvationist nor even a member or visitor of the organization. He was however an admirer of the Salvation Army and its music. He honored The Salvation Army therefore with a musical tribute entitled 'Banners and Bonnets'.

Important composition

Banners and Bonnets (GS1546) 1965

WOOD, DAVID

David was born in Leeds, West Yorkshire in 1947 and was educated at the Leeds Modern Grammar School for Boys. When eight years of age he started playing the cornet at Leeds Burley Corps. He enlisted as a bandsman in 1964 into the Kings Own Yorkshire Light Infantry playing euphonium. During his military service he played euphonium, oboe, and French horn. Later, David attended the Royal Military School of Music in 1969/70 where he was awarded the Worshipful Company of Musicians 'Cassel' Prize for the best musician of the year (Awarded Annually to students at the Royal Marines School of Music (RM), the Royal Military School of Music (RMSM) and the Royal Air Force Music Services (RAF)) and later after attending the Student Bandmasters course (again at RMSM 1975-78) he was appointed as Bandmaster to the 1st Battalion The Royal Hampshire Regiment. After Military service he joined his brother James and opened and ran music shops in Ripon and Harrogate for 17 years. David served as Young People's Bandleader at Leeds Central from 1993 until 1998. Incidentally his eldest brother (of three) is Lieutenant Colonel Peter Wood who prior to retirement was Executive Officer with the International Staff Band.

Important composition

Leeds Central Young People (US0190) 1995

WOOD, T

One of the early composers (late 1800).

No further information could be retrieved about him.

Important composition

The Happy Land (GS0402) 1900

WOODLAND, CRAIG

Craig is currently the principal cornet with the world renowned London Citadel Band (Canada). He studied Music at The University of Western OntarioLives in London, Ontario. He origins from Mount Pearl, Newfoundland and Labrador and was born on July 5, 1975 Craig grew up in the Salvation Army and attended the St. John's Citadel Corps (New Foundland). He is a member of the band and songsters and served as songster leader and deputy bandmaster. He received much of his early musical training in the Salvation Army band and choral programs. Craig completed Bachelor degree programs in Music Performance (Trumpet) and Music Education at Memorial University of Newfoundland. He moved to London, Ontario in 1998 to complete a Master's degree in Music Performance at the University of Western Ontario and currently teaches instrumental and vocal music in the London public school system and plays trumpet professionally with orchestras and other professional ensembles in Southern Ontario. Craig has served as director for Young People music groups at the corps bandmaster for the former Ontario West Divisional Youth Band and frequently serves on faculty or as guest conductor for Salvation Army music camps

Important compositions

Don't Doubt Him Now (GS2034) 2005

WOODS, GEORGE HENRY

Born in Millfield, Sunderland in 1904, out of Salvationist parents, George Henry was better known as Harry, a name which he used throughout his life. It was obviously that he soon would join the banding fraternity of the Salvation Army. After showing interest in music, he was taught by the Reverend R. Witty, a local vicar, on the organ. When the First World War broke out, this tuition was ended. However before they parted company, the vicar gave Harry some homework, which was to practice *'God save the King'*. On the vicar's return from active service, Harry was able to play this tune in every key possible. A career at an organ builders company was soon ended after he had to pump the bellows at a concert which made him instantly deaf for a fortnight.

When still a teenager he composed his first piece of music, and got it published by the Salvation Army. Over the years nine brass band compositions where published by the Army, but also over a dozen choral works. During this time as a teenager he was commissioned as bandmaster of the Sunderland Millfield Band but had to move to the south of England during the depression. He returned to the Sunderland area and worked for the rest of his life in the shipbuilding industry. In the late 1920's he was asked to be the new Songster Leader of the Sunderland Millfield Songsters, a position he held for twenty five years.

During WWII, shipyard workers were necessary at home for building ships. Harry found time during these years to teach youngsters and so form a Young People's Band. During this time he continued to lead the corps songsters as well as playing principal cornet for the Sunderland Millfield Band. After the war he decided to qualify in music and tried to obtain a B.B.C.M (British Bandsman College of Music). He failed the first time as he left for the practical side of the exam, his cornet in the train to the exam. The second time was more successful as he asked his son to join him on the train, so that of he would fall in sleep, he could be awaked by his son. 1953 saw the request again to lead the Sunderland Millfield Band as bandmaster. He hesitated, but within seven years had the band in top form in such a way that they performed in the Royal Albert Hall in London. After fifteen years in the role as bandmaster he resigned from this position but this was only for a short while, as soon after he was asked to become Divisional Bandmaster for the Northern Division of the Salvation Army. In 1976, at the age of seventy two, George Henry (Harry) Woods, was Promoted to Glory. A man of rare musical ability, in teaching as well as in playing (cornet, piano, organ).

Important compositions

Horsham (TS0348) 1943, The Hylton March (GS0914) 1923, Mercy's Call (TS0049) 1924, Millfield (TS0392) 1946, Newcastle City Temple (GS1434) 1956

WORTHINGTON, TREVOR

Trevor (29 September 1929) was brought up in a home with a strong love of music, his parents were Salvationists and his father was Deputy Bandmaster of the Hinckley Temple Band. Hinckley is a small town in England in the Midlands and the Corps had very strong music sections. Trevor's father taught him to play the cornet and he started to have piano lessons at age nine. There were twelve young boys in the Corps band and they formed into a group called the 'Singspirators'. They soon started to receive invitations to take part in away weekends. That is when Trevor started to write music, as the leader of the group said they needed some original music for the group to play. So he wrote his first piece, a march called *'Hinckley Temple'* at the age of fifteen. Not even knowing how to write music correctly, but that was his beginning. Then he decided he needed some lessons in composition and took a correspondence course in Harmony and Counterpoint with a well known brass band professional. At age eighteen Trevor recieved some very valuable tuition and experience playing in a Military Band as he did his National Conscription Service. After that he applied for a part-time course at the Birmingham Conservatoire and he was still writing songs and band music constantly, several of which have been published by The Salvation Army.

He has also been heavily involved in Salvation Army Music Camps and has always been inspired to write music for these. Most of his life has been spent in leadership of bands and choirs which again has inspired him to write music for them. He has also spent some years teaching music in Senior Schools and again has always been inspired to write something special for the students. The latter part of his work life was spent in the USA as Director of Music and Youth at the Sacramento Corps and again was inspired to write music for the Groups there. Trevor has had the honour of having one of his songs chosen by the famous Kings Singers to be used in their latest album 'The Quiet Heart' which was called *'Sweet Hour Of Prayer'*. At age 82 he is still writing and still getting excited when he find different harmonies and phrases and hearing good music. Some music titles he has written included *'It's a great day', 'Christmas Collage', 'A robe of white', 'Daniel', Cornet Trio '3 Images', 'In the bleak mid-winter', 'Cantilena'* and *'Scherzo'*.

Important compositions

For I'm Building a People of Power (US0335) 2007, In the Cross (US0357) 2009, It's a Great Day! (US0220) 1997 King of Kings, Majesty (US0342) 2008

WRIEDEN, WILLIAM

Was a soprano player and solo cornet player in the New York Staff Band during the period of the late 1930s through the early 1940s. He was featured at least one time as a soprano cornet soloist, but in the main was included as part of cornet trios (along with other players such as Fred Farrar and William Parkins) during the time he played solo cornet.

He wrote and arranged items for the band, as well during the time that he was in the band, particularly marches. He left the New York Staff Band in the early 1940s to play in a band organized by Erik Leidzén in New York City during World War II called the 'Arma' band. Apparently this was not uncommon during that time in the band's history as he was not the only player to do this, but occasionally still 'guested' with the band as needed for a time during the war years.

'The Musician', 1942:

'William Wierden was born in Yonkers, New York, U.S.A., in 1911 to a Salvationist mother. At twelve years of age he was placed in the Young People's Band by the Corps Officer who constantly encouraged him to study and practice faithfully. From his early day he had as his goal the Eastern Territorial Staff Band. As a Junior Soldier and later in the Senior Corps he rendered service in Yonkers, Pittsburgh, Pennsylvania and New York Bands. Upon leaving school he went to the New York Telephone Company, where he was employed a draftsman. Seven years ago, when opportunity for employment in The Salvation Army became possible. He accepted the offer with a view to attaining his goal membership of the Eastern Territorial Staff Band. For six years now he has been playing in the Band and is at present on soprano cornet. For the past seven years he has been studying with Professor Erik W. Leidzén, to whom he is greatly indebted. He is also attending New York University from which he hopes to obtain a degree in music. Staff-Bandsman Wrieden last summer instructed in harmony at The Salvation Army Star Lake Music Camp. His wife, Isabelle, is the daughter of Bandmaster James Ryans, of Schenectady, New York,

formerly cornet soloist of Govan Band, Scotland. A sister, Major Jane Wrieden, is Social Welfare Secretary of Buffalo, New York, Divisional Headquarters'.

Important composition

Onward America

WRIGHT, JAMES

James was born in Lincoln on 2 august 1948 and attended Lincoln Citadel. He learnt to play a brass instrument (euphonium) in the Young People's Band and was Singing Company Leader. Although he attended a few piano lessons he mainly developed his own skills as a pianist with the advantage of being able to play by ear as well as with music. He was Singing Company pianist, songster pianist and corps pianist, both at Lincoln and later at Sheffield Citadel. He entered the Training College for officers and was the sessional pianist for the Evangelists Session. He transferred to Sheffield Citadel in 1973 and played trombone and bass in the senior band and held the position of Young People's Sergeant Major, Deputy Bandmaster and then Bandmaster of the Sheffield Citadel Band and was also the leader of the South Yorkshire Divisional Youth Band. James never attended music college or gained any degrees in music but he was always willing to learn and listen to improve his musical skills. It was when he met George Thomson, a well known conducter in the brass band world, that he started to seriously consider arranging and composing brass band music and James' attributes to George the encouragement and knowledge he needed at that time. He always wanted people to enjoy playing his music whether it be in a small band or larger band. When he heard the International Staff Band playing his *'Fantasia for Children'* at Doncaster Citadel, he was thrilled. He wanted his music to bless and challenge its listeners. He had a wonderful sense of humour and many bands and congregation collapse into fits of laughter as he would observe and see the humorous side of situations. James Wright didn't often play many of his own pieces when he was bandmaster so it was good that the Salvation Army published quite a number of his arrangements. Sadly he was Promoted to Glory on 1st June 2006, but he left a legacy of brass band music and the influence and encouragement he gave to those around him.

Important compositions

Fantasia for Children (GS1834) 1989, It is Jesus (TS995) 1992

WRIGHT, G

One of the early composers (first half of 19th century).

No further information could be retrieved about him.

Important composition

Freedom (TS0148) 1930

WRIGHT, W.H

One of the early composers (first half of 19th century).

No further information could be retrieved about him.

Important compositions

Courageous (TS0032) 1923, Mersey (TS0043) 1924

YOUNG, ARTHUR

Arthur Young was a composer from Christchurch in New Zealand and for a time it's bandmaster. He won third prize in the 1905 composition competition. Sometimes referred to as 'J. Young', it is the same person.

Arthur Young won third prize in the 1905 IMED competition with 'The Christchurch March' and was Bandmaster of Christchurch Citadel Band at the turn of last century. Henry Goffin, a subsequent prizewinner emigrated to NZ in 1913. Harold Scotney also immigrated to New Zealand about this time.

Both Goffin and Scotney appeared in other journals. Scotney initially appeared in the Australian Band Journal published in Melbourne. Goffin, never one for kow-towing to authority, created the New Zealand Band Brass Band Journal in the 1920s. It is significant that Arthur Young does not appear in any of these: he is a one piece wonder. That is not to say he did not compose other music: it is highly likely that he did. George Jackson started the initial New Zealand Band Journal and was still working on it at his death in 1893. The only part book that was found of this journal was from the Oamaru Corps, a 2nd Baritone part book. It was not until after the Second World War that New Zealand bands fully complied with using only Salvation Army published music. Wellington City had Scotney and Goffin writing music for them, a tradition carried on by Dean Goffin at Wellington South, Arthur Millard in Dunedin, Tom Rive at Auckland Congress Hall and Herbert Rive and various others who contributed to the old Black Books of the New Zealand Band Journal (also filled with one piece wonders).

Arthur Young's output is verified by only one competition piece and was the first New Zealander to have success in the international journal forum. Arthur Young's bandmastering career would seem to have overlapped the pioneering careers of George Jackson and the wave of immigration with Scotney and Harry Goffin. That Arthur Young's name appears nowhere else suggests he was either a minor composer (unlikely given the paucity of Salvation Army published music available in New Zealand at that time because of its expense) or that his creative period was nearing its end when he finally had a piece published and so he missed Goffin's New Zealand Brass Band Journal.

Important compositions

The Christchurch March (GS0507) 1905, The Wearside March (GS0628) 1910

YOUNG, HERBERT

Songster Leader of the Portland Citadel Songsters, Herbert Young, was a well known composer for his useful contributions to the vocal repertoire of Salvation Army music, made his first appearance in the band journals of the Army with *'Without One Plea'*.

Important compositions

Without One Plea (TS0654) 1964

YOUNG, TERENCE

One of the early composers (late 1800, early 1900). Research could not clarify whether or not this person is the same as the earlier mentioned Arthur Young of Australia although some says it is the same person. No records were kept to find the truth about this.

Important compositions

Army Heroes (GS0822) 1919, The Commonwealth (GS0728) 1915, Second (GS0535) 1907

ZEALLEY, HAROLD

Salvation Army officer (amongst other occupations, he was a Divisional Commander) who, while stationed in the USA was active in the musical scene of the Salvation Army and a member of the New York Staff Band, especially when serving as Divisional Commander in Southwest Ohio Northeast Kentucky—called SWONEKY, which is also the name of one of his marches, a prize-winner in the 1948 contest. While only a handful of his works survive, he made as great an impact as a conductor and an encourager of various Salvation Army bands that he led.

Important compositions

Meditation - O Boundless Salvation (ABJ1-1) 1948, March – SWONEKY (ABJ1-5) 1948, Selection - Songs of Testimony (ABJ1-9) 1948, March - New Jersey (ABJ1-11) 1948

ZHURAVLYOV, SERGEI

When the Salvation Army opened fire in Russia, soon after the first musical forces were inaugerated and it didn't take a long time before the first Salvation Army composer from Russia announced his first piece of music. When Russian musical groups were invited as special guests as the Music Councils in the United Kingdom, a cassette tape *'From Russia with Love'* was produced containing the music of Sergei Shuravlyov (25 April, 1971). Sergei is now a Salvation Army officer and still in demand as a composer of Salvation Army music. Captain Sergej Zhuravlyov has written a brilliant march *'Who is on the Lord's side'* which was distributed to the bandsmen oft he Oslo Temple Band and rehearsed for 10 to 15 minutes the day before it was performed for the first time during the festival at the Salvation Army 20th anniversary congress for the Eastern Europe Territory in Kiev May 28th 2011.

Important compositions

Call of the Heavenly Trumpet (m/s), Let Your Light So Shine (m/s), Return to Russia (GS 1894) 1994, My Soul Thirsts for God (m/s)

ZIMMERMANN, MARTIN

Although Martin doesn't consider himself a composer, he actually wrote several songs and band pieces, in particular for Sunday morning purposes. His parents are Salvation Army officers and therefore he grew up, like so many others in these circumstances, with the beauty of Salvation Army brass music. A part of his musical raising was by the use and listening to the records coming from the United Kingdom. Martin played cornet in the Switzerland Staff Band 'Brass of Praise'. Several years later he became the bandmaster of the Zurich Zentral Band. It was here that he really started to write music. He has studied languages and has a PhD in French Literature and is the head of a high school.

Important compositions

All Night, All Day (m/s), Gott ist Nahe (m/s)

IS MUSIC HEREDITARY?

Can the art of composing (or common interest in music?) be hereditary? When we look to all the people included in this book, there are some remarkable examples that this might be the case. However, as with all hobbies and avid performers of such a hobby, as well as with dedicated people to the jobs they are doing, it is obvious that descendants get 'something' which they will never loose the rest of their lives. Call it a heritage if you like. Who doesn't remember the 'stamp collection' of their father, or the 'thimble collection' of their mother? Once you have seen that during childhood, you will never forget it. The difference however with such a noted subject as music, *in any form*, is that this is so often a kind of addiction and therefore it looks like it is in the genes, in the genealogical tree, so *in the blood.*

When the Hendon Citadel Band some years back planned a new recording, the idea was launched to include a 'solo' for fathers and sons, and *'The Inheritors'* became a fact, played by Roland and Stephen Cobb, Derek and Philip Smith. Nowadays the youngest son of Stephen Cobb is even the principal trumpet of the London Philharmonic Orchestra. So yes, there must be something like a *transfer of interest* between family members. When I look around me, it is hard to believe that if certain fathers did not have their children introduced in the brass band fraternity from a very young age, these people would never have become as far as a composer/arranger.

When I take my good friend Olaf Ritman, currently the Amsterdam Staff Bandmaster in The Netherlands, as an example it is obvious that composing, or the love for music in the first place, is hereditary. His grandfathers were strongly involved in Salvation Army banding. His grandfather on mother's side became the principal cornet of the then National Band of the Salvation Army (forerunners of the Amsterdam Staff Band). The family of this well known man, Alewijn van Gulik, emigrated to Canada, became a well established and firm family in Ottawa, and 'delivered' great musicians including some noted professionals. Olaf's father was for years a Salvation Army bandmaster and an avid bass trombone player. His uncles were noted musicians, so in principle his whole family was *soaked* in music. However, he got the chance to develop into a composer and arranger and succeeded in this, and now his name is also in the journals of Salvation Army publications and he continues to compose and arrange great music! This is just but one example and very close by, but there are countless other examples of great people that have inherited their skills and competencies from their ancestors.

Just go through the names mentioned in the above chapters and you can find some father-son 'composing' combinations for example:

- Kenneth Smith and Jeremy Smith (Canada)
- Robert Venables and Marcus Venables (Canada)
- Erik Silfverberg and Niels Silfverberg (Denmark)
- Norman Bearcroft and Marc Bearcroft (United Kingdom)
- Ray Brooks and Noel Brooks (Canada)

History shows us that each of these gentlemen came under the influence of their father after which they decided to start putting music on paper and they are currently completely in the 'system', being a fully accepted composer

Father-grandson combinations can also be found such as Walter Thomas and Martyn Thomas (United Kingdom), and what about the world famous brothers, William and Bruce Broughton (USA), who both became involved, impressed and introduced to music by their grandfather, Brigadier William Broughton Sr? Or the brothers Keith (Canada) and Kenneth (UK) Ketteringham, who although separated by thousands of nautical miles, still both seem to provide the Army journals with new works. David Rowsell and Jonathan Rowsell (New Foundland, Canada) can be even more highlighted, as Jonathan's granddad, Dr. Eric Abbot, was also a Salvation Army composer, which makes it no less than three generations of composers and arrangers, just like William Spencer, father-in-law of Fredrick Cooper, and grandfather of Maurice Cooper, all three composers. An odd one out is perhaps the father – daughter combination Ray Steadman-Allen and Barbara Steadman-Allen! Quite unique!

So, is composing hereditary? It must be somehow. Of course the love for objects, activities, hobbies etc can or had to be 'transmitted' by the fact that a person has always taken his child(ren) with him or her to the relevant happenings, but there should somehow be a connection between the love from parents for a certain activity and the interest in it by their children.

INFLUENCING EACH OTHER

Although composers and arrangers always will try to be original, it is no secret that sometimes they can be of example to each other or will give one another great ideas. They listen and study each others scores and music, and try to learn from it.

Torchbearers

An example of this is the brilliant march *'The Torchbearers'*, played countless times over the years by also countless bands and written by the doyen of all (Salvation Army and secular brass movement) composers, Eric Ball, a one time bandmaster of the International Staff Band but even more known for his work as bandmaster with the Salvationist Publishing & Supplies Band (SP&S Band). It was written to show how (great) a band of a small number of players can sound. He was of great example to many and still today many composers and arrangers are using his material to copy, arrange, transcribe and even better, to learn from.

Torchbearer

When Dr. Peter Graham was asked to write a new contest piece for the National Brass Band Championship in the United Kingdom, he came up with the great idea to use this march as theme for his new works appropriately named *'The Torchbearer' (note the missing 's' at the end).* His work had nothing to do with a march as such, but the theme was used as basis for his brilliant test piece.

Torch Swingers

Another composer, the American Glenn Welch, used it for a completely different purpose. The march was used for real Salvation Army purposes, for use on the streets, while Peter Graham's work should test the very best bands to its limits, Glenn gave the army an arrangement what was strongly influenced by Eric Ball's march, but put it in a more present age form - *'The Torchswingers'* was born, first in sextet form, later being transcribed and adjusted for full brass band.

Song of the Brother versus **A Joy Untold**

Another example of such influence was when Terry Camsey wanted a *'Flight of the Bumble Bee'* type of solo and opened it with a bit of *'Song of the brother'* as an element of surprise (a joke to mislead the listener then surprise them). When Albert Jakeway first heard it on the radio he said something to the effect that Terry had stolen Erik Leidzén's music! Many composers since have since written similar fast moving solos.

Composers might even influence themselves by writing a piece which creates other ideas for the so called *accompanying compositions*. Think about Dean Goffin's *'The Light of the World'* with *'Wonderful Healer'* as 'parallel' piece. What about Eric Ball's *'Songs of the Morning'* and his ideas to also compose *'Songs of the Evening'* although this last piece never came into being but was started in his brilliant mind. Fact is that influence on what composers write is of huge importance.

When talking about influencing each other one immediately also thinks about married couples. Composers Ian and Isobel Robinson, currently Salvation Army officers in the United States of America are probably the most well known example, but also Paul Sharman and his wife Charlotte Sharman (who has published under her maiden name – Charlotte Pitteway) are excellent examples. The difference between these people is that Ian and Isobel really works closely together while Paul and Charlotte compose independently. Coincidentally they are both featured on the Kettering Citadel Young People's Band recording (in cooperation with the Chatham Citadel Singing Company) 'Do Something Beautiful' which was released in 2011. Paul is a much recorded composer so it is no surprise that his music is used on this disc, but the output of Charlotte is rather limited, but still on this disc. Another variant on composer influences is when you look is for example Wilfred Heaton's world famous festival march *'Praise'*. One of the most recorded marches in the Salvation Army history, fellow composer Dr. Kenneth Downie payed tribute to Wilfred Heaton by writing the march *'Praise Tribute'* of which the text in the booklet of the International Staff Band recording 'St. Magnus' says; '*… a deliberate acknowledgement of the late Wilfred Heaton's march Praise, which was the source for this new march…*'. Not only is this new march of great quality, as we are used to seeing with compositions by Ken Downie, but here he writes in exactly the same style and scoring as Wilfred Heaton. Composers also often pay tribute to each other by using each others tunes as centrepoint for another piece. An example of this is when Terry Camsey wrote his well know Christmas tune, several years later Ray Bowes used this tune as main tune in one of his best known compositions, his timeless cornet solo *'Rhapsody for Cornet and Band'* which Terry also performed and recorded (amongst others).

COMPOSER OR CONDUCTOR?

It is remarkable that so many well known composers also have been (or are) outstanding conductors and bandmasters. So if we look a bit closer the question immediately arises - is a good composer by definition also always a good conductor, or bandmaster? Past and even current appointments have shown that good or even great players, who because of their outstanding playing skills and abilities have been asked to take over the baton, have not always ended in a good way. This might be because these outstanding players, who are in most cases the bands soloist, could have developed also a soloist's character. They often think that the whole band knows what they mean and also have equal playing skills. Of course this is only but an assumption. Compare this to how composers (could/might) think. Composers write music with the/a whole band in mind, and often composers also write with a particular band in mind so can write music for strong players, but also adjust parts for the lesser qualitative musicians.

Some significant composers and the bands they conduct(ed):

Robert Redhead (*Canadian Staff Band, International Staff Band, Melbourne Staff Band*), Dick Krommenhoek (*Amsterdam Staff Band*), William Himes (*Flint Citadel Band, Chicago Staff Band*), Erik Silfverberg (*Valby Corps Band*), William Gordon (*Pasadena Tabernacle Band*), Barrie Gott (*Pasadena Tabernacle Band, Sydney Congress Hall Band, Brisbane City Temple Band*), Ray Ogg (*Chicago Staff Band, Los Angeles Tabernacle Band*), Peter Graham (*Regent Hall Band*), Arthur Gullidge (*Brunswick Citadel Band*), Eric Ball (*International Staff Band, SP&S Band*), Ray Bowes (*International Staff Band*), Leslie Condon (*Croydon Citadel Band*), Howard Evans (*Boscombe Citadel Band, Amsterdam Staff Band*), Brian Bowen (*Staines Corps Band, New York Staff Band*), Olaf Ritman (*Amsterdam Staff Band, Valleistreek Citadel Band*) are just a *small* enumeration of the composers who were or are also on active service as leader of a music group.

Also take into account that many other composers on a more modest (senior band, youth band, division youth band, divisional band, fellowship band) level have conducted or are conducting Salvation Army bands. People such as Noel Jones (*Ringwood Citadel Band*), David Rowsell (*St. John's Citadel Band*) and Orville Payton (*Port Huron Citadel Band*) just to name but three deserve credit for their tireless and well structured gift of music for the benefit of these Salvation Army bands. So, are composers in the first place a composer or are they primarily a conductor (or musician for that matter) rather than a composer. It is probably a combination of both; however, it *always* starts with the (a) composer. Without him or her, no music would become available. Only then, when after loads of effort, thinking, creating, shaping and reshaping, a composition will see daylight after which the performers can enjoy the new creation.

RECOMMENDED BOOKS ABOUT COMPOSERS (and related subjects)

In Good Company - Norman Bearcroft

In Good Company covers a wide expanse of time and space in Salvation Army history. The author, Lieut-Colonel Norman Bearcroft, was born in the UK in 1926 and now in retirement serves his Lord in the USA. His memoirs take the reader on a fascinating journey from Wallsend to New York via Alderney, London, Canada, Ukraine, Zimbabwe and Australia, to name just a few stops along the way. The book covers such ground as the first National School of Music, the re-formation of the Canadian Staff Band, the founding of The International Staff Songsters and much more besides. His personal insights and powers of storytelling bring historical events to life.

The Best of Both Worlds - Brindley Boon

In The Best of Both Worlds, Salvation Army officer Colonel Brindley Boon delves deep into memories covering nine decades to provide a record of an extraordinary life. His twin loves of music and journalism provide the framework for this fascinating autobiography. But, more than that, every experience he recollects seems to shine with his love for God and his desire to serve Him. Colonel Boon died in March 2009.

Leslie Condon - He just couldn't say no – by Dot Condon

Major Leslie Condon did much to develop the role of the tuba within The Salvation Army before his untimely Promotion to glory whilst carolling with Croydon Citadel Band. His daughter Dorothy has recently produced a memoir of her father with the *title 'He just couldn't say no'* to raise money for the Leslie Condon Trust, which funds places for young people at music schools.

'Aspiration . . .Anecdotal Snapshots of Genius' Biography of Dr. Emil Soderstrom!

Historic Manuscripts & Rare Music Music Illustrations. Treasury of Little-known Facts Inner Thoughts in Emil's Own Words Excerpts from Hundreds of Letters Unique Soderstrom Music Style Revealed Emil & Leidzen's Long Shadow NBC . . .**Compiled and written by Robert Getz (R).**

Sympony of Thanksgiving - The music of Commissioner Sir Dean Goffin - by Cyril R Bradwell

This is a fascinating story of Sir Dean Goffin that tells of his musical masterpiece and personal testimony that has had an influence around the world.

Erik Leidzén; Band arranger and composer - by Ronald W. Holz

This great book deals with the life of Erik Leidzen, a band arranger and composer for the Salvation Army who was among the first generation of American musicians to be able to maintain a profession as a writer/arranger of band music.

Erik Leidzén – This man Leidzén – by Leslie Fossey

Stories from the life of Erik Leidzén, an American Salvationist Musican

Triumph of Faith (George Marshall) - by Arch R Wiggins

Triumph of Faith--The author tells the story of his collaboration with the 'great Bandmaster', George Marshall.

Eric Ball, his words and his wisdom - by Peter M Cooke

A most interesting book, compiled by Peter Cooke but really written by Eric Ball himself as it contains many thoughts, letters and discussions about music.

Eric Ball, The man and his music - by Peter M Cooke

In this absorbing biography, Peter M. Cooke traces the story of his this iconic composer, conductor compere and pianist; through his early years with the Salvation Army, and the years of crisis in his personal life, then into the calmer waters of ever-widening influence as a world musical figure.

In the Firing Line (Bramwell Coles) – by Wally Court

Eighty years after its publication as a march in 1926, In the Firing Line is receiving renewed attention, this time as the title of Colonel Bramwell Coles' biography. The newly released biography, by Wally Court, firmly establishes Coles in the pantheon of Salvation Army composers.

Brave and True (Arthur Gulldige) - by Lindsey C. Cox

In 1942, the biggest single loss of life suffered by Australia happened in one single wartime act. The number of lives lost was two-and-a-half times the total number of Australian soldiers killed in Vietnam. Amongst those who perished were 22 Salvation Army Bandsmen who enlisted in the AIF under renowned Bandmaster Arthur Gullidge to form the 2/22nd Battalion Band. Just one bandsman survived the invasion of Rabaul.

Tuned to the Celestial Pitch (Arthur Gulldige) - by Leslie Rusher

It is timely to recognise the life and work of Salvationist composer and Bandmaster, Arthur Gullidge. At the age of 33, Arthur lost his life when the prisoner of war vessel on which he was being held was torpedoed. Twenty-one other Salvation Army bandsmen who were part of the 2/22nd battalion were lost on that day. This book will evoke tender memories of their service.

Father of Salvation Army Music - by Arch R. Wiggins

'Father of Salvation Music' was General Bramwell Booth's description of Richard Slater, O.F. whose story, together with much of the early history of Salvation Army music is given in this book. Slater was foremost among the many music makers of a Movement whose playing has encircled the globe.

The Heritage of the North East Brass Band Movement - By Dennis Taylor

Brass bands hold an important place in the British music culture, and some writers have characterized bands as one of the great achievements of the working class. This book is a tribute to the development of the Brass Band Movement in the North East of England.

The Story of the Chalk Farm Band 1882-1932

Author unknown.

Fighting for the Lord – The History of the Danish Staff Band – by Niels Silfverberg

Due to the everlasting interest in the history of Salvation Army bands, Amsterdam Staff Bandsman William Sprokkereef requested much information about the Danish Staff Band

and eventually triggered composer Niels Silfverberg to write a complete book about this fascinating, inspiring and encouraging band.

'The Musical Salvationist' – by Gordon Cox

'The Musical Salvationist' frames the musical history of the Salvation Army through the life story of Richard Slater, popularly known as the 'Father of Salvation Army Music'. This book focuses upon the significant contribution of the Salvation Army to British musical life from the late Victorian era until the outbreak of the Second World War in 1939. It demonstrates links between the Army's music-making and working class popular culture, education and religion.

EPILOGUE

One of the sayings of the Founder of the Salvation Army, William Booth, is '*Music is for the soul, what wind is for the sail*'. Nothing could be further from the truth. A soul without music would go nowhere, just like a sail without any wind.

Although this is certainly not an academic book, -apart from the chapter written by my valued colleague, Prof. Dr. Garmt Dijksterhuis, and even he wrote it from an amateur musician's perspective rather than from his profession, it is also not intend to be one. It has cost me a considerable amount of time putting it together. Think on reading existing books, going through numerous ancient 'Musicians', 'Salvationists', 'The Bandsman and Songster' etc, interviewing people, sending thousands of emails and reminders, replying again, investigating, research etc. The idea from the beginning has always been to give a simple but yet clear answer to the everlasting question, being a avid bandsman myself, who that '*person on the right top of the sheetmusic*' was, or is.

I really hope that this book gives a bit of an answer to that and that you have been able to relate to these people. Music –any music for that matter- is of vital importance in the lives of countless people. Many can't do without. But if there weren't any composers, the story would have stopped here. Fortunately there are many. The reasons that many titles of compositions have been named in this book are 1. Just to show you what is written by various composers and perhaps even more important 2. To trigger bandmasters and conductors alike to dig into this often old music, motivate them to recognize the significance of it and hopefully, when they have a chance dust it off, play it over and over again, and hopefully record it with their bands.

I am also very sure that not all the past and current composers and arrangers have been described in this book but I have tried to make it as complete as possible as time, source, information and assistance let me. If I have forgotten anyone who 'should' be in it, please don't be offended, but keep writing for the Lord and the Salvation Army!

O yes, a last word… there is an everlasting discussion about what is the best piece ever written… if you have a hundred people, you get a hundred opinions of course but to give the final answer on this, it is Eric Ball's '*Songs in Exile*'! Why? Because '*I am the child of a King*'!

My Father is rich in houses and lands;
He holdeth the wealth of the world in His hands!
Of rubies and diamonds, of silver and gold,
His coffers are full-He has riches untold.

My Father's own Son, the Savior of men,
Once wandered o'er earth as the poorest of them;
But now He is reigning forever on high,
And will give me a home in heav'n by and by.

I once was an outcast stranger on earth,
A sinner by choice and an alien by birth;
But I've been adopted; my name's written down-
An heir to a mansion, a robe, and a crown.

A tent or a cottage, why should I care?
They're building a palace for me over there!
Though exiled from home, yet still I may sing:
All glory to God, I'm a child of the King.

Chorus:

I'm a child of the King, a child of the King!
With Jesus my Savior, I'm a child of the King!

Harriett E. Buell (1834-1910)

SOURCES AND LITERATURE USED IN THIS BOOK

Brass Bands of the Salvation Army (vol.1) – Their Mission and Music

by Dr. Ronald W. Holz,

Streets Publishers, England SG5 4AF,

ISBN 0-9551988-4-4, 978-0-9551988-4-7

Ever Heard the Sound?

By Steef Klepke Jr

Boekscout.nl

ISBN 978-94-6089-797-9

Play the Music, Play!

By Brindley Boon

Salvationist Publishing and Supplies Ltd

ISBN 0-85412-322-9

Companion to the Songbook oft he Salvation Army

By Gordon Taylor

Salvationist Publishing and Supplies Ltd

ISBN 0 85412 531 0

The Proclaimers – the History of the New York Staff Band

by Dr. Ronald W. Holz

The Salvation Army, New York Staff Band

440 West Nyack Road

West Nyack, New York 10994

ISBN 978-0-89216-110-2

The Heritage of the North East Brass Band Movement

By Dennis Taylor

Research Fellow, Durham University

8, Butsfield Gardens, Sunderland

Tyne and Wear

SR3 1PN England

Companion to the Song Book of the Salvation Army

Compiled by Gordon Taylor

Copyright © The General of the Salvation Army

First published 1989

ISBN 0 85412 531 0

Krigstrumpetens klara toner.

Otto Lundahl och Frälsningsarméns stabsmusikkår.

FA-Press 1999

By Lars-Erik Lingström

Frälsningssång och Stridsmusik.

Frälsningsarméns sånger och sångböcker 1882-1990.

FA-press 2000

By Karin Hartman

Med tusen tungors ljud.

Frälsningsarméns vokalmusik under ett sekel.

FA-Press 2002

By Mildred Österberg

www.BrassLink.nl

The Salvationist

The Salvation Army

101 Newington Causeway

London, United Kingdom

SE1 6BN

PUBLISHERS OF THE SALVATION ARMY

Salvationist Publishing & Supplies

66-78 Denington Road
Deningon Industrial Estate
Wellingborough, Northants
NN8 2QH, England
Telephone: +44 (0)1933 441807
Fax: +44 (0)1933 445415

Salvation Army Supplies

95 - 99 Railway Road
Blackburn VIC 3130
Phone: +61 3 8878 4700
Fax: +61 3 8878 4824
Email: trade@aus.salvationarmy.org

The Salvation Army

USA East Music Department
440 West Nyack Road
PO Box C-635
West Nyack, NY 10994-1739
Tel: +01(914)-620-7443
Fax: +01(914)-620-7777

The Salvation Army

USA Southern Territorial Music Department
1424 Northeast Expressway
Atlanta, GA 30329
Tel: +01(404)-728-1344
Fax: +01(404)-728-1373